The Playbill® Broadway Yearbook

Ninth Annual Edition
2012-2013

Robert Viagas
Editor

Amy Asch
Assistant Editor

Frank Dain
Production Coordinator

Kesler Thibert
Art Director

Brian Mapp   Joseph Marzullo
Photographers

The Playbill Broadway Yearbook: Ninth Annual Edition, June 1, 2012–May 31, 2013
Robert Viagas, Editor

©2013 PLAYBILL® Incorporated

ISBN 978-1-48034-159-3
HL00119141
ISSN 1932-1945

Published by PLAYBILL® BOOKS
525 Seventh Avenue, Suite 1801
New York, NY 10018
Email: yearbook@playbill.com
Internet: www.playbill.com

Published in 2013 by Applause Theatre & Cinema Books
An Imprint of Hal Leonard Corporation
7777 West Bluemound Road
Milwaukee, WI 53213

Trade Book Division Editorial Offices
33 Plymouth St., Montclair, NJ 07042

Printed in the United States of America

Book design by Kesler Thibert
Cover photo of Bob Crowley's set for *Once* on the Bernard B. Jacobs Theatre stage by Brian Mapp.

www.applausebooks.com

Preface to the Ninth Edition

This year's season summaries were fond of quoting comedian W.C. Fields' dictum that actors should never work with animals or children. Broadway ostentatiously flouted that advice in 2012-2013, with many productions that showcased one or the other—or both. Equity reported that more tha two dozen actors under the age of 18 had Broadway contracts this year. On the 2013 Tony Awards broadcast, host Neil Patrick Harris clucked that with shows like *Matilda, Annie, A Christmas Story, Newsies* and others, Broadway began to resemble Chuck E. Cheese, a regional birthday party franchise.

Four-legged (or even winged) thespians also strutted and sometimes fretted. When *Breakfast at Tiffany's* had to fire one of its cats (it employed three—two "regular" puddies and one understudy), the cast change made the evening news.

Grownup humans also did some things this season. And they did a lot of them. The ninth edition of *The Playbill Broadway Yearbook,* which you hold in your hands, contains information on all 81 shows that played on Broadway at some point between June 1, 2012 and May 31, 2013—the most shows in the history of the *Yearbook,* and a considerable jump over the 65 that played during our inaugural season. Here are the totals for the nine seasons the Yearbook has been in existence:

2004-05 = 65	2009-10 = 71
2005-06 = 71	2010-11 = 77
2006-07 = 67	2011-12 = 72
2007-08 = 70	2012-13 = 81
2008-09 = 78	

Those figures reflect not only that the pace of new shows continues to blister, but the number of shows settling in for long runs also continues to burgeon. One blogger this season warned semi-seriously that Broadway may be heading toward a singularity when ALL theatres will be booked with long-running hits, preventing the opening of any new shows at all. Real estate people may need to start building new playhouses in the skyscrapers shooting up around Times Square, something that hasn't happened since the 2010 opening of the Sondheim Theatre on 43rd Street.

Another boost to those numbers was the opposite of a long run: limited engagements of singers, comedians, rock groups and other curiosities. Theatres used to stand dark for months between bookings. This year, theatre owners filled those hiatuses with brief, vaudeville-style engagements of specialty acts including crooner Barry Manilow, funnyman Lewis Black, a reunion of the 1960s group The Rascals, and even former heavyweight boxing champ turned tabloid novelty Mike Tyson, who was later invited to sing and dance on the 2013 Tony Awards.

The proliferation of these extra productions went on undeterred by Hurricane Sandy, which hit the New York metropolitan area squarely in late October, flooding large swathes of the city and causing a multi-day blackout in many places south of midtown. Despite being built on marshy land that was a small pond in the pre-Columbian era, Times Square was spared the worst of damage from the storm. Other areas, closer to the waterfront, were not so lucky. The storm was blamed for depressing attendance figures, which dropped to 11.57 million, the lowest level in eight years. However, premium ticket

YOUR 2012-2013 YEARBOOK COMMITTEE
Standing (L-R): photographers Joseph Marzullo, Monica Simoes and Brian Mapp.
Seated (L-R): Editor Robert Viagas and production coordinator Frank Dain.
Bottom: Assistant Editor Amy Asch.
Not pictured: Art Director Kesler Thibert

Photo by Kari Otero

Photo by Matt Blank

prices pushing $500 in one case helped keep the overall boxoffice total nearly identical to last year's.

Summer and fall 2012 were comparatively quiet, highlighted by *Chaplin,* a musical biography of silent film clown Charlie Chaplin, and *Bring It On,* a youthful musical about high school cheerleaders that was a collaboration between two award-winning songwriters, Lin-Manuel Miranda (*In the Heights*) and Tom Kitt (*Next to Normal*), plus Amanda Green.

The battle of the Christmas shows was unusually fierce this year with *Elf, A Christmas Story* and *Annie* competing with *How the Grinch Stole Christmas!* (at the Theatre at Madison Square Garden) and perennial *The Radio City Christmas Spectacular.* The winner appears to have been *A Christmas Story,* a musicalization of a film hit that was boosted by a sterling cast and a flavorful score by the tyro songwriting team of Benj Pasek and Justin Paul, which was nominated for a Best Score Tony Award. The show as a whole was nominated for Best Musical.

During the slow months of January and February many theatre fans found themselves turning to their TV sets for the cult NBC series "Smash," about the writing, tryout and Broadway opening of a musical biography of film goddess Marilyn Monroe. It was packed with Broadway stars and original Broadway-style tunes, but fans despaired as the show's scripts caused it to slide inexorably to cancellation at season's end.

However, starting in March, Broadway itself wrapped up the season with a fireworks display of major openings. Fifteen shows bowed in the thirty days of April, including Nathan Lane's memorable portrait of a closeted Burlesque-era

comedian, *The Nance;* Christopher Durang's tribute to actors' egos and Anton Chekhov, *Vanya and Sonia and Masha and Spike;* and a lavish adaptation of Rodgers and Hammerstein's onetime TV special, *Cinderella.* Broadway also saw several powerful solo (or near-solo) shows including Alan Cumming's *Macbeth,* Fiona Shaw's *The Testament of Mary* and Bette Midler's *I'll Eat You Last.* Surprisingly enough for their fans, those three stars earned nary a Tony Award nomination among them.

The same was definitely NOT true for the two main Tony contenders, *Matilda* (12 nominations) and *Kinky Boots* (13 nominations), which spent the late spring battling for Best Musical and other top honors. *Matilda,* which seemed a shoo-in, hung back primly as the cast and creators of *Kinky Boots* sang, danced, quipped and dished on every talk show and every Broadway event, every Facebook wall and in every store window. Even the Times Square subway turnstiles were festooned with images of the show's signature sparkly red thigh boots. Best Musical went to *Kinky Boots,* but after the dust settled the winner at the box office proved to be…*Motown,* a jukebox salute to vintage R&B, written by Motown founder Berry Gordy, which earned not a single Tony.

The Playbill Broadway Yearbook's parent company, Playbill Inc., continued its evolution from a theatre program company to a broader theatre information company by rolling out a family of new websites including the Playbill Vault (PlaybillVault.com), a place to look up program information on all Broadway shows going back to the turn of the 20th century; Playbill Memory Bank (PlaybillMB.com), a place to store and share personal memories of shows you've seen; PlaybillVIP (PlaybillVIP.com), which stands for Virtual Internet Playbill and allows anyone to create an online Playbill program for school and community theatre productions; and the most ambitious of all, PlaybillEDU (PlaybillEDU.com), the single largest online resource for college programs in theatre, music and dance, scheduled for debut in summer 2013. All these sites were created and/or compiled by some of the same people who assemble this Yearbook.

Speaking of which, new in the *Yearbook* this year: livelier layouts for the Scrapbook pages, a clearer look for the Faculty table of contents, and brighter photos throughout. Our back cover collage of Playbill images (assembled each spring by designer Kesler Thibert) has been sold through the PlaybillStore.com as a poster and a puzzle. This year, in answer to popular request, we're also making it available on a t-shirt.

In the meantime we've already begun work on the special tenth edition of the Yearbook. See you in 2014!

Robert Viagas
June 2013

Special Thanks

Special thanks to Amy Asch, Frank Dain, Brian Mapp, Joseph Marzullo, Monica Simoes, Kesler Thibert, David Gewirtzman, Pam Karr, Matt Blank, Andrew Gans, Adam Hetrick, Jean Kroeper Murphy, Nick Viagas and Debra Candela Novack, whose help made this year's edition possible.

We also thank the Ninth Edition *Yearbook* Correspondents who shared their stories with such wit and insight: Alicia Albright, Genevieve Angelson, Donna Marie Asbury, Emily Bergl, Teddy Bergman, Lewis Black, Lauren Blumenfeld, John Bolton, Kye Brackett, Jared Bradshaw, Patrick R. Brown, Molly Campbell, Allyson Carr, Stephen Carrasco, Tracee Chimo, Jill Cordle (for the third time), Robert Creighton, Trevon R. Davis, Crystal Dickinson, Madison Dirks, Kevin Duda, Timothy Eaker, Tom Edden, Brad Fleischer, Merwin Foard, Kelly Jeanne Grant, John Arthur Greene, Andy Grotelueschen, Ann Harada, James Harker, Roy Harris (for the seventh time), Ellen Harvey, Satomi Hofman, Marin Ireland, Dominique Johnson, Jay Armstrong Johnson, Amanda Dekker Kaus, Isabel Keating, Benjamin Klein, Kris Koop Ouellette (for the ninth time), Bill Kux, Josh Lamon, James Lecesne, Raymond J. Lee (for the second time), Deirdre Lovejoy, Laird Mackintosh, Melanie Marshall, Alexi Melvin, Carolyn D. Miller, Jonny Orsini, Zoe Perry, Christopher Pineda, Hayley Podschun, Josephine Rose Roberts, Kate Cullen Roberts, Tory Ross (for the second time), Jon Rua, Bethany Russell, Chris Shin, Amy Spanger, Holland Taylor, Brendan Titley, Daniel Torres, Jonathan Warren, James Waterston and Katrina Yaukey.

And we thank the folks on each show who shared their photographs and other artwork that lent extra sparkle to the Scrapbook pages: George Lee Andrews, Jimmy Asnes, Lewis Black, Jared Bradshaw, Allyson Carr, Robert Creighton, Jeremy Daniel, Brad Fleischer, Heidi Gutman, Tim Hughes, Hayley Podschun, Kate Cullen Roberts, Alicia Albright, and many others.

Also the Broadway press agents who helped set up interviews and photo sessions and helped track down the names of all the people in the crew photos: especially Chris Boneau, Adrian Bryan-Brown, Michael Hartman, Richard Kornberg, Matt Polk, Jeffrey Richards, Keith Sherman, Marc Thibodeau, Philip Rinaldi, Sam Rudy, Tony Origlio, Rick Miramontez, Glenn Schwartz and their respective staffs.

Plus Joan Marcus, Paul Kolnik, Carol Rosegg, Jeremy Daniel, Chad Batka, Chris Bennion, Ave Bonar, Scott Landis, Brinkoff-Mögenburg, Sunshine Sachs, Jacob Cohl, Andrew Cole, Deen Van Meer, William Ngai, Richard Termine, Tristram Kenton, Matthew Murphy, Michael Brosilow, Nathan Johnson, and all the fine professional photographers whose work appears on these pages.

And, most of all, thanks to the great show people of Broadway who got into the spirit of the Yearbook and took time out of their busy days to pose for our cameras. There's no people like them.

Frequently-Asked Questions

Which Shows Are Included? *The Playbill Broadway Yearbook 2012-2013* covers the Broadway season that ran, as per tradition, from June 1, 2012 to May 31, 2013. Each of the eighty-one shows that played at a Broadway theatre under a Broadway contract during that time are spotlighted in this edition. That includes new shows that opened during that time, like *Matilda*; shows from last season that ran into this season, like *Once*; older shows from seasons past that closed during this season, like *Mary Poppins*; and older shows from seasons past that ran throughout this season and continue into the future (and into the next *Yearbook*), like *Wicked*.

How Is It Decided Which Credits Page Will Be Featured? Each show's credits page (which PLAYBILL calls a "billboard page") changes over the year as cast members come and go. We use the opening-night billboard page for most new shows. For most shows that carry over from the previous season we use the billboard page from the first week in October.

Occasionally, sometimes at the request of the producer, we use a billboard page from another part of the season, especially when a major new star joins the cast.

What Are "Alumni" and "Transfer Students"? Over the course of a season some actors leave a production; others take their place. To follow our *Yearbook* concept, the ones who left a show before the date of the billboard page are listed as "Alumni"; the ones who joined the cast are called "Transfer Students." If you see a photo appearing in both "Alumni" and "Transfer Students" sections, it's not a mistake; it just means that they went in and out of the show during the season and were not present on the billboard date.

What Is a "Correspondent" and How Is One Chosen? We ask each show to appoint a Correspondent to record anecdotes of backstage life at their production. Sometimes the show's press agent picks the Correspondent; sometimes the company manager, the stage manager or the producer does the choosing. Each show gets to decide for itself. A few shows

decline to provide a correspondent, fail to respond to our request, or miss the deadline. Correspondents bring a richness of experience to the job and help tell the story of backstage life on Broadway from many different points of view.

Who Gets Their Picture in the Yearbook? Anyone who works on Broadway can get their picture in the *Yearbook*. That includes actors, producers, writers, designers, assistants, stagehands, ushers, box office personnel, stage doormen and anyone else employed at a Broadway show or a support organization. PLAYBILL maintains a database of headshots of all Broadway actors and most creators. We send our staff photographers to all opening nights and all major Broadway-related events. We also offer to schedule in-theatre photo shoots at every production. No one is required to appear in the *Yearbook*, but all are invited. A few shows declined to host a photo shoot this year or were unable to provide material by our deadline. We hope the ones that are still running will join us in 2014.

TABLE OF CONTENTS

Timeline 2012-2013

Opening Nights, News Headlines and Other Significant Milestones of the Season

June 10, 2012 At the 66th Annual Tony Awards, *Once* is named Best Musical and *Clybourne Park* is named Best Play.

June 14, 2012 Jim Parsons of TV's "The Big Bang Theory" stars with Charles Kimbrough and Jessica Hecht in a revival of *Harvey*, the classic comedy about a gentle alcoholic who hallucinates the six-foot talking rabbit of the title.

Summer 2012 A vacant lot on West 45th Street across from the Jacobs Theatre, the former site of several small brownstones with restaurants on their ground floors, spends summer 2012 occupied by a European-style tent circus called Spiegelworld, which presents a New Vaudeville display of acrobatics titled *Empire* (technically an Off-Broadway show though it was situated in the center of the Broadway theatre district). Passersby see an entry façade that looks like it was pieced together from bits of scrap metal and discarded signs.

July 9, 2012 *Fela!*, the Afro-beat musical biography of Nigerian political dissident/musician Fela Kuti, begins a summer-long return engagement on Broadway.

July 11, 2012 Mayor Michael Bloomberg proclaims today "*Peter and the Starcatcher* Day" to mark the show's 100th performance.

July 14 and 15, 2012 First Lady Michelle Obama and her two daughters hit New York for a two-day theatregoing trip. Saturday night the First Daughters see *Sister Act* while Mrs. Obama goes to *Porgy and Bess*. Sunday all three attend a matinee of *Spider-Man: Turn Off the Dark*. Secret Service and the NYPD bomb-squad are summoned to the Foxwoods Theatre when Ross Mandell of North Carolina jokes to baggage checker that if the show is bad, his bags will blow up. It is later determined that there was no bomb and that he apparently was unaware that the First Family was at the theatre that day.

July 18, 2012 A severe midsummer lightning storm knocks out the Belasco Theatre stage lights fifteen minutes before the end of the matinee of *End of the Rainbow*, in which Tracie

The orphans of *Annie* jump for reporters' cameras in Duffy Square across from the entrance to the Palace Theatre in a season that will feature a bumper crop of children in many shows. See November 8, 2012.

Bennett is playing Judy Garland. Bennett finishes the performance with the help of house lights and a follow spot during the storm, bringing extra poignancy to her final number, "Over the Rainbow."

July 30, 2012 Broadway's Child Actor Guardians, known colloquially as "child wranglers," ratify a four-year contract—the first for the wranglers—with the Broadway League, under the aegis of IATSE Local 764. The timing is right for the people who oversee the welfare of child actors. This season an unprecented 80 under-18 actors will be employed on Broadway.

July 31, 2012 Former World Heavyweight Champ and convicted rapist Mike Tyson recounts his eventful life in and out of the ring in a solo show, *Mike Tyson: Undisputed Truth*, that attracts fans, friends and family members, often prompting Tyson to draw familiar members of the audience into his monologues.

Week of July 31, 2012 An unidentified Tweeter upset with Tyson's show threatens to rampage at the Longacre Theatre, recreating a similar recent fatal attack at an Aurora, Colorado movie theatre. Police provide enhanced security at the theatre for the remaining week of the limited run, and there is no further incident.

August 1, 2012 The world of competitive high school cheerleading is celebrated in *Bring It On*, a new musical with a score by Tony-winning songwriters Tom Kitt and Lin-Manuel Miranda, plus Amanda Green. Originally scheduled for a limited run until early fall, the show finds its audience and gets extended through December.

August 15, 2012 Disney's musical *The Lion King* plays its 6138th performance, surpassing *A Chorus Line* to become the fifth longest running show in Broadway history.

September 6, 2012 Nearly three years after

creator Gerard Alessandrini suspended the popular *Forbidden Broadway* parody revue series, he returns with a new edition, *Forbidden Broadway: Alive and Kicking*. He tells interviewers that the current Broadway scene offered too many tempting targets to resist.

September 10, 2012 The new musical *Chaplin* traces the life of silent film icon Charlie Chaplin, with music and lyrics by Christopher Curtis (Broadway debut), book by Curtis and Thomas Meehan, and a notable performance by Rob McClure in the title role. The show caps decades of efforts to bring Chaplin's story to the stage, by actors including Anthony Newley and Larry Kert.

September 13, 2012 New York City's Board of Health votes to ban the sale of sugary soft drinks in cups and bottles bigger than sixteen ounces. Broadway concessions are among the venues targeted, though in practice few sell drinks of that size.

September 16, 2012 Colony Records, the theatre-district landmark at the corner of Broadway and 49th Street where many theatre lovers had been buying their cast albums and sheet music since 1948, has its last day of business. A crowd of one hundred people is on hand at 6 PM to take one last look at the store's leaping-bobbysoxer logo and applaud owner Richard Turk as he locks the door for the last time.

September/October 2012 Plans for the Broadway musical *Rebecca* go up in flames in the glare of national media attention as it is first announced that a major investor has died, and then it is revealed that the investor never existed at all, but was part of an oddball scam against the lead producer, Ben Sprecher. The marquee was up at the Broadhurst Theatre, and the actors were about to start rehearsal. The cast of the

The marquee was up, the actors were ready to rehearse but *Rebecca* never got to play a Broadway performance. See September/October 2012.

Timeline 2012-2013

show that was to have featured a spectacular Act II conflagration, had even recorded their track for the annual "Carols for a Cure" AIDS fundraising album. Their chosen song was "Keep the Home Fires Burning." By season's end, however, Sprecher announced he was again assembling financing for another shot at Broadway next season.

September 23, 2012 Glenn Weiss, director of the June 2011 broadcast of the 65th Annual Tony Awards, wins a Primetime Emmy Award for Outstanding Directing for a Variety Special. The 2011 Tony broadcast also won three Creative Arts Emmys the previous week: Outstanding Special Class Program—Ricky Kirshner, Executive Producer, Glenn Weiss Executive Producer and Neil Patrick Harris, Host/Producer; Outstanding Original Music and Lyrics: "It's Not Just For Gays Anymore"— Music by Adam Schlesinger, Lyrics by David

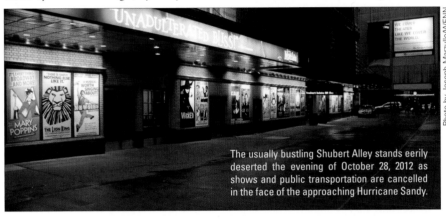

The usually bustling Shubert Alley stands eerily deserted the evening of October 28, 2012 as shows and public transportation are cancelled in the face of the approaching Hurricane Sandy.

Photo by Joseph Marzullo/WENN

Javerbaum; and Outstanding Art Direction for Variety or Nonfiction Programming—Steve Bass, Production Designer, Seth Easter, Art Director.

September 27, 2012 Richard Thomas and Boyd Gaines play brothers who battle over the eerily timely issue of public health versus public jobs in a revival of Henrik Ibsen's 19th century drama *An Enemy of the People*, directed by Doug Hughes.

September 30, 2012 Hundreds of little girls and their parents converge on Pearl Studios on Eighth Avenue where producers of the hit London musical *Matilda* hold a rare open call for four young actresses to share the leading role in the planned spring Broadway transfer.

October 4, 2012 Two fundamentalist Christians (Paul Rudd and Kate Arrington) go out on a financial limb to start a chain of Bible-themed hotels in Craig Wright's new play *Grace*—only to find that faith and finance don't always make a good mix. Michael Shannon plays a disfigured neighbor and Ed Asner plays a philosophical exterminator.

October 11, 2012 Douglas Hodge dons the hypertrophied proboscis in Jamie Lloyd's revival of Edmond Rostand's poetic *Cyrano de Bergerac*. Clémence Poésy and Patrick Page are on hand to help him deliver Ranjit Bolt's new translation of the 1897 classic. The production is memorable

partly for Hodge's entrance—bursting in the side doors from 43rd Street.

October 13, 2012 Tracy Letts, the Pulitzer-winning author of *August: Osage County*, crosses the footlights to co-star with *A:OC* actress Amy Morton in a revival of *Edward Albee's Who's Afraid of Virginia Woolf?* Pam MacKinnon directs the savage portrait of a curdled marriage in this 50th anniversary production that transfers to Broadway from Chicago's Steppenwolf Theatre Company.

October 22, 2012 The TKTS discount booth in Times Square begins testing two new services. Evening and matinee tickets, which used to be sold at separate times, are now to be sold simultaneously on the same day of performance. Also, one window is set aside to sell full-price tickets for any show on any day.

October 28-31, 2012 Hurricane Sandy clobbers the eastern seaboard causing New York's and New Jersey's Metropolitan Transportation Authority to suspend all public transportation starting 7 PM Sunday the 28th. Amid the storm's destruction and chaos, all Broadway shows cancel performances Sunday night, Monday and Tuesday, October 28-30, with all but a handful returning Wednesday, October 31. A full schedule of performances resumes November 1. On Wednesday afternoon, actor Patrick Page of Broadway's *Cyrano de Bergerac* posts this on Facebook: "Curtain going up on the matinee of *Cyrano*. So proud of my cast. Some of them walked three hours to get here today. Others came in despite homes and families without power, heat or hot water. We are Broadway."

November 1, 2012 Film star Jessica Chastain makes her Broadway debut in the title role of *The Heiress*, Ruth and Augustus Goetz's 1947 story about a wealthy girl who is loved only for her money. Broadway veterans David Strathairn and Judith Ivey are on hand to play her relatives, and Dan Stevens plays her suitor. The production benefits from the three stars' concurrent appearances in other media during the run: Strathairn is featured in the movie *Lincoln*, Dan Stevens melts hearts in the TV series "Downton Abbey," and Chastain is nominated for an Oscar in *Zero Dark Thirty*.

November 6, 2012 Election Day. Several

Broadway shows adjust their performance schedule so the casts (and potential audiences) have a chance today to cast ballots in the closely-contested presidential race between Barack Obama and Mitt Romney. These shows include *Chicago*, *Virginia Woolf* and *Nice Work If You Can Get It*.

November 8, 2012 James Lapine directs a full-scale revival of *Annie*, the classic 1977 musical about an ever-optimistic Depression-era orphan whose single-minded hunt for her long-lost parents leads to her getting adopted by a billionaire and helping to launch President Franklin Roosevelt's New Deal. Stars Lilla Crawford, Katie Finneran and Anthony Warlow.

November 9, 2012 A return Christmas season engagement of *Elf: The Musical,* a stage adaptation of the popular film comedy about a man who sets out to find his true family in New York after he is raised as an elf by Santa Claus at the North Pole. Jordan Gelber plays Buddy the Elf, Wayne Knight plays Santa, with original cast members Beth Leavel and Mark Jacoby recreating their roles as the folks Buddy meets on his quest.

November 13, 2012 The first Broadway revival of 1986 Tony winning musical *The Mystery of Edwin Drood* is a starry affair, with Chita Rivera as Princess Puffer leading a cast that includes Stephanie J. Block, Will Chase, Gregg Edelman, Jessie Mueller and Jim Norton. As before, the audience votes each night to determine the identity of the murderer and others in Charles Dickens' unfinished story, as completed in multiple ways by composer/lyricist/librettist/orchestrator Rupert Holmes.

November 13, 2012 Also today, Disney's *The Lion King* marks fifteen years on Broadway with a celebration that brings in cast members from throughout its run and from companies around the world.

November 14, 2012 Playwright David West Read sets his romantic comedy *The Performers* in the seemingly unlikely world of pornographic films. The cast: Henry Winkler, Cheyenne Jackson, Daniel Breaker, Alicia Silverstone, Ari Graynor and Jenni Barber.

November 15, 2012 Capping a twelve-year gestation, *Scandalous: The Life and Trials of Aimee Semple McPherson*, Kathie Lee Gifford's musical retelling of the life of the multi-media 1920s evangelist, finally gets its Broadway debut. Carolee Carmello stars in the title role. Deep-pocketed producers keep the show running for three weeks after dismissive reviews becalm the box office. The show's failure also rocks McPherson's real-life Foursquare Church Foundation, which had invested $2 million in the musical, according to the *Los Angeles Times*. Within days of the show's closing, Foursquare Executive Director Greg Campbell resigns and the church subsequently replaces all but one member of the foundation's board.

November 19, 2012 Beloved holiday movie *A Christmas Story* becomes a Broadway musical with a score by newcomers Benj Pasek (music and lyrics) and Justin Paul (music and lyrics). As before, the story involves young Ralphie's

Timeline 2012-2013

single-minded quest to convince his parents to get him a BB-gun for Christmas. Dan Lauria plays Ralphie as a grownup, narrating the story, which is enacted by a cast that includes John Bolton, Erin Dilly and Caroline O'Connor.

Thanksgiving Week, 2012 House records are broken at several Broadway box offices for the week ending November 25. These include *Annie*, which sells $1,499,879 worth of tickets at the Palace Theatre, and *Book of Mormon*, which breaks the O'Neill Theatre weekly house record for the 42nd time since the show's opening, selling $1,801,672 worth of tickets.

Thanksgiving Weekend, 2012 Times Square Hot Bagels closes its doors for the last time. The tiny storefront on 44th Street across from the entrance to Shubert Alley had been a go-to spot for Broadway's blue-collar workers for a quick and cheap early-morning snack/breakfast, but had struggled as that section of the block moved upmarket during the past few seasons.

November 29, 2012 Just a few days later another landmark Theatre District eatery bites the dust. The Stage Deli, which stood on Seventh Avenue near 54th Street since 1937, plates its last order of stuffed derma. Rising rents are blamed for the closing.

November 29, 2012 Also today, Katie Holmes, recently in headlines owing to her divorce from actor Tom Cruise, picks up her acting career by co-starring with Norbert Leo Butz in Theresa Rebeck's *Dead Accounts,* a drama about a hyperkinetic New York embezzler who returns to his small-town Ohio family to sort out his life.

November 30, 2012 A demographic study of Broadway theatregoers finds that 63.4 percent of the 12.3 million Broadway tickets sold during the 2011-2012 season were bought by tourists from across America and around the world, up slightly from 61.7 percent during the previous season—a new record. In another ongoing trend, the number of tickets bought over the internet climbed from 44 percent of the total to a new high of 47 percent. Some two-thirds of all ticket holders were women and the average age of Broadway theatregoers was 43.5 years.

December 2, 2012 Patti LuPone and Debra Winger star in *The Anarchist*, David Mamet's all-new jailhouse drama about a convicted cop-killer who tries to convince the authorities that she has found Jesus, mended her ways and deserves to be turned loose after decades behind bars. When producers opt to shutter the critically panned play after just 17 performances, The New York Times puts LuPone's reaction on the front page. She is "not happy" that they had "pulled the plug."

December 4, 2012 In honor of *The Lion King*'s fifteenth anniversary on Broadway, the Empire State Building lights up yellow, the color of the show's logo.

December 6, 2012 Seth Numrich plays a man torn between careers as a classical musician and a brutal prizefighter in the 75th anniversary revival of Clifford Odets' *Golden Boy*. The supporting cast of this drama is full of actors

Colony Records, a Broadway landmark in the Brill Building at 49th Street, sold its last page of sheet music and went out of business. See September 16, 2012.

who previously played lead roles, including Tony Shalhoub, Danny Burstein, Jonathan Hadary and Daniel Jenkins, all directed by Bartlett Sher for Lincoln Center Theater.

December 8, 2012 Al Pacino plays end-of-his-rope real-estate salesman Shelly Levene in Daniel Sullivan's revival of Pulitzer Prize winner *Glengarry Glen Ross*, the second Mamet play to open this week. Among those also in the cast: Bobby Cannavale, David Harbour, Richard Schiff and Jeremy Shamos.

December 17, 2012 The Broadway League reaches a new three-year contract deal with 32BJ Local SEIU, the union representing Broadway's porters, cleaners, elevator operators and matrons, averting a threatened holiday-season job action.

December 20, 2012 The revival of *Chicago* surpasses the Tony-winning musical *Les Misérables* to become the third-longest running show in Broadway history.

December 25, 2012 The film version of *Les Misérables* opens in the U.S., starring Hugh Jackman as Jean Valjean, Russell Crowe as Javert and Anne Hathaway as Fantine.

January 10, 2013 Laurie Metcalf earns raves in Manhattan Theatre Club's transfer of MCC's 2011 Off-Broadway hit, *The Other Place*, in which she plays a hard-charging neurologist dealing with the loss of her daughter and the onset of dementia.

January 13, 2013 An ensemble cast led by Sebastian Stan reanimates William Inge's 1953 classic *Picnic*, about a handsome young ne'er-do-well who gets a small Kansas town all hot and bothered one torrid summer.

January 17, 2013 In the third Broadway revival of Tennessee Williams' *Cat on a Hot Tin Roof* in just ten years, Scarlett Johansson lolls on the bed as Maggie, with Benjamin Walker as Brick and Ciarán Hinds as Big Daddy.

January 28, 2013 The Theater Hall of Fame at the Gershwin Theatre inducts actors Betty Buckley and Sam Waterston, directors Trevor Nunn and Michael Kahn, producer/director André Bishop, playwrights Paula Vogel and

Christopher Durang and, posthumously, costume designer Martin Pakledinaz.

January 29, 2013 Barry Manilow opens his concert show after a week's delay caused by a bout of the same illness that struck many performers and audience members this winter. "This flu thing really was a bear," he tells the crowd at the premiere. "But for me it wasn't just the flu part, it was the Jewish guilt part that got me."

February 5, 2013 TV's Broadway soap opera "Smash" makes its season debut to unexpectedly low ratings.

February 6, 2013 Tony-winning Best Actor in a Musical Steve Kazee suffers what he later describes as a "vocal injury" and plays his final performance as "Guy" in *Once*.

February 8-9, 2013 As if Hurricane Sandy hadn't been enough, a freezing nor'easter named Nemo buries Broadway under about 11 inches of snow, and up to 30 inches in parts of the metro area. Nevertheless, the theatres stay open and the shows go on.

February 20, 2013 Film actor Shia LaBeouf, who was to have made his Broadway debut with the upcoming *Orphans*, withdraws from the project, citing "creative differences."

February 24, 2013 The annual Academy Awards ceremony salutes movie musicals of the past decade, leading to performers and performances from the film versions of *Chicago, Les Misérables, Dreamgirls* and other film adaptations of Broadway shows.

March 3, 2013 Written for a 1957 TV special, *Rodgers + Hammerstein's Cinderella* makes its Broadway debut with several R&H trunk songs, a new libretto by Douglas Carter Beane, and a cast that includes Laura Osnes as the enchanted heroine and Victoria Clark as the Fairy Godmother.

March 3, 2013 Also on this date, *Mary Poppins* closes after 2,619 performances.

March 7, 2013 Holland Taylor wrote and stars in *Ann*, a solo portrait of charismatic Texas governor Ann Richards.

March 11, 2013 The U.S. 9th Circuit Court of Appeals rules that the Broadway musical

Timeline 2012-2013

Jersey Boys did not violate copyright law by using a short clip from TV's "The Ed Sullivan Show." "Being selected by Ed Sullivan to perform on his show was evidence of the band's enduring prominence in American music," Judge Stephen S. Trott wrote for the three-judge panel. "By using it as a biographical anchor, Dodger put the clip to its own transformative ends." Plaintiff SOFA Entertainment, which brought the suit, was further ordered to pay *Jersey Boys* $155,000 for the cost of defending itself.

March 14, 2013 Sigourney Weaver and David Hyde Pierce are featured in the Broadway transfer of Christopher Durang's hit Off-Broadway comedy *Vanya and Sonia and Masha and Spike*, which parodies show business and Chekhov.

March 19, 2013 Montie, a cat, gets fired from *Breakfast at Tiffany's* for "failure to take direction," prompting a flurry of media attention. Montie, who alternates in the role with another cat, Vito Vincent, is replaced by his understudy, Moo.

March 20, 2013 Richard Greenberg's new adaptation of Truman Capote's whimsical novel *Breakfast at Tiffany's* stars Emilia Clarke of TV's "Game of Thrones" as Manhattan good-time girl Holly Golightly, and Cory Michael Smith as the Southern writer who becomes fascinated with her.

March 21, 2013 Ten down-on-their-luck Texans compete to win a new flatbed truck in *Hands on a Hardbody*, a musical adaptation of the 1997 documentary film, with a book by Doug Wright, music and lyrics by Amanda Green, and music co-written by Trey Anastasio. Cast includes Keith Carradine, Dale Soules and Hunter Foster.

March 26, 2013 Protesters picket the first preview of Colm Tóibín's *The Testament of Mary*, across 48th Street from where it is playing at the Walter Kerr Theatre. The American Society for the Defense of Tradition, Family and Property, a non-profit Catholic organization based in Pennsylvania, objects to the depiction of the mother of Jesus in the play. Numbering about fifty, the group carries banners reading, "Stop blaspheming our Lord NOW!," "We offer God this public act of reparation and vehemently protest against the blasphemous play" and "Blasphemers believe free speech is absolute. But there is no such thing as a right to lie... to defame... to offend God!" The protesters returned periodically, including opening night.

April 1, 2013 Tom Hanks makes his Broadway debut playing newspaper columnist Mike McAlary in the late Nora Ephron's biographical play, *Lucky Guy*.

April 4, 2013 Pop composer/singer Cyndi Lauper makes her Broadway writing debut with an original score for *Kinky Boots*, a musical based on the film about a shoe manufacturer who turns around his fortunes by switching to footwear designed for drag queens. Libretto by Harvey Fierstein. Stars Stark Sands and Billy Porter.

April 7, 2013 A man dressed as Cookie Monster from TV's "Sesame Street"—one of dozens of unauthorized costumed figures who have become ubiquitous in Times Square since it was turned into a pedestrian mall—is arrested and charged with shoving a 2 1/2-year-old child when his parents were too slow to pay a "tip" after being photographed with him. In the

A group protests across the street from the play *The Testament of Mary*. See March 26, 2013.

following weeks, the New York City Council considers a measure to ban or restrict the increasingly aggressive characters.

April 11, 2013 The hit London musical *Matilda*, based on Roald Dahl's book about an abused little girl with a secret power, transfers to Broadway with Bertie Carvel recreating his role as the demonic Miss Trunchbull, and four little girls alternating performances in the title role.

April 14, 2013 The R&B and soul music given mass popularity in the 1960s and 1970s by Berry Gordy's Motown Records is recreated in *Motown*, a revue featuring songs made famous by the likes of The Supremes, Stevie Wonder, the Jackson Five, Marvin Gaye and Smokey Robinson.

April 15, 2013 Nathan Lane stars in *The Nance*, Douglas Carter Beane's new play about a gay comedian in the homophobic world of 1930s Burlesque.

April 15, 2013 Also today, the Off-Broadway play *Disgraced* wins the Pulitzer Prize for Drama.

April 16, 2013 Also today, playwright Clifford Odets gets his second Broadway revival of the season with *The Big Knife*, another of his parables about the corrupting influence of success, this time set in Hollywood. Features Bobby Cannavale, Marin Ireland, Richard Kind and Chip Zien.

April 16, 2013 The concert show *The Rascals: Once Upon a Dream* features music by original members of the 1960s pop group.

April 17, 2013 *The Assembled Parties*, Richard Greenberg's new play about a family's holiday dinner that goes awry, stars Jessica Hecht, Judith Light, Jeremy Shamos and Mark Blum. It's Greenberg's second Broadway opening in a month.

April 18, 2013 Alec Baldwin stars in the Broadway premiere of Lyle Kessler's 1983 drama *Orphans*, about a pair of street kids who kidnap a rich older man. It's also the third show in four days to feature a set by designer John Lee Beatty.

April 18, 2013 Also on this date, Constantine Maroulis and Deborah Cox star in the first Broadway revival of Frank Wildhorn's cult hit musical, *Jekyll & Hyde*. This marks the sixth Broadway opening in five days.

April 21, 2013 Actor Alan Cumming recreates his one-man version of Shakespeare's *Macbeth* following sold-out runs in Scotland and at Lincoln Center.

April 22, 2013 Fiona Shaw stars in *The Testament of Mary*, Colm Tóibín's drama about the life of the Blessed Virgin Mary in the period after the crucifixion of Jesus.

April 23, 2013 Cicely Tyson, Cuba Gooding Jr., Vanessa Williams and Condola Rashad lead the ensemble in a revival of Horton Foote's *The Trip to Bountiful*, about an elderly woman's odyssey to revisit her childhood home.

April 24, 2013 Bette Midler returns to Broadway for the first time in 38 years playing a legendary Hollywood talent agent in John Logan's solo play, *I'll Eat You Last: A Chat with Sue Mengers*.

April 25, 2013 Tony eligibility comes to a close with a revival of the 1972 Stephen Schwartz musical *Pippin*, with circus-themed direction by Diane Paulus.

April 30, 2013 Fans of Bette Midler and Fiona Shaw decry their omission from today's Tony Award nominations. Shaw's play closes May 5.

May 20, 2013 Ambassador Theatre Group, the UK's largest theatre owner/operator announces that it has taken over the lease to Broadway's Foxwoods Theatre, previously held by Live Nation Entertainment. Insiders reported it was a $60 million deal.

May 26, 2013 100th anniversary of the founding of Actors' Equity Association, the national stage actors' union.

May 31, 2013 The aftereffects of Hurricane Sandy are blamed for a decline in both attendance and boxoffice income during the 2012-2013 Broadway season, which ends today. The Broadway League reports that shows sold $1.138 billion worth of tickets, down 0.1 percent from last year's record $1.139 billion. Total attendance was 11.57 million, down 6 percent from the 12.33 million in 2011-2012.

June 9, 2013 The 67th Annual Tony Awards are given at Radio City Music Hall. *Vanya and Sonia and Masha and Spike* is named Best Play and *Kinky Boots* is named Best Musical.

—Robert Viagas

Head of the Class

Trends, Extraordinary Achievements and Peculiar Coincidences of the Season

Most Tony Awards to a Play: (tie) *The Nance* and *Edward Albee's Who's Afraid of Virginia Woolf?* (3).

Most Tony Awards to a Musical: *Kinky Boots* (6).

Shortest Run: *The Performers* (6 performances).

Long Runs Say Farewell: *Mary Poppins* (2619 performances), *War Horse* (718 performances), *Priscilla Queen of the Desert* (526 performances). *Anything Goes* (521 performances).

Stars You Could Have Seen on Broadway This Season: Alec Baldwin, Norbert Leo Butz, Michael Cerveris, Jessica Chastain, James Corden, Alan Cumming, Tom Hanks, Scarlett Johansson, Nathan Lane, Jane Lynch, Constantine Maroulis, Laurie Metcalf, Bette Midler, David Hyde Pierce, Chita Rivera, Fiona Shaw, Sigourney Weaver, among many more.

Kids! At one point during the season, nearly half the shows on Broadway had cast members under the age of 18: *Annie, The Assembled Parties, Cat on a Hot Tin Roof, A Christmas Story, Elf, Kinky Boots, The Lion King, Mary Poppins, Matilda, Motown, The Mystery of Edwin Drood, Newsies, Once, Orphans, Picnic, Pippin.*

Awards They Should Give: #1 Best New Showtune: Our nominees: "When I Grow Up" from *Matilda*, "Joy of the Lord" in *Hands on a Hardbody*, "Sex Is in the Heel" from *Kinky Boots*, "The Life That You Wished For" from *Chaplin*, "You'll Shoot Your Eye Out" from *A Christmas Story.*

"We Are All Shirtless Now" (Men With Their Shirts Off): *Breakfast at Tiffany's; Cat on a Hot Tin Roof; Fela, Ghost; Golden Boy; Kinky Boots; Macbeth; Mamma Mia!; The Nance; Newsies; The Performers, Picnic; Pippin; Scandalous; A Streetcar Named Desire; Vanya and Sonia and Masha and Spike* (but not, for some reason, *Evita*). Honorable mention: Fiona Shaw in *Testament of Mary.*

Live Animals: *Annie* (dog), *Drood* (dog), *A Christmas Story* (dogs), *Breakfast at Tiffany's* (cat), *Pippin* (dog), *The Testament of Mary* (vulture). Honorable Mention: *Cat on a Hot Tin Roof.*

Awards They Should Give: #2 Best Special Effect: Our nominees: Costumes in *Cinderella*, Harvey in *Harvey*, Matilda makes the chalk move with her mind in *Matilda*,

Goodbye Cruel World: Leading man kills himself: *The Big Knife, Jekyll & Hyde, Golden Boy.* Honorable Mention to Show Where Leading Man Is Supposed to Kill Himself But Doesn't: *Pippin.*

Journalists Are Scum: *The Big Knife; Breakfast at Tiffany's; Chaplin; Hands on a Hardbody; I'll Eat You Last; Lucky Guy; Motown; Scandalous.*

Awards They Should Give: #3 Best New Rendition of an Old Song in a Revival or Jukebox Musical: Our nominees: "The Wages of Sin" in *The Mystery of Edwin Drood*, "I Don't Need Anything But You" in *Annie*, "Ten Minutes Ago" in *Cinderella*, "No Time at All" in *Pippin*, "Ain't No Mountain High Enough" in *Motown.*

Times Is Hard (People Desperate for Money) *The Assembled Parties, Chaplin, Hands on a Hardbody, Kinky Boots, Annie, Breakfast at Tiffany's, Cat on a Hot Tin Roof, Matilda, The Trip to Bountiful*

Broadway's Longest Runs

By number of performances
(2,500 or more).
Asterisk (*) indicates show still running
as of May 31, 2013. Totals are for original
runs except where otherwise noted.

**The Phantom of the Opera* 10,543
Cats 7485
*Chicago (Revival) 6869
Les Misérables 6680
*The Lion King 6471
A Chorus Line 6137
Oh! Calcutta! (Revival) 5959
Beauty and the Beast 5461
Rent 5123
**Mamma Mia!* 4819
Miss Saigon 4097
*Wicked 3983
42nd Street 3486
Grease 3388
Fiddler on the Roof 3242
Life With Father 3224
Tobacco Road 3182
*Jersey Boys 3132
Hello, Dolly! 2844
My Fair Lady 2717
Hairspray 2641
Mary Poppins 2619
Avenue Q 2534
The Producers 2502

Footwear Can Change Your Life *Cinderella* (glass slippers), *Kinky Boots* (big red boots), *Wicked* (magic slippers).

Awards They Should Give #4 Best Acting Ensemble: Our nominees: *Hands on a Hardbody*; drag queens in *Kinky Boots;* kids in *Matilda*; the Burlesque troupe in *The Nance.*

Four Hats...and Four Staircases John Lee Beatty designed sets for four new shows, *An Enemy of the People, The Nance, The Big Knife* and *Orphans*, the latter three of which opened within a single four-day period April 15-18, 2013.

Awards They Should Give: #5 Best Dancer: Our nominees: Charlie Sutton in *Kinky Boots*, Luke Spring in *A Christmas Story*, Patina Miller in *Pippin*, Eric LaJuan Summers in *Motown*, Taylor Louderman in *Bring It On.*

Orphans *Annie, Breakfast at Tiffany's, Newsies, Cinderella* and, of course, *Orphans.*

Young Woman Being Oppressed by an Authority Figure: *Wicked, Annie, Matilda, Cinderella*

Awards They Should Give: #6 Best Prop: Our nominees: Leg lamp in *A Christmas Story*, magic coach in *Cinderella*, the big red boots in *Kinky Boots*, giant cake in *Matilda*, big gavel in *The Nance*. the truck in *Hands on a Hardbody.*

Coups de Théâtre: The whole cast of *Kinky Boots* emerges wearing the show's iconic red thigh boots to sing the show's finale. Prompted by her Fairy Godmother, Cinderella whirls at stage center as her plain brown farm dress is transformed into a dazzling white ball gown

---

thanks to designer William Ivey Long's costume magic in *Rodgers + Hammerstein's Cinderella.* As columnist Mike McAlary, Tom Hanks teaches himself how to walk again after a car accident in *Lucky Guy*. Bobby Cannavale slices right through Richard Kind's avuncular manipulation in their Act III confrontation in *The Big Knife*. A late-life suitor calls to ask Kristine Nielsen out and she can't quite remember the right way to respond in the instantly classic "Phone Call Speech" from *Vanya and Sonia and Masha and Spike*. Nine-year-old wunderkind Luke Spring stops the show in *A Christmas Story* with a virtuoso tap break in the song "You'll Shoot Your Eye Out." Andrea Martin stops her own show, *Pippin*, with an unexpectedly expert trapeze turn during the song "No Time at All." Former classical violinist-turned-boxer Seth Numrich emits an eerie laugh when he realizes he has destroyed his hands permanently in *Golden Boy*. Norbert Leo Butz tries to justify embezzling a fortune with a manic speech in *Dead Accounts*. In *Chaplin*, Rob McClure enacts the evening Charlie Chaplin made his first transformation into his immortal screen alter ego, The Little Tramp. Valisia LeKae evolves from a mousy backup singer into the soul diva Diana Ross in *Motown*. Laurie Metcalf is horrified when she realizes that the mysterious bikini blonde in *The Other Place* is the product of her own imagination. Elizabeth Marvel plays a brash older woman in *Picnic*, who, in a private moment, breaks down and begs her longtime boyfriend to marry her. As an elderly exterminator, Ed Asner recalls the nightmare of his youth during the Holocaust in *Grace*. The school kids of *Matilda* spell out the horrors of Crunchem Hall in Tim Minchin's alphabet-based "School Song." Also in *Matilda*, the Hall's chief horror, Miss Trunchbull, leads the kids in a grueling phys-ed workout that ends with a flourish as she performs an acrobatic leap and somersault of her own from a trampoline through a hoop. Acrobatics of a different kind take place in *Macbeth*, where all the characters of Shakespeare's tragedy are embodied by a single patient in a mental institution, played by Alan Cumming, who makes the audience believe he is drowning himself in a tub in the show's finale. Keala Settle starts with a quiet chuckle, and builds to full-out laughter and a show-stopping spiritual "Joy of the Lord" around a shiny new pickup truck in *Hands on a Hardbody*. The first cheerleader is flung skyward in *Bring It On*. The previously unflappable Charles Kimbrough makes his Act II entrance disheveled and wild-eyed after he starts to see for himself the eponymous six-foot rabbit in *Harvey*. Chita Rivera and Nicholas Barasch react when they are elected by the audience as unlikely lovers in *The Mystery of Edwin Drood*. Nathan Lane's little breakdown when he realizes that his self-loathing is costing him the possibility of true love in *The Nance*. The audience is invited onstage to view Fiona Shaw posing behind glass as a living embodiment of the traditional Blessed Virgin Mary—an image she will later demolish in *The Testament of Mary.*

The Anarchist

First Preview: November 13, 2012. Opened: December 2, 2012.
Closed December 16, 2012 after 23 Previews and 17 Performances.

David Mamet's sixty-five-minute drama presents a battle of wits between a long-imprisoned and supposedly reformed 1960s domestic terrorist and the authority figure she hopes will finally set her free. The play becomes a personal portrait of two women on different kinds of spiritual quests. But is the anarchist's jailhouse embrace of Jesus real? Or is it just another mask she has assumed in a very long game?

CAST

Cathy ....PATTI LuPONE
Ann ....DEBRA WINGER

UNDERSTUDY
GORDANA RASHOVICH

⊛ GOLDEN THEATRE
A Shubert Organization Theatre
Philip J. Smith, *Chairman*   Robert E. Wankel, *President*

JEFFREY RICHARDS   JERRY FRANKEL   HOWARD & JANET KAGAN

CATHERINE SCHREIBER   JAM THEATRICALS

LUIGI & ROSE CAIOLA   GUTTERMAN CHERNOFF MXKC   KIT SEIDEL   BROADWAY ACROSS AMERICA

AMY & PHIL MICKELSON   JAMES FULD JR.   CARLOS ARANA/BARD THEATRICALS   WILL TRICE

PRESENT

PATTI LUPONE   DEBRA WINGER

IN

THE ANARCHIST

WRITTEN AND DIRECTED BY

DAVID MAMET

SCENIC & COSTUME DESIGN
PATRIZIA VON BRANDENSTEIN

LIGHTING DESIGN
JEFF CROITER

PRODUCTION STAGE MANAGER
WILLIAM JOSEPH BARNES

CASTING
**TELSEY + COMPANY
WILLIAM CANTLER, C.S.A.**
AND
SHARON BIALY & SHERRY THOMAS, C.S.A.

TECHNICAL SUPERVISION
**HUDSON THEATRICAL
ASSOCIATES**

PRESS REPRESENTATIVE
IRENE GANDY/ALANA KARPOFF

COMPANY MANAGER
JENNIFER HINDMAN KEMP

GENERAL MANAGER
RICHARDS/CLIMAN, INC.

The Producers wish to express their appreciation to the Theatre Development Fund for its support of this production.

THEANARCHISTBROADWAY.COM

12/2/12

SETTING
An office

Patti LuPone
as Cathy

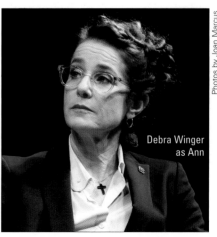

Debra Winger
as Ann

Photos by Joan Marcus

The Anarchist

Patti LuPone
Cathy

Debra Winger
Ann

Gordana Rashovich
Understudy

David Mamet
Playwright/Director

Patrizia von
Brandenstein
*Scenic and
Costume Designer*

Jeff Croiter
Lighting Designer

Bernard Telsey
Telsey + Company
Casting

Sharon Bialy/Sherry Thomas
Casting

Neil A. Mazzella
Hudson Theatrical
Associates
*Technical
Supervision*

Kathy Fabian
Props Coordinator

David R. Richards
Richards/Climan, Inc.
General Manager

Tamar Haimes
Richards/Climan, Inc.
General Manager

Jeffrey Richards
Producer

Jerry Frankel
Producer

Howard & Janet Kagan
Producer

Catherine Schreiber
Producer

Arny Granat
Jam Theatricals
Producer

Steve Traxler
Jam Theatricals
Producer

Luigi and Rose Caiola
Producers

Jay Gutterman
Producer

Cindy Gutterman
Producer

Cathy Chernoff
Producer

Kit Seidel
Producer

John Gore
CEO
Broadway Across
America
Producer

Thomas B. McGrath
Chairman
Broadway Across
America
Producer

James Fuld, Jr.
Producer

Carlos Arana
Producer

Annette Jolles
Bard Theatricals
Producer

Jim van Bergen
Bard Theatricals
Producer

Laurence Holzman
Bard Theatricals
Producer

Lara Holzman
Bard Theatricals
Producer

The Anarchist

David Stern
Bard Theatricals
Producer

Linda Hamil
Bard Theatricals
Producer

Will Trice
Producer

CREW
(L-R): Maeve Fiona Butler (Dresser to Patti LuPone),
Brendan O'Neal (Hair/Wig Supervisor)

CREW
(L-R): Tommy Mitchell, William Joseph Barnes (Production Stage Manager), Ashley Singh,
Chris Zaccardi (Stage Manager), Terry McGarty, Sylvia Yoshioka, Brad Gyorgak

STAGE DOOR
John Green

FRONT OF HOUSE
Front Row (L-R): Sheila Staffney, Cookie Harlin, Julia Gonzales
Back Row (L-R): Pat Byrne, Andrew Sanford, Karen Banyai, Helen Bentley

BOX OFFICE
(L-R): Chip Jorgensen, Gary Powers

The Anarchist
SCRAPBOOK

At a press conference (L-R): Patti LuPone and Debra Winger

STAFF FOR *THE ANARCHIST*

GENERAL MANAGEMENT
RICHARDS/CLIMAN, INC.
David R. Richards   Tamar Haimes
Michael Sag   Kyle Bonder
Jessica Fried   Ashley Rodbro

COMPANY MANAGER
Jennifer Hindman Kemp

GENERAL PRESS REPRESENTATIVE
JEFFREY RICHARDS ASSOCIATES
Irene Gandy   Alana Karpoff
Thomas Raynor   Christopher Pineda
Laura Kaplow-Goldman

TECHNICAL SUPERVISION
HUDSON THEATRICAL ASSOCIATES
Neil A. Mazzella   Sam Ellis
Caitlin McInerney   Irene Wang

CASTING
TELSEY + COMPANY
Bernie Telsey CSA, Will Cantler CSA,
David Vaccari CSA, Bethany Knox CSA,
Craig Burns CSA, Tiffany Little Canfield CSA,
Rachel Hoffman CSA, Justin Huff CSA,
Patrick Goodwin CSA, Abbie Brady-Dalton CSA,
David Morris, Cesar A. Rocha,
Andrew Femenella, Karyn Casl,
Kristina Bramhall, Jessie Malone

Production Stage Manager ....William Joseph Barnes
Stage Manager ....Chris Zaccardi
Assistants to the Director ....Justin Fair, Eli Linnetz
Assistant Scenic Designer ....Fredda Slavin
Assistant Costume Designer ....Aileen Abercrombie
Associate Lighting Designer ....Wilburn Bonnell
Assistant to the Lighting Designer ....Ken Wills
Bialy/Thomas Casting Associate ....Gohar Gazayan

Production Carpenter ....Terry McGarty
Production Electrician ....James Maloney
Props Coordinator ....Kathy Fabian/Propstar
Associate Props Coordinators ....John Estep,
Carrie Mossman
Make-up Designer ....Angelina Avallone
Wardrobe Supervisor/Dresser
to Debra Winger ....Mary Ann Oberpriller
Dresser to Patti LuPone ....Maeve Fiona Butler
Hair/Wig Supervisor ....Brendan O'Neal
Production Assistants ....Rebecca Esquivel,
Ashley Singh
Assistant Producers ....Michael Crea, PJ Miller
Advertising & Marketing ....aka/Elizabeth Furze,
Scott A. Moore, Melissa Marano,
Bashan Aquart, Adam Jay,
Janette Roush, Jennifer Sims,
Trevor Sponseller, Sara Rosenzweig,
Danielle Barchetto
Digital Marketing Strategy ....Tomris Laffly,
Flora Pei
Interactive Marketing
Service ....Broadway's Best Shows/
Andy Drachenberg, Steven Strauss,
Layne McNish
Merchandise ....Max Merchandising, LLC
Producing Assistant ....Wally Hays
General Management Interns ....Rose Bochner,
Joanna Levinger
Banking ....City National Bank/
Michele Gibbons, Erik Piecuch
Insurance ....DeWitt Stern Group/
Peter Shoemaker, Anthony Pittari
Accountants ....Fried & Kowgios CPAs LLP
Comptroller ....Elliott Aronstam
Legal Counsel ....Lazarus and Harris LLP/
Scott Lazarus, Esq., Robert C. Harris, Esq.
Payroll..............................Castellana Services, Inc.
Production Photographers ....Brigitte Lacombe,
Joan Marcus
Company Mascots ....Skye, Franco

CREDITS
Scenery constructed by Hudson Scenic Studio, Inc. Lighting equipment by Hudson Sound & Light, LLC. Sound equipment by Sound Associates. Costumes built by Euroco. Shoes by Oscar Navarro. Patti LuPone's wig by Paul Huntley. Debra Winger's hairstyle by Toni Ann Walker.

Rehearsed at the Davenport Studios, the Ruskin Theatre and the New 42nd Street Studios

Special thanks to
Peter Fitzgerald and American Airlines

THE SHUBERT ORGANIZATION, INC.
Board of Directors

Philip J. Smith	**Robert E. Wankel**
Chairman	President
Wyche Fowler, Jr.	**Diana Phillips**
Lee J. Seidler	**Michael I. Sovern**

Stuart Subotnick

Chief Financial Officer ....Elliot Greene
Sr. Vice President, Ticketing ....David Andrews
Vice President, Finance ....Juan Calvo
Vice President, Human Resources ....Cathy Cozens
Vice President, Facilities ....John Darby
Vice President, Theatre Operations ....Peter Entin
Vice President, Marketing ....Charles Flateman
Vice President, Audit ....Anthony LaMattina
Vice President, Ticket Sales ....Brian Mahoney
Vice President, Creative Projects ...........D.S. Moynihan
Vice President, Real Estate ....Julio Peterson

House Manager ....Carolyne A. Jones-Barnes

Ann

First Preview: February 18, 2013. Opened: March 7, 2013.
Still running as of May 31, 2013.

Actress Holland Taylor wrote and starred in this more-or-less solo portrait of onetime Texas governor Ann Richards. With a halo of white hair and a good-old-girl tough love, Richards was a gritty progressive who was elected boss of her conservative state from 1991 to 1995 after gaining national stature at the 1988 Democratic convention. The play shows her addressing a college graduating class, and fielding overlapping personal and political phone calls at the governor's desk in Austin.

CAST

Ann Richards ....HOLLAND TAYLOR
Voice of Nancy Kohler ....JULIE WHITE

SETTING

ACT ONE

The school auditorium at an imaginary college
in the middle of Texas.
The Present.

ACT TWO

The same.

VIVIAN BEAUMONT THEATER

Bob Boyett   Harriet Newman Leve
Jane Dubin   Jack Thomas/Mark Johannes and Amy Danis
Sarahbeth Grossman   Jon Cryer/Lisa Joyner   Minerva Productions   Lary Brandt/Brian Dorsey
Kate Hathaway/Allison Thomas   Jennifer Isaacson   Kevin Bailey

IN ASSOCIATION WITH
Lincoln Center Theater

PRESENT

Holland Taylor

IN

SCENIC DESIGNER	COSTUME DESIGNER	LIGHTING DESIGNER	SOUND DESIGNER	PROJECTION DESIGNER
Michael Fagin	Julie Weiss	Matthew Richards	Ken Huncovsky	Zachary Borovay

WIG DESIGNER	PRESS REPRESENTATIVE	PRODUCTION MANAGER	PRODUCTION STAGE MANAGER
Paul Huntley	The Hartman Group	Peter Fulbright	J. P. Elins

MARKETING	ADVERTISING	GENERAL MANAGEMENT
Leanne Schanzer Promotions, Inc.	SpotCo	101 Productions, Ltd.

ASSOCIATE PRODUCERS
Colleen Barrett   Francesca Zambello and Faith Gay   Nancy T. Beren/Patrick Terry
Marcy Adelman/Paula Kaminsky Davis   Campbell Spencer/Gasparian Suisman   Bonnie Levinson

WRITTEN BY
Holland Taylor

DIRECTED BY
Benjamin Endsley Klein

The Producers wish to express their appreciation to Theatre Development Fund for its support of this production.

3/7/13

Holland Taylor as
Ann Richards

Photo by Ave Bonar

Ann

There is no way to convey my love and appreciation for the hundred or so friends, associates and members of Ann Richards' family who helped me understand her in a way that would have been utterly impossible without them.

I was compelled to write this play…the notion to do it at all, the idea for *how* to write it — its shape and style — came all in a rush, leaving me wide-eyed with surprise. And in I plunged. During the darkest hours of trying to shape a tumultuous mountain of material, in a daydream I would see Ann in the fifth row, beaming happily and elbowing our mutual old friend, Liz Smith. Six years of work later, I have made a journey I could never have imagined. But I went in whole hog, and stayed in — working hard and doing the best I could — which gave me a hint of how I'll bet Ann Richards felt every single day.

I hope Ann would like this. People loved to please her…one of her children said to please her was to get hit with a million suns. So, of course, now I want to please her, too.

Texans have welcomed me in my endeavor, which I find incredibly generous

Governor Ann Richards
September 1, 1933 – September 13, 2006

(Yankee that I am), and I will always be grateful for their affection and fun and open hearts.

As this is a piece of writing based on research, I should say something about the text itself. I had intended by now to annotate it, to say who told the story something was based on, what chunk was cobbled from this, what sliver was taken from that and what large sections were stitched up out of whole cloth, though based on sure and certain knowledge of my subject. But, of course, the tide sweeps me along, and I haven't done that yet. (I never did master footnotes in school.)

Most of the play is based on years of overlapping stories told me in significant detail, including fragments of fabulous dialogue, by the players themselves.

The office scenes in the play have been created based on many, many anecdotes and, in some areas, profound and lengthy study — though the play's ending, for obvious reasons, is purely a dream — about someone I do think of now as a friend I know pretty well, and love.

Holland Taylor

Holland Taylor
Ann Richards and Playwright

Julie White
Voice of Nancy Kohler

Benjamin Endsley Klein
Director

Ken Huncovsky
Sound Designer

Zachary Borovay
Projection Designer

Julie Weiss
Costume Design

Paul Huntley
Wig Design and Fabrication

Wendy Orshan
101 Productions, Ltd.
General Management

Kevin Bailey
Executive Producer

Sandra Castellanos
Consultant

Barbara Chapman
Consultant

Ave Bonar
Documentary Photographer

Bob Boyett
Producer

Harriet Newman Leve
Producer

Ann

Jack Thomas
Co-Producer

Mark Johannes
Mars Theatricals
Co-Producers

Amy Danis
Mars Theatricals
Co-Producers

Sarahbeth Grossman
Co-Producer

Jon Cryer
Co-Producer

Lisa Joyner
Co-Producer

Anne O'Shea
Minerva Productions
LLC
Co-Producer

Lary Brandt
Co-Producer

Brian Dorsey
Co-Producer

Kate Hathaway
Co-Producer

Allison Thomas
Co-Producer

Jennifer Isaacson
Co-Producer

André Bishop
*Artistic Director
Lincoln Center
Theater*

Bernard Gersten
*Artistic Director
Lincoln Center
Theater*

Colleen Barrett
Associate Producer

Francesca Zambello
Associate Producer

Faith Gay
Associate Producer

Nancy T. Beren
Associate Producer

Marcy Adelman
Associate Producer

Paula Kaminsky
Davis
Associate Producer

Elsa Suisman
Associate Producer

CREW
Sitting: J.P. Elins (Production Stage Manager)
Standing (L-R): Ray Skillin, Brant Underwood, Karl Rausenberger, Robert Tolaro (Stage Manager), Joe Pizzuto, Bill Nagle, Bruce Rubin, John Weingart

Ann

FRONT OF HOUSE
Front Row (L-R): Amy Yedowitz, Barbara Hart,
Denise Bergen, Donna Zurich
Second Row (L-R): Paula Gallo-Kcira, Diana Lounsbury,
Susan Lehman, Eleanor Rooks
Third Row (L-R): Mildred Terrero, Jeff Goldstein,
Margie Blair, Bru Dye
Fourth Row (L-R): Rheba Flegelman, Catherine Thorpe,
Nick Andors, Steve Bratton, Officer Charles
Top Row (L-R): Judith Fanelli, Philip Condenzio

WARDROBE SUPERVISOR
Barry Doss

STAFF FOR *ANN*

GENERAL MANAGEMENT
101 PRODUCTIONS, LTD.
Wendy Orshan   Jeffrey M. Wilson
Elie Landau
Ron Gubin
Chris Morey

COMPANY MANAGER
Thom Clay

GENERAL PRESS REPRESENTATIVE
THE HARTMAN GROUP
Michael Hartman   Wayne Wolfe
Nicole Capatasto

PRODUCTION MANAGEMENT
TECH PRODUCTION SERVICES, INC.
Peter Fulbright   Mary Duffe
Shaminda Amarakoon   Zoe Hoarty

Production Stage Manager .........................J.P. Elins
Stage Manager ....Robert Tolaro

Associate Scenic Designer ....Michael Carnahan
Assistant Scenic Designer ....Aimee Dombo
Associate Sound Designer ....David Sanderson
Associate
    Lighting Designer ....G. Benjamin Swope
Associate Projection Designer ....Daniel Vatsky
Assistant Projection Designer ....Driscoll Otto

Production Carpenter ....Bill Nagle
Production Electrician ....Pat Merryman
Production Props ....Karl Rausenberger
Production Sound ....Adam Smolenski
Wardrobe Supervisor ....Barry Doss
Hair Supervisor ....Cindy Demand

Legal Counsel ....Lazarus & Harris LLP/
                                          Scott Lazarus, Esq.,
                                          Robert C. Harris, Esq.
Accountant ....Rosenberg, Neuwirth &
                                          Kuchner/Chris Cacace,
                                          Jana Jevnikar,
                                          Ruthie Wagh
Payroll Services ....Castellana Services, Inc.

Banking ....City National Bank/
                                          Anne McSweeney
Insurance ....Dewitt Stern Group/
                                          Peter Shoemaker
Assistant to Ms. Taylor ....Jeremiah Maestas
101 Productions, Ltd. Staff ....Beth Blitzer,
                                          Kathy Kim, Mike McLinden,
                                          Michael Rudd, Mary-Six Rupert,
                                          Steve Supeck
101 Productions,
    Ltd. Interns ....Serene Lim, Caroline Watters
Production Photographer ....Ave Bonar
Dramaturg ....Stephanie Faracy
Dialect Coach ....Jessica Drake
Advertising ....SpotCo/Drew Hodges,
                                          Jim Edwards, Tom Greenwald,
                                          Beth Watson, Ryan Zatcoff
Website Design/
    Interactive Marketing ....SpotCo/
                                          Sheila Collins, Marc Mettler,
                                          Kristen Bardwill, Callie Goff,
                                          Shelby Ladd, Amanda Baker,
                                          Rebecca Cohen

Ann

SCRAPBOOK

Correspondents: Benjamin Endsley Klein (Director) and Holland Taylor, "Ann"

Opening Night Party Gifts: Party for five hundred souls in honor of Ann Richards and *Ann* the Play at the PLAZA HOTEL!

The play and life and duties took off at such a wild pace that I haven't even opened all the first night presents and letters yet. (Not complaining. I'll get there, and all "thank yous," too, when the creek goes down.)

Director Benjamin Endsley Klein gave everyone *Ann*-engraved boot jacks (special tool for pulling off your cowboy boots).

Most Exciting Celebrity Visitors: Bill Clinton, Hillary Clinton, Gabby Giffords, Mark Kelly (her astronaut husband), and Meryl Streep. All on the same night! There have been many others, but this evening was extra special.

My favorite, really, was Meryl. How could she not be? Well, she and my darling Tom Hanks, who came to an audience-filled dress rehearsal. Tom thrilled me with his excitement—and Meryl thrilled me by holding my arms as I held hers (as I later noted in pictures taken) as we talked about...acting. And about the enormous honor, glory, and burden of playing an actual person... a person of SIZE and depth. Actually we talked a lot. I'll never get over it. Lucky me.

Special Backstage Rituals: I make the same four requests of the universe every single performance of *Ann*, as I wait in the dark, up on a platform, to begin the Keynote—my face only inches away from the scrim.

Memorable Press Encounter: Holland's interview with Wayne Slater, great Dallas Morning News journalist who covered Ann Richards and was her friend.

Memorable Stage Door Fan Encounter: A man waited a very long time on a freezing night having just seen the show after driving a long haul from Massachusetts. He was wearing what appeared to be hunting gear and flannel plaid pants and boots and a deer stalker.

Favorite Moment During Each Performance: In this play? Every moment. All moments.

Memorable Directorial Note: "Be brave."—Mr. Directly (a.k.a. Benjamin Endsley Klein).

Company In-Jokes: April Fools joke on Holland (and others) where the "understudy" auditions were announced in the post show report.

I was completely snookered by this and will not live it down. Why would I want to?

Favorite In-Theatre Gathering Place: We have hardly slowed down to sit anywhere.

Favorite Off-Site Hangout: Bar Centrale.

Favorite Snack Food: I eat so healthily that it's revolting. My big cheat? Carrot cake, serious butter icing.

Mascot: Sandra Castellanos. Ann Richards' executive assistant during her New York years. Keeps coming back and coming back. Ushers just show her to her usual seat.

Favorite Therapy: ALLLL of 'em. NO time for massage... need to be on damn computer too much. Live two blocks from Central Park, and now that spring is sneaking in, I WILL make time to walk there. One of the glories of life in New York.

Most Memorable Ad-Lib: "I'm the Boss of the Applesauce." I'm allowed to ad lib. I do so with caution, when I have a light bulb moment. About half the time, I keep them in.

Record Number of Cell Phone Rings, Cell Phone Photos, Tweeting or Texting Incidents During a Performance: Vaguely heard two or three rings... saw a few screens texting a few times. If anyone does that up front, close enough to me—he/she will get the surprise of his/her life.

Ghostly Encounters Backstage: Once in a rare while I feel Ann drift by me. Such a brief, dimly felt moment. Hell, if she did any more than that I would be wobbly. She knows best. And no, I'm neither religious, nor spiritual, nor woo-woo.

Superstitions That Turned Out to Be True: That a special star shone on this play from day one, six years ago.

What Did You Think of the Web Buzz on Your Show: I have a lot of fun on Twitter and the responses there are fantastic.

Fastest Costume Change: Ann's change from the opening keynote speech blue dress to Ann's white suit she wears for the rest of the show. It happens in seconds flat. Most people don't even believe that Holland does the keynote speech live because the illusion is so great, but also because the change seems impossible. But thanks to Barry Doss (wardrobe supervisor) it is possible and wonderful!

Catchphrase Only the Company Would Recognize: "Well, shit, Nancy."

Company Legends: We're working on it.

Understudy Anecdote: Oh, God. Don't start. (See Company In-jokes.)

Coolest Thing About Being In This Show: Well...just that—Being in this show. With Julie White as Ann's secretary. Acting with Julie is a joy and she is a living being WITH me, up there...just snap! And, man, she ALWAYS gets her laughs.

2012-2013 AWARD

OUTER CRITICS CIRCLE AWARD
Outstanding Solo Performance
(Holland Taylor)

Marketing . . . . SpotCo/Nick Pramik,
Kristen Rathbun, Julie Wechsler
Marketing . . . . Leanne Schanzer Promotions, Inc./
Leanne Schanzer, Justin Schanzer,
Kara Laviola, Michael Schanzer,
Chelsey Berger, Ekaterina Zaitseva
Housing Coordination . . . . Maison International/
Marie-Claire Martineau
Community Outreach . . . . Donna Walker-Kuhne
Assistant to Mr. Boyett . . . . Diane Murphy
Assistant to Ms. Leve . . . . Caitlin Clements
Theatre Displays . . . . King Displays/
Wayne Snapper
Tour Booking . . . . Broadway Booking Office/
Steve Schnepp, Temah Higgins

LINCOLN CENTER THEATER

André Bishop, *Artistic Director*
Bernard Gersten, *Executive Producer*
Adam Siegel, *Managing Director*
Jeff Hamlin, *Production Manager*
Hattie Jutagir, *Executive Director of*
Development & Planning
David Brown, *Director of Finance*
Linda Mason Ross, *Director of Marketing*
Jessica Niebanck, *General Manager*

Manager . . . . Rheba Flegelman
Box Office Treasurer . . . . Fred Bonis
Assistant Treasurer . . . . Bob Belkin

CREDITS

Scenery fabrication by PRG-Scenic Technologies, a division of Production Resource Group, LLC, New Windsor, NY. Lighting equipment from PRG Lighting. Sound equipment from Masque Sound. Video projection system engineered and provided by Worldstage. Props by Dove Huntley and Rob Corn.

The production acknowledges and thanks Alan Pogue for use of the final photographic image, "Ann Richards, Serenity."

The production greatly acknowledges the support of the Dolph Briscoe Center for American History for the usage of archival photographs.

The Ann Richards School for Young Women Leaders is a unique all-girls public school founded to educate young women and give them the confidence and skills necessary to succeed in college, in their careers and in their communities. Our mission is to prepare young women to attend and graduate from college, commit to a healthy and well-balanced lifestyle, lead with courage and compassion and solve problems creatively and ethically in support of our global community. Donate, volunteer, or learn more at www.annrichardsschool.org

SPECIAL THANKS

Lynne Fredrichsen, Miles Marek, Rich Affannato, Doug Suisman, Moye Thompson, Deborah Taylor, JoDee Winterhof, Shamina Singh, Ann Mound, Emily Conner, Margery Tabankin, Laura Wagner, Michele Crowley, Martha Blalock, Christine Delucchi, Kim Hoover, Lynn Hackney, Ashley Bell, Andrea Sharrin, Mary Tucker, Amy S. Layton

We would like to thank our *ANN* Ambassadors for their continued enthusiasm and support:
Atiba Moss, Deborah Parchment, Kaz Mitchell, Kwame Jackson, Laurence Pinckney, Lori Armstrong, Lynn Rutledge, Marci McCall, Marguerite Greene, Norma Jean Darden, Princess Jenkins, Gwendolyn Quinn, Randreta Ward-Evans, Sandy Berger.

Annie

First Preview: October 3, 2012. Opened: November 8, 2012.
Still running as of May 31, 2013.

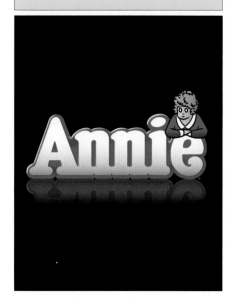

Red-headed moppet Annie suffers through life at an oppressive Depression-era orphanage run by the tyrannical Miss Hannigan. Through a lucky break Annie is chosen to spend Christmas with billionaire Oliver Warbucks, who develops a strong affection for the child and decides he wants to adopt her. She resists, insisting that her parents are alive somewhere. Miss Hannigan and her crooked brother Rooster concoct a scheme to pretend to be Annie's folks, with the aim of collecting money from Warbucks and then killing Annie. Their plot is foiled and Annie is saved—only to learn that the FBI has discovered her parents are no longer living. Warbucks steps up and adopts Annie, at last becoming her "Daddy Warbucks."

CAST
(in order of appearance)

Annie	LILLA CRAWFORD
Molly	EMILY ROSENFELD
Pepper	GEORGI JAMES
Duffy	TAYLOR RICHARDSON
July	MADI RAE DiPIETRO
Tessie	JUNAH JANG
Kate	TYRAH SKYE ODOMS
Miss Hannigan	KATIE FINNERAN
Bundles	JEREMY DAVIS
Apple Seller	JANE BLASS
Dog Catcher	GAVIN LODGE
Asst. Dog Catcher	RYAN VANDENBOOM
Stray Dog	CASEY
Sandy	SUNNY
Lt. Ward	DENNIS STOWE
Eddie	JEREMY DAVIS
Sophie the Kettle	AMANDA LEA LaVERGNE

Continued on next page

PALACE THEATRE
UNDER THE DIRECTION OF
STEWART F. LANE, JAMES M. NEDERLANDER AND JAMES L. NEDERLANDER

Arielle Tepper Madover   Roger Horchow   Sally Horchow   Roger Berlind   Roy Furman
Debbie Bisno   Stacey Mindich   James M. Nederlander
Jane Bergère/Daryl Roth   Eva Price/Christina Papagjika

PRESENT

Annie
THE MUSICAL

BOOK BY	MUSIC BY	LYRICS BY
Thomas Meehan	Charles Strouse	Martin Charnin

BASED ON THE COMIC STRIP "LITTLE ORPHAN ANNIE" BY HAROLD GRAY
"ANNIE" AND "LITTLE ORPHAN ANNIE" USED BY PERMISSION OF TRIBUNE MEDIA SERVICES, INC.

STARRING

Katie Finneran   Anthony Warlow
AND
Lilla Crawford

WITH

Brynn O'Malley   Clarke Thorell   J. Elaine Marcos

AND

Madi Rae DiPietro   Georgi James   Junah Jang   Tyrah Skye Odoms
Taylor Richardson   Emily Rosenfeld   Sadie Sink   Jaidyn Young

Ashley Blanchet   Jane Blass   Jeremy Davis   Merwin Foard   Joel Hatch   Fred Inkley
Amanda Lea LaVergne   Gavin Lodge   Liz McCartney   Desi Oakley   Keven Quillon
David Rossetti   Sarah Solie   Dennis Stowe   Ryan VanDenBoom

SCENIC DESIGN	COSTUME DESIGN	LIGHTING DESIGN	SOUND DESIGN
David Korins	Susan Hilferty	Donald Holder	Brian Ronan

PROJECTION DESIGN	HAIR DESIGN	ANIMAL TRAINER	CASTING
Wendall K. Harrington	Tom Watson	William Berloni	Telsey + Company Patrick Goodwin, CSA

MUSIC DIRECTOR & VOCAL ARRANGEMENTS	ORCHESTRATIONS	DANCE MUSIC ARRANGEMENTS	MUSIC COORDINATOR
Todd Ellison	Michael Starobin	Alex Lacamoire	Patrick Vaccariello

ADVERTISING	PRESS REPRESENTATIVE	MARKETING	SPONSORSHIP	EXECUTIVE PRODUCER
Serino/Coyne	Boneau/Bryan-Brown	bdb marketing	Rose Polidoro	101 Productions, Ltd.

PRODUCTION SUPERVISOR	PRODUCTION MANAGER	ASSOCIATE DIRECTOR	ASSOCIATE CHOREOGRAPHER	COMPANY MANAGER
Peter Lawrence	David Benken	Mark Schneider	Rachel Bress	Heidi Neven

CHOREOGRAPHY BY
Andy Blankenbuehler

DIRECTED BY
James Lapine

ORIGINALLY PRODUCED BY THE GOODSPEED OPERA HOUSE
MICHAEL P. PRICE, EXECUTIVE PRODUCER

11/8/12

Lilla Crawford as Annie
with Sunny as Sandy

Photo by Joan Marcus

Annie

MUSICAL NUMBERS

ACT I

OVERTURE

"Maybe" ....Annie
"It's the Hard Knock Life" ....Annie, Orphans
"It's the Hard Knock Life" (Reprise) ....Orphans
"Tomorrow" ....Annie
"We'd Like to Thank You" ....Annie, Ensemble
"Little Girls" ....Miss Hannigan
"Little Girls" (Reprise) ....Miss Hannigan
"I Think I'm Gonna Like It Here" ....Annie, Grace, Ensemble
"N.Y.C." ....Oliver Warbucks, Grace, Annie, Lily, Ensemble
"Easy Street" ....Miss Hannigan, Rooster, Lily
"You Won't Be an Orphan for Long" ....Oliver Warbucks, Grace, Annie, Ensemble

ACT II

ENTR'ACTE

"Maybe" (Reprise) ....Annie
"You're Never Fully Dressed Without a Smile" ....Bert Healy, The Boylan Sisters
"You're Never Fully Dressed Without a Smile" (Reprise) ....Orphans
"Easy Street" (Reprise) ....Miss Hannigan, Rooster, Lily
"Tomorrow" (Reprise) ....Annie, Oliver Warbucks, F.D.R., Cabinet
"Something Was Missing" ....Oliver Warbucks
"Annie" ....Grace, Ensemble
"I Don't Need Anything But You"* ....Annie, Oliver Warbucks, Grace, Ensemble
"Maybe" (Reprise) ....Annie
"New Deal for Christmas" ....Annie, Oliver Warbucks, Grace, Orphans, Ensemble

ORCHESTRA

Conductor:
TODD ELLISON
Associate Conductor:
JOEY CHANCEY
Reed 1:
STEVE KENYON
Reed 2:
DAVID YOUNG
Reed 3:
DAVE NOLAND
Reed 4:
RONALD JANELLI
Lead Trumpet:
TREVOR NEUMANN
Trumpets:
SCOTT WENDHOLT, EARL GARDNER
Trombone:
MARK PATTERSON
Bass Trombone:
JEFF NELSON
Guitar/Banjo:
SCOTT KUNEY
Bass:
DAVE KUHN

Drums:
ERIC POLAND
Percussion:
JOE NERO
Piano/Keyboard:
JOEY CHANCEY
Keyboard 2/Accordion:
MAGGIE TORRE
Violin:
SEAN CARNEY
Cello:
DIANE BARERE
Music Coordinator:
PATRICK VACCARIELLO

Music Copying: Emily Grishman Music Preparation
EMILY GRISHMAN/KATHARINE EDMONDS

Keyboard Programmer: RANDY COHEN

Additional Orchestrations by
DOUG BESTERMAN* and ALEX LACAMOIRE

Cast Continued

Grace Farrell ....BRYNN O'MALLEY
Drake ....JOEL HATCH
Mrs. Greer ....JANE BLASS
Mrs. Pugh ....LIZ McCARTNEY
Cecile ....ASHLEY BLANCHET
Annette................................SARAH SOLIE
Oliver Warbucks ....ANTHONY WARLOW
Star to Be ....ASHLEY BLANCHET
Rooster Hannigan ....CLARKE THORELL
Lily ....J. ELAINE MARCOS
Bert Healy ....JEREMY DAVIS
Fred McCracken ....JOEL HATCH
Jimmy Johnson ....DENNIS STOWE
Sound Effects Man ....KEVEN QUILLON
Bonnie Boylan ....SARAH SOLIE
Connie Boylan ....AMANDA LEA LaVERGNE
Ronnie Boylan ....ASHLEY BLANCHET
Ickes ....GAVIN LODGE
Perkins ....JANE BLASS
Hull ....JEREMY DAVIS
Morganthau ....DENNIS STOWE
F.D.R. ....MERWIN FOARD
Howe ....KEVEN QUILLON
Judge Brandeis ....GAVIN LODGE

UNDERSTUDIES

For Annie: TAYLOR RICHARDSON
For Warbucks: MERWIN FOARD, JOEL HATCH
For Miss Hannigan: JANE BLASS,
        LIZ McCARTNEY
For Grace: AMANDA LEA LaVERGNE,
        DESI OAKLEY
For Rooster: JEREMY DAVIS, DAVID ROSSETTI
For Lily: ASHLEY BLANCHET, DESI OAKLEY
For Kate: MADI RAE DiPIETRO
For Molly: JUNAH JANG,
        TYRAH SKYE ODOMS
For Sandy: CASEY

SWINGS

FRED INKLEY, DESI OAKLEY,
DAVID ROSSETTI

Dance Captain: DAVID ROSSETTI

Standby for Annie, Pepper, Duffy, July & Tessie:
JAIDYN YOUNG

Standby for Annie, Tessie, Duffy, July & Kate:
SADIE SINK

Anthony Warlow is appearing with the permission of
Actors' Equity Association.

SETTING

New York City, December 1933

Annie

Katie Finneran
Miss Hannigan

Anthony Warlow
Oliver Warbucks

Lilla Crawford
Annie

Brynn O'Malley
Grace Farrell

Clarke Thorell
Rooster Hannigan

J. Elaine Marcos
Lily

Madi Rae DiPietro
July

Georgi James
Pepper

Junah Jang
Tessie

Tyrah Skye Odoms
Kate

Taylor Richardson
Duffy, u/s Annie

Emily Rosenfeld
Molly

Sadie Sink
Standby for Annie, Tessie, Duffy, July & Kate

Jaidyn Young
Standby for Annie, Pepper, Duffy, July, & Tessie

Sunny
Sandy

Ashley Blanchet
Cecile, Star to Be, Ronnie Boylan

Jane Blass
Apple Seller, Mrs. Greer, Perkins

Jeremy Davis
Bundles, Bert Healy, Hull, Eddie

Merwin Foard
F.D.R.

Joel Hatch
Drake, Fred McCracken

Fred Inkley
Swing, u/s FDR, Drake

Amanda Lea LaVergne
Connie Boylan, Sophie the Kettle; u/s Grace

Gavin Lodge
Dog Catcher, Ickes, Judge Brandeis

Liz McCartney
Mrs. Pugh

Desi Oakley
Swing; u/s Grace, Lily

Keven Quillon
Sound Effects Man, Howe

David Rossetti
Swing; u/s Rooster

Sarah Solie
Annette, Bonnie Boylan

Dennis Stowe
Lt. Ward, Jimmy Johnson, Morganthau

Ryan VanDenBoom
Asst. Dog Catcher

Casey
Stray Dog, u/s Sandy

Thomas Meehan
Book

Charles Strouse
Music

Martin Charnin
Lyrics

James Lapine
Director

Annie

Andy Blankenbuehler
Choreographer

Todd Ellison
Music Director/Vocal Arrangements

David Korins
Set Design

Susan Hilferty
Costume Design

Donald Holder
Lighting Design

Brian Ronan
Sound Design

Wendall K. Harrington
Projecton Design

Tom Watson
Hair Design

Ashley Ryan
Make-up Design

William Berloni
Animal Trainer

Michael Starobin
Orchestrations

Alex Lacamoire
Dance Music Arrangements

Patrick Vaccariello
Music Coordinator

Rick Sordelet
Fight Director

Mark Schneider
Associate Director

Rachel Bress
Associate Choreographer

Bernard Telsey
Telsey + Company
Casting

Peter Lawrence
Production Supervisor

David Benken
Production Management

Wendy Orshan
101 Productions, Ltd.
General Manager

Betsy Bernstein
BDB Marketing
Marketing

Arielle Tepper Madover
Producer

Roger Horchow
Producer

Sally Horchow
Producer

Roger Berlind
Producer

Roy Furman
Producer

Debbie Bisno
Producer

Stacey Mindich
Producer

James M. Nederlander
Producer

Jane Bergère
Producer

Daryl Roth
Producer

Eva Price
Producer

Christina Papagjika
Producer

2012-2013
Transfer Students

Mary Callanan
Mrs. Pugh

Annie

Danette Holden
Swing

Jane Lynch
Miss Hannigan

Mikey
Stray Dog; u/s Sandy

Brooklyn Shuck
Standby for Molly, Kate, Tessie, July, Duffy

Matt Wall
Ensemble

Photo by Joan Marcus

(L-R): Lilla Crawford as Annie and Jane Lynch as Miss Hannigan

Photo by Brian Mapp

USHERS
(L-R): Maria Agurto, Lorraine O'Sullivan

Photo by Brian Mapp

CREW
Front Row (L-R): Ron Hiatt, Graziella Zapata, Angela Simpson, Jesse Hancox, Roseanna Sharrow, Stuart Metcalf, Mary Kathryn Flynt (Assistant Stage Manager), Heidi Neven, James Cariot, Rachel A. Wolff (Stage Manager)
Second Row (L-R): Taylor Michael, Polly Noble, Meredith Benson, Amanda Grundy, Dustin J. Harder, Scott Westervelt, Jill Valentine, Bryan Odar, Patrick Eviston, Scott Anderson, Michael Carey, Shannon Slaton
Stairway (L-R): Hector Lugo, Mia Mel Rose, Douglas Earl, Cecilia Cruz, Ryan Oslak, Barry C. Hoff, Brendan O'Neal, Julienne Schubert-Blechman, Joshua Gericke

Annie

STAFF FOR *ANNIE*

GENERAL MANAGEMENT
101 PRODUCTIONS, LTD.
Wendy Orshan   Jeffrey M. Wilson
Elie Landau
Chris Morey
Ron Gubin

COMPANY MANAGER
Heidi Neven
Associate Company Manager: Roseanna Sharrow

GENERAL PRESS REPRESENTATIVE
BONEAU/BRYAN-BROWN
Adrian Bryan-Brown   Jim Byk
Emily Meagher   Christine Olver

PRODUCTION MANAGEMENT
BenRo PRODUCTIONS
David Benken, Rose Palombo

CASTING
TELSEY + COMPANY
Bernie Telsey CSA, Will Cantler CSA,
David Vaccari CSA,
Bethany Knox CSA, Craig Burns CSA,
Tiffany Little Canfield CSA, Rachel Hoffman CSA,
Justin Huff CSA, Patrick Goodwin CSA,
Abbie Brady-Dalton CSA,
David Morris, Cesar A. Rocha, Andrew Femenella,
Karyn Casl, Kristina Bramhall, Jessie Malone

Production Supervisor	Peter Lawrence
Stage Manager	Rachel A. Wolff
Assistant Stage Manager	Mary Kathryn Flynt
Associate Company Manager	Roseanna Sharrow
Fight Captain	David Rossetti
Associate Scenic Designer	Rod Lemmond
Assistant Scenic Designer	Amanda Stephens
Associate Costume Designer	Tricia Barsamian
Assistant Costume Designers	Rebecca Lasky, Anna Lacivita
Associate Lighting Designer	Michael P. Jones
Assistant Lighting Designer	Carolyn Wong
Associate Sound Designer	Cody Spencer
Associate Projection Designers	Daniel Brodie, Michael Clark
Moving Light Programmer	Richard Tyndall
Moving Lighting Tracking	Sarah Bullock
Projection Programmer	Paul Vershbow
Projection Researchers	Mary Recine, Anya Klepikov, Susan Hormuth
Projection Graphics	Bo G. Eriksson

FIGHT DIRECTOR
Rick Sordelet

Head Carpenter	Patrick Eviston
Automation Carpenters	Michael L. Shepp Jr., Jeff Zink
Production Electrician	Jimmy Maloney
Head Electrician	Vince Goga
Assistant Electrician	Jesse Hancox
Production Sound	Nicholas Borisjuk
Head Sound Engineer	Shannon Slaton

Production Props	Jerry Marshall
Assistant Properties Supervisor	James Cariot
Wardrobe Supervisor	Scott Westervelt
Assistant Wardrobe Supervisor	Angela Simpson
Dressers	Meredith Benson, Cecilia Cruz, Barry Hoff, Hector Lugo, Polly Noble, Ryan Oslak, Julienne Schubert-Blechman
Costume Interns	Bernadette Banner, Amanda Shafran
Hair Supervisor	Thomas Augustine
Hair Assistants	Josh Gericke, Mia Mel Rose
Makeup Designer	Ashley Ryan
Assistant Makeup Designer	Eli Aguirre
Animal Trainer	William Berloni
Animal Handler	Dustin Harder
Vocal Coach	Deborah Hecht
Music Coordinator	Patrick Vaccariello
Music Department Production Assistant	Scott Wasserman
Physical Therapist	PhysioArts, Jennifer Green, Ryanne Glasper
Keyboard Programmer	Randy Cohen
Technical Production Assistant	Morgan Holbrook
Production Assistants	Michelle Heller, Derric Nolte, Ellen Mezzera, Taylor Michael, Max Pescherine
Head Child Guardian	Jill A. Valentine
Child Guardian	Amanda Grundy
Children's Tutoring	On Location Education/ Alan Simon, Jodi Green
Tutors	Lisa Chasin, Irene Karasik
Producer's Associate	Holly Ferguson
ATM Productions Staff	Sam Levy, David Loughner, Gabby Dasilva
Producers' Apprentice	John Mara, Jr.
Strouse IP CEO	Ben Strouse
Executive Producer	Carolyn Rossi Copeland
Assistant to Mr. Strouse	Katy Wadsworth
Assistants to Mr. Korins	Stephen Edwards, Emily Inglis, Sarah Weede
Legal Counsel	Lazarus & Harris LLP/ Scott Lazarus, Robert Harris, Emily Lawson
Accountant	Fried & Kowgios, LLP
Comptroller	Galbraith & Co./ Sarah Galbraith, Kenny Noth
Advertising	Serino/Coyne/ Nancy Coyne, Angelo Desimini, Tom Callahan, Matt Upshaw, Lauren Houlberg, Christina Hernandez
Marketing	bdb marketing/ Betsy Bernstein, Livie Cohn
Interactive Marketing	Situation Marketing/ Damian Bazadona, Chris Powers, Jeremy Kraus, Maris Smith, Mollie Shapiro
101 Productions, Ltd. Staff	Beth Blitzer, Kit Ingui, Kathy Kim, Mike McLinden, Michael Rudd, David van Zyll de Jong
101 Productions, Ltd. Interns	Simon Pincus, Sarah Springborn
Production Photographer	Joan Marcus
Insurance	DeWitt Stern Group, Inc.
Immigration	David King, Lisa Carr
Opening Night Coordination	Serino Coyne/ Suzanne Tobak

Merchandising	Creative Goods/Pete Milano
Banking	City National Bank/Anne McSweeney
Payroll Services	Checks and Balances
Theatre Displays	King Displays, Inc.
Group Sales	Nederlander Group Sales

www.anniethemusical.com

CREDITS
Scenery provided by PRG Scenic Technologies, Proof Productions Inc., Daedalus Design & Production Inc. Props provided by Gerrard Studios, Tom Carroll Scenery. Video projection system engineered and provided by Worldstages. Costume construction by Eric Winterling, Inc.; Tricorne, Inc.; Arel Studio, Inc.; Giliberto Designs; and Maria Ficalora Knitwear. Custom fabric printing by Gene Mignola, Inc. Custom fabric painting and distressing by Hochi Asiatico. Custom fur pieces by Fur & Furgery. Millinery by Lynne Mackey Studio and Arnold Levine, Inc. Custom footwear by LaDuca Shoes and Worldtone Dance. Undergarments and hosiery by Bra*Tenders. Newsreel footage by Historic Films Archive LLC.

SPONSORSHIPS
The PEDIGREE® Brand, Sergeants

SPECIAL THANKS
Dave Auster, Beverly Randolph, David van Zyll de Jong, Helen Uffner Vintage Clothing and Illisa's Vintage Lingerie, Lizzie Levin, Al Roker Entertainment, Thirteen, the PEDIGREE Brand, Arren Spence, Judy Grant, Tracie Brennan, Al Roker, Shana Scott, Bruce Kallner, Sabrina Lopez, Charles Compagnone, Justin Black

NEDERLANDER

Chairman	**James M. Nederlander**
President	**James L. Nederlander**

Executive Vice President
Nick Scandalios

Vice President	Senior Vice President
Corporate Development	Labor Relations
Charlene S. Nederlander	**Herschel Waxman**

Vice President	Chief Financial Officer
Jim Boese	**Freida Sawyer Belviso**

STAFF FOR THE PALACE THEATRE

Theatre Manager	Austin Nathaniel
Treasurer	Cissy Caspare
Assistant Treasurer	Richard Aubrey
Carpenter	Thomas K. Phillips
Flyman	Robert W. Kelly
Electrician	Eddie Webber
Property Master	Steve Camus
Engineer	Rob O'Connor
Chief Usher	Gloria Hill

Annie
Scrapbook

Correspondent: Merwin Foard, "F.D.R."

Most Exciting Celebrity Visitors: Rep. Gabrielle Giffords and her husband Mark Kelly came to see the show and requested to meet with the cast afterward for a group photo. She was so gracious and wanted us to know how much this show means to her and her family. Her husband Mark recognized one of our orphan stand-bys, Sadie Sink, as having played Annie at Theatre Under the Stars in Houston recently. Watching Gabby and him speak with Sadie about that experience was truly moving. Then, when we realized that Gabby's mom had worked with Gabby at her bedside following the shooting, and they would sing "Tomorrow" together... well... I think that speaks for itself.

Actor Who Performed the Most Roles in This Show: Gavin Lodge: Delivery guy, dog catcher, Hooverville-ian, chef, chauffeur, Bergdorf shopper, Hannigan admirer, homeless guy, Santa, footman, Harold Ickes, and Judge Brandeis. Twelve tracks in every show! Twelve...

Actor Who Has Done the Most Shows: It looks as if I have done the most Broadway shows, as I was honored to receive the Gypsy Robe on opening night. Fourteen Broadway contracts spanning 30 years, as of this writing.

Special Backstage Rituals: Two of our youngest orphans, Emily (8) and Tyrah (7) have an adorable preshow dance/cheer that they made up and do together before every show at five minute call.

Mascots: Sunny and Casey, duh!

Favorite Moments During Each Performance: ONSTAGE: My favorite moment is leading the Cabinet members, Annie and Warbucks in singing the "Tomorrow" reprise.

OFFSTAGE: Connecting with cast members. We are big fans of one another.

Favorite In-Theatre Gathering Place: Possibly the best place to be is Brynn O'Malley's dressing room after the show on Saturday nights. A group of the adults gather there for an end of the week toast. It is certainly one of the highlights of our work week!

Favorite Off-Site Hangout: Langan's! It's right next door and the orphans have a regular table there. Awesome!

Favorite Therapies: Gum (this theatre is dry), tea, massage, "Dexter," "Breaking Bad" and red wine.

Memorable Ad-Lib: As F.D.R., upon the completion of our Cabinet scene where we

Front row (L-R): J. Elaine Marcos, Clarke Thorell, Anthony Warlow, Lilla Crawford, Sunny, Katie Finneran, Brynn O'Malley and Taylor Richardson. Back row center: *Yearbook* Correspondent Merwin Foard

reprise "Tomorrow," I am wheeled off in my wheelchair by Keven Quillon who plays my aide, Louis Howe. Every night, I try to say something witty to make him laugh. So far, "I want some cream of tomato soup with those little oysterette crackers that you know how to crumble up so well" is a stand-out! That and "Tomorrow... that's the day after Today!"

Record Number of Cell Phone Rings, Cell Phone Photos or Texting Incidents during a Performance: Too many to count. Mostly pictures and video being taken with cell phones.

Memorable Press Encounter: Having [Playbill reporter] Harry Haun put a digital recorder in my face the moment I arrived inside the

At the opening night party (L-R): choreographer Andy Blankenbuehler, librettist Thomas Meehan, composer Charles Strouse, producer Arielle Tepper Madover, lyricist Martin Charnin, director James Lapine

opening night party with my family to get a quote. Priceless!

Latest Audience Arrival: *Annie* draws a large number of first-time theatregoers, which is wonderful. However, sometimes they think every matinee is at 3 p.m. Nope, just Sundays.

Fastest Costume Change: Many of us do incredibly quick costume changes during the "NYC" number. Changes that are timed in seconds. It's a whirlwind backstage.

Busiest Day at the Box Office: It has to have been the day after opening and then the day after we appeared on the Macy's Thanksgiving Day Parade.

Heaviest/Hottest Costume: Probably a tossup

between Gavin Lodge in his Santa costume or Liz McCartney as the fortune teller. Both costumes are seen during "NYC."

Who Wore the Least: Sandy! Only a rope leash and a red bow/collar for the finale! Other than that, I'd say Sarah Solie as a sexy Roxy usherette.

Favorite Snack Food: Trail Mix!

Catchphrase Only the Company Would Recognize: "No, it's kackety kackety kack kack kuh kacketykack."

Sweethearts Within the Company: All of us. We are still in the honeymoon phase of this show and are all in love still.

Orchestra Members Who Play the Most Instruments: Four woodwind players play 19 instruments. From bass saxophone to piccolo. Steve Kenyon, David Young, Dave Noland and Ron Janelli.

In-House Parody Lyrics: The orphans make up "NYC" lyrics specific to cast members. Most recently, they sang to Anthony Warlow on his birthday, "An-tho-nyyyy, he is an Australian."

Memorable Directorial Notes: "I don't know what this says" or "What the hell are you doing up there?" Both said with great humor.

Company In-Jokes: Lilla has a thing about people throwing up, so we torture her with stories and sounds of puking. Thanks GRACE!

Company Legends: Anthony Warlow, Katie Finneran, James Lapine, Andy Blankenbuehler, Susan Hilferty, Michael Starobin, Brian Ronan and a few others.

"Gypsy of the Year" Skit: Not really a skit, but Lilla Crawford sang "Tomorrow" with original Annie, Andrea McArdle.

Superstition That Turned Out To Be True: Sometimes a flu shot can give you flu-like symptoms.

Coolest Thing About Being in This Show: Getting to hear the squeals of all those children, who likely are at their first Broadway show, when Lilla comes out for her bow is one of the coolest things about being in the cast of *Annie*.

Also: I'd only like to add that this production has been a labor of love from every department. Getting to perform this show eight times a week is a gift, and when you add in the loving, supportive and talented cast, crew, orchestra, house staff both backstage and front of house, it makes coming to work so rich. We should all be this fortunate in our chosen careers.

Anything Goes

First Preview: March 10, 2011. Opened: April 7, 2011.
Closed July 8, 2012 after 32 Previews and 521 Performances.

When Billy Crocker learns that the girl of his dreams, Hope Harcourt, is sailing off to Europe to marry a rich twit, Billy stows away and adopts a series of disguises in hopes of winning her away from her fiancé and her disapproving mother. Along the way Billy gets help from gangster Moonface Martin and nightclub singer Reno Sweeney in a series of farcical plots that eventually win Hope's heart and hand.

CAST

(in order of appearance)

Elisha Whitney	JOHN McMARTIN
Fred, a bartender	DEREK HANSON
Billy Crocker	BILL ENGLISH
Reno Sweeney	STEPHANIE J. BLOCK
Captain	ED DIXON
Ship's Purser	ROBERT CREIGHTON
Crew	LAWRENCE ALEXANDER, BRANDON BIEBER, WARD BILLEISEN, DANIEL J. EDWARDS, DEREK HANSON, KEVIN MUNHALL, BRANDON RUBENDALL, WILLIAM RYALL
A Reporter	LAWRENCE ALEXANDER
A Photographer	BRANDON BIEBER
Henry T. Dobson, a minister	WILLIAM RYALL
Luke	ANDREW CAO
John	RAYMOND J. LEE
Angels	
Purity	SHINA ANN MORRIS
Chastity	BRITTANY MARCIN
Charity	JENNIFER SAVELLI
Virtue	KAITLIN MESH

Continued on next page

STEPHEN SONDHEIM THEATRE

ROUNDABOUTTHEATRECOMPANY

Todd Haimes, Artistic Director
Harold Wolpert, Managing Director
Julia C. Levy, Executive Director

Presents

Stephanie J. Block *and* Joel Grey

in

Music & Lyrics by
Cole Porter

Original Book by
P.G. Wodehouse & Guy Bolton
and Howard Lindsay & Russel Crouse

New Book by
Timothy Crouse & John Weidman

with

Bill English   Erin Mackey   Robert Petkoff   Jessica Stone
Robert Creighton   Andrew Cao   Ed Dixon   Raymond J. Lee

Lawrence Alexander   Leslie Becker   Brandon Bieber   Ward Billeison   Janine DiVita
Daniel J. Edwards   Justin Greer   Derek Hanson   Michelle Loucadoux   Brittany Marcin
Kaitlin Mesh   Shina Ann Morris   Kevin Munhall   Mary Michael Patterson
Brandon Rubendall   William Ryall   Jennifer Savelli   Kiira Schmidt   Vanessa Sonon

with

John McMartin

and

Julie Halston

Set Design	*Costume Design*	*Lighting Design*	*Sound Design*
Derek McLane	Martin Pakledinaz	Peter Kaczorowski	Brian Ronan
Additional Orchestrations	*Original Orchestrations*	*Dance Arrangements*	*Music Director/Conductor*	*Music Coordinator*
Bill Elliott	Michael Gibson	David Chase	James Lowe	Seymour Red Press
Hair & Wig Design	*Makeup Design*	*Production Stage Manager*	*Casting*
Paul Huntley	Angelina Avallone	Peter Hanson	Jim Carnahan, C.S.A. & Stephen Kopel
Associate Director	*Associate Choreographer*	*Technical Supervisor*	*Executive Producer*
Marc Bruni	Vince Pesce	Steve Beers	Sydney Beers
Press Representative	*Director of Marketing & Sales Promotion*	*Director of Development*	*Founding Director*	*Associate Artistic Director*
Boneau-Bryan/Brown	Thomas Mygatt	Lynne Gugenheim Gregory	Gene Feist	Scott Ellis

Music Supervisor/Vocal Arranger
Rob Fisher

Directed and Choreographed by
Kathleen Marshall

Proud Sponsor BANK OF AMERICA
Anything Goes benefits from Roundabout's Musical Theatre Fund with gifts from Marty and Perry Granoff, HRH Foundation, Ted and Mary Jo Shen,
Peter and Leni May, Tom and Diane Tuft, The Kaplen Foundation, and one anonymous donor.
Roundabout thanks the Henry Nias Foundation, courtesy of Dr. Stanley Edelman, for their support of Anything Goes.
*Generously underwritten by Margot Adams, in memory of Mason Adams.

Anything Goes was produced by Lincoln Center Theater in 1987.

6/4/12

Stephanie J. Block as Reno Sweeney, with Sailors (L-R): Adam Perry, Kevin Munhall, Anthony Wayne, Clyde Alves, Ward Billeisen, Josh Franklin

Photo by Joan Marcus

Anything Goes

SCENES & MUSICAL NUMBERS

ACT ONE

Overture

Scene 1: **A Smoky Manhattan Bar**
"I Get a Kick Out of You" ....Reno Sweeney

Scene 2: **The Afterdeck of an Ocean Liner**
"There's No Cure Like Travel" ....Captain, Purser and Sailors
"Bon Voyage" ....Sailors and Passengers

Scene 3: **On Deck, that evening**
"You're the Top" ....Reno Sweeney and Billy Crocker
"Easy to Love" ....Billy Crocker
Reprise: "Easy to Love" ....Hope Harcourt

Scene 4: **Whitney's Stateroom/Moon's Adjacent Cabin**
"The Crew Song" ....Elisha Whitney

Scene 5: **On Deck, mid-morning**
"There'll Always Be a Lady Fair" (Sailor's Chantey) ....Quartet
"Friendship" ....Moonface Martin and Reno Sweeney

Scene 6: **Evelyn's Stateroom**

Scene 7: **On Deck, at twilight**
"It's De-lovely" ....Billy Crocker and Hope Harcourt

Scene 8: **On Deck, early the following morning**
"Anything Goes" ....Reno Sweeney, Sailors and Passengers

ACT TWO

Entr'Acte

Scene 1: **The Ship's Nightclub**
"Public Enemy Number One" ....Captain, Purser and Passengers
"Blow, Gabriel, Blow" ....Reno Sweeney, Angels and Passengers
"Goodbye, Little Dream, Goodbye" ....Hope Harcourt

Scene 2: **The Ship's Brig**
"Be Like the Blue Bird" ....Moonface Martin
"All Through the Night" ....Billy Crocker, Hope Harcourt and Quartet

Scene 3: **On Deck, later that night**
"The Gypsy in Me" ....Lord Evelyn Oakleigh and Reno Sweeney

Scene 4: **The Ship's Brig**

Scene 5: **On Deck**
"Buddie, Beware" ....Erma and Sailors
Finale ....Full Company

ORCHESTRA

Conductor:
JAMES LOWE

Associate Conductor:
DAVID GURSKY

Music Coordinator:
SEYMOUR RED PRESS

Reeds:
GIUSEPPE FUSCO, RON JANNELLI,
DAVE YOUNG, JOHN WINDER

Trumpets:
EARL GARDNER, KEN RAMPTON,
STU SATALOF

Trombone:
LARRY FARRELL, ROB FOURNIER,
MARK PATTERSON

Piano:
DAVID GURSKY

Bass:
JEFF CARNEY

Drums:
JOHN REDSECKER

Percussion:
BILL HAYES

Guitar:
ANDREW SCHWARTZ

Synthesizer Programmer:
BRUCE SAMUELS

Music Copying:
EMILY GRISHMAN MUSIC PREPARATION—
KATHARINE EDMONDS/EMILY GRISHMAN

Cast Continued

Hope Harcourt ....ERIN MACKEY
Mrs. Evangeline Harcourt ....JULIE HALSTON
Lord Evelyn Oakleigh ....ROBERT PETKOFF
FBI Agents ....KEVIN MUNHALL,
 BRANDON RUBENDALL
Erma ....JESSICA STONE
Moonface Martin ....JOEL GREY
Old Lady in a Wheelchair ....LESLIE BECKER
Quartet ....WARD BILLEISEN,
 DANIEL J. EDWARDS, DEREK HANSON,
 WILLIAM RYALL
Ship's Passengers ......LAWRENCE ALEXANDER,
 LESLIE BECKER, BRANDON BIEBER,
 WARD BILLEISEN, JANINE DiVITA,
 DANIEL J. EDWARDS, DEREK HANSON,
 KEVIN MUNHALL,
 MARY MICHAEL PATTERSON,
 BRANDON RUBENDALL,
 WILLIAM RYALL, KIIRA SCHMIDT

SWINGS

JUSTIN GREER, MICHELLE LOUCADOUX,
VANESSA SONON

UNDERSTUDIES

For Reno Sweeney:
JANINE DiVITA, KIIRA SCHMIDT
For Billy Crocker & Evelyn Oakleigh:
DEREK HANSON
For Moonface Martin:
ROBERT CREIGHTON
For Hope Harcourt:
MICHELLE LOUCADOUX,
 MARY MICHAEL PATTERSON
For Mrs. Evangeline Harcourt:
LESLIE BECKER
For Elisha Whitney & Captain:
WILLIAM RYALL
For the Purser:
BRANDON BIEBER, JUSTIN GREER
For Erma:
SHINA ANN MORRIS, VANESSA SONON
For Luke:
BRANDON BIEBER, DANIEL J. EDWARDS
For John:
ANDREW CAO, DANIEL J. EDWARDS

Dance Captain: JENNIFER SAVELLI
Assistant Dance Captain: JUSTIN GREER

Production Stage Manager: PETER HANSON
Stage Manager: JON KRAUSE
Assistant Stage Manager: RACHEL BAUDER

Anything Goes

Stephanie J. Block
Reno Sweeney

Joel Grey
Moonface Martin

John McMartin
Elisha Whitney

Julie Halston
Mrs. Evangeline Harcourt

Bill English
Billy Crocker

Erin Mackey
Hope Harcourt

Robert Petkoff
Lord Evelyn Oakleigh

Jessica Stone
Erma

Robert Creighton
Ship's Purser; u/s Moonface Martin

Andrew Cao
Luke; u/s John

Ed Dixon
Captain

Raymond J. Lee
John

Lawrence Alexander
Crew, Reporter, Passenger

Leslie Becker
Old Lady in a Wheelchair, Passenger

Brandon Bieber
Crew, Photographer, Passenger; u/s Purser, Luke

Ward Billeisen
Crew, Passenger, Quartet

Janine DiVita
Passenger; u/s Reno Sweeney

Daniel J. Edwards
Crew, Quartet; u/s Luke, John

Justin Greer
Swing; u/s Purser

Derek Hanson
Fred, Crew, Passenger, Quartet; u/s Lord Evelyn, Billy Crocker

Michelle Loucadoux
Swing; u/s Hope Harcourt

Brittany Marcin
Chastity

Kaitlin Mesh
Virtue

Shina Ann Morris
Purity; u/s Erma

Kevin Munhall
FBI Agent, Passenger

Mary Michael Patterson
Passenger; u/s Hope Harcourt

Brandon Rubendall
Crew, Passenger

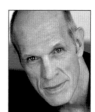
William Ryall
Crew, Henry T. Dobson, Passenger, Quartet; u/s Elisha Whitney, Captain

Jennifer Savelli
Charity, Dance Captain

Kiira Schmidt
Passenger

Vanessa Sonon
Swing; u/s Erma

Cole Porter
Music & Lyrics

Guy Bolton
Original Book

P.G. Wodehouse
Original Book

Russel Crouse & Howard Lindsay
Original Book

Anything Goes

Timothy Crouse
*Co-Author of the
New Book*

John Weidman
New Book

Kathleen Marshall
*Director &
Choreographer*

Derek McLane
Scenic Design

Martin Pakledinaz
Costume Design

Peter Kaczorowski
Lighting Design

Brian Ronan
Sound Design

Rob Fisher
*Musical Supervisor,
Vocal Arranger*

Bill Elliott
*Additional
Orchestrations*

Seymour Red Press
Musical Coordinator

David Chase
Dance Arranger

James Lowe
*Musical Director/
Conductor*

Paul Huntley
Hair & Wig Design

Angelina Avallone
Make-Up Design

Kathy Fabian/
Propstar
*Properties
Coordinator*

Marc Bruni
Associate Director

Vince Pesce
*Associate
Choreographer*

Jim Carnahan
Casting

Gene Feist
*Founding Director,
Roundabout Theatre
Company*

Todd Haimes
*Artistic Director,
Roundabout Theatre
Company*

TRANSFER
STUDENTS
2012-2013

Joyce Chittick
Erma

Gary Lindemann
*Henry T. Dobson,
Crew, Passenger,
Quartet*

Anything Goes

Script Readers .... Jay Cohen, Shannon Deep, Ben Izzo, Alexis Roblan

Artistic Apprentice .... Joshua M. Feder

EDUCATION STAFF
EDUCATION DIRECTOR .... Greg McCaslin
Associate Education Director .... Jennifer DiBella
Education Program Manager .... Aliza Greenberg
Education Program Associate .... Sarah Malone
Education Assistant .... Holly Sansom
Education Dramaturg .... Ted Sod
Teaching Artists .... Josh Allen, Cynthia Babak, Victor Barbella, LaTonya Borsay, Mark Bruckner, Eric C. Dente, Joe Doran, Elizabeth Dunn-Ruiz, Carrie Ellman-Larsen, Deanna Frieman, Sheri Graubert, Melissa Gregus, Adam Gwon, Devin Haqq, Carrie Heitman, Karla Hendrick, Jason Jacobs, Alana Jacoby, Lisa Renee Jordan, Jamie Kalama Wood, Alvin Keith, Erin McCready, James Miles, Nick Moore, Meghan O'Neil, Nicole Press, Leah Reddy, Amanda Rehbein, Nick Simone, Joe Skowronski, Heidi Stallings, Daniel Sullivan, Carl Tallent, Vickie Tanner, Laurine Towler, Jennifer Varbalow, Leese Walker, Gail Winar, Chad Yarborough
Teaching Artist Emeritus .... Reneé Flemings
Education Apprentice .... Kimberley Oria

EXECUTIVE ADMINISTRATIVE STAFF
ASSOCIATE MANAGING
DIRECTOR .... Greg Backstrom
Assistant Managing Director .... Katharine Croke
Assistant to the
Managing Director .... Christina Pezzello
Assistant to the Executive Director .... Nicole Tingir

MANAGEMENT/ADMINISTRATIVE STAFF
GENERAL MANAGER .... Sydney Beers
General Manager,
American Airlines Theatre .... Denise Cooper
General Manager,
Steinberg Center .... Nicholas J. Caccavo
Human Resources Director .... Stephen Deutsch
Operations Manager .... Valerie D. Simmons
Associate General Manager .... Maggie Cantrick
Office Manager .... Scott Kelly
Archivist .... Tiffany Nixon
Receptionists .... Dee Beider, Emily Frohnhoefer, Elisa Papa, Allison Patrick
Messenger .... Darnell Franklin
Management Apprentice .... Christina Pezzello

FINANCE STAFF
DIRECTOR OF FINANCE .... Susan Neiman
Payroll Director .... John LaBarbera
Accounts Payable Manager .... Frank Surdi
Payroll Benefits Administrator .... Yonit Kafka
Manager Financial Reporting .... Joshua Cohen
Business Office Assistant .... Jackie Verbitski
Business Apprentice .... Kimberly Lucia

DEVELOPMENT STAFF
DIRECTOR OF
DEVELOPMENT .... Lynne Gugenheim Gregory
Assistant to the
Director of Development .... Liz Malta
Director, Institutional Giving .... Liz S. Alsina

Director, Individual Giving .... Christopher Nave
Director, Special Events .... Lane Hosmer
Associate Director, Individual Giving .... Tyler Ennis
Manager, Telefundraising .... Gavin Brown
Manager, Corporate Relations .... Sohyun Kim
Manager, Friends of Roundabout .... Marisa Perry
Manager, Donor Information Systems .... Lise Speidel
Special Events Associate .... Natalie Corr
Individual Giving Officer .... Joseph Foster
Institutional Giving Assistant .... Brett Barbour
Development Assistant .... Martin Giannini
Development Apprentice .... Julie Erhart
Special Events Apprentice .... Genevieve Carroll

INFORMATION TECHNOLOGY STAFF
DIRECTOR OF
INFORMATION TECHNOLOGY .. Daniel V. Gomez
Information Systems Manager .... Dale Aucoin
System Administrator .... Jim Roma
IT Associate .... Cary Kim

MARKETING STAFF
DIRECTOR OF MARKETING AND
SALES PROMOTION .... Thomas Mygatt
Associate Director of Marketing .... Tom O'Connor
Marketing Associate, Graphic Design .... Eric Emch
Marketing Assistant .... Bradley Sanchez
Web Producer .... Mark Cajigao
Director of Telesales
Special Promotions .... Marco Frezza
Telesales Manager .... Patrick Pastor
Telesales Office Coordinator .... Nicholas Ronan
Marketing Apprentices .... Christina Pezzello, Bethany Nothstein

AUDIENCE SERVICES STAFF
DIRECTOR OF AUDIENCE
SERVICES .... Wendy Hutton
Associate Director of Audience Services .... Bill Klemm
Box Office Managers .... Edward P. Osborne, Jaime Perlman, Krystin MacRitchie, Nicole Nicholson
Group Sales Manager .... Jeff Monteith
Assistant Box Office Managers .... Robert Morgan, Joseph Clark, Andrew Clements, Catherine Fitzpatrick
Assistant Audience Services Managers .... Robert Kane, Lindsay Ericson, Jessica Pruett-Barnett
Customer Services Coordinator .... Thomas Walsh
Audience Services .... Solangel Bido, Michael Bultman, Jay Bush, Lauren Cartelli, Adam Elsberry, Joe Gallina, Ashley Gezana, Alanna Harms, Kara Harrington, Jennifer Hlinka, Lindsay Hoffman, Nicki Ishmael, Kiah Johnson, Kate Longosky, Michelle Maccarone, Mead Margulies, Laura Marshall, Chuck Migliaccio, Carlos Morris, Sarah Olsen, Kaia Rafoss, Josh Rozett, Ben Schneider, Heather Siebert, Nalane Singh, Ron Tobia, Michael Valentine, Hannah Weitzman
Audience Services Apprentice .... Jennifer Almgreen

SERVICES
Counsel .... Paul, Weiss,

Rifkind, Wharton and Garrison LLP, Charles H. Googe Jr., Carol M. Kaplan
Counsel .... Rosenberg & Estis
Counsel .... Andrew Lance, Gibson, Dunn, & Crutcher, LLP
Counsel .... Harry H. Weintraub, Glick and Weintraub, P.C.
Counsel .... Stroock & Stroock & Lavan LLP
Counsel .... Daniel S. Dokos, Weil, Gotshal & Manges LLP
Counsel .... Claudia Wagner/ Manatt, Phelps & Phillips, LLP
Immigration Counsel .... Mark D. Koestler and Theodore Ruthizer
House Physicians .... Dr. Theodore Tyberg, Dr. Lawrence Katz
House Dentist .... Neil Kanner, D.M.D.
Insurance .... DeWitt Stern Group, Inc.
Accountant .... Lutz & Carr CPAs, LLP
Advertising .... Spotco/ Drew Hodges, Jim Edwards, Tom Greenwald, Kyle Hall, Josh Fraenkel
Interactive Marketing .... Situation Interactive/ Damian Bazadona, John Lanasa, Eric Bornemann, Mollie Shapiro, Danielle Migliaccio
Events Photography .... Anita and Steve Shevett
Production Photographer .... Joan Marcus
Theatre Displays .... King Displays, Wayne Sapper
Lobby Refreshments .... Sweet Concessions
Merchandising .... Spotco Merch/ James Decker

MANAGING DIRECTOR
EMERITUS .... Ellen Richard

Roundabout Theatre Company
231 West 39th Street, New York, NY 10018
(212) 719-9393.

GENERAL PRESS REPRESENTATIVE
BONEAU/BRYAN-BROWN
Adrian Bryan-Brown
Matt Polk   Jessica Johnson   Amy Kass

CREDITS FOR *ANYTHING GOES*
Company Manager .... Karl Baudendistel
Assistant Company Manager .... David Solomon
Production Stage Manager .... Peter Hanson
Assistant Stage Manager .... Rachel Bauder
Stage Manager .... Jon Krause
Dance Captain .... Jennifer Savelli
Assistant Dance Captain .... Justin Greer
Assistant Choreographer .... David Eggers
Assistant Set Designer .... Erica Hemminger
Associate Costume Designer .... Sara Jean Tosetti
Costume Design Assistant .... Carisa Kelly
Assistant to the
Costume Designer .... Justin Hall
Costume Interns .... Hannah Kittel, Shannon Smith, Heather Mathiesen
Associate Lighting Designer .... Paul Toben
Assistant Lighting Designer .... Gina Scherr
Associate Wig and
Hair Designer .... Giovanna Calabretta
Makeup Design Associate .... Jorge Vargas
Assistant Sound Designer .... John Emmett O'Brien

Anything Goes
SCRAPBOOK

Photo by Joseph Marzullo/WENN

The cast flings hats in the air on the stage of the Sondheim Theatre at the 500th performance.

Correspondent: Raymond J. Lee, "John"
Closing Night: We started off our final *Anything Goes* show on a warm Sunday afternoon on July 8, 2012. We all got to the theatre with our closing cards and gifts in hand and got to our dressing rooms, which had been slowly brought to their first-visit glory the previous week.

Earlier that morning we had learned that our brilliant and wonderful costume designer Martin Pakledinaz had passed away, so the air at the theatre was definitely affected with the news. We all went to the green room to see all of his beautiful, original *Anything Goes* sketches and took a moment to reflect. There was also a table full of tasty sweets and we made sure to relish some gluttonous pastry behavior before our show.

It was a half hour full of cards, hugs, reminiscences, and a commitment to do the show for ourselves and for Marty. It all still felt surreal that today would be our last voyage on the SS American, only because we had had such a wonderful time together. We had all made so many warm memories and many new friendships that will carry on to our next contracts.

The show was electric and filled with memories of all sorts of wonderful backstage moments including Poker Saturdays, Donut Sundays, Birthday Celebrations, Baby Showers, Secret Santa, Door Decorating Contests...and those are just a few!

The amazing thing about our show (and something I tell people all the time) is that there is just as good a show backstage as there is onstage. The entire cast and crew find moments to entertain each other and crack jokes and that is something I will definitely miss. Our closing show was no exception as people made sure to leave a lasting impression on each other as we all completed our final *Anything Goes* tracks.

One of the most amazing moments we will all remember, as a cast, is the end of the Act I, the "Anything Goes" tap. Our stage manager held the curtain for us for a couple minutes at the end so we could hear and see the audience rise and cheer. It meant the world to us and I think tears were streaming down all of our faces.

After the show, we made sure to clean up our dressing rooms, pack our bags full of gifts and last dressing room remnants, give our final tours, and head to the closing party, which was being held at Tony's DiNapoli right across the street (and that chicken parmigiana was absolutely mouth-watering).

As with any show I finish, I waited until everybody was out, looked back at my wonderful dressing room, blew a kiss to it, turned out the lights, closed the door, and said goodbye to it and goodbye to this amazing journey.

We were all blessed to be a part of this experience and will remember it for the rest of our lives.

Editor's Note: A wonderful farewell YouTube video can be viewed at: www.youtube.com/watch?v=WL9O2_o4PHU.

Production Sound Engineer ....Shannon Slaton
Music Department
    Interns ....Molly Gachignard, Ian Weinberger
Production Carpenter ....Steve Beers
Automation Operator ....Paul Ashton
Flyman ....William Craven
Deck Carpenters ....Donald Roberts, John Patrick Nord
Production Electrician/
    Moving Light Programmer ....Josh Weitzman
Assistant Production Electricians ....John Wooding,
Jocelyn Smith
Sound Mixer......................................Shannon Slaton
Followspot Operators ....Dorion Fuchs,
Erika Warmbrunn, Jessica Morton
Deck Electricians ....Jocelyn Smith,
Francis Elers
House Properties ....Andrew Forste
Properties Running Crew ....Dan Mendeloff,
Nelson Vaughn
Associate Production Properties ....Carrie Mossman
Prop Artisans.....................Mike Billings, Tim Ferro,
Cathy Small, Mary Wilson
Wardrobe Supervisor ....Nadine Hettel
Dressers ....Sam Brooks, Steve Chazaro,
Tara Delahunt, Kyle LaColla,

Emily Merriweather, Pamela Pierzina,
Stacy Sarmiento
Hair and Wig Supervisor ....Kelly Reid
Hair Assistants ....Barry Lee Moe, Jessie Mojica,
Shanah-Ann Kendall
SDC Observer ....Adam Cates
Production Assistant ....Hannah Dorfman
Physical Therapy ....Performing Arts Physical Therapy

CREDITS
Scenery fabrication by Hudson Scenic Studio, Inc. Scenic elements constructed by global scenic services, inc., Bridgeport, CT. Lighting equipment by PRG Lighting. Audio equipment by PRG Audio. Costumes by Arel Studio Inc.; Artur & Tailors Ltd.; Carelli Costumes Inc.; Helen Uffner Vintage Clothing, LLC; Krostyne Studio; Parson-Meares, Ltd; Paul Chang Custom Tailors; Tricorne, Inc. Millinery by Lynne Mackey Studio, Rodney Gordon, Inc. Men's hats by J.J. Hatts Center. Furs by Sharnelle Furs. Shoes by JC Theatrical, LaDuca, Worldtone Dance. Shoe repair by Rostelle Shoe Repair. Mr. McMartin's glasses provided by Myoptics. Special thanks to Bra*Tenders for hosiery and undergarments. Softgoods by I. Weiss. Specialty prop construction by Cigar Box Studios, Inc.; Costume Amour; Craig Grigg; Anne Guay; Aardvark Interiors. Flame treatment by Turning Star, Inc.

Flying by Foy

STEPHEN SONDHEIM THEATRE
SYDNEY BEERS   GREG BACKSTROM
General Manager   Associate Managing Director
VALERIE SIMMONS
Operations Manager

Make-up provided by M•A•C

STEPHEN SONDHEIM THEATRE STAFF
Operations Manager ....Valerie D. Simmons
House Manager ....Johannah-Joy G. Magyawe
Assistant House Manager ....Molly McQuilkin
Head Treasurer ....Jaime Perlman
Associate Treasurer ....Andrew Clements
Assistant Treasurers ....Kiah Johnson, Carlos Morris,
Ronnie Tobia
House Carpenter ....Steve Beers
House Electrician ....Josh Weitzman
House Properties ....Andrew Forste
Engineer ....Deosarran
Security ....Gotham Security
Maintenance ....C+W Cleaning Services Inc.
Lobby Refreshments by ....Sweet Concessions

The Assembled Parties

First Preview: March 21, 2013. Opened: April 17, 2013.
Still running as of May 31, 2013.

THE ASSEMBLED PARTIES

Richard Greenberg's new drama is a portrait of four generations in the life of an Upper West Side Manhattan Jewish family. Over the course of two Christmases (that's right) two decades apart, they come together, break apart, then come together again in a new and unexpected way, bound by a palatial 14-room apartment on Central Park West, a ruby necklace that may or may not be genuine, and a love (or hate) for the central character, Julie.

CAST

(in order of appearance)

Julie .... JESSICA HECHT
Jeff .... JEREMY SHAMOS
Ben .... JONATHAN WALKER
Mort .... MARK BLUM
Shelley .... LAUREN BLUMENFELD
Faye .... JUDITH LIGHT
Scotty/Tim .... JAKE SILBERMANN
Timmy .... ALEX DREIER
Voice of Hector .... GABRIEL SLOYER

TIME

Act One: Christmas Day 1980
Act Two: Christmas Day 2000

PLACE

A fourteen-room apartment on Central Park West

Stage Manager .... KELLY BEAULIEU

Continued on next page

Manhattan Theatre Club
Samuel J. Friedman Theatre

ARTISTIC DIRECTOR
Lynne Meadow

EXECUTIVE PRODUCER
Barry Grove

PRESENTS

THE ASSEMBLED PARTIES

BY
Richard Greenberg

WITH

Jessica Hecht   Judith Light   Jeremy Shamos

Mark Blum   Lauren Blumenfeld
Alex Dreier   Jake Silbermann   Jonathan Walker

SCENIC DESIGN	COSTUME DESIGN	LIGHTING DESIGN	ORIGINAL MUSIC & SOUND DESIGN
Santo Loquasto	**Jane Greenwood**	**Peter Kaczorowski**	**Obadiah Eaves**

HAIR & WIG DESIGN	PRODUCTION STAGE MANAGER	CASTING
Tom Watson	**Barclay Stiff**	**Nancy Piccione**

DIRECTED BY
Lynne Meadow

ARTISTIC PRODUCER
Mandy Greenfield

GENERAL MANAGER
Florie Seery

DIRECTOR OF ARTISTIC DEVELOPMENT	DIRECTOR OF MARKETING	PRESS REPRESENTATIVE
Jerry Patch	**Debra Waxman-Pilla**	**Boneau/Bryan-Brown**

PRODUCTION MANAGER	ARTISTIC LINE PRODUCER	DIRECTOR OF DEVELOPMENT
Joshua Helman	**Lisa McNulty**	**Lynne Randall**

The Assembled Parties was commissioned through the U.S. Trust New American Play Commissioning Program.
Special thanks to the Harold and Mimi Steinberg Charitable Trust for supporting Manhattan Theatre Club.
Manhattan Theatre Club wishes to express its appreciation to Theatre Development Fund for its support of this production.

4/17/13

(L-R): Mark Blum, Lauren Blumenfeld, Judith Light, Jessica Hecht, Jeremy Shamos, Jake Silbermann, Jonathan Walker

Photo by Joan Marcus

The Assembled Parties

Jessica Hecht
Julie

Judith Light
Faye

Jeremy Shamos
Jeff

Mark Blum
Mort

Cast Continued

UNDERSTUDIES

For Ben/Mort: TONY CARLIN
For Timmy: STEPHEN McGAHAN
For Scotty/Tim/Jeff: JED ORLEMANN
For Julie/Faye/Shelley: LORI WILNER

Lauren Blumenfeld
Shelley

Alex Dreier
Timmy

Jake Silbermann
Scotty/Tim

Jonathan Walker
Ben

Tony Carlin
u/s Ben/Mort

Stephen McGahan
u/s Timmy

Jed Orlemann
u/s Scotty/Tim/Jeff

Lori Wilner
u/s Julie/Faye/Shelley

Richard Greenberg
Playwright

Lynne Meadow
Director/Artistic Director Manhattan Theatre Club

Santo Loquasto
Scenic Design

Jane Greenwood
Costume Design

Peter Kaczorowski
Lighting Design

Obadiah Eaves
Original Music & Sound Design

Photo by Joan Marcus

(L-R): Jessica Hecht, Jeremy Shamos and Judith Light

Tom Watson
Hair & Wig Design

Barclay Stiff
Production Stage Manager

Kelly Beaulieu
Stage Manager

Barry Grove
Executive Producer Manhattan Theatre Club

The Assembled Parties

MANHATTAN THEATRE CLUB STAFF

Artistic Director	**Lynne Meadow**
Executive Producer	**Barry Grove**
General Manager	**Florie Seery**
Artistic Producer	**Mandy Greenfield**
Director of Artistic Development	**Jerry Patch**
Director of Artistic Operations	**Amy Gilkes Loe**
Artistic Line Producer	Lisa McNulty
Assistant to the Artistic Director	Nicki Hunter
Assistant to the Executive Producer	Melanie Sovern
Assistant to the Artistic Producer	Ben Ferber
Director of Casting	**Nancy Piccione**
Associate Casting Director	Kelly Gillespie
Casting Assistant	Darragh Garvey
Literary Manager/ Sloan Project Manager	Annie MacRae
Artistic Development Associate	Elizabeth Rothman
Artistic Development Assistant	Scott Kaplan
Director of Development	**Lynne Randall**
Director, Individual Giving & Major Gifts	Emily Fleisher
Director, Institutional Giving	Patricia Leonard
Director, Special Events	Laura Stuart Wood
Associate Director of Individual Giving	Josh Martinez-Nelson
Manager, Individual Giving	Aubrie Fennecken
Development Associate/ Individual Giving	Laura Petrucci
Development Associate/ Special Events	Molly Clarke
Development Associate/ Institutional Giving	Heather Gallagher
Patrons' Liaison	Emily Yowell
Database Associate	Katie Fergerson
Director of Marketing	**Debra Waxman-Pilla**
Assistant Marketing Director	Becca Goland-Van Ryn
Marketing Manager	Caitlin Baird
Director of Finance	**Jessica Adler**
Director of Human Resources	**Stephanie Dolce**
Business Manager	Ryan Guhde
Business & HR Associate	Mallory Triest
Business Assistant	Sarah DeStefano
IT Manager	Mendy Sudranski
Systems Analyst	Jason Fritzsch
Studio Manager/Receptionist	Thatcher Stevens
Associate General Manager	**Lindsey Sag**
Company Manager/ NY City Center	Samantha Kindler
General Management Assistant	Derrick Olson
Director of Subscriber Services	**Robert Allenberg**
Subscriber Services Manager	Kevin Sullivan
Subscriber Services Representatives	Mark Bowers, Tim Salamandyk, Rosanna Consalvo Sarto, Amber Wilkerson
Director of Telesales and Telefunding	**George Tetlow**
Telesales and Telefunding Manager	Terrence Burnett
Telefunding Staff	Alex Gould, Kel Haney, Dan McCabe, Jeff Ronan, Tom Trimble
Director of Education	**David Shookhoff**

Assistant Education Director/ Coordinator, Paul A. Kaplan Theatre Management Program	Amy Harris
Education Programs Coordinator	Kimberley Oria
MTC Teaching Artists	Stephanie Alston, David Auburn, Chris Ceraso, Charlotte Colavin, Dominic Colon, Allison Daugherty, Andy Goldberg, Kel Haney, Elise Hernandez, Jeffrey Joseph, Bridget Leak, Julie Leedes, Kate Long, Victor Maog, Andres Munar, Melissa Murray, Angela Pietropinto, Carmen Rivera, Judy Tate, Candido Tirado, Liam Torres, Joe White
Theatre Management Interns	Cressa Amundsen, Lanie Bayless, Hunter Chancellor, Danielle Doherty, Dylan Evans, Ariana Georgulas, Mary Heatwole, Kathryn Pamula, Jessica Penzias, Kaitria Resetar, Elizabeth Sharpe-Levine, Joanne Schwartzberg

Production Manager	**Joshua Helman**
Associate Production Manager	Bethany Weinstein
Assistant Production Manager	Kevin Service
Properties Supervisor	**Scott Laule**
Assistant Properties Supervisor	Lily Fairbanks
Props Carpenters	Christine Gat, Peter Grimes
Costume Supervisor	**Erin Hennessy Dean**

GENERAL PRESS REPRESENTATION
BONEAU/BRYAN-BROWN

Chris Boneau	Aaron Meier
Christine Olver	Emily Meagher

Script Readers	Alex Barron, Aaron Grunfeld, Clifford Lee Johnson III, Rachel Lerner-Ley, Thomas Park, Rachel Slaven

SERVICES

Accountants	Fried & Kowgios CPAs, LLP
Advertising	SpotCo/Drew Hodges, Tom Greenwald, Jim Edwards, Ilene Rosen, Michael Crowley, Corey Schwitz
Web Design	SpotCo Interactive
Legal Counsel	Charles H. Googe, Jr.; Carol M. Kaplan/ Paul, Weiss, Rifkind, Wharton and Garrison LLP
Real Estate Counsel	Marcus Attorneys
Labor Counsel	Harry H. Weintraub/ Glick and Weintraub, P.C.
Immigration Counsel	Theodore Ruthizer/ Kramer, Levin, Naftalis & Frankel, LLP
Insurance	DeWitt Stern Group, Inc./ Anthony Pittari
Media Counsel	Cameron Stracher
Maintenance	Reliable Cleaning
Production Photographer	Joan Marcus
Event Photography	Bruce Glikas
Artwork Photography	Andrew Eccles
Cover Design	SpotCo
Theatre Displays	King Displays

PRODUCTION STAFF FOR
THE ASSEMBLED PARTIES

Company Manager	**Erin Moeller**
Production Stage Manager	**Barclay Stiff**
Stage Manager	Kelly Beaulieu
Assistant Director	Kimberly Faith Hickman
Make-Up Designer	Angelina Avallone
Associate Scenic Designer	Jisun Kim
Associate Costume Designer	Daniel Urlie
Assistant Lighting Designer	Nick Flinn
Associate Sound Designer	Jessica Paz
Photographic Images	Christie Mullen
Hair/Make-Up Supervisor	Natasha Steinhagen
Lighting Programmer	Marc Polimeni
Automation Operator	Vaughn Preston
Flyman	John Fullum
Deck Hands	Rich Klinger, Andrew Belits
Dresser	David Oliver
Costume Shopper	Mark Nagle
Production Assistants	Catherine Lynch, Stephen Ravet
Child Guardian	Nikki Kelly
Children's Tutoring	On Location Education/ Kathleen Kenney

CREDITS

Scenery fabrication by Hudson Scenic Studio. Lighting equipment provided by PRG Lighting. Sound equipment provided by Masque Sound. Costumes executed by Eric Winterling. Makeup provided by M•A•C.

SPECIAL THANKS

Special thanks to our friend Tim Monich.

MANHATTAN THEATRE CLUB
SAMUEL J. FRIEDMAN THEATRE STAFF

Theatre Manager	**Jim Joseph**
Assistant House Manager	Richard Ponce
Box Office Treasurer	**David Dillon**
Assistant Box Office Treasurers	Rachel James, Geoffrey Nixon
Head Carpenter	Chris Wiggins
Head Propertyman	Timothy Walters
Sound Engineer	Louis Shapiro
Master Electrician	Jeff Dodson
Wardrobe Supervisor	Leah Redmond
Apprentices	Andrew Braggs, Jeremy Von Deck
Chief Engineer	Deosarran
Maintenance Engineers	Ricky Deosarran, Maximo Perez
Security	Allied Barton
Lobby Refreshments	Sweet Hospitality Group

2012-2013 AWARDS

Tony Award
Best Performance by an Actress
in a Featured Role in a Play
(Judith Light)

Drama Desk Award
Outstanding Featured Actress in a Play
(Judith Light)

The Assembled Parties
SCRAPBOOK

Correspondent: Lauren Blumenfeld, "Shelley"

Opening Night Gifts: Lynne Meadow, director extraordinaire, gave us each a small statue of Ganesh—the Hindu god of wisdom, prophecy, good luck and success. The god who removes obstacles. This was particularly meaningful because Judith Light had brought a statue of Ganesh from India to our first rehearsal and it remained in the rehearsal room and then backstage throughout our entire process. My gift to the cast and crew was far less spiritual. I got everyone potholders because the character I play (Shelley) has a homemade potholder business—a strange, but hopefully useful gift?

Special Backstage Rituals: Before we enter, Judith Light, Mark Blum and I do a little dance backstage. At the top of the show, our characters are supposed to be driving to the Bascovs' home from Roslyn, New York, so we do a ridiculous pantomime-driving dance. It has gotten more absurd with each performance. We look like morons, but it effectively pumps us up.

Favorite In-Theatre Gathering Place: Alex Dreier (age 9, who plays young Timmy) and Stephen McGahan (also 9, his

understudy) opened up one of the finest restaurants backstage. It's called "Alex & Stephen's *Assembled Parties* Drive/Walk Thru." Before the show or at intermission, the cast and crew can choose from a variety of dishes and call down to Alex and Stephen's dressing room to order food for delivery. (The food is drawn on and cut out of paper.) I personally recommend the pizza with lettuce, the pickle, and the cookies and cream shake. Alex and Stephen also accept non-food orders. Lori Wilner (who covers Jessica, Judith and me... She's amazing!) ordered a collection of cats. The young lads have also started a pretty successful investment banking business. I don't quite understand the details of this endeavor, but I support their entrepreneurial skills!

Favorite Off-Site Hangout: This is a real Edison Café cast. Perhaps Richard Greenberg's Jewish play has caused us all to crave Jewish comfort food. I like the split pea soup, but I quickly learned to order a cup instead of a bowl. The bowl is like a swimming pool—it's huge! After the show, we often go to the Glass House Tavern. The staff is amazing there! I will also never forget the first time Jessica, Jeremy and Mark took me to Green Symphony, and later to Joe Allen. It was like a rite of passage for me, a new actor on Broadway.

Mascot: Ganesh—the Hindu god of wisdom, luck, success and the remover of obstacles. Also, maybe calamari? Long story.

Memorable Press Encounter: I have always been a big AndrewAndrew fan. They are dynamic theatre critics and DJs who dress exactly alike in the most dapper of styles. AndrewAndrew interviewed me for their podcast. It was surreal to have these two fabulous gents sitting in my dressing room, dressed in the exact same blue spectacles, gingham shirts and red ties. I have no idea what I said in this interview because I was so transfixed by their outfits and dazzled by their full commitment to details.

Catchphrases Only the Company Would Recognize: "Show enough to win." (The punchline to a pretty hilarious story about Milton Berle, compliments of Mark Blum.)

Understudy Anecdote: On Tuesday May 7, 2013, the great Jed Orlemann went on for the amazing Jeremy Shamos (who was filming a movie!). Jed stepped into the high stress situation with such grace and ease. He did a truly outstanding job. We were all blown away. *The Assembled Parties* has some of the most talented actors understudying: Tony Carlin (covering Mort and Ben); Lori Wilner (covering Julie, Faye and Shelley); Jed Orlemann (covering Scott/Tim and Jeff;) and Stephen McGahan (covering young Timmy). They are truly brilliant.

Sweethearts Within the Company: We are all sweethearts.

Coolest Thing About Being in This Show: I know that it sounds cheesy, but it's totally the truth: The coolest thing about being in this show is getting to work with such generous, loving, talented and supportive people. I feel like the luckiest actor on the planet to be making my Broadway debut with the great Jake Silbermann, in a Richard Greenberg play, in the company of my favorite veteran actors. Everyone has shown me such kindness. Each

day feels like a master class on acting.

Other Stories and Memories: Two weeks into the rehearsal process I mentioned wanting to take a little trip to Roslyn, New York where the Rappaport family lives in the play. Judith immediately asked if I wanted to go with her. I was a little nervous because Judith Light is one of my favorite actresses on the planet. But I said to myself, when else in my life will I have the opportunity to cruise around Bed Stuy Brooklyn in a town car with Judith Light? So I went and I'm so thankful that I did. She picked me up early in the morning and we visited the neighborhood where Faye and Ben grew up. Later, we schlepped on the LIRR to Roslyn and visited the Roosevelt Field Mall where my character (Shelley) works. It was a day I will never forget. This is just one of the many stories demonstrating the kindness and generosity of this extraordinary ensemble of actors. Jessica was constantly baking for us. Jeremy was always brightening the room with videos of his awesome kids doing crazy songs and dances. Mark's jokes at the dinner table scene made even the most high stress previews a delight. Jonathan brought delicious dark chocolate and tons of positivity to rehearsals, and Jake consistently brought tremendous heart and kindness to the room. It's such a special ensemble and I feel so lucky to be a part of *The Assembled Parties* family.

1. Cast member and *Yearbook* correspondent Lauren Blumenfeld, at the opening night party.
2. Curtain call, opening night, (L-R): Mark Blum, Jonathan Walker, Jeremy Shamos, Jessica Hecht, Judith Light, Jake Silbermann, Lauren Blumenfeld and Alex Dreier.
3. The proprietors of "Alex & Stephen's *Assembled Parties* Drive/Walk Thru" (L-R): Stephen McGahan and Alex Dreier.

The Big Knife

First Preview: March 22, 2013. Opened: April 16, 2013.
Limited run closed June 2, 2013 after 29 Previews and 56 Performances.

PLAYBILL®

Revival of Clifford Odets' 1949 drama about a successful Hollywood movie star who tears his personal and professional life to pieces when he tries to get out of a long-term contract in order to save his marriage. Another of Odets' morality tales about the conflict between art and commerce and the corrupting effects of money on the integrity of the human spirit.

CAST

(in order of appearance)

Russell	BILLY EUGENE JONES
Buddy Bliss	JOEY SLOTNICK
Charlie Castle	BOBBY CANNAVALE
Patty Benedict	BRENDA WEHLE
Marion Castle	MARIN IRELAND
Nat Danziger	CHIP ZIEN
Marcus Hoff	RICHARD KIND
Smiley Coy	REG ROGERS
Connie Bliss	ANA REEDER
Hank Teagle	C.J. WILSON
Dixie Evans	RACHEL BROSNAHAN

TIME

July, 1948

PLACE

The "playroom" of Charlie Castle's
Beverly Hills house

Continued on next page

AMERICAN AIRLINES THEATRE

ROUNDABOUT THEATRE COMPANY

Todd Haimes, Artistic Director
Harold Wolpert, Managing Director
Julia C. Levy, Executive Director

presents

THE BIG KNIFE

By

Clifford Odets

with

Rachel Brosnahan   Bobby Cannavale   Marin Ireland
Billy Eugene Jones   Richard Kind   Ana Reeder   Reg Rogers
Joey Slotnick   Brenda Wehle   C.J. Wilson   Chip Zien

Set Design John Lee Beatty	*Costume Design* Catherine Zuber	*Lighting Design* James F. Ingalls	*Original Music & Sound Design* David Van Tieghem
Hair & Wig Design Tom Watson	*Production Stage Manager* Winnie Y. Lok	*Production Management* Aurora Productions	
Casting Jim Carnahan, C.S.A.	*The Big Knife General Manager* Denise Cooper	*Press Representative* Polk & Co.	
Associate Managing Director Greg Backstrom	*Director of Marketing & Audience Development* Tom O'Connor	*Director of Development* Lynne Gugenheim Gregory	
General Manager Sydney Beers	*Founding Director* Gene Feist	*Adams Associate Artistic Director** Scott Ellis	

Directed by

Doug Hughes

*Generously underwritten by Margot Adams, in memory of Mason Adams.

Roundabout Theatre Company is a member of the League of Resident Theatres.
www.roundabouttheatre.org

4/16/13

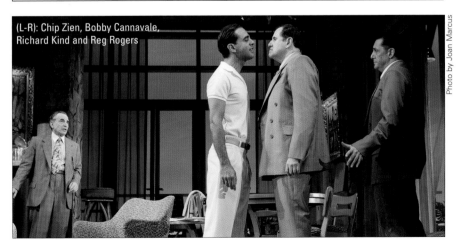

(L-R): Chip Zien, Bobby Cannavale, Richard Kind and Reg Rogers

Photo by Joan Marcus

27

The Big Knife

Photo by Joan Marcus

(L-R): Bobby Cannavale and Ana Reeder

Cast Continued

SCENES

Act One
Mid-afternoon
Act Two
Late one night, the following week
Act Three
Scene One: Late afternoon, a few days later
Scene Two: An hour later

UNDERSTUDIES

For Connie Bliss, Dixie Evans:
KATYA CAMPBELL
For Marion Castle, Patty Benedict:
ERIKA ROLFSRUD
For Charlie Castle, Smiley Coy:
LEE AARON ROSEN
For Hank Teagle, Buddy Bliss, Russell:
BAYLEN THOMAS
For Nat Danziger, Marcus Hoff: MARK ZEISLER
Production Stage Manager: WINNIE Y. LOK
Stage Manager: CARLOS MAISONET

2012-2013 AWARD

DRAMA DESK AWARD
Outstanding Featured Actor in a Play
(Richard Kind)

Rachel Brosnahan
Dixie Evans

Bobby Cannavale
Charlie Castle

Marin Ireland
Marion Castle

Billy Eugene Jones
Russell

Richard Kind
Marcus Hoff

Ana Reeder
Connie Bliss

Reg Rogers
Smiley Coy

Joey Slotnick
Buddy Bliss

Brenda Wehle
Patty Benedict

C.J. Wilson
Hank Teagle

Chip Zien
Nat Danziger

Katya Campbell
u/s Connie Bliss, Dixie Evans

Erika Rolfsrud
u/s Marion Castle, Patty Benedict

Lee Aaron Rosen
u/s Charlie Castle, Smiley Coy

Baylen Thomas
u/s Hank Teagle, Buddy Bliss, Russell

Mark Zeisler
u/s Nat Danziger, Marcus Hoff

Clifford Odets
Playwright

Doug Hughes
Director

John Lee Beatty
Set Design

Catherine Zuber
Costume Design

James F. Ingalls
Lighting Design

The Big Knife

     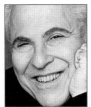 

David Van Tieghem
*Original Music and
Sound Design*

Matthew Hodges
*Properties
Supervisor*

Jim Carnahan, CSA
Casting

Gene O'Donovan
Aurora Productions
*Production
Management*

Ben Heller
Aurora Productions
*Production
Management*

Gene Feist
*Founding Director
Roundabout Theatre
Company*

Todd Haimes
*Artistic Director
Roundabout Theatre
Company*

BOX OFFICE
(L-R): Ted Osborne, Solangel Bido, Mead Margulies

Photos by Brian Mapp

FRONT OF HOUSE
Front Row (L-R): Zipporah Aguasvivas, Crystal Suarez
Middle Row (L-R): Dominga Veloz Rivera,
Sheila Portorreal, Enrika Nicholas
Top Row (L-R): Jim Lynch, Oscar Castillo, David Cross

CREW
Sitting (L-R): Winnie Y. Lok (Production Stage Manager), Carlos Maisonet (Stage Manager), Barbara Morse
Standing Center (L-R): Manuela LaPorte, Paul Ludick, Pamela Short, Susan Fallon, Carly DiFulvio and dog Dempsey Allen
Back Row (L-R): Dann Wojnar, Glenn Merwede, Brian Maiuri, Hannah Overton, Robert W. Dowling II

The Big Knife

ROUNDABOUT THEATRE COMPANY STAFF
ARTISTIC DIRECTOR ....**TODD HAIMES**
MANAGING DIRECTOR ....**HAROLD WOLPERT**
EXECUTIVE DIRECTOR ....**JULIA C. LEVY**
ADAMS ASSOCIATE
   ARTISTIC DIRECTOR ....**SCOTT ELLIS**

ARTISTIC STAFF

DIRECTOR OF ARTISTIC DEVELOPMENT/
  DIRECTOR OF CASTING ....Jim Carnahan
Artistic Consultant ....Robyn Goodman
Resident Directors ....Doug Hughes, Sam Gold
Associate Artists ....Mark Brokaw, Scott Elliott,
                    Bill Irwin, Joe Mantello,
        Kathleen Marshall, Theresa Rebeck
Literary Manager ....Jill Rafson
Senior Casting Director ....Carrie Gardner
Casting Director ....Stephen Kopel
Casting Associate ....Jillian Cimini
Casting Assistants ....Lain Kunin, Logan Reid
Artistic Associate ....Amy Ashton
Literary Associate ....Josh Fiedler
Educational Foundation of
  America Commissions ....Bekah Brunstetter,
         Lydia Diamond, Diana Fithian,
                 Julie Marie Myatt
Roundabout Commissions.............Helen Edmundson,
        Adam Gwon & Michael Mitnick,
        Joshua Harmon, Andrew Hinderaker,
        Stephen Karam, Matthew Lopez,
                 Kim Rosenstock
Casting Interns ....Joyah Spangler, Steven Laing,
                    Ragan Rhodes
Script Readers ....Shannon Deep, Liz Malta,
         Michael Perlman, Alexis Roblan
Artistic Apprentice ....Nikki DiLoreto

EDUCATION STAFF

EDUCATION DIRECTOR ....Greg McCaslin
Associate Education Director ....Jennifer DiBella
Senior Education Program Associate ....Sarah Malone
Education Program Associate ....Paul Brewster
Education Assistant ....Lou-Lou Igbokwe
Education Dramaturg ....Ted Sod
Teaching Artists ....Josh Allen, Cynthia Babak,
        Victor Barbella, LaTonya Borsay,
        Mark Bruckner, Chloe Chapin,
        Joe Doran, Elizabeth Dunn-Ruiz,
        Mathilde Dratwa, Carrie Ellman-Larsen,
        Theresa Flanagan, Deanna Frieman,
        Sheri Graubert, Adam Gwon, Creighton Irons,
        Devin Haqq, Carrie Heitman, Karla Hendrick,
        Jason Jacobs, Alana Jacoby,
        Hannah Johnson-Walsh, Lisa Renee Jordan,
        Boo Killebrew, Anya Klepikov,
        Erin McCready, James Miles, Nick Moore,
        Meghan O'Neil, Drew Peterson,
        Nicole Press, Leah Reddy, Amanda Rehbein,
        Nick Simone, Heidi Stallings,
        Daniel Sullivan, Carl Tallent,
        Vickie Tanner, Laurine Towler,
        Jennifer Varbalow, Kathryn Veillette,
        Leese Walker, Christopher Weston,
        Gail Winar, Jamie Kalama Wood,
                Chad Yarborough
Teaching Artist Emeritus ....Reneé Flemings

Education Apprentices ....Maia Collier,
                    Will Hudson

EXECUTIVE ADMINISTRATIVE STAFF

ASSOCIATE MANAGING
  DIRECTOR............................Greg Backstrom
Assistant Managing Director ....Katharine Croke
Assistant to the Managing Director .....Christina Pezzello
Assistant to the Executive Director ....Nicole Tingir

MANAGEMENT/ADMINISTRATIVE STAFF

GENERAL MANAGER ....Sydney Beers
General Manager,
  American Airlines Theatre ....Denise Cooper
General Manager,
  Steinberg Center ....Nicholas J. Caccavo
Human Resources Director ....Stephen Deutsch
Operations Manager ....Valerie D. Simmons
Associate General Manager ....Maggie Cantrick
Office Manager ....Scott Kelly
Archivist ....Tiffany Nixon
Receptionists ....Dee Beider, Emily Frohnhoefer,
         Elisa Papa, Allison Patrick
Messenger ....Darnell Franklin
Management Apprentice ....Holli Campbell

FINANCE STAFF

DIRECTOR OF FINANCE.................Susan Neiman
Payroll Director ....John LaBarbera
Accounts Payable Manager ....Frank Surdi
Payroll Benefits Administrator ....Yonit Kafka
Manager Financial Reporting ....Joshua Cohen
Business Office Assistant ....Jackie Verbitski
Business Office Apprentice ....Mara Abeleda

DEVELOPMENT STAFF

DIRECTOR OF
  DEVELOPMENT ....Lynne Gugenheim Gregory
Assistant to the Director of Development ....Liz Malta
Director, Special Events.......................Lane Hosmer
Director, Individual Giving ....Christopher Nave
Director, Institutional Giving ....Erica Raven
Associate Director, Individual Giving ....Tyler Ennis
Manager, Telefundraising ....Gavin Brown
Manager, Special Events ....Natalie Corr
Manager, Friends of Roundabout ....Marisa Perry
Manager, Donor Information Systems ....Lise Speidel
Institutional Giving Officer,
  Solicitations and Special Projects ....Brett Barbour
Individual Giving Officer ....Jordan Frausto
Individual Giving Officer ....Toni Rosenbaum
Institutional Giving Officer,
  Stewardship and Prospect
  Development ....Kimberly Sidey
Special Events Assistant ....Genevieve Carroll
Development Assistant ....Martin Giannini
Special Events Apprentice ....Alayna George
Development Apprentice ....Haley Tanenbaum

INFORMATION TECHNOLOGY STAFF

DIRECTOR OF
  INFORMATION TECHNOLOGY ..Daniel V. Gomez
Systems Administrator ....Jim Roma
Tessitura &
  Applications Administrator ....Yelena Ingberg
Database Administrator/Developer ....Rajan Eddy

Web Administrator ....Robert Parmelee
IT Associate ....Cary Kim

MARKETING STAFF

DIRECTOR OF MARKETING &
  AUDIENCE DEVELOPMENT ....Tom O'Connor
Senior Marketing Manager ....Rani Haywood
Manager, Design & Production ....Eric Emch
Digital Content Producer ....Mark Cajigao
Marketing Associate,
  Events & Promotions..............Rachel LeFevre-Snee
Marketing Associate, Digital ....Alex Barber
Marketing Assistant ....Dayna Johnson
Director of Telesales
  Special Promotions ....Marco Frezza
Telesales Manager ....Patrick Pastor
Telesales Office Coordinator ....Adam Unze
Marketing Apprentices ....Tyler Beddoe,
                   Maureen Keleher
Digital Marketing Apprentice ....Laura Abbott

AUDIENCE SERVICES STAFF

DIRECTOR OF AUDIENCE
  SERVICES ....Wendy Hutton
Associate Director of Audience Services.........Bill Klemm
Customer Care Manager ....Robert Kane
Box Office Managers ....Edward P. Osborne,
        Jaime Perlman, Krystin MacRitchie,
              Catherine Fitzpatrick
Group Sales Manager ....Jeff Monteith
Assistant Box Office Managers ....Robert Morgan,
        Joseph Clark, Andrew Clements,
                Nicki Ishmael
Assistant Audience
  Services Managers ....Lindsay Ericson,
          Jessica Pruett-Barnett,
         Kaia Lay Rafoss, Joe Gallina
Customer Care Associate ....Thomas Walsh
Audience Services ....Jennifer Almgreen, Solangel Bido,
        Jay Bush, Lauren Cartelli, Adam Elsberry,
        Ashley Gezana, Alanna Harms, Kara Harrington,
        Kiah Johnson, Mark Lavey, Rebecca Lewis-Whitson,
        Michelle Maccarone, Mead Margulies,
        Laura Marshall, Chuck Migliaccio, Carlos Morris,
        Katie Mueller, Sarah Olsen, Tom Protulipac,
        Josh Rozett, Austin Ruffer, Heather Seibert,
        Nalane Singh, Ron Tobia, Hannah Weitzman
Audience Services Apprentice ....Blair Laurie

SERVICES

Counsel ....Paul, Weiss,
        Rifkind, Wharton and Garrison LLP,
        Charles H. Googe Jr., Carol M. Kaplan
Counsel ....Rosenberg & Estis
Counsel ....Andrew Lance,
        Gibson, Dunn, & Crutcher, LLP
Counsel ....Harry H. Weintraub,
        Glick and Weintraub, P.C.
Counsel ....Strook & Strook & Lavan LLP
Counsel ....Daniel S. Dokos,
        Weil, Gotshal & Manges LLP
Counsel ....Claudia Wagner/
        Manatt, Phelps & Phillips, LLP
Immigration Counsel ....Mark D. Koestler and
               Theodore Ruthizer

The Big Knife

House Physicians ....Dr. Theodore Tyberg,
Dr. Lawrence Katz
House Dentist ....Neil Kanner, D.M.D.
Insurance ....DeWitt Stern Group, Inc.
Accountant ....Lutz & Carr CPAs, LLP
Advertising ....Spotco/
Drew Hodges, Jim Edwards,
Tom Greenwald, Ilene Rosen,
Josh Fraenkel, Hillary Wilson
Interactive Marketing..................Situation Interactive/
Damian Bazadona, Eric Bornemann,
Elizabeth Kandel, Mollie Shapiro,
Danielle Migliaccio
Events Photography.................Anita and Steve Shevett
Production Photographer ....Joan Marcus
Theatre Displays.............King Displays, Wayne Sapper
Lobby Refreshments....................Sweet Concessions
Merchandising ....Spotco Merch/
James Decker

MANAGING DIRECTOR
EMERITUS ....Ellen Richard

Roundabout Theatre Company
231 West 39th Street, New York, NY 10018
(212) 719-9393.

GENERAL PRESS REPRESENTATIVE
POLK & CO.

| Matt Polk | Jessica Johnson |
| Layne McNish | Steven Pipps |

STAFF FOR THE BIG KNIFE
Company Manager ....Carly DiFulvio
Production Stage Manager ....Winnie Y. Lok

(L-R): Marin Ireland and Bobby Cannavale

Bobby Cannavale

Photos by Joan Marcus

Stage Manager.............................Carlos Maisonet
Production Management .... Aurora Productions Inc./
Gene O'Donovan, Ben Heller,
Stephanie Sherline, Anthony Jusino,
Jarid Sumner, Anita Shah, Liza Luxenberg,
G. Garrett Ellison, Troy Pepicelli,
Gayle Riess, Cat Nelson, Melissa Mazdra
Assistant Directors ....Alexander Greenfield,
Steven P. Nemphos
Makeup Design ....Ashley Ryan
Fight Consultant ....J. David Brimmer
Associate Scenic Designer ....Kacie Hultgren
Associate Costume Designer ....Ryan Park
Associate Lighting Designer ....Peter West
Assistant Lighting Designer ....Aaron Porter
Associate Sound Designer ....Brandon Wolcott
Production Properties Supervisor .... Matthew Hodges
Production Carpenter ....Glenn Merwede
Production Electrician ....Brian Maiuri
Running Properties ....Robert W. Dowling II
Sound Operator ....Dann Wojnar
Wardrobe Supervisor ....Susan Fallon
Dressers ....Dale Carman, Paul Ludick
Wardrobe Dayworker ....Pamela Short
Hair and Wig Supervisor ....Nellie LaPorte
Production Assistant ....Rebecca Spinac

CREDITS
Scenery fabricated and painted by Global Scenic Services, Inc. Bridgeport, CT. Lighting equipment by PRG Lighting. Audio equipment by PRG Audio. Costumes constructed by EuroCo Costumes and John Cowles. Millinery by

Rodney Gordon. Men's tailoring by Brian Hemesath and Angels the Costumiers. Special effect by Craig Grigg. Props artisan: Sarah Bird, Gloria Sun, Jeremy Lydic. Upholstery by V. Ramos Upholstery. Carpet installation by Halls Carpet. Special thanks to Bra*Tenders for hosiery and undergarments.

Makeup provided by M•A•C Cosmetics.

AMERICAN AIRLINES THEATRE STAFF
Company Manager ....Carly DiFulvio
House Carpenter ....Glenn Merwede
House Electrician ....Brian Maiuri
House Properties....................Robert W. Dowling II
House Sound ....Dann Wojnar
IA Apprentice ....Hannah Overton
Wardrobe Supervisor ....Susan J. Fallon
Box Office Manager ....Ted Osborne
Assistant Box Office Manager ....Robert Morgan
House Manager ....Stephen Ryan
Associate House Manager ....Zipporah Aguasvivas
Head Usher ....Crystal Suarez
House Staff ....Christopher Busch, Oscar Castillo,
Anne Ezell, Saira Flores,
Rebecca Knell, Enrika Nicholas,
Sheila Portorreal, CharDia Reynolds,
Celia Torres, Dominga Veloz Rivera
Security ....Julious Russell
Additional Security ....Gotham Security

For more information on *The Big Knife*, including exclusive interviews with the artists and a note from Roundabout Artistic Director Todd Haimes, visit www.thebigknifebroadway.com/upstage.htm.

(L-R): Richard Kind and Bobby Cannavale

The Big Knife
Scrapbook

Correspondents: Marin Ireland, "Marion Castle" and Joey Slotnick, "Buddy Bliss"

Memorable Opening Night Letter, Fax or Note: Joey wrote everybody a card as though it was written from a character that's mentioned in the play but never seen. For Marin, the card came from the butcher she speaks to in the second act. For Reg, it was from Tommy Murdoch (Reg's character had seen his new movie and wasn't a fan).

Opening Night Gifts: We each got white tulips from Walt Whitman Odets, Clifford's son, who was with us for about two weeks during previews. That was pretty special. Almost as sweet as that Bobby bought us all gift certificates from Long Room so we could all go one night and get stinko.

hard-boiled egg snack.

Favorite In-Theatre Gathering Place: Sunday brunch in the trap room! The most elaborate, beautiful spread you've ever seen, hosted by the incomparable wardrobe mistress,

Susan Fallon—bacon, French toast, smoothies, a different entrée every week! Astonishing.

Favorite Off-Site Hangout: Usually it's been Long Room. On two-show days, Kodama or Joe Allen. Although, during rehearsals, the whole company ordered from Chop't EVERY DAY.

Favorite Snack Food: Joey's wife, Talya Cousins, makes incredible granola, so we're

lucky whenever that's backstage.

Favorite Therapy: Grether's Blackcurrant Pastilles. Duh!

Most Memorable Ad-Lib: One night, Reg blanked on the name 'Tommy Murdoch' and instead, in that blink of a second, came up with the name 'Lester Hughes'. Nobody was the wiser. That was kind of awesome. Bobby has a line, "Isn't it time we learned to bear living with the strains of silence?" One night: "Isn't it time we learned to live with the bears?....In silence?"

What Did You Think of the Internet Buzz on Your Show?: I don't go into those chat rooms. They usually smell like cat piss.

Busiest Day at the Box Office: Hmmmm. For tickets, you can always call the Roundabout or log on to their website. I don't

Photos by Joseph Marzullo/WENN

Most Exciting Celebrity Visitor and What They Did/Said: James Gandolfini. He was really moved by the whole thing and found it extremely prescient.

Who Has Done the Most Shows in Their Career: The unsinkable Chip Zien.

Special Backstage Rituals: Joey and Bobby have to light cigarettes at the top of the show so those guys are flipping their Zippos and lighting them a million times before they go on. Joey, ever the gentleman, pours a cup of water for himself and Brenda Wehle before they call places, whether they're thirsty or not. Bobby has to do his impression of Rich's recorded curtain speech about two seconds before we hear it, at least the "Hello." And Bobby and Marin have to share a wink before he goes on, from her perch on the stairs.

Favorite Moment During Each Performance: For those of us backstage at places, it's probably Bobby's Rich impression. Dead on. Also, the group of us waiting behind the curtain (Ana, Marin, Joey, Bobby) while the "movie" is heard before Odets's Act Two begins (our scene two), have a great secret party, saying the lines along with the movie, cheering and air-kissing each other. Brenda's favorite moment is hearing Bobby's "OW! OW!" at the same moment Rachel is unpeeling her traditional

think you'll have a problem.

Catchphrases Only the Company Would Recognize: "Thanks. And thanks." "Suck them with the wrapper on."

Memorable Directorial Note: "Slotnick! Whatever you're doing up there.....Stop." After our final dress rehearsal, we were told all was going alright, and we could "sleep the sleep of the just" that night. That was a memorable one. Seriously, Doug Hughes is so damn eloquent and smart that you can't possibly choose one thing. He's an incredible director and human being.

Company Legend: Chip Zien.

Nicknames: There's a band called Low-Cut Connie, so that one's stuck to...Ana.

Sweethearts Within the Company: They're not very secretive about it, but Chip and Richard have had a pretty hot and heavy thing going ever since tech.

Coolest Thing About Being in This Show: Says Joey: "It's my Broadway debut, so everything about it is cool."

1. Curtain call on opening night with Bobby Cannavale (c) alongside *Yearbook* correspondents Joey Slotnick (L) and Marin Ireland.
2. The cast meets the press March 1, 2013.
3. Ana Reeder, nicknamed "Low Cut" by the cast, takes a bow.

The Book of Mormon

First Preview: February 24, 2011. Opened: March 24, 2011.
Still running as of May 31, 2013.

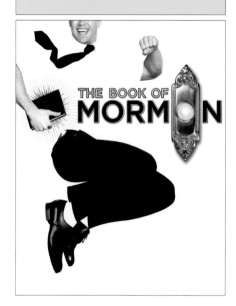

PLAYBILL®

Elder Price, the smartest, most devout and most handsome young Mormon in missionary school, is stunned to find himself assigned, not to Orlando, Florida, as he had prayed, but to a small, miserable village in Africa. He's also shocked to find himself partnered with the dorkiest missionary student, Elder Cunningham. Things go from bad to worse—until Cunningham starts making up his own additions to the Mormon Bible.

CAST
(in order of appearance)

Mormon	JASON MICHAEL SNOW
Moroni	RORY O'MALLEY
Elder Price	NIC ROULEAU
Elder Cunningham	CALE KRISE
Missionary Training Center Voice	LEWIS CLEALE
Price's Dad	LEWIS CLEALE
Cunningham's Dad	KEVIN DUDA
Mrs. Brown	TAMIKA SONJA LAWRENCE
Guards	JOHN ERIC PARKER, TOMMAR WILSON
Mafala Hatimbi	MICHAEL POTTS
Nabulungi	NIKKI M. JAMES
Elder McKinley	RORY O'MALLEY
Joseph Smith	LEWIS CLEALE
General	BRIAN TYREE HENRY
Doctor	MICHAEL JAMES SCOTT
Mission President	LEWIS CLEALE
Ensemble	SCOTT BARNHARDT, JUSTIN BOHON, DARLESIA CEARCY, KEVIN DUDA, ASMERET GHEBREMICHAEL, CLARK JOHNSEN,

Continued on next page

⊙ EUGENE O'NEILL THEATRE
A JUJAMCYN THEATRE

JORDAN ROTH
President

PAUL LIBIN
Executive Vice President

JACK VIERTEL
Senior Vice President

ANNE GAREFINO   SCOTT RUDIN

ROGER BERLIND   SCOTT M. DELMAN   JEAN DOUMANIAN
ROY FURMAN   IMPORTANT MUSICALS   STEPHANIE P. McCLELLAND
KEVIN MORRIS   JON B. PLATT   SONIA FRIEDMAN PRODUCTIONS

EXECUTIVE PRODUCER STUART THOMPSON

PRESENT

THE BOOK OF MORMON

BOOK, MUSIC AND LYRICS BY
TREY PARKER, ROBERT LOPEZ AND MATT STONE

WITH
CALE KRISE   NIC ROULEAU

NIKKI M. JAMES   RORY O'MALLEY   MICHAEL POTTS

LEWIS CLEALE   BRIAN TYREE HENRY   SCOTT BARNHARDT   JUSTIN BOHON
GRAHAM BOWEN   DARLESIA CEARCY   DELIUS DOHERTY   KEVIN DUDA
ASMERET GHEBREMICHAEL   TYSON JENNETTE   CLARK JOHNSEN   TAMIKA SONJA LAWRENCE
STEPHEN MARK LUKAS   JOHN ERIC PARKER   TRAVIS ROBERTSON   BENJAMIN SCHRADER
MICHAEL JAMES SCOTT   BRIAN SEARS   ALLISON SEMMES   JASON MICHAEL SNOW
NICK SPANGLER   LAWRENCE STALLINGS   MAIA NKENGE WILSON   TOMMAR WILSON

SCENIC DESIGN	COSTUME DESIGN	LIGHTING DESIGN	SOUND DESIGN
SCOTT PASK	**ANN ROTH**	**BRIAN MacDEVITT**	**BRIAN RONAN**

HAIR DESIGN	CASTING	PRODUCTION STAGE MANAGER
JOSH MARQUETTE	**CARRIE GARDNER**	**KAREN MOORE**

ORCHESTRATIONS	DANCE MUSIC ARRANGEMENTS	MUSIC COORDINATOR
LARRY HOCHMAN & STEPHEN OREMUS	**GLEN KELLY**	**MICHAEL KELLER**

ASSOCIATE PRODUCER	PRESS REPRESENTATIVE	PRODUCTION MANAGEMENT	GENERAL MANAGEMENT
ELI BUSH	**BONEAU/ BRYAN-BROWN**	**AURORA PRODUCTIONS**	**STP/DAVID TURNER**

MUSIC DIRECTION AND VOCAL ARRANGEMENTS
STEPHEN OREMUS

CHOREOGRAPHED BY
CASEY NICHOLAW

DIRECTED BY
CASEY NICHOLAW AND TREY PARKER

10/9/12

Rory O'Malley (C)
with ensemble

Photo by Joan Marcus

The Book of Mormon

Cast Continued

TAMIKA SONJA LAWRENCE,
JOHN ERIC PARKER, BENJAMIN SCHRADER,
MICHAEL JAMES SCOTT, BRIAN SEARS,
JASON MICHAEL SNOW,
LAWRENCE STALLINGS,
MAIA NKENGE WILSON, TOMMAR WILSON

UNDERSTUDIES

For Elder Price:
KEVIN DUDA, NICK SPANGLER
For Elder Cunningham:
BENJAMIN SCHRADER
For Missionary Training Center Voice/
Price's Dad/Joseph Smith/Mission President:
GRAHAM BOWEN, KEVIN DUDA,
BENJAMIN SCHRADER
For Mafala Hatimbi:
TYSON JENNETTE, JOHN ERIC PARKER
For Nabulungi:
ASMERET GHEBREMICHAEL,
ALLISON SEMMES
For Elder McKinley:
SCOTT BARNHARDT, GRAHAM BOWEN,
BRIAN SEARS
For The General:
DELIUS DOHERTY, TYSON JENNETTE,
JOHN ERIC PARKER

Standby For Elder Price:
STEPHEN MARK LUKAS

Nikki M. James
as Nabulungi

Photo by Joan Marcus

SWINGS
GRAHAM BOWEN, DELIUS DOHERTY,
TYSON JENNETTE, TRAVIS ROBERTSON,
ALLISON SEMMES, NICK SPANGLER

Dance Captain:
GRAHAM BOWEN
Assistant Dance Captain:
ASMERET GHEBREMICHAEL

ORCHESTRA
Conductor:
STEPHEN OREMUS
Associate Conductor:
ADAM BEN-DAVID

Keyboards:
STEPHEN OREMUS, ADAM BEN-DAVID
Guitars:
JAKE SCHWARTZ
Bass:
DAVE PHILLIPS
Drums/Percussion:
SEAN McDANIEL
Reeds:
BRYAN CROOK
Trumpet:
RAUL AGRAZ
Trombone:
RANDY ANDOS
Violin/Viola:
ENTCHO TODOROV

Music Coordinator:
MICHAEL KELLER
Keyboard Programmer:
RANDY COHEN
Copyist:
EMILY GRISHMAN MUSIC PREPARATION

Cale Krise
*Elder Cunningham
(alternate)*

Will Blum
*Elder Cunningham
(alternate)*

Nic Rouleau
Elder Price

Nikki M. James
Nabulungi

Rory O'Malley
Elder McKinley

Michael Potts
Mafala Hatimbi

Lewis Cleale
*Missionary Training
Center Voice/Price's
Dad/Joseph
Smith/Mission
President*

Brian Tyree Henry
General

Scott Barnhardt
Ensemble

Justin Bohon
Ensemble

Graham Bowen
*Swing, Dance
Captain*

Darlesia Cearcy
Ensemble

Delius Doherty
Swing

Kevin Duda
Ensemble

The Book of Mormon

Asmeret Ghebremichael
Ensemble, Assistant Dance Captain

Tyson Jennette
Swing

Clark Johnsen
Ensemble

Tamika Sonja Lawrence
Ensemble

Stephen Mark Lukas
Standby Elder Price

John Eric Parker
Ensemble

Travis Robertson
Swing

Benjamin Schrader
Ensemble

Michael James Scott
Ensemble

Brian Sears
Ensemble

Allison Semmes
Swing

Jason Michael Snow
Ensemble

Nick Spangler
Swing

Lawrence Stallings
Ensemble

Maia Nkenge Wilson
Ensemble

Tommar Wilson
Ensemble

Trey Parker
Co-Director, Book, Music, Lyrics

Robert Lopez
Book, Music, Lyrics

Matt Stone
Book, Music and Lyrics

Casey Nicholaw
Co-Director and Choreographer

Scott Pask
Scenic Design

Ann Roth
Costume Design

Brian MacDevitt
Lighting Design

Brian Ronan
Sound Design

Stephen Oremus
Music Director/ Vocal Arrranger/ Co-Orchestrator

Larry Hochman
Co-Orchestrator

Josh Marquette
Hair Design

Randy Houston Mercer
Makeup Design

Carrie Gardner, C.S.A.
Casting

Glen Kelly
Dance Arrangements

Michael Keller
Music Coordinator

Jennifer Werner
Associate Director

John MacInnis
Associate Choreographer

Gene O'Donovan
Aurora Productions
Production Management

Ben Heller
Aurora Productions
Production Management

The Book of Mormon

Brian Usifer
Associate Music Supervisor

David Turner
General Manager

Anne Garefino
Producer

Scott Rudin
Producer

Roger Berlind
Producer

Scott M. Delman
Producer

Jean Doumanian
Producer

Sonia Friedman
Sonia Friedman Productions
Producer

Roy Furman
Producer

Stephanie P. McClelland
Producer

Jon B. Platt
Producer

Stuart Thompson
Producer

David Aron Damane
General

Josh Gad
Elder Cunningham

Jared Gertner
Elder Cunningham

Douglas Lyons
Swing

Andrew Rannells
Elder Price

Samantha Marie Ware
Nabulungi

Jon Bass
Elder Cunningham

Christian Delcroix
Ensemble

Matt Doyle
Elder Price

Jeff Heimbrock
Swing

K.J. Hippensteel
Standby for Elder Price

Carly Hughes
Ensemble, Mrs. Brown

David Hull
Ensemble

Matt Loehr
Elder McKinley, Moroni

Matthew Marks
Swing

Stanley Wayne Mathis
Mafala Hatimbi

Christopher Rice
Swing

Cody Jamison Strand
Elder Cunningham

Candice Marie Woods
Ensemble

The Book of Mormon

MANAGEMENT
(L-R): Mike Zaleski (Assistant Stage Manager),
Rachel S. McCutchen (Stage Manager),
Karen Moore (Production Stage Manager)

BOX OFFICE
(L-R): Joe Kane,
Keith Stephenson,
Harry Jaffie,
Russell Owen

FRONT OF HOUSE
Standing, Front (L-R):
Byron Vargas (Head Porter),
Michael Composto
Standing, Back (L-R):
Michael Hyde, Michael Gregorek,
Scott Rippe
On Stairs:
Front Row (L-R): Kristen Vaphides,
Saime Hodzic (Head Usher),
Emily Hare (Theatre Manager)
Second Row (L-R): Bruce Lucoff,
Verna Hobson, Lorraine Wheeler,
Dorothy Lennon
Third Row (L-R): Stephen Jones,
Jay Levy, Lesley Ryder,
Martine Sigue
Fourth Row (L-R):
Giovanni Monserrate (Director),
Irene Vincent, Raymond Millan,
Ying Le
Fifth Row (L-R):
Pamela F. Martin (Director),
Sandra Palmer, Claire Newhouse,
Mili Vela (Director)
Back Row (L-R): Chris "Lotto Dude"
Catalano, Jared St. Gelais,
Alana Linchner, Sid Solomon

The Book of Mormon

WARDROBE
(L-R): Tasha Cowd, Roy Seiler, Frank Scaccia (Dresser), Elise Tolefson, Eugene Nicks (Dresser), Fred Castner (Assistant Wardrobe Supervisor),
Dolly Williams (Wardrobe Supervisor), James Martin Williams Gunn, Jamie Friday, D'Ambrose Boyd (Dresser), Melanie McClintock (Dresser), Michael Harrell (Dresser)

STAGE CREW
Front Row (L-R): Kevin Maher (Flyman), Scott Dixon (Fly Automation), Drew Lanzarotta (Deck Automation), Mike Martinez (Carpenter),
Damian Caza-Cleypool (Lead Front Electrics), Jake Mooney (Carpenter), Chris Sloan (Sound Engineer)
Back Row (L-R): Max Mooney, Chris Beck (Head Propertyman), Drayton Allison (Head Electrician), Vinnie Valvo, Don Robinson (Head Carpenter),
Ken Keneally (Props), Greg Fedigan (Propertyman), Kevin Crawford, Mary McGregor (House Sound Engineer), Kurt Fischer, Todd D'Aiuto (Head Electrician)

Photos by Brian Mapp

The Book of Mormon

STAFF FOR *THE BOOK OF MORMON*

GENERAL MANAGEMENT
STUART THOMPSON PRODUCTIONS
Stuart Thompson   David Turner   Patrick Gracey
Gregg Arst   Kevin Emrick   Andrew Lowy
Brittany Weber   James Yandoli

COMPANY MANAGER
Adam J. Miller

PRODUCTION MANAGEMENT
AURORA PRODUCTIONS
Gene O'Donovan   Ben Heller
Stephanie Sherline   Jarid Sumner   Anthony Jusino
Anita Shah   Liza Luxenberg   G. Garrett Ellison
Troy Pepicelli   Gayle Riess   Catherine Nelson
Melissa Mazdra

PRESS REPRESENTATIVE
BONEAU/BRYAN-BROWN
Chris Boneau   Jim Byk   Christine Olver

MAKEUP DESIGNER
Randy Houston Mercer

ASSOCIATE DIRECTOR
Jennifer Werner

ASSOCIATE CHOREOGRAPHER
John MacInnis

SCOTT RUDIN PRODUCTIONS
Peter Cron   Nick Reimond
Jason Sack   Chelsea Salyer   Dan Sarrow
John Schoenfelder   Jason Shrier   Jeff Stern

Production Stage Manager	**Karen Moore**
Stage Manager	Rachel S. McCutchen
Assistant Stage Manager	Michael P. Zaleski
Assistant Company Manager	Christopher Taggart
Associate Music Supervisor	Brian Usifer
Dance Captain	Graham Bowen
Assistant Dance Captain	Asmeret Ghebremichael
Associate Scenic Designer	Frank McCullough
Assistant Scenic Designers	Lauren Alvarez, Christine Peters
Associate Costume Designers	Matthew Pachtman, Michelle Matland
Costume Design Assistant	Irma Escobar
Associate Lighting Designer	Benjamin C. Travis
Assistant Lighting Designer	Carl Faber
Associate Sound Designer	Ashley Hanson
Production Carpenter	Mike Martinez
Production Electrician	Dan Coey
Head Electrician	Drayton Allison
Production Sound Engineer	Chris Sloan
Moving Light Programmer	David John Arch
Lead Front Electrics	Damian Caza-Cleypool
Sound Engineer	Jason McKenna
Deck Automation	Andrew Lanzarotta
Fly Automation	Scott Dixon
Production Props	Ken Keneally
Properties Coordinator	Pete Sarafin
Wardrobe Supervisor	Dolly Williams
Assistant Wardrobe Supervisor	Fred Castner

Hair Supervisor	Tod L. McKim
Assistant Hair Supervisor	Matthew Wilson
Dressers	D'Ambrose Boyd, Michael Harrell, Eugene Nicks, Melanie McClintock, Virginia Neinenger, Virginia Ohnesorge, Frank Scaccia, Veneda Truesdale
Hair Dresser	Joel Hawkins
Associate Musical Director	Adam Ben-David
Electronic Music Programmer	Randy Cohen
Drum Programmer	Sean McDaniel
Assistants to the Producers	Kurt Nickels, Jack Zegarski
Production Assistants	Sara Cox Bradley, Derek DiGregorio
Music Department Assistant	Matthew Aument
Costume Shoppers	Brenda Abbandandolo, Kate Friedberg
Assistant to Ms. Roth	Jonathan Schwartz
Research Assistant to Ms. Roth	Debbe DuPerrieu
Assistants to Mr. MacDevitt	Ariel Benjamin, Jonathan Dillard
Prop Shopper	Buist Bickley
Casting Associate	Kate S. Boka
Company Management Assistant	Matthew L. Wright
General Management Intern	Zachary Spitzer
Marketing Director	Steven Cardwell
Banking	City National Bank/ Erik Piecuch, Michele Gibbons
Payroll	Castellana Services, Inc.
Accountant	Fried & Kowgios CPA's LLP/ Robert Fried, CPA
Controller	J.S. Kubala
Insurance	DeWitt Stern Group
Legal Counsel	Lazarus & Harris LLP/ Scott Lazarus, Esq., Robert C. Harris, Esq.
Advertising	Serino/Coyne/ Nancy Coyne, Sandy Block, Greg Corradetti, William Bell, Jason Zammit
Digital Outreach	Serino/Coyne/ Kevin Keating, Laurie Connor, Chip Meyrelles, Crystal Chase, Jacqui Kaiser
Marketing	Serino/Coyne/ Leslie Barrett, Mike Rafael, Diana Salameh
Website Design	South Park Digital Studios/aka
Production Photographer	Joan Marcus
Vocal Coach	Liz Caplan
Company Physical Therapists	PhysioArts
Company Orthopaedist	David S. Weiss, M.D.
Theatre Displays	BAM Signs, Inc.
Transportation	IBA Limousines

CREDITS
Scenery fabrication by PRG-Scenic Technologies, a division of Production Resource Groups, LLC, New Windsor, NY. Lighting equipment provided by PRG Lighting, Secaucus, NJ. Sound equipment provided by Masque Sound. Costumes by Eric Winterling, Inc.; Gilberto Designs, Inc.; Katrina Patterns; Izquierdo Studios, Ltd.; Studio Rouge, Inc. Millinery by Rodney Gordon, Inc. Military clothing provided by Kaufman's Army & Navy. Custom military ammunition by Weapons Specialists, Ltd. Custom fabric printing by First 2 Print LLC. Custom fabric dyeing and

painting by Jeff Fender. Eyewear provided by Dr. Wayne Goldberg. Custom footwear by LaDuca Shoes, Inc.; Worldtone Dance. Props executed by Cigar Box Studios, Tom Carroll Scenery, Jerard Studios, Daedalus Design and Production, Joe Cairo, J&M Special Effects, Jeremy Lydic, Josh Yoccom. Wigs made by Hudson Wigs. Makeup provided by M•A•C Cosmetics. Keyboards from Yamaha Corporation of America.

SPECIAL THANKS
John Barlow, Lisa Gajda, Angela Howard, Bruce Howell, Beth Johnson-Nicely, Sarah Kooperkamp, Kristen Anderson-Lopez, Katie Lopez, Annie Lopez, Kathy Lopez, Frank Lopez, Billy Lopez, Brian Shepherd, Eric Stough, Boogie Tillmon, The Vineyard Theatre, Darlene Wilson

Souvenir merchandise designed and created by
The Araca Group.

Rehearsed at the New 42nd Street Studios

JUJAMCYN THEATERS

JORDAN ROTH
President

PAUL LIBIN	**JACK VIERTEL**
Executive Vice President	Senior Vice President
MEREDITH VILLATORE	**JENNIFER HERSHEY**
Chief Financial Officer	Vice President, Building Operations
MICAH HOLLINGWORTH	**HAL GOLDBERG**
Vice President, Company Operations	Vice President, Theatre Operations

Director of Business Affairs	Albert Kim
Director of Human Resources	Michele Louhisdon
Director of Ticketing Services	Justin Karr
Theatre Operations Managers	Willa Burke, Susan Elrod, Emily Hare, Jeff Hubbard, Albert Kim
Theatre Operations Associates	Carrie Brinker, Brian Busby, Michael Composto, Anah Jyoti Klate
Accounting	Cathy Cerge, Amy Frank, Tariq Hamami, Alexander Parra
Executive Producer, Red Awning	Nicole Kastrinos
Director of Sales, Givenik.com	Karen Freidus
Building Operations Associate	Erich Bussing
Executive Coordinator	Ed Lefferson
Executive Assistants	Clark Mims Tedesco, Beth Given, Julia Kraus
Receptionist	Lisa Perchinske
Maintenance	Ralph Santos, Ramon Zapata
Security	Rasim Hodzic, John Acero
Interns	Kayla Burgett, Estefania Fadul, Taylor Kurpiel, Amy Larrowe, Matthew Robertson, Brandon Smithey

STAFF FOR THE EUGENE O'NEILL THEATRE FOR *THE BOOK OF MORMON*

Theatre Manager	Emily Hare
Associate Theatre Manager	Brian Busby
Treasurer	Stanley Shaffer
Head Carpenter	Donald E. Robinson
Head Propertyman	Christopher Beck

The Book of Mormon

SCRAPBOOK

Correspondent: Kevin Duda, "Cunningham's Dad"

Milestones: On June 6, 2012, we again celebrated the *BOM* Super Fans by having our "Fan Appreciation Performance." We opened up the Tony Awards Telecast from the Beacon Theatre on Sunday, June 10! On February 24, 2013 we celebrated our 800th show, which was coincidentally also the two-year anniversary of our first preview. On March 24, 2013 we celebrated *BOM*'s two-year anniversary from Opening Day! This year we celebrated the ever-growing *Mormon* family, with the opening of three companies around the globe! The National Tour launched in Denver in August 2012, followed closely by our Chicago company in December 2012 and lastly our London family—which opened in March 2013!! We have had a wedding (Brian Sears & Jenny Fellner), we will have a baby (Graham Bowen & Cara Cooper) and we're excited for more announcements and surprises in year three!!

Most Exciting Celebrity Visitor: Our first year was PACKED with celebs and so many amazing folks, as was our second year. But I think special mention should still go to Keith Olbermann, who saw our show a whopping 13 times over the course of two years.

Actor Who Performed the Most Roles: Tyson Jennette, our amazing African Male Swing, still holds this title as he not only covers Mafala, the General and all the African Males, but he also covers all of the African Females, except Nabulungi. But give him another six months and I'm sure he'll be understudying that as well.

Special Backstage Rituals: The Mormon Boys have a "circle-up" before "Turn It Off" nightly, which consists of a number of superstitious add-ons created to remember new choreography, iconic moments or our own stupidity. Maia continues to have her "Vestibule Cabaret" at intermission many nights. Michael James Scott is our official SIP Photographer providing both hilarious moments (the *BOM* cast in "The New Normal" poses) and some sad moments (the departure of Rory O'Malley.) Nikki James still kicks those shoes down the stairs before "Hasa Diga." Our newest McKinley, Matt Loehr, has started his own ritual of some amazing Solid Gold Dancing during his off-stage time during "All American."

Favorite Moments: The boys breakup scene at the end of Act I. It hits me every time I watch it. I think that, along with Nikki's performance, and the African's line "If you don't like what we say, try living here a couple days" is the emotional glue in the show. But Maia's Vestibule Cabaret— found on Stage Right during selected performances—continues to be a highlight for all who can enjoy. Get your tickets early, though—not much seating on those stairwells.

Favorite In-Theatre Gathering Place: Coffee time in the Stage Management office in between a two-show day, where we watched *Kid President* a million times. Also the Birthday Club in the SM office—singing Happy Birthday in some rather questionable keys.

Favorite Off-Site Hangouts: We love The Palm on 50th—Brian, Alex, David and staff always treat us right! Other faves are the INC Lounge at The Time Hotel, Hurley's for our crew, Molloy's & Shorty's around bowling or softball seasons.

Favorite Snacks: With new cast members coming in, we've had a few more sweet deliveries at the door to celebrate their arrival. Schmackary's Cookies & Donna Bell's Bake Shop always show up at the perfect time. Our newest Cunningham & Price, Jon Bass & Matt Doyle have started Boys Bagel Sunday—providing us with much needed nourishment before our final two-show day of the week.

Mascots: Our "jumping Mormon" still is the iconic mascot for *BOM*, as is our "doorbell" which can be seen clear down 49th Street.

Favorite Therapy: Nikki continues to love her pastilles, and Stage Left continues to plow through Altoids like they're a meal. We are grateful to the fine folks at PhysioArts for providing our amazing physical therapy: Ryanne, Laura, Maura, Hector, Jenny & the crew! Thank you!!

Memorable Ad-Lib: Darlesia Cearcy, who brilliantly plays one of the Afican villagers, has a line at the end of the show: "You must not talk like that, Nabulungi." Well, one night she went up, as we all do from time to time. She just squeezed Nabulungi's cheeks and said "Nabulungi...ah...you know!" And scene.

Texting Incidents During a Performance: We are still lucky that we don't have too many cell phones going off. However there was a girl in the FRONT ROW in January 2013 who was our biggest offender yet...texting and checking her emails the ENTIRE show. John Eric Parker is great at giving them all "the look that kills," especially if a camera is involved.

Memorable Stage Door Fan Encounter: We had a fan follow a cast member to his subway stop once. Is that enough?

Fastest Costume Change: The Mormon Boys "pink vest" reveal is still the fastest, timing out at seven seconds!

Heaviest/Hottest Costume: The demon costumes in "Hell" win the prize. Other than that, whoever is inside the Monster costume also carries a heavy burden. Hmmm...who could that be? Is it BTH?

Who Wore the Least: Nikki James' LAD holds the title of "Lightest Costume." Never heard of an LAD? It's the African version of an LBD.

Catchphrases Only the Company Would Recognize: "Jumamosi Jackpot!" "GTI," "LYLQ," "It's Broadway Boo!"

Orchestra Member Who Played the Most Instruments: Bryan, our resident "reed doubler," logs in the most with a whopping TEN INSTRUMENTS!

Memorable Directorial Note: "Be Better."

Company In-Jokes: So many....and most involve yours truly (Duda) in some type of situation, deal, wager or strategized friendship with a cast member, crew member, management member or Superfan. Thanks to you all for the well-deserved ribbing for the past two years.

Understudy Anecdote: Our standbys and swings have become synonymous with room #601. It is a magical place where mysteries get solved, puzzles get finished, Girl Scout cookies get eaten, movies get watched and life questions are answered. Many have tried to unlock #601...few have succeeded, many have failed. Here's to you Will, KJ, Alison, Tyson, Matthew, Chris, Delius & vacation swings Jablonski, Daxton, Taprena & Jeff!

Nicknames: Sears = Brah. Michael James Scott = Boo. Nikki = Diva. Michael Potts = POTTS! Graham = G.

Coolest Thing About Being in This Show: *Mormon* is still the hottest ticket on Broadway and we are all grateful daily for that. Getting someone a "house seat" still requires a lot of notice, but gives you instant superstar status!

Iconic Story That Proves How Much Love Is Within the *BOM* Family: Brian Sears and Nick Spangler (rest in peace, who has defected to *Cinderella*) trained together to run the NYC Marathon in support of Broadway Impact, of which our very own Rory O'Malley (rest in peace) was a founding member. When Hurricane Sandy hit and they had to cancel the marathon, Sears and Spangler were crushed. So Rory, Asmeret (rest in peace), MJS and their wives, along with Jenny from Broadway Impact and many cast members, helped stage a mock finish line in our mezzanine between shows. They ran around the 50th Street block, visited *Wicked, Jersey Boys* and a few favorite hangouts, and ended with the entire cast cheering them on with signs and banners. It was a standout day at *BOM*! Congrats boys—you deserve it for all of your hard work!

Head Electrician	Todd J. D'Aiuto
Flyman	Kevin Maher
Engineer	Brian DiNapoli
Assistant Treasurers	Garry Kenny, Russell P. Owen, Keith Stephenson, Sonia Vazquez
Carpenters	Jake Mooney, Guy Patria
Propertyman	Gregory Fedigan
Electrician	James Gardner
House Sound Engineer	Mary McGregor
Head Usher	Saime Hodzic

Ticket-Takers	Dorothy Lennon, Scott Rippe
Ushers	Charlotte Brauer, Verna Hobson, Bruce Lucoff, Raymond Millan, John Nascenti, Claire Newhouse, Sandra Palmer, Irene Vincent, Lorraine Wheeler
Doorman	Emir Hodzic
Directors	Pamela F. Martin, Giovanni Monserrate, Mili Vela
Head Porter	Byron Vargas

Porter	Francisco Lopez
Head Cleaner	Mara Mijat
Cleaners	Mujesira Bicic, Maribel Cabrera

Lobby refreshments by Sweet Concessions.

Security provided by GBA Consulting, Inc.

Energy efficient washer/dryer courtesy of LG Electronics.

Breakfast at Tiffany's

First Preview: March 4, 2013. Opened: March 20, 2013.
Closed April 21, 2013 after 17 Previews and 38 Performances.

PLAYBILL

A Southern writer comes to New York and discovers a world of eccentric Manhattanites led by Holly Golightly, a devil-may-care call girl who escaped a poverty-stricken childhood and is determined to find and marry a millionaire. The writer narrates a series of alcohol-fueled romantic adventures with Holly as she strives to have as much fun as possible en route to her dream life. But then her gossamer dream world starts to crumble.

CAST
(in order of appearance)

Fred	CORY MICHAEL SMITH
Joe Bell	GEORGE WENDT
I.Y. Yunioshi	JAMES YAEGASHI
Madame Spanella	SUZANNE BERTISH
Holly Golightly	EMILIA CLARKE
Sid Arbuck	JOHN ROTHMAN
Editor	JOHN ROTHMAN
OJ Berman	LEE WILKOF
Rusty Trawler	TONY TORN
Mag Wildwood	KATE CULLEN ROBERTS
Air Force Colonel	MURPHY GUYER
Department Store Owner	EDDIE KORBICH
Journalist	ELISABETH ANTHONY GRAY
José	PEDRO CARMO
Doc	MURPHY GUYER
Stern Lady Boss	SUZANNE BERTISH
Dr. Goldman	EDDIE KORBICH
Reporter	DANNY BINSTOCK
Cop	ELISABETH ANTHONY GRAY
Rusty's Servant	PAOLO MONTALBAN

Continued on next page

⑥ CORT THEATRE
138 West 48th Street
A Shubert Organization Theatre

Philip J. Smith, *Chairman*   **Robert E. Wankel,** *President*

COLIN INGRAM & DONOVAN MANNATO   GEOFFREY THOMAS   DOMINIC IANNO

IN ASSOCIATION WITH
ROBERT L. HUTT   MICHAEL FONG/JOHN SCHMIDT   MAY CHU   ILENE STARGER

PRESENT

TRUMAN CAPOTE'S

Breakfast at Tiffany's

STAGE ADAPTATION BY
RICHARD GREENBERG

STARRING

EMILIA CLARKE   **CORY MICHAEL SMITH**

SUZANNE BERTISH   DANNY BINSTOCK   PEDRO CARMO
ELISABETH ANTHONY GRAY   MURPHY GUYER   EDDIE KORBICH
PAOLO MONTALBAN   KATE CULLEN ROBERTS   JOHN ROTHMAN
TONY TORN   LEE WILKOF   JAMES YAEGASHI

AND

GEORGE WENDT

SCENIC DESIGN	COSTUME DESIGN	LIGHTING DESIGN
DEREK McLANE	COLLEEN ATWOOD	PETER KACZOROWSKI

PROJECTION DESIGN	ORIGINAL MUSIC & SOUND DESIGN
WENDALL K. HARRINGTON	ROB MILBURN & MICHAEL BODEEN

HAIR DESIGN	MAKEUP DESIGN	ASSOCIATE DIRECTOR
DAVID BRIAN BROWN	J. ROY HELLAND	SCOTT FARIS

GENERAL MANAGER	CASTING	TECHNICAL SUPERVISOR
BESPOKE THEATRICALS	ILENE STARGER, C.S.A. ZOE E. ROTTER, C.S.A.	NEIL A. MAZZELLA

ADVERTISING & MARKETING	INTEGRATED MARKETING & SPONSORSHIPS	PRESS REPRESENTATIVE
SPOTCO	INDOMITABLE ENTERTAINMENT	O&M CO.

DIRECTED BY
SEAN MATHIAS

3/20/13

(L-R): Cory Michael Smith and Emilia Clarke

Photo by Nathan Johnson

Breakfast at Tiffany's

Cast Continued

UNDERSTUDIES

For Fred, José:
DANNY BINSTOCK
For Holly Golightly, Mag Wildwood,
Madame Spanella/Stern Lady Boss:
ELISABETH ANTHONY GRAY
For Joe Bell, OJ Berman, Rusty Trawler,
Doc, Editor/Sid Arbuck:
EDDIE KORBICH
For I.Y. Yunioshi, José, Dr. Goldman:
PAOLO MONTALBAN
For Joe Bell, OJ Berman:
JOHN ROTHMAN

The action takes place in New York City
in 1943, 1944 and 1957.

Emilia Clarke
Holly Golightly

Cory Michael Smith
Fred

George Wendt
Joe Bell

Suzanne Bertish
Madame Spanella

Danny Binstock
*Reporter and others;
Understudy*

Pedro Carmo
José

Elisabeth Anthony
Gray
*Cop and others;
Understudy*

Murphy Guyer
Doc

Eddie Korbich
*Dr. Goldman and
others; Understudy*

Paolo Montalban
*Rusty's Servant and
others; Understudy*

Kate Cullen Roberts
Mag Wildwood

John Rothman
Editor, Sid Arbuck

Tony Torn
Rusty Trawler

Lee Wilkof
OJ Berman

James Yaegashi
I.Y. Yunioshi

Montie
Cat

Moo
Cat

Vito Vincent
Cat

Truman Capote
Original Novella

Richard Greenberg
Playwright

Sean Mathias
Director

Derek McLane
Scenic Designer

Colleen Atwood
Costume Designer

Peter Kaczorowski
Lighting Designer

Wendall K.
Harrington
Projection Designer

Rod Milburn
*Original Music and
Sound Design*

Michael Bodeen
*Original Music and
Sound Design*

David Brian Brown
Hair Design

Kate Wilson
Dialect Coach

Breakfast at Tiffany's

Kate Dunn
Choreographer

Ilene Starger
Casting Director

Zoe E. Rotter
Casting Director

Scott Faris
Associate Director

J. Philip Bassett
Stage Manager

Michelle Heller
Assistant Stage Manager

Maggie Brohn
Bespoke Theatricals
General Management

Amy Jacobs
Bespoke Theatricals
General Management

Devin Keudell
Bespoke Theatricals
General Management

Nina Lannan
Bespoke Theatricals
General Management

Neil A. Mazzella
Hudson Theatrical Associates
Technical Supervisor

Kathy Fabian
Props Supervisor

Bambi Brook
Dawn Animal Agency
Animal Trainers

Colin Ingram
Lead Producer

Donovan Mannato
Producer

Dominic Ianno
Producer

BOX OFFICE
(L-R): Jose Hernandez, Julie Lui

Photos by Brian Mapp

WARDROBE/HAIR
(L-R): Philip Heckman, Lolly Totero (Dresser for Ms. Clarke), Steve Chazaro, Irene L. Bunis (Wardrobe Supervisor), Katie Chick, Kevin O'Brien, Karen Dickenson (Hair Supervisor)

Breakfast at Tiffany's

CREW
(L-R): Dave Levenberg (Head Props), Lonnie Gaddy, Jennifer Diaz, Scott DeVerna, Jens McVoy (Sound Engineer), Justin Freeman (Head Electrician)

Photo by Brian Mapp

STAFF FOR *BREAKFAST AT TIFFANY'S*

GENERAL MANAGEMENT
BESPOKE THEATRICALS
Devin Keudell · Nina Lannan
Maggie Brohn · Amy Jacobs
Associate General Manager ....Steve Dow

COMPANY MANAGER
Kate Egan

GENERAL PRESS REPRESENTATIVES
O&M CO.
Rick Miramontez · Ryan Ratelle · Michael Jorgensen

TECHNICAL SUPERVISOR
HUDSON THEATRICAL ASSOCIATES
Neil A. Mazzella
Sam Ellis · Caitlin McInerney · Irene Wang

CASTING
Ilene Starger, CSA
Zoe E. Rotter, CSA

COLIN INGRAM PRODUCTIONS
Producer ....Colin Ingram
Associate General Manager ....Simon Ash
Production Associate ....Lee Henderson

Breakfast at Tiffany's would like to thank its sponsor:
TARGET®

Special thanks for collaboration from Target® Beauty
makeup and hair partners
SONIA KASHUK and UMBERTO

Stage Manager ....J. Philip Bassett
Assistant Stage Manager ....Michelle Heller
Choreography ....Kate Dunn
Dialect Coach ....Kate Wilson
Cat Trainers ....Dawn Animal Agency
Associate Set Designer ....Erica Hemminger

Set Assistant ....Nicholas Richardson
Associate Costume Designer ....Scott Traugott
Assistant Costume Designer ....Angela Kahler
Costume Assistant ....Justin Hall
Associate Lighting Designer ....Gina Scherr
Moving Light Programmer ....Marc Polimeni
Associate Projection Designer ....Michael Clark
Assistant Projection Designer ....Olivia Sebesky
Projection Graphics ....Bo G. Eriksson
Projection Researchers ....Anya Klepikov,
Susan Hormuth
Projection Programmer ....Paul Vershbow
Associate Sound Designer ....Chris Cronin
Production Carpenter ....Ed Diaz
Production Automation Carpenter ....McBrian Dunbar
Production Electrician ....Jimmy Maloney
Head Electrician ....Justin Freeman
Sound Engineer ....Jens McVoy
Head Props ....David Levenberg
Props Supervisor ....Kathy Fabian
Wardrobe Supervisor ....Irene L. Bunis
Dresser for Ms. Clarke ....Lolly Totero
Wardrobe Staff ....Philip Heckman, Charlie Catanese,
Katie Chick, Kevin O'Brien
Hair Supervisor ....Karen Dickenson
SDC Directing Observer ....Andrew Britt
General Management Associates ....Danielle Saks,
Jimmy Wilson
General Management Interns ....Johnny Lloyd,
Brent Winzek
Press Associates ....Sarah Babin, Molly Barnett,
Scott Braun, Philip Carrubba,
Jon Dimond, Yufen Kung,
Chelsea Nachman, Pete Sanders,
Andy Snyder, Marie Pace
Press Interns ....Valentina Berger, Clio McConnell
Advertising ....SpotCo/
Drew Hodges, Tom Greenwald,
Jim Edwards, Christopher Scherer,
Stephen Sosnowski, Stephen Santore,
Ryan Zatcoff

Marketing..SpotCo/
Nick Pramik, Kristen Rathbun,
Julie Weschler
Website/Interactive Marketing ....SpotCo/
Sheila Collins, Marc Mettler,
Callie Goff
Legal Counsel (UK) ....Harbottle & Lewis LLP/
Neil Adleman
Legal Counsel ....Davis Wright Tremaine LLP/
M. Graham Coleman, Robert J. Driscoll
Immigration
Legal Counsel ....Kramer, Levin & Franklin LLP/
Mark D. Koestler
Accountant ....FK Partners/Robert Fried
Controller ....Galbraith & Co./Sarah Galbraith
Banking ....City National Bank/Michele Gibbons
Insurance ....AON/Albert G. Ruben, Claudia Kaufman
Payroll Services ....Checks and Balances/
Anthony Walker
Travel Agent ....Tzell Travel/
The "A" Team, Andi Henig
Housing Services ....ABA IDEAL/Elizabeth Helke
Merchandising ....The Araca Group
Music Clearances ....Chris Robertson

CREDITS
Scenery and automation by Hudson Scenic Studio, Inc.
Lighting by Hudson Sound and Light, LLC. Sound
equipment by Sound Associates. Video projection system
engineered and provided by Worldstage. Costumes by
EuroCo Costumes, Artur & Tailors, Arel Tailoring and
Sylvia's Costumes. Custom knitwear by Adele Recklies.
Shirts by L. Allmeier Shirts and Anto Custom Shirtmakers.
Custom millinery by Sean Barrett, London. Men's hats by
Optimo Hats, Chicago. Vintage clothing from Western
Costume, Helen Uffner, Steppin' Out, Ian Drummond,
The Archives and Palace Costume.

BREAKFAST AT TIFFANY'S BAND
Piano ....Benjamin Lewis
Saxophones ....Jim Gailloreto
Trumpet ....Benjamin Cord

Breakfast at Tiffany's

Trombone ....Andy Baker
Bass ....Larry Kohut
Drums ....Andre Beasley
Piano Arrangements ....Benjamin Lewis
Dance Sequence Arrangements ....Jim Gailloreto
Recording Engineer ....Jeff Breakey/
                            Hinge Studios, Chicago
Original Music Composed,
   Arranged and Mixed by ....Milburn & Bodeen

MUSIC CREDITS

"Velvet Moon" written by Edgar De Lange/Josef Myrow. Published by WB Music Corp and Shapiro, Bernstein & Co., Inc. (ASCAP). Performed by Harry James & His Orchestra. Courtesy of Columbia Records, a division of Sony Music Entertainment. By arrangement with Sony Music Licensing. And performed by the *Breakfast at Tiffany's* Band. "Perfidia" written by Alberto Dominguez. Published by Peer International (BMI). Performed by the *Breakfast at Tiffany's* Band. "Stardust (instrumental version)" written by Hoagy Carmichael. Published by Peer International (ASCAP). Performed by the *Breakfast at Tiffany's* Band. "Why Don't You Do Right" written by Jo McCoy. Published by Morley Music/MPL Communications (ASCAP). Performed by the American Patrol Orchestra. "Well, Git It!" written by Sy Oliver. Published by Embassy Music/Music Sales Corp (BMI). Performed by Tommy Dorsey & His Orchestra. Courtesy of RCA Records, a division of Sony Music Entertainment. By arrangement with Sony Music Licensing. "It Started All Over Again" written by Bill Carey/Carl Fischer. Published by Music Sales Corp./Songwriters Guild of America (ASCAP). Performed by Tommy Dorsey & His Orchestra. Courtesy of RCA Records, a division of Sony Music Entertainment. By arrangement with Sony Music Licensing. "Boogie Woogie" written by Clarence Smith. Published by MPL Communications (ASCAP). Performed by Tommy Dorsey & His Orchestra. Courtesy of RCA Records, a division of Sony Music Entertainment. By arrangement with Sony Music Licensing. "Strictly Instrumental" written by Edgar Battle/Bennie Benjamin/Sol Marcus/Edward Seiler. Published by Bennie Benjamin Music, Inc. Administered by Chappell & Co./MPL Communications/BMG Gold Songs on behalf of Eddie Durham Swing Music Publishing (ASCAP). Performed by Harry James & His Orchestra. Courtesy of Columbia Records, a division of Sony Music Entertainment. By arrangement with Sony Music Licensing. "A Nightingale Sang in Berkeley Square" written by Eric Maschwitz/Manning Sherwin. Published by Shapiro, Bernstein & Co., Inc. (ASCAP). Performed by Glenn Miller Orchestra. Courtesy of RCA/Sony Music. "Don't Get Around Much Anymore" written by Duke Ellington/Sidney Russell. Published by Music Sales Corp./Sony ATV Music (ASCAP). Performed by the *Breakfast at Tiffany's* Band. "Take the A Train" written by Billy Strayhorn. Published by Billy Strayhorn Songs (ASCAP). Performed by the *Breakfast at Tiffany's* Band. "Winter Wonderland" written by Felix Bernard/Richard Smith. Published by WB Music Corp (ASCAP). Performed by The Andrews Sisters. Courtesy of Geffen Records under license from Universal Music Enterprises. "Dime Adios" written by Armando Orfiche. Published by Peer International (ASCAP). Performed by Lecuona Cuban Boys. "One O'Clock Jump" written by William Count Basie. Published by Sony ATV-EMI Music Publishing (ASCAP). Performed by Tommy Dorsey. Courtesy of Geffen Records under license from Universal Music Enterprises. "I Had the Craziest Dream" written by Mack Gordon/Harry Warren. Published by WB Music Corp. (ASCAP). Performed by Harry James & His Orchestra. Courtesy of Columbia Records, a division of Sony Music Entertainment. By arrangement with Sony Music Licensing. "Serenade in Blue" written by Mack Gordon/Harry Warren. Published by WB Music Corp. (ASCAP). Performed by Glenn Miller & His Orchestra. Courtesy of RCA Records, a division of Sony Music Entertainment. By arrangement with Sony Music Licensing. "Don't Sit Under the Apple Tree (With Anyone Else But Me)" written by Lew Brown/Sam Stept/Charles Tobias. Published by Ched Music Corporation administered by WB Music Corp./Sony ATV-EMI Music Publishing (ASCAP). Performed by Glenn Miller & His Orchestra. Courtesy of RCA Records, a division of Sony Music Entertainment. By arrangement with Sony Music Licensing. "Blue Champagne" written by Jimmy Eaton/Frank Ryerson/H. Grady Watts. Published by Music Sales Corp. (ASCAP). Performed by Jimmy Dorsey & His Orchestra with Bob Eberly. Courtesy of Geffen Records under license from Universal Music Enterprises. "Sentimental Lady" written by Duke Ellington. Published by Sony ATV Music (ASCAP). Performed by Duke Ellington. Courtesy of Columbia Records, a division of Sony Music Entertainment. By arrangement with Sony Music Licensing.

PROJECTION CREDITS

Library of Congress, National Archive, The Municipal Archive of New York City, New York Historical Society, Museum of the City of New York

Breakfast at Tiffany's rehearsed at the
New 42nd Street Studios

Holly Golightly's fur provided by DENNIS BASSO.

SPECIAL THANKS

Nick Archer, John & Sarah Banks, Randy Caruso, Robert Deege, Evan & Maryann Denner, Thomas Fallon, Richard Fields, Marie Gray, Robert & Clare Gray, Joshua Heintz, Victor Ianno, Steve Kalalian, Ed Koller, Philip Kuntz, Charles Levinsohn, Chris Mirosevic, Adam Parr, Stuart Pollok, William Stuart Price, Daryl Roth, Lynn Smith, Francis Stinziano and Michael Turpen.

THE SHUBERT ORGANIZATION, INC.
Board of Directors

Philip J. Smith	**Robert E. Wankel**
Chairman	President
Wyche Fowler, Jr.	**Diana Phillips**
Lee J. Seidler	**Michael I. Sovern**
Stuart Subotnick	

Chief Financial Officer ....Elliot Greene
Sr. Vice President, Ticketing ....David Andrews
Vice President, Finance ....Juan Calvo
Vice President, Human Resources ....Cathy Cozens
Vice President, Facilities ....John Darby
Vice President, Theatre Operations ....Peter Entin
Vice President, Marketing ....Charles Flateman
Vice President, Audit ....Anthony LaMattina
Vice President, Ticket Sales ....Brian Mahoney
Vice President, Creative Projects ...........D.S. Moynihan
Vice President, Real Estate ....Julio Peterson

CORT THEATRE

House Manager ....Joseph Traina

The Shubert Organization is a proud member of the
Broadway Green Alliance

Emilia Clarke

Chessie the understudy
and mascot

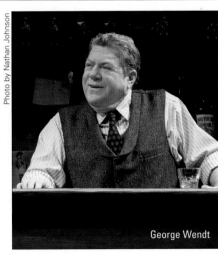

George Wendt

Breakfast at Tiffany's
SCRAPBOOK

Correspondent: Kate Cullen Roberts, "Mag Wildwood"

Opening Night Gifts: Tony Torn gave all of us a coupon for a Tarot Card reading done by himself "to be redeemed on a two-show day." Some of us were a little nervous about doing it, but the readings he gave me were really cool and exciting! Tony definitely has a second career as a Tarot Card Reader if he ever wants to leave the "biz." John Rothman gave us all a framed image of an amazing painting by Paul Cadmus. John brought a book of Cadmus paintings to rehearsal which depict these crazy 1940's drunken parties with all sorts of characters. It gave us inspiration for the party scenes in our play.

Most Exciting Celebrity Visitors: You mean other than George Wendt and Emilia Clarke?!?! Debbie Harry, Ian McKellen, Anna Wintour and Joan Rivers were some exciting visitors. Ms. Rivers sent the sweetest card to the cast, "I was happy that you would retell the original dark, moving story of the original piece and you did it in spades."

Who Has Done the Most Shows in Their Career: Suzanne Bertish, Lee Wilkof, Murphy Guyer or John Rothman. But this is Eddie Korbich's 9th Broadway show! So let's call it a five-way tie. We pretty much have a company of theatre legends. It's awesome.

Special Backstage Rituals: I like to watch Lee Wilkof perform his hilarious Act I monologue in its entirety from stage left before my entrance every show. A little dancing happens backstage before the first party scene. And in Act II, George Wendt likes me to update him on the status of the cat's performance from my vantage point in the wing. I give him a thumbs up or a thumbs down every night.

Favorite Moment During Each Performance: I love the cab ride scene where Holly leaves the cat and shoos him away and then panics and runs to find him. I get a little teary every time...even when I hear it over the monitors.

Favorite In-Theatre Gathering Places: The greenroom in the Cort is teeny weeny but we manage small magazine-reading gatherings there throughout the show. Most of us also like to make the rounds from dressing room to dressing room. The stage left water cooler is also a popular gathering place.

Favorite Off-Site Hangouts: The Rum House next to the Edison Hotel was a huge surprise to me when we first went—"This place is in midtown?!?!" There are several fellow whiskey fans in the cast. Also, the Glass House Tavern.

Mascot: Well, this used to be Vito Vincent and his handler. And now that Vito's left the show, our new cat star, Chessie.

Favorite Therapy: Paolo Montalban's magical hands.

Photos courtesy of Kate Cullen Roberts

In addition to being a studly actor (I mean, among other things, he was the Prince in Brandy's *Cinderella*!), he's also a licensed massage therapist! There has been more than one occasion when I've witnessed him healing someone's aches in the cast. He also owns the best foam roller I have ever used.

Memorable Ad-Libs: Lee Wilkof's list of his character's movie titles every night. Near the end, you never know what will come out. Also, Tony Torn and I had to do our entire dance scene with his jacket buttons stuck to my wig. Somehow that awkwardness worked for Mag and Rusty, though.

Memorable Press Encounter: We had our big press event at the Carlyle Hotel. (Incidentally, in the suite where Princess Diana would stay.) Don't tell, but everyone in the cast helped themselves to some Kiehl's toiletries in the bathrooms.

Memorable Stage Door Fan Encounter: Well, personally, I always get a sea of disappointed faces staring back at me when I leave the theatre— understandably. I myself am also personally devastated

that I'm not Emilia Clarke! There are always throngs of really thrilled "Game of Thrones" fans waiting to see her. And Emilia is, by the way, probably the sweetest and most beautiful person I have ever met. Inside and out. And she has amazing eyebrows. So jealous of those eyebrows.

What Did You Think of the Internet Buzz on Your Show: CATS!

Fastest Costume Change: It's got to be one of Emilia's 20+ costume changes...she's a pro.

Catchphrases Only the Company Would Recognize: "Die Cousin!" from the Pedro's cut scene, and Tony Torn's lines, "Alright, alright." and "Yup, yup!"

Memorable Directorial Note: Um, this would be inappropriate for public consumption.

Ghostly Encounters Backstage: I think that John Rothman's mustache from his first character "Sid Arbuck" has gone missing backstage several times, never to return. But I think I stepped on it once and it flew away. Those mustache ghosts can be really hard to exorcise.

1. A Playbill signed by the cast.
2. An opening night gift from cast member John Rothman of a copy of a Paul Cadmus painting.
3. (L-R): Our correspondent, Kate Cullen Roberts, and Elisabeth Gray in their dressing room taking out pin-curls.
4. The cast and creative team of *Breakfast at Tiffany's* taken on the last day in the rehearsal room before moving to the Cort Theatre.
5. Eddie Korbich signing in as James Yaegashi waits his turn.

Bring It On: The Musical

First Preview: July 12, 2012. Opened: August 1, 2012.
Limited Engagement. Closed December 30, 2012 after 21 Previews and 171 Performances.

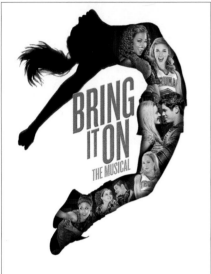

Pretty blonde teenager Campbell expects to fulfill her life dream of becoming captain of the Truman High School cheerleading squad when she finds herself transferred to the multi-ethnic Jackson High where they—gasp!—don't even have a cheerleading squad. To rebuild her dream and show up her rival at her old school, Campbell organizes her new classmates and points them at the annual national cheerleading championship. This musical is inspired by—but not based on—the 2000 movie of the same title.

CAST

(in order of appearance)

Campbell	TAYLOR LOUDERMAN
Skylar	KATE ROCKWELL
Kylar	JANET KRUPIN
Bridget	RYANN REDMOND
Steven	NEIL HASKELL
Eva	ELLE McLEMORE
Twig	NICOLAS WOMACK
Cameron	DOMINIQUE JOHNSON
Randall	JASON GOTAY
Nautica	ARIANA DeBOSE
La Cienega	GREGORY HANEY
Danielle	ADRIENNE WARREN
Burger Pagoda Girls	CALLI ALDEN, HALEY HANNAH
"Legendary" Soloist	ALYSHA UMPHRESS
"Cross the Line" Soloist	JOSHUA HENRY

Continued on next page

✪ ST. JAMES THEATRE
A JUJAMCYN THEATRE

JORDAN ROTH
President

PAUL LIBIN
Executive Vice President

JACK VIERTEL
Senior Vice President

Universal Pictures
Stage Productions/Glenn Ross

Beacon Communications/
Armyan Bernstein & Charlie Lyons

and

Kristin Caskey & Mike Isaacson
Executive Producers

present

BRING IT ON THE MUSICAL

Libretto By	Music by	Lyrics by
Jeff Whitty	Tom Kitt & Lin-Manuel Miranda	Amanda Green & Lin-Manuel Miranda

Inspired by the Motion Picture Bring It On Written by Jessica Bendinger

Starring

Taylor Louderman   Adrienne Warren

Jason Gotay   Elle McLemore   Ryann Redmond

Ariana DeBose   Gregory Haney   Neil Haskell
Dominique Johnson   Janet Krupin   Kate Rockwell   Nicolas Womack

Calli Alden   Antwan Bethea   AJ Blankenship   Nikki Bohne   Danielle Carlacci   Dexter Carr
Courtney Corbeille   Dahlston Delgado   Brooklyn Alexis Freitag   Shonica Gooden
Keith Gross   Haley Hannah   Rod Harrelson   Casey Jamerson   Melody Mills
Michael Mindlin   Michael Naone-Carter   Adrianna Parson   David Ranck
Bettis Richardson   Billie Sue Roe   Sheldon Tucker   Lauren Whitt

Set Design	Costume Design	Lighting Design	Sound Design
David Korins	Andrea Lauer	Jason Lyons	Brian Ronan

Video Design	Hair & Wig Design	Casting	Production Stage Manager
Jeff Sugg	Charles G. LaPointe	Telsey + Company Rachel Hoffman, CSA	Bonnie Panson

Technical Supervisor	Production Supervisor	Press	Marketing Direction
Jake Bell	Lisa Dawn Cave	The Hartman Group	Type A Marketing Anne Rippey

Arrangements & Orchestrations	Music Coordinator	Music Director	General Management
Alex Lacamoire & Tom Kitt	Michael Keller	Dave Pepin	321 Theatrical Management

Music Supervision & Dance Arrangements
Alex Lacamoire

Directed and Choreographed by
Andy Blankenbuehler

World premiere produced by Alliance Theatre, Atlanta, GA, Susan V. Booth, Artistic Director.
The producers wish to express their appreciation to Theatre Development Fund for its support of this production.

8/1/12

The cast of *Bring It On* in "Cross the Line"

Photo by Joan Marcus

Bring It On: The Musical

MUSICAL NUMBERS

ACT I
Overture
"What I Was Born to Do"
"Tryouts"
"One Perfect Moment"
"What I Was Born to Do" (Reprise)
"One Perfect Moment" (Reprise)
"Do Your Own Thing"
"We Ain't No Cheerleaders"
"Friday Night Jackson"
"Something Isn't Right Here"
"Bring It On"

ACT II
Entr'Acte
"It's All Happening"
"Better"
"It Ain't No Thing"
"What Was I Thinking?"
"Enjoy the Trip"
"Killer Instinct"
"We're Not Done"
"Legendary"
"Eva's Rant"
"Cross the Line"
"I Got You"

BAND
Conductor/Keyboard:
DAVE PEPIN
Associate Conductor/Keyboard:
KURT CROWLEY
Bass:
CARL CARTER
Drums:
ANDRÉS FORERO
Guitars:
RALPH AGRESTA, JOSH WEINSTEIN
Percussion:
TREY FILES
Synthesizer Programming:
RANDY COHEN

The cast of *Bring It On* in "It's All Happening."

Cast Continued

ENSEMBLE
CALLI ALDEN, ANTWAN BETHEA,
DEXTER CARR, COURTNEY CORBEILLE,
BROOKLYN ALEXIS FREITAG,
SHONICA GOODEN, HALEY HANNAH,
MELODY MILLS, MICHAEL MINDLIN,
MICHAEL NAONE-CARTER, DAVID RANCK,
BETTIS RICHARDSON, SHELDON TUCKER,
LAUREN WHITT

STANDBY
For Campbell, Eva:
NIKKI BOHNE

UNDERSTUDIES
For Campbell:
HALEY HANNAH
For Skylar:
CALLI ALDEN
For Kylar:
CALLI ALDEN, HALEY HANNAH
For Steven:
MICHAEL MINDLIN, BETTIS RICHARDSON
For Bridget:
CALLI ALDEN, JANET KRUPIN
For Eva:
HALEY HANNAH
For Twig:
DEXTER CARR, MICHAEL MINDLIN

For Randall:
NEIL HASKELL, BETTIS RICHARDSON
For Nautica:
SHONICA GOODEN, JANET KRUPIN,
ADRIANNA PARSON
For La Cienega:
MICHAEL MINDLIN, BETTIS RICHARDSON
For Danielle:
ARIANA DeBOSE, SHONICA GOODEN,
ADRIANNA PARSON
For Cameron:
DEXTER CARR, ROD HARRELSON

SWINGS
AJ BLANKENSHIP, DANIELLE CARLACCI,
DAHLSTON DELGADO, KEITH GROSS,
ROD HARRELSON, CASEY JAMERSON,
ADRIANNA PARSON, BILLIE SUE ROE

DANCE AND STUNT CAPTAIN
ROD HARRELSON

ASSISTANT DANCE CAPTAIN
ADRIANNA PARSON

ASSISTANT STUNT CAPTAIN
BILLIE SUE ROE

Taylor Louderman
Campbell

Adrienne Warren
Danielle

Jason Gotay
Randall

Elle McLemore
Eva

Ryann Redmond
Bridget

Ariana DeBose
Nautica

Gregory Haney
La Cienega

Bring It On: The Musical

Neil Haskell
Steven

Dominique Johnson
Cameron

Janet Krupin
Kylar

Kate Rockwell
Skylar

Nicolas Womack
Twig

Nikki Bohne
Standby for Campbell, Eva

Calli Alden
Ensemble

Antwan Bethea
Ensemble

AJ Blankenship
Swing

Danielle Carlacci
Swing

Dexter Carr
Ensemble

Courtney Corbeille
Ensemble

Dahlston Delgado
Swing

Brooklyn Alexis Freitag
Ensemble

Shonica Gooden
Ensemble

Keith Gross
Ensemble

Haley Hannah
Ensemble

Rod Harrelson
Dance and Stunt Captain, Swing

Casey Jamerson
Swing

Melody Mills
Ensemble

Michael Mindlin
Ensemble

Michael Naone-Carter
Ensemble

Adrianna Parson
Assistant Dance Captain, Swing

David Ranck
Ensemble

Bettis Richardson
Ensemble

Billie Sue Roe
Assistant Stunt Captain, Swing

Sheldon Tucker
Ensemble

Lauren Whitt
Ensemble

Alysha Umphress
"Legendary" Soloist

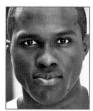
Joshua Henry
"Cross the Line" Soloist

Jeff Whitty
Librettist

Tom Kitt
Co-Composer, Co-Arranger/ Orchestrator

Lin-Manuel Miranda
Co-Composer, Co-Lyricist

Amanda Green
Co-Lyricist

Andy Blankenbuehler
Director, Choreographer

Bring It On: The Musical

David Korins
Scenic Designer

Andrea Lauer
Costume Designer

Jason Lyons
Lighting Designer

Brian Ronan
Sound Designer

Jeff Sugg
Video Design

Charles G. LaPointe
Hair and Wig Design

Bernard Telsey
Telsey + Company
Casting

Holly-Anne Ruggiero
Assistant Director

Stephanie Klemons
Associate Choreographer

Jessica Colombo
Cheer Consultant

Jake Bell
Technical Supervisor

Alex Lacamoire
Music Supervisor, Co-Arranger/ Orchestrator

Michael Keller
Music Coordinator

Dave Pepin
Music Director/ Conductor

Marcia Goldberg, Nancy Nagel Gibbs and Nina Essman
321 Theatrical Management
General Management

Kristin Caskey
Executive Producer

Mike Isaacson
Executive Producer

Armyan Bernstein
Beacon Entertainment
Producer

Charlie Lyons
Beacon Entertainment
Producer

Susan V. Booth
Alliance Theatre

Zach Pennix
Ensemble

Lindsey Brett Carothers
Ensemble

Teddy Toye
Swing

BOX OFFICE
(L-R): Vincent Sclafani (Treasurer), Carmine Loiacono (Assistant Treasurer)

STAGE MANAGEMENT
(L-R): R.L. Campbell (Assistant Stage Manager), Bonnie Panson (Production Stage Manager), Ryan J. Bell (Stage Manager)

Photos by Brian Mapp

Bring It On: The Musical

Photos by Brian Mapp

CREW
Front Row (L-R): Laura Horner (Dresser), Amy Micallef (Dresser), Bonnie Prather (Dresser), Shonté Walker (Dresser), Sue Pelkofer (Electrician), Carin Ford (Sound Engineer), Dawn Marcoccia (Dresser), Claire Ore (Hair).
Second Row (L-R): Brandon Bolton (Hair Supervisor), Sara Darneille (Dresser), Fritz Frisell (Follow Spot Operator), David Brown (Flyman), Emile LaFargue (Electrician), Paul Coltoff (Electrician), Tommy Vercetti (Carpenter), Greg Tassinaro (Head Props), Tom Sharkey (Dresser).
Back Row (L-R): Gabby Vincent (Hair Assistant), Susan Cook (Dresser), Renee Borys (Dresser), Kimberly Baird (Asst. Wardrobe Supervisor), Cate Goetschius (Dresser), Jason Muldrow (Propertyman), Justin Borowinski (Propertyman), Robert Guy (Wardrobe Supervisor), Tim McDonough, Sr. (Head Carpenter), Tim McDonough, Jr. (Head Propertyman), Keith A. Keene (Automation), Al Sayers (Head Electrician), Matthew Raudabaugh (Assistant Sound Engineer), Steve LaPlante (Electrician), Mike Farfalla (Production Sound Engineer), Ryan McDonough (Carpenter)

FRONT OF HOUSE STAFF
Front Row (L-R): Jeff Hubbard, Kendra McDuffie, Katia Koziara, Colleen Gallagher, Rochelle Rogers
Second Row (L-R): Len Baron, Andrew Mackay, Rita Richardson, Caroline Choi, Rebecca Segarra, Leslie Morgenstern, Barbara Carroll, Brian Busby
Back Row (L-R): Cynthia Lopiano, Heather Jewels, Christine Snyder, Peter Hanson

---

STAFF FOR *BRING IT ON: THE MUSICAL*

GENERAL MANAGEMENT
321 THEATRICAL MANAGEMENT
Nina Essman   Nancy Nagel Gibbs
Marcia Goldberg   Ken Silverman

CASTING
TELSEY + COMPANY
Bernie Telsey CSA, Will Cantler CSA,
David Vaccari CSA,
Bethany Knox CSA, Craig Burns CSA,
Tiffany Little Canfield CSA,
Rachel Hoffman CSA, Justin Huff CSA,
Patrick Goodwin CSA, Abbie Brady-Dalton CSA,
David Morris, Cesar A. Rocha,
Andrew Femenella, Karyn Casl,
Kristina Bramhall, Jessie Malone

GENERAL PRESS REPRESENTATIVE
THE HARTMAN GROUP
Michael Hartman   Leslie Papa
Matt Ross   Whitney Holden Gore
Nicole Capatasto

MARKETING DIRECTION
TYPE A MARKETING
Anne Rippey   Elyce Henkin
John McCoy   Robin Steinthal

ASSOCIATE PRODUCER
Megan Larche

TECHNICAL SUPERVISOR
Jake Bell

COMPANY MANAGER
Michael Bolgar

PRODUCTION STAGE MANAGER
Bonnie Panson

Stage Manager	Ryan J. Bell
Assistant Stage Manager	RL Campbell
Assistant Company Manager	Tammie Ward
Associate Choreographer	Stephanie Klemons
Assistant Director	Holly-Anne Ruggiero
Cheer Consultant	Jessica Colombo
Dance Captain/Stunt Captain	Rod Harrelson

Assistant Dance Captain	Adrianna Parson
Assistant Stunt Captain	Billie Sue Roe
Announcer Voices	Joshua Henry, Alysha Umphress
Associate Scenic Designer	Amanda Stephens
Assistant to the Scenic Designer	Stephen Edwards
Associate Costume Designer	Amanda Whidden
Assistant Costume Designer	Tristan Raines
Costume Intern	Jenna Weinstein
Assistant Hair Designer	Leah Loukas
Associate Lighting Designer	Peter Hoerburger
Assistant Lighting Designer	Grant Wilcoxen
Assistant to the Lighting Designer	Jamie Roderick
Lighting Programmer	Timothy F. Rogers
Lighting Intern	Jamie Roderick
Associate Sound Designers	Keith Caggiano, Cody Spencer
Video Supervisor	Arianna Knapp, SenovvA, Inc.
Associate Video Designer	Daniel Brodie
Video Programmer	Matthew Mellinger
Video Animators	Gabriel Aronson, Michael Bell-Smith
Video Assistant	Bart Cortright
Video Intern	Jackson Gallagher

Bring It On: The Musical

Production Carpenter ....Rick Howard
Advance Carpenter ....Randy Deboer
Head Carpenter ....Kevin Hoekstra
Automation ....Keith A. Keene
Production Electrician ....J. Michael Pitzer
Assistant Production Electrician ....Shannon January
Head Electrician ....Steve LaPlante
Production Props ....J. Marvin Crosland
Advance Props ....Courtney O'Neill
Head Props ....Gregory Tassinaro
Advance Sound ....Nick Borisjuk
Production Sound Engineer ....Mike Farfalla
Assistant Sound Engineer ....Matt Raudabaugh
Advance Wardrobe Supervisor ....Marcia VanKuiken
Wardrobe Supervisor ....Robert Guy
Assistant Wardrobe Supervisor ....Kimberly Baird
Dressers ....Shonté Walker, Cate Goetschius,
     Sara Darneille, Susan Cook,
     Bonnie Prather, Dawn Marcoccia,
     Laura Horner, Thomas Sharkey,
     Renee Borys
Hair Supervisor ....Brandon Claflin
Assistant Hair Supervisor ....Katie Beatty
Hair Assistant ....Gabby Vincent
Make Up Consultant ....Leah Loukas
Synthesizer Programming ....Randy Cohen
Music Track Editor ....Derik Lee
Music Preparation ....Emily Grishman/
     Emily Grishman Music Preparation, Inc.
Music Assistant ....Cherie Tay
Production Assistants ....Tom Casserly,
     Chandler Corbeille, Johnny Milani,
     Samantha Preiss
NBC Universal Brand
  Marketing Director ....Lori Nahama
Assistant to Ms. Caskey ....Kate Cofran
Advertising ....Serino/Coyne, Inc.
     Sandy Block, Tom Callahan,
     Joe Alesi, Zack Kinney, Roger Micone,
     Nick Nolte, Alex Rubin
Digital Marketing ....Situation Interactive
Production Photography ....Paul Aresu,
     Michael Lamont, Joan Marcus
     Craig Schwartz
Merchandise ....The Araca Group, Peter Hansen
Press Representative Staff ....Tom D'Ambrosio,
     Juliana Hannett, Bethany Larsen,
     Emily McGill, Colgan McNeill,
     Frances White, Wayne Wolfe
Banking ....City National Bank/Michele Gibbons
Director of Finance ....John DiMeglio
Payroll Service ....Checks and Balances/
     Sarah Galbraith and Anthony Walker
Accounting ....Fried and Kowgios Partners, LLP/
     Robert Fried, CPA
Insurance ....AON/Claudia Kaufman
Legal Counsel ....Brooks & Distler/Tom Distler
Physical Therapy ....Neuro Tour, LLC
Physical Therapist ....Lisa Basarab

UNIVERSAL PICTURES

President & COO,
  Universal Studios ....Ron Meyer
Chairman ....Adam Fogelson
Co-Chairman ....Donna Langley
Vice-Chairman & COO ....Rick Finkelstein

President ....Jimmy Horowitz
SVP & CFO Productions,
  Theater, Music ....Arturo Barquet
Legal Affairs ....Keith Blau
Executive, Live Theatricals ....Chris Herzberger

321 THEATRICAL MANAGEMENT

Bob Brinkerhoff, Susan Brumley,
Patrick Catullo, Mattea Cogliano-Benedict,
Eric Cornell, John DiMeglio, Tara Geesaman,
Tracy Geltman, Aaron Glick, Jason Haft,
Andrew Hartman, Adam Jackson, Andrew Karp,
Brent McCreary, Alex Owen, Rebecca Peterson,
Susan Sampliner, Nathan Vernon, Haley Ward

ALLIANCE THEATRE

Susan V. Booth ....Artistic Director
Max Leventhal ....General Manager
Brian Shively ....Finance Director
Christopher Moses ....Education Director
Kristin Hathaway-Hansen ....Development Director
Gary Sayers ....Marketing Director
Jody Feldman ....Alliance Casting Director
Victor Smith ....Director of Production
Carol Hammond ....Costume Manager
Robert Elliott ....Properties Master
Pete Shinn ....Master Electrician
Clay Benning ....Resident Sound Designer

EXCLUSIVE TOUR DIRECTION

Stephen Lindsay, Brett Sirota
The Road Company

Proud Partner—Varsity

CREDITS

Apparel sponsors: Nfinity, Levi's, Jordana Silver. Scenery
fabrication and show control and scenic motion control
featuring Stage Command Systems® by PRG–Scenic
Technologies. Lighting equipment by Christie Lites. Sound
equipment by Sound Associates. Video equipment by
SenovvA, Inc. Andrés Forero uses Yamaha drums, Sabian
cymbals, REMO drum heads and Vic Firth drumsticks
exclusively. Electronic keyboards by Yamaha. Steve
Lobemeier, D'Addario Strings and Larry Fitzgerald,
Fitzgerald Guitars. Custom costumes executed by John
Kristiansen New York Inc. Custom costume crafts by Jeff
Fender Studio. Makeup provided by M•A•C. Hair products
by Schwarzkopf Professional. Rehearsed at the Harlem Stage
Gatehouse and DiMenna Center for Classical Music. Special
thanks to those who helped us on the road to Broadway —
Phillip Aleman, Laura Baeumel, Sandy Keslar, Debbie
Burkman-Margolies, Nicole Laeger, Amy Neswald and
Patrick Harrington.

JUJAMCYN THEATERS

JORDAN ROTH
President

PAUL LIBIN
Executive Vice President

JACK VIERTEL
Senior Vice President

MEREDITH VILLATORE
Chief Financial Officer

JENNIFER HERSHEY
Vice President,
Building Operations

MICAH HOLLINGWORTH
Vice President,
Company Operations

HAL GOLDBERG
Vice President,
Theatre Operations

Director of Business Affairs ....Albert T. Kim
Director of Human Resources ....Michele Louhisdon
Director of Ticketing Services ....Justin Karr
Theatre Operations Managers ....Willa Burke,
     Susan Elrod, Emily Hare,
     Jeff Hubbard, Albert T. Kim
Theatre Operations Associates ....Carrie Jo Brinker,
     Brian Busby, Michael Composto,
     Anah Jyoti Klate
Accounting ....Cathy Cerge, Amy Frank, Tariq Hamami
Executive Producer, Red Awning ....Nicole Kastrinos
Director of Marketing, Givenik.com ....Joe Tropia
Building Operations Associate ....Erich Bussing
Executive Coordinator ....Ed Lefferson
Executive Assistants ....Clark Mims Tedesco,
     Beth Given, Julia Kraus
Receptionist ....Lisa Perchinske
Maintenance ....Ralph Santos, Ramon Zapata
Security ....Rasim Hodzic, John Acero
Interns ....Maggie Baker, Sarah Collins, Colin Geary,
     Emily Goeler, Taylor Kurpiel,
     Will Sarratt, Lena Stein

Staff for the St. James Theatre for
Bring It On: The Musical

Manager ....Jeff Hubbard
Associate Manager ....Michael Composto
Treasurer ....Vincent Sclafani
Head Carpenter ....Timothy B. McDonough
Head Propertyman ....Timothy M. McDonough
Head Electrician ....Albert Sayers
Flyman ....David Brown
Engineer ....David Neville
Assistant Treasurers ....Katie Fearon,
     Carmine Loiacono, Thomas Motylenski,
     Vincent Siniscalchi
Propertymen ....Justin Borowinski, Jason Muldrow
Electricians ....Paul Coltoff, Emile LaFargue,
     Bob Miller, Susan Pelkofer
Carpenters ....Ryan McDonough, Thomas Vercetti
Head Usher ....Cynthia Lopiano
Ticket-takers/Directors/Ushers ....Leonard Baron,
     Jim Barry, Murray Bradley,
     Barbara Carroll, Caroline Choi,
     Heather Jewels, Barbara Kagan,
     Andrew Mackay, Kendra McDuffie,
     Margaret McElroy, Leslie Morgenstern,
     Rebecca Segarra, Jessica Theisen,
     Donna Vanderlinden, Sean Zimmerman
Doormen ....Russell Buenteo, Adam Hodzic
Head Porter ....Jacobo Medrano
Porters ....Rafael Liriano, Francisco Medina,
     Donnette Niles
Head Cleaner ....Carmela Tenebruso
Cleaners ....Benita Aliberti, Juana Medrano,
     Antonia Moreno

Lobby refreshments by Sweet Concessions.

Security provided by GBA Consulting, Inc.

Bring It On: The Musical
SCRAPBOOK

Correspondent: Dominique Johnson, "Cameron"

Opening Night Gifts/Party: Our Broadway opening night was great, but we had a really big one when we opened the tour. The producers got us all iPods with the show's logo on the back. And that was not just the cast, but the entire company. Everyone was screaming and crying. The Broadway opening part was just as nice. Everyone dressed up and it was a lot of fun.

Most Exciting Celebrity Visitors: We recently had Rosie O'Donnell come to visit. When the Women's U.S. Olympic Gymnastics Team came I did not expect it would be that big of a deal. But because we have so many former gymnasts in the cast, everyone was super excited.

Who Got the Gypsy Robe: Rod Harrelson. We put two little cheer skirts on it, one red for Truman and one green for Jackson. And we bedazzled them with a lot of sparkles and pompoms.

"Gypsy of the Year" Sketch: "Feel Ur Beat" written by Janet Krupin and Rod Harrelson, choreography by Dexter Carr, Dahlston Delgado, Neil Haskel and Rod Harrelson. We were First Runner-Up for Best Stage Presentation.

"Carols for a Cure" Carol: "Angels We Have Heard on High."

Actor Who Has Done the Most Shows: Rod has done the most: *The Lion King, Chitty Chitty Bang Bang, Legally Blonde* and others.

Special Backstage Rituals: Before each performance we have a Cheer Call where other shows would have a Fight Call. We come together and run through the stunts. We also do what we call runway walks in one of the hallways backstage. We put on high-energy music, strip down to our skivvies and do a fashion show. We pretend to be models and everyone claps. It usually happens on two-show days when everyone is so tired and we need something to get the blood pumping. Personally, I like to turn on my iPod and sing very loudly in my dressing room.

Favorite Moments During Each Performance: Most definitely when Adrienne and Taylor sing "We're Not Done" and then go into the Nationals scenes. It's the first full-out cheer number the audience sees. Just the sight and the sound of it—it gives me chills. The other moment I most look forward to is when we go out of the stage door and see all the young boys and girls waiting for us. They are so enthusiastic!

Favorite In-Theatre Gathering Place: Instead of a greenroom, our theatre has a place

Curtain call on opening night.

Creative team at debut (L-R): Lin-Manuel Miranda, Tom Kitt, Amanda Green, Jeff Whitty, Alex Lacamoire

we call the Red Room. It was created by Tim McDonough and his son, Timmy Junior. We call them The Timmys. They painted a room red, and they always have food in there for us. That's the room where we sing "Happy Birthday," and where they have a TV so we can watch football games. There are a lot of athletes and former cheerleaders in our cast so there is a higher-than-usual interest in football.

Favorite Off-Site Hangout: During the summer we spent a lot of time at Blockheads on 50th between Eighth and Ninth. Since then we've been going to the downstairs lounge at Southern Hospitality.

Favorite Snack Foods: Usually Bonnie Panson, our stage manager, brings bagels on weekends. The Timmys and a few of the girls are in the habit of bringing things, so our Red Room is usually filled with food. After Thanksgiving the number of cakes and pies was ridiculous!

Mascot: We have two actual team mascots in the show: Bucky the Parrot and Lucky McClover the Leprechaun.

Favorite Therapies: For the throat everyone is pretty much sucking on pastilles, and drinking the occasional cup of tea. And, oh my gosh, PT! It's really nice that the producers have a PT

person who's with the show. We all take therapy almost every day because our bodies get so banged up.

Memorable Ad-Libs: I am a rapper in the show, but whenever I forget a line, I freeze. Taylor, on the other hand, is the best freestyler. She'll come up with the most clever lyric or clever thing to say and it makes perfect sense.

Memorable Press Encounters: We got an ice cream sundae named after our show at Serendipity. Whenever we get interviewed, everybody asks, "Are you real cheerleaders?" And we have to tell them, no, we're not real cheerleaders. They just taught us how to do it.

Memorable Stage Door Fan Encounter: We get a lot of girls coming to the show, but one day there was a father and his 6-year-old son. The little boy was so excited to meet me because he thought I was a real-life basketball player. He said, "I want to be in the NBA when I grow up." It was so adorable, it warmed my heart.

Catchphrase Only the Company Would Recognize: "Werq." We say that a lot.

Memorable Directorial Note: Andy Blankenbuehler gave us a group note on a dance number: "That wasn't what it was. Fix it." We all laughed. Thanks a lot, Andy!

Understudy Anecdote: Oh my God, our show probably has had more flop-outs than any show ever! We have so much tumbling that the boys, especially, get injured pretty often. Almost every day at intermission we hear the announcement that a swing will be going on for somebody in Act II. Our swings cover at least four tracks each. But it keeps things exciting.

Nicknames: I get called "Dom." Antwan is "Twon." Everyone calls Elle "Bambi" because she's so little.

Ghostly Encounters Backstage: I'm not sure, but I do know that I will leave my dressing room window closed, but when I come back it's wide open, and my dresser says he did not touch that window.

Coolest Thing About Being in This Show: About 95 percent of our cast is making our Broadway debuts, so we're all excited about the same things, like performing in the Macy's parade, or recording our cast album. Everyone's so young and so talented and the same age, and we all get to share this experience with each other. So it's SO FUN.

Cat on a Hot Tin Roof

First Preview: December 18, 2012. Opened: January 17, 2013.
Limited Engagement. Closed March 30, 2013 after 34 Previews and 84 Performances.

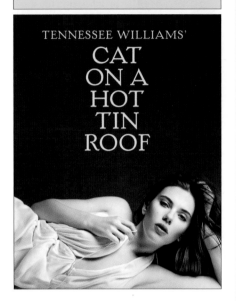

PLAYBILL

TENNESSEE WILLIAMS'
CAT ON A HOT TIN ROOF

A revival of Tennessee Williams' Pulitzer-winning classic about Big Daddy Pollitt, a wealthy Mississippi plantation owner who is dying from cancer and must decide which of his two flawed sons will inherit "28,000 acres of the richest land this side of the valley Nile." The older son, Gooper, an attorney, would seem to be the likelier candidate. But Big Daddy can't stand him. He prefers his younger son, Brick. But Brick is a drunk who harbors a terrible secret and refuses to make a child with his wife, Margaret (a.k.a. Maggie the Cat). In the end, Maggie turns out to be a stronger and more determined character than any of them.

CAST

(in order of appearance)

Margaret .... SCARLETT JOHANSSON
Daisy .... TANYA BIRL
Brick .... BENJAMIN WALKER
Mae .... EMILY BERGL
Gooper .... MICHAEL PARK
Big Mama .... DEBRA MONK
Sookey .... CHERENE SNOW
Dixie .... VICTORIA LEIGH
Big Daddy .... CIARÁN HINDS
Lacey .... LANCE ROBERTS
Brightie .... WILL COBBS
Reverend Tooker .... VIN KNIGHT
Doctor Baugh .... BRIAN REDDY
Buster .... NOAH UNGER
Trixie .... CHARLOTTE ROSE MASI
Polly .... LAUREL GRIGGS
Sonny .... GEORGE PORTEOUS

Continued on next page

RICHARD RODGERS THEATRE

UNDER THE DIRECTION OF JAMES M. NEDERLANDER AND JAMES L. NEDERLANDER

STUART THOMPSON
JON B. PLATT   THE ARACA GROUP   ROGER BERLIND
SCOTT M. DELMAN   ROY FURMAN   RUTH HENDEL   CARL MOELLENBERG
SCOTT & BRIAN ZEILINGER   NEDERLANDER PRESENTATIONS, INC.
TULCHIN/BARTNER PRODUCTIONS   SCOTT RUDIN

PRESENT

SCARLETT JOHANSSON
CIARÁN HINDS   BENJAMIN WALKER

TENNESSEE WILLIAMS'
CAT ON A
HOT TIN ROOF

WITH

DEBRA MONK

EMILY BERGL   MICHAEL PARK
VIN KNIGHT   BRIAN REDDY
TANYA BIRL   WILL COBBS   LANCE ROBERTS   CHERENE SNOW
LAUREL GRIGGS   VICTORIA LEIGH   CHARLOTTE ROSE MASI   GEORGE PORTEOUS   NOAH UNGER

SCENIC DESIGN	COSTUME DESIGN	LIGHTING DESIGN	COMPOSER & SOUND DESIGN
CHRISTOPHER ORAM	JULIE WEISS	NEIL AUSTIN	ADAM CORK

HAIR & WIG DESIGN	CASTING BY	FIGHT DIRECTOR	PRODUCTION STAGE MANAGER
PAUL HUNTLEY	DANIEL SWEE	RICK SORDELET	LISA DAWN CAVE

PRODUCTION MANAGEMENT	PRESS REPRESENTATIVE	ASSOCIATE PRODUCER	GENERAL MANAGEMENTT
AURORA PRODUCTIONS	BONEAU/BRYAN-BROWN	KEVIN EMRICK	STP / PATRICK GRACEY

DIRECTED BY
ROB ASHFORD

Cat on a Hot Tin Roof is presented by special arrangement with The University of the South, Sewanee, Tennessee.

The Producers wish to express their appreciation to Theatre Development Fund for its support of this production.

1/17/13

(L-R): Ciarán Hinds and Benjamin Walker

Photo by Joan Marcus

Cat on a Hot Tin Roof

Benjamin Walker and
Scarlett Johansson

Scarlett Johansson
Margaret

Ciarán Hinds
Big Daddy

Benjamin Walker
Brick

Debra Monk
Big Mama

Emily Bergl
Mae

Michael Park
Gooper

Vin Knight
Reverend Tooker

Brian Reddy
Doctor Baugh

Tanya Birl
Daisy; u/s Sookey

Will Cobbs
Brightie; u/s Lacey

Lance Roberts
Lacey

Cherene Snow
Sookey

Laurel Griggs
Polly

Victoria Leigh
Dixie

Cast Continued

UNDERSTUDIES

For Margaret, Mae: LEIGHTON BRYAN
For Big Daddy: TERRY LAYMAN
For Brick, Gooper: ALEX HURT
For Big Mama: AMELIA WHITE
For Doctor Baugh, Reverend Tooker,
    Brightie: T.J. KENNEALLY
For Lacey: WILL COBBS, T.J. KENNEALLY
For Sookey: TANYA BIRL, AMELIA WHITE
For Dixie: ALEXA SHAE NIZIAK,
    GEORGE PORTEOUS
For Sonny: VICTORIA LEIGH,
    ALEXA SHAE NIZIAK
For Buster, Trixie, Polly: ALEXA SHAE NIZIAK

TIME AND PLACE

An evening gathering at the
Pollitt family estate in Mississippi

MUSICIANS

Alto Sax, Clarinet, Bass Clarinet:
HIDEAKI AOMORI
Baritone Sax, Clarinet, Bass Clarinet:
ALDEN C. BANTA III
Guitar, Ukulele:
THAD C. DeBROCK
Tenor Sax, Clarinet, Bass Clarinet:
ALLEN S. SADIGURSKY

Ciarán Hinds is appearing with the
permission of Actors' Equity Association.

Cat on a Hot Tin Roof

Charlotte Rose Masi
Trixie

George Porteous
Sonny

Noah Unger
Buster

Leighton Bryan
u/s Maggie, Mae

Alex Hurt
u/s Brick, Gooper

T.J. Kenneally
u/s Baugh, Tooker, Lacey, Brightie

Terry Layman
u/s Big Daddy

Amelia White
u/s Big Mama, Sookey

Alexa Shae Niziak
u/s Dixie, Buster, Trixie, Polly, Sonny

Tennessee Williams
Playwright

Rob Ashford
Director

Christopher Oram
Scenic Designer

Julie Weiss
Costume Designer

Neil Austin
Lighting Designer

Adam Cork
Composer and Sound Design

Paul Huntley
Wig and Hair Design

Angelina Avallone
Make-up Design

Daniel Swee
Casting Director

Rick Sordelet
Fight Director

Deborah Hecht
Dialect & Vocal Coach

Stephen Sposito
Associate Director

Gene O'Donovan
Aurora Productions
Production Management

Ben Heller
Aurora Productions
Production Management

Patrick Gracey
General Manager

Stuart Thompson
Producer

Jon B. Platt
Producer

Michael Rego, Hank Unger, Matthew Rego
The Araca Group
Producers

Roger Berlind
Producer

Scott M. Delman
Producer

Roy Furman
Producer

Ruth Hendel
Producer

Carl Moellenberg
Producer

Scott Zeilinger
Producer

Brian Zeilinger
Producer

Cat on a Hot Tin Roof

James M.
Nederlander
Producer

James L.
Nederlander
Producer

Norman Tulchin
Tulchin/Bartner
Productions
Producer

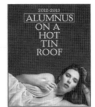

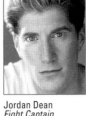
Jordan Dean
Fight Captain

Photos by Brian Mapp

CREW
Front Row (L-R): Kimberly Prentice (Dresser), Natasha Harper (Child Guardian), Lisa Dawn Cave (Production Stage Manager), Richard Fabris (Hair & Wig Assistant),
Edward DeJesus (Sub, Head Properties), Christopher Taggart (General Management Assistant), Steve Carver (House Electrician)
Middle Row (L-R): Renee Borys (Dresser), Carol M. Oune (Company Manager), Laura Ellington (Dresser), Robert Presley (Head Properties)
Back Row (L-R): Patricia Marcus (Hair/Wig Supervisor), Paul J. Smith (Stage Manager), Stephen F. DeVerna (House Propertymaster),
Kevin Camus (House Carpenter), Michael Ward (Head Electrician)

DOORMAN
James Russell

BOX OFFICE TREASURERS
(L-R): Erich Stollber, Corinne Russ

FRONT OF HOUSE
Front Row (L-R): Frances Eppy (Usher), Ray Ramos (Bar Manager), Rosanne Kelly (Matron)
Middle Row (L-R): Timothy Pettolina (House Manager), Siobhan Dunne (Usher), Ivan Rodriguez (Usher)
Back Row (L-R): Dorothy Darby (Directress), Destiny Bivona (Usher), Beverly Thornton (Usher)

Cat on a Hot Tin Roof
SCRAPBOOK

Correspondent: Emily Bergl, "Mae"

Memorable Opening Night Fax: We all swooned to see Dan Stevens' signature on the fax from *The Heiress*.

Opening Night Gift: I made red velvet Cat on a Hot Tin Cupcakes.

Who Has Done the Most Shows in Their Career: The honorable Debra Monk.

Special Backstage Ritual: Everyone LOVES it when I tune my mandolin.

Favorite In-Theatre Gathering Place: Floor 3 parties!

Favorite Off-Site Hangout: O'Flaherty's—we're working with an Irishman.

Favorite Therapy: Barry's Tea.

Most Memorable Ad-Lib: Ya don't really do that in Tennessee Williams.

Internet Buzz: You have to stay away from that stuff because you won't stop reading until you find something horrible about yourself.

(L-R): Alexa Shae Niziak, Victoria Leigh, George Porteous, Noah Unger, Charlotte Rose Masi and Laurel Griggs at the opening night party at the Lighthouse at Chelsea Piers.

Fastest Costume Change: Scarlett's dress wouldn't zip so she changed into a prop dress ON STAGE!

Heaviest/Hottest Costume: It's a hot Mississippi night and Michael Park is in a wool suit.

Who Wore the Least: Ben Walker hands down, and everyone was happy about it.

Company In-Joke: Hevening Mr. Politttt (the honorable Mr. Lance Roberts).

Company Legend: Charlotte Rose Masi.

Nickname: "50 Shades of Cherene."

Sweethearts Within the Company: Ben Walker and the Green Symphony Deli.

Embarrassing Moments: Almost every night my onstage daughter Victoria Leigh tells me I have bright pink lipstick on my teeth.

Ghostly Encounters Backstage: Laurel Griggs' Barbie was haunted by the ghost of Richard Rodgers.

Superstition That Turned Out to Be True: Not signing in IS bad luck.

Coolest Thing About Being in This Show: Being with this company on and off stage every single night.

STAFF FOR *CAT ON A HOT TIN ROOF*

GENERAL MANAGEMENT
STUART THOMPSON PRODUCTIONS
Stuart Thompson   Patrick Gracey
Marshall Purdy   David Turner
Kevin Emrick   Christopher Taggart
Andrew Lowy   Brittany Weber
Matthew Wright   James Yandoli

COMPANY MANAGER
Carol M. Oune

PRODUCTION MANAGEMENT
AURORA PRODUCTIONS
Gene O'Donovan   Ben Heller
Stephanie Sherline   Anita Shah   Jarid Sumner
Anthony Jusino   Liza Luxenberg
G. Garrett Ellison   Troy Pepicelli   Gayle Riess
Cat Nelson   Melissa Mazdra

PRESS REPRESENTATIVE
BONEAU/BRYAN-BROWN
Chris Boneau   Susanne Tighe   Christine Olver

Production Stage Manager . . . . Lisa Dawn Cave
Stage Manager . . . . .Paul J. Smith
Associate Director . . . . .Stephen Sposito
Makeup Design . . . . .Angelina Avallone
Dialect & Vocal Coach . . . . .Deborah Hecht
Associate Scenic Designer . . . . .Timothy R. Mackabee
Associate Costume Designer . . . . .Justin Hall
Associate Lighting Designer . . . . .Dan Walker
Associate Sound Designer . . . . .Chris Cronin
U.K. Scenic Associates . . . . .Lee Newby,
David Woodhead
Assistant to the Costume Designer . . . . . .Heather Lockard
Production Electrician . . . . .Jimmy Maloney
Production Props . . . . .Buist Bickley
Moving Light Programmer . . . . .Sean Beach
Head Properties . . . . .Robert Presley
Head Electrician . . . . .Justin Freeman
Production Sound Engineer . . . . .Ed Chapman
Wardrobe Supervisor . . . . .Kay Grunder
Hair Supervisor .Pat Marcus
Hair & Wig Assistant . . . . .Rich Fabris

Dressers . . . . .Renee Borys, Laura Ellington,
Kim Prentice
Child Guardian . . . . .Natasha Harper
Music Contractor . . . . .Carmen Camerieri
Production Assistant . . . . .Colyn Fiendel
Casting Associate . . . . .Camille Hickman
General Management Intern . . . . Zachary Spitzer
SDC Foundation Director Observer . . . .Pilar Castro Kiltz

Advertising . . . . .SpotCo/
Drew Hodges, Jim Edwards,
Tom Greenwald, Jim Aquino, Ryan Zatcoff
Website Design & Online Marketing . . . . .SpotCo/
Marc Mettler, Christina Sees,
Marisa Delmore
Production Photographer . . . . .Joan Marcus
Accountant . . . . .Fried & Kowgios CPA's LLP/
Robert Fried, CPA
Controller . . . . .J.S. Kubala
Insurance . . . . .DeWitt Stern Group
Legal Counsel . . . . .Davis Wright Tremaine LLP/
M. Graham Coleman, Andrew Owens
Banking . . . . .City National Bank/Michele Gibbons
Payroll . . . . .Castellana Services, Inc.
Theatre Displays . . . . .BAM Signs/Adam Miller
Transportation . . . . .IBA Limousine
Children's Tutoring . . . . .On Location Education
Children's Tutor . . . . .Muriel Kester

---

PRODUCTION CREDITS

Scenery and scenic effects built, painted, electrified and automated by Show Motion, Inc., Milford, CT. Automation and show control by Show Motion, Inc. Milford, CT. using the AC2 Computerized Motion Control System. Lighting equipment from PRG Lighting, a division of Production Resource Group, LLC, New Windsor, NY. Sound equipment by Sound Associates. Costumes by Artur & Tailors, Donna Langman Costumes and Eric Winterling, Inc. Special thanks to Bra*Tenders for hosiery and undergarments. Custom shirts by Cego. Special thanks to David Chase, Jim Hershman, Brenda Murphy, Early Halloween, Hero Wardrobe, Palace Costumes, Sichel Embroidery Studio, Western Costume.

MUSIC CREDITS

"I'm Looking Over a Four Leaf Clover" written by Mort Dixon and Harry M. Woods. Published by Olde Clover Leaf Music (ASCAP) administered by BMG Rights Management (U.S.) LLC and Callicoon Music (ASCAP). "Beautiful Dreamer" written by Stephen Foster (PD). "Happy Birthday to You" by Mildred J. Hill and Patty Smith Hill. Summy-Birchard Company (ASCAP). "Skinamarink" (Traditional, PD). "Forward Rebels (Ole Miss Fight Song)" written by E.F. Yerby. "Pick a Bale of Cotton" written by Raymond Edward Dorset; DP. Courtesy of Universal PolyGram Int. Publishing, Inc. on behalf of In the Summertime Ltd. (ASCAP). "By the Light of the Silvery Moon" written by Gus Edwards and Edward Madden (PD). "I Just Can't Stay Here by Myself" (Traditional, PD). "The Ballad of John Henry" (Traditional, PD).

Souvenir merchandise designed and created by
The Araca Group

Rehearsed at the New 42nd Street Studios.

---

www.catonahottinroofbroadway.com

➤N➤
NEDERLANDER

Chairman . . . .**James M. Nederlander**
President . . . .**James L. Nederlander**
Executive Vice President
Nick Scandalios

Vice President	Senior Vice President
Corporate Development	Labor Relations
Charlene S. Nederlander	**Herschel Waxman**
Vice President	Chief Financial Officer
Jim Boese	**Freida Sawyer Belviso**

HOUSE STAFF FOR
THE RICHARD RODGERS THEATRE

House Manager . . . . .Timothy Pettolina
Box Office Treasurer . . . . .Fred Santore Jr.
Assistant Treasurer . . . . .Corinne Russ
Electrician . . . . .Steve Carver
Carpenter . . . . .Kevin Camus
Propertymaster . . . . .Stephen F. DeVerna
Engineer . . . . .Sean Quinn

Chaplin: The Musical

First Preview: August 21, 2012. Opened: September 10, 2012.
Closed January 6, 2013 after 24 Previews and 135 Performances.

PLAYBILL®

Musical biography of pioneering silent film comedian Charlie Chaplin, from his childhood in England with a mentally unstable single mother through his introduction to the stage, his journey to America, his discovery of film, his early work with director Mack Sennett, the creation of his signature "Little Tramp" character, his ascent to superstardom in the earliest days of Hollywood, his failed marriages, his flirtation with politics, his time in the tabloid spotlight, his self-exile to Switzerland, and his eventual return to the U.S. with honors.

CAST

Charlie Chaplin	ROB McCLURE
Hannah Chaplin	CHRISTIANE NOLL
Young Charlie Chaplin, Jackie Coogan	ZACHARY UNGER
Sydney Chaplin	WAYNE ALAN WILCOX
Alf Reeves	JIM BORSTELMANN
Mack Sennett, Charlie Chaplin Sr., McGranery	MICHAEL McCORMICK
Hedda Hopper	JENN COLELLA
Oona O'Neill	ERIN MACKEY
Mr. Karno	WILLIAM RYALL
Usher	ETHAN KHUSIDMAN
Mildred Harris	HAYLEY PODSCHUN
Joan Barry	EMILEE DUPRÉ

Londoners, Music Hall Patrons, Film Crew, Starlets,
    Reporters and Hollywood Elite ....
        JUSTIN BOWEN, EMILEE DUPRÉ,
        SARA EDWARDS, LISA GAJDA,
        TIMOTHY HUGHES,

Continued on next page

☺ ETHEL BARRYMORE THEATRE

243 West 47th Street
A Shubert Organization Theatre

Philip J. Smith, *Chairman*   Robert E. Wankel, *President*

Rich Entertainment Group   John & Claire Caudwell   Roy Gabay
Viertel Routh Frankel Baruch Group   Chunsoo Shin/Waxman-Dokton   Broadway Across America

By special arrangement with Bubbles Incorporated, S.A. & Roy Export, S.A.S.

PRESENT

CHAPLIN
THE MUSICAL

BOOK BY
Christopher Curtis & Thomas Meehan

MUSIC & LYRICS BY
Christopher Curtis

INTRODUCING
ROB McCLURE
AS "Charlie Chaplin"

STARRING

**Jim Borstelmann   Jenn Colella   Erin Mackey
Michael McCormick   Christiane Noll
Zachary Unger   Wayne Alan Wilcox**

WITH

Justin Bowen   Emilee Dupré   Sara Edwards   Leslie Donna Flesner   Lisa Gajda   Timothy Hughes
Ethan Khusidman   Ian Liberto   Renée Marino   Michael Mendez   Sarah O'Gleby
Hayley Podschun   Adam Rogers   William Ryall   Eric Santagata   Emily Tyra

SET DESIGN	COSTUME DESIGN	LIGHTING DESIGN	SOUND DESIGN	VIDEO/PROJECTION DESIGN
Beowulf Boritt	Amy Clark Martin Pakledinaz	Ken Billington	Scott Lehrer Drew Levy	Jon Driscoll

WIG/HAIR DESIGN	MAKE-UP DESIGN	CASTING	VOCAL & DIALECT COACH
Paul Huntley	Angelina Avallone	Telsey + Company Patrick Goodwin, C.S.A.	Beth McGuire

PRODUCTION STAGE MANAGER	PRESS REPRESENTATIVE	COMPANY MANAGER
Kim Vernace	Boneau/Bryan-Brown	Bruce Kagel

TECHNICAL SUPERVISOR	FLYING EFFECTS	GENERAL MANAGER
Chris Smith/Smitty	Flying by Foy	Roy Gabay Productions

MUSIC DIRECTOR/ VOCAL ARRANGEMENTS	ORCHESTRATIONS	MUSIC COORDINATOR	DANCE ARRANGEMENTS
Bryan Perri	Larry Hochman	Howard Joines	Bryan Perri & Christopher Curtis

ASSOCIATE PRODUCERS
**Richard & Emily Smucker
Jon Luther**

DIRECTED & CHOREOGRAPHED BY
Warren Carlyle

World Premiere of "Chaplin" produced by La Jolla Playhouse
Christopher Ashley, Artistic Director & Michael S. Rosenberg, Managing Director
Originally presented in the 2006 New York Musical Theatre Festival
The producers wish to express their appreciation to the Theatre Development Fund for its support of this production.

Zachary Unger
(Young Charlie Chaplin)
and Rob McClure
(Charlie Chaplin)

Photo by Joan Marcus

Chaplin: The Musical

MUSICAL NUMBERS

ACT I
London, 1894-1913   Hollywood, 1913-1925

Overture/Prologue	Full Company
"Look At All the People"	Hannah
"What'cha Gonna Do?"	Hannah, Young Charlie, Charlie, Ensemble
"If I Left London"	Charlie
"Sennett Song"	Mack Sennett
"Look At All the People" (Reprise)/"Tramp Discovery"	Charlie, Hannah
"Tramp Shuffle, Pt. 1"	Charlie, Mack Sennett, Usher
"Tramp Shuffle, Pt. 2"	Reporters, Charlie, Usher, Ensemble
"Life Can Be Like the Movies"	Charlie, Sydney, Mildred, Ensemble
"The Look-a-Like Contest"	Charlie, Ensemble

ACT II
Hollywood, 1925-1972

"Just Another Day in Hollywood"	Charlie, Hedda, Ensemble
"The Life That You Wished For"	Charlie
"All Falls Down"	Hedda
"Man of All Countries"	Hedda, McGranery
"What Only Love Can See"	Oona
"Pre-Exile"	Hedda, McGranery, Ensemble
"The Exile"	Hedda, Ensemble
"Where Are All the People?"	Charlie
"What Only Love Can See" (Reprise)	Oona, Charlie
"This Man"	Full Company
Finale/Tramp Reprise	Full Company

Cast Continued

ETHAN KHUSIDMAN, IAN LIBERTO,
RENÉE MARINO, MICHAEL MENDEZ,
SARAH O'GLEBY, HAYLEY PODSCHUN,
ADAM ROGERS, WILLIAM RYALL, EMILY TYRA

SWINGS
LESLIE DONNA FLESNER, ERIC SANTAGATA

DANCE CAPTAIN
SARA EDWARDS

UNDERSTUDIES
For Charlie Chaplin:
JUSTIN BOWEN, ERIC SANTAGATA
For Hannah Chaplin:
EMILEE DUPRÉ, LESLIE DONNA FLESNER
For Young Charlie and Jackie Coogan:
ETHAN KHUSIDMAN
For Sydney Chaplin:
IAN LIBERTO, ERIC SANTAGATA
For Alf Reeves:
MICHAEL MENDEZ, ERIC SANTAGATA
For Mack Sennett, Chaplin Sr., McGranery:
WILLIAM RYALL, ERIC SANTAGATA
For Hedda Hopper:
LISA GAJDA, LESLIE DONNA FLESNER
For Oona O'Neill:
EMILY TYRA, LESLIE DONNA FLESNER

ORCHESTRA
Music Director/Piano:
BRYAN PERRI
Associate Conductor/Keyboard, Violin
DAVID GARDOS
Music Coordinator:
HOWARD JOINES
Reed 1:
CHARLES PILLOW
Reed 2:
ALDEN BANTA
Trumpet:
DAN URNESS
Horn:
DAVID PEEL
Bass:
MICHAEL BLANCO
Drums/Percussion
SHANNON FORD
Violin:
ERIN BENIM
Cello:
TARA CHAMBERS
Keyboard Programmer:
RANDY COHEN

Rob McClure and
Erin Mackey

Photo by Joan Marcus

Chaplin: The Musical

Rob McClure
Charlie Chaplin

Jim Borstelmann
Alf Reeves

Jenn Colella
Hedda Hopper

Erin Mackey
Oona O'Neill

Michael McCormick
*Mack Sennett,
Charlie Chaplin Sr.,
McGranery*

Christiane Noll
Hannah Chaplin

Zachary Unger
*Young Charlie
Chaplin, Jackie
Coogan*

Wayne Alan Wilcox
Sydney Chaplin

Justin Bowen
Ensemble

Emilee Dupré
Joan Barry

Sara Edwards
*Mabel, Dance
Captain*

Leslie Donna Flesner
Swing

Lisa Gajda
*Hedda's Secretary,
Hanwell Nurse*

Timothy Hughes
*John Frueler,
Hanwell Guard, Cop,
Car Thief*

Ethan Khusidman
Boy, Usher

Ian Liberto
Ensemble

Renée Marino
Fifteen-Year-Old Girl

Michael Mendez
*Fatty Arbuckle,
Thomas Tally*

Sarah O'Gleby
*Paulette Goddard,
Mrs. Coogan,
Chorus Girl*

Hayley Podschun
*Mildred Harris,
Gloria*

Adam Rogers
Ensemble

William Ryall
*Mr. Karno, Villain,
Jesse Robbins,
Car Thief*

Eric Santagata
Swing

Emily Tyra
*Lita Grey, Molly,
Chorus Girl*

Christopher Curtis
*Music & Lyrics,
Book*

Thomas Meehan
Book

Warren Carlyle
*Director/
Choreographer*

Bryan Perri
Musical Director

Beowulf Boritt
Scenic Design

Amy Clark
Costume Design

Martin Pakledinaz
Costume Design

Ken Billington
Lighting Design

Scott Lehrer
Sound Design

Jon Driscoll
*Video/Projection
Design*

Paul Huntley
Hair & Wig Design

Chaplin: The Musical

Angelina Avallone
Make-up Design

Larry Hochman
Orchestrations

Beth McGuire
Vocal & Dialect Coach

Bobby Hedglin-Taylor
Tightrope Trainer

Howard Joines
Music Coordinator

Tanya Birl
Associate Choreographer

Bernard Telsey
Telsey + Company
Casting

Chris Smith
Theatresmith, Inc.
Technical Supervisor

Mindy Rich
Rich Entertainment Group
Producer

Bob Rich
Rich Entertainment Group
Producer

John & Claire Caudwell
Producers

Roy Gabay
Producer/ General Manager

Thomas Viertel
Viertel/Routh/ Frankel/Baruch Group
Producer

Marc Routh
Viertel/Routh/ Frankel/Baruch Group
Producer

Richard Frankel
Viertel/Routh/ Frankel/Baruch Group
Producer

Steven Baruch
Viertel/Routh/ Frankel/Baruch Group
Producer

John Gore
CEO
Broadway Across America
Producer

Thomas B. McGrath
Chairman
Broadway Across America
Producer

Chunsoo Shin
Producer

Anita Waxman
Producer

Dan Kamin
Chaplin Consultant

Photos by Brian Mapp

BOX OFFICE
(L-R): Chuck Loesche (Treasurer),
Karen Winer (Treasurer)

CREW
Seated (L-R): Joan Weiss (Dresser), Steven Kirkham (Asst. Hair Supervisor), Edward J. Wilson (Hair Supervisor), Maureen George (Dresser), Mandy Tate (Asst. Company Manager), Bruce Kagel (Company Manager), Stephanie Vetter (Asst. Sound Mixer), Megan J. Schneid (Stage Manager), Chris Pantuso (Production Props)
Standing (L-R): David J. Elmer (Fly/Automation), Philip Feller (House Props), Michael Rico Cohen (Asst. Stage Manager), John Barbaretti (Ticket Taker), Jeanette Harrington (Hairdresser), Maurice Vancooten (Theatre Doorman), Dan Landon (House Manager), Tara Delahunt (Dresser), Sandy Binion (Dresser), Dora Bonilla (Dresser), Ben Horrigan (Deck/Automation), Roy Gabay (General Manager), Mark Gagliardi (Children's Guardian), Kim Vernace (Production Stage Manager), Patrick Pummill (Sound Mixer), Jason Clark (Production Carpenter)

Chaplin: The Musical

Photo by Joan Marcus

Rob McClure as Chaplin's Little Tramp

2012-2013 AWARDS

DRAMA DESK AWARD
Outstanding Sound Design in a Musical
(Scott Lehrer and Drew Levy)

THEATRE WORLD AWARD
For Outstanding Broadway
or Off-Broadway Debut
(Rob McClure)

The authors, with the blessings of the Chaplin family,
wish it to be known that a certain amount of dramatic
license was taken in the course of turning the long and
enormously complicated life of Charles Chaplin into a
musical play. However, the spirit and true essence of the
great man's remarkable career has been scrupulously
retained. Chaplin films made from 1923 onwards,
Copyright ©Roy Export S.A.S. All Rights Reserved. Charles
Chaplin and the Little Tramp character are trademarks
and/or service marks of Bubbles Inc. S.A. and/or Roy
Export, used with permission. Roy Export S.A.S owns and
licenses the rights to the films made by Charles Chaplin at
his studios on La Brea Avenue in Los Angeles, and A King
in New York, which was shot in the UK. Bubbles
Incorporated S.A. was set up by Charles Chaplin in the early
1970s and continues to manage and license the rights to his
name and image. www.charliechaplin.com

Chaplin: The Musical
SCRAPBOOK

Correspondent: Hayley Podschun, "Mildred Harris"

Parties and Gifts: We LOVE celebrating everyone's birthdays. Rob McClure (Charlie Chaplin) is nice enough to open up his dressing room for the cake and pie cutting. Sara Edwards (Mabel Normand, Dance Captain) hosted a lovely brunch at her apartment for her birthday for the entire cast. It was awesome!

Also, every Thursday we have TH.N.O.B. (Thursday Night on Broadway). Ian Liberto brought this tradition over from *How to Succeed....* Every week a new dressing room hosts a party for about an hour then we head to Broadway Bowling. Thursdays are definitely our favorite days of the week.

Celebrity Visitors: Our celebrity list has been super exciting so far. We've been visited by The Duchess of York-Sarah Ferguson, Nathan Lane, Anthony Warlow, Monty Hall, Susan Stroman, Dr. Ruth, Adam Shankman, and of course The Jonas Brothers who are close friends with Rob.

Actor Who Performed the Most Roles in This Show: William Ryall has 11 characters in the show. 11! They are: Karno, Master of Ceremonies, Crewman, Villain, Reporter, Jesse Robbins, Waiter, Car Thief, Tramp Look-a-Like, Ring Master, Flag Man.

Actor Who Has Done the Most Shows in Their Career: The Gypsy Robe winner on this show was Miss Lisa Gajda. She has done fifteen Broadway shows. Bill Ryall is a close runner up with thirteen shows.

Special Backstage Rituals: We're so lucky to start and end the show all together as a company. So, when the show starts, and we're in our places, we all do a little "spirit fingers" raise. Jenn Colella will also hug everyone and say "Break it!" before the curtain rises.

Another ritual happens after the big 'Circus' number at the top of Act II. We girls like to eat our dinners and have a picnic in our dressing room.

Memorable Stage Door Fan Encounters: Seeing fans wear the Chaplin bowler hats at the stage door is pretty awesome.

Favorite Moments During Each Performance (On Stage or Off):

ON: *The beginning of the show at places because we're all together.

*At the end of intermission, once "places" is called, because we all scurry like mice to our spots once the orchestra starts playing.

*A majority of us love doing the party scene because we all get to dance so many different styles in one number. And, it's just fun!!!

OFF: *Broadway Bowling!!

*Filming all of the Chaplin videos that you see in the show was pretty neat too. We all went to a studio with a green screen and reenacted scenes from *The Gold Rush, Mabel's Strange Predicament, The Kid,* et cetera.

Favorite In-Theatre Gathering Place: The girls' dressing room is a popular place because it's right by the call board and easy to get to.

Favorite Off-Site Hangouts: We love The Glass House Tavern and Café Edison because they're right across the street and super delicious. Fuel is also a popular place to eat

between shows. My favorite place in the world is Schmackary's. I'm cookie-obsessed.

Favorite Snack Foods: Trader Joe's COOKIE BUTTER!!! Tzatziki sauce with veggies, ginger chews, thinkThin Protein Bars, and chocolate.

Mascot: Jenn and I both wear furs in the show so I guess we could say Edwaaard and Jessica are our mascots.

Favorite Therapies: Intense deep-tissue mas-sages!! Leslie Flesner (our female swing) has a secret of wearing lavender oil whenever she goes on. It keeps her calm and focused.

Memorable Ad-Lib: Hands down, this goes to Wayne Wilcox (Sydney Chaplin). We're in the scene where my character, Mildred Harris, is forced by Sydney to tell Charlie that she lied about her pregnancy. Wayne is supposed to say "Yes, Mildred. Tell him there is no baby." And instead of that, he said "Yes, Mildred. Tell him there IS a baby."

1. Snacking during Act II, one of our favorite rituals (clockwise from top): Sara Edwards, Renée Marino, Emily Tyra, Hayley Podschun.
2. Mustache-on-a-stick opening night gifts from cast member, Tim Hughes.
(L-R) Podschun, Rob McClure, Marino.
3. One of our many "#SIPs" ("Saturday Intermission Pics.")

Chaplin: The Musical
SCRAPBOOK

…No baby." Let's just say it was hard for all of us to keep a straight face. I don't know how we did it, but we succeeded.

Memorable Press Encounter: Jenn, Rob, Sandy Binion (Rob's dresser), Steven Kirkham (Hair), and our amazing band were lucky enough to take a trip to Philadelphia, PA for a 'Broadway Inbound' press event. Philly also happens to be where Rob, and his wife, Maggie, call home. Everyone spoke about what fun they had not only at the event but being able to spend time at Rob's favorite hang-out spots.

"Carols for a Cure" Carol: "You Don't Have to Be Alone on Christmas."

Fastest Costume Change: There are two and they both go to Rob McClure. His first quick-quick change is 20 seconds out of the three-piece outfit into a four-piece outfit. The second quick-quick change is actually onstage during "The Circus." He puts on a flying harness followed by a tramp "onesie" behind the mirrors ONSTAGE. Thanks to Emily Tyra and Lisa Gajda he makes it every time.

Who Wore the Heaviest/Hottest Costume: Michael Mendez's hobo costume is pretty intense. The fabrics are very heavy. He also has a full beard on and a long wig. Lots of layers. Another contender for the heaviest/ hottest costumes is Rob. He wears three costumes all at the beginning of

act two for "The Circus." THREE!

Best In-House Parody Lyrics: Tim Hughes and I have a moment in the show (backstage) during "Man of All Countries" where we improv a dance, then Tim freestyles different lyrics with country themes to the underscoring. We call ourselves "Pangea." One of Tim's favorite improv lyrics was: "I heard that Antarctica is unbelievably cold. The only people that can live there are the elves of the North Pole. Is it even possible for Charlie to live there? Hardly. But it would be a funny picture: Polar Bears, Santa Claus, Charlie." Keep in mind, this is not written out beforehand. It's amazing!

Catchphrases Only the Company Would Recognize: "This. Show. Has. Everything." "Gooooooood."

① Rob McClure participates in First Skate at The Rink at Rockefeller Center.

Musical Director), and Bryan Perri (Musical Director) have all yet to miss a show.

Understudy Anecdote: "Familiarize yourself with the animal props before you go on. Edwaaard and I had a fight when I went on for Hedda."
– Leslie Flesner
"Specifically to me when I go on for Hannah: When in doubt, spin, laugh, cry, or push some scenery on stage. And don't kill Rob!" –Emilee Dupré

Nicknames: Warren Carlyle, our director/ choreographer, likes to nickname people. Here are our favorites: "Pocket" (Renée Marino), "Apple" (Sara Edwards), "Sally Bowles" (Emilee Dupré), "Dentist" (Adam Rogers), "Hugh Jackman" (Emily Tyra).

Embarrassing Moments: One of my embarrassing moments was when my "Circus" mirror got re-hooked during the number and starting flying up in the air. It was a little scary and definitely a little embarrassing.

Coolest Thing About Being in This Show: Just being a part of it! We all have so much fun and love coming to work. Most of the times, we hang out together on our days off. Our rehearsal process was awesome as well. We had only nineteen days to put the show together and, because of that, everyone came in with a "yes" attitude and was ready to play.

Fan Club: Our #1 fan is a lovely girl named Katie. She saw the show nine times within one month.

"Devotion."
"Life can be like the scoopies."
"And you will knooow…oops!"
"I KNOW IT!"
"Zoo!"
"I want it. I desire it."
"Carpet. Carpet."
"Hello Mr. Napkin"
"Aaaaactive, active, active, active."

Orchestra Member Who Played the Most Instruments: Shannon Ford, our drummer, plays 12 instruments during the show.

Orchestra Members Who Played the Most Consecutive Performances Without a Sub: Erin Benim (Violin), David Gardos (Assoc.

② Cast and creators in rehearsal.
③ Green-screen shoot day, recreating a scene from Charlie Chaplin's film, *The Kid*.
(L-R): Emily Tyra, Sarah O'Gleby, Hayley Podschun.

Chicago

First Preview: October 23, 1996. Opened: November 14, 1996.
Still running as of May 31, 2013.

Aspiring vaudeville performer Roxie Hart kills her lover and finds herself plunged into the corrupt legal system of late 1920s Chicago. As fast-talking lawyer Billy Flynn and fellow murderess Velma Kelly teach her that razzle-dazzle outdoes justice, Roxie's whole world starts to look more and more like show business.

THE CAST
(in order of appearance)

Velma Kelly .... AMRA-FAYE WRIGHT
Roxie Hart .... AMY SPANGER
Fred Casely .... JASON PATRICK SANDS
Sergeant Fogarty .... RYAN WORSING
Amos Hart .... CORY ENGLISH
Liz .... NICOLE BRIDGEWATER
Annie .... CRISTY CANDLER
June .... DONNA MARIE ASBURY
Hunyak .... TONYA WATHEN
Mona .... DYLIS CROMAN
Matron "Mama" Morton .... CAROL WOODS
Billy Flynn .... BILLY RAY CYRUS
Mary Sunshine .... R. LOWE
Go-To-Hell Kitty .... RACHEL BICKERTON
Harry .... PETER NELSON
Doctor .... EDDIE BENNETT
Aaron .... DENNY PASCHALL
The Judge .... EDDIE BENNETT
Bailiff .... AMOS WOLFF
Martin Harrison .... PETER NELSON
Court Clerk .... AMOS WOLFF
The Jury .... MICHAEL CUSUMANO

Continued on next page

⑤ AMBASSADOR THEATRE

A Shubert Organization Theatre

Philip J. Smith, *Chairman*   Robert E. Wankel, *President*

Barry & Fran Weissler
in association with
Kardana/Hart Sharp Entertainment
present

Amy Spanger   Amra-Faye Wright
Billy Ray Cyrus
Cory English

in

CHICAGO

Lyrics by   Music By   Book by
Fred Ebb   John Kander   Fred Ebb & Bob Fosse

Original Production Directed and Choreographed by **Bob Fosse**

Based on the play by Maurine Dallas Watkins

with

Carol Woods   R. Lowe

and

Donna Marie Asbury   Eddie Bennett   Rachel Bickerton   Nicole Bridgewater
Cristy Candler   Dylis Croman   Michael Cusumano   Jennifer Dunne
David Kent   J. Loeffelholz   Sharon Moore   Peter Nelson   Denny Paschall
Jason Patrick Sands   Brian Spitulnik   Tonya Wathen   Amos Wolff   Ryan Worsing

Supervising Music Director   Music Director
Rob Fisher   **Leslie Stifelman**

Scenic Design   Costume Design   Lighting Design
John Lee Beatty   **William Ivey Long**   **Ken Billington**

Sound Design   Orchestrations   Dance Music Arrangements
Scott Lehrer   **Ralph Burns**   **Peter Howard**

Script Adaptation   Musical Coordinator   Hair Design
David Thompson   **Seymour Red Press**   **David Brian Brown**

Casting   Original Casting
Duncan Stewart and Company   **Jay Binder**

Technical Supervisor   Dance Supervisor   Production Stage Manager
Arthur Siccardi   **Gary Chryst**   **David Hyslop**

Executive Producer   Presented in association with
Alecia Parker   **Broadway Across America**

General Manager   Press Representative
B.J. Holt   **Jeremy Shaffer**
                        The Publicity Office

Based on the presentation by City Center's Encores!℠

Choreography by
Ann Reinking
in the style of Bob Fosse

Directed by
Walter Bobbie

Cast Recording on RCA Victor

11/5/12

Billy Ray Cyrus as Billy Flynn with Dylis Croman (L) and Cristy Candler

Photo by Andrew Eccles

Chicago

MUSICAL NUMBERS

ACT I

"All That Jazz"	Velma and Company
"Funny Honey"	Roxie
"Cell Block Tango"	Velma and the Girls
"When You're Good to Mama"	Matron
"Tap Dance"	Roxie, Amos and Boys
"All I Care About"	Billy and Girls
"A Little Bit of Good"	Mary Sunshine
"We Both Reached for the Gun"	Billy, Roxie, Mary Sunshine and Company
"Roxie"	Roxie and Boys
"I Can't Do It Alone"	Velma
"My Own Best Friend"	Roxie and Velma

ACT II

Entr'acte	The Band
"I Know a Girl"	Velma
"Me and My Baby"	Roxie and Boys
"Mister Cellophane"	Amos
"When Velma Takes the Stand"	Velma and Boys
"Razzle Dazzle"	Billy and Company
"Class"	Velma and Matron
"Nowadays"	Roxie and Velma
"Hot Honey Rag"	Roxie and Velma
Finale	Company

ORCHESTRA

Orchestra Conducted by
LESLIE STIFELMAN
Associate Conductor:
SCOTT CADY
Assistant Conductor:
JOHN JOHNSON
Woodwinds:
SEYMOUR RED PRESS, JACK STUCKEY,
RICHARD CENTALONZA
Trumpets:
GLENN DREWES, DARRYL SHAW
Trombones:
DAVE BARGERON, BRUCE BONVISSUTO

Piano:
SCOTT CADY
Piano, Accordion:
JOHN JOHNSON
Banjo:
JAY BERLINER
Bass, Tuba:
DAN PECK
Violin:
MARSHALL COID
Drums, Percussion:
RONALD ZITO

Cast Continued

THE SCENE

Chicago, Illinois. The Late 1920s.

UNDERSTUDIES

For Roxie Hart:
DYLIS CROMAN, TONYA WATHEN
For Velma Kelly and Matron "Mama" Morton:
DONNA MARIE ASBURY,
    NICOLE BRIDGEWATER
For Billy Flynn and Amos Hart:
DENNY PASCHALL, JASON PATRICK SANDS
For Mary Sunshine:
J. LOEFFELHOLZ
For Fred Casely:
DAVID KENT, JASON PATRICK SANDS,
    BRIAN SPITULNIK
For "Me and My Baby":
DAVID KENT, BRIAN SPITULNIK,
    AMOS WOLFF

For All Other Roles:
JENNIFER DUNNE, DAVID KENT,
SHARON MOORE, BRIAN SPITULNIK

Dance Captain:
DAVID KENT

"Tap Dance" specialty performed by
EDDIE BENNETT, DENNY PASCHALL
and AMOS WOLFF.

"Me and My Baby" specialty performed by
MICHAEL CUSUMANO
and DENNY PASCHALL.

"Nowadays" whistle performed by
JASON PATRICK SANDS.

Original Choreography for "Hot Honey Rag" by
BOB FOSSE

Amy Spanger
Roxie Hart

Amra-Faye Wright
Velma Kelly

Billy Ray Cyrus
Billy Flynn

Cory English
Amos Hart

Carol Woods
Matron "Mama" Morton

R. Lowe
Mary Sunshine

Donna Marie Asbury
June

Chicago

Eddie Bennett
Doctor/The Judge

Rachel Bickerton
Go-to-Hell Kitty

Nicole Bridgewater
Liz

Cristy Candler
Annie

Dylis Croman
Mona

Michael Cusumano
The Jury

Jennifer Dunne
Swing

David Kent
Swing/Dance Captain

J. Loeffelholz
Standby Mary Sunshine

Sharon Moore
Swing

Peter Nelson
Harry/Martin Harrison

Denny Paschall
Aaron

Jason Patrick Sands
Fred Casely

Brian Spitulnik
Swing

Tonya Wathen
Hunyak

Amos Wolff
Bailiff/Court Clerk

Ryan Worsing
Sergeant Fogarty

John Kander & Fred Ebb
Music; Book/Lyrics

Bob Fosse
Book

Walter Bobbie
Director

Ann Reinking
Choreographer

John Lee Beatty
Set Design

William Ivey Long
Costume Designer

Ken Billington
Lighting Designer

Scott Lehrer
Sound Design

David Thompson
Script Adaptation

Rob Fisher
Supervising Music Director

Leslie Stifelman
Musical Director

Seymour Red Press
Music Coordinator

Duncan Stewart
Duncan Stewart and Company
Casting

Benton Whitley
Duncan Stewart and Company
Casting

Arthur Siccardi
Theatrical Services, Inc.
Technical Supervisor

Gary Chryst
Dance Supervisor

David Hyslop
Production Stage Manager

68

Chicago

Alecia Parker
Executive Producer

Fran and Barry Weissler
Producers

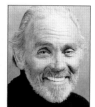
John H. Hart
Evamere
Entertainment
Producer

Morton Swinsky
Kardana Productions
Producer

John Gore
Broadway Across
America
Producer

Thomas B. McGrath
Broadway Across
America
Producer

Brent Barrett
Billy Flynn

Nili Bassman
Hunyak

Raymond Bokhour
Amos Hart

Terra C. MacLeod
Velma Kelly

Melissa Rae Mahon
Go-to-Hell Kitty

Bianca Marroquin
Roxie Hart

C. Newcomer
Mary Sunshine

Brian O'Brien
Fred Casely

Tracy Shayne
Roxie Hart

T.W. Smith
*Standby for Mary
Sunshine*

Tony Yazbeck
Billy Flynn

Ryoko Yonekura
Roxie Hart

Adam Zotovich
Sergeant Fogarty

Raymond Bokhour
Amos Hart

Paige Davis
Roxie Hart

Anne Horak
Mona

Nathan Madden
*Harry/Martin
Harrison*

D. Micciche
*Standby for Mary
Sunshine*

Brian O'Brien
Fred Casely

Adam Pascal
Billy Flynn

Christine Pedi
*Matron "Mama"
Morton*

Angel Reda
Go-to-Hell Kitty

Christopher Sieber
Billy Flynn

Adam Zotovich
Sergeant Fogarty

Adam Pascal as Billy Flynn
and Christine Pedi as
Matron "Mama" Morton

Photo by Joseph Marzullo/WENN

Chicago

Photos by Jeremy Shaffer

FRONT OF HOUSE STAFF
Front Row (L-R): Ellen Cogan, Timothy Newsome, Arlene Peters, Manuel Levine (House Manager), Allison Martin, Matthew Rodriguez
Second Row (L-R): Lori McElroy, Olga Campos
Third Row (L-R): Subhadra Robert, Dorothea Bentley, Tasha Allen
Back Row (L-R): Kasha Williams, Michael Heitzler, Jack Donaghy, Belen Bekker, Beatrice Carney

WARDROBE AND HAIR
Front Row (L-R): Sue Stepnik (Dresser), Cleopatra Matheos (Dresser)
Back Row (L-R): Patrick Rinn (Dresser), Kevin Woodworth (Wardrobe Supervisor), Jeff Silverman (Hair), Rick Meadows (Dresser)

CREW
Front Row (L-R):
John Montgomery (Sound Engineer),
Tim McIntyre (Stage Crew),
Fred Phelan (Props),
Mike Guggino (Front Light Op.),
Mike Phillips (Stage Crew)
Back Row (L-R):
Lee Iwanski (House Electrician),
Jim Werner (Front Light Op.),
Luciana Fusco (Head Electrician),
Bob Hale (Front Light Op.)

STAGE MANAGEMENT AND COMPANY MANAGEMENT
(L-R): Terrence J. Witter (Stage Manager), Mindy Farbrother (Stage Manager), Rina Saltzman (Company Manager), Rolt Smith (Production Stage Manager)

STAFF FOR *CHICAGO*

GENERAL MANAGEMENT
B.J. Holt, General Manager
Nina Skriloff, International Manager
Matthew Rimmer, Associate General Manager

PRESS REPRESENTATIVE
THE PUBLICITY OFFICE
Jeremy Shaffer   Marc Thibodeau   Michael Borowski

CASTING
DUNCAN STEWART AND COMPANY
Duncan Stewart, C.S.A.; Benton Whitley, C.S.A.;
Andrea Zee

COMPANY MANAGER
Rina L. Saltzman

Production Stage Manager	**David Hyslop**
Stage Managers	Terrence J. Witter,
	Mindy Farbrother, Mahlon Kruse

General Management	
Associate	Stephen Spadaro
Assistant Director	Jonathan Bernstein
Associate Lighting Designer	John McKernon
Assistant Choreographer	Debra McWaters
Assistant Set Designers	Eric Renschler,
	Shelley Barclay
Wardrobe Supervisor	Kevin Woodworth
Hair Supervisor	Jenna Brauer
Costume Assistant	Donald Sanders
Personal Asst to Mr. Billington	Jon Kusner

Chicago
SCRAPBOOK

(L-R): Amra-Faye Wright, Olympic Gold Medalist Gabby Douglas and *Yearbook* Correspondent Amy Spanger do a split.

Photo by Jeremy Daniel

Correspondent: Amy Spanger, "Roxie Hart"

Memorable Fan Letter: I received a caricature of myself playing Roxie recently from a fan who's studying animation at Parsons. It was brilliant!

Anniversary Parties and/or Gifts: This year, our Christmas gift from our producers was a donation to the Red Cross for Hurricane Sandy.

Most Exciting Celebrity Visitor: Olympic Gold medalist Gabby Douglas came to our show recently and afterward Amra-Faye Wright and I got our picture taken with her. The three of us were doing the splits!

Actor Who Performed the Most Roles in This Show:: Our wonderful swings do the most roles in *Chicago*. They are Sharon Moore, Brian Spitulnik, David Kent and Jennifer Dunne.

Special Backstage Rituals: Right before she makes her first entrance, Amra-Faye does push ups in her room, she then sings "Jazz" on a very high and loud note, and I say "You got it!". Then we begin...

Favorite Moment During Each Performance: Too many favorite moments to narrow down to one. I love this show.

Favorite In-Theatre Gathering Place: We hang out in the wardrobe room. There's always chocolate!

Favorite Off-Site Hangout: Our current favorite is E&E Grill. It's two doors down, they treat us great and the burgers are amazing!

Favorite Snack Foods: We love birthdays or anniversaries cuz there's cake in the wardrobe room.

"Gypsy of the Year" Skit: "Forever Fosse" by Dylis Croman, Jennifer Dunne, Tonya Wathen, Leslie Stifelman and Brian O'Brien.

Favorite Therapy: Ibuprofen. It's crack for musical theatre actors.

Memorable Ad-Lib: I recently said "Wait For It..." during "Roxie" when I had to wait for a vamp to come around before I say "I'm gonna get me a whole bunch a boys!" It's not appropriate for the period, and I haven't used it again but it got a big laugh in the moment.

Record Number of Cell Phone Rings, Cell Phone Photos or Texting Incidents During a Performance: I saw someone filming Amra-Faye and me during "Nowadays" with an iPad the other day. Now that's ballsy!

Fastest Costume Change: We're lucky at *Chicago* in that most of the company has no costume changes.

Busiest Day at the Box Office: We have many busy days and sold-out performances throughout the year — but Thanksgiving, Christmas and New Year's Day are always the most crazy.

Who Wore the Heaviest/Hottest Costume?: Ray Bokhour, who plays Amos Hart, wears a sweater.

Who Wore the Least?: The rest of us are practically naked.

Catchphrase Only the Company Would Recognize: "Poughkeepsie!"

Sweethearts Within the Company: Leslie Stifelman and Melissa Rae Mahon. They have a baby on the way!

Orchestra Members Who Played the Most Instruments: Seymour "Red" Press, Richard Centalonza and Jack Stuckey. They are our fabulous woodwind section.

Orchestra Member Who Played the Most Consecutive Performances Without a Sub: Jay Berliner, our banjo player.

Memorable Directorial Note: During a recent note session, Walter Bobbie told Amra-Faye and I to "Go Minnelli" in the song "My Own Best Friend"—which he translated as "starting at 10 and finishing in the hospital."

Company Legends: Amra-Faye Wright had played Velma all over the world for the past 12 years, including in Japan in Japanese! Donna Marie Asbury has played the role of June on Broadway for the past 15 years!

Nicknames: Jason Patrick Sands calls me "Spangladesh." I really like that. He also calls Cristy Candler "Crispy Chandler."

Coolest Thing About Being in This Show: *Chicago* has played a vital role in musical theatre history. We just celebrated 16 years on Broadway and we are now the third longest running musical in musical theatre history!

Assistant to Mr. Lehrer	Thom Mohrman
Production Carpenter	Joseph Mooneyham
Production Electrician	James Fedigan
Head Electrician	Luciana Fusco
Front Lite Operator	Michael Guggino
Production Sound Engineer	John Montgomery
Production Props	Fred Phelan
Dressers	Jo-Ann Bethell, Kathy Dacey,
	Cleopatra Matheos, Rick Meadows, Patrick Rinn
Banking	City National Bank,
	Stephanie Dalton, Michele Gibbons
Music Prep	Chelsea Music Services, Inc.
Payroll	Castellana Services, Inc.
Accountants	Rosenberg, Neuwirth & Kuchner
	Mark D'Ambrosi, Marina Flom
Insurance	Industrial Risk Specialists
Counsel	Seth Gelblum/Loeb & Loeb
Art Design	Spot Design
Advertising	SpotCo: Drew Hodges,
	Jim Edwards, Michelle Haines,
	Stephen Sosnowski, Tim Falotico
Merchandising	Dewynters Advertising Inc.
Displays	King Display

NATIONAL ARTISTS MANAGEMENT CO.

Chief Financial Officer	Bob Williams

Head of Marketing Strategy	Clint Bond Jr.
Manager of Accounting/Admin	Marian Albarracin
Associate to the Weisslers	Brett England
Assistant to Mrs. Weissler	Nikki Pelazza
Executive Assistant	Laura Sisk
Director of Marketing	Ken Sperr

SPECIAL THANKS

Additional legal services provided by Jay Goldberg, Esq. and Michael Berger, Esq. Tuxedos by Brioni.

CREDITS

Lighting equipment by PRG Lighting. Scenery built and painted by Hudson Scenic Studios. Specialty Rigging by United Staging & Rigging. Sound equipment by PRG Audio. Shoulder holster courtesy of DeSantis Holster and Leather Goods Co. Period cameras and flash units by George Fenmore, Inc. Colibri lighters used. Bible courtesy of Chiarelli's Religious Goods, Inc. Black pencils by Dixon-Ticonderoga. Gavel courtesy of The Gavel Co. Zippo lighters used. Garcia y Vega cigars used. Shoes by T.O. Dey. Orthopaedic Consultant, David S. Weiss, M.D.

Energy-efficient washer/dryer courtesy of LG Electronics.

A Christmas Story, The Musical

First Preview: November 7, 2012. Opened: November 19, 2012.
Limited Engagement. Closed December 30, 2012 after 15 Previews and 51 Performances.

PLAYBILL

Based on the 1983 film comedy of the same name, this musical tells the story of young Ralphie and his quest to persuade his parents to give him a coveted Red Ryder Air Rifle for Christmas. Along the way he must overcome bullies, an unsympathetic school teacher, a contest-obsessed father, an uncooperative department store Santa and a protective mother who is certain that Ralphie will "shoot your eye out" if he gets the gun.

CAST

(in order of appearance)

Jean Shepherd	DAN LAURIA
Ralphie	JOHNNY RABE
Ralphie (at certain performances)	JOE WEST
Mother	ERIN DILLY
Randy	ZAC BALLARD
The Old Man	JOHN BOLTON
The Bumpus Hounds	PETE AND LILY
Schwartz	J.D. RODRIGUEZ
Flick	JEREMY SHINDER
Esther Jane	ANALISE SCARPACI
Mary Beth	BEATRICE TULCHIN
Scut Farkus	JACK MASTRIANNI
Grover Dill	JOHN BABBO
Other Children	GRACE CAPELESS, SARAH MIN-KYUNG PARK, LUKE SPRING
Miss Shields	CAROLINE O'CONNOR
Fantasy Villain	MARK LEDBETTER
Delivery Men	THAY FLOYD, MARK LEDBETTER

Continued on next page

⇒N⇐ LUNT–FONTANNE THEATRE

UNDER THE DIRECTION OF
JAMES M. NEDERLANDER AND JAMES L. NEDERLANDER

Gerald Goehring   Roy Miller   Michael F. Mitri   Pat Flicker Addiss   Peter Billingsley
Timothy Laczynski   Mariano Tolentino, Jr.   Louise H. Beard   Michael Filerman   Scott Hart
Alison Eckert   Bob Bartner   Michael Jenkins   Angela Milonas   Bradford W. Smith

present

A CHRISTMAS STORY
the Musical

Book by
Joseph Robinette

Music and Lyrics by
Benj Pasek and **Justin Paul**

Based upon the motion picture "A Christmas Story"
© 1983 Turner Entertainment Co., distributed by **Warner Bros.**
written by **Jean Shepherd, Leigh Brown** and **Bob Clark**
and "In God We Trust All Others Pay Cash" by **Jean Shepherd**
Produced with permission of **Warner Bros. Theatre Ventures, Inc.** and **Dalfie Entertainment, Inc.**

Starring
Dan Lauria

John Bolton
Johnny Rabe   Zac Ballard
and **Erin Dilly**

with

Tia Altinay   John Babbo   Charissa Bertels   Grace Capeless   Zoe Considine
Andrew Cristi   Mathew deGuzman   Thay Floyd   George Franklin   Nick Gaswirth
Mark Ledbetter   Jose Luaces   Jack Mastrianni   Mara Newbery   Lindsay O'Neil
Sarah Min-Kyung Park   J.D. Rodriguez   Analise Scarpaci   Lara Seibert   Jeremy Shinder
Luke Spring   Beatrice Tulchin   Joe West   Kirsten Wyatt   and Eddie Korbich as Santa

and

Caroline O'Connor as Miss Shields

Set Design	Costume Design	Lighting Design	Sound Design
Walt Spangler	**Elizabeth Hope Clancy**	**Howell Binkley**	**Ken Travis**

Hair & Wig Design	Animals Trained by	Associate Choreographer	Casting
Tom Watson	**William Berloni**	**James Gray**	**Stephanie Klapper, CSA**

Vocal Arrangements	Music Coordinator	Production Stage Manager	Technical Supervisor
Justin Paul	**Talitha Fehr**	**Peter Wolf**	**Fred Gallo**

General Management	Press Representative	Advertising & Marketing	Associate Producers
Corker Group, LLC **John S. Corker**	**Keith Sherman** **& Associates**	**aka**	**Vincent G. Palumbo** **Dancap Productions, Inc.** **Jeffrey Jackson Ric Zivic**

Orchestrations	Music Direction and Supervision	Dance Music Arrangements
Larry Blank	**Ian Eisendrath**	**Glen Kelly**

Choreographed by
Warren Carlyle

Directed by
John Rando

World premiere produced by Kansas City Repertory Theatre, Eric Rosen, Artistic Director;
Jerry Genochio, Producing Director; Cynthia Rider, Managing Director
Subsequently produced by The 5th Avenue Theatre, Seattle, Washington; David Armstrong, Executive Producer and Artistic Director;
Bernadine C. Griffin, Managing Director and Bill Berry, Producing Director

11/19/12

(L-R): John Bolton, Johnny Rabe, Erin Dilly and Zac Ballard

Photo by Carol Rosegg

A Christmas Story, The Musical

SCENES AND MUSICAL NUMBERS

ACT I

Overture ....Orchestra
Prologue: A street corner outside radio station WOR, New York City/
   the radio studio desk — Christmas Eve, several years ago
Scene 1: The Parker Family House and Higbee's Department Store — December 1, 1940
  "It All Comes Down to Christmas" ....Ralphie, The Parkers and Ensemble
  "Red Ryder Carbine Action BB Gun" ....Ralphie and Jean
  "It All Comes Down to Christmas" (Reprise) ....Ralphie and Company
Scene 2: The Parker Family House — The Next Day
  "The Genius on Cleveland Street" ....The Old Man, Mother
Scene 3: A Path Leading to School — Soon Afterward
  "When You're a Wimp" ....Kids
Scene 4: The Classroom — A Few Minutes Later
  "Ralphie to the Rescue!" ....Ralphie, Miss Shields, The Old Man, Mother,
                                           Randy and Ensemble
Scene 5: The Parker Family House — A Week Later
  "What a Mother Does" ....Mother
  "A Major Award" ....The Old Man, Mother and Neighbors
Scene 6: The Parker Family House — Early Evening of December 13
Scene 7: On the Road — Immediately Following
  "Parker Family Singalong" ....The Parkers
Scene 8: The Parker Family House — Late That Night
  "Act I Finale" ....Ralphie and Ensemble

ACT II

Entr'Acte ....Orchestra
Scene 1: The Schoolyard and the Classroom
  "Sticky Situation" ....Ralphie, Flick, Schwartz, Kids, Miss Shields,
                     Nurse, Flick's Mom, Fireman, Policeman and Doctor
Scene 2: Fantasy 1930's Speakeasy
  "You'll Shoot Your Eye Out" ....Miss Shields and Kids
Scene 3: A Path From School — Immediately Following
Scene 4: The Parker Family House — a Few Minutes Later
  "Just Like That" ....Mother
Scene 5: Santa's Station at Higbee's — Christmas Eve
  "At Higbee's" ....Elves
  "Up on Santa's Lap" ....Santa, Elves, Ralphie, Randy and Kids
Scene 6: The Parker Family House — Christmas Eve
  "Before the Old Man Comes Home" ....The Parkers
Scene 7: The Boys' Bedroom
  "Somewhere Hovering Over Indiana" ....Ralphie, Randy and Kids
Scene 8: The Parker Family House, a Chinese Restaurant
  and the Town — Christmas Morning
  "Ralphie to the Rescue" (Reprise) ....Ralphie and Ensemble
  "A Christmas Story" ....The Parkers and Full Company

Cast Continued

Policeman ....MARK LEDBETTER
Fireman ....THAY FLOYD
Doctor ....EDDIE KORBICH
Nurse ....KIRSTEN WYATT
Flick's Mother ....LINDSAY O'NEIL
Mrs. Schwartz ....KIRSTEN WYATT
Santa Claus ....EDDIE KORBICH
Chief Elves ....ANDREW CRISTI,
              KIRSTEN WYATT
Nancy ....GRACE CAPELESS
Goggles Kid ....JOHN BABBO
Waiter ....ANDREW CRISTI
Waitress ....SARAH MIN-KYUNG PARK
Neighbors, Shoppers, Parents, Students,
  Townspeople, Elves and Others ...TIA ALTINAY,
    JOHN BABBO, CHARISSA BERTELS,
    GRACE CAPELESS, ANDREW CRISTI,
    THAY FLOYD, NICK GASWIRTH,
    EDDIE KORBICH, MARK LEDBETTER,
    JOSE LUACES, JACK MASTRIANNI,
  LINDSAY O'NEIL, SARAH MIN-KYUNG PARK,
    J.D. RODRIGUEZ, ANALISE SCARPACI,
    LARA SEIBERT, JEREMY SHINDER,
    LUKE SPRING, BEATRICE TULCHIN,
    KIRSTEN WYATT

UNDERSTUDIES

For Ralphie Parker: JOE WEST
For The Old Man: EDDIE KORBICH
For Jean Shepherd: MARK LEDBETTER
For Mother: LINDSAY O'NEIL
For Randy: JOHN BABBO
For Miss Shields: CHARISSA BERTELS

SWINGS

MATHEW deGUZMAN, MARA NEWBERY
Child Swings: GEORGE FRANKLIN
and ZOE CONSIDINE

Dance Captain: MARA NEWBERY
Assistant Dance Captain: MATHEW deGUZMAN

ORCHESTRA

Conductor: IAN EISENDRATH
Associate Conductor/Keyboard II:
  CYNTHIA KORTMAN WESTPHAL
Keys I: MICHAEL GACETTA
Reeds: DANE ANDERSEN, JIM ERCOLE,
  CHARLES PILLOW, CHAD SMITH,
  BRADEN TOAN

Trumpets: JOHN CHUDOBA,
  JAMES DE LA GARZA
Trombones: ALAN FERBER,
  MARC DONATELLE, VINNY FANUELE
Bass, Acoustic: JOE BONGIORNO
Harp: LYNETTE WARDLE
Guitar/Banjo: ANDY SCHWARTZ

Percussion: PAUL HANSEN
Drums: LARRY LELLI

Music Coordinator: TALITHA FEHR, TL MUSIC
INTERNATIONAL
Music Preparation: DONALD OLIVER and
PAUL HOLDERBAUM/CHELSEA MUSIC, INC.

A Christmas Story, The Musical

Dan Lauria
Jean Shepherd

John Bolton
The Old Man

Erin Dilly
Mother

Johnny Rabe
Ralphie

Zac Ballard
Randy

Joe West
Ralphie Standby

Caroline O'Connor
Miss Shields

Tia Altinay
Ensemble

John Babbo
Ensemble, u/s Randy

Charissa Bertels
*Ensemble,
u/s Miss Shields*

Grace Capeless
Ensemble

Zoe Considine
Swing

Andrew Cristi
Ensemble

Mathew deGuzman
*Assistant Dance
Captain/Swing*

Thay Floyd
Ensemble

George Franklin
Swing

Nick Gaswirth
Ensemble

Eddie Korbich
*Ensemble,
u/s The Old Man*

Mark Ledbetter
*Ensemble,
u/s Jean Shepherd*

Jose Luaces
Ensemble

Jack Mastrianni
Ensemble

Mara Newbery
*Dance Captain/
Swing*

Lindsay O'Neil
*Ensemble,
u/s Mother*

Sarah Min-Kyung
Park
Ensemble

J.D. Rodriguez
Ensemble

Analise Scarpaci
Ensemble

Lara Seibert
Ensemble

Jeremy Shinder
Ensemble

Luke Spring
Ensemble

Beatrice Tulchin
Ensemble

Kirsten Wyatt
Ensemble

Pete & Lily
The Bumpus Hounds

Jean Shepherd
Originating Author

Benjamin "Bob"
Clark
*Motion Picture
Director/
Co-Screenwriter*

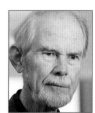

Joseph Robinette
Book

A Christmas Story, The Musical

Benj Pasek
Lyrics/Music

Justin Paul
Lyrics/Music

John Rando
Director

Warren Carlyle
Choreographer

Ian Eisendrath
Music Supervisor and Conductor

Larry Blank
Orchestrations

Walt Spangler
Scenic Design

Elizabeth Hope Clancy
Costume Designer

Howell Binkley
Lighting Designer

Ken Travis
Sound Designer

Tom Watson
Hair and Wig Designer

William Berloni
Animal Trainer

James Gray
Associate Choreographer

Cynthia Kortman Westphal
Associate Conductor

Glen Kelly
Dance Arrangements

Brandon Ivie
Assistant Director

Talitha Fehr
Music Coordinator

Fred Gallo
Technical Supervisor

John S. Corker
General Manager

**Brett Oberman
Keith Sherman & Associates**
National Press Representative

Stephanie Klapper
Casting

Luke Spring stops the show with his tap specialty in "You'll Shoot Your Eye Out."

Photo by Carol Rosegg

Gerald Goehring
Producer

Roy Miller
Producer

Pat Flicker Addiss
Producer

Peter Billingsley
Producer

Mariano Tolentino, Jr.
Producer

Louise H. Beard
Producer

Michael Filerman
Producer

Scott Hart
Producer

Alison Eckert
Producer

Michael A. Jenkins
Producer

A Christmas Story, The Musical

Vincent G. Palumbo
Associate Producer

Aubrey Dan
Dancap Productions,
Inc.
Associate Producer

Jeffrey Jackson
Associate Producer

Ric Zivic
Associate Producer

Eric Rosen
*Artistic Director
Kansas City
Repertory Theatre*

David Armstrong
*Executive Producer
and Artistic Director
5th Avenue Theatre*

Bernadine C. Griffin
*Managing Director
5th Avenue Theatre*

Bill Berry
*Producing Director
5th Avenue Theatre*

Alexa Shae Niziak
Ensemble

STAGE AND COMPANY MANAGEMENT, CHILD GUARDIANS
(L-R): Jim Brady, Peter Wolf (Production Stage Manager), Jenn McNeil (Assistant Stage Manager), Amy Gornet (Stage Manager), Alissa Zulvergold, John Mara. Not Pictured: Barbara Crompton

Photos by Brian Mapp

FRONT OF HOUSE
Standing (L-R): Barry Jenkins, Tracey Malinowski
Bottom Row (L-R): Dennis Cintron, Angalic Cortes, Paul Perez,
Second Row (L-R): Evelyn Fernandez, Madeline Flores, Stephanie Martinez, Stephanie Colon
Third Row (L-R): Lauren Banyai, Kirstin DeCicco, Richard Darbasie, Philip Zhang
Fourth Row (L-R): Melissa Ocasio, Joanne DeCicco, Spencer Cordiero, Charles Thompson
Top Row (L-R): Anthony Marcello, Roberto Calderon, Benilda Cortez, Marienell Clavano

A Christmas Story, The Musical

CREW
Sitting (L-R): Alan Schuster, Joe Valentino
Standing (L-R): Joe Pfifferling, Scott Butler, Mike Wojchik,
Stephen Clem, David Cohen, Jim Wilkinson, Kurchta Harding
On Stairs (L-R): Joe Giordano, Greg Davis

ORCHESTRA
Front (R): Vinny Fanuele
Standing (L-R): Alan Ferber, John Chudoba, Braden Toan,
Cynthia Kortman Westphal, Michael Gacetta
On Stairs (L-R): James De La Garza, Larry Lelli, Paul Hansen,
Marc Donatelle, Ian Eisendrath

STAFF FOR
A CHRISTMAS STORY, THE MUSICAL

GENERAL MANAGEMENT
CORKER GROUP, LLC
John S. Corker

GENERAL PRESS REPRESENTATIVE
KEITH SHERMAN & ASSOCIATES
Brett Oberman
Scott Klein   Logan Metzler   Chuck Mirarchi

CASTING
STEPHANIE KLAPPER CASTING
Stephanie Klapper, CSA
Tyler Albright   Lauren O'Connell

TECHNICAL SUPERVISOR
Fred Gallo

ASSOCIATE TECHNICAL SUPERVISOR
Chad Woerner

COMPANY MANAGER
Barbara Crompton

PRODUCTION STAGE MANAGER
Peter Wolf

Stage Manager ....Amy Gornet
Assistant Stage Manager ....Jenn McNeil

Associate Music Director ....Cynthia Kortman Westphal
Assistant Director ....Brandon Ivie
Dance Captain ....Mara Newbery
Assistant Dance Captain ....Mathew deGuzman
Fight Captain.... ....Mathew deGuzman
Creative Consultant ....Red Awning/Jack Viertel
Consultant ....Chizner & Co. LLC, CPAs
General Management Associate ....Kristina Wicke
Assistant Company Manager ....Jim Brady
Assistant to General Manager ....James Viggiano
Assistant Set Designer ....Jisun Kim
Assistant Costume Designer ....Lisa Zinni
Costume Assistant/Shopper ....Abigail Dana Hahn
Costume Shopper ....Sarafina Bush
Costume Interns ....Mahalah King Sltutzsky,
                                       Tina McCartney
Associate Lighting Designer ....Ryan O'Gara
Assistant Lighting Designer ....Amanda Zieve
Moving Light Programmer ....Chris Herman
Associate Sound Designer ....Alex Hawthorn
Animal
   Trainer ....William Berloni Theatrical Animals, Inc./
                                       Bill Berloni
Animal Handler ....Patrick Peavy
Assistant Animal Handler ....Kristen Sobanki
Production Electrician ....Randy Zaibek
Production Sound Supervisor ....Phil Lojo
Advance Sound ....Darren Shaw
Production Properties Supervisor ....Chris Pantuso
Head Carpenter ....David Cohen
Assistant Carpenter ....Joe Valentino Jr.

Head Properties ....Greg Davis
Assistant Properties ....Kurchta Harding
Head Electrician ....Alan Schuster
Assistant Electrician/
   Spot Operator ....Scott Butler
Head Sound ....Mike Wojchik
Assistant Sound ....Bill Ruger
Wardrobe Supervisor/
   Costume Coordinator ....Jessica Worsnop
Assistant Wardrobe Supervisor ....Jason Bishop
Dressers ....Elizabeth Brady, Cathy Cline,
                              Tracey Diebold, John Furrow,
                              Victoria Grecki, Scott Harrington,
                              Gregory Holtz, Bryen Shannon,
                                       Amanda Zane
Laundry ....Nancy Ronan
Stitcher ....Angela Lehrer
Day Workers ....Barry Doss, William Hubner,
                                       Judy Kahn
Hair Supervisor ....Susan Corrado
Assistant Hair Supervisor ....Jenna Barrios
House Contractor ....Marc Donatelle
Assistant Music Director/
   Rehearsal Pianist ....Michael Gacetta
Music
   Preparation ....Donald Oliver & Paul Holderbaum/
                                       Chelsea Music, Inc.
Music Preparation Assistant ....Calvin Brown
Keyboard Programmer ....Jim Harp/Synthlink
Associate Keyboard Programmer ....Gary Georgett/
                                       Synthlink

A Christmas Story, The Musical

Music PA ....Chris Ranney
Librarian ....Braden Toan
Music Department Intern ....Han Park
Advertising & Marketing ....aka/
Scott A. Moore, Liz Furze,
Joshua Lee Poole, Meghan Bartley,
Jen Taylor, Sara Rosenzweig,
Trevor Sponseller
Media & Marketing ....Curio Productions/
Jeff Jackson
Press Rep for Peter Billingsley ....Nicole Chabot
Sports Press Agent ....Joe Favorito
Tour Booking ....AWA Touring Services/
Alison Spiriti, Matt Chin, Sean Mackey
Merchandise Company ....Patriot Promotions, LLC
Merchandise Manager ....Ali Roach
Production Photography ....Carol Rosegg
Legal ....Beigelman, Feiner, Feldman, P.C./
Pamela Golinski, Esq.
Legal Consultant on behalf of
Dalfie Entertainment, Inc. ....Richard Agins
Banking ....Signature Bank/Margaret Monigan
Payroll Services ....Castellana Services
Group Sales ....Group Sales Box Office/
Broadway.com
Accountant ....Rosenberg, Neuwirth & Kuchner/
Mark D'Ambrosi
Comptroller ....Rosenberg, Neuwirth & Kuchner/
Patricia Pedersen

Insurance ....C&S International
Insurance Brokers, Inc./Debra Kozee
Production Assistants ....Cassandra Flowers,
Jeff Siebert, Gary Shackleford
Press Intern ....Amber Rodriguez
Casting Interns ....Jackie Dimitrief,
Anthony Sullivan, Krystal Worrell
Child Actor Guardians ....John Mara,
Alissa Zulvergold
Children's Tutoring ....On Location Education;
Jodi Green
Tutors ....Bernadette Jusinski, Amy Wolk
Foreign Language Tutors ....Nancy Van Ness,
Alla Markova, James Donohue

achristmasstorythemusical.com

CREDITS

Scenery construction by Production Resource Group, RA Reed Productions. Automation systems by PRG Scenic Technologies. Lighting equipment provided by PRG Lighting. Sound equipment provided by Masque Sound. Additional property construction by Prop N Spoon. Costume construction by Euroco Costumes, Giliberto Designs, Martin Izquierdo Studio, David Menkes, George Hudacko, Michele Richmond, Theodore Stark, Ann Wingate, Marian Grealish, Rachel Navarro, Jana Jessee, Barry Doss, John Furrow, Erin Roth, Carol Brookover.

American Airlines is the official airline of
A Christmas Story, The Musical.

RED RYDER® is a registered trademark of Red Ryder Entertainment, Inc. and is used with permission.

SPECIAL THANKS

Dramatic Publishing Company; Kansas City Repertory; the 5th Ave. Theatre, Seattle; Irwin Zwilling; Chris Sergel; Mark Kaufman; Raymond Wu; Michael Schall and the KC Rep Prop Shop; Maria Balboa; Lena Sands; Eva Maciek; Chris Meyers; 5th Ave. Theatre Costume Shop; Jason Frank at Archive Vintage; Maureen McGill at Daybreak Vintage; Mitch Speight at Autumn Olive Vintage; What Goes Around Comes Around; Laura Callanan; James Harrington; Chicago Custom Costumes; Gayla Voss and KC Rep Costume Shop; Ballyhoo Vintage; Brian Kohler; Jeanine Wilson/MadCreek Advertising; Janet Lauer and Carol Dibo of Wilmett Children's Theatre. And a very special thank you to Gildai and Sal Mitri.

Rehearsed at the New 42nd Street Studios, NY

NEDERLANDER

Chairman ....**James M. Nederlander**
President ....**James L. Nederlander**

Executive Vice President
Nick Scandalios

Vice President Corporate Development **Charlene S. Nederlander**	Senior Vice President Labor Relations **Herschel Waxman**
Vice President **Jim Boese**	Chief Financial Officer **Freida Sawyer Belviso**

STAFF FOR THE LUNT-FONTANNE

House Manager ....**Tracey Malinowski**
Treasurer ....Joe Olcese
Assistant Treasurer ....Kevin Lynch
House Carpenter ....Terry Taylor
House Electrician ....Dennis Boyle
House Propertyman ....Andrew Bentz
House Flyman ....Matt Walters
House Engineers ....Robert MacMahon,
Joseph Riccio III

Photo by Brian Mapp

WARDROBE AND HAIR
Sitting (L-R): Bryen Shannon,
Angela Lehrer,
Amanda Zane
Standing (L-R): Susan Corrado,
Jenna Barrios,
Liz Brady
On Stairs (L-R): Victoria Grecki,
Jason Bishop,
Scott Harrington, Jessica Worsnop,
Greg Holtz, Cathy Cline, John Furrow

A Christmas Story, The Musical

SCRAPBOOK

Curtain call on opening night.

Yearbook correspondent
John Bolton with Lily and Pete

Correspondent: John Bolton, "The Old Man"
Memorable Opening Night Gifts/Party: Awesome robes/dressing gowns and leg lamp artwork prints from producers; "wimp" t-shirts to the kids from wranglers John and Alissa; Cake Boss cake; Fantastic party at Lucky Strike Lanes.
Most Exciting Celebrity Visitors: Whoopi Goldberg told Johnny Rabe that he made her want to perform on stage again. Michael Bublé was so genuine and personable, appreciated every single cast member and took photos with all of us. Katy Perry and John Mayer.
Who Got the Gypsy Robe: Kirsten Wyatt. She added a leg lamp that lights up!
Actor Who Performed the Most Roles: John Babbo played four different kids in his regular track and also went on for Randy. Members of the male ensemble each played about six different roles.
Special Backstage Rituals: Ladies' dressing room dance party at five-minute call. Sparkle Saturday. The elves always "cling" their bells before going on stage. Lots of handshakes, energy circles and 'arrivals' on stage right during "Before the Old Man Comes Home." "Mister Melody." John and Erin's marriage ritual ("with this ring, I thee wed." Ah-oooo-gah).
Favorite Moments: Luke's tap solo, Chinese restaurant scene, doggy time.
Favorite In-Theatre Gathering Places: The wranglers' room, or, as the kids know it, "the room with the X-Box." Dan's room for coffee and tea. Erin and John's rooms for hanging out. Caroline's room for champagne and chocolates. The ladies' Winter Wonderland dressing room. The TV in the underpass for Sunday football watching.
Favorite Off-Site Hangouts: Sardi's, Glass House, Bar Centrale.
Favorite Snack Foods: White cheddar Cheez-its, bananas, Jose's firecrackers, Charissa's husband's cookies. We did not have a day without home-made cookies.
Mascots: Zac. Pete and Lily.
Favorite Therapies: Talent Juice (hot water with honey). Tea with honey and lemon—and

not sipped out of a teacup, but inhaled from a bottle. By the gallon. Grether's Pastilles. Ricola. Our amazing physical therapist, Sean. Foam rollers. Lara's purple spikey ball.
Memorable Ad-Libs: Erin Dilly: "You made me so mad my shoe came off."
In "Up on Santa's Lap," Andrew accidentally fed Kirsten an old lyric. Undeterred, Kirsten made up her own lyric on the spot that rhymed. All other elves disintegrated into laughter and were then unable to sing.
Memorable Press Encounters: We loved doing Broadway In Bryant Park, Broadway Rocks Times Square, NASDAQ, "GMA," "The View," et cetera.
Memorable Directorial Notes: When John Rando showed Zac exactly how to "show Mommy how the piggies eat." Warren Carlyle's "Your bruises will spell out Broadway!" and "It won't hurt if you get a laugh."
Fastest Costume Changes: The ensemble into "A Major Award" Busby Berkeley outfits. The kids into "You'll Shoot Your Eye Out" gangster clothes.
Who Wore the Heaviest/Hottest Costumes: Mark Ledbetter completely underdressed a full winter outdoor look under another full winter outdoor look.

Zac Ballard, who, as Randy, endured hours and hours of rehearsal in the 'Can't put my arms down' snowsuit, hat, mittens and scarf.
Who Wore the Least: Pete and Lily. The ladies in "Major Award."
Catchphrases Only the Company Would Recognize: A "comedy" anything; "spin the lamp/catch the b*%@#!"; "Is this organic?" (Zac asking about the food he was about to mash his face into); "Text text text"; "I'm 50!"; Squirrel; Girl!; "I have arrived"; "We love you Mr. James."
Orchestra Member Who Played the Most Instruments: Paul Hansen, our very busy percussionist, who also happens to be a Jean Shepherd scholar.
Best In-House Parody Lyrics: The ladies like to make up their own alternate ending to "Before the Old Man Comes Home" when Mother says "What I mean to say...I'm sorry" substituting "I'm sorry" with filth du jour.
Hidden Talent: Caroline O'Connor can make animals out of towels. Do not leave this life until you have seen her make a chicken.
Company In-Jokes: "Aaahn-semble" (said as nasally as possible). "Sir, sir!" "That's not dog drool."
Nicknames: Fifi Lamour, Zac Attack, Limp Lou, Vera, Miss Patalonia (Panty) Shields.
Sweethearts Within the Company: Babbo and Beatrice (we actually have no proof of this, just wishful thinking); Andrew Cristi and his dressing room mirror; Pete and anybody's leg.
Embarrassing Moments: Lara Seibert biffing a cartwheel. Elves and prairie folk forgetting bloomers and trunks. Kirsten realizing she forgot her kneepads just as she was going down for her big knee slide.
Superstition That Turned Out to Be True: Mashed potatoes don't taste as good when you have to eat a plate full of them every single performance.
Superstition That Turned Out to Be False: Never work with children, animals or fishnet stockings. Untrue. All three are a joy.
Coolest Thing About Being In This Show: It's fun from start to finish. And it's a hit!

Clybourne Park

First Preview: March 26, 2012. Opened: April 19, 2012.
Closed September 2, 2012 after 27 Previews and 157 Performances.

The Pulitzer Prize-winning "sequel" to Lorraine Hansberry's 1959 classic A Raisin in the Sun, *which was about the black Younger family, and the mother's resolve to move into a house in an all-white Chicago suburb despite racist pressure to stay out. Act I of* Clybourne Park *shows what was happening in the lives of the white family living in the house that made them decide to sell their home to the Youngers over the objections of their neighbors. Act II of* Clybourne Park *jumps ahead to 2009 to show what happens when a white family tries to buy the same house and move into what has now become an all-black neighborhood.*

CAST

(in alphabetical order)

Francine/Lena ....CRYSTAL A. DICKINSON
Jim/Tom/Kenneth ....BRENDAN GRIFFIN
Albert/Kevin ....DAMON GUPTON
Bev/Kathy ....CHRISTINA KIRK
Betsy/Lindsey ....ANNIE PARISSE
Karl/Steve ....JEREMY SHAMOS
Russ/Dan ....FRANK WOOD

TIME:

ACT ONE: 1959
ACT TWO: 2009

Continued on next page

❾ WALTER KERR THEATRE

A JUJAMCYN THEATRE

JORDAN ROTH
President

PAUL LIBIN
Executive Vice President

JACK VIERTEL
Senior Vice President

JUJAMCYN THEATERS

JANE BERGÈRE   ROGER BERLIND/QUINTET PRODUCTIONS   ERIC FALKENSTEIN/DAN FRISHWASSER

RUTH HENDEL/HARRIS KARMA PRODUCTIONS   JTG THEATRICALS

DARYL ROTH   JON B. PLATT   CENTER THEATRE GROUP

in association with

LINCOLN CENTER THEATER

Present

THE PLAYWRIGHTS HORIZONS PRODUCTION OF

By

BRUCE NORRIS

With

CRYSTAL A. DICKINSON   BRENDAN GRIFFIN   DAMON GUPTON
CHRISTINA KIRK   ANNIE PARISSE   JEREMY SHAMOS   FRANK WOOD

Scenic Design	Costume Design	Lighting Design	Sound Design
DANIEL OSTLING	ILONA SOMOGYI	ALLEN LEE HUGHES	JOHN GROMADA

Hair & Wig Design	Casting	Production Management	Production Stage Manager
CHARLES LaPOINTE	ALAINE ALLDAFFER	AURORA PRODUCTIONS	C.A. CLARK

General Manager	Press Representative	Advertising	Executive Producer
BESPOKE THEATRICALS	O&M CO.	SERINO/COYNE	RED AWNING

Directed by

PAM MacKINNON

The Producers wish to express their appreciation to Theatre Development Fund for its support of this production.

6/4/12

(L-R): Jeremy Shamos, Damon Gupton and Crystal A. Dickinson

Photo by Nathan Johnson

Clybourne Park

**UNDERSTUDIES
AND STANDBYS**

For Francine/Lena:
APRIL YVETTE THOMPSON
For Jim/Tom/Kenneth:
RICHARD THIERIOT
For Albert/Kevin:
BRANDON J. DIRDEN
For Bev/Kathy:
CARLY STREET
For Betsy/Lindsey:
CARLY STREET
For Karl/Steve:
RICHARD THIERIOT
For Russ/Dan:
GREG STUHR

Scrapbook

Correspondent: Crystal A. Dickinson, "Francine/Lena"

Memories of Closing Night: Over two years ago, I auditioned for *Clybourne Park* in front of Pam MacKinnon and Bruce Norris. Who knew where this play would take us all? I believe our Closing Night was just as triumphant as our Opening. There were smiles all around.

Of course some bumps and bruises were acquired along the way, but I believe there was a satisfaction that we all shared—front of house, box office, production, cast, crew, management—all, in doing a piece of theatre that we felt so relevant and necessary to what is sometimes referred to as "Post-Racial America." We gave people a chance to look at our American selves and laugh and shake our heads and cry and boo and hiss and laugh again.

Many people along this ride have told me that long after they saw *Clybourne Park*, they were still thinking about it. Who could ask for more than that when it is all said and done?

At the closing night party, they had to flicker the lights and nearly force us out of the Lambs Club. We all wanted to say that final thank you and good bye. However when finally I stepped out of the door I felt a complete satisfaction as I am certain many of us did that final night. No tears. Just joy for a job we all felt was well done.

Crystal A. Dickinson
Francine/Lena

Brendan Griffin
Jim/Tom/Kenneth

Damon Gupton
Albert/Kevin

Christina Kirk
Bev/Kathy

Annie Parisse
Betsy/Lindsey

Jeremy Shamos
Karl/Steve

Frank Wood
Russ/Dan

Brandon J. Dirden
u/s Albert/Kevin

Richard Thieriot
u/s Karl/Steve and Jim/Tom

Carly Street
u/s Bev/Kathy and Betsy Lindsey

April Yvette Thompson
u/s Francine/Lena

Greg Stuhr
u/s Russ/Dan

Bruce Norris
Playwright

Pam MacKinnon
Director

Daniel Ostling
Scenic Designer

Ilona Somogyi
Costume Designer

Allen Lee Hughes
Lighting Designer

John Gromada
Sound Designer

Charles LaPointe
Hair and Wig Designer

Alaine Alldaffer
Casting

Clybourne Park

Gene O'Donovan
Aurora Productions
Production Management

Ben Heller
Aurora Productions
Production Management

Maggie Brohn
Bespoke Theatricals
General Manager

Amy Jacobs
Bespoke Theatricals
General Manager

Devin Keudell
Bespoke Theatricals
General Manager

Nina Lannan
Bespoke Theatricals
General Manager

Jordan Roth
President
Jujamcyn Theaters
Producer

Jane Bergère
Producer

Roger Berlind
Producer

Sue Vaccaro
Quintet Productions
Producer

Ricky Stevens
Quintet Productions
Producer

Catherine Schreiber
Quintet Productions
Producer

Bruce Robert Harris
Quintet Productions
Producer

Jack W. Batman
Quintet Productions
Producer

Wendell Pierce
Quintet Productions
Producer

Eric Falkenstein
Producer

Dan Frishwasser
Producer

Ruth Hendel
Producer

Dede Harris
Harris Karma
Productions
Producer

Sharon Karmazin
Harris Karma
Productions
Producer

John Pinckard
JTG Theatricals
Producer

Terry Schnuck
JTG Theatricals
Producer

Gregory Rae
JTG Theatricals
Producer

Daryl Roth
Producer

Jon B. Platt
Producer

Michael Ritchie
Artistic Director
Center Theatre
Group
Producer

Edward L. Rada
Managing Director
Center Theatre
Group
Producer

Douglas C. Baker
Producing Director
Center Theatre
Group
Producer

André Bishop and Bernard Gersten
Artistic Director and Executive Producer
Lincoln Center Theater
Producer

Tim Sanford
Artistic Director
Playwrights Horizons
Originating Theatre

Leslie Marcus
Managing Director
Playwrights Horizons
Originating Theatre

Nicole Kastrinos
Red Awning
Executive Producer

Sarah Goldberg
Betsy/Lindsey

Clybourne Park

Photos by Brian Mapp

FRONT OF HOUSE
Front Row (L-R): Robert Zwaschka, Michelle Fleury, T.J. D'Angelo
Second Row (L-R): Juliett Cipriati, Katie Siegmund, Alison Traynor
Third Row (L-R): Ilir Velovich, Mallory Sims, Aaron Kendall
Top Row (L-R): Martine Sigue, Manuel Sandridge

BOX OFFICE TREASURERS
(L-R): Michael Loiacono, Joe Smith

CREW
Front Row (Seated L-R): Ed Chapman, Christina Ainge
Middle Row (L-R): Ron Fleming, Vincent J. Valvo, George E. Fullum, Timothy Bennet, Peter J. Iacoviello
Back Row (L-R): Carol Clark, Francine Schwartz-Buryiak, Chad Heulitt, Moose Johnson, Heidi Neven, Pat Marcus, James Latus, Jill Johnson

Clybourne Park

STAFF FOR *CLYBOURNE PARK*

GENERAL MANAGEMENT
BESPOKE THEATRICALS
Amy Jacobs, Nina Lannan
Maggie Brohn, Devin Keudell

COMPANY MANAGER
Heidi Neven

PRESS REPRESENTATIVE
O&M CO.
Rick Miramontez
Joyce Friedmann   Ryan Ratelle
Andy Snyder   Michael Jorgensen

PRODUCTION MANAGEMENT
AURORA PRODUCTIONS
Gene O'Donovan, Ben Heller,
Stephanie Sherline, Anita Shah, Jarid Sumner,
Liza Luxenberg, Anthony Jusino, Steven Dalton,
Eugenio Saenz Flores, Isaac Katzanek,
Melissa Mazdra

CASTING
Alaine Alldaffer, CSA
Associate Casting Director .... Lisa Donadio

Production Stage Manager .... C.A. Clark
Stage Manager .... James Latus
Assistant Director .... Kimberly Faith Hickman
Associate Costume Designer .... Jessica Wegener Shay
Associate Lighting Designer .... Xavier Pierce
Assistant Lighting Designer .... Miriam Crowe
Associate Sound Designer .... Chris Cronin
Associate Hair Designer .... Leah Loukas
Production Carpenter .... Chad Heulitt
Production Electrician .... Michael Pitzer
Production Props Supervisor .... Faye Armon
Production Props .... Jill Johnson
Production Sound Engineer .... Ed Chapman
Wardrobe Supervisor .... Christina Ainge
Dressers .... Ron Fleming, Francine Schwartz-Buryiak
Hair Supervisor .... Pat Marcus
Moving Light Programmer .... Jeremy Wahlers
Scenic Consultant .... Brenda Sabatka-Davis
Advertising .... Serino/Coyne/
Greg Corradetti, Tom Callahan,
Danielle Boyle, Drew Nebrig, Doug Ensign
Digital Outreach & Website .... Serino/Coyne/
Jim Glaub, Chip Meyrelles,
Laurie Connor, Kevin Keating, Mark Seeley
Marketing .... Serino/Coyne/
Leslie Barrett, Diana Salameh
Legal Counsel .... Sendroff & Baruch/
Jason Baruch, Esq.
Accountant .... FK Partners/Robert Fried
Comptroller .... Galbraith and Co./
Sarah Galbraith, Kenny Noth
General Management Associates .... Steve Dow,
Ryan Conway, Libby Fox,
David Roth, Danielle Saks
General Management Interns .... Michelle Heller,
Jimmy Wilson, Sean Coughlin
Production Assistant .... Matthew Lutz
Costume Shopper .... Kristina Makowski

Press Associates .... Sarah Babin, Molly Barnett,
Jaron Caldwell, Philip Carrubba,
Jon Dimond, Richard Hillman,
Yufen Kung, Chelsea Nachman,
Elizabeth Wagner
Payroll Services .... Checks and Balances Payroll Inc.
Travel Agent .... Tzell Travel/
The "A" Team, Andi Henig
Banking .... City National Bank/Michele Gibbons
Insurance .... Dewitt Stern Group, Inc./
Peter Shoemaker
Theatre Displays .... King Displays, Inc.
Merchandise .... Max Merchandising

CREDITS

Scenery constructed by F&D Scene Changes. Lighting equipment supplied by PRG. Sound equipment supplied by Sound Associates. Costumes by the Center Theatre Group Costume Shop; Paul Chang Custom Tailors & Shirtmakers; Tiia Torchia; Eric Winterling, Inc.; Sarah Reever; Bobby Tilley; Harry Johnson. Props from Lincoln Center Theater. Special thanks to Bra*Tenders for hosiery and undergarments.

MUSIC CREDITS

"Catch a Falling Star" by Perry Como.
"Confidential" by the Fleetwoods.
"It's Too Soon to Know" by Pat Boone.

To learn more about the production, please visit
www.ClybournePark.com

CENTER THEATRE GROUP

Michael Ritchie, *Artistic Director*
Edward L. Rada, *Managing Director*
Douglas C. Baker, *Producing Director*
Kelley Kirkpatrick and Neel Keller,
Associate Artistic Directors
Nausica Stergiou, *General Manager,*
Mark Taper Forum

LINCOLN CENTER THEATER

André Bishop, *Artistic Director*
Bernard Gersten, *Executive Director*
Adam Siegel, *Managing Director*
Hattie Jutagir, *Executive Director of*
Development & Planning
Linda Mason Ross, *Director of Marketing*

PLAYWRIGHTS HORIZONS

Tim Sanford, *Artistic Director*
Leslie Marcus, *Managing Director*
Carol Fishman, *General Manager*

JORDAN ROTH
President

PAUL LIBIN   **JACK VIERTEL**
Executive Vice President   Senior Vice President
MEREDITH VILLATORE   **JENNIFER HERSHEY**
Chief Financial Officer   Vice President,
Building Operations

MICAH HOLLINGWORTH   **HAL GOLDBERG**
Vice President,   Vice President,
Company Operations   Theatre Operations

Director of Business Affairs .... Albert T. Kim
Director of Human Resources .... Michele Louhisdon
Director of Ticketing Services .... Justin Karr
Theatre Operations Managers .... Willa Burke,
Susan Elrod, Emily Hare,
Jeff Hubbard, Albert T. Kim
Theatre Operations Associates .... Carrie Jo Brinker,
Brian Busby, Michael Composto,
Anah Jyoti Klate
Accounting .... Cathy Cerge, Erin Dooley,
Amy Frank
Executive Producer, Red Awning .... Nicole Kastrinos
Director of Marketing, Givenik.com .... Joe Tropia
Marketing Associate, Givenik.com .... Ben Cohen
Building Operations Associate .... Erich Bussing
Executive Coordinator .... Ed Lefferson
Executive Assistants .... Clark Mims Tedesco,
Beth Given, Julia Kraus
Receptionist .... Lisa Perchinske
Maintenance .... Ralph Santos, Ramon Zapata
Security .... Rasim Hodzic, John Acero
Interns .... Maggie Baker, Alaina Bono,
Hunter Chancellor, Sarah Collins,
Cindy Vargas, Kelvin Veras,
Luke Weidner, Margaret White

STAFF FOR THE WALTER KERR THEATRE FOR
CLYBOURNE PARK
Theatre Manager .... Susan Elrod
Treasurer .... Harry Jaffie
Head Carpenter .... George E. Fullum
Head Propertyman .... Timothy Bennet
Head Electrician .... Vincent J. Valvo
Flyman .... Peter J. Iacoviello
Propertyman .... Moose Johnson
Engineer .... Brian DiNapoli
Assistant Treasurers .... Michael Loiacono,
Joseph Smith, Gail Yerkovich
Head Usher .... T.J. D'Angelo
Director .... Michelle Fleury
Ticket Takers .... Alison Traynor, Robert Zwaschka
Ushers .... Jason Aguirre, Florence Arcaro,
Juliett Cipriati, Aaron Kendall,
Victoria Lauzun, Ilir Velovich
Doormen .... Brandon Houghton, Kevin Wallace
Head Porter .... Marcio Martinez
Porter .... Rudy Martinez
Head Cleaner .... Sevdija Pasukanovic
Cleaner .... Lourdes Perez

Lobby refreshments by Sweet Concessions.

Security provided by GBA Consulting, Inc.

Cyrano de Bergerac

First Preview: September 14, 2012. Opened: October 11, 2012.
Limited Engagement. Closed November 25, 2012 after 32 Previews and 52 Performances.

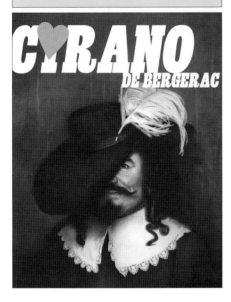

PLAYBILL

Cyrano, a soldier from the French province of Gascony is a fearless swordsman and a fearless poet but there is one thing he does fear: a word of derision about his oversized nose from Roxane, the girl he loves. Roxane is in love with another man, the handsome Christian. But Christian is as tongue-tied as Cyrano is eloquent, so Cyrano agrees to lend his rival his wit, his heart and his unquenchable panache in this classic romantic tragedy.

CAST

(in order of appearance)

Cuigy	JACK CUTMORE-SCOTT
Lignière	TIM McGEEVER
Christian	KYLE SOLLER
Amélie	FRANCES MERCANTI-ANTHONY
Ragueneau	BILL BUELL
Le Bret	MAX BAKER
Roxane	CLÉMENCE POÉSY
Duenna	GERALDINE HUGHES
Comte de Guiche	PATRICK PAGE
Valvert	SAMUEL ROUKIN
Pickpocket	PETER BRADBURY
Montfleury	ANDY GROTELUESCHEN
Cyrano de Bergerac	DOUGLAS HODGE
Musketeer	BEN STEINFELD
Pastry Cooks	PETER BRADBURY, ANDY GROTELUESCHEN, DREW McVETY, OKIERIETE ONAODOWAN, SAMUEL ROUKIN
Lise	FRANCES MERCANTI-ANTHONY
Carbon de Castel-Jaloux	PETER BRADBURY

Continued on next page

Continued on next page

AMERICAN AIRLINES THEATRE

ROUNDABOUT THEATRE COMPANY

Todd Haimes, Artistic Director
Harold Wolpert, Managing Director
Julia C. Levy, Executive Director

Presents

Douglas Hodge
Clémence Poésy   Patrick Page

in

CYRANO DE BERGERAC

By
Edmond Rostand

Translation by
Ranjit Bolt

with

Max Baker   Bill Buell   Geraldine Hughes

Peter Bradbury   Jack Cutmore-Scott   Mikaela Feely-Lehmann   Andy Grotelueschen
Tim McGeever   Drew McVety   Frances Mercanti-Anthony   Okcrieté Onaodowan
Samuel Roukin   Ben Steinfeld

introducing
Kyle Soller

Set & Costume Design	*Lighting Design*	*Sound Design*	*Music*
Soutra Gilmour	Japhy Weideman	Dan Moses Schreier	Charlie Rosen
Hair & Wig Design	*Movement*	*Fight Director*	*Dialect Coach*
Amanda Miller	Chris Bailey	Jacob Grigolia-Rosenbaum	Kate Wilson

Production Stage Manager	*Production Management*	*Casting*	*Cyrano de Bergerac General Manager*	*Press Representative*
Nevin Hedley	Aurora Productions	Jim Carnahan, C.S.A. & Carrie Gardner, C.S.A.	Denise Cooper	Boneau/Bryan-Brown

Associate Managing Director	*Director of Marketing & Audience Development*	*Director of Development*
Greg Backstrom	Tom O'Connor	Lynne Gugenheim Gregory

General Manager	*Founding Director*	*Adams Associate Artistic Director**
Sydney Beers	Gene Feist	Scott Ellis

Directed by
Jamie Lloyd

Major support for this production provided by Beth and Ravenel Curry.
*Generously underwritten by Margot Adams, in memory of Mason Adams.
Roundabout Theatre Company is a member of the League of Resident Theatres.
www.roundabouttheatre.org

10/11/12

Douglas Hodge and Clémence Poésy

Photo by Joan Marcus

Cyrano de Bergerac

Cast Continued

Cadets .... ANDY GROTELUESCHEN,
TIM McGEEVER, DREW McVETY,
OKIERIETE ONAODOWAN,
SAMUEL ROUKIN, BEN STEINFELD
Poets .... JACK CUTMORE-SCOTT,
TIM McGEEVER
Sentries .... DREW McVETY,
OKIERIETE ONAODOWAN
Friar .... ANDY GROTELUESCHEN
Sister Marguérite .... FRANCES
MERCANTI-ANTHONY
Sister Marthe .... GERALDINE HUGHES
Sister Claire .... MIKAELA FEELY-LEHMANN

TIME	PLACE
1640-1655	Paris and Arras

Douglas Hodge and Clémence Poésy are appearing
with the permission of Actors' Equity Association. Ms.
Poésy is appearing pursuant to an exchange program
between American Equity and UK Equity.

UNDERSTUDIES/STANDBYS
Standby for Douglas Hodge:
GRAHAM WINTON
For Comte de Guiche:
PETER BRADBURY
For Christian, Valvert, Sister Claire:
JACK CUTMORE-SCOTT
For Roxane, Duenna/Marthe,
Amélie/Lise/Marguérite:
MIKAELA FEELY-LEHMANN
For Ragueneau:
TIM McGEEVER
For Le Bret, Montfleury/Friar, Lignière
DREW McVETY
For Cuigy, Musketeer, Carbon de Castel-Jaloux:
OKIERIETE ONAODOWAN

Production Stage Manager: NEVIN HEDLEY
Stage Manager: DAVIN DE SANTIS

Douglas Hodge
Cyrano de Bergerac

Clémence Poésy
Roxane

Patrick Page
Comte de Guiche

Kyle Soller
Christian

Max Baker
Le Bret

Bill Buell
Ragueneau

Geraldine Hughes
*Duenna, Sister
Marthe*

Peter Bradbury
*Pickpocket, Carbon
de Castel-Jaloux,
Pastry Cook;
u/s Comte de Guiche*

Jack Cutmore-Scott
*Cuigy, Poet;
u/s Christian, Valvert,
Sister Claire*

Mikaela
Feely-Lehmann
*Sister Claire;
u/s Roxane, Duenna/
Marthe, Lise/
Marguerite/Amélie*

Andy Grotelueschen
*Montfleury,
Cadet/Pastry Cook/
Friar*

Tim McGeever
*Lignière, Cadet/Poet;
u/s Ragueneau*

Drew McVety
*Pastry Cook/Cadet/
Sentry/Violin;
u/s Le Bret,
Montfleury/Friar,
Lignière*

Frances
Mercanti-Anthony
*Amélie/Lise/Sister
Marguérite*

Okieriete Onaodowan
*Pastry Cook/
Cadet/ Sentry;
u/s Cuigy, Musketeer,
Carbon de
Castel-Jaloux*

Samuel Roukin
*Valvert, Pastry
Cook/Cadet*

Ben Steinfeld
Musketeer, Cadet

Jamie Lloyd
Director

Edmond Rostand
Playwright

Ranjit Bolt
Translation

Soutra Gilmour
*Set & Costume
Design*

Japhy Weideman
Lighting Design

Dan Moses Schreier
Sound Design

Cyrano de Bergerac

Charlie Rosen
Music

Chris Bailey
Movement

Jacob Grigolia-
Rosenbaum
Fight Director

Amanda Miller
*Wig, Hair & Makeup
Designer*

Matthew Hodges
*Properties
Supervisor*

Kate Wilson
Dialect Coach

Gene O'Donovan
Aurora Productions
*Production
Management*

Ben Heller
Aurora Productions
*Production
Management*

Jim Carnahan, CSA
Casting

Carrie Gardner, CSA
Casting

Gene Feist
*Founding Director
Roundabout Theatre
Company*

Todd Haimes
*Artistic Director
Roundabout Theatre
Company*

(L-R): Kyle Soller
and Douglas Hodge

Photo by Joan Marcus

Photo by Brian Mapp

HOUSE STAFF
(L-R): Jazmine Perez, Zipporah Aguasvivas, James Miller, Enrika Nicholas

Photo by Brian Mapp

BOX OFFICE
(L-R): Heather Siebert, Mead Margulies,
Robert Morgan

Cyrano de Bergerac

ROUNDABOUT THEATRE COMPANY STAFF
ARTISTIC DIRECTOR ....TODD HAIMES
MANAGING DIRECTOR ....HAROLD WOLPERT
EXECUTIVE DIRECTOR ....JULIA C. LEVY
ADAMS ASSOCIATE
   ARTISTIC DIRECTOR ....SCOTT ELLIS

ARTISTIC STAFF

DIRECTOR OF ARTISTIC DEVELOPMENT/
   DIRECTOR OF CASTING ....Jim Carnahan
Artistic Consultant ....Robyn Goodman
Resident Directors ....Doug Hughes, Sam Gold
Associate Artists ....Mark Brokaw, Scott Elliott,
   Sam Gold, Bill Irwin, Joe Mantello,
   Kathleen Marshall, Theresa Rebeck
Literary Manager ....Jill Rafson
Senior Casting Director ....Carrie Gardner
Casting Director ....Stephen Kopel
Casting Associate ....Jillian Cimini
Casting Assistants ....Michael Morlani,
   Rachel Reichblum
Artistic Associate ....Amy Ashton
Literary Associate ....Josh Fiedler
The Blanche and Irving Laurie Foundation
   Theatre Visions Fund
   Commissions ....David West Read
Educational Foundation of
   America Commissions ....Bekah Brunstetter,
   Lydia Diamond, Diana Fithian,
   Julie Marie Myatt
Roundabout Commissions.............Helen Edmundson,
   Andrew Hinderaker, Stephen Karam,
   Steven Levenson, Matthew Lopez,
   Kim Rosenstock
Casting Interns ....Eric Byrd, Cat Gagliotti,
   Rebecca Henin, Krystal Rowley
Script Readers ....Shannon Deep, Ben Izzo,
   Liz Malta, Alexis Roblan
Artistic Apprentice ....Nikki DiLoreto

EDUCATION STAFF

EDUCATION DIRECTOR ....Greg McCaslin
Associate Education Director ....Jennifer DiBella
Education Program Manager ....Aliza Greenberg
Education Program Associate ....Sarah Malone
Education Assistant ....Lou-Lou Igbokwe
Education Dramaturg ....Ted Sod
Teaching Artists ....Josh Allen, Cynthia Babak,
   Victor Barbella, LaTonya Borsay,
   Mark Bruckner, Chloe Chapin, Joe Doran,
   Elizabeth Dunn-Ruiz, Carrie Ellman-Larsen,
   Theresa Flanagan, Deanna Frieman,
   Sheri Graubert, Adam Gwon, Devin Haqq,
   Carrie Heitman, Karla Hendrick, Jason Jacobs,
   Alana Jacoby, Lisa Renee Jordan, Jamie Kalama,
   Alvin Keith, Erin McCready, James Miles,
   Nick Moore, Meghan O'Neil, Drew Peterson,
   Nicole Press, Leah Reddy, Amanda Rehbein,
   Nick Simone, Heidi Stallings, Daniel Sullivan,
   Carl Tallent, Vickie Tanner, Larine Towler,
   Jennifer Varbalow, Kathryn Veillette,
   Leese Walker, Gail Winar, Chad Yarborough
Teaching Artist Emeritus ....Reneé Flemings
Education Apprentices ....Maia Collier, Betsy Huggins

EXECUTIVE ADMINISTRATIVE STAFF

ASSOCIATE MANAGING
   DIRECTOR.......................Greg Backstrom
Assistant Managing Director ....Katharine Croke
Assistant to the Managing Director ......Christina Pezzello
Assistant to the Executive Director ....Nicole Tingir

MANAGEMENT/ADMINISTRATIVE STAFF

GENERAL MANAGER ....Sydney Beers
General Manager,
   American Airlines Theatre ....Denise Cooper
General Manager,
   Steinberg Center ....Nicholas J. Caccavo
Human Resources Director ....Stephen Deutsch
Operations Manager ....Valerie D. Simmons
Associate General Manager ....Maggie Cantrick
Office Manager ....Scott Kelly
Archivist ....Tiffany Nixon
Receptionists ....Dee Beider, Emily Frohnhoefer,
   Elisa Papa, Allison Patrick
Messenger ....Darnell Franklin
Management Apprentice ....Holli Campbell

FINANCE STAFF

DIRECTOR OF FINANCE.................Susan Neiman
Payroll Director ....John LaBarbera
Accounts Payable Manager ....Frank Surdi
Payroll Benefits Administrator ....Yonit Kafka
Manager Financial Reporting ....Joshua Cohen
Business Office Assistant ....Jackie Verbitski
Business Office Apprentice ....Mara Abeleda

DEVELOPMENT STAFF

DIRECTOR OF
   DEVELOPMENT ....Lynne Gugenheim Gregory
Assistant to the
   Director of Development ....Liz Malta
Director, Institutional Giving ....Liz S. Alsina
Director, Individual Giving ....Christopher Nave
Director, Special Events ....Lane Hosmer
Associate Director, Individual Giving ....Tyler Ennis
Manager, Telefundraising ....Gavin Brown
Manager, Friends of Roundabout ....Marisa Perry
Manager, Donor Information Systems ....Lise Speidel
Special Events Associate ....Natalie Corr
Individual Giving Officers ....Joseph Foster,
   Toni Rosenbaum
Institutional Giving Officer,
   Stewardship and Prospect
   Development ....Kim Sidey
Institutional Giving Assistant ....Brett Barbour
Development Assistant ....Martin Giannini
Special Events Assistant ....Genevieve Carroll
Development Apprentice ....Haley Tanenbaum
Special Projects Apprentice ....Alayna George

INFORMATION TECHNOLOGY STAFF

DIRECTOR OF
   INFORMATION TECHNOLOGY ..Daniel V. Gomez
System Administrator ....Jim Roma
DBA/Developer ....Rajan Eddy
Web Administrator ....Robert Parmelee
IT Associate ....Cary Kim

MARKETING STAFF

DIRECTOR OF MARKETING &
   AUDIENCE DEVELOPMENT ....Tom O'Connor
Manager, Design & Production ....Eric Emch
Digital Content Producer ....Mark Cajigao
Marketing Associate,
   Events & Promotions..............Rachel LeFevre-Snee
Marketing Associate, Digital ....Alex Barber
Marketing Assistant ....Dayna Johnson
Director of Telesales
   Special Promotions ....Marco Frezza
Telesales Manager ....Patrick Pastor
Telesales Office Coordinator ....Adam Unze
Marketing Apprentices ....Tyler Beddoe,
   Maureen Keleher
Digital Marketing Apprentice ....Laura Abbott

AUDIENCE SERVICES STAFF

DIRECTOR OF AUDIENCE
   SERVICES ....Wendy Hutton
Associate Director of Audience Services.........Bill Klemm
Box Office Managers ....Edward P. Osborne,
   Jaime Perlman, Krystin MacRitchie,
   Nicole Nicholson
Group Sales Manager ....Jeff Monteith
Assistant Box Office Managers ....Robert Morgan,
   Joseph Clark, Andrew Clements,
   Catherine Fitzpatrick
Assistant Audience Services Managers ....Robert Kane,
   Lindsay Ericson,
   Jessica Pruett-Barnett,
   Kaia Lay Rafoss
Customer Services Coordinator ....Thomas Walsh
Audience Services ....Jennifer Almgreen,
   Solangel Bido, Jay Bush,
   Lauren Cartelli, Adam Elsberry,
   Joe Gallina, Ashley Gezana,
   Alanna Harms, Kara Harrington,
   Nicki Ishmael, Kiah Johnson,
   Rebecca Lewis-Whitson,
   Kate Longosky, Michelle Maccarone,
   Mead Margulies, Laura Marshall,
   Chuck Migliaccio, Carlos Morris,
   Katie Mueller, Sarah Olsen, Josh Rozett,
   Heather Siebert, Nalane Singh,
   Ron Tobia, Hannah Weitzman
Audience Services Apprentice ....Blair Laurie

SERVICES

Counsel ....Paul, Weiss,
   Rifkind, Wharton and Garrison LLP,
   Charles H. Googe Jr., Carol M. Kaplan
Counsel ....Rosenberg & Estis
Counsel ....Andrew Lance,
   Gibson, Dunn, & Crutcher, LLP
Counsel ....Harry H. Weintraub,
   Glick and Weintraub, P.C.
Counsel ....Stroock & Stroock & Lavan LLP
Counsel ....Daniel S. Dokos,
   Weil, Gotshal & Manges LLP
Counsel ....Claudia Wagner/
   Manatt, Phelps & Phillips, LLP
Immigration Counsel ....Mark D. Koestler and
   Theodore Ruthizer
House Physicians ....Dr. Theodore Tyberg,
   Dr. Lawrence Katz

Cyrano de Bergerac

Photo by Brian Mapp

CREW

Seated (L-R): Carly DiFulvio, Manuela LaPorte, Kimberly Mark, Hannah Overton, Susan Fallon, Glenn Merwede, Kat Martin, Brian Maiuri, Robert W. Dowling II
Standing (L-R): Dann Wojnar, Cynthia O'Rourke, Enrique Vega, Bobbi Morse, Dale Carman, Emily Ockenfels, Barb Bartel, Nevin Hedley, Amy Kaskeski, Davin De Santis

House Dentist ....Neil Kanner, D.M.D.
Insurance ....DeWitt Stern Group, Inc.
Accountant ....Lutz & Carr CPAs, LLP
Advertising ....Spotco/
Drew Hodges, Jim Edwards,
Tom Greenwald, Josh Fraenkel
Interactive Marketing.................Situation Interactive/
Damian Bazadona, John Lanasa,
Eric Bornemann, Mollie Shapiro,
Danielle Migliaccio
Events Photography.................Anita and Steve Shevett
Production Photographer ....Joan Marcus
Theatre Displays..............King Displays, Wayne Sapper
Lobby Refreshments....................Sweet Concessions
Merchandising................................Spotco Merch/
James Decker

MANAGING DIRECTOR
EMERITUS ....Ellen Richard

Roundabout Theatre Company
231 West 39th Street, New York, NY 10018
(212) 719-9393.

GENERAL PRESS REPRESENTATIVE
BONEAU/BRYAN-BROWN
Adrian Bryan-Brown
Matt Polk   Jessica Johnson   Amy Kass

CREDITS FOR *CYRANO DE BERGERAC*
Company Manager.........................Carly DiFulvio
Production Stage Manager ....Nevin Hedley
Stage Manager ....Davin De Santis
Production Management by ......Aurora Productions Inc./
Gene O'Donovan, Ben Heller,

Stephanie Sherline, Jarid Sumner,
Anthony Jusino, Anita Shah,
Liza Luxenberg, Garrett Ellison,
Troy Pepicelli, Gayle Riess, Melissa Mazdra
Assistant Director ....Chris Bailey
Additional Music ....Drew McVety
Associate Scenic Designer ....Michael Carnahan
Assistant to the Scenic Designer ....Jason Sherwood
Associate Costume Designer ....Brian J. Bustos
Assistant Costume Designer ....Angela M. Kahler
Assistant to the Costume Designer ....Lisa Loen
Costume Intern ....Corey Hummerston
UK Costume Supervisor ....Chris Cahill
Associate Lighting Designer ....Peter Bragg
Associate Sound Designer ....Jana Hoglund
Make-Up Designer ....Amanda Miller
Prosthetic Nose Design ....Christal Schanes
Production Properties Supervisor ....Matthew Hodges
Prop Artisans ....Sarah Bird, Gloria Sun
Associate Fight Director ....John Gardner
Production Carpenter ....Glenn Merwede
Production Electrician ....Brian Maiuri
Running Properties ....Robert W. Dowling II
Sound Operator ....Dann Wojnar
Wardrobe Supervisor ....Susan J. Fallon
Dressers ....Dale Carman, Kimberly Mark,
Kat Martin
Wardrobe Dayworker ....Emily Ockenfels
Hair and Wig Supervisor ....Manuela Laporte
Production Assistants ....Cody Renard Richard,
Sara Sahin
Vocal Wellness & Physical Therapy ....Sean Gallagher

CREDITS
Scenery constructed and automated by Showman

Fabricators, Inc., Long Island City, NY. Lighting equipment by PRG Lighting. Sound equipment by Sound Associates. Custom costumes constructed by Tricorne, Inc. Additional costumes by Angels the Costumiers and the Royal Shakespeare Company. Custom millinery by Arnold Levine. Custom shoes by Capri Shoes. Custom wardrobe painting by Hochi Asiatico. Special thanks to Bra*Tenders for hosiery and undergarments.

SPECIAL THANKS
Barrie Gower, BGFX

Makeup provided by M•A•C Cosmetics.

AMERICAN AIRLINES THEATRE STAFF
Company Manager ....Carly DiFulvio
House Carpenter ....Glenn Merwede
House Electrician ....Brian Maiuri
House Properties ....Robert W. Dowling II
House Sound ....Dann Wojnar
IA Apprentice ....Hannah Overton
Wardrobe Supervisor ....Susan J. Fallon
Box Office Manager ....Ted Osborne
Assistant Box Office Manager ....Robert Morgan
House Manager ....Stephen Ryan
Associate House Manager ....Zipporah Aguasvivas
Head Usher ....Crystal Suarez
House Staff ....Lance Andrade,
Christopher Busch, Jeanne Coutant,
Anne Ezell, Denise Furbert, Maria Graves,
Lee Henry, Rebecca Knell, Taylor Martin,
Enrika Nicholas, Jazmine Perez,
Samantha Rivera, Celia Torres,
Alvin Vega, Felisha Whatts
Security ....Julious Russell

Cyrano de Bergerac
SCRAPBOOK

Correspondent: Andy Grotelueschen, "Mont-fleury/Cadet/Pastry Cook/ Friar"

Opening Night Gifts: Our English director, Jamie Lloyd, upon Opening, received a bottle of Bulleit bourbon that he safely stowed in the Stage Management office until his return to NYC. A week ago, Drew McVety conducted a formal search for this bottle and reclaimed it for the cast.

Opening Night Party: It was at B.B. King's, next door to the AA Theatre. They put us up on the marquee!

Most Exciting Celebrity Visitors: Brooke Shields (blam!), Sam Mendes (blam!), Naomi Watts (blam! blam!), Emily Mortimer (blam!).

Actors Who Performed the Most Roles in This Show: This was a huge ensemble show, so a number of us (myself included) played up to four parts. This translated to a LOT of stairs and a TON of wigs, dreadlocks included.

Who Has Done the Most Broadway Shows in Their Career: We hypothesize that Bill Buell's got it, but Patrick Page is also a strong contender.

Special Backstage Rituals: We do a group warm-up before every show, fifteen minutes before the house opens. It's something to bring

(L-R) *Yearbook* correspondent Andy Grotelueschen with dressing room-mate Ben Steinfeld.

us all together as an ensemble every night. We play theatre games! We never know what we're going to do, so someone just volunteers an exercise or game and everybody jumps in. We have our favorites—Murder, This is a Tick, Zip Zap Boing!, Pinch the Butts, One Word Story—but we always finish with a group impulse exercise which goes like this: Everybody stands in a circle for a really long time just waiting and listening...until everyone, as a group, at the exact same time, steps forward and says "panache," which is absolutely our word of the show. We've even done this one with our eyes closed.

Favorite Moment During Each Performance: Mine has got to be sitting in the wings each night, waiting to go on as the Friar just before intermission. It's the balcony scene onstage with Doug, Clémence, and Kyle. At this point of the show, everything's quieted down, and stage right, there's nobody but me sitting there. And I get to sit and listen, not fifteen feet from Doug

(Cyrano), and hear some of the most beautiful writing I've ever heard. It's a classic thing.

Favorite In-Theatre Gathering Place: Each night, during Act V, the final 20 minutes of the play, the Secret Supper Club/Liquor Lounge convenes in my, Ben Steinfeld's, and Samuel Roukin's dressing room. The featured guest of the evening is always Mr. McVety, alter ego of Drew McVety. Samuel Roukin is Pat, the owner, and I'm Andy, the bartender. We discuss wives, babies, girlfriends, careers...and some nights, if you're lucky, Mr. McVety, also an accomplished chef, will treat you to a tasting! Check out those ribs.

Favorite Off-Site Hangout: St. Andrews is right around the corner from our rehearsal studios, so that became the go-to. The waitstaff knows us and takes care of us well.

Favorite Snack Food: Bourbon.

Mascot: Tim McGeever.

Favorite Therapies: Physio. Bourbon.

Most Memorable Ad-Lib: One night, during the sword fight between Cyrano (Douglas Hodge) and Valvert (Samuel Roukin), Sam's sword just fell apart. The thing just went to pieces. In a brilliant ad-lib (of which he had many), Patrick Page exclaimed "Give him a sword!" Jack Cutmore-Scott (our fight captain) was at the ready and tossed a sword into the mix, and the scene was saved.

Cell Phone Incident During a Performance: Once, in a scene between Kyle and Doug, an insistent cellphone kept interrupting. Both actors paused, listened a moment, and put their hands on their swords as if to draw.

Least Busy Day at the Box Office: Without question our first show following Hurricane (Superstorm) Sandy. All of Broadway canceled Tuesday night performances, but Wednesday, most shows were back up with the matinee. I believe we had 137 people that day. It was surreal doing the show that day.

Catchphrase Only the Company Would Recognize: "Gritty, sweaty, cinematic."

Memorable Directorial Note: In previews, our utterly fearless director, Jamie Lloyd, gave this note to the ensemble: "Don't worry about pulling focus." A dangerous freedom to give to actors, but we ran with that note till the very end.

Coolest Things About Being in This Show: I

The whole *Cyrano* family.

couldn't have asked for a better experience in my Broadway debut! The Roundabout, the American Airlines Theatre, the cast, the crew. An amazing time!

Every time there is a birthday, our wardrobe head, Susan Fallon, makes a birthday cake. These cakes are amazing! She decorates each one for whomever's birthday it is, and after the candles are blown out, she cuts that cake like a drunk surgeon! I've never seen someone tear through a cake like that. And not only are they some of the loveliest cakes to look at, they taste even better!

Also: Absolutely one of the defining aspects of this production of *Cyrano* was Hurricane Sandy in October 2012. Riding my bike to Broadway for our Wednesday matinee after the storm was surreal. Over the Brooklyn Bridge, into Lower Manhattan with no power, and rolling up to the lights in Times Square where the power had not gone out. Other cast members had driven in from their homes. Some people even walked from Queens. Our matinee audience was small, as I said above, but they were appreciative. That whole week we had smaller houses, but I think some people were really happy to have a play to go to. It was a crazy time for everyone in the region—the recovery is on-going—and it's been amazing to see communities pull together, including the Broadway community. Each year, during the holiday season, Broadway Cares/Equity Fights Aids collects money after the shows. This year, part of the donations are going to help victims of the hurricane. To date, over $250,000 has been raised and it's not even Thanksgiving yet!

Fun with a prop (L-R): Tim McGeever, Samuel Roukin, Okieriete Onaodowan.

Dead Accounts

First Preview: November 5, 2012. Opened: November 29, 2012.
Closed January 6, 2013 after 27 Previews and 44 Performances.

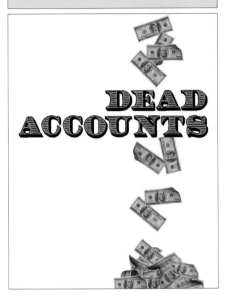

After embezzling $27 million from a New York bank and seeing his marriage fall apart, a man retreats to his boyhood home in Ohio where he hopes to find sanctuary, forgiveness, peace, and perhaps a new start on life with his mother and sister. But things aren't that simple and before long his sins start catching up with him.

CAST

(in order of appearance)

Jack	NORBERT LEO BUTZ
Lorna	KATIE HOLMES
Barbara	JAYNE HOUDYSHELL
Phil	JOSH HAMILTON
Jenny	JUDY GREER

UNDERSTUDIES

For Jack, Phil: HAYNES THIGPEN
For Lorna, Jenny: SUZY JANE HUNT
For Barbara: DARRIE LAWRENCE

TIME

Present

SETTING

Cincinnati, Ohio

---

⑤ THE MUSIC BOX

239 W. 45th Street
A Shubert Organization Theatre

Philip J. Smith, *Chairman*   Robert E. Wankel, *President*

Jeffrey Finn   John N. Hart, Jr.
David Mirvish   Amy Nauiokas   Ergo Entertainment
Harriet Newman Leve   Double Gemini Productions   3toGo Entertainment
and
The Shubert Organization

present

NORBERT LEO BUTZ   KATIE HOLMES

in

DEAD ACCOUNTS

by

THERESA REBECK

with

JUDY GREER   JOSH HAMILTON

and

JAYNE HOUDYSHELL

Scenic Design	Costume Design	Lighting Design	Composition/ Sound Design
David Rockwell	Catherine Zuber	David Weiner	Mark Bennett

Hair Design	Casting
Tom Watson	Caparelliotis Casting

Press Representative	Advertising & Marketing	Technical Supervisor
Boneau/Bryan-Brown	Serino/Coyne	Peter Fulbright Tech Production Services, Inc.

Production Stage Manager	Associate Producers	General Manager
Rolt Smith	Jamie Kaye-Phillips Charles Stone	101 Productions, Ltd.

Directed by

JACK O'BRIEN

Commissioned and originally Produced by Cincinnati Playhouse in the Park
Edward Stern, Producing Artistic Director; Buzz Ward, Executive Director

11/29/12

(L-R): Norbert Leo Butz, Katie Holmes and Jayne Houdyshell

Photo by Joan Marcus

Dead Accounts

Norbert Leo Butz
Jack

Katie Holmes
Lorna

Judy Greer
Jenny

Josh Hamilton
Phil

Jayne Houdyshell
Barbara

Haynes Thigpen
u/s Jack, Phil

Suzy Jane Hunt
u/s Lorna, Jenny

Darrie Lawrence
u/s Barbara

Theresa Rebeck
Playwright

Jack O'Brien
Director

David Rockwell
Scenic Design

Catherine Zuber
Costume Design

David Weiner
Lighting Design

Mark Bennett
*Composition/
Sound Design*

Tom Watson
Hair Design

Ashley Ryan
Make-up Design

David Caparelliotis
Caparelliotis Casting
Casting

Adrienne
Campbell-Holt
Assistant Director

Rolt Smith
*Production Stage
Manager*

Julia P. Jones
Stage Manager

Peter Fulbright/
Tech Production
Services
Production Manager

Wendy Orshan
101 Productions Ltd.
*General
Management*

Jeffrey Finn
Producer

John N. Hart, Jr.
Producer

Philip J. Smith
Chairman
The Shubert
Organization
Producer

Robert E. Wankel
President
The Shubert
Organization
Producer

David Mirvish
Producer

Donny Epstein
Ergo Entertainment
Producer

Yeeshai Gross
Ergo Entertainment
Producer

Elie Landau
Ergo Entertainment
Producer

Harriet Newman
Leve
Producer

Carl Moellenberg
Double Gemini
Productions
Producer

Wendy Federman
Double Gemini
Productions
Producer

Jennifer
Manocherian
3toGo Entertainment
Producer

Peg McFeeley
Golden
3toGo Entertainment
Producer

Dead Accounts

Candy Kosow Gold
3toGo Entertainment
Producer

Charles Stone
Associate Producer

Curtain call on opening night (L–R):
Josh Hamilton, Katie Holmes, Norbert Leo Butz,
Jayne Houdyshell and Judy Greer

Photo by Joseph Marzullo/WENN

STAFF FOR *DEAD ACCOUNTS*

GENERAL MANAGEMENT
101 PRODUCTIONS, LTD.
Wendy Orshan   Jeffrey M. Wilson
Elie Landau
Ron Gubin
Chris Morey

COMPANY MANAGER
- Jeff Klein

GENERAL PRESS REPRESENTATIVE
BONEAU/BRYAN-BROWN
Chris Boneau
Aaron Meier   Kelly Guiod

PRODUCTION MANAGER
TECH PRODUCTION SERVICES, INC.
Peter Fulbright   Mary Duffe
Shaminda Amarakoon   Melanie Ganim
Erica Gambino

CASTING
CAPARELLIOTIS CASTING
David Caparelliotis, Casting Director
Lauren Port, Miriam Mintz

Production Stage Manager ....Rolt Smith
Stage Manager ....Julia P. Jones
Assistant Director ....Adrienne Campbell-Holt
Associate Scenic Designer....................Edward Pierce
Assistant Scenic Designers ....Nick Francone,
Richard Jarvis, T.J. Greenway,
Jennifer Price
Assistant Costume Designers ....Patrick Bevilacqua,
Ryan Park, David Newell
Associate Lighting Designer ....Vivien Leone
Associate Sound Designer ....Christopher Cronin
Composition Associate........................Curtis Moore
Production Carpenter ....Tony Menditto
Production Electrician ....Jon Lawson
Production Props Coordinator ....Buist Bickley
Assistant Props Coordinator ....Susan Barras

Prop Shopper ....Anna C. Goller
Prop Painter ....Emily Walsh
Sound Engineer/Mixer ....Wayne Smith
Makeup Design ....Ashley Ryan
Wardrobe Supervisor ....Meghan Carsella
Dressers ....Ray Panelli, Tree Sarvay
Hair/Makeup Supervisor ....John Mendola
Scenic Studio Assistants ....Nick Francone,
Jennifer Price
Production Assistants ....Mitchell Anderson,
Kate Croasdale
Legal Counsel ....Sendroff & Baruch LLC/
Jason Baruch
Accountant ....FK Partners, Robert Fried
Comptroller ....Galbraith & Co./Kenny Noth
Advertising ....Serino/Coyne/
Nancy Coyne, Angelo Desimini,
Matt Upshaw, Lauren Houlberg,
Tom Callahan, Joe Alesi
Marketing ....Serino/Coyne/
Leslie Barrett, Diana Salameh
Digital Outreach & Website ....Serino/Coyne/
Jim Glaub, Chip Meyrelles,
Laurie Connor, Kevin Keating,
Mark Seeley, Andrea Cuevas
101 Productions, Ltd. Staff ....Christina Boursiquot,
Beth Blitzer, Kit Ingui, Kathy Kim,
Mike McLinden, Michael Rudd,
Mary-Six Rupert, Steve Supeck,
David van Zyll de Jong
101 Productions, Ltd. Interns ....Erik Kaiko,
Simon Pincus, Sarah Springborn
Banking ....City National Bank/Anne McSweeney
Insurance ....Insurance Office of America/
Carol Bressi-Cilona
Opening Night Coordinator ....Serino/Coyne/
Suzanne Tobak
Merchandising ....The Araca Group
Production Photographer ....Joan Marcus
Payroll Services ....Checks & Balances Payroll, Inc.
Theatre Displays ....King Displays, Inc.
Group Sales ....Telecharge.com Group Sales

To learn more about the production, please visit

www.DeadAccountsOnBroadway.com

CREDITS
Scenery and scenic effects built, painted and electrified by
Show Motion, Inc., Milford, CT. Lighting equipment from
Hudson Sound and Light LLC. Sound equipment provided
by Sound Associates, Inc. Special thanks to Bra*Tenders for
hosiery and undergarments. Special thanks to Yamaha
Pianos. Household props provided by D'Agostino's. Pizza
provided by John's Pizzeria Times Square.

This production was rehearsed at
the New 42nd Street Studios.

Accounts was further developed at the 2011 New
ny Project playwriting workshop.

THE SHUBERT ORGANIZATION, INC.
Board of Directors

Philip J. Smith   **Robert E. Wankel**
Chairman   President

Wyche Fowler, Jr.   **Diana Phillips**

Lee J. Seidler   **Michael I. Sovern**

Stuart Subotnick

Chief Financial Officer........................Elliot Greene
Sr. Vice President, Ticketing ....David Andrews
Vice President, Finance ....Juan Calvo
Vice President, Human Resources ....Cathy Cozens
Vice President, Facilities ....John Darby
Vice President, Theatre Operations ....Peter Entin
Vice President, Marketing ....Charles Flateman
Vice President, Audit ....Anthony LaMattina
Vice President, Ticket Sales ....Brian Mahoney
Vice President, Creative Projects ...........D.S. Moynihan
Vice President, Real Estate ....Julio Peterson

House Manager ....Jonathan Shulman

Edward Albee's Who's Afraid of Virginia Woolf?

First Preview: September 27, 2012. Opened: October 13, 2012.
Limited Engagement. Closed March 3, 2013 after 17 Previews and 142 Performances.

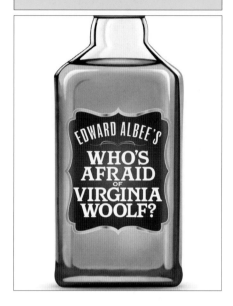

PLAYBILL

George is a middle-aged college history professor; his wife Martha is the daughter of the college president. She thinks he's a failure, he thinks she's a bitch. And on one alcohol-fueled night, in front of two younger guests, all their anger and bitterness spills out in the form of a series of deadly-serious parlor games: "Get the Guests," "Hump the Hostess" and the most vicious of them all, "Bringing Up Baby."

CAST
(in order of appearance)

Martha ....AMY MORTON
George ....TRACY LETTS
Nick ....MADISON DIRKS
Honey ....CARRIE COON

STANDBYS

For George: TONY WARD
For Martha: DEIRDRE MADIGAN
For Nick: ZACH SHAFFER
For Honey: NICOLE LOWRANCE

SETTING

The living room at a house on the campus
of a small New England college

TIME

Fall, 1962

⑤ BOOTH THEATRE
222 West 45th Street
A Shubert Organization Theatre

Philip J. Smith, *Chairman*   Robert E. Wankel, *President*

Jeffrey Richards   Jerry Frankel   Susan Quint Gallin   Mary Lu Roffe
Kit Seidel   Amy Danis & Mark Johannes   Patty Baker   Mark S. Golub & David S. Golub
Richard Gross   Jam Theatricals   Cheryl Lachowicz   Michael Palitz
Dramatic Forces/Angelina Fiordellisi   Luigi & Rose Caiola   Ken Greiner   Kathleen K. Johnson
Kirmser Ponturo Fund   Will Trice   GFour Productions

present

Tracy Letts   Amy Morton

in

Steppenwolf Theatre Company's

production of

Edward Albee's
Who's Afraid of Virginia Woolf?

with

Carrie Coon   Madison Dirks

Scenic Design	Costume Design	Lighting Design	Sound Design
Todd Rosenthal	**Nan Cibula-Jenkins**	**Allen Lee Hughes**	**Rob Milburn & Michael Bodeen**

Casting	Technical Supervision	Production Stage Manager
Erica Daniels, C.S.A.	**Hudson Theatrical Associates**	**Malcolm Ewen**

Press Representative	General Manager
Irene Gandy/Alana Karpoff	**Richards/Climan, Inc.**

Directed by
Pam MacKinnon

This production was first produced and presented at Chicago's Steppenwolf Theatre Company, Martha Lavey, Artistic Director, David Hawkanson, Executive Director. It was subsequently presented in Washington, D.C. at Arena Stage, Molly Smith, Artistic Director, Edgar Dobie, Executive Director.

The producers wish to express their appreciation to the Theatre Development Fund for its support of this production.

www.virginiawoolfonbroadway.com

10/13/12

(L-R): Tracy Letts, Carrie Coon, Amy Morton and Madison Dirks

Photo by Michael Brosilow

Edward Albee's Who's Afraid of Virginia Woolf?

Tracy Letts
George

Amy Morton
Martha

Carrie Coon
Honey, Fight Captain

Madison Dirks
Nick

Nicole Lowrance
Standby Honey

Deirdre Madigan
Standby Martha

Zach Shaffer
Standby Nick

Tony Ward
Standby George

Edward Albee
Playwright

Pam MacKinnon
Director

Todd Rosenthal
Set Design

Nan Cibula-Jenkins
Costume Design

Allen Lee Hughes
Lighting Design

Rob Milburn
Sound Design

Michael Bodeen
Sound Design

Nick Sandys
Fight Director

Erica Daniels
Casting

Martha Lavey
*Artistic Director
Steppenwolf Theatre
Company*

David Hawkanson
*Executive Director
Steppenwolf Theatre
Company*

Neil A. Mazzella
Hudson Theatrical
Associates
*Technical
Supervision*

David R. Richards
Richards/Climan, Inc.
*General
Management*

Tamar Haimes
Richards/Climan, Inc.
General Management

Jeffrey Richards
Producer

Jerry Frankel
Producer

Susan Quint Gallin
Producer

Mary Lu Roffe
Producer

Kit Seidel
Producer

Amy Danis
Producer

Mark Johannes
Producer

Patty Baker
Good Productions
Producer

Mark S. Golub
Producer

David S. Golub
Producer

Richard Gross
Producer

Arny Granat
Jam Theatricals
Producer

Steve Traxler
Jam Theatricals
Producer

Edward Albee's Who's Afraid of Virginia Woolf?

Cheryl Lachowicz
Producer

Michael Palitz
Producer

Dori Berinstein
Dramatic Forces
Producer

Angelina Fiordellisi
Producer

Luigi & Rose Caiola
Producers

Ken Greiner
Producer

Kathleen K. Johnson
Producer

Fran Kirmser
Kirmser Ponturo
Fund
Producer

Tony Ponturo
Kirmser Ponturo
Fund
Producer

Will Trice
Producer

Kenneth Greenblatt
GFour Productions
Producer

Seth Greenleaf
GFour Productions
Producer

Alan Glist
GFour Productions
Producer

David Beckerman
GFour Productions
Producer

CREW
Seated (L-R): Malcolm Ewen
(Production Stage Manager),
Susan Bennett-Goulet
(House Electrician),
Beth Berkeley (Sound Operator),
James Latus (Assistant Stage Manager),
Andy Jones (Company Manager)
Standing (L-R):
Rob Bevenger (Wardrobe Supervisor),
David Marquez (Dresser),
Jimmy Keane (House Props),
Carmel Vargyas (Hair/Wig Supervisor)

Photos by Brian Mapp

Marc Goldman
GFour Productions
Producer

BOX OFFICE
(L-R): Dennis Vogelgesang, Vigi Cadunz, Kathy Cadunz

FRONT OF HOUSE
(L-R): Daniel Rosario, Catherine Tavares, BeeBee, Nadine Space, Larry Hincher

---

2012-2013 AWARDS

TONY AWARDS
Best Revival of a Play
Best Performance by an Actor
in a Leading Role in a Play
(Tracy Letts)
Best Direction of a Play
(Pam MacKinnon)

DRAMA LEAGUE AWARD
Distinguished Revival of a Play

Photo: Michael Brosilow
Tracy Letts

OUTER CRITICS CIRCLE AWARD
Outstanding Revival of a Play
(Broadway or Off-Broadway)

DRAMA DESK AWARDS
Outstanding Revival of a Play
Outstanding Actor in a Play
(Tracy Letts)
Outstanding Director of a Play
(Pam MacKinnon)

THEATRE WORLD AWARD
For Outstanding Broadway
or Off-Broadway Debut
(Carrie Coon)

Edward Albee's Who's Afraid of Virginia Woolf?
Scrapbook

Correspondent: Madison Dirks, "Nick"
Opening Night Gifts: Our stage managers gave us bar towels with "Hump the Hostess" stenciled on them.
Actor Who Has Done the Most Shows: I think Amy Morton takes that honor.
Special Backstage Ritual: Before Carrie and I re-enter in the middle of Act III with her hopping like a bunny, Carrie cycles through different animals backstage before settling on a bunny.
Favorite Moment During Each Performance: As painful as it is, the end of Act III is something to see every single time.
Favorite In-Theatre Gathering Place: The Stage Management office. That's where the sweets are.
Favorite Off-Site Hangout: I can't get enough of The Rum House at the Hotel Edison.
Favorite Therapy: Gotta have that Ricola. Every intermission!

Record Number of Cell Phone Rings During a Performance: Amazingly, we've been very lucky so far. We haven't had many cell phones go off at all (as I'm knocking on a piece of wood the size of the Intrepid).
Memorable Press Encounter: There is an older woman who writes a blog about New York Theatre and she waited to talk to us after a performance. She held an impromptu interview with us at the stage door. Tenacious. And lovely.
Memorable Stage Door Fan Encounter: The high school/college students are the best. They go nuts for the show and they make sure to let you know it.
What Did You Think of the Internet Buzz on Your Show: It was exciting and daunting. It really made me feel like we had to deliver the goods on this one. The production had been a hit in Chicago and Washington DC, but you never know what will happen in New York.

Thankfully, we got it done!
Latest Audience Arrival: One performance, we had people coming in a good 40 minutes into Act I.
Catchphrases Only the Company Would Recognize: Tracy and I have pretty dirty mouths, so I don't think I can repeat some of our catchphrases.
Embarrassing Moments: The umbrella gun has been known not to work on occasion. And once, during the fight in Act II, I almost fell over on the couch. That would have left Tracy standing up all alone and given us nowhere to go afterwards.
Ghostly Encounters Backstage: There haven't been any. God, I hope there won't be any in the future.
Coolest Thing About Being in This Show: It's the 50th anniversary of Who's Afraid of Virginia Woolf? That's pretty cool.

STAFF FOR
EDWARD ALBEE'S
WHO'S AFRAID OF VIRGINIA WOOLF?

GENERAL MANAGEMENT
RICHARDS/CLIMAN, INC.

David R. Richards	Tamar Haimes
Michael Sag	Kyle Bonder
Jessica Fried	Ashley Rodbro

COMPANY MANAGER
Andy Jones

GENERAL PRESS REPRESENTATIVE

Irene Gandy	Alana Karpoff
Thomas Raynor	Christopher Pineda

PRODUCTION MANAGEMENT
HUDSON THEATRICAL ASSOCIATES

Neil A. Mazzella	Sam Ellis
Canara Price	Irene Wang

CASTING
Erica Daniels, CSA

PRODUCTION
STAGE MANAGER ....MALCOLM EWEN
Stage Manager ....James Latus
Assistant Director ....Lori Wolter Hudson
Fight Director ....Nick Sandys
Fight Captain ....Carrie Coon
Scenic Designer Assistants....................Sean Renfro, Scott A. Davis
Assistant Costume Designer ....Angela R. Harner
Associate Lighting Designer ....Joshua Benghiat
Associate Sound Designer ....Chris Cronin
Production Carpenter ....Adam Braunstein
Production Electrician ....Jimmy Maloney
Lighting Programmer ....Jay Penfield
Advance Sound ....Jim Van Bergen
New York Prop Coordinator ....Noah Pilipski
Wardrobe Supervisor ....Rob Bevenger
Hair/Wig Supervisor ....Monica Costea
Dresser ....David Marquez
Production Assistant ....Ashley Singh

Assistant Producers ....Michael Crea, PJ Miller
Advertising ....Serino/Coyne/
Greg Corradetti, Tom Callahan,
Danielle Boyle, Drew Nebrig,
Andrei Oleinik
Digital Outreach & Website ....Serino/Coyne/
Jim Glaub, Laurie Connor,
Kevin Keating, Whitney Manalio Creighton,
Mark Seeley
Interactive Marketing
Service ....Broadway's Best Shows/
Andy Drachenberg, Steven Strauss,
Layne McNish
General Management Interns ....Rose Bochner,
Joanna Levinger
Banking.................................City National Bank/
Michele Gibbons, Erik Piecuch
Insurance ....DeWitt Stern Group/
Jolyon Stern, Peter Shoemaker,
Anthony Pittari
Accountants ....Fried & Kowgios CPAs LLP/
Robert Fried, Anthony Moore
Comptroller ....Elliott Aronstam
Legal Counsel ....Lazarus and Harris LLP/
Scott Lazarus, Esq., Robert C. Harris, Esq.
Payroll ....Checks & Balances, Inc.
Production Photographer ....Michael Brosilow
Company Mascots ....Skye, Franco

STEPPENWOLF THEATRE COMPANY
Nora Daley, Trustee Chair
Martha Lavey, Artistic Director
David Hawkanson, Executive Director
Erica Daniels, Associate Artistic Director
David M. Schmitz, Managing Director
Associate Artists: Tracy Letts, Amy Morton,
Anna D. Shapiro, Jessica Thebus
Founders: Terry Kinney, Jeff Perry, Gary Sinise

CREDITS
Scenery constructed by Hudson Scenic Studio, Inc. Lighting equipment by Hudson Sound & Light LLC. Sound equipment by Sound Associates. Costumes built by Steppenwolf Theatre Company.

MUSIC CREDITS
"When First I Love" by Martin Denny ©1964, renewed 1992. Exotica Publishing Company/ASCAP. All rights reserved. Used by permission.

"Who's Afraid of the Big Bad Wolf?" by Frank Churchill. Additional lyric by Ann Ronell. ©Copyright by Bourne Co. Copyright renewed. All rights reserved. International copyright secured ASCAP.

"Just a Gigolo" written by Julius Brammer, Irving Caesar, Nello Casucci. ©1930 (renewed), Irving Caesar Music Corp. (ASCAP) and Chappell & Co., Inc. (ASCAP). All rights on behalf of Irving Caesar Music Corp. Administered by WB Music Corp. All rights reserved.

Rehearsed at Steppenwolf Theatre Company in Chicago, Illinois

 THE SHUBERT ORGANIZATION, INC.
Board of Directors

Elf: The Musical

No previews. Opened November 9, 2012.
Limited Engagement. Closed January 6, 2013 after 74 Performances.

PLAYBILL®

The Musical

Up at the North Pole, Buddy, one of Santa's perkiest toymakers, gets the shocking news that he's not really an elf at all, but is actually a human who was raised from babyhood by elves. The news launches him on an odyssey to New York City to find his real family—and eventually to reawaken true Christmas spirit in the jaded New Yorkers.

CAST

(in order of appearance)

Santa .... WAYNE KNIGHT
Mrs. Claus .... NANCY JOHNSTON
Buddy .... JORDAN GELBER
Charlie .... JONATHAN SCHWARTZ
Shawanda .... ARIEL REID
Walter Hobbs .... MARK JACOBY
Sam .... JONATHAN SCHWARTZ
Matthews .... DAVID HIBBARD
Chadwick .... JOSH LAMON
Emily .... BETH LEAVEL
Michael .... MITCHELL SINK
Deb .... VALERIE WRIGHT
Sales Woman .... CATHERINE BRUNELL
Macy's Manager .... MICHAEL MANDELL
Jovie .... LESLIE KRITZER
Fake Santa .... TIMOTHY J. ALEX
Little Boy .... JASON ERIC TESTA
Policemen .... JONATHAN SCHWARTZ,
                                   LEE A. WILKINS
Mr. Greenway .... ADAM HELLER
Charlotte Dennon .... EMILY HSU

Continued on next page

(L-R): Mitchell Sink and Jordan Gelber

Photo by Joan Marcus

---

9 AL HIRSCHFELD THEATRE
A JUJAMCYN THEATRE

JORDAN ROTH
President

PAUL LIBIN
Executive Vice President

JACK VIERTEL
Senior Vice President

Warner Bros. Theatre Ventures, Inc.
in association with
Unique Features and Jujamcyn Theaters

Present

elf
The Musical

Book by
Thomas Meehan and **Bob Martin**

Music by
Matthew Sklar

Lyrics by
Chad Beguelin

Based upon the New Line Cinema film written by David Berenbaum

Starring
Jordan Gelber
Leslie Kritzer
Mark Jacoby

Adam Heller   Michael Mandell   Valerie Wright
Mitchell Sink   Rory Donovan   Jason Eric Testa

With
Timothy J. Alex   Catherine Brunell   Callie Carter   Andrea Chamberlain
Jay Douglas   David Hibbard   Jenny Hill   Stacey Todd Holt
Emily Hsu   Nancy Johnston   Josh Lamon   Ariel Reid
Jonathan Schwartz   Eric LaJuan Summers   Jen Taylor   Lee A. Wilkins

Also Starring
Beth Leavel

And
Wayne Knight
as
Santa

Scenic Design	Costume Design	Lighting Design	Sound Design
David Rockwell	Gregg Barnes	Natasha Katz	Peter Hylenski

Casting	Projection Design	Hair Design	Dance Arrangements
Telsey + Company Bethany Knox, CSA	Zachary Borovay	Josh Marquette	David Chase

Production Stage Manager	Associate Director	Associate Choreographer	Music Coordinator	Technical Supervisor
Joshua Halperin	Casey Hushion	Callie Carter	John Miller	Chris Smith/Smitty

Executive Producers	Advertising & Marketing	Press Representative	General Manager
Mark Kaufman Raymond Wu	Serino/Coyne	The Hartman Group	The Charlotte Wilcox Company

Orchestrations
Doug Besterman

Music Direction & Vocal Arrangements
Phil Reno

Directed and Choreographed by
Casey Nicholaw

Original Broadway Cast Recording Available on Ghostlight Records

11/9/12

Elf: The Musical

MUSICAL NUMBERS

ACT I

Overture	Orchestra
"Happy All the Time"	Santa, Buddy & Company
"World's Greatest Dad"	Buddy
"In the Way"	Deb, Walter, Emily, Michael & Company
"Sparklejollytwinklejingley"	Buddy, Store Manager & Company
"I'll Believe in You"	Michael & Emily
"In the Way" (Reprise)	Emily & Walter
"Just Like Him"	Buddy, Deb & Company
"A Christmas Song"	Buddy, Jovie & Company
"World's Greatest Dad" (Reprise)	Buddy & Company

ACT II

Entr'Acte	Orchestra
"Nobody Cares About Santa"	Fake Santas, Store Manager & Buddy
"Never Fall in Love"	Jovie
"There Is a Santa Claus"	Michael & Emily
"The Story of Buddy"	Buddy, Michael, Walter, Greenway, Emily, Deb & Company
"Nobody Cares About Santa" (Reprise)	Santa
"A Christmas Song" (Reprise)	Jovie, Buddy, Emily, Michael, Walter & Company
Finale	Company

Cast Continued

Ensemble ....TIMOTHY J. ALEX, CATHERINE BRUNELL, ANDREA CHAMBERLAIN, DAVID HIBBARD, JENNY HILL, EMILY HSU, NANCY JOHNSTON, JOSH LAMON, ARIEL REID, JONATHAN SCHWARTZ, ERIC LAJUAN SUMMERS, LEE A. WILKINS

UNDERSTUDIES

For Santa: STACEY TODD HOLT, JOSH LAMON
For Buddy: JAY DOUGLAS
For Walter: TIMOTHY J. ALEX, STACEY TODD HOLT
For Emily: ANDREA CHAMBERLAIN, NANCY JOHNSTON
For Deb: ANDREA CHAMBERLAIN, JENNY HILL
For Macy's Manager: JOSH LAMON, ERIC LAJUAN SUMMERS
For Jovie: CATHERINE BRUNELL, JENNY HILL
For Mr. Greenway: TIMOTHY J. ALEX, JOSH LAMON

Standby For Buddy: RORY DONOVAN
Standby For Michael: JASON ERIC TESTA

SWINGS

CALLIE CARTER, JAY DOUGLAS, STACEY TODD HOLT, JEN TAYLOR

Dance Captain: CALLIE CARTER
Assistant Dance Captain: STACEY TODD HOLT

ORCHESTRA

Conductor: PHIL RENO
Associate Conductor: MAT EISENSTEIN

Concert Master: RICK DOLAN
Violin: BELINDA WHITNEY
Cello: SARAH HEWITT-ROTH
Bass: MICHAEL KUENNEN
Woodwinds: TOM MURRAY, RICK HECKMAN, FRANK SANTAGATA
Trumpets: CRAIG JOHNSON, SCOTT HARRELL
Trombones: LARRY FARRELL, JOE BARATI
Percussion: CHARLES DESCARFINO
Drums: PERRY CAVARI
Keyboards: MAT EISENSTEIN, SUE ANSCHUTZ, PHIL RENO
Music Coordinator: JOHN MILLER

Jordan Gelber
Buddy

Leslie Kritzer
Jovie

Beth Leavel
Emily

Wayne Knight
Santa

Mark Jacoby
Walter

Adam Heller
Mr. Greenway

Michael Mandell
Macy's Manager

Valerie Wright
Deb

Mitchell Sink
Michael

Rory Donovan
Buddy Standby

Elf: The Musical

Jason Eric Testa
*Michael Standby/
Little Boy*

Timothy J. Alex
*Ensemble/Fake
Santa; u/s Walter,
Mr. Greenway*

Catherine Brunell
*Ensemble/Sales
Woman; u/s Jovie*

Callie Carter
*Associate
Choreographer/
Dance Captain/
Swing*

Andrea Chamberlain
*Ensemble; u/s Emily,
Deb*

Jay Douglas
Swing; u/s Buddy

David Hibbard
Ensemble/Matthews

Jenny Hill
*Ensemble; u/s Deb,
Jovie*

Stacey Todd Holt
Swing; u/s Santa

Emily Hsu
*Ensemble/Charlotte
Dennon*

Nancy Johnston
*Ensemble/Mrs.
Claus; u/s Emily*

Josh Lamon
*Ensemble/Chadwick;
u/s Santa, Macy's
Manager, Mr.
Greenaway*

Ariel Reid
Ensemble/Shawanda

Jonathan Schwartz
*Ensemble/Charlie/
Sam/Policeman*

Eric LaJuan
Summers
*Ensemble; u/s
Macy's Manager*

Jen Taylor
Swing

Lee A. Wilkins
Ensemble/Policeman

Thomas Meehan
Book

Bob Martin
Book

Matthew Sklar
Music

Chad Beguelin
Lyrics

Casey Nicholaw
*Director/
Choreographer*

David Rockwell
Scenic Designer

Gregg Barnes
Costume Designer

Natasha Katz
Lighting Designer

Peter Hylenski
Sound Designer

Zachary Borovay
Projection Designer

Josh Marquette
Hair Designer

Bernard Telsey
Telsey + Company
Casting

Doug Besterman
Orchestrations

Phil Reno
*Music Director/
Vocal Arranger*

David Chase
Dance Arranger

Casey Hushion
Associate Director

John Miller
Music Coordinator

Chris Smith/
Theatersmith, Inc.
Technical Supervisor

Elf: The Musical

Charlotte Wilcox
The Charlotte Wilcox
Company
General Manager

Robert Shaye
Unique Features
Producer

Michael Lynne
Unique Features
Producer

Jordan Roth
President
Jujamcyn Theaters
Producer

Mark Kaufman
*Warner Bros.
Theatre Ventures*
Executive Producer

Raymond Wu
*Warner Bros.
Theatre Ventures*
Executive Producer

Photos by Brian Mapp

FRONT OF HOUSE
Front Row (L-R): Mark Maciejewski,
Julie Burnham, Lorraine Feeks,
Jose Nunez, Albert T. Kim
Second Row (L-R): Heather Gilles,
Christina Ruiz, Lawrence Levens, Bill Meyers
Third Row (L-R): Theresa Lopez, Chris Cannon,
Janice Rodriguez, Lisé Greaves
Fourth Row (L-R): Michael Mattie,
Rachel Broadwell, Joseph Sims
Fifth Row (L-R): Michael Wirsch, Clifford Ray Berry,
Bart Ryan, Donald Royal
Back Row (L-R): Terry Monahan, Nicole Corrales,
Elizabeth Meck, Jeremiah Hernandez

CREW
First Row (L-R): Mitchell Beck, Sarah Levine, Brian Dawson, Bob Griffin, Joe Mooneyham, Ginny Hounsel, Richie Anderson, Rob Brenner, Michele Gutierrez,
Gabe Harris, Hank Hale, Megan Bowers
Back Row (L-R): Susan Kroeter, Joe Manoy, Jason Strangfeld, Noah Pilipski, Lisa Preston, Vangeli Kaseluris, John Blixt, Tom Burke, Rocco Williams, Pete Drummond,
Dan Foss, Chris Conrad, Lou Kringle, Josh Burns, Jeff Johnson

Elf: The Musical

STAGE MANAGEMENT
(L-R): Karyn Meek, Brian Bogin (Stage Manager), Rachel Miller Davis (Assistant Stage Manager),
Joshua Halperin (Production Stage Manager)

DOORMAN
Neil Perez

Photos by Brian Mapp

STAFF for *ELF*

FOR WARNER BROS.
Chairman & CEO Barry Meyer

WARNER BROS. THEATRE VENTURES
Executive Vice President .... Raymond Wu
Executive Vice President .... Mark Kaufman
Head of Finance .... Laura Valan
Head of Business and Legal Affairs .... Jess Wittenberg
Senior Vice President, Finance .... Mark Coker
Vice President, Business and
    Legal Affairs .... Nicole Nagel
Director, Finance .... Maria Gonzalez
Manager, Business Planning .... Matt Zarider
Senior Financial Analyst .... Arthur Yang
Business and Legal Affairs .... Susan de Christofaro,
    Elena Cahalan, Courtney Anders
Staff .... Jennifer Kim, Kathryn Pellegrini,
    Briana Rimicci, Rachel Spenst,
    Michael O'Shea, Susan Gary

FOR UNIQUE FEATURES
Michael Lynne, Principal
Bob Shaye, Principal
Christina Delgado Zach Keach Sarah Victor

GENERAL MANAGEMENT
CHARLOTTE WILCOX COMPANY
Charlotte W. Wilcox
Scott M. Ellis Matthew W. Krawiec Dina S. Friedler
Chantel Hopper Margaret Wilcox Stephen Donovan
Todd Piskin Joshua Black

COMPANY MANAGER
Scott M. Ellis

ASSOCIATE COMPANY MANAGER
Michelle H. Tamagawa

GENERAL PRESS REPRESENTATIVE
THE HARTMAN GROUP
Michael Hartman   Juliana Hannett
Emily McGill

CASTING
TELSEY + COMPANY
Bernie Telsey CSA, Will Cantler CSA,
David Vaccari CSA, Bethany Knox CSA,
Craig Burns CSA, Tiffany Little Canfield CSA,
Rachel Hoffman CSA, Justin Huff CSA,
Patrick Goodwin CSA, Abbie Brady-Dalton CSA,
David Morris, Cesar A. Rocha,
Andrew Femenella, Karyn Casl,
Kristina Bramhall, Jessie Malone

Production Stage Manager .... Joshua Halperin
1st Assistant Stage Manager .... Brian Bogin
2nd Assistant Stage Manager .... Rachel Miller Davis
Associate Director .... Casey Hushion
Associate Choreographer/
    Dance Captain .... Callie Carter
Associate Costume Designer .... Matthew Pachtman
Assistant Costume Designer .... Irma Brainard
Associate Lighting Designer .... Peter Hoerburger
Assistant Lighting Designer .... Jon Goldman
Moving Light Programmer .... Hillary Knox
Associate Sound Designer .... Francis Elers
Associate Projection Designer .... Driscoll Otto
Production Electrician .... James Fedigan
Production Property Supervisor .... Emiliano Pares
Production Sound .... Jesse Stevens
Head Carpenter .... Hank Hale
Automation Carpenter .... Bob Griffin
Head Electrician .... Brian Dawson
Front Light .... Steve Long
Head Props .... Pete Drummond
Assistant Props .... Noah Pilipski
Head Sound .... Jason Strangfeld
Wardrobe Supervisor .... James Hall
Assistant Wardrobe Supervisor .... Jesse Galvan

Dressers .... Josh Burns, Dan Foss,
    Kaye Gowenlock, Ginny Hounsel,
    Jeff Johnson, Vangeli Kaseluris,
    Kurt Kielmann, Susan Kroeter,
    Lisa Preston
Hair and Wig Supervisor .... Mitchell Beck
Assistant Hair Supervisor .... Sarah Levine
Hair Dressers .... Barry Ernst, Kevin Phillips
Assistant to John Miller .... Nichole Jennino
Production Assistants .... Sarah Testerman,
    McKenzie Murphy
Legal Counsel .... Loeb & Loeb LLP/Seth Gelblum
Accountant .... Rosenberg, Neuwirth & Kushner,
    CPA's/Mark D'Ambrosi, Jana Jevnikar
Advertising .... Serino/Coyne–
    Greg Corradetti, Tom Callahan,
    Joe Alesi, Sarah Marcus,
    Adina Levin, Ryan McPhee
Digital Outreach & Website .... Serino/Coyne–
    Jim Glaub, Chip Meyrelles,
    Laurie Connor, Kevin Keating,
    Crystal Chase, Sumeet Bharati
Marketing & Ticketing Analytics .... Serino/Coyne–
    Leslie Barrett,
    Uma McCrosson,
    Mike Rafael
Payroll Services .... Castellana Services Inc.
Production Photographer .... Joan Marcus
Banking .... JP Morgan Chase Bank/Grace Correa
Insurance .... Dewitt Stern Group Inc./
    Peter Shoemaker
Physiotherapist .... Mark Hunter Hall
Massage Therapist .... Russ Beasley
Children's Tutoring .... On Location Education
Children's Tutor .... Muriel Kester
Children's Guardian .... Robert Wilson
Merchandising .... The Araca Group
Information Management
    Services .... Marion Finkler Taylor
Travel Services .... Tzell Travel/Andi Henig
Theatre Displays .... King Displays

Elf: The Musical
SCRAPBOOK

Correspondent: Josh Lamon, "Chadwick"

Memorable Note, Fax or Fan Letter: Not sure, but Wayne Knight gets an insane amount of fan mail.

Most Exciting Celebrity Visitor: For the two boys (Mitchell Sink and Jason Eric Testa) it was a HUGE deal when One Direction came. The rest of us are too old to know who they were.

Actor Who Performed the Most Roles in This Show: Josh Lamon played nine parts. Most of the ensemble plays six or seven.

Tales From the Put-in of the Two New Stars: We didn't need one cause we are a seasonal show! Yay for no put-ins!

Special Backstage Ritual: Group prayer.

Favorite Off-Site Hangout: Our cast is mainly made up of Moms and Dads. So we didn't really hang out outside of the show.

Favorite Snack Foods: Jonathan Schwartz and his bag of raw cauliflower.

Mascot: Raw cauliflower.

Favorite Therapy Physical Therapy and Massage. For the most part we did nine shows a week (thank you Equity) and were all pretty broken by show five.

Memorable Ad-Lib: Jordan changed a line to "All I have is chocolate money, but I spent most of that playing dreidel." Funny stuff.

Columnist Perez Hilton backstage with Leslie Kritzer.
Photo by Joseph Marzullo/WENN

Technological Interruptions During a Performance: People are always on their phones during the show. It's the sad reality of the times.

Memorable Stage Door Fan Encounter: The stage door opened before the show and a kid saw an "Elf" heading downstairs and exclaimed "OOO LA LA!!! An Elf!"

What Did You Think of the Web Buzz on Your Show: We are old-school. We don't pay much attention to the Web Buzz. We come to work. We do our job and we have a great time doing it.

Fastest Costume Change: Josh Lamon changes from Santa look-alike to a tap dancing elf in a few seconds. Pretty magical stuff.

Busiest Day at the Box Office: Every single day. People were storming the theatre for tickets. Rioting at Chicken Bar if they didn't get them.

Who Wore the Heaviest/Hottest Costume: Poor Wayne Knight. That Santa costume is no joke.

Who Wore the Least: Naughty naughty. I will never tell.

Catchphrase Only the Company Would Recognize: "Sell It!!!" (Often exclaimed during dance numbers.)

Sweethearts Within the Company: EVERYONE. Nicest cast on Broadway.

Best In-House Parody Lyrics: I would tell you, but they're filthy.

Embarrassing Moment: During the "angry Santa" opening of Act II, a line came out wrong. The line is supposed to be: "Now all they do is SIT on your lap and text each other." One day it accidentally came out: "Now all they do is s*#& on your lap and text each other." Oops!

Ghostly Encounters Backstage: So many. This theatre is HAUNTED ya'll.

CREDITS

Scenery by Hudson Scenic and Showman Fabrication. Video projection system engineered and provided by Worldstage. Automation by Hudson Scenic. Costumes by Arel Studios; Barbara Matera, Ltd.; Carelli Costumes; Eric Winterling, Inc.; Giliberto Designs, Inc.; Katrina Patterns, Inc.; Shafton, Inc.; Tricorne, Inc. Millinery by Carelli Costumes. Custom footwear by LaDuca Shoes; Rodney Gordon, Inc.; Worldtone Dance. Ice skates by Klingbeil Shoe Labs, Inc. Custom fabric printing by First2Print and Gene Mignola, Inc. Custom fabric dyeing and painting by Eric Winterling, Inc.; Jeff Fender. Fur by Fur & Furgery, Inc. Hair products provided by L'Oreal Professionell. Eyewear by Dr. Wayne Goldberg. Undergarments and hosiery provided by Bra*Tenders, On Stage Dancewear. Lighting and sound equipment from Production Resource Group.

SPECIAL THANKS
Amanda Hicks
Karen Moore

To learn more about the production,
please visit
ELFMUSICAL.com

Rehearsed at Lincoln Center Studios

JUJAMCYN THEATERS

JORDAN ROTH
President

PAUL LIBIN
Executive Vice President

JACK VIERTEL
Senior Vice President

MEREDITH VILLATORE	**JENNIFER HERSHEY**
Chief Financial Officer	Vice President,
	Building Operations
MICAH HOLLINGWORTH	**HAL GOLDBERG**
Vice President,	Vice President,
Company Operations	Theatre Operations

Director of Business Affairs ....Albert T. Kim
Director of Human Resources ....Michele Louhisdon
Director of Ticketing Services ....Justin Karr
Theatre Operations
  Managers ....Willa Burke, Susan Elrod,
    Emily Hare, Jeff Hubbard, Albert T. Kim
Theatre Operations
  Associates ....Carrie Jo Brinker, Brian Busby,
    Michael Composto, Anah Jyoti Klate
Accounting ....Cathy Cerge, Amy Frank,
    Tariq Hamami, Alexander Parra
Executive Producer, Red Awning ....Nicole Kastrinos
Director of Sales, Givenik.com ....Karen Freidus
Building Operations Associate ....Erich Bussing
Ticketing and Pricing Associate ....Jonathon Scott
Executive Coordinator ....Ed Lefferson
Executive Assistants ....Clark Mims Tedesco,
    Beth Given, Julia Kraus
Receptionist ....Lisa Perchinske
Maintenance ....Ralph Santos, Ramon Zapata
Security ....Rasim Hodzic, John Acero
Interns ....Kayla Burgett, Estefania Fadul,
    Taylor Kurpiel, Amy Larrowe,
    Matthew Robertson, Brandon Smithey

Staff for the Al Hirschfeld Theatre for
Elf
Theatre Manager ....Albert T. Kim

Associate Theatre Manager ....Carrie Jo Brinker
Treasurer ....Carmine LaMendola
Head Carpenter ....Joseph J. Maher, Jr.
Head Propertyperson ....Richard Anderson
Head Electrician ....Michele Gutierrez
Flyman ....Gabe Harris
Engineer ....David Neville
Assistant Treasurers ....Vicci Stanton,
    Gloria Diabo, Jeffrey Nevin,
    Janette Wernegreen
Carpenters ....Joe Mooneyham, Mike Maher,
    Joe Manoy
Propertyperson ....Rob Brenner
Electricians ....John Blixt, Tom Burke,
    Joe Lenihan, Rocco Williams
Head Usher ....Janice Rodriguez
Ticket-Takers ....Tristan Blacer, Lorraine Feeks
Doormen ....Henry E. Menendez, Neil Perez
Front of House Directors ....Julie Burnham,
    Lawrence Levens, William Meyers
Head Porter ....Jose Nunez
Head Cleaner ....Bethania Alvarez
Ushers ....Peter Davino, Jennifer DiDonato,
    Heather Gilles, Lisé Greaves,
    Theresa Lopez, Mark Maciejewski,
    Mary Marzan, Hollis Miller,
    Donald Royal, Bart Ryan
Porters ....Tereso Avila, Roberto Ellington
Cleaners ....Michelina Annarumma, Mirjan Aquino

Lobby refreshments by Sweet Concessions.

Security provided by GBA Consulting, Inc.

An Enemy of the People

First Preview: September 4, 2012. Opened: September 27, 2012.
Limited Engagement. Closed November 18, 2012 after 26 Previews and 59 Performances.

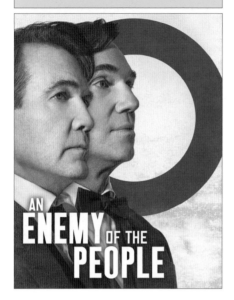

PLAYBILL

Respected doctor Thomas Stockmann expects to be praised and honored when he discovers that the local spa is polluted and harming visitors instead of helping them. But because the spa is the economic mainstay of his village he immediately finds himself locking horns with his brother, the mayor, who believes that the expensive repairs and bad publicity would be financially ruinous. The scene is set for a political battle royal between the two fiery siblings to do what each thinks is right.

CAST

(in order of appearance)

Billing .... JAMES WATERSTON
Catherine Stockmann ..... KATHLEEN McNENNY
Peter Stockmann .... RICHARD THOMAS
Hovstad .... JOHN PROCACCINO
Dr. Thomas Stockmann .... BOYD GAINES
Captain Horster .... RANDALL NEWSOME
Petra Stockmann .... MAÏTÉ ALINA
Morten Kiil .... MICHAEL SIBERRY
Aslaksen .... GERRY BAMMAN
The Drunk .... JOHN ROBERT TILLOTSON
Townspeople .... MIKE BOLAND,
VICTORIA FRINGS,
ANDREW HOVELSON, RAY VIRTA

The action takes place in a coastal town
in southern Norway.

Stage Manager .... CARLOS MAISONET

Continued on next page

Continued on next page

MANHATTAN THEATRE CLUB
SAMUEL J. FRIEDMAN THEATRE

ARTISTIC DIRECTOR
LYNNE MEADOW

EXECUTIVE PRODUCER
BARRY GROVE

PRESENTS

AN ENEMY OF THE PEOPLE

BY
HENRIK IBSEN

A NEW VERSION BY
REBECCA LENKIEWICZ

WITH

BOYD GAINES   RICHARD THOMAS

MAÏTÉ ALINA   GERRY BAMMAN   KATHLEEN McNENNY
RANDALL NEWSOME   JOHN PROCACCINO   MICHAEL SIBERRY   JAMES WATERSTON
MIKE BOLAND   VICTORIA FRINGS   ANDREW HOVELSON
JOHN ROBERT TILLOTSON   RAY VIRTA

SCENIC DESIGN
JOHN LEE BEATTY

COSTUME DESIGN
CATHERINE ZUBER

LIGHTING DESIGN
BEN STANTON

ORIGINAL MUSIC & SOUND DESIGN
DAVID VAN TIEGHEM

HAIR & WIG DESIGN
TOM WATSON

FIGHT DIRECTOR
J. DAVID BRIMMER

PRODUCTION STAGE MANAGER
WINNIE Y. LOK

DIRECTED BY
DOUG HUGHES

ARTISTIC PRODUCER
MANDY GREENFIELD

GENERAL MANAGER
FLORIE SEERY

DIRECTOR OF ARTISTIC DEVELOPMENT
JERRY PATCH

DIRECTOR OF MARKETING
DEBRA WAXMAN-PILLA

PRESS REPRESENTATIVE
BONEAU/BRYAN-BROWN

PRODUCTION MANAGER
JOSHUA HELMAN

DIRECTOR OF CASTING
NANCY PICCIONE

ARTISTIC LINE PRODUCER
LISA McNULTY

DIRECTOR OF DEVELOPMENT
LYNNE RANDALL

PRODUCTION SUPPORT PROVIDED BY THE ALFRED P. SLOAN FOUNDATION AS PART OF THE MTC/SLOAN SCIENCE THEATRE INITIATIVE.
THIS VERSION WAS COMMISSIONED AND FIRST PRODUCED BY THE ARCOLA THEATRE, LONDON ON 4TH APRIL 2008.
LITERAL TRANSLATION BY CHARLOTTE BARSLUND.
MANHATTAN THEATRE CLUB WISHES TO EXPRESS ITS APPRECIATION TO THEATRE DEVELOPMENT FUND FOR ITS SUPPORT OF THIS PRODUCTION.

9/27/12

Kathleen McNenny, Richard Thomas
and Boyd Gaines

Photo by Joan Marcus

An Enemy of the People

Cast Continued

UNDERSTUDIES

For Captain Horster, Hovstad and The Drunk:
MIKE BOLAND
For Catherine Stockmann and Petra Stockmann:
VICTORIA FRINGS
For Billing and Townspeople:
ANDREW HOVELSON
For Aslaksen and Morten Kiil:
JOHN ROBERT TILLOTSON
For Dr. Thomas Stockmann:
RAY VIRTA

James Waterston
Billing

Kathleen McNenny
Catherine Stockmann

Richard Thomas
Peter Stockmann

John Procaccino
Hovstad

Boyd Gaines
Dr. Thomas Stockmann

Randall Newsome
Captain Horster

Maïté Alina
Petra Stockmann

Michael Siberry
Morten Kiil

Richard Thomas as Peter Stockmann

Photo by Joan Marcus

Gerry Bamman
Aslaksen

John Robert Tillotson
*The Drunk;
u/s Morten Kiil,
Aslaksen,*

Mike Boland
*Townsperson;
u/s Captain Horster,
Hovstad, The Drunk*

Victoria Frings
*Townsperson;
u/s Catherine
Stockmann, Petra
Stockmann*

Andrew Hovelson
*Townsperson;
u/s Billing,
Townspeople*

Ray Virta
*Townsperson;
u/s Dr. Thomas
Stockmann*

An Enemy of the People

Henrik Ibsen
Playwright

Rebecca Lenkiewicz
Adaptation

Doug Hughes
Director

John Lee Beatty
Scenic Design

Catherine Zuber
Costume Design

David Van Tieghem
*Original Music &
Sound Design*

Tom Watson
Hair & Wig Design

J. David Brimmer
Fight Director

Lynne Meadow
*Artistic Director
Manhattan Theatre
Club, Inc.*

Barry Grove
*Executive Producer,
Manhattan Theatre
Club*

Photos by Brian Mapp

BOX OFFICE
(L-R): Rachel James, David Dillon, Geoffrey Nixon

FRONT OF HOUSE
Front Row (L-R):
Wendy Wright,
Patricia Polhill,
Lyanna Alvarado,
Nikki Kelly,
Blake Ricciardi,
Selena Nelson
Back Row (L-R):
Dinah Glorioso,
Jackson Ero, Ed Brashear,
Jim Joseph, Richard Ponce,
Joe Spezzano

CREW
Front Row (L-R): Winnie Y. Lok,
Erin Moeller, Carlos Maisonet,
Catherine Lynch, Natasha Steinhagen,
Leah Redmond, Andrew Braggs
Back Row (L-R): Savana Leveille,
David Grevengoed, Jeremy Von Deck,
Chris Wiggins, Vaughn Preston,
Timothy Walters, Jeff Dodson, Louis Shapiro

An Enemy of the People

Artistic Director ....**Lynne Meadow**
Executive Producer ....**Barry Grove**
General Manager ....**Florie Seery**
Artistic Producer ....**Mandy Greenfield**
Director of Artistic Development ....**Jerry Patch**
Director of Artistic Operations ....**Amy Gilkes Loe**
Artistic Line Producer ....Lisa McNulty
Assistant to the Artistic Director ....Nicki Hunter
Assistant to the
    Executive Producer ....Emily Hammond
Assistant to the Artistic Producer ....Ryan McGlone
Director of Casting ....**Nancy Piccione**
Casting Associate ....Kelly Gillespie
Casting Assistant ....Darragh Garvey
Literary Manager/
    Sloan Project Manager ....Annie MacRae
Artistic Development Associate ....Elizabeth Rothman
Artistic Delelopment Assistant ....Scott Kaplan
Director of Development ....**Lynne Randall**
Director, Individual Giving ....Emily Fleisher
Director, Institutional Giving ....Patricia Leonard
Director, Special Events ....Kristina Hoge
Manager, Individual Giving ....Josh Martinez-Nelson
Manager, Institutional Giving ....Andrea Gorzell
Development Associate/
    Individual Giving ....Laura Petrucci
Development Associate,
    Special Events ....Molly Clarke
Development Associate/
    Institutional Giving ....Heather Gallagher
Patrons' Liaison ....Kaity Neagle
Director of Marketing ....**Debra Waxman-Pilla**
Assistant Marketing Director ....Becca Goland-Van Ryn
Marketing Manager ....Caitlin Baird
Director of Finance ....**Jessica Adler**
Director of Human Resources ....**Stephanie Dolce**
Business Manager ....Ryan Guhde
Business & HR Associate ....Mallory Triest
Business Assistant ....Sarah DeStefano
IT Manager ....Mendy Sudranski
Systems Analyst ....Jason Fritzsch
Studio Manager/Receptionist ....Thatcher Stevens
Associate General Manager ....**Lindsey Sag**
Company Manager/
    NY City Center ....Samantha Kindler
General Management Assistant ....Derrick Olson
Director of
    Subscriber Services ....**Robert Allenberg**
Subscriber Services Manager ....Kevin Sullivan
Subscriber Services
    Representatives...........................Mark Bowers,
                                              Tim Salamandyk,
                                        Rosanna Consalvo Sarto,
                                              Amber Wilkerson
Director of Telesales and
    Telefunding ....**George Tetlow**
Telesales and Telefunding Manager ....Terrence Burnett
Telesales and Telefunding Staff ....Stephen Brown,
                                       Kel Haney, Molly Thomas,
                                          Allison Zajac-Batell
Director of Education ....**David Shookhoff**
Assistant Education Director/
    Coordinator, Paul A. Kaplan Theatre
        Management Program ....Amy Harris
Education Programs Coordinator ....Kimberley Oria

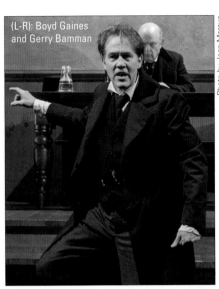

(L-R): Boyd Gaines and Gerry Bamman

Photo by Joan Marcus

MTC Teaching Artists....................Stephanie Alston,
                                    David Auburn, Chris Ceraso,
                                 Charlotte Colavin, Dominic Colon,
                                 Allison Daugherty, Andy Goldberg,
                                      Kel Haney, Elise Hernandez,
                             Jeffrey Joseph, Julie Leedes, Kate Long,
                                   Andres Munar, Melissa Murray,
                            Angela Pietropinto, Carmen Rivera, Judy Tate,
                              Candido Tirado, Liam Torres, Joe White
Theatre Management Interns ....Claire Dyrud,
                                    Sanam Emami, Drew Factor,
                                     Ben Ferber, Rachel Friedman,
                                      Nicole Kelly, Roman Micevic,
                                   Kathryn Pamula, Blake Riccardi,
                            Elizabeth Sharpe-Levine, Elizabeth Stern

Production Manager ....**Joshua Helman**
Associate Production Manager ....Bethany Weinstein
Assistant Production Manager ....Kevin Service
Properties Supervisor ....**Scott Laule**
Assistant Properties Supervisor ....Lily Fairbanks
Props Carpenter ....Peter Grimes
Costume Supervisor ....**Erin Hennessy Dean**

GENERAL PRESS REPRESENTATION
BONEAU/BRYAN-BROWN
Chris Boneau   Aaron Meier
Christine Olver   Emily Meagher

Script Readers ....Alex Barron, Aaron Grunfeld,
                                     Clifford Lee Johnson III,
                                Rachel Lerner-Ley, Thomas Park,
                                              Rachel Slaven

SERVICES
Accountants ....ERE, LLP
Advertising ....SpotCo/Drew Hodges,
                                   Tom Greenwald, Jim Edwards,
                                  Michael Crowley, Tim Falotico,
                                   Marc Mettler, Brandon Stansell
Web Design ....SpotCo Interactive
Legal Counsel ....Charles H. Googe, Jr.;
                                        Carol M. Kaplan/
                                     Paul, Weiss, Rifkind,
                                   Wharton and Garrison LLP

Real Estate Counsel ....Marcus Attorneys
Labor Counsel ....Harry H. Weintraub/
                                        Glick and Weintraub, P.C.
Immigration Counsel ....Theodore Ruthizer/
                                    Kramer, Levin, Naftalis & Frankel, LLP
Insurance ....DeWitt Stern Group, Inc./
                                              Anthony Pittari
Maintenance ....Reliable Cleaning
Production Photographer ....Joan Marcus
Event Photography ....Bruce Glikas
Cover Photograph ....Henry Leutwyler
Cover Design ....SPOTCO
Theatre Displays ....King Displays

PRODUCTION STAFF FOR
AN ENEMY OF THE PEOPLE
Company Manager ....**Erin Moeller**
Production Stage Manager ....**Winnie Y. Lok**
Stage Manager ....Carlos Maisonet
Assistant Director ....Alexander Greenfield
Production Dramaturg ....Mark Bly
Make-Up Designer ....Angelina Avallone
Associate Scenic Designer ....Kacie Hultgren
Assistant Costume Designers ....Patrick Bevilacqua,
                                       Ryan Park, Cole McCarty,
                                              David Newell
Assistant Lighting Designer ....Ken Elliott
Associate Sound Designer ....David Sanderson
Hair/Make-Up Supervisor ....Natasha Steinhagen
Moving Light Programmer ....Marc Polimeni
Automation Operator ....Vaughn Preston
Dressers ....David Grevengoed, Savana Leveille
Production Assistant ....Catherine Lynch

CREDITS
Deck built, painted, electrified and automated by Show
Motion, Inc., Milford, CT. Scenery fabrication by Great
Lakes Scenic Studios. Lighting equipment provided by
PRG Lighting. Sound equipment provided by Masque
Sound. Men's and women's costumes provided by Angels,
the Costumiers. Women's clothes by John Cowles. Men's
tailoring by Brian Hemesath. Tailoring by Ed Dawson.
Millinery by Wil Crowther/Centerstage. Makeup provided
by M•A•C.

For more information visit
www.ManhattanTheatreClub.org

An Enemy of the People
SCRAPBOOK

Correspondent: James Waterston, "Billing"

Memorable Opening Night Note: A note to me from David Henry Hwang—a feast of superlatives!

Memorable Opening Night Gift: A distinguished cast member received a floral arrangement from his representative which essentially featured a bunch of carnations dressed up to look like a pilgrim, surrounded by small plastic pumpkins.

Most Exciting Celebrity Visitor: Keith Carradine—he didn't have to do or say anything (although he couldn't have been more complimentary).

Special Backstage Ritual: Staring at the mirror, applying makeup, questioning all the choices I've made in my life.

Favorite Moment During Each Performance: Trying to read John Procaccino's mind as we sit at the dinner table in Act I and eat cold meat and potatoes night after night.

Favorite In-Theatre Gathering Place: Boyd and Richard's, for a post-show "assessment" and maybe a drink.

Favorite Off-Site Hangout: Glass House Tavern.

Mascot: Jingles. (That's the floral arrangement/pilgrim)

Favorite Therapy: I'm not aware of a lot of folks getting massages, although I'll bet they wouldn't turn them down.

Most Memorable Ad-Lib: "You gotta get that door fixed!"

Memorable Stage Door Fan Encounter: A fan raved, "Great enunciation!"

Internet Buzz on the Show: I don't read about "le buzz."

Fastest Costume Change: It's between Boyd and Kathleen.

Busiest Day at the Box Office: NOT the matinee after Hurricane Sandy—but bless their souls for managing to get here!

Heaviest/Hottest Costume: Johnny Pro wore a leather coat made from the hide of at least eleven cows.

Who Wore the Least: Certain naughty people backstage.

Catchphrase Only the Company Would Recognize: "Yes. Yes. He's Alone. ....Randeen!! (curtain)."

Memorable Directorial Note: Let's give the audience an experience and not a lesson.

Sweethearts Within the Company: The Stockmanns are all I know about.

Embarrassing Moment: Arriving for the first day's rehearsal, proudly sporting a spanking new mustache, only to sense immediately from Doug that I would be shaving that sucker before the second day's rehearsal.

Coolest Thing About Being in This Show: Being a part of this fabulous story, being a part of sharing this play with NYC during elections—although it would be relevant any time! Being a part of MTC's daring dream to have this little-produced brilliant play on Broadway! And best of all, like any show, those magic nights when the audience really enjoys and absorbs the show!

Fan Club Info: All fan mail should be sent in care of: The Baths Nowheresville Southern Norway

1. Director Doug Hughes (far L) and the cast of *An Enemy of the People* in the rehearsal studio August 2012.
2. (L-R): Richard Thomas and Boyd Gaines pal around for the press.
3. Cast members on opening night (L-R): Victoria Frings, Kathleen McNenny and Maïté Alina.
4. Cast party at Copacabana (L-R): John Procaccino, Rebecca Lenkiewicz, Randall Newsome.
5. Richard Thomas reunites with his TV mom from "The Waltons," Michael Learned, at the cast party.

Evita

First Preview: March 12, 2012. Opened: April 5, 2012.
Closed January 26, 2013 after 26 Previews and 337 Performances.

Beautiful, passionate and ambitious Eva Duarte grows up in poverty in backwater Argentina. She tries to improve her lot in life by bedding a series of powerful men, eventually allying herself with army colonel Juan Perón. Using the mass media to touch the common people, the descamisados ("shirtless ones"), who call her "Evita," she builds a powerful political base to get Perón elected president. However, the real power behind his throne is Evita, whose dreams for enriching herself, Perón and Argentina know no bounds. Is this woman a gangster, a saint— or a combination of both?

CAST
(in order of appearance)

Che .... RICKY MARTIN
Eva .... ELENA ROGER
Eva (At Wed. Eve and Sat.
   Mat. Performances) .... CHRISTINA DeCICCO
Magaldi .... MAX VON ESSEN
Perón .... MICHAEL CERVERIS
Mistress .... RACHEL POTTER
Cabinet Members ...... GEORGE LEE ANDREWS,
          BRADLEY DEAN, BRAD LITTLE
Priest .... GEORGE LEE ANDREWS
Italian Admiral .... BRAD LITTLE
Child .... AVA DeMARY
          or MAVIS SIMPSON-ERNST
Nurses .... MARGOT DE LA BARRE,
          MELANIE FIELD

Eva's Family
MARGOT DE LA BARRE, BRADLEY DEAN,

Continued on next page

N **MARQUIS THEATRE**
UNDER THE DIRECTION OF JAMES M. NEDERLANDER AND JAMES L. NEDERLANDER

HAL LUFTIG   SCOTT SANDERS PRODUCTIONS
ROY FURMAN   YASUHIRO KAWANA   ALLAN S. GORDON/ADAM S. GORDON   JAMES L. NEDERLANDER
TERRY ALLEN KRAMER   GUTTERMAN FULD CHERNOFF/PITTSBURGH CLO   THOUSAND STARS PRODUCTIONS
ADAM BLANSHAY   ADAM ZOTOVICH   ROBERT AHRENS   STEPHANIE P. McCLELLAND   CAROLE L. HABER
RICARDO HORNOS   CAROL FINEMAN   BRIAN SMITH   WARREN & JÂLÉ TREPP

RICKY MARTIN   ELENA ROGER   MICHAEL CERVERIS

EVITA

Lyrics by   Music by
TIM RICE   **ANDREW LLOYD WEBBER**

MAX VON ESSEN   with   **RACHEL POTTER**

and at certain performances
CHRISTINA DeCICCO
plays the role of "Eva"

ASHLEY AMBER   GEORGE LEE ANDREWS   WENDI BERGAMINI   CALLIE CARTER   ERIC L. CHRISTIAN   KRISTINE COVILLO
MARGOT DE LA BARRE   BRADLEY DEAN   AVA DeMARY   REBECCA EICHENBERGER   J. AUSTIN EYER   MELANIE FIELD
JENNIE FORD   JASON LEE GARRETT   CONSTANTINE GERMANACOS   LAUREL HARRIS   BAHIYAH HIBAH   NICK KENKEL
BRAD LITTLE   MATT LOEHR   ERICA MANSFIELD   EMILY MECHLER   SYDNEY MORTON   JESSICA LEA PATTY
KRISTIE DALE SANDERS   TIMOTHY SHEW   MAVIS SIMPSON-ERNST   MICHAELJON SLINGER
JOHNNY STELLARD   ALEX MICHAEL STOLL   DANIEL TORRES   MATT WALL

Scenic & Costume Design	Lighting Design	Sound Design
CHRISTOPHER ORAM	NEIL AUSTIN	MICK POTTER

Wig & Hair Design	Projection Design	Casting
RICHARD MAWBEY	ZACHARY BOROVAY	TELSEY + COMPANY

Technical Supervisor	Production Stage Manager	Associate Director	Associate Choreographer
CHRISTOPHER C. SMITH	MICHAEL J. PASSARO	SETH SKLAR-HEYN	CHRIS BAILEY

Advertising	Press	Marketing Services	General Management
SPOTCO	THE HARTMAN GROUP	TYPE A MARKETING / ANNE RIPPEY	BESPOKE THEATRICALS

Music Supervisor/Conductor	Orchestrations	Dance Arrangements	Music Coordinator
KRISTEN BLODGETTE	ANDREW LLOYD WEBBER & DAVID CULLEN	DAVID CHASE	DAVID LAI

Choreographed by
ROB ASHFORD

Directed by
MICHAEL GRANDAGE

ORIGINALLY PRODUCED BY ANDRÉ PTASZYNSKI FOR THE REALLY USEFUL THEATRE COMPANY.
WORLD PREMIERE OF *EVITA* DIRECTED BY HAROLD PRINCE IN 1978.

10/8/12

(L-R): Michael Cerveris as Perón and Elena Roger as Eva

Photo by Richard Termine

Evita

MUSICAL NUMBERS

ACT I

"Requiem"	The Company
"Oh, What a Circus"	Che, Quartet and Company
"On This Night of a Thousand Stars"	Magaldi
"Eva, Beware of the City"	Magaldi, Eva, Che and Family
"Buenos Aires"	Eva, Che and Company
"Goodnight and Thank You"	Che, Eva and Lovers
"The Art of the Possible"	Perón, Eva and Generals
"Charity Concert"	Magaldi, Che, Perón and Company
"I'd Be Surprisingly Good for You"	Eva and Perón
"Another Suitcase in Another Hall"	Mistress
"Perón's Latest Flame"	Che and Company
"A New Argentina"	Perón, Eva, Che and Company

ACT II

"On the Balcony of the Casa Rosada"	Perón and Company
"Don't Cry for Me Argentina"	Eva
"High Flying, Adored"	Che and Eva
"Rainbow High"	Eva and Valets
"Rainbow Tour"	Perón, Che, Eva and Company
"The Chorus Girl Hasn't Learned"	Eva and Company
"And the Money Kept Rolling In"	Che and Company
"Santa Evita"	Child and Company
"Waltz for Eva and Che"	Eva and Che
"You Must Love Me"	Eva
"She Is a Diamond"	Perón and Military
"Dice Are Rolling"	Perón and Eva
"Eva's Final Broadcast"	Eva
"Montage"	The Company
"Lament"	Eva

ORCHESTRA

Conductor: KRISTEN BLODGETTE
Associate Conductor: WILLIAM WALDROP
Woodwinds: JAMES ERCOLE,
    KATHLEEN NESTER
Trumpets: JAMES DE LA GARZA,
    ALEX HOLTON
Trombone: TIM ALBRIGHT
French Horn: SHELAGH ABATE
Guitar: MICHAEL AARONS
Bass: JEFF COOPER
Drums: BILL LANHAM
Percussion: DAVE ROTH
Keyboards: ANDY EINHORN,
    WILLIAM WALDROP
Keyboards/Accordion: EDDIE MONTEIRO
Violins: VICTOR COSTANZI,
    KATHERINE LIVOLSI-LANDAU,
    SUZY PERELMAN
Viola: DAVID BLINN
Cello: MAIRI DORMAN-PHANEUF
Music Coordinator: DAVID LAI
Synthesizer Programmer: STUART ANDREWS
Music Copyist: ROB MEFFE

Photo by Richard Termine

Elena Roger and company perform "And the Money Kept Rolling In"

Cast Continued

REBECCA EICHENBERGER,
J. AUSTIN EYER, SYDNEY MORTON

Eva's Lovers
MATT LOEHR, J. AUSTIN EYER,
GEORGE LEE ANDREWS,
JOHNNY STELLARD, ALEX MICHAEL STOLL

Generals
BRADLEY DEAN,
CONSTANTINE GERMANACOS,
BRAD LITTLE, DANIEL TORRES

ENSEMBLE

ASHLEY AMBER, GEORGE LEE ANDREWS,
ERIC L. CHRISTIAN, KRISTINE COVILLO,
MARGOT DE LA BARRE, BRADLEY DEAN,
REBECCA EICHENBERGER,
J. AUSTIN EYER, MELANIE FIELD,
CONSTANTINE GERMANACOS,
LAUREL HARRIS, BAHIYAH HIBAH,
NICK KENKEL, BRAD LITTLE,
MATT LOEHR, ERICA MANSFIELD,
EMILY MECHLER, SYDNEY MORTON,
JESSICA LEA PATTY, RACHEL POTTER,
KRISTIE DALE SANDERS, TIMOTHY SHEW,
JOHNNY STELLARD,
ALEX MICHAEL STOLL, DANIEL TORRES

UNDERSTUDIES

For Eva: CHRISTINA DeCICCO,
    LAUREL HARRIS, JESSICA LEA PATTY
For Che: MAX VON ESSEN, DANIEL TORRES
For Perón: BRADLEY DEAN, BRAD LITTLE
For Magaldi: BRADLEY DEAN,
    CONSTANTINE GERMANACOS,
    MATT WALL
For Mistress: EMILY MECHLER,
    SYDNEY MORTON

SWINGS

WENDI BERGAMINI, CALLIE CARTER,
JENNIE FORD, JASON LEE GARRETT,
MICHAELJON SLINGER, MATT WALL

Assistant Dance Captain
MATT WALL
Dance Captain
JENNIE FORD

Elena Roger appears courtesy of Actors' Equity Association.

SETTING

Junin and Buenos Aires, Argentina, 1934-1952

Evita

Ricky Martin
Che

Elena Roger
Eva

Michael Cerveris
Perón

Christina DeCicco
Eva Alternate

Max von Essen
Magaldi

Rachel Potter
Mistress/Ensemble

Ashley Amber
Ensemble

George Lee Andrews
Ensemble

Wendi Bergamini
Swing

Callie Carter
Swing

Eric L. Christian
Ensemble

Kristine Covillo
Ensemble

Margot de la Barre
Ensemble

Bradley Dean
Ensemble

Ava DeMary
Child

Rebecca Eichenberger
Ensemble

J. Austin Eyer
Ensemble

Melanie Field
Ensemble

Jennie Ford
Swing/Dance Captain

Jason Lee Garrett
Swing

Constantine Germanacos
Ensemble

Laurel Harris
Ensemble

Bahiyah Hibah
Ensemble

Nick Kenkel
Ensemble

Brad Little
Ensemble

Matt Loehr
Ensemble

Erica Mansfield
Ensemble

Emily Mechler
Ensemble

Sydney Morton
Ensemble

Jessica Lea Patty
Ensemble

Kristie Dale Sanders
Ensemble

Timothy Shew
Ensemble

Mavis Simpson-Ernst
Child

Michaeljon Slinger
Swing

Johnny Stellard
Ensemble

Evita

Alex Michael Stoll
Ensemble

Daniel Torres
Ensemble

Matt Wall
Swing/Assistant Dance Captain

Andrew Lloyd Webber
The Really Useful Group
Licensor, Music and Orchestrations

Tim Rice
Book and Lyrics

Michael Grandage
Director

Rob Ashford
Choreographer

Christopher Oram
Scenic and Costume Design

Neil Austin
Lighting Design

Mick Potter
Sound Design

Richard Mawbey
Wig and Hair Design

Zachary Borovay
Projection Design

Bernard Telsey
Telsey + Company
Casting

Jason Goldsberry
Make-up Design

David Cullen
Co-Orchestrator

Kristen Blodgette
Music Supervisor/ Conductor

David Chase
Dance Arrangements

Seth Sklar-Heyn
Associate Director

Chris Bailey
Associate Choreographer

David Lai
Music Coordinator

Christopher C. Smith
Technical Supervisor

Maggie Brohn
Bespoke Theatricals
General Management

Amy Jacobs
Bespoke Theatricals
General Management

Devin Keudell
Bespoke Theatricals
General Management

Nina Lannan
Bespoke Theatricals
General Management

Hal Luftig
Producer

Scott Sanders
Scott Sanders Productions
Producer

Roy Furman
Producer

Yasuhiro Kawana
Producer

Allan S. Gordon
Producer

Adam S. Gordon
Producer

James L. Nederlander
Producer

Terry Allen Kramer
Producer

Jay Gutterman
Gutterman Fuld Chernoff/ Pittsburgh CLO
Producer

Evita

Cindy Gutterman
Gutterman Fuld
Chernoff/
Pittsburgh CLO
Producer

James Fuld, Jr.
Gutterman Fuld
Chernoff/
Pittsburgh CLO
Producer

Cathy Chernoff
Gutterman Fuld
Chernoff/
Pittsburgh CLO
Producer

Van Kaplan
Executive Producer
Pittsburg CLO
Producer

Van Dean, Kenny Howard
The Broadway Consortium
Thousand Stars Productions
Producers

Wendy Federman
Thousand Stars
Productions
Producer

Carl Moellenberg
Thousand Stars
Productions
Producer

Antonio Marion
Thousand Stars
Productions
Producer

Barbara
Manocherian
Thousand Stars
Productions
Producer

Michael A. Alden
Thousand Stars
Productions
Producer

Adam Blanshay
Producer

Adam Zotovich
Producer

Robert Ahrens
Producer

Stephanie P.
McClelland
Producer

Carole L. Haber
Producer

Ricardo Hornos
Producer

Carol Fineman
Producer

Brian Smith
Producer

Jâlé and Warren Trepp
Producers

Colin Cunliffe
Ensemble

Maya Jade Frank
Child

Isabela Moner
Child

Aleks Pevec
Ensemble

John Cudia
Ensemble

Ava-Riley Miles
Child

Aleks Pevec
Ensemble

Gabrielle Ruiz
Ensemble

Evita

CREW/WARDROBE/HAIR
Front Row (L-R): Scotty R. Cain, Jeannie Naughton, Vera Pizzarelli, Jay Woods, Katie Chick, Sean McMahon
Middle Row (L-R): Douglas Petitjean, Samantha Lawrence, Adam Girardet, Kathleen Mack, Rick Caroto, Jake Fry, Joe Valentino
Back Row (L-R): Kenny Sheehan, Brian Aman, Joe Sardo, Scott Mecionis, Derek Healy, Emilia Martin, Nathan Gehan, Jenny Pendergraft, Tanya Guercy-Blue, Deirdre LaBarre, Erick Medinilla, Freddy Mecionis

FRONT OF HOUSE STAFF
Front Row (L-R): Rosaire Caso, Phyllis Weinsaft, Barbara Newsome, Jesse White
Middle Row (L-R): George Fitze, Michael Mejias, David Calhoun, Stanley Seidman, Iskritsa Ognianova, Mariea Crainiciuc
Back Row (L-R): Mamie Spruell, Sonia Torres, Heidi Giovine, Odalis Concepcion

STAGE DOOR
Juan Garcia

BOX OFFICE
(L-R): Gary Flynn, Nick Kapovic

STAGE MANAGEMENT TEAM
(L-R): Pat Sosnow (Stage Manager), Michael J. Passaro (Production Stage Manager), Jim Athens (Assistant Stage Manager), Seth Sklar-Heyn (Associate Director)

Evita

STAFF FOR *EVITA*

GENERAL MANAGEMENT
BESPOKE THEATRICALS
Amy Jacobs
Maggie Brohn Devin Keudell Nina Lannan
Associate General Manager ....David Roth

COMPANY MANAGER
Nathan Gehan
Associate Company Manager ....Kate Egan

GENERAL PRESS REPRESENTATIVE
THE HARTMAN GROUP
Michael Hartman
Leslie Baden Papa Whitney Holden Gore

CASTING
TELSEY + COMPANY
Bernie Telsey CSA, Will Cantler CSA,
David Vaccari CSA, Bethany Knox CSA,
Craig Burns CSA, Tiffany Little Canfield CSA,
Rachel Hoffman CSA, Justin Huff CSA,
Patrick Goodwin CSA, Abbie Brady-Dalton CSA,
David Morris, Cesar A. Rocha, Andrew Femenella,
Karyn Casl, Kristina Bramhall, Jessie Malone

MARKETING SERVICES
TYPE A MARKETING
Anne Rippey Elyce Henkin Melissa Cohen

PRODUCTION STAGE
  MANAGER ....Michael J. Passaro
Stage Manager ....Pat Sosnow
Assistant Stage Manager ....Jim Athens
Associate Director ....Seth Sklar-Heyn
Associate Choreographer ....Chris Bailey
Dance Captain ....Jennie Ford
Assistant Dance Captain ....Matt Wall
Associate Scenic Designer ....Bryan Johnson
UK Scenic Associate ....Richard Kent
UK Scenic Assistants ....David Woodhead,
  Andrew Riley, Simon Anthony Wells
Associate Costume Designer ....Barry Doss
Assistant Costume Designers ....Christina Cocchiara,
  Robert J. Martin
Associate Lighting Designer ....Dan Walker
Assistant Lighting Designer ....Kristina Kloss
Lighting Programmer ....Rob Halliday
Associate Sound Designer ....Anthony Smolenski
Associate Projection Designer ....Driscoll A. Otto
Assistant Projection Designer ....Daniel Vatsky
Assistant to the Hair Designer ....Susan Pedersen
Makeup Designer ....Jason Goldsberry
Production Carpenter ....Donald J. Oberpriller
Fly Automation ....Chad Hershey
Production Electrician ....Jimmy Maloney
Associate Production Electrician ....Kevin Barry
Head Followspot ....Matthew Gratz
Production Sound ....Paul Delcioppo, Phil Lojo
Head Sound ....George Huckins
Assistant Sound ....John Dory
Production Properties ....Vera Pizzarelli
Head Properties ....Jill Johnson
Wardrobe Supervisor ....Douglas Petitjean
Assistant Wardrobe Supervisor ....Deirdre LaBarre
Dresser for Mr. Martin ....Scotty R. Cain
Dresser for Ms. Roger ....Jeannie Naughton
Dresser for Mr. Cerveris ....Erick Medinilla

Dressers ....Tracey Diebold, Jake Fry,
  Adam Girardet, Tanya Guercy-Blue,
  Samantha Lawrence, Kathleen Mack,
  Herb Ouellette
Hair Supervisor ....Wanda Gregory
Hair Assistants ....Rick Caroto,
  Jenny Pendergraft, Emilia Martin
Assistant Synthesizer Programmer ....Dave Weiser
Children's Guardian ....Bridget Mills
Projection Research ....Sheila Maniar
Costume Production Assistant ....Carly J. Price
Costume Shoppers ....Adam Adelman,
  Edgar Contreras
UK Costume Design Liaison ....Stephanie Arditti
Costume Stitchers/
  Construction ....Katie Chick, Adam Girardet,
  Jamie Englehart, Libby Villanova,
  Erin Brooke Roth, Sandy Vojta
Costume Interns ....Kayla Quiter, Jana Violante,
  Aaron Simms, Cim Roesener,
  Elizabeth Gleason, Anne Liberman,
  Ryan Dodson, Todd Phillips, Maggie Ronck
Production Assistants ....Lee Micklin,
  Derric Nolte, Michael Ulreich
SDC Observer ....Stephen Kaliski
Assistant to Mr. Luftig ....Scott Sinclair
Assistant to Mr. Sanders ....Jamie Quiroz
Children's Tutoring ....On Location Education/
  Alan Simon, Jodi Green
Physical Therapy ....Mark Hunter Hall
Orthopaedist ....David S. Weiss, M.D.
Production Photographer ....Richard Termine
Advertising ....SpotCo/Drew Hodges,
  Jim Edwards, Tom Greenwald,
  Tom McCann, Laura Ellis
Website & Online Marketing ....SpotCo/
  Sara Fitzpatrick, Marc Mettler,
  Michael Crowley, Meghan Ownbey
Accountant ....Robert Fried CPA/
  Fried & Kowgios CPAS LLP
Comptroller ....Galbraith & Company/
  Sarah Galbraith
General Management Associates ....Jimmy Wilson
General Management Intern ....Lisa Jaeger
Press Representative Staff ....Nicole Capatasto,
  Tom D'Ambrosio, Juliana Hannett,
  Bethany Larsen, Emily McGill, Colgan McNeil,
  Matt Ross, Frances White, Wayne Wolfe
Insurance ....AON/Albert G. Ruben Insurance
  Services, Inc./Claudia Kaufman
Banking ....City National Bank/Michele Gibbons
Payroll ....Checks and Balances Payroll Inc.
Travel Agent ....Tzell Travel/The "A" Team,
  Andi Henig
Legal Counsel ....Franklin, Weinrib, Rudell &
  Vassallo, P.C.
Immigration Counsel ....Kramer Levin Naftalis &
  Frankel, LLP
Visa Consultant ....Lisa Carr
Merchandising ....Broadway Merchandising, LLC/
  Adam S. Gordon, David Eck
Opening Night
  Coordination ....The Lawrence Company
Opening Night Creative Consultant ....Susan Holland

Official Airline of *Evita* ....Delta

www.EvitaOnBroadway.com

CREDITS
Scenery and automation constructed by Show Motion. Set built by Terry Murphy Scenery. Costumes by Siobhan Nestor; Artur & Tailors; Cygnet Studio, Inc.; John Kristiansen; Sarah Timberlake; Jennifer Love; House of Savoia; Scafati; Jared B. Leese, Jodek International Ltd. - David Douek, Daniel Webster; Costume Armour; Kaufman's Army & Navy; Beckenstein's Men's Fabric Czar. Handmade shoes by Fred Longtin, J.C. Theatrical, T.O. Dey custom made shoes, Worldtone Dance Shoes, Capezio Theatricals, LaDuca Shoes. Eva Perón's jewelry by Marcelo Toledo. Millinery by Anne Guay & Stetson Hats, Arnold S. Levine. Lighting equipment by PRG Lighting, Inc. Sound equipment by Sound Associates. Projection equipment by Scharff Weisberg, Inc. Props by Props Is Tops, Propstar, Tom Carroll Scenery, John Creech Design & Production. Soft goods by iWeiss Theatrical Solutions. Wigs made by Wig Specialities, London. Additional costume support provided by Tony Craney, Melissa Crawford, Shahnaz Khan, Alyce Gilbert, Kevin Hucke. Housing by ABA-Elizabeth Helke. Historical footage provided by Associated Press, ArenaPAL, Fondo Documental Museo Evita/Archivo General de la Nacion and Producers Library. Yamaha pianos provided courtesy of Yamaha Artist Services, New York. Drum heads provided by Remo, Inc. Drum sticks and mallets provided by Vic Firth Inc. Cymbals provided by Paiste America. Makeup provided by M•A•C Cosmetics. Event photography provided by Bruce Glikas.

SPECIAL THANKS
Diagio Americas, Inc., Swarovski Elements and
Steven Rivellino/8th Sea Inc.

Evita rehearsed at the
New 42nd Street Studios

Performance rights to *Evita*
are licensed by R&H Theatricals:
www.rnh.com

N•E•D•E•R•L•A•N•D•E•R

Chairman ....**James M. Nederlander**	
President ....**James L. Nederlander**	

Executive Vice President
Nick Scandalios

Vice President Corporate Development	Senior Vice President Labor Relations
Charlene S. Nederlander	**Herschel Waxman**

Vice President	Chief Financial Officer
Jim Boese	**Freida Sawyer Belviso**

STAFF FOR THE MARQUIS THEATRE
Manager ....David Calhoun
Associate Manager ....Sean Coughlin
Treasurer ....Rick Waxman
Assistant Treasurer ....John Rooney
Carpenter ....Joseph P. Valentino
Electrician ....James Mayo
Property Man ....Scott Mecionis

Evita
SCRAPBOOK

Correspondent: Daniel Torres, Ensemble, Ricky Martin's Understudy

Memorable Note, Fax or Fan Letter: One night during bows we noticed a young audience member giving a very enthusiastic standing ovation in the front row. The entire cast was so moved by this young man's joy, that we actually pulled him out of the audience as he was exiting the theatre and brought him backstage for a tour and a chance to meet Ricky Martin and the rest of the cast. As you can imagine, he was shocked and overjoyed. The next day we received a beautiful thank-you note from him which we kept on the callboard. It served as an inspiration and a constant reminder for us that we in the theatre have the power to truly impact our audience.

Most Exciting Celebrity Visitor: The entire theatre was abuzz when Jennifer Lopez came to see the show. A group of us waited around in the hopes we would get the chance to meet her. After visiting with Ricky she came out of his dressing room and congratulated us all on a great show. Jason Lee Garrett may have cried… but you didn't hear that from me.

Actor Who Performs the Most Roles: Ricky Martin, as Che, got to play the most roles in the show. Che is the show's narrator but he gets to jump into the action by becoming a waiter, sound guy, pub patron, et cetera.

Who Has Done the Most Shows: Our Gypsy Robe recipient, Mr. Matt Wall. *Evita* marks Matt's eleventh Broadway show.

Special Backstage Ritual: Hand sanitizing. With the plague of 2013 ravaging most of NYC, using hand sanitizer backstage became a very special/important ritual for us all.

Favorite Pastime Dur-ing Intermission: Sat-urday Intermission Pics (#SIP) was actually started by Andrew Keenan-Bolger and our very own "Magaldi," Max von Essen. We had a blast each week coming up with new themes and fun poses.

Favorite Moment During Each Performance: The "Lament." It's the most haunting bit of music and Elena Roger sings it just beautifully. The rest of the cast is singing underneath her while circling the stage, each taking their moment with Eva's coffin. It's a very moving scene and I love that the entire company is onstage experiencing it together.

Favorite In-Theatre Gathering Place: The greenroom was defi-nitely our favorite hang-out during the show and for our "Saturday Night On Broadway" parties. The wardrobe room became our favorite hangout for "Tuesday Wine Nights!"

Favorite Off-Site Hangout: Elena Roger's apartment.

Favorite Snack Foods: "Baked by Melissa" cupcakes and cookies from Schmackary's.

Mascot: Stephen Bunt-rock.

Favorite Therapy: Foam rollers and Emergen-C.

Memorable Ad-Libs: "Johnny!" "Standing back!" "We're almost outta this one!" "Lead with the left!" Pretty much anything that came out of

Tim Shew's mouth.

Did your company collect for Broadway Cares: Yes! We were very motivated to raise as much money for BC/EFA as we possibly could. We held a live auction each night for a chance to meet Ricky and take home a signed handkerchief he used in the show. We also put together an amazing Halloween Benefit called BROADWAY SCARES: NIGHT OF THE SINGING DEAD but it was unfortunately canceled due to Hurricane Sandy. In the end we raised $224,105 in only six weeks.

"Gypsy of the Year" Skit: Rachel Potter, Ava DeMary and Mavis Simpson-Ernst performed "Live the Dream" from Rachel's debut Country album of the same title. We took home First Runner Up for Top Fundraiser so I'm glad the girls could be there to represent us!

Memorable Fan Encounter: During our full company bow at the end of the show, a fan in the front row hoisted herself up on the stage and wrapped her arms around Ricky Martin. After the hug, she bowed with the company and re-turned to her seat.

The entire cast was shocked by what had just happened. From that moment on the theatre hired guards to stand in the au-dience to make sure that never happened again.

Fastest Costume Change: The ensemble had many quick costume changes throughout the show. We didn't have enough time to make it to our dressing room, so all ensemble costume changes took place backstage. But I'd say the FASTEST costume change in the show occurred onstage when, behind a group of ensemble dancers, the cast quickly stripped down and redressed Eva during the song "And the Money Kept Rolling In."

Who Wore the Least: Elena Roger, who, with the help of many a chambermaid, stripped down to her skivvies during "High Flying Adored."

Catchphrases Only the Company Would Recognize: "Love and Light. Success and Freedom."

Best In-House Parody Lyrics: "Dice are rolling. The knives are out!" became "Rice-a-Roni. The San Francisco Treat!"

Memorable Directorial Note: The note that always came back to haunt us was to not speak during the Charity Concert. The ensemble was staged to be schmoozing at a party but any amount of talking was disruptive to the very intimate scene happening downstage. We tried and tried but it was near impossible to keep quiet and chatter always found its way back in.

Company Pranks: Ricky had a tradition of smearing cake on the face of whoever's birthday we were celebrating. For his birthday, I bought him a large red velvet cake from Make My Cake in Harlem. You

better believe he got a taste of his own medicine.

Company Legend: Having performed 9,382 performances of *The Phantom of the Opera*, company legend definitely goes to George Lee Andrews who is in the "Guinness Book of World Records" for "Most Performances in the Same Broadway Show." One night, he was even an answer on the TV show "Who Wants to Be a Millionaire." He turned 70 years old during our run of *Evita* and yet he was onstage each night kicking his face with the rest of us.

Understudy Anecdote: Getting to understudy Ricky Martin in the role of Che was such an amazing experience. As an understudy you never know if you will get the opportunity to go on. But halfway through our run the producers announced that Max von Essen and I would be alternating in the role at Monday night performances. This gave us both an ample opportunity to play the role of Che and to invite our family and friends to our scheduled shows. I will never forget my father making an announcement at a party I was throwing after one of my performances: "Daniel, I swear if you recorded 'High Flying Adored' you would make a million dollars!" I didn't have the heart to tell him Ricky had already recorded it and even HE didn't make a million dollars!

Nickname: Ricky definitely answers to the name…"Kiki."

Superstitions That Turned Out to Be True: Christina DeCicco broke a mirror onstage and we closed three weeks later! (To be fair, we got our closing notice BEFORE Christina's turn of bad luck.)

Coolest Thing About Being in This Show: Getting to work with this amazing and creative group of individuals. Michael Grandage, Rob Ashford, Michael Cerveris, Elena Roger, Ricky Martin…does it get any "cooler" then that!? Getting to do the first-ever revival of *Evita* on Broadway was a pretty nifty experience as well!

What Was It Like Working With Ricky Martin: It was amazing! He is an incredible co-worker and just a beautiful human being. I am from Puerto Rico, where Ricky Martin ranks right up there with Jesus Christ. Haha! To get to know and work with one of my childhood heroes was such an amazing experience. He was humble and kind from the very first day of rehearsals all the way through to the end of the run. He acted like any other member of the company hanging out with us in the greenroom and even deejaying Elena Roger's fantastic Saturday night parties. He's an attentive and loving father, bringing his beautiful boys to the theatre and letting them hang out in his dressing room on our two-show days and he is a caring friend, always texting get-well wishes if you were too sick to make a performance. He's an inspiration to me—to be the best performer, co-worker, friend and father that I can be. I hope we get him back on Broadway very soon!

Recording the Masterworks Broadway cast album.
1. The women of the ensemble.
2. The men of the ensemble.

Photos courtesy of George Lee Andrews

Fela!

First Preview: July 9, 2012. Opened: July 12, 2012.
Limited Engagement. Closed August 4, 2012 after 4 Previews and 28 Performances.

PLAYBILL

A kaleidoscopic chronicle of the short, intense, musical and political life of real-life activist Fela Anikulapo Kuti and his fight for freedom from oppression in his native Nigeria during the 1960s and 1970s. The story is told in the form of an evening's concert at Kuti's legendary Lagos commune/nightclub, the Afrika Shrine, with a score consisting mainly of Kuti's own Afrobeat hits.

CAST
(in order of appearance)

Fela Anikulapo Kuti ....SAHR NGAUJAH,
                ADESOLA OSAKALUMI*
Funmilayo ....MELANIE MARSHALL
Sandra ....PAULETTE IVORY
Ismael.............................ISMAEL KOUYATÉ
J.K. Braimah (Tap Dancer),
   Egungun........................GELAN LAMBERT
Djembe—
  "Mustafa" ...RASAAN-ELIJAH "TALU" GREEN
Ensemble ....SHERINNE KAYRA ANDERSON,
        JONATHAN ANDRE, CINDY BELLIOT,
        NANDI BHEBHE, CATIA MOTA DA CRUZ,
        NICOLE CHANTAL DE WEEVER,
                 JACQUI DUBOIS,
        POUNDO "SWEET" GOMIS,
        SHAKIRA MARSHALL, JEFFREY PAGE,
        ONEIKA PHILLIPS, THIERRY PICAUT,
        DUAIN RICHMOND, JERMAINE ROWE,
        DANIEL SOTO, JILL MARIE VALLERY,
                    IRIS WILSON,
        AIMEE GRAHAM WODOBODE

Continued on next page

♪ AL HIRSCHFELD THEATRE
A JUJAMCYN THEATRE

JORDAN ROTH
President

PAUL LIBIN
Executive Vice President

JACK VIERTEL
Senior Vice President

SHAWN "JAY-Z" CARTER AND **WILL & JADA PINKETT SMITH**
RUTH & STEPHEN HENDEL, THE NATIONAL THEATRE OF GREAT BRITAIN,
AHMIR "QUESTLOVE" THOMPSON, SONY PICTURES ENTERTAINMENT, FELA LLC,
ROY GABAY, EDWARD TYLER NAHEM, SLAVA SMOLOKOWSKI, CHIP MEYRELLES/KEN GREINER,
DOUGLAS G. SMITH, STEVE SEMLITZ/CATHY GLASER, DARYL ROTH/TRUE LOVE PRODUCTIONS,
SUSAN DIETZ/M. SWINSKY/J. DEITCH, KNITTING FACTORY ENTERTAINMENT

PRESENT

FELA!

A BROADWAY/NATIONAL THEATRE OF LONDON PRODUCTION

BOOK
JIM LEWIS & BILL T. JONES

MUSIC AND LYRICS
FELA ANIKULAPO-KUTI

ADDITIONAL LYRICS BY
JIM LEWIS

ADDITIONAL MUSIC BY
AARON JOHNSON & JORDAN McLEAN

BASED ON THE LIFE OF
FELA ANIKULAPO-KUTI

CONCEIVED BY
BILL T. JONES, JIM LEWIS & STEPHEN HENDEL

INSPIRED BY
THE AUTHORIZED BIOGRAPHY *FELA: THIS BITCH OF A LIFE* BY CARLOS MOORE

SAHR NGAUJAH   **ADESOLA OSAKALUMI**
PAULETTE IVORY

RASAAN-ELIJAH "TALU" GREEN   **ISMAEL KOUYATE**   **GELAN LAMBERT**

SHERINNE KAYRA ANDERSON, JONATHAN ANDRE, CINDY BELLIOT, NANDI BHEBHE, CATIA MOTA DA CRUZ, NICOLE CHANTAL de WEEVER, JACQUI DUBOIS, POUNDO GOMIS, WANJIRU KAMUYU,
SHAKIRA MARSHALL, JEFFREY PAGE, ONEIKA PHILLIPS, THIERRY PICAUT, DUAIN RICHMOND, JERMAINE ROWE, DANIEL SOTO, ADÉ CHIKÉ TORBERT, JILL MARIE VALLERY, IRIS WILSON, AIMEE GRAHAM WODOBODE

AND

MELANIE MARSHALL

SCENIC & COSTUME DESIGNER **MARINA DRAGHICI**	LIGHTING DESIGNER **ROBERT WIERZEL**	SOUND DESIGNER **ROBERT KAPLOWITZ**	PROJECTION DESIGNER **PETER NIGRINI**
WIG, HAIR & MAKEUP DESIGNER **COOKIE JORDAN**	PRODUCTION STAGE MANAGER **JOHN M. ATHERLAY**	CASTING **ARNOLD J. MUNGIOLI, CSA** **PIPPA AILION, CDG**	GENERAL MANAGER **ROY GABAY**
GENERAL PRESS REPRESENTATIVE **RICHARD KORNBERG & ASSOCIATES**	TECHNICAL SUPERVISION **PAUL RAMBACHER**	COMPANY MANAGER **JUDI WILFORE**	MUSIC DIRECTION & COORDINATOR/ ORCHESTRATIONS/ARRANGEMENTS **AARON JOHNSON**
TOUR PRESENTATION **CAMI SPECTRUM/** **COLUMBIA ARTIST THEATRICALS**	MARKETING MANAGER **ELLEN JACOBS**	MUSICAL ARRANGEMENTS **JORDAN McLEAN**	MUSIC CONSULTANT **ANTIBALAS**

CREATIVE DIRECTOR/ASSOCIATE CHOREOGRAPHER
MAIJA GARCIA

ASSOCIATE DIRECTOR
NIEGEL SMITH

DIRECTED AND CHOREOGRAPHED BY
BILL T. JONES

7/12/12

Sahr Ngaujah as Fela and company

Photo by Raymond Hagans

Fela!

MUSICAL NUMBERS

ACT I

Welcome Na De Shrine
"Everything Scatter" ....Fela and Company

B.I.D. (Breaking It Down)
"Iba Orisa": Traditional Yoruba chant .... Ismael, Fela and Company
Hymn by Reverend J.J. Ransome-Kuti ....Fela, Company and Band
"Medzi Medzi" by E.T. Mensah ....Company and Band
"Manteca" by Chano Pozo ....Company and Band
"I Got the Feeling" by James Brown ....Ismael and Company

Underground Spiritual Game (The Clock)
"Originality/Yellow Fever" ....Fela and Company

Trouble
"Trouble Sleep" ....Fela, Funmilayo and Company

Black President
"Lover"* ....Fela and Sandra
"Upside Down" ....Fela, Sandra and Company
"Expensive Shit" ....Fela and Company
"Pipeline"*/"I.T.T. (International Thief Thief)" ....Fela and Company
"Kere Kay" ....Fela and Company

ACT II

Water
"Water No Get Enemy" ....Fela, Sandra and Company
"Egbe Mio" ....Fela, Queens and Funmilayo

The Game
"Zombie" ....Fela and Company
"Trouble Sleep" (reprise) ....Fela, Funmilayo and Queens

Wedding
"Na Poi" ....Fela and Queens

The Storming of Kalakuta
"Sorrow Tears and Blood" ....Fela and Company

Dance of the Orisas
"Iba Orisa/Shakara" ....Company and Band
"Rain"** ....Funmilayo and Company

B.Y.O.C. (Bring Your Own Coffin)
"Coffin for Head of State" ....Fela and Company
"Kere Kay" (reprise) ....Fela and Company

*"Lover" and "Pipeline," lyrics by Jim Lewis
**"Rain" music by Aaron Johnson and Jordan McLean, lyrics by Bill T. Jones and Jim Lewis

Sahr Ngaujah
Fela Anikulapo Kuti

Adesola Osakalumi
Fela Anikulapo Kuti Alternate

Melanie Marshall
Funmilayo

Paulette Ivory
Sandra

Cast Continued

SWINGS
WANJIRU KAMUYU, ADÉ CHIKÉ TORBERT

DANCE CAPTAINS
WANJIRU KAMUYU, JILL MARIE VALLERY

ASSISTANT DANCE CAPTAIN
JERMAINE ROWE

*At certain performances, the role of Fela Anikulapo-Kuti will be played by ADESOLA OSAKALUMI or DUAIN RICHMOND.

UNDERSTUDIES
For Funmilayo:
JACQUI DUBOIS
For Sandra:
ONEIKA PHILLIPS, CINDY BELLIOT

SETTING
A concert at Fela's Shrine. Lagos, Nigeria. Several months after the death of Fela's mother, Funmilayo.

The company of *Fela!* is appearing with the permission of Actors' Equity Association and UK Equity.

BAND
Conductor/Trombone/Keyboard:
AARON JOHNSON
Assistant Conductor/Drums:
GREG GONZALEZ
Trumpet:
JEFF PIERCE
Bass/Keyboards/Percussion:
JEREMY WILMS
Guitar/Percussion:
RICARDO QUINONES
Guitar/Percussion:
BRYAN VARGAS

Congas/Percussion:
YOSHIHIRO TAKEMASA
Baritone Saxophone/Percussion:
ALEX HARDING
Tenor Saxophone/Percussion:
MORGAN PRICE
Percussion:
DYLAN FUSILLO
Music Coordinator:
AARON JOHNSON

Fela!

Rasaan-Elijah "Talu" Green
Djembe—"Mustafa"

Ismael Kouyaté
Ismael

Gelan Lambert
J.K. Braimah/Tap Dancer/ Egungun

Sherinne Kayra Anderson
Ensemble

Jonathan Andre
Ensemble

Cindy Belliot
u/s Sandra/Ensemble

Nandi Bhebhe
Ensemble

Catia Mota Da Cruz
Ensemble

Nicole Chantal de Weever,

Ensemble

Jacqui Dubois
u/s Funmilayo/ Ensemble

Poundo "Sweets" Gomis
Ensemble

Wanjiru Kamuyu
Dance Captain/ Swing

Shakira Marshall
Ensemble

Jeffrey Page
Ensemble/ u/s Ismael

Oneika Phillips
u/s Sandra/ Ensemble

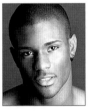
Thierry Picaut
Ensemble/Swing/ u/s Ismael

Duain Richmond
Fela Anikulapo-Kuti Alternate/Ensemble

Jermaine Rowe
Ensemble/ Asst. Dance Captain

Daniel Soto
Ensemble

Adé Chiké Torbert
Swing

Jill Marie Vallery
Ensemble/ Dance Captain

Iris Wilson
Ensemble

Aimee Graham Wodobode
Ensemble

Fela Anikulapo-Kuti
Music/Lyrics

Bill T. Jones
Co-Conception/ Director/ Choreographer/ Book Writer

Jim Lewis
Book/Co-Conception/ Additional Lyrics

Marina Draghici
Scenic & Costume Designer

Robert Wierzel
Lighting Designer

Robert Kaplowitz
Sound Director

Peter Nigrini
Projection Designer

Cookie Jordan
Wigs, Hair & Make-up Designer

Aaron Johnson
Additional Music/Music Supervisor/ Arrangements

Jordan McLean
Additional Music/Associate Musical Director

Maija Garcia
Creative Director/ Associate Choreographer

Niegel Smith
Associate Director

Fela!

Pippa Ailion
UK Casting

Arnold J. Mungioli
Mungioli Theatricals,
Inc.
U.S. Casting

Richard Kornberg &
Associates
*General Press
Representative*

Shawn "Jay-Z"
Carter
Producer

Will Smith
Producer

Jada Pinkett Smith
Producer

Ruth Hendel
Producer

Stephen Hendel
*Co-Conceiver and
Producer*

Ahmir "Questlove"
Thompson
Producer

Roy Gabay
*Producer/
General Manager*

Edward Tyler Nahem
Producer

DOORMAN
Neil Perez

FRONT OF HOUSE STAFF
Seated (L-R): Jose Nunez, Bart Ryan, Clifford Ray Berry, Tristan Blacer, Donald Royal, Hollis Miller, Janice Rodriguez, Lorraine Feeks
Standing (L-R): Theresa Lopez, Mark Maciejewski, Terry Monahan, Lisé Greaves, Heather Gilles, Jennifer DiDonato, Lawrence Levens, Julie Burnham,
William Meyers, Albert T. Kim

CREW
Front Row (L-R): Dale Carman, Gretchen Metzloff, Richard Anderson, John Blixt, David Barnathan, Gardner Friscia, Francoise Herard,
Hannah Dorfman, Liz Goodrum, Angie Simpson
Sitting on Chairs (L-R): Patrick Harrington, Ashton Jones, Susie Ghebresillassie, Wes Shaffer
Standing (L-R): Dora Bonilla, Randy Moreland, Robert Brenner, Tom Burke, Dustin Adams, Jonathan Parke, Joe Lenihan, Josh Moberly,
Michele Gutierrez, Judi Wilfore, John M. Atherlay, William Gilinsky, Rashida Poole, Ruth Goya

Fela!

STAFF FOR FELA!

GENERAL MANAGEMENT
ROY GABAY THEATRICAL
PRODUCTION & MANAGEMENT
Roy Gabay, Chris Aniello,
Daniel Kuney, Mandy Tate, Mark Gagliardi

COMPANY MANAGER
Judi Wilfore
Assistant Company Manager: David Barnathan

EXCLUSIVE TOUR REPRESENTATION
Margaret Selby, CAMI SPECTRUM
Gary McAvay, COLUMBIA ARTISTS THEATRICALS

GENERAL PRESS REPRESENTATIVE
RICHARD KORNBERG & ASSOCIATES
Richard Kornberg, Don Summa, Billy Zavelson,
Danielle McGarry

U.S. CASTING BY MUNGIOLI THEATRICALS
Arnold J. Mungioli, CSA

UK CASTING BY PIPPA AILION, CDG

PRODUCTION COORDINATOR
PROFESSIONAL MANAGEMENT & RESOURCES
Paul M. Rambacher

PRODUCTION STAGE
MANAGER . . . . .JOHN M. ATHERLAY
Stage Manager . . . . .William Gilinsky
Assistant Stage Manager . . . . .Hannah Dorfman
Creative Director/
Associate Choreographer . . . . .Maija Garcia
Associate Director . . . . .Niegel Smith
Associate Set Designer . . . . .Timothy R. Mackabee
Associate Costume Designer . . . . .Amy Clark
Assistant Costume Designer . . . . .Mike Floyd
Associate Lighting Designer . . . . . . .Paul Hackenmueller
Assistant Lighting Designer . . . . . . .G. Benjamin Swope
Lighting Programmer . . . . .John McGarrigle
Original Mural and Scenic Art . . . . .IRLO,
Omar and Nuclear Fairy
Associate Sound Designer . . . . .Jessica Paz
Assistant Sound Designer . . . . . . .John Emmett O'Brien
Associate Projection Designer,
Content .C. Andrew Bauer
Associate Projection Designer,
System . . . . .Dan Scully
Projection Programmer . . . . .Steve Parkinson
Liquid Light Projection Footage . . . . . . .Rainbow Puddle
Additional Content and Editing . . . . .Mirit Tal
Production Carpenter . . . . .Randy Moreland
Assistant Carpenter .Todd Frank
Advance Carpenter . . . . .Marc Mannoni
Production Electrician/
Video . . . . .Josh "Big Frank" Moberly
Head Electrician . . . . .Dustin Adams
Assistant Electrician . . . . .Patrick Harrington
Production Props . . . . .Gardner Friscia
Head Sound . . . . .Jonathan Parke
Assistant Sound . . . . .Walter E. Shaffer
Head Wardrobe . . . . .Susie Ghebresillassie
Assistant Wardrobe . . . . .Andrea Matura
Head Hair .Francoise Herard
Assistant Hair . . . . .Jerome Shavers
Physical
Therapy . . . . . .NEUROTOUR Physical Therapy, Inc.

Physical Therapist . . . . .Ashton Leigh Jones, DPT
Medical Director . . . . .Thomas R. Myers, MD
Casting Associates . . . . . . .Alex Hanna, Melanie Lockyer
Marketing and Advertising Director . . . . .Ellen M. Jacobs
Advertising, Digital Outreach,
Marketing . . . . .Serino/Coyne/
Jim Glaub, Uma McCrosson,
Nicole Francois, David Barrineau,
Chip Meyrelles, Laurie Connor,
Kevin Keating, Leslie Barrett,
Crystal Chase, Sumeet Bharati
Marketing and Community
Relations . . . . .Adero-Zaire Green
Marketing and Promotions . . . . . .The Viney Group, LLC
Audience Development . . . . .WTGP, Inc./
Marcia Pendelton
Merchandise Director . . . . .Victor Bloise
Consultants to the Production . . . . . .Rikki Stein, Misani
Legal . . . . .Susan Mindell/
Levine, Plotkin & Menin LLP
Accounting . . . . .Fried & Kowgios Partners, LLP/
Robert Fried, Sarah Galbraith
Payroll .Castellana Services, Inc.
Insurance . . . . .Ventura Insurance Brokerage, Inc./
Jessica Brown
Marketing and Advertising Director . . . . .Ellen M. Jacobs
Marketing and Community
Relations . . . . .Adero-Zaire Green
Consultant to the Production . . . . .Rikki Stein

CREDITS
Lighting equipment from PRG Lighting. Sound and
projection equipment from Sound Associates. Costumes
constructed by Tricorne, John Scheeman Studios, Izquierdo
Studios, Jennifer Love Costumes, Monica Vianni
Custom Millinery.

MUSIC RIGHTS
"I Got the Feeling" by James Brown. By arrangement with
Fort Knox Music Inc. c/o Carlin America Inc. (BMI).
"Manteca" by Dizzy Gillespie, Walter Gil Fuller and Chano
Pozo. By arrangement with Boosey & Hawkes, Inc. o/b/o
Twenty-Eighth Street Music (ASCAP) and with Music Sales
Corporation (ASCAP). "Medzi Medzi" by E.T. Mensah. By
arrangement with RetroAfric Music (PRS). "Mr. Syms" by
John Coltrane. By arrangement with Jowcol Music (BMI).
"Nice 'N Easy" by Alan and Marilyn Bergman and Lew
Spence. By arrangement with Spirit Two Music, Inc. o/b/o
Lew Spence Music (ASCAP) and with Threesome Music
Company (ASCAP). Frank Sinatra video clip from "The
Edsel Show" (1957). Produced by CBS Television Network.

SPECIAL THANKS
Romanian Cultural Institute in New York, Actors' Equity
Association, Link TV, LAByrinth Theater, Culture Project,
Atlantic Theater Company, Bill T. Jones/Arnie Zane Dance
Company, the Joyce Theater, Public Theater, the New
Group, Sean Barlow/AFROPOP, Joe's Pub, S.O.B.'s

The producers gratefully acknowledge Carlos Moore's
valuable work Fela: This Bitch of a Life for the inspiration and
understanding that it provided for the development of Fela!

The producers also gratefully acknowledge Trevor
Schoonmaker's Fela: From West Africa to West Broadway and
Black President: The Art and Legacy of Fela Anikulapo Kuti for
inspiration and understanding of the life and times of Fela
Kuti.

JUJAMCYN THEATERS

JORDAN ROTH
President

PAUL LIBIN
Executive Vice President

JACK VIERTEL
Senior Vice President

MEREDITH VILLATORE
Chief Financial Officer

JENNIFER HERSHEY
Vice President,
Building Operations

MICAH HOLLINGWORTH
Vice President,
Company Operations

HAL GOLDBERG
Vice President,
Theatre Operations

Director of Business Affairs . . . . .Albert T. Kim
Director of Human Resources . . . . . . .Michele Louhisdon
Director of Ticketing Services . . . . .Justin Karr
Theatre Operations Managers . . . . .Willa Burke,
Susan Elrod, Emily Hare,
Jeff Hubbard, Albert T. Kim
Theatre Operations Associates . . . . . . .Carrie Jo Brinker,
Brian Busby, Michael Composto,
Anah Jyoti Klate
Accounting . . . . .Cathy Cerge, Amy Frank, Tariq Hamami
Executive Producer, Red Awning . . . . . . .Nicole Kastrinos
Director of Marketing, Givenik.com . . . . .Joe Tropia
Building Operations Associate . . . . .Erich Bussing
Executive Coordinator . . . . .Ed Lefferson
Executive Assistants . . . . .Clark Mims Tedesco,
Julia Kraus, Beth Given
Receptionist .Lisa Perchinske
Maintenance . . . . .Ralph Santos, Ramon Zapata
Security . . . . .Rasim Hodzic, John Acero
Interns . . . . .Maggie Baker, Sarah Collins,
Colin Geary, Emily Goeler, Taylor Kurpiel,
Will Sarratt, Lena Stein

Staff for the Al Hirschfeld Theatre
for Fela!

Theatre Manager .Albert T. Kim
Associate Theatre Manager . . . . .Carrie Jo Brinker
Treasurer . . . . .Carmine LaMendola
Head Carpenter . . . . .Joseph J. Maher, Jr.
Head Propertyman . . . . .Sal Sclafani
Head Electrician . . . . .Michele Gutierrez
Flyman . . . . .Gabe Harris
Engineer . . . . .Kevin Farrelly
Assistant Treasurers . . . . .Vicci Stanton, Gloria Diabo,
Jeffrey Nevin, Janette Wernegreen
Propertyperson .Will Sweeney
Electricians . . . . .John Blixt, Tom Burke,
Joe Lenihan, Gretchen Metzloff
Head Usher .Janice Rodriguez
Ticket-Takers . . . . .Tristan Blacer, Lorraine Feeks
Doormen . . . . .Henry E. Menendez, Neil Perez
Front of House Directors . . . . .Julie Burnham,
Lawrence Levens, William Meyers
Head Porter . . . . .Jose Nunez
Head Cleaner . . . . .Bethania Alvarez
Ushers . . . . .Peter Davino, Jennifer DiDonato,
Heather Gilles, Lisé Greaves, Theresa Lopez,
Mark Maciejewski, Mary Marzan,
Hollis Miller, Donald Royal, Bart Ryan
Porters . . . . .Tereso Avila, Roberto Ellington
Cleaners . . . . . . .Michelina Annarumma, Mirjan Aquino

Lobby refreshments by Sweet Concessions.

Security provided by GBA Consulting, Inc.

Fela!
SCRAPBOOK

Correspondent: Melanie Marshall, "Funmilayo"

Memorable Fans: A lady suffering from cancer in L.A. who found the strength and spirit to get up and join the ensemble on stage with her walking stick during Act I. And a lady called Dawn who must have seen the show about eight times on Broadway who wrote the most beautiful cards and sent cakes and biscuits (cookies!!) for the cast, who looked on the show as a therapy. And a lady who came to the last matinee on Broadway who had lost her daughter two years before and finally found joy in her life after seeing the show.

Memorable Cast Party: Melanie Marshall's 50th Birthday Party in Detroit! Deejay, food, booze sponsored by Rémy Martin! Generosity of the theatre staff, and every single person coming to help me celebrate!

Most Exciting Celebrity Visitors: So many!! Quincy Jones, Rita Marley, Ziggy Marley, Jesse Jackson, Busta Rhymes, Jessye Norman, Nas, Laurence Fishburne, Halle Berry, Stevie Wonder, Smokey Robinson, Dennis Haysbert, Taye Diggs, Gary Dourdan...to mention a few. And they ALL loved the show and most took the time to say hello and have pictures taken with the cast...also the real Sandra Izsadore, Femi, Seun and Yeni Kuti, Fela's children. When the Reverend Jesse Jackson came onto the stage at the end of the show and after the audience had left, he prayed with the whole cast, band and company. Wonderful. Also, I sent a message to Dennis Haysbert that unless he agreed to come backstage and say hello to me and the cast at the end of the show, I would refuse to do Act II! He agreed and came!! The Power of a Woman! Yeah Yeah!

Actor Who Performed the Most Roles in This Show: That would probably be Ismael Kouyaté who plays many roles in addition to chorus dancer and singer. He gives a call to prayer, honoring Fela as a rising star.

Four of Fela's "Queens" acknowledge the audience on opening night.

Sahr Ngaujah and *Yearbook* correspondent Melanie Marshall take bows on opening night.

Who Has Done the Most Shows: That may be me, Melanie Marshall!! Too many to mention!!

Special Backstage Rituals: I always sing a harmony during Act I's "High Life"...a great vocal warm up! Gelan Lambert warming up and Jermaine Rowe doing a ballet barre warm-up, both wearing headsets.

Favorite Moments During Each Performance: The whole of the "Orisas" culminating in my aria, "Rain," and of course, "Yellow Fever"!!

Favorite In-Theatre Gathering Place: Backstage at the Sound desk! (One place for all the chocolates and sweets.)

Favorite Snack Foods: That would be fresh pineapple, as it contains an enzyme that is beneficial for the voice. Otherwise, any miniature chocolate or sweet that the stage management have at the side of the stage. And of course water—the life blood!

Favorite Therapies: See Above. Ginger tea crystals. Also, the healing hands of our PT, Ashton. Tiger Balm and the foam rollers!! Homemade cakes (Barbados rum cake!) and cupcakes for special occasions. Finding "Massage Envy" in most cities. Great free memberships at gyms. Equinox, we thank you!! Parties, outings on our days off.

Memorable Ad-Lib: During "Expensive Shit," Adesola Osakalumi (Fela) was speaking about "igbo" (grass/weed) and how expensive it is and a man walked from the back of the theatre and put money on the stage!!

Technology/Cell Phone Interruptions: Unbelievable! People who just blatantly tape the show... sometimes using their iPad!

Memorable Press Encounter: Africa Channel revealing the true genealogy results for Iris Wilson and Gelan Lambert.

Memorable Stage Door Fan Encounter: A lady in Chicago who was waiting for "The Mother" to come out, and I had been standing next to her for at least 15 minutes!

What Did You Think of the Web Buzz on Your Show: Great coverage on Facebook and Twitter and stamp of approvals from celebrities who posted on those sites.

Latest Audience Arrival: The last five minutes before the end of Act I!! Unbelievable!!

Fastest Costume Change: That would be Fela. About 20 seconds, changing into the role of the General.

Busiest Day at the Box Office: The last three shows of the Broadway run.

Who Wore the Heaviest/Hottest Costume: That would be the character of the Egungun, played by Gelan Lambert (and Adé Chiké Torbert).

Who Wore the Least: All of the beautiful Queens.

Catchphrases Only the Company Would Recognize: "A-go" and "A-me."

Orchestra Member Who Played the Most Instruments: Dylan Fusillo who plays percussion. Too many instruments to mention, but without him it doesn't sound "whole."

Orchestra Member Who Played the Most Consecutive Performances Without a Sub: That would be the incomparable Bryan Vargas, guitar.

Company In-Jokes: Knowing that during the show various Stage Management people are imitating us!

Paulette Ivory takes a curtain call at the premiere.

Tales From the Put-in: Poor Jeremy Wilms breaking his finger...but then being so unbelievably professional and playing the bass guitar for the show that same night flawlessly *but in so much pain.*

Nicknames: "Sexy-O" for Thierry Picaut, Ismael Kouyaté calling Jermaine "Cap-i-taine," Sahr Ngaujah calling me "Mellie Mel."

Embarrassing Moments: When Iris Wilson's mohawk wig came off during "Yellow Fever," the improvisational dance in Act I, and Jeffrey Page's wig coming off during the James Brown moment!! Priceless!

Coolest Things About Being in This Show: Portraying a TRUE story of a powerful Black man and his family, and educating people on a part of Black history that was perhaps unknown to them, proudly continuing this amazing legacy.

Frankie Valli and the Four Seasons

Opened: October 19, 2012.
Limited Engagement. Closed October 27, 2012 after 7 Perfomances.

Concert show featuring real-life Frankie Valli, whose life story is told in the musical Jersey Boys.

PROGRAM NOTE: ABOUT FRANKIE VALLI

Oh, what a story. Frankie Valli, who came to fame in 1962 as the lead singer of the Four Seasons, is hotter than ever in the twenty-first century. Thanks to the volcanic success of the Tony-winning musical *Jersey Boys*, which chronicles the life and times of Frankie and his legendary group, such classic songs as "Big Girls Don't Cry," "Walk Like a Man," "Rag Doll," "Can't Take My Eyes Off You" and "December 1963 (Oh, What a Night)" are all the rage all over again. As the 2005 play begins its eighth blockbuster year on Broadway, and six other casts perform *Jersey Boys* nightly around the world, the real Frankie Valli is globetrotting as well. To mark the 50th anniversary of the Seasons' first hit, "Sherry," Frankie has toured the United Kingdom, Australia and New Zealand in 2012. And to top off the anniversary tour, he's making his first-ever appearance on Broadway, a seven-show run at the Broadway Theatre (conveniently located around the corner from *Jersey Boys*).

Born on May 3, 1934, Valli grew up on the tough streets of Newark, New Jersey, and dreamed of being a singer from the time his mother took him at age seven to see Frank Sinatra at New York City's Paramount Theatre. After cutting his first record, "My Mother's Eyes," in 1953, Valli joined a nightclub act called the Variety Trio, which evolved into the Four Lovers. In 1956, they had the minor hit "You're the Apple of My Eye" and appeared on "The Ed Sullivan Show" (eight years prior to the Beatles!) before falling back into obscurity. Things didn't start really happening until the early 1960s, when songwriting prodigy Bob Gaudio (who co-wrote "Short Shorts" at age 15 as a member of the Royal Teens) joined the Lovers, and they began to work with producer Bob Crewe. The Lovers flunked an audition to play at the cocktail lounge of a bowling alley in Union, NJ, but

Continued on next page

⊗ BROADWAY THEATRE

1681 Broadway
A Shubert Organization Theatre

Philip J. Smith, *Chairman*   **Robert E. Wankel,** *President*

A BROADWAY CONCERT EVENT • LIVE NATION ENTERTAINMENT
ROBERT AHRENS, EVA PRICE, MANNY KLADITIS, JASON STONE

PRESENT

THE ONE. THE ONLY. THE ORIGINAL.

MUSIC DIRECTOR
ROBBY ROBINSON

WITH
**LANDON BEARD   BRANDON BRIGHAM
BRIAN BRIGHAM   TODD FOURNIER**

**ROBERTO ANGELUCCI   RICHIE GAJATE GARCIA   RICK KELLER
JOHN MENZANO   CRAIG PILO   JOHN SCHROEDER**

TOUR MANAGEMENT & DESIGN	SOUND	ASSOCIATE TOUR MANAGER
DEAN EGNATER	**JIM SANDERS** **MIKE O'MALLEY**	**ANDY TYLER**

MOVEMENT	TECHNICAL SUPERVISOR	PRESS REPRESENTATIVE
RAYMOND DEL BARRIO	**HILLARY BLANKEN** **GUY KWAN**	**THE HARTMAN GROUP**

ADVERTISING	GENERAL MANAGEMENT
SPOTCO	**NIKO COMPANIES**

10/19/12

Frankie Valli

Photo courtesy of the production

MUSICIANS

ROBBY ROBINSON	........**MUSIC DIRECTOR**
LANDON BEARD	..............Background Vocals
BRANDON BRIGHAM	.........Background Vocals
BRIAN BRIGHAM	...............Background Vocals
TODD FOURNIER	..............Background Vocals
ROBERTO ANGELUCCI	.....................Guitar
RICHIE GAJATE GARCIA	.................Percussion
RICK KELLER	....................................Sax
JOHN SCHROEDER	..........................Guitar
CRAIG PILO	....................................Drums
JOHN MENZANO	................................Bass

123

Frankie Valli and the Four Seasons

they decided the lounge's name would make a classy moniker for a singing group: the Four Seasons.

In 1962 Gaudio came up with a song that made full use of Frankie's remarkable range, from baritone to falsetto. When the unknown Seasons sang "Sherry" on "American Bandstand," they suddenly became the hottest band in the land, and after nine years as a recording artist, Frankie Valli became an "overnight" sensation with a No. 1 record. The sound of "Sherry" was unlike anything else on the airwaves. "Many R&B groups had used falsetto as part of their background harmonies," explains Frankie, "but we were different because we put the falsetto out front and made it the lead."

Determined not to be a one-hit wonder again, Gaudio collaborated with Crewe, and the duo quickly composed two more No. 1 hits for the Seasons: "Big Girls Don't Cry" and "Walk Like a Man." Gaudio and Crewe went on to become one of the most successful songwriting teams in pop-music history. Around the same time, Gaudio also formed a special partnership with Valli. With a handshake, Bob agreed to give Frankie half of everything Bob earned as a writer and producer, and Frankie agreed to give Bob half of Frankie's earnings from performances outside the group. That partnership remains in force 50 years later, still sealed only with a handshake.

The fateful year of 1964 brought the British invasion, but that didn't stall the Four Seasons. With the Gaudio-Crewe engine firing on all cylinders, the group released one smash after another: "Dawn (Go Away)," "Ronnie," "Rag Doll,"

"Save It for Me," "Big Man in Town" and, in early 1965, "Bye Bye Baby (Baby, Goodbye)."

From late 1965 to 1967, Gaudio and Crewe began working on songs that Frankie could sing solo — adult-oriented songs that didn't rely on his famous falsetto. Songwriting for the group was largely turned over to the team of Denny Randell and Sandy Linzer, who produced three straight giant hits: "Let's Hang On," "Working My Way Back to You" and "Opus 17 (Don't You Worry 'Bout Me)." Gaudio's main contribution to the group during this period was "Beggin'," written with Peggy Farina of the Angels.

In 1967 Gaudio and Crewe finally fashioned a signature song that would make Frankie a solo superstar, even as he kept up his parallel career as the Four Seasons' lead singer. "Can't Take My Eyes Off You" went to No. 2 in Billboard and No. 1 in Cash Box and Record World. With the popularity of the original record and at least 200 cover versions, "Can't Take My Eyes Off You" has become one of the top ten most-played songs in the history of BMI, one of the two major companies that collect royalties for songwriters.

After a brief cold spell, Frankie came roaring back in 1975 with "My Eyes Adored You," which reached No. 1, "Swearin' to God" and a cover of "Our Day Will Come." That burst of success spurred Gaudio to put together a new Four Seasons, led by Frankie of course. With his future wife Judy Parker, Gaudio wrote "Who Loves You" and "December 1963 (Oh, What a Night)," two of the biggest hits in the Seasons' history. And in 1978 Frankie scored

another No. 1 with his solo performance of "Grease."

In a career on the pop charts running all the way from 1962 to 2007, Frankie Valli and the Four Seasons have racked up an amazing 77 hits in the U.S. and Britain, including 48 in the Top 40, 24 in the Top 10 and nine No. 1 records. They were inducted into the Rock and Roll Hall of Fame in 1990.

But who could have imagined in 1990 that so much more was coming? Since the turn of the twenty-first century, Valli has released a new album, Romancing the '60s, had a No. 1 dance record in Britain (a remix of "Beggin'") and launched a clone army of Jersey Boys around the globe. In 2009 Jersey Boys established itself in the Southern Hemisphere by having a successful run in Australia, then moving to New Zealand, and then back to Australia again by popular demand. In 2013 a new cast will open in South Africa after previewing in Singapore. Meanwhile back in the Northern Hemisphere, there are two different North American tours of the play, while fixed companies continue performances on Broadway and in Las Vegas and London. GK Films, producers of Martin Scorsese's Hugo, is now making a Jersey Boys movie.

For as far into the future as anyone can see, Jersey Boys will introduce the music of Frankie Valli to new generations. And Frankie himself? As his character says at the end of Jersey Boys: "Like that bunny on TV with the battery, I just keep going and going and going." For as long as he wants to sing, people will want to listen.

— Charles Alexander

Frankie Valli

Robby Robinson
*Music Director/
Keyboards*

Landon Beard
Background Singer

Brandon Brigham
Background Singer

Brian Brigham
Background Singer

Todd Fournier
Background Singer

Roberto Angelucci
Guitar

Richie Gajate Garcia
Percussion

John Schroeder
Guitar

Rick Keller
Sax

Craig Pilo
Drums

John Menzano
Bass

Jim Sanders
Sound Engineer

Raymond del Barrio
*Stage Direction/
Choreography*

Robert Ahrens
Presenter

Eva Price
Maximum
Entertainment
Presenter

Manny Kladitis
Presenter

Jason Stone
Live Nation
Entertainment
Presenter

Jason Vanderwoude
Company Manager

Frankie Valli and the Four Seasons

DOORMAN
Guy Ennis

Photos by Brian Mapp

FRONT OF HOUSE
Front Row (L-R): Mattie Robinson, Jorge Colon, Mae Park, Karen Banyai, David Grote, Russ Ramsey (standing)
Second Row (L-R): William Phelan, Svetlana Pinkhaus, Lori Bokun, Jaime Wilhelm
Third Row (L-R): Troy Scarborough, Luis Santiago, Nancy Reyes
Fourth Row (L-R): Ishmael Tirado, Carmen Walker
Back Row (L-R): Janise Beckwith, Selena Nelson, Freddy Matos, Nathaniel Wright

BAND AND CREW
Front Row (L-R): Brandon Brigham, Landon Beard, Brian Brigham, Frankie Valli, Robby Robinson, Dean Egnater, Andy Tyler, Mike O'Malley, Jim Sanders
Back Row (L-R): Todd Fournier, Rick Keller, John Schroeder, Craig Pilo, Richie Gajate Garcia, John Menzano, Roberto Angelucci, unidentified, unidentified

STAFF FOR
FRANKIE VALLI AND THE FOUR SEASONS:
THE ONE. THE ONLY. THE ORIGINAL.

GENERAL MANAGEMENT
NIKO COMPANIES
Manny Kladitis
Jason T. Vanderwoude

BOOKING AGENCY
INTERNATIONAL CREATIVE MANAGEMENT (ICM)
Steve Levine

GENERAL PRESS REPRESENTATIVE
THE HARTMAN GROUP
Michael Hartman   Wayne Wolfe   Nicole Capatasto

PRODUCTION MANAGER
JUNIPER STREET PRODUCTIONS
Hillary Blanken   Joe DeLuise
Guy Kwan   Ana Rose Greene

Production Carpenter ....Alan Grudzinski
Production Electrician ....Jimmy Fedigan
Sound Designer/Production Sound ....Keith Caggiano
Wardrobe Supervisor ....John Furrow
Assistant to Mr. Ahrens ....Collin Schulbaum
Assistant to Ms. Price ....Taylor James
Advertising ....SpotCo/
Drew Hodges, Jim Edwards,
Tom Greenwald, Ilene Rosen,
Michael Crowley, Cory Spinney
Website ....SpotCo Interactive

Technical Supervisor ....Juniper Street Productions/
Hillary Blanken, Guy Kwan,
Joe DeLuise
Banking ....JPMorgan Chase/
Padmini Sivaprakasam
Insurance ....Insurance Office of America/
Carol Bressi-Cilona
Legal ....Screwvala LLC/
Erach F. Screwvala, Esq.
Accounting ....Rosenberg, Neuwirth & Kuchner,
Mark D'Ambrosi, Jana Javnikar

LIVE NATION ENTERTAINMENT, INC.
Michael Rapino ....President & Chief Executive Officer
Irving Azoff ....Executive Chairman
Joe Berchtold ....Chief Operating Officer
Ron Bension ....Chief Executive Officer,
House of Blues Entertainment
Ben Weeden ....Chief Operating Officer
Jason Stone ....Senior Vice President New York

CREDITS
Lighting equipment provided by PRG Lighting. Scenery provided by Global Scenic Services. Video equipment provided by Scharff Weisberg/WorldStage – East Coast.

Mr. Ahrens would like to thank Bill Griffin.
Ms. Price would like to thank Holly Sutton.
Mr. Kladitis would like to dedicate
this engagement to Clarence.

SPECIAL THANKS
Mr. Valli would like to thank Emilo, Brando, Francesco and

Toni, Olivia and Dario, Bob Gaudio, Peter Bennett, Barry Siegel, Rosa Grimes, Dodger Theatricals and all my friends too numerous to mention. And above all…to the fans who have supported the Four Seasons for five fabulous decades.

The Gershwins' Porgy and Bess

First Preview: December 17, 2011. Opened: January 12, 2012.
Closed September 23, 2012 after 28 Previews and 293 Performances.

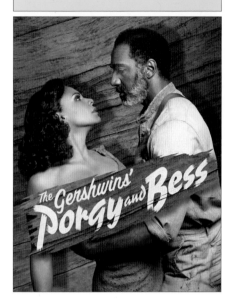

In the Charleston, South Carolina ghetto of Catfish Row poor beggar Porgy falls in love with Bess, a scarlet woman who is the consort of the powerful and murderous bully Crown. Bess finds herself falling in love with the kind goodness of Porgy, and she tries to turn her back on her old life, especially after it appears that Crown has died in a hurricane. But when Crown returns to claim her, Porgy knows he has to find a way to fight for the woman he loves, or lose her forever.

CAST

(in order of appearance)

Clara	NIKKI RENÉE DANIELS
Jake	JOSHUA HENRY
Mariah	NaTASHA YVETTE WILLIAMS
Sporting Life	DAVID ALAN GRIER
Mingo, The Undertaker	J.D. WEBSTER
Serena	BRYONHA MARIE PARHAM
Robbins	NATHANIEL STAMPLEY
Porgy	NORM LEWIS
Crown	PHILLIP BOYKIN
Bess	AUDRA McDONALD
Detective	CHRISTOPHER INNVAR
Policeman	JOSEPH DELLGER
The Strawberry Woman	ANDREA JONES-SOJOLA
Peter, The Honey Man	PHUMZILE SOJOLA
The Crab Man	CEDRIC NEAL
Fishermen	ROOSEVELT ANDRÉ CREDIT, TREVON DAVIS, WILKIE FERGUSON III
Women of Catfish Row	ALLISON BLACKWELL, HEATHER HILL, ALICIA HALL MORAN, LISA NICOLE WILKERSON

Continued on next page

RICHARD RODGERS THEATRE

UNDER THE DIRECTION OF JAMES M. NEDERLANDER AND JAMES L. NEDERLANDER

Jeffrey Richards   Jerry Frankel   Rebecca Gold   Howard Kagan
Cheryl Wiesenfeld/Brunish Trinchero/Lucio Simons TBC   Joseph & Matthew Deitch
Mark S. Golub & David S. Golub   Terry Schnuck   Freitag Productions/Koenigsberg Filerman
The Leonore S. Gershwin 1987 Trust   Universal Pictures Stage Productions   Ken Mahoney
Judith Resnick   Tulchin/Bartner/ATG   Paper Boy Productions   Christopher Hart   Alden Badway
Broadway Across America   Irene Gandy   Will Trice

PRESENT

AUDRA McDONALD   NORM LEWIS   DAVID ALAN GRIER

in the AMERICAN REPERTORY THEATER production of

THE GERSHWINS'®
PORGY AND BESS®

by
George Gershwin, DuBose and Dorothy Heyward and Ira Gershwin

Musical Book Adapted by
Suzan-Lori Parks

Musical Score Adapted by
Diedre L. Murray

with

Phillip Boykin   Nikki Renée Daniels   Joshua Henry
Christopher Innvar   Bryonha Marie Parham   NaTasha Yvette Williams

Sumayya Ali   Allison Blackwell   Roosevelt André Credit   Trevon Davis   Joseph Dellger   Wilkie Ferguson III   Carmen Ruby Floyd
Gavin Gregory   Heather Hill   David Hughey   Andrea Jones-Sojola   Alicia Hall Moran   Cedric Neal   Phumzile Sojola
Nathaniel Stampley   Julius Thomas III   J.D. Webster   Lisa Nicole Wilkerson

Scenic Design	Costume Design	Lighting Design	Sound Design
Riccardo Hernandez	ESosa	Christopher Akerlind	Acme Sound Partners

Wig/Hair/Makeup Design	Music Supervisor	Music Director and Conductor	Music Coordinator
J. Jared Janas and Rob Greene	David Loud	Constantine Kitsopoulos	John Miller

Casting	Associate Director/Production Stage Manager	Technical Supervision
Telsey + Company Justin Huff, CSA	Nancy Harrington	Hudson Theatrical Associates

Press Representative	Company Manager	General Management
Jeffrey Richards Associates Irene Gandy/Alana Karpoff	Bruce Klinger	Richards/Climan, Inc.

Associate Producers
Ronald Frankel   James Fuld Jr.   Allan S. Gordon   INFINITY Stages
Shorenstein Hays-Nederlander Theatres LLC   David & Barbara Stoller   Michael & Jean Strunsky   Theresa Wozunk

Orchestrations by
William David Brohn and Christopher Jahnke

Choreographed by
Ronald K. Brown

Directed by
Diane Paulus

First performed at the American Repertory Theater August 17, 2011
Diane Paulus, Artistic Director and Diane Borger, Producer
The worldwide copyrights in the works of George Gershwin and Ira Gershwin for this presentation are licensed by the Gershwin Family.

6/4/12

(L-R): Audra McDonald as Bess and Norm Lewis as Porgy

Photo by Michael J. Lutch

The Gershwins' Porgy and Bess

MUSICAL NUMBERS

ACT I

"Overture"

"Summertime" .... Clara and Jake

"A Woman Is a Sometime Thing" .... Jake and Ensemble

"Crap Game" .... Ensemble

"Gone, Gone, Gone" .... Ensemble

"My Man's Gone Now" .... Serena

"Leaving for the Promised Land" .... Bess and Ensemble

"It Takes a Long Pull" .... Jake and the Fishermen

"I Got Plenty of Nothing" .... Porgy

"I Hates Your Strutting Style" .... Mariah

"Bess, You Is My Woman Now" .... Porgy and Bess

"Oh, I Can't Sit Down" .... Ensemble

ACT II

"Entr'acte"

"It Ain't Necessarily So" .... Sporting Life and Ensemble

"What You Want With Bess?" .... Bess and Crown

"It Takes a Long Pull" (Reprise) .... Jake and the Fishermen

"Oh, Doctor Jesus" .... Serena and Ensemble

"Street Cries" .... Strawberry Woman, Honey Man, Crab Man

"I Loves You, Porgy" .... Bess and Porgy

"Oh, The Lord Shake the Heaven" .... Ensemble

"A Red Headed Woman" .... Crown and Ensemble

"Clara, Don't You Be Downhearted" .... Ensemble

"There's a Boat That's Leaving Soon" .... Sporting Life

"Where's My Bess?" .... Porgy, Mariah, Serena

"I'm on My Way" .... Porgy and Ensemble

ORCHESTRA

Conductor:
CONSTANTINE KITSOPOULOS

Associate Conductor:
PAUL MASSE

Woodwinds:
KATHY FINK, LYNNE COHEN,
STEVE KENYON, JONATHAN LEVINE,
JILL M. COLLURA

Trumpets:
NICK MARCHIONE, DAN URNESS

Trombone:
KEITH O'QUINN

Bass Trombone/Tuba:
JENNIFER WHARTON

French Horns:
R.J. KELLEY, ERIC DAVIS

Concert Master:
BELINDA WHITNEY

Violins:
ORLANDO WELLS, KARL KAWAHARA,
PHILIP PAYTON

Violas:
CRYSTAL GARNER, LIUH-WEN TING

Cellos:
SARAH SEIVER, SUMMER BOGGESS

Bass:
BILL ELLISON

Drums/Percussion:
CHARLES DESCARFINO

Piano/Celeste/Accordion:
PAUL MASSE

Music Coordinator:
JOHN MILLER

Cast Continued

SWINGS
SUMAYYA ALI, CARMEN RUBY FLOYD,
GAVIN GREGORY, DAVID HUGHEY,
JULIUS THOMAS III

UNDERSTUDIES
For Porgy:
PHUMZILE SOJOLA, NATHANIEL STAMPLEY
For Bess:
SUMAYYA ALI, ALICIA HALL MORAN
For Sporting Life:
DAVID HUGHEY, CEDRIC NEAL
For Crown:
GAVIN GREGORY, NATHANIEL STAMPLEY
For Clara:
SUMAYYA ALI, ANDREA JONES-SOJOLA
For Jake:
TREVON DAVIS, DAVID HUGHEY
For Detective:
JOSEPH DELLGER
For Serena:
SUMAYYA ALI, ANDREA JONES-SOJOLA
For Mariah:
ALLISON BLACKWELL,
CARMEN RUBY FLOYD
For The Crab Man:
WILKIE FERGUSON III, JULIUS THOMAS III
For Mingo:
JULIUS THOMAS III
For Robbins:
WILKIE FERGUSON III, DAVID HUGHEY,
PHUMZILE SOJOLA
For Peter:
JULIUS THOMAS III
For The Strawberry Woman:
SUMAYYA ALI, HEATHER HILL
For Fishermen:
GAVIN GREGORY, DAVID HUGHEY,
JULIUS HOMAS III

DANCE CAPTAIN
LISA NICOLE WILKERSON

SETTING
Time: Late 1930s
Place: Catfish Row and Kittawah Island
Charleston, South Carolina

The Gershwins' Porgy and Bess

Audra McDonald
Bess

Norm Lewis
Porgy

David Alan Grier
Sporting Life

Phillip Boykin
Crown

Nikki Renée Daniels
Clara

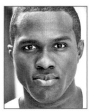
Joshua Henry
Jake

Christopher Innvar
Detective

Bryonha Marie
Parham
Serena

NaTasha Yvette
Williams
Mariah

Sumayya Ali
*Swing, u/s Bess,
Clara, Serena, The
Strawberry Woman*

Allison Blackwell
*Woman of Catfish
Row, u/s Mariah*

Roosevelt André
Credit
Fisherman

Trevon Davis
*Fisherman
u/s Jake*

Joseph Dellger
*Policeman
u/s Detective*

Wilkie Ferguson III
*Fisherman,
u/s The Crab Man,
Robbins*

Carmen Ruby Floyd
Swing, u/s Mariah

Gavin Gregory
*Swing, u/s Crown,
Fisherman*

Heather Hill
*Woman of Catfish
Row; u/s The
Strawberry Woman*

David Hughey
*Swing; u/s Sporting
Life, Jake, Robbins,
Fisherman*

Andrea Jones-Sojola
*The Strawberry
Woman, u/s Clara,
Serena*

Alicia Hall Moran
*Woman of Catfish
Row, u/s Bess*

Cedric Neal
*The Crab Man,
u/s Sporting Life*

Phumzile Sojola
*Peter, the Honey
Man, u/s Porgy,
Robbins*

Nathaniel Stampley
*Robbins, u/s Porgy,
Crown*

Julius Thomas III
*Swing; u/s The Crab
Man, Mingo, the
Undertaker, Peter
the Honey Man*

J.D. Webster
*Mingo, the
Undertaker*

Lisa Nicole
Wilkerson
*Woman of Catfish
Row, Dance Captain,
Fight Captain*

George Gershwin
Music

DuBose & Dorothy Heyward
Libretto/Lyrics

Ira Gershwin
Lyrics

Diane Paulus
Director

Suzan-Lori Parks
*Musical Book
Adapter*

Diedre L. Murray
*Musical Score
Adapter*

Ronald K. Brown
Choreographer

The Gershwins' Porgy and Bess

Riccardo Hernandez
Scenic Design

ESosa
Costume Design

Christopher Akerlind
Lighting Design

Sten Severson, Tom Clark, Mark Menard and Nevin Steinberg
Acme Sound Partners
Sound Design

J. Jared Janas
Wig/Hair/Make-up Design

Rob Greene
Wig/Hair/Make-up Design

David Loud
Music Supervisor

Constantine Kitsopoulos
Music Director and Conductor

John Miller
Music Coordinator

William David Brohn
Orchestrations

Christopher Jahnke
Orchestrations

Bernard Telsey
Telsey + Company
Casting

Mia Walker
Assistant Director

Denise Woods
Dialect Coach

J. Steven White
Fight Consultant

Neil A. Mazzella
Hudson Theatrical Associates
Technical Supervision

David R. Richards, Tamar Haimes
Richards/Climan, Inc
General Management

Jeffrey Richards
Producer

Jerry Frankel
Producer

Rebecca Gold
Producer

Howard Kagan
Producer

Cheryl Wiesenfeld
Producer

Brisa Trinchero
Producer

Meredith Lucio
Producer

Ron Simons
Producer

Van Dean and Kenny Howard
The Broadway Consortium
Producers

Joseph Deitch
Producer

Matthew Deitch
Producer

Mark S. Golub
Producer

David S. Golub
Producer

Terry Schnuck
Producer

The Gershwins' Porgy and Bess

Barbara and Buddy
Freitag
Freitag Productions
Producers

Heni Koenigsberg
Producer

Michael Filerman
Producer

Ken Mahoney
Producer

Judith Resnick
Producer

Will Dombrowski
Paper Boy
Productions
Producer

Bruston Kade
Manuel
Paper Boy
Productions
Producer

Michael A. Alden
Producer

Dale Badway
Producer

John Gore
Broadway Across
America
Producer

Thomas B. McGrath
Broadway Across
America
Producer

Christopher Hart
Christopher Hart
Productions
Producer

Irene Gandy
Producer

Will Trice
Producer

Dan Barnhill
*Policeman,
u/s Detective*

Photos by Lisa Pacino

COMPANY MANAGEMENT
(L-R): Bruce Klinger, Caitlin Fahey

ORCHESTRA
(L-R): Constantine Kitsopoulos, Lynne Cohen, Rob Shaw, Summer Boggess, Liuh-Wen Ting, Laura Bontrager, Katherine Fink, Orlando Wells, Fred Lassen, Charles Descarfino, Crystal Garner, Eric Davis, Bill Ellison, Janet Lantz, Keith O'Quinn, Karl Kawahara, Philip Payton, Don McGeen, Steve Kenyon, Jonathan Levine, Dan Urness, Max Seigel

The Gershwins' Porgy and Bess

FRONT OF HOUSE STAFF
Front Row (L-R): Carla Cherry (Concessions), Barbara Rodell, Lori Miata, Derrick Darby, Carmen Frank (Ushers), Dorothy Darby (Directress),
Destiny Bivona (Usher), Rosanne Kelly (Matron)
Middle Row (L-R): Larry Purvis (Concessions), Brenda Schwarz, Roxanne Gayol (Ushers), Timothy Pettolina (House Manager)
Back Row (L-R): Colum Meehan (Usher), Richard Lester (Concessions), Maureen Gonzalez, Frank Holmes, Beverly Thornton, Giovanny Lopez (Ushers)

CREW
Front Row (L-R): Julie Baldauff (Stage Manager), Brendan O'Neal, Justin Rathbun, Steve Carver, Sharika Niles (Assistant Stage Manager), Vangeli Kaseluris
Middle Row (L-R): Worth Strecker, Nancy Harrington (Associate Director/Production Stage Manager)
Back Row (L-R): Kate Sorg, Stephen F. DeVerna, Yleana Nuñez, Thomas Augustine, James Wilkinson, Kevin Camus, Justin Freeman, Tim Rossi

The Gershwins' Porgy and Bess

Audra McDonald (C) and Cast

Photo by Michael J. Lutch

STAFF FOR *THE GERSHWINS' PORGY AND BESS*

GENERAL MANAGEMENT
RICHARDS/CLIMAN, INC.
David R. Richards   Tamar Haimes
Michael Sag   Kyle Bonder
Jessica Fried   Jacqueline Kolek

COMPANY MANAGER
Bruce Klinger

GENERAL PRESS REPRESENTATIVE
JEFFREY RICHARDS ASSOCIATES
Irene Gandy/Alana Karpoff
Ryan Hallett   Elon Rutberg

PRODUCTION MANAGEMENT
HUDSON THEATRICAL ASSOCIATES
Neil Mazzella   Sam Ellis   Irene Wang
Walter Murphy   Corky Boyd

CASTING
TELSEY + COMPANY
Bernie Telsey CSA, Will Cantler CSA,
David Vaccari CSA, Bethany Knox CSA,
Craig Burns CSA, Tiffany Little Canfield CSA,
Rachel Hoffman CSA, Justin Huff CSA,
Patrick Goodwin CSA, Abbie Brady-Dalton CSA,
David Morris, Cesar A. Rocha, Andrew Femenella,
Karyn Casl, Kristina Bramhall, Jessie Malone

PRODUCTION STAGE
    MANAGER ....NANCY HARRINGTON
Stage Manager ....Julie Baldauff
Assistant Stage Manager ....Sharika Niles
Assistant Company Manager ....Caitlin Fahey
Assistant Director ....Mia Walker
Assistant Choreographer ....Arcell Cabuag
Dance Captain/Fight Captain ....Lisa Nicole Wilkerson
Assistant Producer ....Michael Crea
Dialect Coach ....Denise Woods
Fight Director ....J. Steven White
Associate Scenic Designer ....Maruti Evans
Associate Costume Designer ....Cathy Parrott
Associate Lighting Designer ....Caroline Chao
Assistant to Mr. Akerlind ....Seth Reiser
Lighting Programmer ....Warren Flynn
Video Programmers ....C. Andrew Bauer,
                                    Daniel Brodie
Associate Sound Designer ....Jason Crystal
Production Assistant ....Christopher Windom
Production Carpenter ....Francis Rapp

Head Carpenter ....Tim Rossi
Flyman ....Ronald Knox
Production Electrician ....Jimmy Maloney
Head Electrician.............................Justin Freeman
Followspot Operators ....William Walters, John Carton,
                                    Brian Frankel
Production Properties Supervisor ....Worth Strecker
Sound Engineer ....Justin Rathbun
Deck Audio...............................James Wilkinson
Advance Sound ....Darin Stillman
Wardrobe Supervisor ....Jesse Galvan
Dressers ....Vangeli Kaseluris, Kurt Keilmann,
                    Angela Lehrer, Yleana Nuñez, Kate Sorg
Hair Supervisor ....Thomas Augustine
Hair Dresser ....Brendan O'Neal
Assistant to Diedre L. Murray ....Randall Eng
Music Preparation Services ....Larry H. Abel,
                    Music Preparation International, Inc.
Assistant to the Orchestrators/
    Music Assistant ....Neil Douglas Reilly
Assistant to John Miller ....Nichole Jennino
Music Assistant ....Nehemiah Luckett
Advertising ....Serino Coyne, Inc./
                    Greg Corradetti, Tom Callahan,
                    Danielle Boyle, Peter Gunther, Drew Nebrig
Website Design/Online Marketing ....SpotCo/
                    Michael Crowley, Meghan Ownbey
Interactive Marketing
    Service ....Broadway's Best Shows/
                    Andy Drachenberg, Christopher Pineda
Marketing Services ....Type A Marketing/
                    Anne Rippey, Elyce Henkin,
                                    Allison Morrow
Marketing/
    Press Services ....It Is Done Communications/
                                    Linda J. Stewart
Banking...................................City National Bank/
                    Michele Gibbons, Erik Piecuch
Insurance ....DeWitt Stern Group Inc./
                    Peter Shoemaker, Anthony Pittari
Accountants ....Fried & Kowgios, CPA's LLP,
                                    Robert Fried, CPA
Comptroller ....Elliott Aronstam
Legal Counsel ....Lazarus & Harris LLP./
                                    Scott R. Lazarus, Esq.,
                                    Robert C. Harris, Esq.
Payroll ....CSI/Lance Castellana
Production Photographer ....Michael Lutch
Merchandise.........................Max Merchandising/
                                    Randi Grossman
Company Mascots ....Skye, Franco, Butler, Georgia

CREDITS
Scenery constructed and automated by Hudson Scenic Studio, Inc. Lighting equipment from Hudson Sound & Light LLC. Sound equipment from Sound Associates. Projection equipment from Scharff Weisberg. Costumes constructed by Giliberto Designs, Jennifer Love Costumes, Katrina Patterns, Tricorne, ART Costume Shop. Fabric dying and distressing by Hochi Asiatico. Millinery by Arnold Levine and Denise Wallace. Dance shoes by Worldtone. Undergarments by Bra*Tenders. Makeup provided by M·A·C.

Rehearsed at the New 42nd Street Studios

SPECIAL THANKS
To all at A.R.T., particularly Diane Borger, Chris DeCamillis, Anna Fitzloff, Jared Fine, Kati Mitchell, Brendan Shea, Lauren Antler, Mark Lunsford, Patricia Quinlan, Ryan McKittrick, Jenna Clark Embrey and the production staff. Karmaloop for A.R.T. production sponsorship. The A.R.T. Board of Trustees and Advisors and the Porgy and Bess Leadership Circle. Ashley Farra, Elizabeth Van Buren, Isabelle Simone.

www.PorgyAndBessOnBroadway.com

NEDERLANDER

Chairman	James M. Nederlander
President	James L. Nederlander

Executive Vice President
Nick Scandalios

Vice President	Senior Vice President
Corporate Development	Labor Relations
Charlene S. Nederlander	**Herschel Waxman**

Vice President	Chief Financial Officer
Jim Boese	**Freida Sawyer Belviso**

HOUSE STAFF FOR
THE RICHARD RODGERS THEATRE

House Manager ....Timothy Pettolina
Box Office Treasurer ....Fred Santore Jr.
Assistant Treasurer ....Corinne Dorso
Electrician ....Steve Carver
Carpenter ....Kevin Camus
Propertymaster ....Stephen F. DeVerna
Engineer ....Sean Quinn

The Gershwins' Porgy and Bess
SCRAPBOOK

Correspondents: Christopher Pineda, Press Rep and Trevon Davis, "Fisherman"

Most Vivid Memory of the Final Performance: The special prayer before the final performance. We made a circle of actors, crew, dressers, stage managers, then grasped hands and spoke from the heart. So emotional and heartfelt.

Memorable Quote from Farewell Stage Speech: Diane Paulus speaking of a man who said "my life was forever changed by Bess and her story. I am a deaf, gay black man and watching Bess changed my life for the better." Wow.

Farewell Party: We had it at the James Hotel Rooftop in NYC. Soooooo fun and sooooo what we needed after the final performance.

Most Exciting Celebrity Visitor: Soooo many wonderful legends attended our show throughout the run. One of the most notable: First Lady Michelle Obama. She came on stage and hugged each and every one of us! You could have heard a pin drop.

Special Backstage Rituals: Prayer before each show and various cast members warming up!

Favorite Moment During the Final Weeks (On Stage or Off): Dancing at the top of Act II—Kittawah Island choreography. At the final performance we had never been so vocal and energized!!! It was on fire!!!!

Favorite In-Theatre Gathering Place: Dressing Room 11, the Men's Ensemble Dressing Room. We were the loudest, most fun dressing room. We had just about everyone come up there to visit us and to see "what was going on."

Favorite Snack Foods: WOW! We had snacks galore throughout our run!!! Homemade and store-bought cookies, cup-cakes, peanut butter-filled pretzel bites, et cetera... LOL.

Mascot: Our Catfish Row Water Pump! :-D

Favorite Therapies: Definitely Ricolas and Altoids. We had buckets on each side of the stage.

Memorable Ad-Lib: NaTasha Williams: As

①

②

③

④

Mariah on stage, after multiple line changes for her "rap" to Sporting Life...she merged them all and added her own lyrics!!! All she needed was a beat-boxing person next to her!! LOL.

Technological Interruptions During a Performance: Throughout the show on the most silent moments "ring ring"...or someone in the second row right behind the conductor with a huge, professional-sized lens taking illegal pictures.

Memorable Stage Door Fan Encounters: On more than one occasion an emotional audience member still uncontrollably crying, saying how much the show captured them and took them to Catfish Row!

Orchestra Member Who Played the Most Instruments: Paul Masse served as the conductor for many shows as well as the piano player and accordion player.

Fastest Costume Change: Audra McDonald from "Catfish Row" wear to "Kittawah Island" dress to go to the picnic!

Catchphrases Only the Company Would Recognize: "On The Day..." "Flying In Diane..." "On the wings of Egrets..."

Sweethearts Within the Company: Phumzile Sojola and Andrea Jones-Sojola (Honey Man and The Strawberry Woman who sing arias back to back) are a married couple. Nancy Harrington (Associate Director/Production Stage Manager) and Worth Strecker (Prop Supervisor) have been together for more than 20 years!!!

Memorable Directorial Note: From Diane to Actor: "Okay great. Yes, you can do that. Nate and umm...Puma—what are you doing?"

Understudy Anecdote: Someone fell into a bench of cups and water during a dance at the beginning of the show. Water everywhere. So loud, embarrassing and disorienting! LOL.

Nicknames: Butterscotch, Sweet-Tooth, Cinnamon.

Coolest Thing About Being in This Show: The Catfish Row Family that we truly became!!! We love one another just as a true family.

1. Audra McDonald and Norm Lewis embrace as the curtain falls on the final performance.
2. As the villain Crown, Phillip Boykin takes his bow by flashing a scowl at the audience...
3. ...then quickly dipping into a curtsey.
4. Bows on closing night:
(L-R): NaTasha Yvette Williams, Boykin, McDonald, Lewis, David Alan Grier, Bryonha Marie Parham and cast.

Ghost: The Musical

First Preview: March 15, 2012. Opened: April 23, 2012.
Closed August 18, 2012 after 39 Previews and 136 Performances.

A pop-musical adaptation of the Oscar-winning 1990 film of the same title. This supernatural romance tells the story of a murder victim who returns as a ghost (with the help of an unwilling medium) to discover the plot behind his murder and to stop his killers from visiting a similar fate on his girlfriend. This transfer from London is memorable for its eerie special effects—including a leading man who vanishes from center stage—created by a team of holograph technicians.

CAST

Sam Wheat	RICHARD FLEESHMAN
Molly Jensen	CAISSIE LEVY
Oda Mae Brown	DA'VINE JOY RANDOLPH
Carl Bruner	BRYCE PINKHAM
Willie Lopez	MICHAEL BALDERRAMA
Subway Ghost	TYLER McGEE
Hospital Ghost	LANCE ROBERTS
Clara	MOYA ANGELA
Louise	CARLY HUGHES
Bank Assistant	JENNIFER NOBLE
Minister	JASON BABINSKY
Mrs. Santiago	JENNIFER SANCHEZ
Officer Wallace	MOYA ANGELA
Detective Beiderman	JASON BABINSKY
Orlando	DANIEL J. WATTS
Ortisha	VASTHY MOMPOINT
Bank Officer	ALISON LUFF
Lionel Furgeson	JEREMY DAVIS
Nuns	CARLY HUGHES, ALISON LUFF

Continued on next page

LUNT-FONTANNE THEATRE

UNDER THE DIRECTION OF
JAMES M. NEDERLANDER AND JAMES L. NEDERLANDER

COLIN INGRAM	HELLO ENTERTAINMENT/DAVID GARFINKLE	
DONOVAN MANNATO	MJE PRODUCTIONS	PATRICIA LAMBRECHT
	ADAM SILBERMAN	

in association with

COPPEL/WATT/WITHERS/BEWICK   FIN GRAY/MICHAEL MELNICK   MAYERSON/GOULD HAUSER/TYSOE
RICHARD CHAIFETZ & JILL CHAIFETZ   JEFFREY B. HECKTMAN   LAND LINE PRODUCTIONS
GILBERT PRODUCTIONS/MARION/SHAHAR   FRESH GLORY PRODUCTIONS/BRUCE CARNEGIE-BROWN

by special arrangement with **PARAMOUNT PICTURES**

present

GHOST
THE MUSICAL

Book & Lyrics
BRUCE JOEL RUBIN

Music & Lyrics
DAVE STEWART & GLEN BALLARD

Based on the Paramount Pictures film written by Bruce Joel Rubin

"Unchained Melody" written by Hy Zaret and Alex North
Courtesy of Frank Music Corp. (ASCAP)

General Management	Production Management	Advertising & Marketing
BESPOKE THEATRICALS	**AURORA PRODUCTIONS**	**SPOTCO**
Press Agent	Casting Director (US)	Casting Director (UK)
THE HARTMAN GROUP	**TARA RUBIN CASTING**	**DAVID GRINDROD**
Musical Director	Associate Director	Production Stage Manager
DAVID HOLCENBERG	**THOMAS CARUSO**	**IRA MONT**

Additional Movement Sequences **LIAM STEEL**

Musical Supervisor, Arranger & Orchestrator	Video & Projection Designer
CHRISTOPHER NIGHTINGALE	**JON DRISCOLL**

Lighting	Illusions	Sound
HUGH VANSTONE	**PAUL KIEVE**	**BOBBY AITKEN**

Designer	Choreographer
ROB HOWELL	**ASHLEY WALLEN**

Director
MATTHEW WARCHUS

6/4/12

Caissie Levy and
Richard Fleeshman

Photo by Joan Marcus

Ghost: The Musical

MUSICAL NUMBERS

ACT I

"Here Right Now"	Sam, Molly
"Unchained Melody"	Sam
"More"	Sam, Carl, Ensemble
"Three Little Words"	Sam, Molly
"You Gotta Let Go"	Hospital Ghost, Ensemble
"Are You a Believer?"	Clara, Louise, Oda Mae
"With You"	Molly
"Suspend My Disbelief/I Had a Life"	Molly, Carl, Sam, Ensemble

ACT II

"Rain/Hold On"	Molly, Sam, Ensemble
"Life Turns on a Dime"	Carl, Molly, Sam
"Focus"	Subway Ghost
"Talkin' 'Bout a Miracle"	Hospital Ghost, Oda Mae, Ensemble
"Nothing Stops Another Day"	Molly
"I'm Outta Here"	Oda Mae, Ensemble
"Unchained Melody" (Reprise)	Sam, Molly

Photo by Joan Marcus

Richard Fleeshman, Da'Vine Joy Randolph and Caissie Levy

ORCHESTRA

Conductor:
DAVID HOLCENBERG
Associate Conductor:
ANDY GROBENGIESER
Keyboard 1:
DEBORAH ABRAMSON
Keyboard 2:
ANDY GROBENGIESER
Guitars:
ERIC DAVIS, J.J. McGEEHAN
Bass:
RANDY LANDAU
Drums:
HOWARD JOINES
Trumpet:
JOHN REID
Trombone:
BRUCE EIDEM
Woodwinds:
HIDEAKI AOMORI
Horn:
ZOHAR SCHONDORF
Concertmaster:
ELIZABETH LIM-DUTTON
Violins:
CENOVIA CUMMINS, JIM TSAO,
ROBIN ZEH
Violin/Viola:
JONATHAN DINKLAGE, HIROKO TAGUCHI
Cello:
JEANNE LeBLANC

Music Copying: Emily Grishman Music
Preparation/EMILY GRISHMAN,
KATHARINE EDMONDS
Music Coordinator: HOWARD JOINES

Cast Continued

ENSEMBLE

MOYA ANGELA, JASON BABINSKY,
JEREMY DAVIS, SHARONA D'ORNELLAS,
JOSH FRANKLIN, ALBERT GUERZON,
AFRA HINES, CARLY HUGHES, ALISON
LUFF, TYLER McGEE, VASTHY MOMPOINT,
JENNIFER NOBLE, JOE AARON REID,
LANCE ROBERTS, CONSTANTINE
ROUSOULI, JENNIFER SANCHEZ,
DANIEL J. WATTS

SWINGS

MIKE CANNON, STEPHEN CARRASCO,
KAREN HYLAND, JESSE WILDMAN

DANCE CAPTAIN

JAMES BROWN III

ASSISTANT DANCE CAPTAIN

AFRA HINES

UNDERSTUDIES

For Sam Wheat:
JOSH FRANKLIN,
CONSTANTINE ROUSOULI
For Molly Jensen:
ALISON LUFF, JENNIFER NOBLE
For Oda Mae Brown:
MOYA ANGELA, CARLY HUGHES
For Carl Bruner:
JASON BABINSKY,
CONSTANTINE ROUSOULI
For Willie Lopez:
MIKE CANNON, JOE AARON REID
For Subway Ghost:
JOE AARON REID, DANIEL J. WATTS
For Hospital Ghost:
STEPHEN CARRASCO, DANIEL J. WATTS
For Clara and Louise:
AFRA HINES, VASTHY MOMPOINT

SETTING

New York City, modern day

Richard Fleeshman is appearing with the support of
Actors' Equity Association pursuant to an exchange
program between American Equity and UK Equity.

Ghost: The Musical

Richard Fleeshman
Sam Wheat

Caissie Levy
Molly Jensen

Da'Vine Joy
Randolph
Oda Mae Brown

Bryce Pinkham
Carl Bruner

Michael Balderrama
Willie Lopez

Tyler McGee
*Subway Ghost/
Ensemble*

Lance Roberts
*Hospital Ghost/
Ensemble*

Moya Angela
*Clara/Officer
Wallace/Ensemble,
u/s Oda Mae Brown*

Carly Hughes
*Louise/Nun/
Ensemble;
u/s Oda Mae Brown*

Jason Babinsky
*Detective
Beiderman/
Minister/Ensemble,
u/s Carl Bruner*

James Brown III
*Dance Captain/
Fight Captain*

Mike Cannon
Swing

Stephen Carrasco
Swing

Jeremy Davis
*Lionel Furgeson/
Ensemble*

Sharona D'Ornellas
Ensemble

Josh Franklin
*Ensemble; u/s Sam
Wheat*

Albert Guerzon
Ensemble

Afra Hines
*Ensemble/Assistant
Dance Captain*

Karen Hyland
Swing

Alison Luff
*Bank Officer/
Nun/Ensemble,
u/s Molly Jensen*

Vasthy Mompoint
Ortisha/Ensemble

Jennifer Noble
*Bank Assistant/
Ensemble,
u/s Molly Jensen*

Joe Aaron Reid
Ensemble

Constantine Rousouli
*Ensemble,
u/s Sam Wheat/
Carl Bruner*

Jennifer Sanchez
*Mrs. Santiago/
Ensemble*

Daniel J. Watts
Orlando/Ensemble

Jesse Wildman
Swing

Bruce Joel Rubin
Book & Lyrics

Dave Stewart
Music & Lyrics

Glen Ballard
Music & Lyrics

Ashley Wallen
Choreographer

Christopher
Nightingale
*Musical Supervisor,
Arranger &
Orchestrator*

Hugh Vanstone
Lighting

Jon Driscoll
*Video & Projection
Designer*

Bobby Aitken
Sound Designer

Ghost: The Musical

Paul Kieve
Illusionist

Rob Howell
Designer

Matthew Warchus
Director

Liam Steel
Additional Movement Sequences

Campbell Young and Luc Verschueren
Campbell Young Associates
Hair, Wig & Makeup Designer

Thomas Caruso
Associate Director

David Holcenberg
Music Director/ Conductor

Howard Joines
Music Coordinator

Sunny Walters
Associate Choreographer

Daryl A. Stone
Associate Costume Designer

Tim Lutkin
Associate Lighting Designer

Joel Shier
Associate Lighting Designer

Simon King
Associate Sound Designer

Joanie Spina
Associate Illusionist

Tara Rubin
Tara Rubin Casting
Casting

David Grindrod
UK Casting

Gene O'Donovan
Aurora Productions
Production Management

Ben Heller
Aurora Productions
Production Management

Maggie Brohn
Bespoke Theatricals
General Management

Amy Jacobs
Bespoke Theatricals
General Management

Devin Keudell
Bespoke Theatricals
General Management

Nina Lannan
Bespoke Theatricals
General Management

Colin Ingram
Lead Producer

David Garfinkle
Hello Entertainment
Lead Producer

Michael Edwards
MJE Productions
Producer

Carole Winter
MJE Productions
Producer

Matthew Gordon
MJE Productions
Producer

Adam Silberman
Executive Producer

Michael Coppel
Producer

Michael Watt
Producer

Louise Withers
Producer

Linda Bewick
Producer

Fin Gray
Producer

Frederic H. Mayerson
Producer

Ghost: The Musical

James M. Gould
Producer

Ron Tysoe
Producer

Richard A. Chaifetz
Producer

Jill Chaifetz
Producer

Jeffrey B. Hecktman
Producer

Jordan Scott Gilbert
Gilbert Productions,
LLC
Co-Producer

Liz Torres
Gilbert Productions,
LLC
Co-Producer

Martin Peacock
Gilbert Productions,
LLC
Co-Producer

John Yonover
Gilbert Productions,
LLC
Co-Producer

Antonio R. Marion
Co-Producer

Guy Shahar
Shahar Productions
Co-Producer

Jonathan Shahar
Shahar Productions
Co-Producer

Marc Goldman
Shahar Productions
Co-Producer

David Goldman
Shahar Productions
Co-Producer

Dave Broitman
Shahar Productions
Co-Producer

Rosalind Cressy
Fresh Glory
Productions
Co-Producer

Bruce
Carnegie-Brown
Co-Producer

Photo by Joan Marcus
Richard Fleeshman (R) and cast.

STAFF FOR *GHOST*

GENERAL MANAGEMENT
BESPOKE THEATRICALS
Nina Lannan   Devin Keudell
Maggie Brohn   Amy Jacobs
Associate General Manager ....Steve Dow

COMPANY MANAGEMENT
Company Manager ....Shaun Moorman
Associate Company Manager ....Roseanna Sharrow

PRODUCTION MANAGEMENT
AURORA PRODUCTIONS
Gene O'Donovan, Ben Heller
Stephanie Sherline, Jarid Sumner, Liza Luxenberg,
Anita Shah, Anthony Jusino, Steven Dalton,
Eugenio Saenz Flores, Isaac Katzanek,
Aneta Feld, Melissa Mazdra

GENERAL PRESS REPRESENTATIVE
THE HARTMAN GROUP
Michael Hartman
Juliana Hannett   Emily McGill

CASTING (U.S.)
TARA RUBIN CASTING

Tara Rubin CSA, Eric Woodall CSA
Merri Sugarman CSA, Dale Brown CSA,
Stephanie Yankwitt CSA
Kaitlin Shaw, Lindsay Levine

CASTING (UK)
DAVID GRINDROD
Casting Associates ....Will Burton, Stephen Crockett

COLIN INGRAM PRODUCTIONS
Producer ....Colin Ingram
Associate General Manager ....Simon Ash
Financial Controller ....Louise Waldron
Production Assistant ....Daisy Campey

HELLO ENTERTAINMENT
Producer ....David Garfinkle
Executive Producer ....Adam Silberman
Chief Financial Officer ....Michael Lowen
Executive Assistant ....Clay Martin
Special Projects Director ....PJ Miller

Production Stage Manager ....Ira Mont
Stage Manager ....Julia P. Jones
Assistant Stage Managers ....Matthew Lacey,
Kate Croasdale
Consulting Stage Manager (UK) ....Natalie Wood

Associate Director ....Thomas Caruso
Associate Choreographer ....Sunny Walters
Dance Captain ....James Brown III
Assistant Dance Captain ....Afra Hines
Fight Director ....Terry King
Fight Captain ....James Brown III
Associate Scenic Designer ....Rosalind Coombes
Associate Scenic Designer ....Paul Weimer
Associate Costume Designer ....Daryl A. Stone
Assistant Costume Designer ....Rachel Attridge
Costume Design Assistant ....Audrey Nauman
Associate Lighting Designer ....Tim Lutkin
Associate Lighting Designer ....Joel Shier
Associate Sound Designer ....Simon King
Associate Sound Designer ....Garth Helm
Associate Video &
Projection Designer ....Gemma Carrington
Associate Video &
Projection Designer ....Michael Clark
Associate Illusionist ....Joanie Spina
Hair, Wig & Makeup
Designer ....Campbell Young Associates
Hair, Wig & Makeup Associate ....Luc Verschueren
Head Carpenter ....Francis Rapp
Fly Automation Carpenter ....John Croissant
Deck Automation Carpenter ....Joel DeRuyter
Head Electrician ....Mike Cornell

Ghost: The Musical

Photo by Joan Marcus

(L-R):Caissie Levy and Richard Fleeshman

Production Electricians	Randall Zaibek, Jimmy Fedigan
Moving Light Technician	Steve Long
Moving Light Programmer	David Arch
Production Property Master	David Bornstein
U.K. Props Supervisors	Lisa Buckley, Lizzie Frankl
Props Shopper	Christina Gould
Production Sound Engineer	Mike Wojchik
Assistant Sound Engineer	Colle Bustin
Production Sound Mixer UK	Ben Evans
Advance Sound	Drew Levy
Associate Music Director (UK)	Laurie Perkins
Music Technology	Phij Adams
Music Technology Associate	Andy Grobengieser
Digital Arrangements & Programming	Ned Douglas
Video System Consultant	Alan Cox
Production Video Technician	Jason Lindahl
Video/Projections Programmers	Laura Frank, Emily Harding
Video Technician	Chris Kurtz
Special Effects Coordinators	Randall Zaibek, Jimmy Fedigan
Wardrobe Supervisor	Terri Purcell
Associate Wardrobe Supervisor	Nanette Golia
Dressers	Michael Berglund, Ken Brown, Tina Clifton, Margian Flanagan, Jaymes Gill, Joby Horrigan, Peggie Kurz, Marcia McIntosh, Duduzile Mitall, Lisa Preston, Jessica Scoblick
Hair Supervisor	Susan Corrado
Assistant Hair Supervisor	Monica Costea
Hairdresser	Elisa Acevedo
Music Copying	Emily Grishman
Music Copying (UK)	Tom Kelly
Vocal Coach	Deborah Hecht
Physical Therapy	Performing Arts Physical Therapy, PhysioArts
Production Assistants	Kate Croasdale, Cody Renard Richard, Kristen Torgrimson

SDC Directing Intern	Stephen Brotebeck
SDC Observer	Ryan Emmons
Lottery Administrator	Benny Enfinger
General Management Associates	Libby Fox, Danielle Saks
General Management Interns	Sean Coughlin, Michelle Heller, Jimmy Wilson
Advertising	SPOTCO/ Drew Hodges, Jim Edwards, Tom Greenwald, Stephen Sosnowski, Nora Tillmanns
Marketing	SPOTCO/ Nick Pramik, Kristen Rathbun, Julie Wechsler, Caroline Newhouse
Online/Digital Interactive	SPOTCO/ Kristen Bardwil, Cory Spinney, Rebecca Cohen, Marisa Delmore, Sara Fitzpatrick, Marc Mettler, Jennifer Sacks, Christina Sees, Matt Wilstein
Ticket Services	SPOTCO/Stephen Santore
Production Photographer U.S.	Joan Marcus
Production Photographer UK	Sean Ebsworth Barnes
Accountant	FK Partners/Robert Fried
Controller	Galbraith & Co./Sarah Galbraith
Legal Counsel UK and Worldwide	Harbottle & Lewis LLP/ Neil Adleman
Legal Counsel U.S.	Davis Wright Tremaine LLP/ M. Graham Coleman, Robert J. Driscoll Kramer Levin Naftalis & Frankel LLP/ Mark D. Koestler Biegelman, Feiner and Feldman PC/ Ron Feiner
Payroll Services	Checks & Balances
Banking	Signature Bank/ Barbara Von Borstel, Margaret Monigan
Insurance	Aon/Albert G. Ruben Company/ Claudia Kaufman

Opening Night Coordination	Stamp Event Management Jason Burlingame, Margaret Crisostomo
Merchandise	The Araca Group
Travel Agent	Tzell Travel/The "A" Team/Andi Henig
Housing	ABA/Elizabeth Helke
Hotel Accommodations	The Time/Kanvar Singh

CREDITS

Scenery fabrication and show control and scenic motion control, featuring Stage Command Systems® by PRG - Scenic Technologies, a division of Production Resource Group, LLC. Scenery painted by Scenic Arts Studio. Lighting equipment from PRG Lighting. Sound and video equipment from Sound Associates, Inc. Flying by Foy. Costumes by Tricorne Inc.; Artur & Tailors; Gene Mignola, Inc.; Maria Ficalora Knitwear; Jeff Fender Studios; Arnold Levine Millinery; Barak Stribling; Beckenstein Shirts; Hochi Asiatico. Undergarments and hosiery by Bra*Tenders. Custom dance shoes by LaDuca Shoes and T.O. Dey Shoe Company. Custom shoes by Center Shoes. Makeup provided by M•A•C. Guitar supplies provided by D'Addario Strings and Ernie Ball. Portions of the video used were filmed at New 42nd Street Studios.

SPECIAL THANKS

American Airlines, Totes Isotoner, Mud Sweat and Tears Pottery, The Time Hotel, Frozen Ghost, Harlem Brewery, Hilco, Ivanka Trump Fine Jewelry, Magnolia Bakery, Russell Nardozza and Geoffrey Beene, Joseph P. Harris, Jr., Ruth Carney, and James McKeon

In memory of Tony Adams
In memory of Tom Lambrecht
In memory of Aaron Padric Noone Garfinkle

Rehearsed at the New 42nd Street Studios

NEDERLANDER

Chairman	**James M. Nederlander**
President	**James L. Nederlander**

Executive Vice President
Nick Scandalios

Vice President Corporate Development	Senior Vice President Labor Relations
Charlene S. Nederlander	**Herschel Waxman**

Vice President	Chief Financial Officer
Jim Boese	**Freida Sawyer Belviso**

STAFF FOR THE LUNT-FONTANNE

House Manager	**Tracey Malinowski**
Treasurer	Joe Olcese
Assistant Treasurer	Kevin Lynch
House Carpenter	Terry Taylor
House Electrician	Dennis Boyle
House Propertyman	Andrew Bentz
House Flyman	Matt Walters
House Engineers	Robert MacMahon, Joseph Riccio III

Ghost: The Musical

SCRAPBOOK

Correspondent: Stephen Carrasco, Swing

Most Vivid Memory of the Final Performance: Caissie belting out "Rain" at the top of Act II. With the optional extra-credit high notes. Ridiculously amazing.

Memorable Fan Tribute in the Final Weeks: Someone gave Constantine these cake pop things that were UNREAL. Worth every calorie.

Farewell Party: Our closing party was at a hotel off Times Square. Everyone looked amazing! We had a ball! Such a wonderful group of people. Also, before the last show, Vasthy made a closing video that she showed the whole cast. It was awesome :)

Most Exciting Celebrity Visitor: Beyoncé. Hands down. She was humble, gracious, and unbelievably stunning. That's a class act.

Special Backstage Rituals: The boys singing offstage right during "Believer" always messed around with the ladies on stage. They'd do anything to try and get their attention, and it got pretty hysterical :) It usually involved some booty pops and inappropriate gesturing.

Favorite Moment During the Final Weeks: One of our swings, Karen Hyland, used to send around these Top Ten lists to everyone in the show. They usually had to do with something going on with *Ghost* at the time. But in our final week, our director Matthew made his own Top Ten list that he sent to the theatre. The list touched on the various aspects of our run, some funny memories we had as a cast, and the upcoming closing. It was both funny and heartfelt. Again, a true class act.

Favorite In-Theatre Gathering Place: The boys on the fourth floor had a fun room. They set up a little espresso station, and it routinely became a social gathering place between half hour and curtain.

Favorite Off-Site Hangout: Richard's building on 42nd street. The MIMA. It's GORGEOUS. We had a few parties on their patio courtesy of Mr. Fleeshman, including his 23rd birthday party.

Favorite Snack Foods: Fuel. The doorman was ALWAYS on the PA announcing the arrival of someone's delivery from Fuel. We were obsessed.

Mascot: Vasthy. She may be a cast member, but she was also our team mascot and constant cheerleader.

The cast gathers around a cake, celebrating 100 Broadway performances July 18, 2012.

Favorite Therapies: Ricola and a sensible foam roller.

Memorable Ad-Lib: We stopped the show for almost an hour once due to tech problems. It was in the middle of the first big production number, "More." It takes place in Sam and Carl's office. When we finally resumed the play, our fearless British leader portraying Sam Wheat walked on stage and apologized to his secretary for arriving late. He said something along the lines of "Sorry we're so late, we had trouble with the lift." Aside from fact that that line is NOT in the script of *Ghost the Musical*, Americans hardly ever refer to an elevator as a "lift." Needless to say, this ad-lib was hysterical.

Memorable Press Encounter: My *Playbill Yearbook* interview was really fun ;)

Memorable Stage Door Fan Encounter: A young lady named Heather Card participated via Twitter in the Doodle Contest I put together (I let the company of *Ghost* deface my old headshots for fun). She gave me the drawings in person one day outside the theater.

Sweet girl. And I was so touched that she wanted to participate!

What Did You Think of the Web Buzz on Your Show: We had fun buzz on Twitter. And our cast was great about keeping spirits up via the internet.

Fastest Costume Change: Jeremy Davis, out of Furgeson and into Fantasy Banker for "Outta Here." I'd say it was about 25 seconds.

Catchphrase Only the Company Would Recognize: "Blowies! For everyone!" Courtesy of Vasthy and Connie.

Sweetheart Within the Company: Jen Noble. Sweetest girl on earth. Heart of gold. No couples though.

Orchestra Member Who Played the Most Instruments: Hideaki Aomori (Woodwinds, all of them.)

Orchestra Member Who Played the Most Consecutive Performances Without a Sub: JJ or Eric are our best guesses :)

Best In-House Parody Lyric: Instead of "Shove 'em in your gut. Shove 'em down here..." we preferred "Shove 'em in your butt. Shove 'em down here."

Company In-Jokes: Jeremy Davis was an AMAZING understudy for Carl.

Understudy Anecdote: Swinging this show was always an interesting experience, largely due to the two treadmills that ran the length of our stage. The cast got to practice on them during tech and dress rehearsals. By the time we were running the show, they navigated them like pros. The swings, however, had to learn the hard way. In front of a paying audience. I almost ate it HARD on several occasions. Either that, or we were catapulted offstage by the moving floor. Rough.

Nicknames: Jason Babinsky was routinely mistaken for Jeremy, so we just started calling him "Jeremy." And we called Connie, "Curnty."

Embarrassing Moments: Every time we had to stop and start again due to the tech problems. That was no fun.

Coolest Things About Being in This Show: Being a part of the magic tricks. That was really cool. Also, the whole show felt like we were in a music video. And of course, queening out during "Outta Here." :)

(L-R): Richard Fleeshman, Caissie Levy, Bryce Pinkham and Da'Vine Joy Randolph toast the 100th performance.

Glengarry Glen Ross

First Preview: October 19, 2012. Opened: December 8, 2012.
Limited Engagement. Closed January 20, 2013 after 48 Previews and 45 Performances.

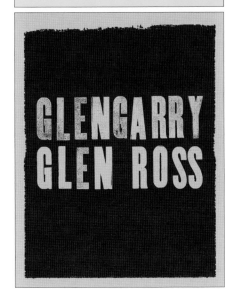

PLAYBILL

A revival of the Pulitzer-winning drama about the sweaty desperation of a group of real estate salesmen who are competing with each other to make the big sale and keep their jobs. Speaking in profane, slice-of-life Mamet dialogue, they hatch a scheme to burglarize their own office, steal their supervisor's sales "leads," and sell them to a competitor.

CAST

(in order of appearance)

Shelly Levene	AL PACINO
John Williamson	DAVID HARBOUR
Dave Moss	JOHN C. McGINLEY
George Aaronow	RICHARD SCHIFF
Richard Roma	BOBBY CANNAVALE
James Lingk	JEREMY SHAMOS
Baylen	MURPHY GUYER

TIME

1983

UNDERSTUDIES

For Levene, Aaronow:
MURPHY GUYER
For Williamson, Moss, Roma,
Lingk and Baylen:
C.J. WILSON

---

⑤ GERALD SCHOENFELD THEATRE

236 West 45th Street
A Shubert Organization Theatre

Philip J. Smith, *Chairman*   Robert E. Wankel, *President*

JEFFREY RICHARDS   JERRY FRANKEL   JAM THEATRICALS

LUIGI & ROSE CAIOLA   GUTTERMAN CHERNOFF   UNIVERSAL PICTURES STAGE PRODUCTIONS
AMY & PHIL MICKELSON   PATTY BAKER   MARK S. GOLUB & DAVID S. GOLUB   KEN GREINER
MEG HERMAN   KATHLEEN K. JOHNSON   STEPHANIE P. McCLELLAND   HARVEY WEINSTEIN
JAMES FULD JR./KIRMSER PONTURO FUND   KIT SEIDEL/MYLA LERNER   WILL TRICE   GFOUR PRODUCTIONS

in association with RPMedia Company

present

AL PACINO

BOBBY CANNAVALE
DAVID HARBOUR   RICHARD SCHIFF

in

GLENGARRY GLEN ROSS

by

DAVID MAMET

with

JOHN C. McGINLEY   JEREMY SHAMOS   MURPHY GUYER

Scenic Design	Costume Design	Lighting Design
EUGENE LEE	JESS GOLDSTEIN	JAMES F. INGALLS

Casting	Technical Supervisor
TELSEY + COMPANY	HUDSON THEATRICAL ASSOCIATES
WILLIAM CANTLER, CSA	

Press Representative	Production Stage Manager	General Manager
IRENE GANDY/ALANA KARPOFF	STEPHEN M. KAUS	RICHARDS/CLIMAN, INC.

Directed by

DANIEL SULLIVAN

Originally Produced on Broadway by Elliot Martin, The Shubert Organization, Arnold Bernhard and the Goodman Theater

12/8/12

Seated (L-R): Bobby Cannavale,
Al Pacino,
John C. McGinley,
Murphy Guyer.
Standing (L-R):
Jeremy Shamos,
David Harbour,
Richard Schiff.

Photo by Scott Landis

Glengarry Glen Ross

Al Pacino
Shelly Levene

Bobby Cannavale
Richard Roma

David Harbour
John Williamson

Richard Schiff
George Aaronow

John C. McGinley
Dave Moss

Jeremy Shamos
James Lingk

Murphy Guyer
Baylen; u/s Levene, Aaronow

C.J. Wilson
u/s Williamson, Moss, Roma, Lingk, Baylen

David Mamet
Playwright

Daniel Sullivan
Director

Eugene Lee
Scenic Designer

Jess Goldstein
Costume Designer

James F. Ingalls
Lighting Designer

Bernard Telsey
*Telsey + Company
Casting*

Neil A. Mazzella
**Hudson Theatrical
Associates**
*Technical
Supervision*

David R. Richards and Tamar Haimes
Richards/Climan, Inc.
General Management

Jeffrey Richards
Producer

Jerry Frankel
Producer

Arny Granat
Jam Theatricals
Producer

Steve Traxler
Jam Theatricals
Producer

Luigi and Rose Caiola
Producers

Jay and Cindy Gutterman
Producers

Cathy Chernoff
Producer

Patty Baker
Good Productions
Producer

Mark S. Golub
Producer

David S. Golub
Producer

Ken Greiner
Producer

Meg Herman
Producer

Kathleen K. Johnson
Producer

**Stephanie P.
McClelland**
Producer

Harvey Weinstein
Producer

James Fuld, Jr.
Producer

Glengarry Glen Ross

Fran Kirmser
Kirmser Ponturo
Fund
Producer

Tony Ponturo
Kirmser Ponturo
Fund
Producer

Kit Seidel
Producer

Myla Lerner
Producer

Will Trice
Producer

Kenneth Greenblatt
GFour Productions
Producer

Seth Greenleaf
GFour Productions
Producer

Alan Glist
GFour Productions
Producer

David Beckerman
GFour Productions
Producer

Marc Goldman
GFour Productions
Producer

Rick Nicita
RPMedia Company
Associate Producer

Paula Wagner
RPMedia Company
Associate Producer

DOORMAN
Dave McGaughran

Photos by Brian Mapp

CREW
Seated (L-R): Ronald Schwier, Leslie Ann Kilian, Steve McDonald, "The Buddha" (representing Stephen M. Kaus, Production Stage Manager), Deanna Weiner, Richard Klinger, Emily Merriweather
Standing (L-R): Paul Ludick, Susan Checklick, Alex Lyu Volckhausen (Stage Manager)

FRONT OF HOUSE
Lying on the Floor: Joe Cabatit
Seated (L-R): Alexandria Williams, Lisa Boyd, Gillian Sheffler, Michael Rhodus, Francine Kramer, Raya Konyk, Karen Diaz, Jonathan Green, Ramona Maben, Amber Lyn Hill
Standing (L-R): Alan Deeb, Pep Speed, Anthony Martinez, Topher McLean, Paul Brown, Malcolm Perry, David Conte

Glengarry Glen Ross

Al Pacino
as Shelly Levene

Richard Schiff
as George Aaronow

Bobby Cannavale
as Richard Roma

Photos by Scott Landis

Golden Boy

First Preview: November 9, 2012. Opened: December 6, 2012.
Limited Engagement. Closed January 20, 2013 after 30 Previews and 53 Performances.

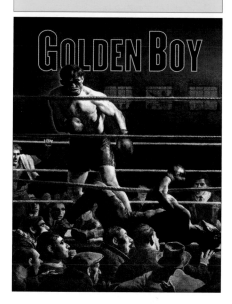

PLAYBILL

A 75th anniversary revival of Clifford Odets' classic about the conflict of art and commerce. Joe Bonaparte has been trained as a classical violinist, but the demons in his heart drive him to pursue the fame and wealth of being a champion prizefighter even if it means the destruction of his skilled and delicate hands—and possibly his soul. Odets surrounds Joe with finely-etched supporting characters: his desperate manager, his grieving father, his lively brother-in-law, his wise trainer, a frightening mobster, and a punch-drunk fellow boxer who has become all the things Joe is most afraid of becoming.

CAST
(in order of speaking)

Tom Moody	DANNY MASTROGIORGIO
Lorna Moon	YVONNE STRAHOVSKI
Joe Bonaparte	SETH NUMRICH
Tokio	DANNY BURSTEIN
Mr. Carp	JONATHAN HADARY
Siggie	MICHAEL ARONOV
Mr. Bonaparte	TONY SHALHOUB
Anna	DAGMARA DOMINCZYK
Frank Bonaparte	LUCAS CALEB ROONEY
Roxy Gottlieb	NED EISENBERG
Eddie Fuseli	ANTHONY CRIVELLO
Pepper White	BRAD FLEISCHER
Mickey	DAVID WOHL
Call Boy	KARL GLUSMAN
Sam	DION MUCCIACITO
Lewis	DEMOSTHENES CHRYSAN
Drake	SEAN CULLEN
Driscoll	VAYU O'DONNELL

Continued on next page

The Playbill Broadway Yearbook 2012-2013

⑧ **BELASCO THEATRE**
111 West 44th Street
A Shubert Organization Theatre
Philip J. Smith, *Chairman*   Robert E. Wankel, *President*

LINCOLN CENTER THEATER
under the direction of
André Bishop and Bernard Gersten
presents

GOLDEN BOY

By
Clifford Odets

with (in alphabetical order)

Michael Aronov   Danny Burstein   Demosthenes Chrysan

Anthony Crivello   Sean Cullen   Dagmara Dominczyk   Ned Eisenberg

Brad Fleischer   Karl Glusman   Jonathan Hadary   Daniel Jenkins

Danny Mastrogiorgio   Dion Mucciacito   Seth Numrich   Vayu O'Donnell

Lucas Caleb Rooney   Tony Shalhoub   Yvonne Strahovski   David Wohl

Sets	Costumes	Lighting
Michael Yeargan	**Catherine Zuber**	**Donald Holder**

Sound	Fight Director	Stage Manager	Casting
Peter John Still and Marc Salzberg	**B.H. Barry**	**Jennifer Rae Moore**	**Daniel Swee**

Executive Director of Development & Planning	Director of Marketing	General Press Agent
Hattie K. Jutagir	**Linda Mason Ross**	**Philip Rinaldi**

Managing Director	Production Manager
Adam Siegel	**Jeff Hamlin**

Directed by
Bartlett Sher

This production is dedicated to the memory of Ben Gazzara.
Sponsored by American Express.
Leadership support provided by The Peter Jay Sharp Foundation's Special Fund for LCT.
Major support provided by The Blanche and Irving Laurie Foundation.
American Airlines is the Official Airline of Lincoln Center Theater.
LCT wishes to express its appreciation to Theatre Development Fund for its support of this production.

12/6/12

(L-R): Tony Shalhoub, Seth Numrich, Dagmara Dominczyk, Michael Aronov

Photo by Paul Kolnik

Golden Boy

Cast Continued

Clifford Odets

Barker ....DANIEL JENKINS
Boxers, Trainers, Gangsters,
    Cops ....BRAD FLEISCHER,
        KARL GLUSMAN, DANIEL JENKINS,
        DION MUCCIACITO, VAYU O'DONNELL,
        LUCAS CALEB ROONEY, DAVID WOHL

TIME AND PLACE
New York City, 1936-1937

Assistant Stage Manager ...LISA ANN CHERNOFF

UNDERSTUDIES
For Tom Moody:
SEAN CULLEN
For Lorna Moon, Anna:
DIANE DAVIS
For Joe Bonaparte, Pepper White:
KARL GLUSMAN
For Tokio:
VAYU O'DONNELL
For Siggie, Frank Bonaparte:
DION MUCCIACITO
For Mr. Bonaparte:
DEMOSTHENES CHRYSAN
For Mickey, Lewis, Drake, Barker:
CHRISTOPHER McHALE
For Call Boy, Sam, Driscoll:
ANDRÉS MUNAR

Photo by Paul Kolnik

(L-R): Seth Numrich, and Yvonne Strahovski

CLIFFORD ODETS
1906–1963

Clifford Odets began his career in 1931 as an actor with The Group Theater, a New York company of which he was a founding member. He shortly turned to writing, and his first play for the Group, *Waiting for Lefty* (1935), immediately launched him as the most celebrated American playwright of the 1930s. *Lefty*, as well as four other major Broadway productions in that decade, introduced theater audiences to subject matter and language that had never before been heard on the American stage. This work deeply influenced generations of American playwrights to follow. Odets' other best-known plays are *Awake and Sing!, Paradise Lost, Rocket to the Moon, Night Music, Clash by Night, The Big Knife, The Country Girl* and *The Flowering Peach*. Screenplay credits include *The General Died at Dawn, None But the Lonely Heart, Humoresque, The Sweet Smell of Success* and *Story on Page One*. Directing credits include both *None But the Lonely Heart* and *Story on Page One*.

Michael Aronov
Siggie

Danny Burstein
Tokio

Demosthenes
Chrysan
Lewis

Anthony Crivello
Eddie Fuseli

Sean Cullen
Drake

Dagmara Dominczyk
Anna

Ned Eisenberg
Roxy Gottlieb

Golden Boy

Brad Fleischer
Pepper White

Karl Glusman
Call Boy

Jonathan Hadary
Mr. Carp

Daniel Jenkins
Barker

Danny Mastrogiorgio
Tom Moody

Dion Mucciacito
Sam

Seth Numrich
Joe Bonaparte

Vayu O'Donnell
Driscoll

Lucas Caleb Rooney
Frank Bonaparte

Tony Shalhoub
Mr. Bonaparte

Yvonne Strahovski
Lorna Moon

David Wohl
Mickey

Diane Davis
Understudy

Christopher McHale
Understudy

Andrés Munar
Understudy

Bartlett Sher
Director

Michael Yeargan
Sets

Catherine Zuber
Costumes

Donald Holder
Lighting

Peter John Still
Sound

Marc Salzberg
Sound

WARDROBE AND HAIR/MAKE-UP
Front Row (L-R):
Adele Miskie,
John McNulty,
Charlie Catanese
Back Row (L-R):
Sara Darneille,
Steve Chazaro,
David Grevengoed

B.H. Barry
Fight Director

André Bishop
*Artistic Director
Lincoln Center
Theater*

Bernard Gersten
*Executive Producer
Lincoln Center
Theater*

Color photos by Brian Mapp

2012-2013 AWARD

THEATRE WORLD AWARD
For Outstanding Broadway
or Off-Broadway Debut
(Yvonne Strahovski)

BOX OFFICE
(L-R): Gary Powers,
Melissa Jorgensen,
Gerard O'Brien

Golden Boy

STAGE AND COMPANY MANAGEMENT
Seated: Jennifer Rae Moore
Standing (L-R): B. Bales Karlin, Lisa Ann Chernoff, Bruce Klinger

FRONT OF HOUSE
Front Row (L-R): Michele Moyna, Marisa Gioffre, Eugenia Raines, Pamela Loetterle
Second Row (L-R): Rene Texeira, Joseph Pittman, Stephanie Wallis (Theatre Manager)
Third Row (L-R): John Hall, Bong Park
Back Row (L-R): Marisol Lugo, Keith Gartner, Maria Lugo, Kathleen Reiter

CREW
Seated (L-R): Carlos Jaramillo, Brad Olson, Mark Diaz, Laura Koch
Standing (L-R): Steve Hills, Erik Yans, Dave Karlson, George Dummitt, Wally Flores, Dylan Foley, Matt Maloney

Golden Boy

ADMINISTRATIVE STAFF

MANAGING DIRECTOR ....ADAM SIEGEL
General Manager ....Jessica Niebanck
Associate General Manager ....Meghan Lantzy
General Management Assistant ....Laura Stuart
Facilities Manager ....Alex Mustelier
Associate Facilities Manager ....Michael Assalone
GENERAL PRESS AGENT ....PHILIP RINALDI
Press Associate ....Amanda Dekker
Press Assistant ....Michael Sanders
PRODUCTION MANAGER ....JEFF HAMLIN
Associate Production Manager ....Paul Smithyman
EXECUTIVE DIRECTOR OF
DEVELOPMENT AND
PLANNING ....HATTIE K. JUTAGIR
Associate Director of Development ......Rachel Norton
Manager of Special Events and Advisor,
LCT Young Angels ....Karin Schall
Grants Writer ....Neal Brilliant
Manager, Patron Program ....Sheilaja Rao
Assistant to the Executive Director of
Development and
Planning ....Raelyn R. Lagerstrom
Development Associate/
LCT Young Angels &
Special Events ....Jenny Rosenbluth-Stoll
Development Assistant/
Patron Program ....Sydney Rais-Sherman
DIRECTOR OF FINANCE ....DAVID S. BROWN
Controller ....Susan Knox
Systems Manager ....Stacy Valentine
Finance Assistant ....Kristen Parker
DIRECTOR
OF MARKETING ....LINDA MASON ROSS
Associate Director of Marketing ....Ashley Dunn
Digital Marketing Associate.............Rebecca Leshin
Marketing Assistant ....David Cannon
DIRECTOR OF EDUCATION ....KATI KOERNER
Associate Director of
Education ....Alexandra Lopez
Education Assistant ....Jennifer Wintzer
Assistant to the
Executive Producer ....Barbara Hourigan
Office Manager ....Brian Hashimoto
Messenger ....Esau Burgess
Reception ....Anna Strasser, Michelle Metcalf

ARTISTIC STAFF

ASSOCIATE DIRECTORS ......GRACIELA DANIELE,
NICHOLAS HYTNER,
JACK O'BRIEN,
SUSAN STROMAN,
DANIEL SULLIVAN
RESIDENT DIRECTOR.............BARTLETT SHER
DRAMATURG and DIRECTOR,
LCT DIRECTORS LAB.........ANNE CATTANEO
CASTING DIRECTOR ....DANIEL SWEE, CSA
MUSICAL THEATER ASSOCIATE
PRODUCER ....IRA WEITZMAN
ARTISTIC DIRECTOR/LCT3 ....PAIGE EVANS
Artistic Administrator ....Julia Judge
Casting Associate ....Camille Hickman

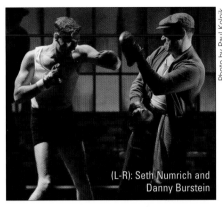

(L-R): Seth Numrich and Danny Burstein

Photo by Paul Kolnik

LCT3 Associate ....Natasha Sinha
Lab Assistant ....Kate Marvin

SPECIAL SERVICES

Advertising ....Serino Coyne/Jim Russek,
Roger Micone, Nick Nolte, Nathaniel Hill
Principal Poster Artist ....James McMullan
Counsel.........................Charles H. Googe, Esq.;
Carol Kaplan, Esq.
and Caroline Barnard, Esq. of
Paul, Weiss, Rifkind, Wharton & Garrison
Immigration Counsel ....Theodore Ruthizer, Esq.;
Mark D. Koestler, Esq.
of Kramer, Levin, Naftalis & Frankel LLP
Labor Counsel ....Michael F. McGahan, Esq.
of Epstein, Becker & Green, P.C.
Auditor..........................Frederick Martens, C.P.A.
Lutz & Carr, L.L.P.
Insurance ....Jennifer Brown of
DeWitt Stern Group
Production Photographer ....Paul Kolnik
Video Services ....Fresh Produce Productions/
Frank Basile
Consulting Architect ....Hugh Hardy,
H3 Hardy Collaboration Architecture
Construction Manager ....Yorke Construction
Payroll Service ....Castellana Services, Inc.
Merchandising ....Marquee Merchandise, LLC/
Matt Murphy

STAFF FOR *GOLDEN BOY*

COMPANY MANAGER ....BRUCE KLINGER
Assistant Director ....Noah Himmelstein
Associate Set Designer ....Mikiko Suzuki MacAdams
Assistant Set Designer ....Jisun Kim
Assistant Costume Designers ....David Newell,
Ryan Park
Assistant Lighting Designers................Caroline Chao,
Jeanne Koenig, Karen Spahn
Assistant Sound Designer ....Benjamin Furiga
Props ....Faye Armon-Troncoso
Props Assistant ....Mallory Paige Marsh
Production Carpenter ....John Weingart
Production Electrician ....David Karlson
Production Propertyman ....Mark Dignam
Production Soundman ....Wallace Flores
Hair and Wig Designer ....Jon Carter
Make-up and Special FX Designer ....Angelina Avallone
Associate Make-up and
Special FX Designer ....Barry Berger
Hair and Make-up Supervisor ....John McNulty

Wardrobe Supervisor ....Patrick Bevilacqua
Dressers ....Charlie Catanese, Steve Chazaro,
Erik Medinilla, Adele Miskie
Production Assistant ....B. Bales Karlin
Columbia Directing Fellow ....Tyne Rafaeli
Fight Captain ....Daniel Jenkins

Dialect Coach ....Deborah Hecht

Technical supervision by
William Nagle and Patrick Merryman

CREDITS

Scenery and scenic effects built, painted, electrified and automated by Show Motion, Inc., Milford, CT. Costumes by Euro Co Costumes, Inc.; John Cowles; Libby Villanova; Center Stage. Men's tailoring by Brian Hemesath; Angels, The Costumiers; and Arel Studio. Custom knitwear by Maria Ficalora. Millinery by Arnold Levine. Custom footwear by T.O. Dey. Lighting equipment from PRG Lighting. Sound equipment by Masque Sound. Special thanks to Steve Farhood, Matt Farrago, Harold Lederman, Tommy Gallagher, Tyrone Jackson, Joe Cortez, Ron Stevens, Jill Diamond, Katie Chew, Ryan Gohsman and Joo Won Lee.

SONG CREDITS

"Kisetsu" by Somei Satoh; "You Took Advantage of Me" Music by Richard Rodgers, Lyrics by Lorenz Hart. This selection is used by special arrangement with Rodgers & Hammerstein: an Imagem Company, www.rnh.com. All Rights Reserved; "Violin Concerto" by Johannes Brahms; "Ridin' Along the Moscowa" by Philippe Brun; "Netcha's Dream" by Coleman Hawkins, Used by permission of The Music of Coleman Hawkins; "Violin Concerto" and "John's Book of Alleged Dances" by John Adams, by arrangement with Hendon Music, Inc., a Boosey & Hawkes company, publisher and copyright owner; "Some of these Days" by Shelton Brooks.

Golden Boy
SCRAPBOOK

Correspondent: Brad Fleischer, "Pepper White."

Memorable Opening Night Letter, Fax or Note: From my buddy Rajiv, reminding me that Tom Brady goes through this every Sunday and comes out on top!

Opening Night Gifts: A bottle of vodka that I had never heard of before... and it's good!

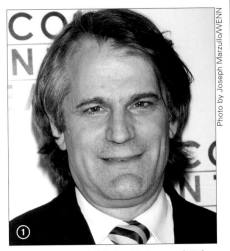

Most Exciting Celebrity Visitor and What They Did/Said: The daughter of John Garfield, who was in the original production of *Golden Boy* and played Joe in the '52 revival. She just loved the show.

Who Has Done the Most Shows in Their Career: Not sure, probably is a 4 or 5 way tie between the three Dans (Burstein, Mastrogiorgio, and Jenkins) and the two Tonys (Shalhoub and Crivello).

Special Backstage Rituals: I always hear "cheers" from Lorna before the start of the second act.

Favorite Moment During Each Performance: There are a bunch, but mine is when Tokio gets Bonaparte ready to fight at the end of act two after his father has left.

Favorite In-Theatre Gathering Place: Probably the stage management office.

Favorite Off-Site Hangout: The Long Room across from the theatre.

Favorite Snack Food: Every candy available.

Favorite Therapy: Gotta be a massage.

Most Memorable Ad-Lib: Too many already.

Record Number of Cell Phone Rings, Cell Phone Photos or Texting Incidents During a Performance: Three in one act.

What Did You Think of the Internet Buzz on Your Show?: From what I understand, people are loving *Golden Boy*. It's great to be a part of something that feels truly special. I personally

think it's amazing to have such an outstanding ensemble of 19 actors in one show. And there isn't a single person who isn't incredible.

Latest Audience Arrival: Probably the end of the second scene, about 30 minutes into the show.

Fastest Costume Change: Has to go to Yvonne and Seth. They have many huge changes that have to be done in under 30 seconds.

Busiest Day at the Box Office: Friday and Saturday night. Although the matinees are selling well too!

Memorable Directorial Note: I want everyone to continue to grow as the show opens. Then, I will come watch and tell you not to do that.

Company In-Jokes: Also...breast notices.... Wish I could elaborate, but then it wouldn't be an inside joke, now would it?

Company Legends: Karl Glusman.

Understudy Anecdote: Too many already... Just that it is a real collaboration!

Nicknames: Franking it up.

Sweethearts Within the Company: No joke, everybody... but top honors go to Jonathan Hadary, Danny Burstein, Captain Dan Jenkins, Ned Eisenberg and Michael Aronov.

Embarrassing Moments: Probably when, during an early preview, the set wouldn't move and people were stuck on stage as the curtain came down early.

Ghostly Encounters Backstage: None so far, although the fifth floor of this theatre is terrifying.

Coolest Thing About Being in This Show: Thirsty Thursdays, and the fact that the whole company truly gets along.

1. Director Bartlett Sher at the opening night party.
2. Together wherever they go: Tyne Daly and Jonathan Hadary, also at the party.
3. Ready to rumble (L-R): Backstage with David Wohl, Brad Fleischer and Karl Glusman.
4. Light the lights! It's opening night.
5. Behing the scenes: Lucas Caleb Rooney (front) sizes up castmate Karl Glusman.
6. Husband and wife Danny Burstein and Rebecca Luker celebrate opening night.
7. Tony Shalhoub and wife Brooke Adams on opening night.

Gore Vidal's The Best Man

First Preview: March 6, 2012. Opened: April 1, 2012.
Closed September 9, 2012 after 31 Previews and 185 Performances.

PLAYBILL®

A starry revival of Vidal's drama, which opens the door on back-room politics during a fictional presidential party convention set in 1960. The ruthless Senator Cantwell will do anything including throw mud to secure his party's nomination. His more thoughtful and restrained opponent, Secretary Russell, wants to win on his merits, but is told that he'll never get the chance to win unless he gets in the gutter with Cantwell. The candidates tell each other "May the best man win," but Vidal's script keeps the audience guessing until the last minute about exactly who will be the title character.

CAST

The Party

Former President
    Arthur "Artie" Hockstader .JAMES EARL JONES
Mrs. Sue-Ellen Gamadge,
    Chairman of the
    Women's Division ....ANGELA LANSBURY
Senator Clyde Carlin ....DAKIN MATTHEWS

The Candidates

Secretary William Russell .JOHN LARROQUETTE
Alice Russell, *his wife* ....CYBILL SHEPHERD
Dick Jensen, *his campaign manager* ...MARK BLUM
Catherine, *a campaign aide* ......ANGELICA PAGE
Senator Joseph Cantwell ....JOHN STAMOS
Mabel Cantwell, *his wife* ....KRISTIN DAVIS
Mrs. Cantwell, *his mother* .....DONNA HANOVER
Don Blades,
    his campaign manager ....COREY BRILL

Continued on next page

---

⑤ GERALD SCHOENFELD THEATRE

236 West 45th Street
A Shubert Organization Theatre

Philip J. Smith, *Chairman*   **Robert E. Wankel,** *President*

Jeffrey Richards   Jerry Frankel   INFINITY Stages

Universal Pictures Stage Productions   Barbara Manocherian/Michael Palitz
Kathleen K. Johnson   Andy Sandberg   Ken Mahoney/The Broadway Consortium
Fifty Church Street Productions   Larry Hirschhorn/Bennu Productions
Patty Baker   Paul Boskind and Martian Entertainment   Wendy Federman
Mark S. Golub & David S. Golub   Cricket Hooper Jiranek   Stewart F. Lane & Bonnie Comley
Carl Moellenberg   Harold Thau   Will Trice

Present

JAMES EARL JONES   JOHN LARROQUETTE
CYBILL SHEPHERD   JOHN STAMOS
KRISTIN DAVIS   JEFFERSON MAYS   MARK BLUM
and ANGELA LANSBURY

in

with

CURTIS BILLINGS   COREY BRILL   TONY CARLIN   DONNA HANOVER
SHERMAN HOWARD   OLJA HRUSTIC   BILL KUX   JAMES LECESNE
ANGELICA PAGE   FRED PARKER   AMY TRIBBEY

and

DAKIN MATTHEWS

Scenic Design	Costume Design	Lighting Design	Original Music/Sound Design	Projection Design
Derek McLane	Ann Roth	Kenneth Posner	John Gromada	Peter Nigrini

Hair Design	Casting	Technical Supervision	Production Stage Manager
Josh Marquette	Telsey + Company Will Cantler, CSA	Hudson Theatrical Productions	Matthew Farrell

Press Representative	Company Manager	General Manager	Associate Producer
Jeffrey Richards Associates Irene Gandy/Alana Karpoff	Brig Berney	Richards/Climan, Inc.	Stephanie Rosenberg

Directed by

MICHAEL WILSON

www.TheBestManOnBroadway.com

7/9/12

(L-R): Kristin Davis, Elizabeth Ashley, Cybill Shepherd, Amy Tribbey, Donna Hanover

Photo by Joan Marcus

Gore Vidal's The Best Man

The Visitors
Dr. Artinian, *a psychiatrist* ....BILL KUX
Sheldon Marcus ....JEFFERSON MAYS

The Press
John Malcolm,
   the News commentator ....SHERMAN HOWARD
Howie Annenberg, *a reporter from*
   the Philadelphia Inquirer ....FRED PARKER
Frank Pearson, *a reporter from*
   the New York Daily Mirror ....TONY CARLIN
Barbara Brinkley, *a reporter from*
   United Press International ..DONNA HANOVER
Mitch Graham, *a reporter from*
   the Washington Post ....JAMES LECESNE

The Hotel Staff
Bellboy ....CURTIS BILLINGS
Cleaning Woman ....AMY TRIBBEY
Security ....TONY CARLIN

Additional Press, Hotel Staff,
   Campaign Workers,
   and Delegates ....CURTIS BILLINGS,
     TONY CARLIN, OLJA HRUSTIC,
     BILL KUX, JAMES LECESNE,
     FRED PARKER, AMY TRIBBEY

UNDERSTUDIES

For Howie Annenberg, a reporter from the
Philadelphia Inquirer; Don Blades, News
Commentator:
CURTIS BILLINGS

For Senator Joseph Cantwell, News Commentator:
TONY CARLIN

For Alice Russell, Mrs. Sue-Ellen Gamadge:
DONNA HANOVER

For Secretary William Russell, Dick Jensen:
SHERMAN HOWARD

For Assistant to Barbara Brinkley, Cleaning Woman:
OLJA HRUSTIC

For Senator Clyde Carlin, Bellboy, Photographer,
Campaign Worker, Bell Person, Cameraperson:
BILL KUX

For Dick Jensen, Sheldon Marcus, Dr. Artinian,
Additional Hotel Staff, Reporter:
JAMES LECESNE

For Ex-President Arthur "Artie" Hockstader:
DAKIN MATTHEWS

John Stamos as Senator Joseph Cantwell

Photo by Joan Marcus

For Frank Pearson, a reporter from the *New York
Daily Mirror*; Security; Mitch Graham, a reporter
from the *Washington Post*:
FRED PARKER

For Barbara Brinkley, a reporter from *United Press
International*; Mrs. Cantwell; Catherine; Additional
Hotel Staff; Reporter; Mabel Cantwell:
AMY TRIBBEY

Photo by Joan Marcus

(L-R): Elizabeth Ashley and Cybill Shepherd

SETTING

TIME: July, 1960

PLACE: The Presidential Convention,
Philadelphia, Pennsylvania

Gore Vidal's The Best Man

James Earl Jones
*Former President
Arthur Hockstader*

Angela Lansbury
*Mrs. Sue-Ellen
Gamadge*

John Larroquette
*Secretary William
Russell*

Cybill Shepherd
Alice Russell

John Stamos
*Senator Joseph
Cantwell*

Kristin Davis
Mabel Cantwell

Jefferson Mays
Sheldon Marcus

Mark Blum
Dick Jensen

Curtis Billings
*Bellboy,
Photographer,
Delegate, Campaign
Worker*

Corey Brill
Don Blades

Tony Carlin
*Frank Pearson,
Delegate, Hotel
Security*

Donna Hanover
*Barbara Brinkley,
Mrs. Cantwell*

Sherman Howard
*John Malcolm, The
News Commentator*

Olja Hrustic
*Bell Person,
Cameraperson*

Bill Kux
*Dr. Artinian,
Delegate*

James Lecesne
*Mitch Graham,
Delegate*

Dakin Matthews
Senator Clyde Carlin

Angelica Page
Catherine

Fred Parker
*Howie Annenberg,
Delegate*

Amy Tribbey
*Assistant to Barbara
Brinkley, Cleaning
Woman*

Gore Vidal
*Playwright
1925-2012*

Michael Wilson
Director

Derek McLane
Set Design

Ann Roth
Costume Design

Kenneth Posner
Lighting Design

John Gromada
*Composer/Sound
Design*

Peter Nigrini
Projection Design

Josh Marquette
Hair Design

Neil A. Mazzella
Hudson Theatrical
Associates
*Technical
Supervision*

Bernard Telsey
Telsey + Company
Casting

David R. Richards, Tamar Haimes
Richards/Climan, Inc.
General Management

Jeffrey Richards
Producer

Jerry Frankel
Producer

Darren Bagert
Infinity Stages
Producer

Gore Vidal's The Best Man

Barbara
Manocherian
Producer

Michael Palitz
Producer

Kathleen K. Johnson
Producer

Andy Sandberg
Producer

Ken Mahoney
Producer

Van Dean, Kenny Howard
The Broadway Consortium
Producers

Rick Costello
Producer

Larry Hirschhorn
Producer

Matthew Masten
Bennu Productions
Producer

Steven Baker
Bennu Productions
Producer

Patty Baker
Producer

Paul Boskind and
Martian
Entertainment
Producer

Wendy Federman
Producer

Mark S. Golub
Producer

David S. Golub
Producer

Cricket Hooper
Jiranek
Producer

Stewart F. Lane,
Bonnie Comley
Producers

Carl Moellenberg
Producer

Harold Thau
Producer

Will Trice
Producer

Candice Bergen
Alice Russell

Kerry Butler
Mabel Cantwell

(L-R): Kristin Davis,
John Stamos

Eric McCormack
*Senator Joseph
Cantwell*

Michael McKean
Dick Jensen

Elizabeth Ashley
*Mrs. Sue-Ellen
Gamadge*

Gore Vidal's The Best Man

Photos by Brian Mapp

FRONT OF HOUSE
Front Row (L-R):
Roz Nyman, Lisa Boyd,
Amber Hill
Second Row (L-R):
David Conte, Raya Konyk,
Rosetta Jlelaty,
Alexandria Williams
Third Row (L-R): Shatail
Williams, Denise DeMirjian
Fourth Row (L-R): Michael
Rhodus, Michael Santoro,
Jennifer Ewing, James Teal
Top Row (L-R): Pep Speed,
Anthony Martinez,
Paul Brown

MANAGEMENT
(L-R): Matthew Farrell,
Ken McGee,
Brig Berney

CREW
Lying Down: Ken McGee
Seated (L-R): Kim Butler-Gilkeson, Lolly Totero, Flynn Earl Jones, Daniel Paul, Andrea Gonzalez, Matthew Farrell
Standing (L-R): Tim McWilliams, Steve McDonald, Wayne Smith, Leslie Ann Kilian, Maeve Fiona Butler, Laura Beattie, Linda Lee, Mark Jones,
Jeanette Harrington, Jay Penfield

STAFF FOR *GORE VIDAL'S THE BEST MAN*

GENERAL MANAGEMENT
RICHARDS/CLIMAN, INC.
David R. Richards   Tamar Haimes
Michael Sag   Kyle Bonder
Jessica Fried   Ashley Rodbro

COMPANY MANAGER
Brig Berney

GENERAL PRESS REPRESENTATIVE
JEFFREY RICHARDS ASSOCIATES
Irene Gandy   Alana Karpoff   Ryan Hallett

PRODUCTION MANAGEMENT
HUDSON THEATRICAL ASSOCIATES
Neil A. Mazzella   Sam Ellis   Irene Wang
Walter Murphy   Corky Boyd   Jillian Oliver

CASTING
TELSEY + COMPANY
Bernie Telsey CSA, Will Cantler CSA,
David Vaccari CSA, Bethany Knox CSA,
Craig Burns CSA, Tiffany Little Canfield CSA,
Rachel Hoffman CSA, Justin Huff CSA,
Patrick Goodwin CSA, Abbie Brady-Dalton CSA,
David Morris, Cesar A. Rocha, Andrew Femenella,
Karyn Casl, Kristina Bramhall, Jessie Malone

PRODUCTION STAGE MANAGER	Matthew Farrell
Stage Manager	Jason Brouillard
Assistant Director	David Alpert
Assistant Producer	Michael Crea
SDC Observer	Jessica Rose McVay
Makeup Designer	Angelina Avallone
Dialect Coach	Kate Wilson
Associate Scenic Designer	Aimee B. Dombo
Assistant Scenic Designer	Erica Hemminger
Associate Costume Designer	Matthew Pachtman
Assistant to Ms. Roth	Irma Escobar
Associate Lighting Designer	John Viesta
Associate Projection Designer	C. Andrew Bauer
Assistant Projection Designer	Dan Scully

Gore Vidal's The Best Man

SCRAPBOOK

Correspondent: James Lecesne, "Mitch Graham"

Most Vivid Memory of the Final Performance: Watching from the wings as James Earl Jones took his final bow and then called us all out onto the stage to join him.

Memorable Quote from Farewell Stage Speech: Michael Wilson (Director) quoting Gore Vidal's words from the play..."But there's hope in this: Every act we make sets off a chain of reaction which—never ends. And if we are reasonably good, well, there is some consolation in that, a kind of immortality."

Memorable Note in the Final Weeks: Eric McCormack, who played Joe Cantwell, sent us all a note with his picture on the floor of the Democratic National Convention. Such a thrill to see how theatre and politics can commingle and inform our actions—even after the curtain comes down.

Farewell Gift: I got to keep my socks!!

Most Exciting Celebrity Visitor: Gore Vidal came to visit us during rehearsal, and that was a thrill. He wasn't that well physically, but he sat with us for two hours regaling us with stories about politics and the theatre and answering all our questions about the play. My favorite quote of his: "The human factor doesn't favor us as Americans."

Special Backstage Rituals: For me, I couldn't properly go on without touching hands with the dressers up and down the stairwell backstage. "Lady-skin" is what I called it and I gathered it every night before I went on—my good fortune in hand. Corey Brill, Fred Parker and I (and occasionally others) executed an impromptu dance routine every night during the Act II scene change—with music.

Favorite Moment During the Final Weeks (On Stage or Off): Angela Lansbury and Kerry Butler returned to see the show during those final weeks. They were both such shining lights, both on stage and off, and to see them in the audience lit us up all over again.

Favorite In-Theatre Gathering Place: The green room in the basement was the scene of much gathering throughout the production. It was just a loose arrangement of sofas and folding chairs, but it became the scene of countless cups of coffee and cakes, where many books got read and then discussed and the place where many laughs were had.

Favorite Off-Site Hangout: The Glass House!!

Favorite Snack Food: Cake. Seemed like someone was always having a birthday or there was some reason to celebrate—with cake!!

Favorite Therapy: The producers generously set it up so that cast members could receive twenty-minute massages. Walking up and down six flights of stairs was no picnic, but the weekly massages and physical therapy made it almost worth it.

Memorable Stage Door Fan Encounter: My best friend from grammar school!! What a surprise!

Memorable Press Encounter: At the first press conference: When Eric McCormack was asked what made him take the part, he replied, "They had me at Earl."

Catchphrase Only the Company Would Recognize: "F#*k that orange."

Sweetheart Within the Company: Kerry Butler, without a doubt. The warmest, kindest, most enthusiastic company member.

Memorable Directorial Note: "Don't eat the olives."

Embarrassing Moment: Not realizing that the sandwich was an actual prop in the show, I ate it one evening. When the time came for its moment, it was missing. I still haven't lived it down. The next day I bought the entire company sandwiches for lunch as my mea culpa. But still...

Coolest Thing About Being in This Show: To work with greats like James Earl Jones and Angela Lansbury was a thrill of my theatrical lifetime. They are the coolest, kindest and most generous of actors. And to watch them every single night summon their great powers and then do their thing so flawlessly was the greatest master class.

Projection Programmer ....Benjamin Keightley
Associate Sound Designer ....Alex Neumann
Sound Intern ....Chet Miller
Production Carpenter ....Robert Griffin
Carpenter/Deck Automation ....McBrien Dunbar
Production Electrician ....James Maloney
Associate Production Electrician ....Brian Maiuri
Electrician ....Jay Penfield
Production Sound Engineer ....Wayne Smith
Production Properties Coordinator ....Peter Sarafin
Assistant Properties Coordinator..............Buist Bickley
Wardrobe Supervisor ....Linda Lee
Dressers ....Laura Beattie, Kimberly Butler,
Maeve Fiona Butler, Andrea Gonzalez,
Victoria Grecki, Mark Jones,
Daniel Paul, Lolly Totero
Hair/Wig Supervisor ....Jeanette Harrington
Assistant Hair Supervisor ....Linda Rice
Production Assistants ....Wade Dooley, Lori Lundquist,
Sean Lyons, Shelley Miles
Assistant to Mr. Bagert ....Matthew Masten
Press Intern ....Thomas Raynor
Advertising ....Serino/Coyne/
Greg Corradetti, Tom Callahan,
Danielle Boyle, Drew Nebrig
Website Design/
Online Marketing Strategy ....Situation Interactive/
Damian Bazadona, John Lanasa,
Brian Hawe, Victoria Gettler,
Tom Lorenzo, Bizzy Coy, Lisa Cecchini
Interactive Marketing
Service ....Broadway's Best Shows/
Andy Drachenberg, Christopher Pineda

Banking ....City National Bank/
Michele Gibbons, Erik Piecuch
Insurance ....DeWitt Stern Group, Peter Shoemaker,
Anthony Pittari
Accountants ....Fried & Kowgios CPAs LLP/
Robert Fried, Anthony Moore
Comptroller ....Elliott Aronstam
Legal Counsel ....Lazarus and Harris LLP/
Scott Lazarus, Esq., Robert C. Harris, Esq.
Legal Clearance and Permissions
provided by ....License It
Payroll ....Castellana Services
Production Photographer ....Joan Marcus
Merchandise ....Max Merchandising
Company Mascots ....Skye, Franco, Jerry, Phyllis

Special Public Relations
Consultant ....Sunshine Sachs

CREDITS

Scenery constructed and automated by Hudson Scenic Studio. Lighting equipment from Hudson Sound and Light LLC. Sound Equipment from Sound Associates. Video projection system provided by Worldstage/Scharff Weisberg, Inc. Costumes by Eric Winterling, Inc. and Giliberto Designs, Inc. Miss Lansbury and Miss Bergen's wigs by Paul Huntley. Other wigs by Hudson Wigs LLC. Millinery by Rodney Gordon, Inc. Prop fabricators: C and R Designs, Joseph Cairo, Jeremy Lydic, Craig Grigg, Enhance a Colour, Anna Light, Joshua Yocum. Furniture painted and finished by Stephanie Dedes.

This production is dedicated to Howard Austen.

Rehearsed at the New 42nd Street Studios

 THE SHUBERT ORGANIZATION, INC.

Board of Directors

Philip J. Smith
Chairman

Robert E. Wankel
President

Wyche Fowler, Jr.

Diana Phillips

Lee J. Seidler

Michael I. Sovern

Stuart Subotnick

Chief Financial Officer ....Elliot Greene
Sr. Vice President, Ticketing ....David Andrews
Vice President, Finance ....Juan Calvo
Vice President, Human Resources ....Cathy Cozens
Vice President, Facilities ....John Darby
Vice President, Theatre Operations ....Peter Entin
Vice President, Marketing ....Charles Flateman
Vice President, Audit ....Anthony LaMattina
Vice President, Ticket Sales ....Brian Mahoney
Vice President, Creative Projects ...........D.S. Moynihan
Vice President, Real Estate ....Julio Peterson

---

Theatre Manager ....David M. Conte

Grace

First Preview: September 13, 2012. Opened: October 4, 2012.
Limited Engagement. Closed January 6, 2013 after 22 Previews and 108 Performances.

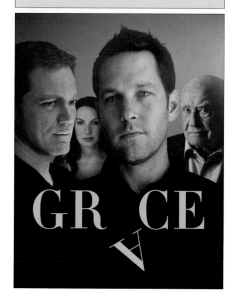

PLAYBILL

A born-again Christian man has his faith challenged when he tries to get the financing to open a chain of religious-themed hotels, only to see his investments, his marriage and his confidence in God unravel when confronted by three people having spiritual crises of their own: his disfigured neighbor, his exterminator and his long-suffering wife. The play is notable for telling its story by moving alternately forward and backward in time.

CAST

Steve	PAUL RUDD
Sam	MICHAEL SHANNON
Sara	KATE ARRINGTON
Karl	ED ASNER

UNDERSTUDIES

Understudy for Steve/Sam:
DANNY McCARTHY
For Sara:
JESSICA LOVE
For Karl:
JACK DAVIDSON

SETTING

The play takes place in two identical, furnished, rental condos next door to one another on the Florida shore. The time is the present.

☺ CORT THEATRE
138 West 48th Street
A Shubert Organization Theatre

Philip J. Smith, *Chairman*   **Robert E. Wankel,** *President*

DEBBIE BISNO   FOX THEATRICALS
PAULA WAGNER   JED BERNSTEIN   JESSICA GENICK

IN ASSOCIATION WITH

CHRISTIAN CHADD TAYLOR   MILES MAREK/PETER MAY
BRUCE BENDELL/SCOTT PRISAND   WILLIAM BERLIND/AMANDA DUBOIS   ALEX DiCLAUDIO/La RUE-NOY

PRESENT

PAUL RUDD AND MICHAEL SHANNON

IN

GRACE

BY
CRAIG WRIGHT

WITH
KATE ARRINGTON

AND
ED ASNER

DIRECTED BY
DEXTER BULLARD

SCENIC DESIGN	COSTUME DESIGN	LIGHTING DESIGN	SOUND DESIGN
BEOWULF BORITT	TIF BULLARD	DAVID WEINER	DARRON L WEST

CASTING	FIGHT DIRECTOR	MAKE UP DESIGNER	TECHNICAL SUPERVISOR
CAPARELLIOTIS CASTING	J. DAVID BRIMMER	NAN ZABRISKIE	NEIL A. MAZZELLA

PRESS REPRESENTATIVE	ADVERTISING	MARKETING SERVICES
O&M CO.	SPOTCO	ABOVE THE TITLE

PRODUCTION STAGE MANAGER	ASSOCIATE PRODUCERS	GENERAL MANAGER
JAMES HARKER	ROBERTA PEREIRA	101 PRODUCTIONS, LTD.
	JUDY PAGE	

*GRACE was originally commissioned and produced by Woolly Mammoth Theatre Company in Washington D.C. Howard Shalwitz, Artistic Director; Kevin Moore, Managing Director.
The producers wish to express their appreciation to the Theatre Development Fund for its support of this production.*

10/4/12

(L-R): Kate Arrington, Paul Rudd and Michael Shannon

Photo by Joan Marcus

Grace

Paul Rudd
Steve

Michael Shannon
Sam

Kate Arrington
Sara

Ed Asner
Karl

Danny McCarthy
u/s Steve/Sam

Jessica Love
u/s Sara

Jack Davidson
u/s Karl

Dexter Bullard
Director

Craig Wright
Playwright

Beowulf Boritt
Scenic Design

Tif Bullard
Costume Design

David Weiner
Lighting Design

Darron L West
Sound Design

Nan Zabriskie
Make-up Design

J. David Brimmer
Fight Director

James Harker
Production Stage Manager

Neil A. Mazzella
Hudson Theatrical
Associates
Technical Supervisor

Wendy Orshan
101 Productions, Ltd.
General Management

Debbie Bisno
Producer

Kristin Caskey
Fox Theatricals
Producer

Mike Isaacson
Fox Theatricals
Producer

Paula Wagner
Producer

Jed Bernstein
Producer

Jessica Genick
Producer

Miles Marek
Producer

Peter May
Producer

Scott Prisand
Producer

Amanda Dubois
Producer

Alex DiClaudio
Producer

Stella La Rue
Producer

Roberta Pereira
Associate Producer

Photo by Brian Mapp

FRONT OF HOUSE
Front Row (L-R): David Callendar, Nicole McIntyre, David Brown, Danielle Smith
Back Row: (L-R): Robert Belafonte, William Denson, Janise Beckwith

Grace
SCRAPBOOK

Correspondents: James Harker and Bethany Russell, Stage Managers
Memorable Opening Night Notes: All of the "Happy Opening" notes from the other Broadway shows
Opening Night Gifts: Engraved scotch glasses.
Most Exciting Celebrity Visitors: James Bond and "Hot Lips" Houlihan (Loretta Swit).

Favorite Off-Site Hangout: Langan's
Favorite Snack Food: Scotch
Mascot: Biscuit
Favorite Therapy: Scotch
Most Memorable Ad-Lib: "I'm not a believer. I'm a knower."
Memorable Press Encounter: Ed Asner getting handsy with Barbara Walters on "The View."

Who Wore the Least: Paul Rudd. Just boxers (when he remembers to put them on).
Memorable Directorial Note: "Well it sounded like you said all the lines."
Company Legend: Ed Asner
Nickname: "Crumbs."
Sweethearts Within the Company: Michael Shannon, Kate Arrington and Sylvie.

STAFF FOR GRACE

GENERAL MANAGEMENT
101 PRODUCTIONS, LTD.
Wendy Orshan   Jeffrey M. Wilson
Elie Landau
Ron Gubin
Chris Morey

COMPANY MANAGER
Bobby Driggers

GENERAL PRESS REPRESENTATIVE
O&M Co.
Rick Miramontez
Molly Barnett   Scott Braun   Sarah Babin

TECHNICAL SUPERVISOR
HUDSON THEATRICAL ASSOCIATES
Neil A. Mazzella
Sam Ellis   Caitlin McInerney   Irene Wang

CASTING
CAPARELLIOTIS CASTING
David Caparelliotis
Lauren Port   Miriam Mintz

ASSOCIATE PRODUCER
Megan Larche

Production Stage Manager ....James Harker
Stage Manager ....Bethany Russell
Assistant Director ....Jessi D. Hill
Assistant to Playwright ....Duncan Riddell
Associate Set Designer ....Alexis Distler
Assistant Set Designer ....Caite Hevner
Associate Costume Designer ....David Kaley
Associate Lighting Designer ....Rob Ross
Associate Sound Designer ....Charles Coes
Moving Light Programmer ....Alex Fogel
Production Carpenter ....Edward Diaz
Production Electrician ....Scott DeVerna
Production Props Supervisor ....Buist Bickley
Production Sound ....Charlie Greico
Automation Operator ....Jennifer Diaz
House Properties ....Lonnie Gaddy
Wardrobe Supervisor ....Eileen Miller

Dresser ....Kevin O'Brien
Production Assistant .........................M.A. Howard
Legal Counsel ....Lazarus & Harris, LLP/
Scott Lazarus, Esq.;
Robert C. Harris, Esq.
Accountant ....Fried & Kowgios
Controller ....Joseph Kubala
Advertising ....SPOTCO/
Drew Hodges, Jim Edwards, Tom Greenwald,
Michelle Haines, Corey Schwitz
Marketing ....Above the Title/
Britt Marden, Yelena Sayko,
Shoshana Kovac Parets
Assistant to Kristin Caskey ....Kate Cofran
Associate Producer,
Bisno Productions ....Roberta Pereira
Bisno Productions Intern ....Laurie Kamens
101 Productions, Ltd. Staff ....Beth Blitzer,
Kathy Kim, Mike McLinden, Michael Rudd,
Mary-Six Rupert, David van Zyll de Jong
101 Productions, Ltd. Interns ....Simon Pincus,
Sarah Springborn, Justin Black
Press Associates ....Philip Carrubba, Jon Dimond,
Michael Jorgensen, Yufen Kung,
Chelsea Nachman, Marie Pace,
Ryan Ratelle, Andy Snyder, Elizabeth Wagner
Press Interns ....Tori Piersanti,
Valentina Berger Maurette
Banking ....City National Bank/Anne McSweeney
Insurance ....Dewitt Stern/
Anthony Pittari, Jennifer Rose Adams
Theatre Displays ....BAM Signs/Adam Miller
Payroll Services ....Castellana Services, Inc.
Production Photographer ....Joan Marcus
Website Design & Online Marketing ....SPOTCO/
Marc Mettler, Cory Spinney
Opening Night Coordinator ....Serino Coyne/
Suzanne Tobak
Music Clearances ....BZ/Rights & Permissions, Inc.

CREDITS
Scenery built by Hudson Scenic, Inc. Lighting by Hudson/ Christie Lighting. Sound equipment by Masque Sound.

MUSIC CREDITS
Husky Rescue's "New Light of Tomorrow" written by Marko

Nyberg and Sam Shingler. Published by Catskills Music Publishing Ltd. (MCPS/PRS). www.husky-rescue.com; www.catskillsrecords.com. "He Reigns" written by Kirk Franklin. ©2008 Lily Mack Music Publishing (BMI), ©2002 Bridge Building Music (BMI) and Kerrion Publishing (BMI). All rights administered by Bridge Building Music (BMI). All rights reserved. Used by permission.

SPECIAL THANKS
Doctor Michael Brown, Senior Minister of Marble Collegiate Church; Elliott Navas of EcoSecur Exterminating; Boris Yendler; David Bickley; David Auster; Beth Blickers; Karen Pritzker; Apple; Byron Wetzel; Joe Machota; Aleen Keshishian; Shani Rosenzweig; Gen Lieber; Blair Kohan; Jodi Gottlieb; Steve Unger; Val Day; Michael Greene; Perry Zimel; Michael Scott Slosar

www.GraceOnBroadway.com

THE SHUBERT ORGANIZATION, INC.
Board of Directors

Philip J. Smith	**Robert E. Wankel**
Chairman	President
Wyche Fowler, Jr.	**Diana Phillips**
Lee J. Seidler	**Michael I. Sovern**

Stuart Subotnick

Chief Financial Officer ....Elliot Greene
Sr. Vice President, Ticketing ....David Andrews
Vice President, Finance ....Juan Calvo
Vice President, Human Resources ....Cathy Cozens
Vice President, Facilities ....John Darby
Vice President, Theatre Operations ....Peter Entin
Vice President, Marketing ....Charles Flateman
Vice President, Audit ....Anthony LaMattina
Vice President, Ticket Sales ....Brian Mahoney
Vice President, Creative Projects ...........D.S. Moynihan
Vice President, Real Estate ....Julio Peterson

CORT THEATRE
House Manager ....Joseph Traina

CREW
Seated (L-R): Bethany Russell (Stage Manager), Jennifer Diaz (Automation Operator), Eileen Miller (Wardrobe Supervisor), Scott DeVerna (House Electrician)
Standing (L-R):
Kevin O'Brien (Dresser), Lonnie Gaddy (House Properties), Jim Harker (Production Stage Manager)

Photos by Brian Mapp

DOORMAN

Smitty Smith

Hands on a Hardbody

First Preview: February 23, 2013. Opened: March 21, 2013.
Closed April 13, 2013 after 28 Previews and 28 Performances.

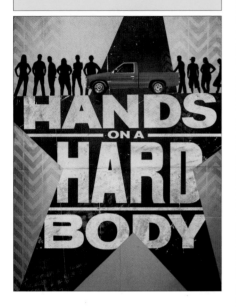

Ten down-on-their-luck Texans compete in a truck dealership contest: They must keep their hands on a beautiful red hardbody pickup for as long as they possibly can—days, if necessary. Last one standing wins the truck. From this A Chorus Line-*like premise comes a portrait of life under a merciless sun during the Great Recession. Based on a documentary film of the same name, the musical helps us to get to know these salt-of-the-earth people who don't just want the truck, they need the truck. The show has a score co-written by Trey Anastasio of the rock band Phish.*

CAST
(in alphabetical order)

JD Drew ....KEITH CARRADINE
Kelli Mangrum ....ALLISON CASE
Benny Perkins ....HUNTER FOSTER
Greg Wilhote ......JAY ARMSTRONG JOHNSON
Chris Alvaro ....DAVID LARSEN
Ronald McCowan ....JACOB MING-TRENT
Heather Stovall ....KATHLEEN ELIZABETH
MONTELEONE
Virginia Drew .... MARY GORDON MURRAY
Mike Ferris ....JIM NEWMAN
Cindy Barnes ....CONNIE RAY
Jesus Peña ....JON RUA
Norma Valverde......................KEALA SETTLE
Janis Curtis ....DALE SOULES
Frank Nugent ....SCOTT WAKEFIELD
Don Curtis/Dr. Stokes ....WILLIAM YOUMANS

Continued on next page

⇥N⇤ BROOKS ATKINSON THEATRE
UNDER THE DIRECTION OF JAMES M. NEDERLANDER AND JAMES L. NEDERLANDER

BROADWAY ACROSS AMERICA - BETH WILLIAMS
BARBARA WHITMAN / LATITUDE LINK   DEDE HARRIS / SHARON KARMAZIN   HOWARD & JANET KAGAN
and
JOHN & CLAIRE CAUDWELL   ROUGH EDGED SOULS   JOYCE PRIMM SCHWEICKERT
PAULA BLACK / BRUCE LONG   OFF THE AISLE PRODUCTIONS / FREITAG-MISHKIN

The La Jolla Playhouse production of

HANDS ON A HARD BODY

Book by
DOUG WRIGHT

Lyrics by
AMANDA GREEN

Music by
TREY ANASTASIO AND AMANDA GREEN

Based on a Film by S.R. Bindler

Starring

KEITH CARRADINE   ALLISON CASE   HUNTER FOSTER   JAY ARMSTRONG JOHNSON
DAVID LARSEN   JACOB MING-TRENT   KATHLEEN ELIZABETH MONTELEONE
MARY GORDON MURRAY   JIM NEWMAN   CONNIE RAY   JON RUA   KEALA SETTLE
DALE SOULES   SCOTT WAKEFIELD   WILLIAM YOUMANS

Scenic Design by	Costume Design by	Lighting Design by	Sound Design by
CHRISTINE JONES	**SUSAN HILFERTY**	**KEVIN ADAMS**	**STEVE CANYON KENNEDY**

Orchestrations by	Music Coordinator	Casting by	Associate Choreographer
TREY ANASTASIO **DON HART**	**MICHAEL KELLER**	**TELSEY + CO** **RACHEL HOFFMAN, CSA**	**LORIN LATARRO**

Press Representative	Marketing	Production Stage Manager	Production Manager
THE HARTMAN GROUP	**TYPE A MARKETING**	**LINDA MARVEL**	**JUNIPER STREET PRODUCTIONS**

Associate Producer	General Management	Executive Producer
DAVID CARPENTER	**FORESIGHT THEATRICAL** **ALLAN WILLIAMS**	**JENNIFER COSTELLO**

Musical Direction and Vocal Arrangements by
CARMEL DEAN

Musical Staging by
SERGIO TRUJILLO

Directed by
NEIL PEPE

Original musical staging for La Jolla Playhouse by Benjamin Millepied
Hands on a Hardbody was commissioned by La Jolla Playhouse
Christopher Ashley, Artistic Director & Michael S. Rosenberg, Managing Director
The Producers wish to express their appreciation to Theatre Development Fund for its support of this production.

3/21/13

The cast performing "Joy of the Lord."

Photo by Chad Batka

Hands on a Hardbody

MUSICAL NUMBERS

ACT I	ACT II
"Human Drama Kind of Thing"	"Hands on a Hardbody"
"If I Had This Truck"	"Born in Laredo"
"If She Don't Sleep"	"Alone With Me" (Reprise)
"My Problem Right There"	"It's a Fix"
"Alone With Me"	"Used to Be"
"Burn That Bridge"	"It's a Fix" (Reprise)
"I'm Gone"	"God Answered My Prayers"
"Joy of the Lord"	"Joy of the Lord" (Reprise)
"Stronger"	"Keep Your Hands on It"
"Hunt with the Big Dogs"	

Jay Armstrong Johnson and Allison Case sing "I'm Gone."

Photo by Chad Batka

STANDBYS

KRISTOFFER CUSICK
for Benny, Jesus, Chris, Greg, Mike, Ronald
RAYANNE GONZALES
for Norma, Janis, Virginia
DAVID JENNINGS
for Ronald, Frank
JANET KRUPIN
for Kelli, Heather
COREY MACH
for Chris, Greg, Jesus
HAPPY McPARTLIN
for Cindy, Janis, Virginia, Norma
CHELSEA PACKARD
for Kelli, Heather, Cindy
BART SHATTO
for Don/Dr. Stokes, Frank, Mike, Benny, JD

DANCE CAPTAIN

JANET KRUPIN

BAND

Conductor/Keyboard 1: CARMEL DEAN
Associate Conductor/Keyboard 2/Organ:
MATT GALLAGHER
Guitar/Mandolin: JON HERINGTON
Guitar/Pedal Steel/Dobro: SKIP KREVENS
Bass: SKIP WARD
Drums: SHANNON FORD
Violin/Mandolin: PAUL WOODIEL
Cello: JENNIFER BAXMEYER
Music Coordinator: MICHAEL KELLER
Music Copyist: STEPHEN LAMB
Synthesizer Programmer: RANDY COHEN

SETTING

The Floyd King Nissan Dealership, Longview, Texas

AUTHOR'S NOTE

Americans thrive on competition; it's innate in our character. Every summer in Spivey's Corner, North Carolina, they hold the National Hollerin' Contest. On Independence Day, Coney Island plays host to Nathan's Famous hot dog eating challenge. Lawn Mower Racing is an established sport in the South, and the annual Redneck Games in Georgia feature hubcap hurling, toilet seat tosses, and mud-pit belly flopping.

In the mid-1990s, documentarian S.R. Bindler captured the Hands on a Hardbody competition in Longview, Texas. In it, contestants placed their hands on a new Nissan "Hardbody" pick-up truck; the entrant who could stand the longest without removing his or her hand from the vehicle won it. The contest garnered international exposure and launched a host of similar promotions across the country. Filmmaker Bindler's achievement lies in his ability to push past the kitschy, absurd premise of the event and hit on deeper truths about the duality of the American Dream. On one hand, anyone with skill and perseverance can triumph, but beneath that bright promise lies a darker one: Darwin's cruel truth about the survival of the fittest.

Amanda Green, Trey Anastasio and I felt the film was ripe for theatrical adaptation. We believe it's more relevant today than it was upon its release; our recent economic tumult has brought age-old fissures of race, class and income inequality to the fore. The truck brings disparate individuals together, who would otherwise never meet, to confront these issues with a startling directness. Implicit in the contest is the American myth of mobility, embodied by an automobile. The truck offers plenty of metaphors; for one contestant, it's a new lease on life; for another, it's his manhood; for a third, it's her religious faith.

For me, the show is a chance to explore my roots in a state that's simultaneously maddening and exhilarating, punch-drunk on its own rich mythology, tongue-in-cheek braggadocio, abundant good humor and boundless sky. For Amanda and Trey, it's an opportunity to forge a score inspired by doggedly individualistic, real-life people and musical idioms from country ballads to southern rock, Americana, swampy funk, gospel and delta blues. We wrote the play in venues across the nation: a writer's retreat in Wyoming, a barn in Vermont and Interstate 20 between Dallas and Shreveport. It all culminated in a premiere run at San Diego's La Jolla Playhouse in the summer of 2012. It's been a joyous enterprise, and now we're on Broadway. It's our portrait of America; we hope it strikes a chord.

— *Doug Wright*

While our musical, *Hands on a Hardbody*, is based upon the events portrayed in a documentary of the same name, certain story points are fictitious. Although some of the characters are based on characters in the documentary, and in some cases bear their names, many of the facts about their lives and much of the dialogue have been invented for dramatic purposes. It is our intention to capture the spirit of the film, and we have freely used dramatic license in trying to accomplish that.

Hands on a Hardbody

Keith Carradine
JD Drew

Allison Case
Kelli Mangrum

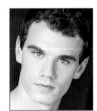
Hunter Foster
Benny Perkins

Jay Armstrong
Johnson
Greg Wilhote

David Larsen
Chris Alvaro

Jacob Ming-Trent
Ronald McCowan

Kathleen Elizabeth
Monteleone
Heather Stovall

Mary Gordon Murray
Virginia Drew

Jim Newman
Mike Ferris

Connie Ray
Cindy Barnes

Jon Rua
Jesus Peña

Keala Settle
Norma Valverde

Dale Soules
Janis Curtis

Scott Wakefield
Frank Nugent

William Youmans
Don Curtis/Dr. Stokes

Kristoffer Cusick
*Standby for Benny,
Jesus, Chris, Greg,
Mike, Ronald*

Rayanne Gonzales
*Standby for Norma,
Janis, Virginia*

David Jennings
*Standby for Ronald,
Frank*

Janet Krupin
*Standby for Kelli,
Heather; Dance
Captain*

Corey Mach
*Standby for Chris,
Greg, Jesus*

Happy McPartlin
*Standby for Cindy,
Janis, Virginia,
Norma*

Chelsea Packard
*Standby for Kelli,
Heather, Cindy*

Bart Shatto
*Standby for Don/
Dr. Stokes, Frank,
Mike, Benny, JD*

Doug Wright
Book

Amanda Green
Lyrics and Music

Trey Anastasio
*Music and
Orchestrations*

Neil Pepe
Director

Sergio Trujillo
Choreographer

Carmel Dean
*Musical Director
and Vocal Arranger*

Christine Jones
Scenic Design

Susan Hilferty
Costume Design

Kevin Adams
Lighting Design

Steve Canyon
Kennedy
Sound Design

Michael Keller
Music Coordinator

Bernard Telsey
Telsey + Company
Casting

Hands on a Hardbody

Akeem Baisden-Folkes
Assistant Director

Lorin Latarro
Associate Choreographer

Ana Rose Greene, Guy Kwan, Joe DeLuise, Hillary Blanken
Juniper Street Productions
Production Manager

Alan Wasser
Foresight Theatrical
General Management

Allan Williams
Foresight Theatrical
General Management

Aaron Lustbader
Foresight Theatrical
General Management

John Gore
CEO
Broadway Across America
Producer

Beth Williams
Producer

Barbara Whitman
Producer

Dede Harris
Producer

Sharon Karmazin
Producer

Howard & Janet Kagan
Producer

John & Claire Caudwell
Producers

Deborah Taylor
Rough Edged Souls
Producer

Carl Moellenberg
Rough Edged Souls
Producer

Wendy Federman
Rough Edged Souls
Producer

Sean Cercone
Rough Edged Souls
Producer

Joyce Primm Schweickert
Producer

Paula Marie Black
Producer

Bruce D. Long
Producer

Orin Wolf
Off the Aisle Productions
Producer

Barbara Freitag
Producer

Photo by Brian Mapp

Chase Mishkin
Producer

Christopher Ashley
Artistic Director
La Jolla Playhouse
Original Producer

Michael S. Rosenberg
Managing Director
La Jolla Playhouse
Original Producer

ORCHESTRA
Front Row (L-R): Paul Woodiel (violin/mandolin),
Skip Krevens (guitar/pedal steel/dobro), Skip Ward (bass)
Back Row (L-R): Matt Gallagher (Keyboard 2/Associate Conductor),
Shannon Ford (drums), Carmel Dean (Keyboard 1/Conductor),
Clay Ruede (cello)

Hands on a Hardbody

2012-2013 AWARDS

DRAMA DESK AWARD
Outstanding Sound Design in a Musical
(Steve Canyon Kennedy)

THEATRE WORLD AWARD
For Outstanding Broadway
or Off-Broadway Debut
(Keala Settle)

BOX OFFICE
Diana Needleman

FRONT OF HOUSE
Standing: Susan Martin
Front Row (L-R): Ilona Figueroa, Hector Aguilar, Jason Burke
Second Row (L-R): Kimberlee Imperato, Brian Aviles
Third Row (L-R): Amy Carcaterra, Doreen Halczak, Tara McCormack
Fourth Row (L-R): Sam Figert, George Vamvoukakis
Top Row (L-R): Jason Mullen, Austin Branda

STAGE MANAGEMENT
(L-R): Linda Marvel (Production Stage Manager),
Matthew Stern (Stage Manager),
Melissa M. Spengler (Assistant Stage Manager)

CREW
Front Row (L-R): Dave Horowitz, Matt Walsh, John H. Paull, III
Back Row (L-R): Joshua First, Shana Albery, Kyle Wesson, Bill Staples, Manuel Becker, Evan Vorono

Hands on a Hardbody

The cast performs "If I Had This Truck"

STAFF FOR *HANDS ON A HARDBODY*

GENERAL MANAGEMENT
FORESIGHT THEATRICAL
Alan Wasser   Allan Williams
Aaron Lustbader   Mark Shacket
Jake Hirzel

COMPANY MANAGER
Cathy Kwon

PRESS REPRESENTATION
THE HARTMAN GROUP
Michael Hartman   Matt Ross   Nicole Capatasto

MARKETING
TYPE A MARKETING
Elyce Henkin   John McCoy   Melissa Cohen

CASTING
TELSEY + COMPANY
Bernie Telsey CSA, Will Cantler CSA,
David Vaccari CSA,
Bethany Knox CSA, Craig Burns CSA,
Tiffany Little Canfield CSA, Rachel Hoffman CSA,
Justin Huff CSA, Patrick Goodwin CSA,
Abbie Brady-Dalton CSA,
David Morris, Cesar A. Rocha CSA, Andrew Femenella,
Karyn Casl CSA, Kristina Bramhall, Jessie Malone,
Conrad Woolfe

PRODUCTION MANAGEMENT
JUNIPER STREET PRODUCTIONS
Hillary Blanken   Guy Kwan
Ana Rose Greene   Joe DeLuise

Production Stage Manager ....Linda Marvel
Stage Manager ....Matthew Stern
Assistant Stage Manager ....Melissa M. Spengler
Associate Company Manager ....Daniel Hoyos
Assistant Director ....Akeem Baisden-Folkes
Associate Scenic Designer ....Brett J. Banakis
Associate Costume Designer ....Tricia Barsamian
Assistant Costume Designer ....Marina Reti
Associate Lighting Designer ....Paul Toben
Assistant Lighting Designer ....Brandon Baker
Moving Lights Programmer ....Jay Penfield
Associate Sound Designer ....Walter Trarbach
Assistant Sound Designer ....Jana Hoglund
Assistant to the Sound Designer ....Stephanie Celustka
Make-Up Designer ....Jimmy Cortés
Dialect Coach ....Deborah Hecht
Fight Consultant ....J. David Brimmer
Production Carpenter ....Erik E. Hansen
Advance Carpenter ....Chad Woerner
Production Electrician ....Gregory Husinko

Head Electrician ....Evan Vorono
Production Properties Supervisor ....Michael Pilipski
Head Properties Supervisor ....John H. Paull III
Production Sound Engineer ....Walter Trarbach
Sound Engineer ....David Horowitz
Assistant Sound Engineer ....Matthew Walsh
Wardrobe Supervisor ....Rory Powers
Dressers ....Shana Albery, Billy Hipkins, Kyle Wesson
Hair Supervisor ....Joshua First
Assistant Synthesizer Programmer ....Tim Crook
Music Copyist ....Stephen Lamb
Music Assistant ....Salomon Lerner
Rehearsal Stage Managers ....Erin Gioia Albrecht,
Emily Hayes
Production Assistant ....Patricia Masera
Advertising ....Serino/Coyne
Nancy Coyne, Greg Corradetti,
Robert Jones, Vanessa Javier,
Carolyn London, Ben Skinner
Digital Outreach/Website/Video ....Serino/Coyne
Jim Glaub, Chip Meyrelles, Laurie Connor,
Kevin Keating, Jeff Carroll, Whitney Creighton,
Mark Seeley, Brian DeVito, Ian Weiss
Theatre Displays ....King Displays
Production Legal
Counsel ....Levine, Plotkin & Menin LLP/
Loren Plotkin, Susan Mindell, Cris Criswell
Associate Producer for BAA ....Erica Rotstein
Production Associate
for BAA ....Rebecca Hengstenberg
Assistant to Ms. Whitman ....Tom Casserly
Accounting ....Rosenberg, Neuwirth & Kuchner/
Chris Cacace
General Management Associates ....Lane Marsh,
Mark Barna
General Management Office ....Kaitlin Boland,
Lauren Friedlander, Nina Lutwick,
Mary Catherine McDonald
Production Photographer ....Chad Batka
Physical Therapist ....Encore Physical Therapy PC/
Marc Hunter Hall
Orthopedist ....David S. Weiss, MD/
NYU Langone Medical Center
Insurance ....Ventura Insurance Brokerage
Banking ....Signature Bank/
Barbara von Borstel, Margaret Monigan
Payroll ....Castellana Services, Inc.
Opening Night Coordination ....Foresight Events/
Jennifer O'Connor, Connie Wilkin
Group Sales ....Group Sales Box Office

CREDITS AND ACKNOWLEDGEMENTS
Scenery construction, show control and scenic motion control featuring Stage Command® Systems by PRG Scenic Technologies, a division of Production Resource Group, LLC, New Windsor, NY. Pickup truck by the Rolling Stock

Company, Sarasota, FL. Lighting equipment from PRG Lighting, Secaucus, NJ. Audio equipment from Sound Associates, Yonkers, NY. Soft goods manufactured by iWeiss, Fairview, NJ. Props by prop N spoon, Rahway, NJ. Wigs by Tom Watson. Special thanks to Bra*Tenders for hosiery and undergarments. Costume distressing by Hochi Asiatico. ElectraDyne and Transatlantic TA 30 guitar amps by Mesa Boogie. TA speaker cabinets by Mesa Boogie.

SPECIAL THANKS
Shipley Do-Nuts, Ellen Pilipski, David McDowell, Ingrid Helton and Erick Sundquist. SansAmp Para Drivers provided by Tech 21. Acoustic guitar provided by Yamaha Guitars. Guitar amp provided by Louis Electric.

A very special thanks to those from the film who inspired and influenced the creation of this show: Donald Curtis, Janis Curtis, J.D. Drew, Virginia Drew, Jan Maynard, Ronald McCowan, Kelli Mestas, Benny Perkins and Norma Valverde.

Makeup provided by M•A•C Cosmetics

Rehearsed at Foxwoods Studios

Souvenir merchandise designed and created by
The Araca Group

www.handsonahardbody.com

Energy-efficient washer/dryer courtesy of
LG Electronics.

NEDERLANDER

Chairman ....**James M. Nederlander**
President ....**James L. Nederlander**

Executive Vice President
Nick Scandalios

Vice President Corporate Development **Charlene S. Nederlander**	Senior Vice President Labor Relations **Herschel Waxman**
Vice President **Jim Boese**	Chief Financial Officer **Freida Sawyer Belviso**

STAFF FOR THE BROOKS ATKINSON THEATRE
Theatre Manager .... Susan Martin
Treasurer .... Peter Attanasio
Associate Treasurer .... Elaine Amplo
House Carpenter .... Thomas A. Lavaia
Flyman .... Joe Maher
House Electrician .... Manuel Becker
House Propman .... Joseph P. DePaulo
House Engineer .... Reynold Barriteau

Hands on a Hardbody

SCRAPBOOK

Correspondent: Jon Rua, "Jesus Peña"

Memorable Opening Night Gifts: Scott Wakefield's paperweights of the state of Texas with a message etched in.

Which Actor Performed the Most Roles in This Show: Bill Youmans. 2.

Who Has Done the Most Shows in Their Career: Bill Youmans and I believe he's done at least 10 Broadway shows. That is enough to determine he has the most shows in comparison to others' careers.

Special Backstage Rituals: I believe there were various ones. We all tapped a Texas Longhorn Iron Piece before the show. Keala Settle, Kathleen Monteleone, and Allison Case listened to Beyoncé before every show. David Larsen, Jay Johnson, Jim Newman, and I would do a "1, 2, 3, hands on" chant at places. Before Act II, part of the cast sings with Keith Carradine upstage stage left to a made-up lyric, "YEAH!!!"

Favorite Moment During Each Performance: When we all laugh during "Joy of the Lord." Beautiful.

Favorite In-Theatre Gathering Places: Either the boys room (Jim Newman, Jay Johnson, David Larsen, Jon Rua) or the girls room (Keala Settle, Allison Case, Kathleen Monteleone). But there was not much gathering since we were all on the truck all the time. So, mainly the last show of the week we gathered.

Favorite Off-Site Hangout: The Glass House Tavern, but to be honest Rock Bottom is where it began.

Favorite Snack Food: Peanut Butter Filled Pretzel Bites!

Mascot: Ashley Connors, David Clement, or Trey Anastasio.

Favorite Therapy: Ricola, physical therapy, steaming.

Most Memorable Ad-Lib: Never had one, but I loved whenever Hunter Foster would repeat certain phrases or words prior to "Joy of the Lord." "INSANITY!"

What Did You Think of the Web Buzz on Your Show: The show was well appreciated and had amazing buzz. There could have been more, but what there was, was great.

Memorable Press Encounter: I loved seeing the real-life contestants being interviewed on opening night.

Memorable Stage Door Fan Encounter:

Two friends of mine, who I had not seen in five years, came to the show and did not inform me. When I exited and saw them there, it was a very special day. So glad they got to see this amazing show.

Who Wore the Least: Allison Case and Kathleen Monteleone.

Catchphrases Only the Company Would Recognize: "Huli Pau," "Keep ya hands on it," "Who put this fan behind this curtain?!," "LAYLA," "YEAH...," "Dalieh, Dalieh," "Musica....Really josa," "That's what I'm fittin' to do," Burp, Elephant noise, "Because if you don't, some other bitch will," "Not a game," "Hezbalando," "I got the note, let's move on," "Is my ****** hanging out?," "I can't...."

Fastest Costume Change: Connie Ray as Cindy Barnes. She did it effortlessly.

Who Wore the Heaviest/Hottest Costume: I would venture to say either David Larsen or me.

Which Orchestra Member Played the Most Instruments and What Were They: Couldn't tell you. But our band is the real deal. Not your normal Broadway orchestra.

Memorable Directorial Note: Too many. Better said with phrases: "Split the differ-ence," "We can have our cake and eat it too," "Nudge to the right, go back, a little more to the right, go back... OK, great, great." "My jury's still out."

Company In-Jokes: TOO MANY.

Sweethearts Within the Company: We all loved each other.

Coolest Thing About Being in This Show: Everything, simply everything. Texas. This music. This book. These people. This story. The cast, the memories, the truths and joys we hold with us at this very moment. The knowing that we, the family of *Hands on a Hardbody,* created art, penetrated the hearts, and en-lightened the minds of anyone who experienced the show. The coolest thing is the entire family of *Hands on a Hardbody.* Nothing will ever be like it again. The energy in the room; the work environment; the comradery. Knowing we did this. It will live forever. BUY THE ALBUM!.

At the opening night party, held at Roseland, the real-life contestants from the documentary film on which the show was based posed with the actors who played them in the show.
1. Keala Settle and Norma Valverde.
2. J.D. Drew and Keith Carradine.
3. Jacob Ming-Trent and Ronald McCowan.
4. Benny Perkins and Hunter Foster.
5. Virginia Drew and Mary Gordon Murray.
6. Allison Case and Kelli Mangrum.
7. Jan Maynard and Connie Ray.

Harvey

First Preview: May 18, 2012. Opened: June 14, 2012.
Limited Engagement. Closed August 5, 2012 after 32 Previews and 62 Performances.

PLAYBILL

Harvey

Elwood P. Dowd seems like a fine fellow, good company, salt of the earth...except for one little quirk. He believes that his best friend in the world is an invisible six-foot talking rabbit named Harvey. Elwood takes Harvey everywhere and chats with him constantly, until finally Elwood's sister and niece have enough and try to have Elwood committed to an asylum. But before long, even the doctor trying to "cure" Elwood starts to think maybe he sees Harvey too!

CAST

(in order of appearance)

Myrtle Mae Simmons	TRACEE CHIMO
Veta Louise Simmons	JESSICA HECHT
Elwood P. Dowd	JIM PARSONS
Mrs. Ethel Chauvenet	ANGELA PATON
Ruth Kelly, R.N.	HOLLEY FAIN
Duane Wilson	RICH SOMMER
Lyman Sanderson, M.D.	MORGAN SPECTOR
William R. Chumley, M.D	
	CHARLES KIMBROUGH
Betty Chumley	CAROL KANE
Judge Omar Gaffney	LARRY BRYGGMAN
E.J. Lofgren	PETER BENSON

UNDERSTUDIES

For Myrtle Mae Simmons, Ruth Kelly, R.N.:
EMILY ALTHAUS
For Veta Louise Simmons, Mrs. Ethel Chauvenet,
Betty Chumley: GLYNIS BELL
For Duane Wilson, Lyman Sanderson, M.D.,
E.J. Lofgren: MATT R. HARRINGTON

Continued on next page

STUDIO 54

ROUNDABOUTTHEATRECOMPANY

Todd Haimes, Artistic Director
Harold Wolpert, Managing Director
Julia C. Levy, Executive Director

In association with

Don Gregory

Presents

Jim Parsons
Jessica Hecht   Charles Kimbrough

in

Harvey

By

Mary Chase

with

Larry Bryggman

Peter Benson Tracee Chimo Holley Fain Angela Paton Rich Sommer Morgan Spector

and

Carol Kane

Set Design	Costume Design	Lighting Design	Original Music & Sound Design	Hair & Wig Design
David Rockwell	Jane Greenwood	Kenneth Posner	Obadiah Eaves	Tom Watson

Production Stage Manager	Casting	Press Representative	Technical Supervisor	General Managers
Arthur Gaffin	Jim Carnahan, CSA Stephen Kopel	Boneau/Bryan-Brown	Steve Beers	Sydney Beers Maggie Cantrick

Associate Managing Director	Director of Marketing & Sales Promotion	Director of Development	Founding Director	Adams Associate Artistic Director*
Greg Backstrom	Thomas Mygatt	Lynne Gugenheim Gregory	Gene Feist	Scott Ellis

Directed by

Scott Ellis

Roundabout gratefully acknowledges partial underwriting from the Petros and Marina Sabatacakis Foundation.
*Generously underwritten by Margot Adams, in memory of Mason Adams.
Roundabout Theatre Company is a member of the League of Resident Theatres.
www.roundabouttheatre.org

6/14/12

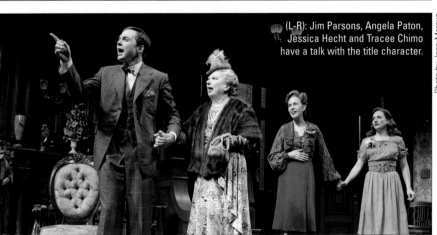

(L-R): Jim Parsons, Angela Paton, Jessica Hecht and Tracee Chimo have a talk with the title character.

Photo by Joan Marcus

Harvey

Cast Continued

For Judge Omar Gaffney,
William R. Chumley, M.D.:
JEFFREY HAYENGA

Production Stage Manager:
ARTHUR GAFFIN
Stage Manager:
JAMIE GREATHOUSE

TIME: 1944

ACT I

Scene 1: The library, late afternoon
Scene 2: Chumley's Rest, two hours later

ACT II

Scene 1: The library, two hours later
Scene 2: Chumley's Rest, four hours later

Jim Parsons
Elwood P. Dowd

Jessica Hecht
Veta Louise Simmons

Charles Kimbrough
William R. Chumley, M.D.

Larry Bryggman
Judge Omar Gaffney

Carol Kane
Betty Chumley

Peter Benson
E.J. Lofgren

Tracee Chimo
Myrtle Mae Simmons

Holley Fain
Ruth Kelly, R.N.

Angela Paton
Mrs. Ethel Chauvenet

Rich Sommer
Duane Wilson

Morgan Spector
Lyman Sanderson, M.D.

Emily Althaus
u/s Ruth Kelly, R.N.; Myrtle Mae Simmons

Glynis Bell
u/s Veta Louise Simmons; Betty Chumley; Ethel Chauvenet

Matt R. Harrington
u/s Lyman Sanderson, M.D.; Duane Wilson; E.J. Lofgren

Jeffrey Hayenga
u/s William R. Chumley, M.D.; Judge Omar Gaffney

Mary Chase
Playwright

Scott Ellis
Director

David Rockwell
Set Design

Jane Greenwood
Costume Design

Kenneth Posner
Lighting Design

Obadiah Eaves
Composer and Sound Design

Tom Watson
Hair and Wig Design

Angelina Avallone
Make-up Design

Jim Carnahan
Casting

Stephen Kopel
Casting

Gene Feist
Founding Director Roundabout Theatre Company

Todd Haimes
Artistic Director Roundabout Theatre Company

BOX OFFICE
(L-R): Krystin MacRitchie, Joe Clark, Laura Marshall

Photo by Brian Mapp

Harvey

Photos by Brian Mapp

FRONT OF HOUSE
Seated (L-R): LaConya Robinson,
Samantha Rivera
Standing (L-R): Aaron Netsky, Carlos Ortiz,
Juan Lopez, Linda Gjonbalaj, Essence Mason,
Christopher Burgos, Alvin Vega

CREW
Front Row (L-R): Dan Hoffman, Pete Malbuisson, Erin Delaney, Mike Widmer
Back Row (L-R): Craig Van Tassel, Lawrence Jennino, Steve Jones, Steve Beers,
John Wooding

WARDROBE AND HAIR
(L-R): Yolanda Ramsay, Kat Martin, Melissa Crawford,
Bryen Shannon, Aughra Moon

STAGE MANAGEMENT
(L-R): Arthur Gaffin, Jamie Greathouse

ROUNDABOUT THEATRE COMPANY STAFF
ARTISTIC DIRECTOR ....TODD HAIMES
MANAGING DIRECTOR ....HAROLD WOLPERT
EXECUTIVE DIRECTOR ....JULIA C. LEVY
ADAMS ASSOCIATE
   ARTISTIC DIRECTOR ....SCOTT ELLIS

ARTISTIC STAFF
DIRECTOR OF ARTISTIC DEVELOPMENT/
   DIRECTOR OF CASTING ....Jim Carnahan
Artistic Consultant ....Robyn Goodman
Resident Director ....Doug Hughes
Associate Artists ....Mark Brokaw, Scott Elliott,
   Sam Gold, Bill Irwin, Joe Mantello,
   Kathleen Marshall, Theresa Rebeck
Literary Manager ....Jill Rafson
Senior Casting Director ....Carrie Gardner
Casting Director ....Stephen Kopel
Casting Associate ....Jillian Cimini
Casting Assistant ....Michael Morlani
Artistic Associate ....Amy Ashton
Literary Associate ....Josh Fiedler
The Blanche and Irving Laurie Foundation
   Theatre Visions Fund
   Commissions ....David West Read,
   Nathan Louis Jackson

Educational Foundation of
   America Commissions ....Bekah Brunstetter,
   Lydia Diamond, Diana Fithian,
   Julie Marie Myatt
New York State Council
   on the Arts Commission ....Nathan Louis Jackson
Roundabout Commissions ....Helen Edmundson,
   Andrew Hinderaker, Stephen Karam,
   Steven Levenson, Matthew Lopez,
   Kim Rosenstock
Casting Interns ....Stanzi Davis, Kyle Eberlein,
   Rebecca Henning, Rachel Reichblum,
   Krystal Rowley
Script Readers ....Jay Cohen, Shannon Deep,
   Ben Izzo, Alexis Roblan
Artistic Apprentice ....Joshua M. Feder

EDUCATION STAFF
EDUCATION DIRECTOR ....Greg McCaslin
Associate Education Director ....Jennifer DiBella
Education Program Manager ....Aliza Greenberg
Education Program Associate ....Sarah Malone
Education Assistant ....Holly Sansom
Education Dramaturg ....Ted Sod
Teaching Artists ....Josh Allen, Cynthia Babak,
   Victor Barbella, LaTonya Borsay,
   Mark Bruckner, Chloe Chapin, Joe Doran,

Elizabeth Dunn-Ruiz, Carrie Ellman-Larsen,
   Theresa Flanagan, Deanna Frieman,
   Sheri Graubert, Adam Gwon, Devin Haqq,
   Carrie Heitman, Karla Hendrick, Jason Jacobs,
   Alana Jacoby, Lisa Renee Jordan, Jamie Kalama,
   Alvin Keith, Erin McCready, James Miles,
   Nick Moore, Meghan O'Neil, Drew Peterson,
   Nicole Press, Leah Reddy, Amanda Rehbein,
   Nick Simone, Heidi Stallings, Daniel Sullivan,
   Carl Tallent, Vickie Tanner, Larine Towler,
   Jennifer Varbalow, Kathryn Veillette,
   Leese Walker, Gail Winar, Chad Yarborough
Teaching Artist Emeritus ....Reneé Flemings
Education Apprentice ....Kimberley Oria

EXECUTIVE ADMINISTRATIVE STAFF
ASSOCIATE MANAGING
   DIRECTOR...............................Greg Backstrom
Assistant Managing Director ....Katharine Croke
Assistant to the Managing Director ......Christina Pezzello
Assistant to the Executive Director ....Nicole Tingir

MANAGEMENT/ADMINISTRATIVE STAFF
GENERAL MANAGER.......................Sydney Beers
General Manager,
   American Airlines Theatre ....Denise Cooper

Harvey

General Manager,
  Steinberg Center ....Nicholas J. Caccavo
Human Resources Director ....Stephen Deutsch
Operations Manager ....Valerie D. Simmons
Associate General Manager ....Maggie Cantrick
Office Manager ....Scott Kelly
Archivist ....Tiffany Nixon
Receptionists ....Dee Beider, Emily Frohnhoefer,
                         Elisa Papa, Allison Patrick
Messenger ....Darnell Franklin
Management Apprentice ....Christina Pezzello

FINANCE STAFF
DIRECTOR OF FINANCE ....Susan Neiman
Payroll Director ....John LaBarbera
Accounts Payable Manager ....Frank Surdi
Payroll Benefits Administrator ....Yonit Kafka
Manager Financial Reporting ....Joshua Cohen
Business Office Assistant ....Jackie Verbitski
Business Apprentice ....Kimberly Lucia

DEVELOPMENT STAFF
DIRECTOR OF
  DEVELOPMENT ....Lynne Gugenheim Gregory
Assistant to the
  Director of Development ....Liz Malta
Director, Institutional Giving ....Liz S. Alsina
Director, Individual Giving ....Christopher Nave
Director, Special Events ....Lane Hosmer
Associate Director, Individual Giving ....Tyler Ennis
Manager, Telefundraising ....Gavin Brown
Manager, Corporate Relations.................Sohyun Kim
Manager, Friends of Roundabout ....Marisa Perry
Manager, Donor Information Systems ....Lise Speidel
Special Events Associate ....Natalie Corr
Individual Giving Officer ....Joseph Foster
Institutional Giving Assistant ....Brett Barbour
Development Assistant ....Martin Giannini
Development Apprentice ....Julie Erhart
Special Events Apprentice ....Genevieve Carroll

INFORMATION TECHNOLOGY STAFF
DIRECTOR OF
  INFORMATION TECHNOLOGY ....Daniel V. Gomez
Information Systems Manager ....Dale Aucoin
System Administrator............................Jim Roma
IT Associate ....Cary Kim

MARKETING STAFF
DIRECTOR OF MARKETING AND
  SALES PROMOTION ....Thomas Mygatt
Associate Director of Marketing ....Tom O'Connor
Marketing Associate, Graphic Design ....Eric Emch
Marketing Assistant ....Bradley Sanchez
Web Producer ....Mark Cajigao
Director of Telesales
  Special Promotions ....Marco Frezza
Telesales Manager ....Patrick Pastor
Telesales Office Coordinator ....Nicholas Ronan
Marketing Apprentices..........................Julie Boor,
                                  Bethany Nothstein

AUDIENCE SERVICES STAFF
DIRECTOR OF AUDIENCE
  SERVICES ....Wendy Hutton
Associate Director of Audience Services ....Bill Klemm
Box Office Managers ....Edward P. Osborne,

Jaime Perlman, Krystin MacRitchie,
                          Nicole Nicholson
Group Sales Manager ....Jeff Monteith
Assistant Box Office Managers ....Robert Morgan,
                 Joseph Clark, Andrew Clements,
                          Catherine Fitzpatrick
Assistant Audience Services Managers ....Robert Kane,
                                  Lindsay Ericson,
                            Jessica Pruett-Barnett
Customer Services Coordinator ....Thomas Walsh
Audience Services ....Solangel Bido,
                 Michael Bultman, Jay Bush,
                 Lauren Cartelli, Adam Elsberry,
                 Joe Gallina, Ashley Gezana,
                 Alanna Harms, Kara Harrington,
                 Jennifer Hlinka, Lindsay Hoffman,
         Nicki Ishmael, Kiah Johnson, Kate Longosky,
                 Michelle Maccarone, Mead Margulies,
                 Laura Marshall, Chuck Migliaccio,
                 Carlos Morris, Sarah Olsen, Kaia Rafoss,
                 Josh Rozett, Ben Schneider, Heather Siebert,
                 Nalane Singh, Ron Tobia,
                 Michael Valentine, Hannah Weitzman
Audience Services Apprentice ....Jennifer Almgreen

SERVICES
Counsel ....Paul, Weiss,
          Rifkind, Wharton and Garrison LLP
          Charles H. Googe Jr., Carol M. Kaplan
Counsel ....Rosenberg & Estis
Counsel ....Andrew Lance,
          Gibson, Dunn, & Crutcher, LLP
Counsel ....Harry H. Weintraub,
          Glick and Weintraub, P.C.
Counsel ....Stroock & Stroock & Lavan LLP
Counsel ....Daniel S. Dokos,
          Weil, Gotshal & Manges LLP
Counsel ....Claudia Wagner/
          Manatt, Phelps & Phillips, LLP
Immigration Counsel ....Mark D. Koestler and
                                  Theodore Ruthizer
House Physicians ....Dr. Theodore Tyberg,
                                  Dr. Lawrence Katz
House Dentist ....Neil Kanner, D.M.D.
Insurance ....DeWitt Stern Group, Inc.
Accountant ....Lutz & Carr CPAs, LLP
Advertising ....Spotco/
          Drew Hodges, Jim Edwards,
          Tom Greenwald, Kyle Hall, Josh Fraenkel
Interactive Marketing ....Situation Interactive/
          Damian Bazadona, John Lanasa,
          Eric Bornemann, Mollie Shapiro,
                          Danielle Migliaccio
Events Photography ....Anita and Steve Shevett
Production Photographer ....Joan Marcus
Theatre Displays..............King Displays, Wayne Sapper
Lobby Refreshments ....Sweet Concessions
Merchandising ....Spotco Merch/
                                  James Decker

MANAGING DIRECTOR
  EMERITUS ....Ellen Richard

Roundabout Theatre Company
231 West 39th Street, New York, NY 10018
(212) 719-9393.

GENERAL PRESS REPRESENTATIVE
BONEAU/BRYAN-BROWN
Adrian Bryan-Brown
Matt Polk   Jessica Johnson   Amy Kass

CREDITS FOR *HARVEY*
Company Manager ....James Lawson
Production Stage Manager ....Arthur Gaffin
Stage Manager ....Jamie Greathouse
Assistant Director ....Lee Kasper
Associate Scenic Designer ....Dick Jaris
Assistants to the Scenic Designer ...........T.J. Greenway,
                                  Charles Corcoran
Associate Costume Designer ....Daniel Urlie
Associate Lighting Designer ....Nick Solyom
Associate Sound Designer ....Alex Hawthorn
Make-up Designer ....Angelina Avallone
Dialect Coach ....Kate Wilson
Production Properties Supervisor ....Scott Laule
Assistant Production Properties ....Julie Sandy
Magic Consultant ....Afterglow Group/
                                  Peter Samelson
Magic Effect Construction ....Wellington Enterprise/
                                  Bill Schmeelk
Encyclopedia Effect
  Design and Construction ....Craig Grigg
Production Carpenter ....Dan Hoffman
Production Electrician ....John Wooding
Running Properties ....Lawrence Jennino
Moving Light Programmer ....Alex Fogel
Sound Operator ....Craig Van Tassel
Wardrobe Supervisor ....Melissa Crawford
Dressers ....Bryen Shannon, Kimberly Prentice,
                                  Aughra Moon
Shopper.................................Emily Rose Adams
Hair and Wig Supervisor ....Yolanda Ramsay
Production Assistants........Trisha Henson, Johnny Milani

CREDITS
Scenery built, painted, automated and electrified by Show
Motion, Inc., Milford, Connecticut. Scenery automation
and show control by Show Motion, Inc., Milford, CT, using
the AC2 Computerized Motion Control System. Lighting
equipment by PRG Lighting. Audio equipment by PRG
Audio. Costumes by Eric Winterling, Inc. Original portrait
photography by Jeffrey Lee/Jeffrey's Photos. Millinery by
Lynne Mackey Studio. Special thanks to Lesley Mulholland,
Wendy Orshan and Jeff Wilson, and Debra Monk.

Makeup provided by M•A•C Cosmetics.

STUDIO 54 THEATRE STAFF
Operations Manager ....Valerie D. Simmons
House Manager ....LaConya Robinson
Associate House Manager ....Jack Watanachaiyot
Head Treasurer ....Krystin MacRitchie
Associate Treasurer ....Joe Clark
Assistant Treasurers ....Kara Harrington,
                                  Laura Marshall
House Carpenter ....Dan Hoffman
House Electrician ....John Wooding
House Properties ....Lawrence Jennino
Security ....Gotham Security
Maintenance ....Reliable Cleaning, Jason Battle,
                                  Ralph Mohan
Lobby Refreshments by ....Sweet Concessions

Harvey
Scrapbook

Correspondent: Tracee Chimo, "Myrtle."

Memorable Opening Night Note: The note that Jim Parsons wrote me on opening night is so heartfelt and beautiful. It's up in my dressing room. He is so very generous.

Opening Night Gifts: Rich Sommer gave us all bottles of lovely champagne with the label "Chumley's Rest"—that's name of the sanatorium where we're all trying to lock up Elwood throughout the show. It was such a great gag gift.

Most Exciting Celebrity Visitor: I died inside when Sam Rockwell came to the show. He came backstage and hugged me and said he loved me—and I almost had a STROKE. I used to imagine that he was my husband and I would fantasize that we had children together. How insane is that?

Actor Who Has Done the Most Shows: You might guess Charles Kimbrough because he did those Sondheim shows [*Company* and *Sunday in the Park with George*], and you'd be right: he's done fourteen Broadway shows. Larry Bryggman has done nine and Jessica Hecht has done seven. Her stage career is something incredible. I've looked up to her for years. Getting to work with her has been a dream.

Special Backstage Ritual: Before we go on, Jessica and I both run, in our costumes, across the stage and kiss Artie, our stage manager, and then run back to where we're supposed to stand for "places." Then we jump up and down and rub noses together. We do that every single night.

Favorite Moments During Each Performance: Jessica and I dance together offstage trying to get Jim's attention while he's on the phone in the first scene. In these ridiculous costumes we pretend we're dancing at a club. Also, onstage, Jessica hits the same note that Deb Monk hits in the "party music" (which scores the first scene). She improvised this one night and we died laughing. She's been doing it ever since. And without fail…every night…it makes me laugh.

Favorite In-Theatre Gathering Place: The greenroom. Roundabout just renovated it, and it's very comfy with lots of big cushiony couches and a big monitor so we can all watch the show when we're not on.

Favorite Off-Site Hangouts: We mainly do our own things after the show. We've had a few nights at a pub called Characters right across the street. The boys, Rich and Morgan, sometimes go to Bathtub Gin in Chelsea.

Favorite Snack Foods: There are just bowls and bowls of Tootsie Pops everywhere. We eat them constantly. I often bring sweets to put on the table in the greenroom for everybody, cupcakes and such. One of my close girlfriends owns a chocolate company called Nibmor. It's delicious Raw Chocolate. She sends us lots of treats.

Mascot: Harvey, of course! We've got bunnies everywhere backstage. Candy bunnies, stuffed bunnies, a little string of white Christmas-like lights made of little bunnies. We support the idea that Harvey exists here.

(L-R) Jessica Hecht, Jim Parsons, Larry Bryggman and Carol Kane take bows on opening night.

Photo by Joseph Marzullo/WENN

Favorite Therapies: Hand sanitizer. Jessica is always sucking on a Ricola. We chew on them. Although *Harvey* is not a musical, it is very demanding vocally. We're not miked, and for a show that is so stylized, we feel like we're in a giant musical.

Memorable Ad-Lib: Larry Bryggman has a line where he says to Jessica: "Stop putting your oar in…keep your oar out!" One night he said, "Keep your oar in! Take it out…. Er…uh…LEAVE IT OUT!!!" It was really hard not to break.

Cell Phone Incidents During a Performance: It hasn't been a really big problem, but one went off during a really beautiful moment in the show one day.

Memorable Press Encounter: A lot of people say I play Myrtle like nothing they've ever seen before. I never watched the movie or saw another production, and I did that purposely so I could keep the work original. I was interviewed on opening night by a guy who said, "You play Myrtle very bitchy." I said, "Um, not 'bitchy,' but I would say 'frustrated'." He went on to say, "I'd call it 'bitchy'." I don't know. The word "bitchy" just seems so broad.

Memorable Stage Door Fan Encounter: I had one lovely encounter with a girl who obviously really loved the show. As we were talking her hands started shaking and she started to cry. These beautiful tears were just quietly dripping down her face. It was the most beautiful thing I'd ever seen. That's why I do this: That kid.

Fastest Costume Change: Jessica, from the first scene into the second, from the home to the sanatorium. It's a full costume change in under a minute.

Heaviest/Hottest Costume: Jim wears a three-piece wool suit for the entire show.

Who Wore the Least: Rich Sommer wears that white puffy outfit, white shirt with white pants and white shoes.

Catchphrases Only the Company Would Recognize: "Keep your oar in."

Memorable Directorial Note: Scott said to me, "Don't be afraid to be aggressive." In previews he said: "You were too gentle tonight. You looked like someone gave you a note to not be pissed off. And now you are afraid of being unlikeable. But don't you dare ever be afraid of that." I have to tell you that that bit of advice has stuck, both in the show—and in my life.

Understudy Anecdote: Just the other day, Jeff went on for Charles Kimbrough who had the flu. Jeff was brilliant, brilliant, brilliant. Charles came right back.

Nicknames: Jim is usually "Jimmy," Rich is "Richie," Morgan is "Morgee" and I'm usually "Chimo." But Morgan calls me "TraceNasty."

Embarrassing Moments: Plenty. I've fallen over on stage a couple of times. One night I wasn't paying attention during the last scene when the cab driver is on. I kind of zoned out and fell backward just as Peter was looking at me. We started laughing. I'm not the only one. Rich has fallen on stage a few times. Morgan once shut the office door on his coat. He tried to pull it out subtly, but had no luck. Finally he had to make a bit out of it. The audience loved it. One night, a man bum-rushed the stage at curtain call with a bouquet of roses. Jim accepted them, but the man said, "No! They're for Harvey!" Jim turned bright pink and said, "I'll make sure he gets them."

Coolest Things About Being in This Show: There's nothing cooler than going to work every day on Broadway. And being in a summer hit on Broadway is especially great because we know the house is always going to be full. We never have to ask how we're doing. We know!

The Heiress

First Preview: October 6, 2012. Opened: November 1, 2012.
Limited Engagement. Closed February 9, 2013 after 27 Previews and 117 Performances.

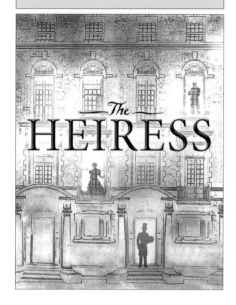

A revival of the American classic about a lonely and socially clumsy heiress whose sudden romance with a handsome, charming young man is opposed by her stern and sour father who believes the suitor is only after her money and could not possibly love her for herself. The fact that the father proves correct only makes the truth more bitter for the heiress, and makes her even more determined to have her personal notion of revenge on them all.

CAST

(in order of appearance)

Maria ....VIRGINIA KULL
Dr. Austin Sloper ....DAVID STRATHAIRN
Lavinia Penniman ....JUDITH IVEY
Catherine Sloper ....JESSICA CHASTAIN
Elizabeth Almond ....CAITLIN O'CONNELL
Arthur Townsend...............KIERAN CAMPION
Marian Almond ....MOLLY CAMP
Morris Townsend ....DAN STEVENS
Mrs. Montgomery ....DEE NELSON
Coachman ....BEN LIVINGSTON

SCENES

The action of the play takes place in the front parlor of Doctor Sloper's house in Washington Square.
The year is 1850.

Continued on next page

WALTER KERR THEATRE
A JUJAMCYN THEATRE

JORDAN ROTH
President

PAUL LIBIN
Executive Vice President

JACK VIERTEL
Senior Vice President

PAULA WAGNER   ROY FURMAN   STEPHANIE P. McCLELLAND
LUIGI CAIOLA/ROSE CAIOLA   JIM HERBERT   TED LIEBOWITZ   STACEY MINDICH
JILL FURMAN   RICARDO HORNOS   JON B. PLATT   ERIC SCHMIDT
MARGO LION/RACHEL WEINSTEIN
and
JUJAMCYN THEATERS

present

JESSICA CHASTAIN   DAVID STRATHAIRN   DAN STEVENS

The HEIRESS

By
RUTH & AUGUSTUS GOETZ

MOLLY CAMP   KIERAN CAMPION   VIRGINIA KULL   MAIRIN LEE

BEN LIVINGSTON   DEE NELSON   CAITLIN O'CONNELL

and

JUDITH IVEY

Scenic Design	Costume Design	Lighting Design	Sound Design
DEREK McLANE	ALBERT WOLSKY	DAVID LANDER	LEON ROTHENBERG

Original Music	Hair & Wig Design	Casting
PETER GOLUB	PAUL HUNTLEY	TARA RUBIN CASTING

Press Representative	Advertising & Marketing	Technical Supervisor
BONEAU/BRYAN-BROWN	SERINO/COYNE	PETER FULBRIGHT

Production Stage Manager	Company Manager	Executive Producer
ARTHUR GAFFIN	PENELOPE DAULTON	101 PRODUCTIONS, LTD.

Directed by
MOISÉS KAUFMAN

11/1/12

(L-R): Judith Ivey, Dan Stevens, David Strathairn, Jessica Chastain

Photo by Joan Marcus

The Heiress

Cast Continued

ACT ONE

Scene 1: An October evening
Scene 2: An afternoon two weeks later
Scene 3: The next morning

ACT TWO

Scene 1: An April night six months later
Scene 2: Two hours later
Scene 3: A morning three days later
Scene 4: A summer evening almost two years later

UNDERSTUDIES

For Maria, Catherine Sloper,
Marian Almond, Mrs. Montgomery:
MAIRIN LEE
For Dr. Austin Sloper, Arthur Townsend:
BEN LIVINGSTON
For Lavinia Penniman:
CAITLIN O'CONNELL
For Elizabeth Almond:
DEE NELSON
For Morris Townsend, Coachman:
KIERAN CAMPION

Dan Stevens is appearing with the support of Actors'
Equity Association pursuant to an exchange program
between American Equity and UK Equity.

Production Stage Manager: ARTHUR GAFFIN
Stage Manager: JAMIE GREATHOUSE

Jessica Chastain
Catherine Sloper

David Strathairn
Dr. Austin Sloper

Dan Stevens
Morris Townsend

Judith Ivey
Lavinia Penniman

Molly Camp
Marian Almond

Kieran Campion
Arthur Townsend;
u/s Morris Townsend,
Coachman

Virginia Kull
Maria

Mairin Lee
u/s Catherine Sloper,
Marian Almond,
Maria,
Mrs. Montgomery

Ben Livingston
Coachman, u/s Dr.
Sloper, Arthur
Townsend

Dee Nelson
Mrs. Montgomery,
u/s Elizabeth Almond

Caitlin O'Connell
Elizabeth Almond,
u/s Lavinia
Penniman

Ruth & Augustus
Goetz
Playwrights

Moisés Kaufman
Director

Derek McLane
Set Design

Albert Wolsky
Costume Design

David Lander
Lighting Design

Leon Rothenberg
Sound Design

Peter Golub
Original Music

Paul Huntley
Hair & Wig Design

Kate Wilson
Dialect Coach

Ashley Ryan
Make-up Design

Tara Rubin
Tara Rubin Casting
Casting

Peter Fulbright
Tech Production
Services
Production Manager

Wendy Orshan
101 Productions, Ltd.
Executive Producer

Paula Wagner
Producer

Roy Furman
Producer

The Heiress

Stephanie P.
McClelland
Producer

Luigi Caiola
Producer

Rose Caiola
Producer

Jill Furman
Producer

Jon B. Platt
Producer

Margo Lion
Producer

Jordan Roth
President
Jujamcyn Theaters
Producer

DOORMAN
Kevin Wallace

WARDROBE/HAIR
Front (L-R): Andrea Gonzalez,
Linda Lee, Laura Beattie
Back (L-R): Daniel Koye,
Terry LaVada

COMPANY AND STAGE MANAGEMENT
Bottom: Penelope Daulton (Company Manager)
Middle (L-R): Johnny Milani (Production
Assistant), Timothy Koch (Assistant Director)
Top (L-R): Arthur Gaffin (Production Stage
Manager), Jamie Greathouse (Stage Manager)

FRONT OF HOUSE STAFF
Bottom Row (L-R): T.J. D'Angelo, Juliett Cipriati
Middle Row (L-R): Robert Zwaschka, Shelby Wong,
Katie Siegmund, Frances Cohen
Top Row (L-R): Phillip Taratula, Shayna Vercillo,
Manuel Sandridge, Mallory Sims

The Heiress

BOX OFFICE
(L-R): Michael Loiacono, Gail Yerkovich, Harry Jaffie

Photos by Brian Mapp

CREW
Front Row (L-R): Vincent J. Valvo, Timothy Bennet, George E. Fullum
Back Row (L-R): David Stollings, Peter J. Iacoviello

STAFF FOR *THE HEIRESS*

GENERAL MANAGEMENT
101 PRODUCTIONS, LTD.
Wendy Orshan   Jeffrey M. Wilson
Elie Landau   Chris Morey   Ron Gubin

COMPANY MANAGER
Penelope Daulton

GENERAL PRESS REPRESENTATIVE
BONEAU/BRYAN-BROWN
Adrian Bryan-Brown
Matt Polk   Heath Schwartz   Amy Kass

CASTING
TARA RUBIN CASTING
Tara Rubin, CSA
Eric Woodall CSA, Merri Sugarman CSA,
Dale Brown CSA, Stephanie Yankwitt CSA
Lindsay Levine, Kaitlin Shaw

TECHNICAL SUPERVISOR
TECH PRODUCTION SERVICES, INC.
Peter Fulbright, Mary Duffe
Shaminda Amarakoon

Production Stage Manager ....Arthur Gaffin
Stage Manager ....Jamie Greathouse
Assistant Director ....Timothy Koch
Associate Scenic Designer ....Erica Hemminger
Associate Costume Designer ....Marina Reti
Associate Lighting Designer ....Travis McHale
Associate Sound Designer ....Danny Erdberg
Production Carpenter ....Brian Munroe
Production Electrician ....Michael S. LoBue
Moving Light Programmer ....Michael S. LoBue
Production Props Coordinator ....Peter Sarafin
Advance Sound ....Danny Erdberg
Sound Engineer ....David Stollings
Make-up Design ....Ashley Ryan
Wardrobe Supervisor ....Linda Lee
Dressers ....Laura Beattie, Andrea Gonzalez,
Terry LaVada
Hair Supervisor ....Daniel Koye
Dialect Coach ....Kate Wilson
Period Style & Etiquette Consultant ....Kevin Connell
Scenic Studio Assistant ....Paul DePoo

Production Assistants ....Lee Micklin, Johnny Milani,
Sophie Quist
Legal Counsel ....Lazarus & Harris/
Scott Lazarus, Robert Harris, Emily Lawson
Accountant ....Rosenberg, Neuwirth & Kuchner/
Chris Cacace, Jana Jevnikar
Advertising ....Serino/Coyne/
Nancy Coyne, Angelo Desimini,
Matt Upshaw, Carolyn London,
Lauren Houlberg, Doug Ensign,
Christina Hernandez
Marketing ....Serino/Coyne/
Leslie Barrett, Abby Wolbe
Digital Outreach & Website ....Serino/Coyne/
Jim Glaub, Chip Meyrelles,
Laurie Connor, Kevin Keating,
Mark Seeley, Andrea Cuevas
101 Productions, Ltd. Staff ....Christina Boursiquot,
Beth Blitzer, Kit Ingui, Kathy Kim,
Mike McLinden, Michael Rudd,
Mary-Six Rupert, David van Zyll de Jong
101 Productions, Ltd. Interns ....Simon Pincus,
Sarah Springborn
Assistant to Paula Wagner ....Jan Bartholemew
Assistant to Roy Furman ....Eileen Williams
Assistant to Stephanie P. McClelland ....Brian Feinstein
Banking ....City National Bank/Anne McSweeney
Insurance ....DeWitt Stern Group, Inc.
Opening Night Coordinator ....Serino/Coyne/
Suzanne Tobak
Merchandising ....Araca Merchandising
Production Photographer ....Joan Marcus
Payroll Services ....Castellana Services, Inc.
Theatre Displays ....King Displays, Inc.
Immigration Services (U.S.) ....Entertainment Visa
Consultants LLC/
David King
Immigration Services (UK) .....Visa Consultants/Lisa Carr
Group Sales ....Telecharge.com Group Sales

To learn more about the production, please visit
www.TheHeiressOnBroadway.com

CREDITS
Scenery fabricated and painted by Global Scenic Services,
Inc., Bridgeport, CT. Scenery automation and show control
by Show Motion, Inc., Milford, CT, using the AC2

computerized motion control system. Lighting and sound
equipment provided by PRG. Costumes by Eric Winterling.
Millinery by Lynne Mackey Studio. Men's hats by Rodney
Gordon. Furniture upholstery and drapes by R. Ramos
Upholstery. Prop electrical wiring by Jeremy Lydic.
Furniture finishing by Liz Schura. Custom furniture builds
by Craig Grigg. Additional drapery sewing and dying by
Anna Light. The producers wish to thank the TDF Costume
Collection for its assistance in this production.

SPECIAL THANKS
Dave Auster, Justin Black and Nick Stern.

This production was rehearsed at the
Pershing Square Signature Center
480 West 42nd Street, NY, NY 10036
www.signaturetheatre.org

JUJAMCYN THEATERS

JORDAN ROTH
President

PAUL LIBIN
Executive Vice President

JACK VIERTEL
Senior Vice President

MEREDITH VILLATORE
Chief Financial Officer

JENNIFER HERSHEY
Vice President,
Building Operations

MICAH HOLLINGWORTH
Vice President,
Company Operations

HAL GOLDBERG
Vice President,
Theatre Operations

Director of Business Affairs ....Albert Kim
Director of Human Resources ....Michele Louhisdon
Director of Ticketing Services ....Justin Karr
Theatre Operations Managers ....Willa Burke,
Susan Elrod, Emily Hare,
Jeff Hubbard, Albert Kim
Theatre Operations Associates ....Carrie Brinker,
Brian Busby, Michael Composto,
Anah Jyoti Klate
Accounting ....Cathy Cerge, Amy Frank,
Tariq Hamami, Alexander Parra
Executive Producer, Red Awning ....Nicole Kastrinos
Director of Sales, Givenik.com ....Karen Freidus
Building Operations Associate ....Erich Bussing
Ticketing and Pricing Associate ....Jonathon Scott

The Heiress
SCRAPBOOK

Correspondent: Molly Camp, "Marian Almond"

Opening Night Gifts: We received a ton of things from the producers, including fancy candy dishes filled with special *Heiress* chocolates wrapped in gold paper. Judy Ivey gave baskets filled with memorabilia including glass Victorian women, fans, and framed samplers she made for each of us. She spends her time between scenes embroidering. David Strathairn, who plays Dr. Sloper, made everyone these little old-fashioned bottles with cork tops filled with an alcoholic drink and labeled "Dr. Sloper's Snake Oil."

Most Exciting Celebrity Visitors: A lot of times when famous people come, I'm afraid to say anything. But James Earl Jones came and was so sweet. Artie Gaffin, our stage manager, said he wanted to meet everybody so we went down and he met every person from the cast and told us he loved the show. His wife told me she had once played my part in an earlier production and we agreed that we sometimes annoy ourselves with how much we have to giggle.

Who Has Done the Most Shows in Their Career: I would say Judith Ivey, with ten Broadway shows.

Special Backstage Ritual: Virginia Kull and I have an open-invitation dance party in our dressing room every night. We try to have a nice balance of classical or musicals or booty-shaking music or whatever we feel like that day. And we take requests.

Favorite Moments During Each Performance (On Stage or Off): I have two. One is for me personally. It occurs in Act II before I go upstairs with Catherine. I have a moment with David Strathairn where he looks at me with these sad eyes and says "Come and visit as often as you can, will you?" It's the only moment that I have with him one-on-one, and in that moment he is so vulnerable and desperate, it breaks my heart. I also love the end of Act I. It's a really powerful scene where you feel empathy for everyone on stage and can empathize with each person's position. It makes you feel bad for everyone on that stage.

Favorite In-Theatre Gathering Place: We don't have a greenroom, so, generally toward the end of the show, about six of us gather and talk on the

The cast and director of *The Heiress* meet the press in their rehearsal studio.
Seated (L-R): *Yearbook* correspondent Molly Camp, Dee Nelson, Kieran Campion, Caitlin O'Connell and Virginia Kull.
Standing (L-R): Ben Livingston, Mairin Lee, Dan Stevens, Jessica Chastain, Judith Ivey, David Strathairn, Moisés Kaufman.

stairs between the first and second levels.

Favorite Off-Site Hangout: We go to Lillie's Bar on 49th between Broadway and Eighth. It's very Victorian so it's appropriate to the show. They have great cocktails, like the Lillie Penny.

Favorite Snack Foods: Artie Gaffin puts out sea-salt chocolate bars which are really good. David brings in great muffins and breads on a regular basis. We also have some amazing cast/crew brunches.

Mascot: There is a fake pigeon that one of the stage crew guys put backstage by the entrance to the house, and every time you go backstage it acquires a new article of clothing. Recently it wore a maid's apron, a cape and a Madonna bra.

Favorite Therapies: I enjoy Ricolas personally. Dan Stevens has a fancy steamer he got from London.

Most Memorable Ad-Lib: One feature of our play is that many people have to make a lot of introductions. There've definitely been a few evenings of misintroductions. One night Kieran Campion, who plays Arthur, introduced Morris as Dr. Sloper and Dr. Sloper as Morris. Poor Caitlin O'Connell makes the most introductions. So she has had her share of slip-ups. :-)

Cell Phone Incidents: During the party scene someone in the first row was playing a game or texting on their phone. A phone also once went off during my scene with Catherine on the couch, and it rang for a while.

Memorable Press Encounters: Judy, Jessica, Dan, and David did a shoot for Vogue with Annie Liebovitz. And then a photographer from New York magazine followed us around for a week and took great photos of us.

Memorable Fan Encounters: I'm usually the one who walks out of the stage door and everyone is very disappointed because they're waiting for Dan and Jessica. One night a girl sitting in the third row got very excited when Dan Stevens came out for his curtain call. She was jumping up and down with her arms in the air. It was very sweet...and a little creepy. On the last day in our rehearsal space Dan, who Tweets a lot, noticed that it was a Chinese holiday on which they like to eat moon pies. He Tweeted "I challenge my fans to bring moon pies to the theatre." Well, three different people brought bags of moon pies to the rehearsal hall for us. They were not very good, haha.

Fastest Costume Change: I would say Jessica. I think she has about two minutes.

Who Wore the Heaviest/Hottest Costume: Probably Caitlin O'Connell. Her first costume is like a carpet—a beautiful carpet, but very heavy.

Who Wore the Least: Possibly David Strathairn. The men don't have as many layers as we do.

Memorable Directorial Note: Moisés liked to use the word "bombuleant." I don't know how it's spelled, or if it's a real word.

Nicknames: Judith Ivey calls me "Molly Girl."

Sweethearts Within the Company: Everybody in our company is married!

Ghostly Encounters Backstage: None in the theatre. But early in our rehearsal process we took a tour of the Merchant's House in Washington Square which is one of the models for the house where the play takes place. It was really cool. It's supposed to be haunted, but we didn't see anything.

Coolest Thing About Being in This Show: We have such a great company. It's a very positive and fun place to be.

Also: We have the most artistic sign-in sheet on Broadway!

Executive Coordinator	Ed Lefferson	
Executive Assistants	Clark Mims Tedesco, Beth Given, Julia Kraus	
Receptionist	Lisa Perchinske	
Maintenance	Ralph Santos, Ramon Zapata	
Security	Rasim Hodzic, John Acero	
Interns	Kayla Burgett, Estefania Fadul, Taylor Kurpiel, Amy Larrowe, Matthew Robertson, Brandon Smithey	

STAFF FOR THE WALTER KERR THEATRE FOR
THE HEIRESS

Theatre Manager ....Susan Elrod

Treasurer	Harry Jaffie
Head Carpenter	George E. Fullum
Head Propertyman	Timothy Bennet
Head Electrician	Vincent J. Valvo
Flyman	Peter J. Iacoviello
Propertyman	Moose Johnson
Engineer	Brian DiNapoli
Assistant Treasurers	Michael Loiacono, Joseph Smith, Gail Yerkovich
Head Usher	T.J. D'Angelo
Director	Michelle Fleury
Tickets Takers	Alison Traynor, Robert Zwaschka

Ushers	Jason Aguirre, Florence Arcaro, Juliett Cipriati, Aaron Kendall, Victoria Lauzun, Ilir Velovich
Doormen	Brandon Houghton, Kevin Wallace
Head Porter	Marcio Martinez
Porter	Rudy Martinez
Head Cleaner	Sevdija Pasukanovic
Cleaner	Lourdes Perez

Lobby refreshments by Sweet Concessions.

Security provided by GBA Consulting, Inc.

I'll Eat You Last: A Chat with Sue Mengers

First Preview: April 5, 2013. Opened: April 24, 2013.
Still running as of May 31, 2013.

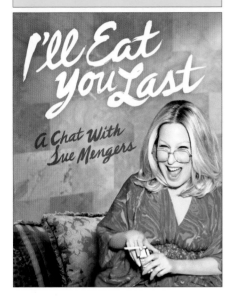

Bette Midler is the entire cast of this solo show about Hollywood super-agent Sue Mengers who breezes through her life story as she dishes the dirt on her stable of stars including Ali McGraw, Julie Harris, Gene Hackman and her über-client Barbra Streisand—who has just fired her. As Mengers lays out her ironclad rules about how to handle clients, she reflects on the transitory nature of stardom, and of life itself: "The credits roll sooner than you think."

CAST

Sue Mengers..........................BETTE MIDLER

SETTING

The living room of Sue Mengers'
Beverly Hills home...1981.

---

⑧ BOOTH THEATRE
222 West 45th Street
A Shubert Organization Theatre

Philip J. Smith, *Chairman*   Robert E. Wankel, *President*

Graydon Carter   Arielle Tepper Madover
James L. Nederlander   The Shubert Organization
Terry Allen Kramer   Stephanie P. McClelland   Jeffrey Finn
Ruth Hendel   Larry Magid   Jon B. Platt   Scott & Brian Zeilinger

Present

Bette Midler

in

I'll Eat you Last
A Chat With Sue Mengers

A New Play By
John Logan

Scenic Designer	Costume Designer	Lighting Designer	Sound Designer
Scott Pask	**Ann Roth**	**Hugh Vanstone**	**Fitz Patton**

Press Representative	Advertising & Marketing	Associate Director	Production Manager
Boneau/Bryan-Brown	**Serino/Coyne**	**William Joseph Barnes**	**Juniper Street Productions, Inc.**

Props	Company Manager	General Manager
Kathy Fabian	**Barbara Crompton**	**101 Productions, Ltd.**

Directed by
Joe Mantello

4/24/13

Bette Midler as
Sue Mengers

Photo by Richard Termine

I'll Eat You Last: A Chat with Sue Mengers

Bette Midler
Sue Mengers

John Logan
Playwright

Joe Mantello
Director

Scott Pask
Scenic Design

Ann Roth
Costume Design

Hugh Vanstone
Lighting Design

Fitz Patton
Sound Design

William Joseph Barnes
Associate Director/ Production Stage Manager

Ana Rose Greene, Guy Kwan, Joe DeLuise, Hillary Blanken
Juniper Street Productions, Inc.
Production Manager

Kathy Fabian
Props

Wendy Orshan
101 Productions, Ltd.
General Manager

Laurie Goldfeder
Stage Manager

Graydon Carter
Producer

Arielle Tepper Madover
Producer

James L. Nederlander
Producer

Philip J. Smith
The Shubert Organization
Producer

Robert E. Wankel
The Shubert Organization
Producer

Terry Allen Kramer
Producer

Stephanie P. McClelland
Producer

Jeffrey Finn
Producer

Ruth Hendel
Producer

Larry Magid
Producer

Jon B. Platt
Producer

Scott Zeilinger
Producer

Brian Zeilinger
Producer

STAGE DOOR
Amanda Tramontozzi

FRONT OF HOUSE
Front Row (L-R):
Marjorie Glover,
Nadine Space,
Beth Naji (Infrared Rep)
Back Row (L-R):
Timothy Wilhelm (Chief Usher),
Alexander MacKay,
Reginald Browne,
Daniel Rosario
Not pictured:
Bernadette Bokun
(Ticket-taker),
Nirmala Sharma (Director),
Chrissie Collins,
Marco Malgiolio

BOX OFFICE
(L-R): Eva Bowen, Kathy Cadunz, Vigi Cadunz
Not pictured: Dennis Vogelgesang

Photos by Brian Mapp

I'll Eat You Last: A Chat with Sue Mengers

Photo by Brian Mapp

CREW

Front (L-R):
Laurel Ann Wilson (House Manager), Susan Bennett-Goulet (House Electrician)

Back (L-R):
Mary Brunetti (Hair Supervisor), Chris "Smitty" Smith (House Carpenter), James Keane (House Props), Oslyn Holder (Make-up Designer), Billy Barnes (Production Stage Manager/Associate Director), Laurie Goldfeder (Stage Manager)

**STAFF FOR *I'LL EAT YOU LAST:*
*A CHAT WITH SUE MENGERS***

GENERAL MANAGEMENT
101 PRODUCTIONS, LTD.
Wendy Orshan   Jeffrey M. Wilson
Elie Landau   Chris Morey   Ron Gubin

COMPANY MANAGER
Barbara Crompton

GENERAL PRESS REPRESENTATIVE
BONEAU/BRYAN-BROWN
Adrian Bryan-Brown
Aaron Meier   Kelly Guiod

PRODUCTION MANAGEMENT
JUNIPER STREET PRODUCTIONS
Hillary Blanken   Joseph DeLuise
Guy Kwan   Ana Rose Greene

Production Stage Manager ....William Joseph Barnes
Stage Manager ....Laurie Goldfeder
Associate Scenic Design ....Orit Jacoby Carroll,
Jeffrey Hinchee
Assistant Scenic Designer ....Lauren Alvarez
Associate Costume Designer ....Michelle Matland
Associate Lighting Designer ....Craig Stelzenmuller
Associate Sound Designer ....Joshua Reid
Production Carpenter ....Erik E. Hansen
Production Electrician ....Jon Lawson
Production Sound ....Josh Maszle
Associate Props Coordinator ....Carrie Mossman
Assistant Props Coordinator ....Will Barrios
Props Artisans ....Mary Wilson, Holly Griffen
Specialty Props ....Propstar, Tom Carroll Scenery
Moving Light Programmer ....Eric Norris
Advance Flyman ....Chad Woerner
Wardrobe Supervisor ....Kay Grunder
Hair Supervisor ....Mary Brunetti
Make-up Supervisor ....Oslyn Holder
Production Assistant ....Devin Day

Advertising ....Serino/Coyne/
Nancy Coyne, Angelo Desimini,
Tom Callahan, Peter Gunther, Matt Upshaw,
Lauren Houlberg, Christina Hernandez
Marketing ....Serino/Coyne/
Leslie Barrett, Diana Salameh
Website Design & Online Marketing ....Serino/Coyne/
Jim Glaub, Chip Meyrelles,
Laurie Connor, Kevin Keating,
Mark Seeley, Andrea Cuevas
Assistant to Ms. Midler ....Jill Hattersley
Assistant to Mr. Logan ....Amanda Crisses
Producing Associate to Mr. Carter ....Annabelle Dunne
Managing Director for ATM
Productions ....Holly Ferguson
Assistant to the General Managers ....Michael Rudd
101 Productions, Ltd. Staff ....Beth Blitzer,
Mark Gagliardi, Kathy Kim,
Mike McLinden, Mary-Six Rupert,
Steve Supeck
101 Productions, Ltd. Interns ....Serene Lim,
Caroline Watters
Legal Counsel ....Lazarus & Harris LLP/
Scott Lazarus, Robert Harris
Accountant ....Marks Paneth & Shron LLP/
Chris Cacace
Controllers.................Patricia Pedersen, Floyd Sklaver
Banking ....City National Bank/Anne McSweeney
Insurance ....DeWitt Stern Group, Inc.
Opening Night Coordinator ....Serino/Coyne/
Suzanne Tobak
Merchandising ....Creative Goods/Pete Milano
Music Clearance ....BZ/Rights & Permissions Inc.
Immigration ....Entertainment Visa Consultants, LLC/
David King
Payroll Services ....Castellana Services, Inc.
Theatre Displays ....King Displays, Inc./Wayne Sapper
Group Sales ....Telecharge.com Group Sales

To learn more about the production, please visit
www.illeatyoulast.com

CREDITS/SPECIAL THANKS
Scenery and scenic effects built, painted and electrified by

PRG Scenic Technologies. Lighting equipment from PRG. Sound equipment from Masque Sound. Handwoven rug by Dilmaghani. Upholstery by Jammal Upholstery and Decor. Special thanks to Elton John, Boaty Boatwright, Barry Diller, Angelica Huston, Ali McGraw, Christopher Walken, Michael Caine, Lorne Michaels, Fran Liebowitz, David Geffen, Cher, Marlo Thomas, Robert Evans.

This production was rehearsed at
The New 42nd Street Studios.

MUSIC CREDITS
"Freeze Frame" written by Peter Wolf and Seth Justman. Courtesy of Universal Music Publishing Group and BMG Rights Management (U.S.) LLC. **"Stoney End"** written by Laura Nyro. Courtesy of EMI Entertainment World, Inc.

 THE SHUBERT ORGANIZATION, INC.
Board of Directors

Philip J. Smith	**Robert E. Wankel**
Chairman	President
Wyche Fowler, Jr.	**Diana Phillips**
Lee J. Seidler	**Michael I. Sovern**

Stuart Subotnick

Chief Financial Officer ....Elliot Greene
Sr. Vice President, Ticketing ....David Andrews
Vice President, Finance ....Juan Calvo
Vice President, Human Resources ....Cathy Cozens
Vice President, Facilities ....John Darby
Vice President, Theatre Operations ....Peter Entin
Vice President, Marketing ....Charles Flateman
Vice President, Audit ....Anthony LaMattina
Vice President, Ticket Sales ....Brian Mahoney
Vice President, Creative Projects ...........D.S. Moynihan
Vice President, Real Estate ....Julio Peterson

House Manager ....Laurel Ann Wilson

Jekyll & Hyde

First Preview: April 5, 2013. Opened: April 18, 2013.
Closed May 12, 2013 after 15 Previews and 30 Performances.

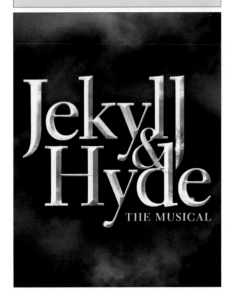

PLAYBILL

Revival of this musical retelling of the Robert Louis Stevenson classic "The Strange Case of Dr. Jekyll and Mr. Hyde," about idealistic Dr. Henry Jekyll who develops a potion that he hopes will enable him to separate man's good nature from his evil nature. Instead, the potion transforms him into the violent Edward Hyde who stalks nighttime London seeking victims. Trying to preserve his relationship with the virginal Emma Carew, Jekyll struggles to win back control as Hyde, who acts out his baser urges with the streetwalker Lucy Harris, works inexorably to take over his life.

CAST

Henry Jekyll/
   Edward Hyde ....CONSTANTINE MAROULIS
Lucy Harris ....DEBORAH COX
Emma Carew ....TEAL WICKS
Sir Danvers Carew...............RICHARD WHITE
John Utterson ....LAIRD MACKINTOSH
The Bishop of Basingstoke/
   Spider ....DAVID BENOIT
Lady Beaconsfield ....BLAIR ROSS
Simon Stride ....JASON WOOTEN
Lord Savage ....BRIAN GALLAGHER
Sir Archibald Proops, Q.C. ....MEL JOHNSON JR.
General Lord Glossop ....AARON RAMEY
Nellie ....DANA COSTELLO
Jekyll's Father/Poole ....JAMES JUDY
Bisset/Minister ....JERRY CHRISTAKOS
People of London ....JERRY CHRISTAKOS,
            DANA COSTELLO, WENDY FOX,

Continued on next page

Continued on next page

⇒N⇐ MARQUIS THEATRE

UNDER THE DIRECTION OF JAMES M. NEDERLANDER AND JAMES L. NEDERLANDER

NEDERLANDER PRESENTATIONS, INC.   INDEPENDENT PRESENTERS NETWORK
CHUNSOO SHIN   LUIGI CAIOLA   STEWART F. LANE / BONNIE COMLEY

present

CONSTANTINE MAROULIS   DEBORAH COX

in

Jekyll & Hyde
THE MUSICAL

Conceived for the stage by Steve Cuden and Frank Wildhorn

**Book and Lyrics by LESLIE BRICUSSE
Music by FRANK WILDHORN**

Also Starring
TEAL WICKS

LAIRD MACKINTOSH   RICHARD WHITE

STEPHEN MITCHELL BROWN   JERRY CHRISTAKOS   DANA COSTELLO   WENDY FOX
BRIAN GALLAGHER   SEAN JENNESS   MEL JOHNSON JR.   JAMES JUDY
ASHLEY LOREN   COURTNEY MARKOWITZ   AARON RAMEY   EMMY RAVER-LAMPMAN
ROB RICHARDSON   BLAIR ROSS   DOUG STORM   HALEY SWINDAL
JASON WOOTEN   and DAVID BENOIT as Bishop/Spider

Scenic & Costume Design	Lighting Design	Sound Design	Projection Design
TOBIN OST	JEFF CROITER	KEN TRAVIS	DANIEL BRODIE

Casting by	Hair & Wig Design	Associate Director/Choreographer
TESLEY + COMPANY JUSTIN HUFF, CSA	CHARLES G. LAPOINTE	RICHARD J. HINDS

Music Director	Music Coordinator	Production Manager	Technical Supervisor
STEVEN LANDAU	DAVID LAI	BUCK MASON	MB PRODUCTIONS NY MIKE BAUDER

National Press Representative	Production Stage Manager	General Manager
THE HARTMAN GROUP	ERIC SPROSTY	THE CHARLOTTE WILCOX COMPANY MATTHEW W. KRAWIEC

Orchestrations	Musical Supervisor/Arrangements
KIM SCHARNBERG	JASON HOWLAND

Directed and Choreographed by
JEFF CALHOUN

This production originally produced by McCoy Rigby Entertainment and La Mirada Theatre for the Performing Arts
Original Broadway Production by PACE Theatrical Group, Inc.

4/18/13

(L-R): Constantine Maroulis and Deborah Cox

Photo by Chris Bennion

Jekyll & Hyde

MUSICAL NUMBERS

ACT I

"Lost in the Darkness"	Jekyll
"I Need to Know"	Jekyll
"Façade"	Company
"Board of Governors"	Jekyll, Danvers, Bishop & Company
"Pursue the Truth"/"Façade" (reprise)	Jekyll, Utterson & Company
"Take Me As I Am"	Jekyll, Emma
"Letting Go"	Danvers, Emma
"Bring on the Men"	Lucy & Company
"This Is the Moment"	Jekyll
"Transformation"	Jekyll, Hyde
"Alive!"	Hyde
"His Work – And Nothing More"	Utterson, Emma, Danvers, Jekyll
"Sympathy, Tenderness"	Lucy
"Someone Like You"	Lucy
"Alive!" (reprise)	Hyde

ACT II

"Murder"	Company
"Once Upon a Dream"	Emma
"Reflections"	Jekyll
"In His Eyes"	Lucy, Emma
"Dangerous Game"	Hyde, Lucy
"The Way Back"	Utterson, Jekyll
"A New Life"	Lucy
"Sympathy, Tenderness" (reprise)	Hyde
"Confrontation"	Jekyll, Hyde
"Letting Go" (reprise)	Danvers, Emma
"The Wedding"	Jekyll, Emma

All Songs feature lyrics by Leslie Bricusse and music by Frank Wildhorn, except "Alive!," "Board of Governors," "Transformation," "His Work – And Nothing More," "Once Upon A Dream" and "Murder," which have lyrics by Steven Cuden, Leslie Bricusse and Frank Wildhorn, and music by Frank Wildhorn.

(L-R): Teal Wicks and Constantine Maroulis

Photo by Chris Bennion

Cast Continued

BRIAN GALLAGHER, SEAN JENNESS,
MEL JOHNSON JR., JAMES JUDY,
ASHLEY LOREN, COURTNEY MARKOWITZ,
AARON RAMEY, EMMY RAVER-LAMPMAN,
BLAIR ROSS, DOUG STORM,
JASON WOOTEN

UNDERSTUDIES
For Jekyll/Hyde:
AARON RAMEY, JASON WOOTEN
For Lucy:
WENDY FOX, EMMY RAVER-LAMPMAN
For Emma:
DANA COSTELLO,
COURTNEY MARKOWITZ
For John Utterson:
BRIAN GALLAGHER, AARON RAMEY
For Sir Danvers Carew:
JERRY CHRISTAKOS, JAMES JUDY
For Bishop/Spider:
STEPHEN MITCHELL BROWN,
ROB RICHARDSON

SWINGS
STEPHEN MITCHELL BROWN,
ROB RICHARDSON, HALEY SWINDAL

Dance Captain: HALEY SWINDAL
Fight Captain: ROB RICHARDSON

ORCHESTRA
Music Supervisor:
JASON HOWLAND
Music Director/Conductor/Keyboard 2:
STEVEN LANDAU
Keyboard 1: JEFF TANSKI
Bass: CHRIS LIGHTCAP
Guitar: NICHOLAS DiFABBIO
Drums: CLINT de GANON
Percussion: BILL LANHAM
Violins: KATHERINE LIVOLSI-LANDAU,
CENOVIA CUMMINS, SUZY PERELMAN
Viola: DAVID BLINN
Cello: MAIRI DORMAN-PHANEUF
Horn: R.J. KELLEY
Woodwinds: DAVID MANN
Bass Trombone: JENNIFER WHARTON
Music Coordinator: DAVID LAI

Jekyll & Hyde

Constantine Maroulis
*Henry Jekyll/
Edward Hyde*

Deborah Cox
Lucy Harris

Teal Wicks
Emma Carew

Laird Mackintosh
John Utterson

Richard White
Sir Danvers Carew

David Benoit
Bishop/Spider

Stephen Mitchell
Brown
Swing

Jerry Christakos
*Bisset/Minister/
Ensemble*

Dana Costello
Nellie/Ensemble

Wendy Fox
Ensemble

Brian Gallagher
Savage/Ensemble

Sean Jenness
Ensemble

Mel Johnson Jr.
Proops/Ensemble

James Judy
*Jekyll's Father/
Poole/Ensemble*

Ashley Loren
Ensemble

Courtney Markowitz
Ensemble

Aaron Ramey
Glossop/Ensemble

Emmy
Raver-Lampman
Ensemble

Rob Richardson
Swing/Fight Captain

Blair Ross
*Lady Beaconsfield/
Ensemble*

Doug Storm
Ensemble

Haley Swindal
*Swing/Dance
Captain*

Jason Wooten
Stride/Ensemble

Leslie Bricusse
Book/Lyrics

Frank Wildhorn
Co-Conceiver/Music

Steve Cuden
Co-Conceiver

Jeff Calhoun
*Director/
Choreographer*

Tobin Ost
*Scenic/Costume
Design*

Jeff Croiter
Lighting Design

Ken Travis
Sound Design

Daniel Brodie
Projection Design

Charles G. LaPointe
Hair/Wig Design

Joe Dulude II
Make-up Design

Jason Howland
*Musical Supervisor/
Arrangements*

Kim Scharnberg
Orchestrations

Jekyll & Hyde

Billy Jay Stein
Electronic Music Designer

Bernard Telsey
Telsey + Company
Casting

Richard J. Hinds
Associate Director/ Choreographer

J. Allen Suddeth
Fight Director

Mike Bauder
MB Productions
Production Supervisor

Charlotte Wilcox
The Charlotte Wilcox Company
General Manager

David Lai
Music Coordinator

James M. Nederlander
Producer

James L. Nederlander
Producer

Luigi Caiola
Producer

Stewart F. Lane/Bonnie Comley
Producer

Photos by Brian Mapp

STAGE MANAGEMENT
(L-R): Eric Sprosty (Production Stage Manager),
Kelly Stillwell (Assistant Stage Manager),
Tom Jeffords (Stage Manager)

CREW
Front Row (L-R): Jessica Reiner,
Samantha Lawrence,
Laura Ellington, Moira Conrad,
Cat Dee, Renee Borys,
Richard Fabris
Middle Row (L-R): Eric McCree,
Andy Miller, Richard Byron,
Justin Stasiw, Chris Lavin
Back Row (L-R): Josh Moberly,
Dan Boesch, Chris Kluth,
Freddy Mecionis,
Scott Mecionis, Joe Sardo,
Dutch Edeburn, Derek Healy,
Matthew Keating,
Adam Lansing, Pat Marcus

Jekyll & Hyde

FRONT OF HOUSE
Front Row (L-R): Mariea Crainiciuc, Carolann Falasca (Assistant Theatre Manager), David Calhoun (Theatre Manager), Daisy Irizarry
Back Row (L-R): Odalis Concepcion, Nancy Diaz, Maxi Abdallah

STAFF FOR *JEKYLL & HYDE*

GENERAL MANAGEMENT
THE CHARLOTTE WILCOX COMPANY
Dina Friedler   Chantel Hopper   Scott Ellis
Margaret Wilcox   Samantha Gloria
Stephen Donovan

GENERAL PRESS REPRESENTATIVE
THE HARTMAN GROUP
Michael Hartman   Matt Ross
Whitney Holden Gore   Nicole Capatasto

CASTING
TELSEY + COMPANY
Bernie Telsey CSA, Will Cantler CSA,
David Vaccari CSA,
Bethany Knox CSA, Craig Burns CSA,
Tiffany Little Canfield CSA, Rachel Hoffman CSA,
Justin Huff CSA, Patrick Goodwin CSA,
Abbie Brady-Dalton CSA,
David Morris, Cesar A. Rocha, Andrew Femenella,
Karyn Casl, Kristina Bramhall, Jessie Malone

COMPANY MANAGER ....**Ryan Lympus**
Assistant Company Manager ....**Claire Trempe**
Stage Manager ....Tom Jeffords
Assistant Stage Manager ....Kelly Stillwell
Dance Captain ....Haley Swindal
Fight Captain ....Rob Richardson
Dialect Coach ....Shane Ann Younts
Properties Designer ....Emiliano Pares
Makeup Designer ....Joe Dulude II
Assistant to the Director ....Derek Hersey
Associate Set Designer ....Christine Peters
Associate Costume Designer ....Leslie Malitz
Costume Intern ....Tony Giruzzi
Associate Lighting Designer ....Wilburn Bonnell
Associate Lighting Designer ....Kenneth Wills
Associate Sound Designer ....Alex Hawthorn
Assistant to Projection Designer ....Aleks Gezentsvey
Assistant to Prop Designer ....Brian Schweppe
Projection Programmer ....Patrick Southern

Moving Light Programmer ....Josh Selander
Head Carpenter ....Chris Kluth
Head Electrician/Projections ....Josh Moberly
Head Sound Engineer ....Justin Stasiw
Head Properties ....Andrew Miller
Wardrobe Supervisor ....Moira Conrad
Hair Supervisor ....Pat Marcus
Deck Carpenter/Automation ....Greg Edeburn
Assistant Electrician ....Adam Lansing
Assistant Sound Engineer ....Eric McCree
Assistant Properties ....Dan Boesch
Assistant Wardrobe Supervisor ....Cat Dee
Assistant Hair Supervisor ....Rich Fabris
Advance Carpenters ....Glenn Jeffords, Jerry Tisdale
Advance Electrician ....Peter Hulin
Advance Properties ....Bobbie Gregory
Advance Sound ....Brett Rothstein
Advance Hair Supervisor ....Patricia LaRocco
Dressers ....Renee Borys, Laura Ellington,
Tree Sarvay, Samantha Lawrence,
Christopher Lavin, Matthew Keating,
Richard Byron, Jessica Reiner
Electronic Music Design ....Billy Jay Stein
Music Preparation ....JoAnn Kane Music Service/
Russ Bartmus

Legal Counsel ....Levine, Plotkin and Menin
Accountant ....Marks Paneth & Shron/
Mark D'Ambrosi, Jana Jevnikar
Advertising ....Serino/Coyne/
Angelo Desimini, Scott Johnson,
Tom Callahan, Kara Weintraub
Payroll Services ....Checks and Balances
Production Photographer ....Chris Bennion
Banking ....City National Bank/
Stephanie Dalton
Merchandise ....Creative Goods
Management Services ....Marion Finkler Taylor

CREDITS AND SPECIAL THANKS
Deborah Cox's wigs designed by Oscar James. Scenery built by Hudson Scenic Studio, Inc. Automation provided by Hudson Scenic Studio Inc. Sound by Sound Associates Inc.

Lighting by PRG. Video by WorldStage Inc. Makeup provided by M•A•C Cosmetics. Costumes by Jennifer Love Costumes, Asolo Repertory Theatre Costume Shop, Susan Eversden, Nancy Malitz, Rebecca Willis, Alysha DeVries, Teri Tavares, CEGO NY. Projection lead animation by Gabriel Aronson. Set mockup by the Spoon Group. Trucking provided by Clark Transfer. Hydrotherapy hallway by Justin Arthur. Image of "Charles" by Jessi Hardesty. Special thanks to Sam Fine, Oscar James, Jef Sharrat, Ryan O'Connor, David Covach, Mütter Museum.

Jekyll & Hyde
rehearsed at the New 42nd Street Studios.

NEDERLANDER

Chairman ....**James M. Nederlander**
President ....**James L. Nederlander**

Executive Vice President
Nick Scandalios

Vice President	Senior Vice President
Corporate Development	Labor Relations
Charlene S. Nederlander	**Herschel Waxman**

Vice President	Chief Financial Officer
Jim Boese	**Freida Sawyer Belviso**

STAFF FOR THE MARQUIS THEATRE
Manager ....David Calhoun
Assistant Managers ....Sean Coughlin,
Carolann Falasca
Treasurer ....Rick Waxman
Assistant Treasurer ....John Rooney
Carpenter................................Joseph P. Valentino
Electrician...James Mayo
Property Man ....Scott Mecionis

Jekyll & Hyde
SCRAPBOOK

Correspondent: Laird Mackintosh, "John Utterson"

Memorable Opening Night Gifts: Our team—Jeff Calhoun (Director), Frank Wildhorn (Composer), Leslie Bricusse (Writer) and Ricky Hinds (Associate Director)—gave us all a bound photo album covering our entire journey, from our first day of rehearsal at the 42nd Street Studios through the tour and finally to our marquee going up on Broadway. It is a great memento of the show and beautifully done. And our Swings (Rob Richardson, Stephen Mitchell Brown and Haley Swindal) gave us one of the coolest opening night presents of all time: Playing cards, custom made, with the *Jekyll & Hyde* logo on one side and a picture of everyone in the cast and creatives on the faces—brilliant!

Most Exciting Celebrity Visitor and What They Did/Said: Ask Clay Aiken...

Who Got the Gypsy Robe? Jason Wooten.

Which Actor Performed the Most Roles in This Show (and how many)?: David Benoit has a double role built into the show: the Bishop/Spider track. Jerry Christakos plays the Valet, the Doctor, the John (!), the Minister and Bisset the Apothecary all in his track. Haley Swindal has been on (at the time of this writing) for 5 of her 6 swing tracks. And of course, Constantine Maroulis—who is Jekyll AND Hyde!!

Who Has Done the Most Shows in Their Career: James Judy lays claim to this one... not exactly sure of the number, but 35 years in the biz with sometimes five or six shows a year... you do the math!

Special Backstage Rituals: Our company managers, Ryan Lympus and Claire Trempe, bought us a Keurig for the tour. It was definitely a pre-show gathering place.

Favorite Moment During Each Performance: Power ballads. That says it all.

Favorite In-Theatre Gathering Place: Green Room, second floor of the Marquis: big table with the cast working on a puzzle.

Favorite Off-Site Hangout: The Starbucks—75 feet from the stage door.

Mascot: We never really had a mascot, but there's a rubber chicken in the pit, and Jason Howland has been known to conduct with it.

Favorite Therapy: We have Ricola and Altoids backstage—couldn't do the show without 'em.

Most Memorable Ad-Lib: Ask Constantine.

Memorable Tweet: Again, ask Clay Aiken!

What Did You Think of the Web Buzz on Your Show: Web buzz for *Jekyll* was always awesome. We have the best fans in the world: the Jekkies!

Memorable Press Encounter: Teal Wicks and I once did a TV interview with a host that wasn't there. She was sick, so the cameraman asked all the questions and they dubbed her voice in later!

Memorable Stage Door Fan Encounter: "Fiction Amy"—probably one of our most intense fans—from loving us to hating us to loving us again, she used to dress up like Deborah Cox

at the stage door and was known to send Constantine some pretty racy "literature."

Fastest Costume Change: I can lay claim to the fastest costume change in the show: Something like 32 seconds to do a complete look change.

Who Wore the Heaviest/Hottest Costume: Blair Ross, who wears a knockout gorgeous dress as Lady B., but it weighs a ton, and she has to hoist

it over her shoulders to get it up the three flights of stairs to her dressing room.

Who Wore the Least: The ladies of the Spider's Web! Skimpy!!

Catchphrases Only the Company Would Recognize: "Airport Pub-crawl," "Bloody-Mary Monday" and "There goes our overage."

Best In-House Parody Lyrics: "Look at this another hair-tie, just like that other hair-tie, that makes them hair-ties three and four!"

Memorable Directorial Notes: In rehearsal: "Best idea wins." Onstage before our first preview: "First previews are like sex with the lights on: you're gonna have a good time, but you're probably going to see something you wish you hadn't."

Company Legend: Mel Johnson Jr.!— original companies of *On the 20th Century, Eubie!, The Rink* and *Big Deal*!!!

Understudy Anecdote: Jason Wooten (u/s Jekyll and Hyde): "I had an amazing time every chance I had to be Jekyll/Hyde and was surrounded by the most supportive group of actors a thespian could hope for." Emmy Raver-Lampman (u/s Lucy): "Like Jason, every time I went on I felt a sense of calm because of the love and support I got from the wonderful cast and crew. Every moment was enjoyable."

Nicknames: James Judy = "Judge Jud."

Sweethearts Within the Company: No sweethearts. Unbelievable!! But we did have two marriages: Jason Wooten married April Berry and Sean Jenness married Linda Zimmerman. Congrats!

Embarrassing Moments: The all-time classic of *J&H* took place on our FIRST preview in La Mirada, CA. Brian Gallagher, who plays Lord Savage, gets dressed (along with all the Board of Governors) onstage—from underwear to full steampunk/Victorian costume. FIRST preview... FIRST time in front of an audience... his dresser (God bless) forgot to set his pants. So Brian did the entire fifteen-minute Board of Governors scene with NO PANTS on! However, he did get the first and only exit-applause of the run for that scene. Also, a funny show story I lived through: James Judy, Teal Wicks and I were just about to make an entrance for one of the "study" scenes and James, who was under the weather and had lost the lower register of his voice, said to me one second before we stepped onstage: "My voice might be a little higher in this scene." He then proceeded to play the MOST serious scene in a Dame Edna falsetto that had all of us—including Richard White, Constantine Maroulis and Deborah Cox, who had come onstage midway through the scene—struggling to contain ourselves. Gold!

Ghostly Encounters Backstage: No ghostly encounters, unless you count Deborah Cox's cardboard standee being placed behind the doors and in the shower stalls of people's dressing rooms. It certainly scared the hell out of people as much as any ghost would!!

Coolest Thing About Being in This Show: The people, of course! Best team (cast, crew and orchestra, both on the road and on Broadway) that anyone could hope for. Many, many fond memories of this one. Special shout-out to Moira Conrad and Cat Dee, our incredible wardrobe team who gave us so many great themed parties ("Robbie Burns Night!," "1st Annual Jekyll and Hyde Awards Ceremonies"), contests, games and who dressed up like superheroes backstage! And... In loving memory of Bill Gregory.

1. Curtain call on opening night with (L-R): Deborah Cox, Constantine Maroulis, Teal Wicks and *Yearbook* correspondent, Laird Mackintosh.
2. (L-R): Robert Cuccioli, the original J&H, with Maroulis at the opening night party.
3. A two-dimensional Cox gets a scream out of Mackintosh.
4. That's a fine how-do-you-do?! Linda Eder, who originated the role of Lucy, with Ms. Cox, her 2013 counterpart, after opening night.

Jersey Boys

First Preview: October 4, 2005. Opened: November 6, 2005.
Still running as of May 31, 2013.

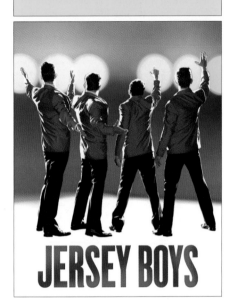

PLAYBILL

JERSEY BOYS

A musical based on the lives and careers of the close-harmony pop group The Four Seasons. We meet founder Tommy DeVito, a bad boy who is constantly in trouble with the law, supportive Nick Massi, songwriter Bob Gaudio, and finally lead singer Frankie Valli, whose soulful falsetto helps loft the foursome to international success. That success, along with DeVito's troubles with the mob and changes in the public's musical taste, helps splinter the original group. But the indefatigable Valli and the prolific Gaudio help make sure that the music lives on.

CAST

(in alphabetical order)

Nick DeVito, Stosh, Billy Dixon, Norman Waxman,
   Charlie Calello (and others) .....MILES AUBREY
Nick Massi ....MATT BOGART
Mary Delgado, Angel
   (and others) ....CARA COOPER
French Rap Star, Detective One, Hal Miller,
   Barry Belson, Police Officer,
   Davis (and others) ....JOHN EDWARDS
Joey, Recording Studio Engineer
   (and others) ....RUSSELL FISCHER
Bob Crewe (and others) ....PETER GREGUS
Tommy DeVito ....ANDY KARL
Gyp DeCarlo (and others) ....MARK LOTITO
Officer Petrillo, Hank Majewski, Crewe's PA,
   Joe Long (and others) ..KRISTOFER McNEELEY
Church Lady, Miss Frankie Nolan, Bob's Party Girl,
   Angel, Lorraine (and others) ......JESSICA RUSH
Frankie Valli (Wed. &
   Sat. Matinees) .....DOMINIC SCAGLIONE JR.

Continued on next page

JORDAN ROTH
President

PAUL LIBIN
Executive Vice President

JACK VIERTEL
Senior Vice President

Dodger Theatricals Joseph J. Grano Tamara and Kevin Kinsella Pelican Group
in association with Latitude Link Rick Steiner/Osher/Staton/Bell/Mayerson Group

present

JERSEY BOYS

The Story of Frankie Valli & The Four Seasons

Book by	Music by	Lyrics by
Marshall Brickman & Rick Elice	**Bob Gaudio**	**Bob Crewe**

with

Matt Bogart Andy Karl Jarrod Spector Quinn VanAntwerp

Miles Aubrey Candi Boyd Jared Bradshaw Cara Cooper Ken Dow John Edwards
Russell Fischer Kristofer McNeeley Katie O'Toole Joe Payne Jessica Rush
Dominic Scaglione Jr. Nathan Scherich Sara Schmidt Taylor Sternberg
with Peter Gregus and Mark Lotito

Scenic Design	Costume Design	Lighting Design	Sound Design
Klara Zieglerova	Jess Goldstein	Howell Binkley	Steve Canyon Kennedy
Projection Design	Wig and Hair Design	Fight Director	Production Supervisor
Michael Clark	Charles LaPointe	Steve Rankin	Richard Hester
Orchestrations	Music Coordinator	Conductor	Production Stage Manager
Steve Orich	John Miller	Andrew Wilder	Michelle Bosch
Technical Supervisor	East Coast Casting	West Coast Casting	Company Manager
Peter Fulbright	Tara Rubin Casting	Sharon Bialy C.S.A. Sherry Thomas C.S.A.	Sandra Carlson
Associate Producers	Executive Producer	Promotions	Press Representative
Lauren Mitchell Rhoda Mayerson Stage Entertainment	Sally Campbell Morse	Red Rising Marketing	Boneau/Bryan-Brown

Music Direction, Vocal Arrangements & Incidental Music
Ron Melrose

Choreography
Sergio Trujillo

Directed by
Des McAnuff

World Premiere Produced by La Jolla Playhouse, La Jolla, CA
Christopher Ashley, Artistic Director & Michael S. Rosenberg, Managing Director

The producers wish to thank Theatre Development Fund for its support of this production.

10/1/12

(L-R): Drew Gehling, Jarrod Spector, Jeremy Kushnier and Matt Bogart

Photo by Joan Marcus

Jersey Boys

MUSICAL NUMBERS

ACT I

"Ces Soirées-La (Oh What a Night)" – Paris, 2000 ....French Rap Star, Backup Group
"Silhouettes" ....Tommy DeVito, Nick Massi, Nick DeVito,
Frankie Castelluccio
"You're the Apple of My Eye" ....Tommy DeVito, Nick Massi, Nick DeVito
"I Can't Give You Anything But Love" ....Frankie Castelluccio
"Earth Angel" ....Tommy DeVito, Full Company
"Sunday Kind of Love" ....Frankie Valli, Tommy DeVito, Nick Massi, Nick's Date
"My Mother's Eyes" ....Frankie Valli
"I Go Ape" ....The Four Lovers
"(Who Wears) Short Shorts" ....The Royal Teens
"I'm in the Mood for Love/Moody's Mood for Love" ....Frankie Valli
"Cry for Me" ....Bob Gaudio, Frankie Valli, Tommy DeVito, Nick Massi
"An Angel Cried" ....Hal Miller and The Rays
"I Still Care" ....Miss Frankie Nolan and The Romans
"Trance" ....Billy Dixon and The Topix
"Sherry" ....The Four Seasons
"Big Girls Don't Cry" ....The Four Seasons
"Walk Like a Man" ....The Four Seasons
"December, 1963 (Oh What a Night)" ....Bob Gaudio, Full Company
"My Boyfriend's Back" ....The Angels
"My Eyes Adored You" ....Frankie Valli, Mary Delgado, The Four Seasons
"Dawn (Go Away)" ....The Four Seasons
"Walk Like a Man" (reprise) ....Full Company

ACT II

"Big Man in Town" ....The Four Seasons
"Beggin'" ....The Four Seasons
"Stay" ....Bob Gaudio, Frankie Valli, Nick Massi
"Let's Hang On (To What We've Got)" ....Bob Gaudio, Frankie Valli
"Opus 17 (Don't You Worry 'Bout Me)" ....Bob Gaudio, Frankie Valli and
The New Seasons
"Bye Bye Baby" ....Frankie Valli and The Four Seasons
"C'mon Marianne" ....Frankie Valli and The Four Seasons
"Can't Take My Eyes Off You" ....Frankie Valli
"Working My Way Back to You" ....Frankie Valli and The Four Seasons
"Fallen Angel" ....Frankie Valli
"Rag Doll" ....The Four Seasons
"Who Loves You" ....The Four Seasons, Full Company

ORCHESTRA

Conductor:
ANDREW WILDER
Associate Conductor:
DEBRA BARSHA
Keyboards:
DEBRA BARSHA,
STEPHEN "HOOPS" SNYDER
Guitars:
JOE PAYNE, STEVE GIBB

Bass:
KEN DOW
Drums:
KEVIN DOW
Reeds:
MATT HONG, BEN KONO
Trumpet:
DAVID SPIER
Music Coordinator
JOHN MILLER

Cast Continued

Frankie's Mother, Nick's Date, Angel,
Francine (and others) ....SARA SCHMIDT
Frankie Valli ....JARROD SPECTOR
Bob Gaudio ....QUINN VanANTWERP
Thugs ....KEN DOW, JOE PAYNE

SWINGS
CANDI BOYD, JARED BRADSHAW,
KATIE O'TOOLE, NATHAN SCHERICH,
TAYLOR STERNBERG

Dance Captain:
KATIE O'TOOLE
Assistant Dance Captain:
CARA COOPER

UNDERSTUDIES
For Tommy DeVito:
JARED BRADSHAW, KRISTOFER McNEELEY
For Nick Massi:
MILES AUBREY, NATHAN SCHERICH
For Frankie Valli:
RUSSELL FISCHER,
DOMINIC SCAGLIONE JR.,
TAYLOR STERNBERG
For Bob Gaudio:
JARED BRADSHAW, NATHAN SCHERICH
For Gyp DeCarlo:
MILES AUBREY, NATHAN SCHERICH
For Bob Crewe:
JARED BRADSHAW, NATHAN SCHERICH

Jarrod Spector
as Frankie Valli
sings "Can't Take
My Eyes Off You"

Photo by Joan Marcus

Jersey Boys

Matt Bogart
Nick Massi

Andy Karl
Tommy DeVito

Jarrod Spector
Frankie Valli

Quinn VanAntwerp
Bob Gaudio

Peter Gregus
Bob Crewe and others

Mark Lotito
Gyp DeCarlo and others

Miles Aubrey
Norm Waxman and others

Candi Boyd
Swing

Jared Bradshaw
Swing

Cara Cooper
Mary Delgado and others

Ken Dow
Thug, Bass

John Edwards
Hal Miller and others

Russell Fischer
Joey, Recording Studio Engineer and others

Kristofer McNeeley
Hank Majewski and others

Katie O'Toole
Swing

Joe Payne
Thug, Guitars

Jessica Rush
Lorraine and others

Dominic Scaglione Jr.
Frankie Valli on Wed. & Sat. matinees

Nathan Scherich
Swing

Sara Schmidt
Francine and others

Taylor Sternberg
Swing

Marshall Brickman
Book

Rick Elice
Book

Bob Gaudio
Composer

Bob Crewe
Lyricist

Des McAnuff
Director

Sergio Trujillo
Choreographer

Ron Melrose
Music Direction, Vocal Arrangements and Incidental Music

Klara Zieglerova
Scenic Design

Jess Goldstein
Costume Design

Howell Binkley
Lighting Design

Steve Canyon Kennedy
Sound Design

Michael Clark
Projection Design

Charles LaPointe
Wig/Hair Design

Steve Rankin
Fight Director

Jersey Boys

Richard Hester
Production Supervisor

Steve Orich
Orchestrations

John Miller
Music Coordinator

Andrew Wilder
Conductor

Peter Fulbright/Tech Production Services
Technical Supervisor

Tara Rubin
Tara Rubin Casting
Casting

Sharon Bialy
West Coast Casting

Sherry Thomas
West Coast Casting

Stephen Gabis
Dialect Coach

Michael David
Dodger Theatricals
Producer

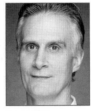
Edward Strong
Dodger Theatricals
Producer

Rocco Landesman
Dodger Theatricals
Producer

Joseph J. Grano
Producer

Kevin Kinsella
Producer

Tamara Kinsella
Producer

Ivor Royston
The Pelican Group
Producer

Rick Steiner
Producer

John and Bonnie Osher
Producer

Dan Staton
Producer

Marc Bell
Producer

Frederic H. Mayerson
Producer

Lauren Mitchell
Associate Producer

Rhoda Mayerson
Associate Producer

Joop van den Ende
Stage Entertainment
Associate Producer

Christopher Ashley
Artistic Director
La Jolla Playhouse
Original Producer

Michael S. Rosenberg
Managing Director
La Jolla Playhouse
Original Producer

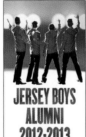
JERSEY BOYS ALUMNI 2012-2013

Erik Bates
Hank Majewski and others

John Lloyd Young
Frankie Valli

JERSEY BOYS TRANSFER STUDENTS 2012-2013

Erik Bates
Hank Majewski, Officer Petrillo, Crewe's PA, Joe Long

Charl Brown
French Rap Star, Detective One, Hal Miller, Barry Belson, Police Officer, Davis, and others

John Michael Dias
Frankie Valli Alternate

Drew Gehling
Bob Gaudio

Andy Karl
Tommy DeVito

Jersey Boys

Jeremy Kushnier
Tommy DeVito

Renée Marino
*Mary Delgado,
Angel and others*

Rashad Naylor
*French Rap Star,
Detective One, Hal
Miller, Barry Belson,
Police Officer, Davis*

Colin Trahan
Swing

John Lloyd Young
Frankie Valli

Photos by Brian Mapp

CREW
(L-R): Ron Fucarino (Fly Automation),
Ann Cavanaugh, Dan Dour (Head Carpenter)
Not pictured: Alex Gutierrez, Peter Wright,
Mike Kelly, Greg Burton

WARDROBE
Clockwise from bottom left: Michelle Sesco, Kristen Gardner,
Shaun Ozminski, Ricky Yates, Davis Duffield, Nick Staub, Kelly Kinsella,
Lee J. Austin (seated)

SOUND AND ELECTRIC
Front (L-R): Jan Nebozenko, Brian Aman, Sean Fedigan
Back (L-R): Dave Shepherd, Mike Lyons, Kevin Fedigan,
Not pictured: Rick Baxter, Gary Marlin, Julie Sloan

STAGE DOOR
Christine Snyder

FRONT OF HOUSE
Front Row (L-R):
Gail Worthman,
Seth Tucker,
Willa Burke,
Katie Schmidt,
Fatima Eljaouhari,
Natividad Nery
Back Row (L-R):
Kelvin Veras,
Carmella Galante,
Robert Fowler,
Raymond Polanco,
Ariel Martinez,
Farah Guzman,
Amy Marquez,
Russell Saylor

Jersey Boys

STAFF FOR *JERSEY BOYS*

GENERAL PRESS REPRESENTATION
BONEAU/BRYAN-BROWN
Adrian Bryan-Brown   Susanne Tighe
Heath Schwartz

COMPANY MANAGER
Sandra Carlson

PRODUCTION STAGE
    MANAGER ....MICHELLE BOSCH
Stage Manager ....Brendan M. Fay
Assistant Stage Manager ....Pamela Remler
Senior Associate
    General Manager ....Jennifer F. Vaughan
Associate General Manager ....Flora Johnstone
General Management Assistant ....Lauren Freed
Production Manager ....Jeff Parvin
Production Management Assistant ....Lyndsey Goode
Associate Company Manager ....Tim Sulka
Technical Supervision ....Tech Production Services/
    Peter Fulbright, Mary Duffe
Music Technical Design ....Deborah N. Hurwitz
Musician Swing ....Steve Gibb
Associate Director ....West Hyler
Assistant Director ....Holly-Anne Ruggiero
Second Assistant Director ....Alex Timbers
Associate Choreographers ....Danny Austin,
    Kelly Devine
Dialect Coach ....Stephen Gabis
Fight Captain ....Kristofer McNeeley
Associate Scenic Designers ....Nancy Thun, Todd Ivins
Assistant Scenic Designers ....Sonoka Gozelski,
    Matthew Myhrum
Associate Costume Designer ....Alejo Vietti
Assistant Costume Designers ....China Lee,
    Elizabeth Flauto
Associate Lighting Designer ....Patricia Nichols
Assistant Lighting Designer ....Sarah E. C. Maines
Associate Sound Designer ....Andrew Keister
Associate Projection Designer ....Jason Thompson
Assistant Projection Designer ....Chris Kateff
Story Board Artist ....Don Hudson
Casting Directors ....Tara Rubin, CSA;
    Merri Sugarman, CSA
Casting Associates ....Eric Woodall, CSA;
    Laura Schutzel, CSA;
    Dale Brown, CSA
Casting Assistants ....Kaitlin Shaw, Lindsay Levine
Automated Lighting Programmer ....Hillary Knox
Projection Programming ....Paul Vershbow
Set Model Builder ....Anne Goelz
Costume Intern ....Jessica Reed
Production Carpenter ....Michael W. Kelly
Deck Automation ....Greg Burton
Production Electrician ....James Fedigan
Head Electrician ....Brian Aman
Assistant Electrician ....Gary L. Marlin
Production Sound Engineer ....Andrew Keister
Head Sound Engineer ....Julie M. Randolph
Production Props ....Emiliano Pares
Assistant Props ....Kenneth Harris Jr.
Production Wardrobe Supervisor ....Lee J. Austin
Assistant Wardrobe Supervisor ....Michelle Sesco

Wardrobe Department ....Davis Duffield,
    Kristen Gardner, Kelly Kinsella,
    Shaun Ozminski, Nicholas Staub, Ricky Yates
Hair Supervisor ....Amy Neswald
Hair Department ....Hazel Higgins, Isaac Gryna
Assistant to John Miller ....Charles Butler
Synthesizer Programming ....Deborah N. Hurwitz,
    Steve Orich
Music Copying ....Anixter Rice Music Service
Music Production Assistant ....Alexandra Melrose
Dramaturg ....Allison Horsley
Associate to Messrs. Michael David
    and Ed Strong ....Pamela Lloyd
Advertising ....Serino Coyne, Inc./
    Scott Johnson, Marci Kaufman,
    Ryan Cunningham, Sarah Marcus
Marketing ....Dodger Marketing/
    Jessica Ludwig, Jessica Morris,
    Ann E. Van Nostrand, Tony Lance
Promotions ....Red Rising Marketing/
    Michael Redman, Nicole Pando
Banking ....Signature Bank/Barbara von Borstel
Payroll ....Castellana Services Inc./
    Lance Castellana, Norman Sewell,
    James Castellana
Accountants ....Schall and Ashenfarb, C.P.A.
Finance Director ....Paula Maldonado
Insurance ......AON/Albert G. Ruben Insurance Services/
    George Walden, Claudia Kaufman
Counsel ....Nan Bases, Esq.
Special Events ....John L. Haber
Travel Arrangements ....The "A" Team at Tzell Travel/
    Andi Henig
Information Technology Management ....ITelagen, Inc.
Web Design ....Curious Minds Media, Inc.
Production Photographer ....Joan Marcus
Theatre Displays ....King Displays

DODGERS
DODGER THEATRICALS
Mark Andrews, Michael Camp, Sandra Carlson, Dhyana Colony, Michael David, Scott Dennis, Anne Ezell, Lauren Freed, Mariann Fresiello, Tyler Gabbard, Lyndsey Goode, John L. Haber, Richard Hester, West Hyler, Flora Johnstone, Deana Marie Kirsch, Daniel Kogan, Abigail Kornet, Tony Lance, Pamela Lloyd, James Elliot Love, Jessica Ludwig, Paula Maldonado, Jennie Mamary, Lauren Mitchell, Jessica Morris, Sally Campbell Morse, Jeff Parvin, Samuel Rivera, R. Doug Rodgers, Maureen Rooney, Andrew Serna, Dana Sherman, Bridget Stegall, Edward Strong, Tim Sulka, Ellen Szorady, Ashley Tracey, Ann E. Van Nostrand, Jennifer F. Vaughan, Laurinda Wilson

Dodger Group Sales 1-877-5DODGER
Exclusive Tour Direction ....Steven Schnepp/
    Broadway Booking Office NYC

CREDITS
Scenery, show control and automation by ShowMotion, Inc., Norwalk, CT. Lighting equipment from PRG Lighting. Sound equipment by Masque Sound. Projection equipment by Sound Associates. Selected men's clothing custom made by Saint Laurie Merchant Tailors, New York City. Costumes executed by Carelli Costumes, Studio Rouge, Carmen Gee, John Kristiansen New York, Inc. Selected menswear by Carlos Campos. Props provided by

The Spoon Group, Downtime Productions, Tessa Dunning. Select guitars provided by Gibson Guitars. Laundry services provided by Ernest Winzer Theatrical Cleaners. Additional set and hand props courtesy of George Fenmore, Inc. Rosebud matches by Diamond Brands, Inc., Zippo lighters used. Rehearsed at the New 42nd Street Studios. Emergen-C by Alacer Corporation. PLAYBILL® cover photo by Chris Callis.

Grammy Award-winning cast album now available on Rhino Records.

www.jerseyboysinfo.com

Scenic drops adapted from *George Tice: Urban Landscapes*/W.W. Norton. Other photographs featured are from *George Tice: Selected Photographs 1953–1999*/David R. Godine. (Photographs courtesy of the Peter Fetterman Gallery/Santa Monica.)

SONG CREDITS
"Ces Soirees-La ("Oh What a Night")" (Bob Gaudio, Judy Parker, Yannick Zolo, Edmond David Bacri). Jobete Music Company Inc., Seasons Music Company (ASCAP). **"Silhouettes"** (Bob Crewe, Frank Slay, Jr.), Regent Music Corporation (BMI). **"You're the Apple of My Eye"** (Otis Blackwell), EMI Unart Catalog Inc. (BMI). **"I Can't Give You Anything But Love"** (Dorothy Fields, Jimmy McHugh), EMI April Music Inc., Aldi Music Company, Cotton Club Publishing (ASCAP). **"Earth Angel"** (Jesse Belvin, Curtis Williams, Gaynel Hodge), Embassy Music Corporation (BMI). **"Sunday Kind of Love"** (Barbara Belle, Anita Leanord Nye, Stan Rhodes, Louis Prima), LGL Music Inc./Larry Spier, Inc. (ASCAP). **"My Mother's Eyes"** (Abel Baer, L. Wolfe Gilbert), Abel Baer Music Company, EMI Feist Catalog Inc. (ASCAP). **"I Go Ape"** (Bob Crewe, Frank Slay, Jr.), MPL Music Publishing Inc. (ASCAP). **"(Who Wears) Short Shorts"** (Bob Gaudio, Bill Crandall, Tom Austin, Bill Dalton), EMI Longitude Music, Admiration Music Inc., Third Story Music Inc., and New Seasons Music (BMI). **"I'm in the Mood for Love"** (Dorothy Fields, Jimmy McHugh), Famous Music Corporation (ASCAP). **"Moody's Mood for Love"** (James Moody, Dorothy Fields, Jimmy McHugh), Famous Music Corporation (ASCAP). **"Cry for Me"** (Bob Gaudio), EMI Longitude Music, Seasons Four Music (BMI). **"An Angel Cried"** (Bob Gaudio), EMI Longitude Music (BMI). **"I Still Care"** (Bob Gaudio), Hearts Delight Music, Seasons Four Music (BMI). **"Trance"** (Bob Gaudio), Hearts Delight Music, Seasons Four Music (BMI). **"Sherry"** (Bob Gaudio), MPL Music Publishing Inc. (ASCAP). **"Big Girls Don't Cry"** (Bob Gaudio, Bob Crewe), MPL Music Publishing Inc. (ASCAP). **"Walk Like a Man"** (Bob Crewe, Bob Gaudio), Gavadima Music, MPL Communications Inc. (ASCAP). **"December, 1963 (Oh What a Night)"** (Bob Gaudio, Judy Parker), Jobete Music Company Inc, Seasons Music Company (ASCAP). **"My Boyfriend's Back"** (Robert Feldman, Gerald Goldstein, Richard Gottehrer), EMI Blackwood Music Inc. (BMI). **"My Eyes Adored You"** (Bob Crewe, Kenny Nolan), Jobete Music Company Inc, Kenny Nolan Publishing (ASCAP), Stone Diamond Music Corporation, Tannyboy Music (BMI). **"Dawn, Go Away"** (Bob Gaudio, Sandy Linzer), EMI Full Keel Music, Gavadima Music, Stebojen Music Company (ASCAP). **"Big Man in Town"** (Bob Gaudio), EMI Longitude Music (BMI), Gavadima Music (ASCAP).

Jersey Boys

Photos by Brian Mapp

STAGE MANAGEMENT
(L-R): Michelle Bosch (Production Stage Manager),
Brendan Fay (Stage Manager),
Pam Remler (Assistant Stage Manager), Leonardo (in tank)

HAIR
Front: Hazel Higgins
Back (L-R): Jodi Jackson, Tim Miller
Not pictured: Amy Neswald

CREW
Top: Scott Mulrain (Head Propertyman)
(L-R): Ken Harris Trevor Ricci, Cathy Prager
Not pictured: John Thomson, Emiliano Pares

"**Beggin'**" (Bob Gaudio, Peggy Farina), EMI Longitude Music, Seasons Four Music (BMI). "**Stay**" (Maurice Williams), Cherio Corporation (BMI). "**Let's Hang On (To What We've Got)**" (Bob Crewe, Denny Randell, Sandy Linzer), EMI Longitude Music, Screen Gems-EMI Music Inc., Seasons Four Music (BMI). "**Opus 17 (Don't You Worry 'Bout Me)**" (Denny Randell, Sandy Linzer) Screen Gems-EMI Music Inc, Seasons Four Music (BMI). "**Everybody Knows My Name**" (Bob Gaudio, Bob Crewe), EMI Longitude Music, Seasons Four Music (BMI). "**Bye Bye Baby**" (Bob Crewe, Bob Gaudio), EMI Longitude Music, Seasons Four Music (BMI). "**C'mon Marianne**" (L. Russell Brown, Ray Bloodworth), EMI Longitude Music and Seasons Four Music (BMI). "**Can't Take My Eyes Off You**" (Bob Gaudio, Bob Crewe), EMI Longitude Music, Seasons Four Music (BMI). "**Working My Way Back to You**" (Denny Randell, Sandy Linzer), Screen Gems–EMI Music Inc, Seasons Four Music (BMI). "**Fallen Angel**" (Guy Fletcher, Doug Flett), Chrysalis Music (ASCAP). "**Rag Doll**" (Bob Crewe, Bob Gaudio), EMI Longitude Music (BMI), Gavadima Music (ASCAP). "**Who Loves You?**" (Bob Gaudio, Judy Parker), Jobete Music Company Inc, Seasons Music Company (ASCAP).

SPECIAL THANKS
Peter Bennett, Elliot Groffman, Karen Pals, Janine Smalls, Chad Woerner, Dan Whitten. The authors, director, cast and company of *Jersey Boys* would like to express their love and thanks to Jordan Ressler.

IN MEMORY
It is difficult to imagine producing anything without the presence of beloved Dodger producing associate James Elliot Love. Friend to everyone he met, James stood at the heart of all that is good about the theatrical community. He will be missed, but his spirit abides.

The producers would like to use this space to remember Mark Fearon, and in the spirit of this production, to contemplate the abiding joy of youth.

In memory of Jairo "Jay" Santos

JUJAMCYN THEATERS

JORDAN ROTH
President

PAUL LIBIN
Executive Vice President

JACK VIERTEL
Senior Vice President

MEREDITH VILLATORE
Chief Financial Officer

JENNIFER HERSHEY
Vice President,
Building Operations

MICAH HOLLINGWORTH
Vice President,
Company Operations

HAL GOLDBERG
Vice President,
Theatre Operations

Director of Business Affairs ....Albert Kim
Director of Human Resources ....Michele Louhisdon
Director of Ticketing Services ....Justin Karr
Theatre Operations Managers ....Willa Burke,
Susan Elrod, Emily Hare,
Jeff Hubbard, Albert Kim
Theatre Operations Associates ....Carrie Brinker,
Brian Busby, Michael Composto,
Anah Jyoti Klate
Accounting ....Cathy Cerge, Amy Frank,
Tariq Hamami, Alexander Parra
Executive Producer, Red Awning ....Nicole Kastrinos
Director of Sales, Givenik.com ....Karen Freidus
Building Operations Associate ....Erich Bussing
Executive Coordinator ....Ed Lefferson
Executive Assistants ....Clark Mims Tedesco,
Beth Given, Julia Kraus
Receptionist ....Lisa Perchinske
Maintenance ....Ralph Santos, Ramon Zapata
Security ....Rasim Hodzic, John Acero
Interns ....Kayla Burgett, Estefania Fadul,
Taylor Kurpiel, Amy Larrowe,
Matthew Robertson, Brandon Smithey

STAFF FOR THE AUGUST WILSON THEATRE
Theatre Manager ....Willa Burke
Associate Theatre Manager ....Anah Jyoti Klate
Treasurer ....Nick Russo
Head Carpenter ....Dan Dour
Head Propertyman ....Scott Mulrain
Head Electrician ....Rick Baxter
Flyman ....Peter Wright
Engineer ....Ralph Santos
Assistant Treasurers ....Kevin Dublynn,
Matthew Fearon, Tara Giebler, Jeanne Halal,
George Licata, James Roeder, John Tobin
Fly Automation ....Ron Fucarino
Carpenter ....Alex Gutierrez
Propertyman...................................John Thomson
Follow Spot Operators ....Andrew Dean, Sean Fedigan,
Michael Lyons
House Sound Engineers ....Jan Nebozenko,
David Shepherd
Head Usher ....Rose Balsamo
Ticket-Takers/Directors/Ushers ....Fatima Eljaouhari,
Helen Flaherty, Robert Fowler, Carmella Galante,
Joan Gilmore, Barbara Hill, Sally Lettieri,
Amy Marquez, J. Ariel Martinez, Eli Phillips,
Raymond Polanco, Russell Saylor, Gail Worthman
Doorpersons ....Gustavo Catuy, Christine Snyder
Line Control ....Nancy Rutter
Head Porter ....Natividad Nery
Porters ....Pedro Martinez, Lourdes Moreno
Head Cleaner ....Maria Giria
Cleaners ....Antonia Duran, Lorraine Feeks

Lobby refreshments by Sweet Concessions.

Security provided by GBA Consulting, Inc.Jujamcyn

Theaters is a proud member of the
Broadway Green Alliance.

Energy efficient washer/dryer courtesy of
LG Electronics.

Jersey Boys
Scrapbook

1. Original company members gather to celebrate the 3,000th Broadway performance (L-R): Sara Schmidt, Richard Hester (production supervisor), Michelle Bosch (PSM), John Lloyd Young, Joe Payne (guitar) and Peter Gregus.
2. Stage door lovebirds Christine and Hoops.
3. Drew Gehling and Jeremy Kushnier (Bob Gaudio and Tommy DeVito) with the "Walk like a MANopoly" themed version of the game Monopoly.

Correspondent: Jared Bradshaw, "Swing" covering "Tommy," "Bob," "Crewe," "Norm," "Hank," "Barry" and "Joey"

Memorable Fan Letters: It's always fun when the stage manager gets a fan note praising her for her work, oh... and, please, can I get a signed PLAYBILL mailed to this address?

Memorable Cast Party: Seventh anniversary party at Copacabana: classy, great food, with the highlight being John Edwards (who plays Barry Belson) clearing the dance floor with an impromptu full-out rendition of Beyoncé's "Single Ladies" step for step.

Most Exciting Celebrity Visitors: Snooki and J-Woww, Kevin Bacon, Berry Gordy, The Village People, Sam Donaldson, Valentino.

Actors Who Performed the Most Roles: Nathan Scherich and Jared Bradshaw have understudied every role in the show but Frankie; 10 roles. That's Tommy, Bob, Nick, Crewe, Gyp, Hank, Norm, Knuckles, Barry, Joey. What's my line?

Actors Who Have Done the Most Performances: Original cast members have clocked in over 3,000 performances in over seven years and remain as fresh as November, 2005: Peter Gregus, Mark Lotito, Sara Schmidt.

"Gypsy of the Year" Skit: *The Hunger Games* goes Broadway! Auditions to the death!

"Carols for a Cure" Carol: "Have You Heard About the Baby/Glory to the Newborn King."

Special Backstage Ritual: "Saturday Night on Broadway." We love celebrating at the "five-minute call" with whatever show is playing at the Neil Simon Theatre across the street from us. This year was *Jesus Christ Superstar* and *Scandalous*. Who's next? I'm hoping something starring Bernadette Peters. That would make my Saturday Night.

Favorite Moment During Each Performance: The third section of "Dawn" when Des McAnuff turns the audience's perspective/view to backstage. The lights really are that bright!

Favorite In-Theatre Gathering Place: The stage manager's office for cold drinks after the show when the air conditioning isn't working well on hot summer night.

Off-Site Hangouts: McHale's, Sosa Borella, Lillie's, Chipotle, and Starbucks on the corner.

Favorite Snack Foods: "Birthday Club" birthday cake, and anything Frankie Valli and Bob Gaudio send over! "No nuts" in the stage management office.

Mascot: Leonardo the Beta fish—in the stage management office .

Favorite Therapy: The "Thera-Cane," made famous by Quinn VanAntwerp (Bob Gaudio).

Memorable Ad-Libs: "Norm Waxman showed up backstage and blew this place right up." "She drops the cash, she does the laundry and I'm the one to drive her to the laundromat." "Call Gyp for the Brill money." "We're going to Atlantic city, we got some money....It's ... It's gonna be fuckin' awesome." "We got Tommy and his boyfriend. They already gave you up numbnuts."

Cell Phone Rings: Our ushers are amazing. If it happens, they nip it in the bud.

Memorable Press Encounter: Adventure Alley at Six Flags in New Jersey. Career high.

Memorable Stage Door Fan Encounter: Our fans come back over and over again. There's a very dedicated lady in a red shirt, from Glenrock, NJ. She has seen the show more than 200 times!

Fastest Costume Change: Cara Cooper out of the "My Boyfriend's Back" dress into the drunken shouting match in Mary Delgado's robe, slippers and drink: 12 seconds.

Heaviest/Hottest Costume: Frankie and Pesci both underdress shirts, otherwise, it's just a lot of warm dancing in slick suits!

Who Wore the Least: Sara Schmidt in the "Oh What a Night" call-girl scene. She's very fit. I'm glad it's not me.

Catchphrases: "Ride the snake." "Pound the veal." "Two Claps."

Sweethearts Within the Company: Christine at the stage door and "Hoops" on the keys.

Best In-House Parody Lyrics: "My boyfriend's black, and my folks are sort of worried... Hey la hey la, my boyfriend's black."

Memorable Directorial Notes: "Do you really do it like that?" "That was almost late." "One more time, faster. OK, again, but even faster."

Embarrassing Moments: An actor knocking his teeth out with a guitar onstage at the end of "Big Girls Don't Cry" and finishing the act.

Coolest Thing About Being in This Show: Getting to play living rock stars, and having these stars come visit the show. Living legends.

Fan Club Info: www.jerseyboysblog.com will keep you up to date on all six worldwide companies. Wait—or are there seven? Broadway, Tour 1, Tour 2, Vegas, South Africa, London, Auckland, Singapore, Brisbane, Adelaide, not to mention the former long running companies in Chicago and Toronto. I vote Hawaii next. A nice long sit-down in Hawaii!

Kinky Boots

First Preview: March 3, 2013. Opened: April 4, 2013.
Still running as of May 31, 2013.

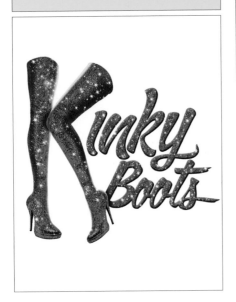

The heir to a failing north England shoe factory revitalizes his business (and his life) when he teams up with a kick line of drag queens to manufacture a fabulous line of sexy women's boots...designed for men. He finds an unexpected soul mate in one of the dragsters, and they both work out their daddy issues as they collaborate to change their respective worlds.

CAST

(in order of appearance)

Mr. Price .... STEPHEN BERGER
Young Charlie ... SEBASTIAN HEDGES THOMAS
Young Lola .... MARQUISE NEAL
Simon Sr. .... EUGENE BARRY-HILL
Nicola .... CELINA CARVAJAL
Charlie Price .... STARK SANDS
George .... MARCUS NEVILLE
Don .... DANIEL STEWART SHERMAN
Lauren .... ANNALEIGH ASHFORD
Pat .... TORY ROSS
Harry .... ANDY KELSO
Lola .... BILLY PORTER
Angels .... PAUL CANAAN,
KEVIN SMITH KIRKWOOD,
KYLE TAYLOR PARKER, KYLE POST,
CHARLIE SUTTON, JOEY TARANTO
Trish .... JENNIFER PERRY
Richard Bailey .... JOHN JEFFREY MARTIN
Milan Stage Manager ..... ADINAH ALEXANDER
Ensemble .... ADINAH ALEXANDER,
ERIC ANDERSON, EUGENE BARRY-HILL,
STEPHEN BERGER, CAROLINE BOWMAN,

Continued on next page

(L-R, front): Stark Sands and Billy Porter with Annaleigh Ashford (C, rear), and cast

Photo by Matthew Murphy

Kinky Boots

MUSICAL NUMBERS

ACT 1

"Price & Son Theme"	Full Company
"The Most Beautiful Thing"	Full Company
"Take What You Got"	Harry, Charlie, Ensemble
"The Land of Lola"	Lola, Angels
"The Land of Lola (Reprise)"	Lola, Angels
"Step One"	Charlie
"Sex Is in the Heel"	Lola, Pat, George, Angels, Ensemble
"The History of Wrong Guys"	Lauren
"I'm Not My Father's Son"	Lola, Charlie
"Everybody Say Yeah"	Charlie, Lola, Angels, Ensemble

ACT 2

"Entr'acte/Price & Son Theme - Reprise"	Full Company
"What a Woman Wants"	Lola, Pat, Don, Ensemble
"In This Corner"	Lola, Don, Pat, Trish, Angels, Ensemble
"The Soul of a Man"	Charlie
"Hold Me in Your Heart"	Lola
"Raise You Up/Just Be"	Full Company

ANDY KELSO, ERIC LEVITON,
ELLYN MARIE MARSH,
JOHN JEFFREY MARTIN,
JENNIFER PERRY, TORY ROSS

STANDBYS AND UNDERSTUDIES

Standby for Young Charlie: JONAH HALPERIN
Standby for Young Lola: COLE BULLOCK

Understudy for Lola: TIMOTHY WARE,
KEVIN SMITH KIRKWOOD
Charlie: ANDY KELSO,
JOHN JEFFREY MARTIN
Lauren: SANDRA DeNISE,
ELLYN MARIE MARSH
Nicola: CAROLINE BOWMAN,
SANDRA DeNISE
Don: ERIC ANDERSON, ERIC LEVITON
George: ERIC ANDERSON, ERIC LEVITON
Mr. Price: ERIC ANDERSON, ERIC LEVITON
Simon Sr.: KEVIN SMITH KIRKWOOD,
TIMOTHY WARE
Trish: ADINAH ALEXANDER, LUCIA SPINA
Pat: ADINAH ALEXANDER,
ELLYN MARIE MARSH, LUCIA SPINA
Harry: JOHN JEFFREY MARTIN, KYLE POST
Richard Bailey: ROBERT PENDILLA,
KYLE POST, CHARLIE SUTTON
Milan Stage Manager: SANDRA DeNISE,
LUCIA SPINA

Dance Captain: NATHAN PECK
Assistant Dance Captain: PAUL CANAAN

SWINGS

SANDRA DeNISE, NATHAN PECK,
ROBERT PENDILLA, LUCIA SPINA,
TIMOTHY WARE

ORCHESTRA

Conductor/Keyboard 1: BRIAN USIFER
Associate Conductor/Keyboard 2:
WILL VAN DYKE
Drums: SAMMY MERENDINO
Bass: MICHAEL VISCEGLIA
Guitars: MICHAEL AARONS, JOHN PUTNAM
Trumpet: JAMES DE LA GARZA
Trombone: KEITH O'QUINN
Reeds: DAN WILLIS
Concertmaster: HIROKO TAGUCHI
Violin: PHILIP PAYTON
Violin/Viola: DENISE STILLWELL
Cello: ALLISON SEIDNER

Synthesizer Programmer: RANDY COHEN
Music Coordination: MICHAEL KELLER
Music Copying: EMILY GRISHMAN MUSIC
PREPARATION–EMILY GRISHMAN/
KATHARINE EDMONDS

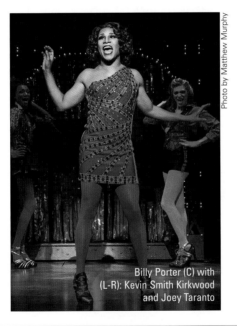

Photo by Matthew Murphy

Billy Porter (C) with
(L-R): Kevin Smith Kirkwood
and Joey Taranto

Stark Sands
Charlie

Billy Porter
Lola

Annaleigh Ashford
Lauren

Celina Carvajal
Nicola

**Daniel Stewart
Sherman**
Don

Marcus Neville
George

Adinah Alexander
*Milan Stage
Manager/Ensemble*

Kinky Boots

Eric Anderson
Ensemble

Eugene Barry-Hill
Simon Sr./Ensemble

Stephen Berger
Mr. Price/Ensemble

Caroline Bowman
Ensemble

Cole Bullock
Young Lola Standby

Paul Canaan
*Angel/Asst. Dance
Captain/Ensemble*

Sandra DeNise
Swing

Jonah Halperin
*Young Charlie
Standby*

Andy Kelso
Harry/Ensemble

Kevin Smith
Kirkwood
Angel/Ensemble

Eric Leviton
Ensemble

Ellyn Marie Marsh
Ensemble

John Jeffrey Martin
*Richard Bailey/
Ensemble*

Marquise Neal
Young Lola

Kyle Taylor Parker
Angel/Ensemble

Nathan Peck
*Dance Captain/
Swing*

Robert Pendilla
Swing

Jennifer Perry
Trish/Ensemble

Kyle Post
Angel/Ensemble

Tory Ross
Pat/Ensemble

Lucia Spina
Swing

Charlie Sutton
Angel/Ensemble

Joey Taranto
Angel/Ensemble

Sebastian Hedges
Thomas
Young Charlie

Timothy Ware
Lola Standby/Swing

Harvey Fierstein
Playwright

Cyndi Lauper
*Composer and
Lyricist*

Jerry Mitchell
*Director/
Choreographer*

Stephen Oremus
*Music Supervisor/
Arranger/
Orchestrator*

David Rockwell
Scenic Design

Gregg Barnes
Costume Design

Kenneth Posner
Lighting Design

John Shivers
Sound Design

Josh Marquette
Hair Design

Randy Houston
Mercer
Make-up Design

Kinky Boots

Kathy Fabian
Propstar
*Properties
Coordinator*

Brian Usifer
Music Director

Michael Keller
Music Coordinator

Rusty Mowery
*Associate
Choreographer*

D.B. Bonds
Associate Director

Amy Jo Jackson
Dialect Coach

Bernard Telsey
Telsey + Company
Casting

Christopher C. Smith
Smitty/
Theatersmith, Inc.
Technical Supervisor

Aaron Lustbader
Foresight Theatrical
General Manager

Daryl Roth
Producer

Hal Luftig
Producer

James L.
Nederlander
Producer

Terry Allen Kramer
Producer

Byeong Seok Kim
CJ E&M Live
Entertainment
Producer

Jayne Baron
Sherman
Producer

Adam Blanshay
CEO Just for Laughs
Theatricals
Producer

Judith Ann Abrams
Producer

Yasuhiro Kawana
Producer

Jane Bergère
Producer

Allan S. Gordon
Producer

Adam S. Gordon
Producer

Ken Davenport
Producer

Hunter Arnold
Producer

Phil and Lucy Suarez
Producer

Bryan Bantry
Producer

Ron Fierstein
Producer

Dorsey Regal
Producer

Jim Kierstead
Producer

Gregory Rae
Producer

Christina Papagjika
Producer

Michael DeSantis
Producer

Patrick Baugh
Producer

Kinky Boots

Brian Smith
Producer

Connie and Tom Walsh
Producer

Jordan Roth
Jujamcyn Theaters
Producer

Stephen Carrasco
Swing

FRONT OF HOUSE
First Row (L-R):
Hollis Miller,
Tristan Blacer
Second Row (L-R):
Christina Ruiz,
Clifford Ray Berry,
Julie Burnham,
Donald Royal
Third Row (L-R):
Theresa Lopez,
Heather Gilles,
Mark Maciejewski
Fourth Row (L-R):
Lisé Greaves,
Rebecca Segarra
Fifth Row (L-R):
John Barker,
Lorraine Feeks,
Janice Rodriguez
Sixth Row (L-R):
Elisa Schneider,
Lawrence Levens
Seventh Row (L-R):
Dan Curley,
Chris Cannon,
Bill Meyers,
Carrie Jo Brinker,
Sarah Ricker
Eighth Row (L-R):
Michael Mattie,
Michael Leibring,
Mike Wirsch
Ninth Row (L-R):
Albert T. Kim,
Bart Ryan, J. Max Baker
Top Row: Terry Monahan

Photos by Brian Mapp

BOX OFFICE
(L-R): Gloria Diabo, Brendan McCaffrey

STAGE MANAGEMENT
Front (L-R): Lois L. Griffing (Production
Stage Manager), Thomas Recktenwald
(Stage Manager)
Back (L-R): Ken McGee (Assistant Stage
Manager), Derek Michael DiGregorio

WARDROBE/HAIR
Front: Ray Ranellone
On Stairs: Pat Shea
Standing (L-R): Jake White, Sabana Majeed, Guy Smith, Jason Blair, Michele Gutierrez, Joshua Burns, James Hall, Ginny Hounsel, Dan Foss, Susan Kroeter,
Megan Bowers, Mary Beth Irons, Richard Anderson

Kinky Boots

STAFF FOR *KINKY BOOTS*

GENERAL MANAGEMENT
FORESIGHT THEATRICAL
Alan Wasser   Allan Williams
Aaron Lustbader   Mark Shacket
Mark Barna

COMPANY MANAGER
Marc Borsak

GENERAL PRESS REPRESENTATIVE
O&M CO.
Rick Miramontez
Molly Barnett   Ryan Ratelle
Chelsea Nachman

CASTING
TELSEY + COMPANY
Bernard Telsey CSA, Will Cantler CSA,
David Vaccari CSA,
Bethany Knox CSA, Craig Burns CSA,
Tiffany Little Canfield CSA, Rachel Hoffman CSA,
Justin Huff CSA, Patrick Goodwin CSA,
Abbie Brady-Dalton CSA,
David Morris, Cesar A. Rocha CSA,
Andrew Femenella, Karyn Casl CSA,
Kristina Bramhall, Jessie Malone, Conrad Woolfe

ASSOCIATE DIRECTOR
D.B. Bonds

Production Stage Manager ....Lois L. Griffing
Stage Manager ....Thomas Recktenwald
Assistant Stage Manager ....Kenneth J. McGee
Associate Company Manager ....Ashley Berman
Dialect Coach ....Amy Jo Jackson
Dance Captain ....Nathan Peck
Assistant Dance Captain ....Paul Canaan
Associate Scenic Designer ....Dick Jaris
Assistant Scenic Designers ...............T.J. Greenway,
Jerome Martin, Michael Carnahan,
Gaetane Bertol
Associate Costume
Designers ....Thomas Charles LeGalley,
Matthew Pachtman
Assistant Costume Designers ....Rachel Attridge,
Dana Burkart
Associate Lighting Designer ....Anthony Pearson
Assistant Lighting Designers ....Jeremy Cunningham,
Keri Thibodeau
Associate Sound Designer ....David Patridge
Additional Arrangements ....Brian Usifer
Associate Synthesizer Programmer ....Tim Crook
Music Track Editor ....Derik Lee
Electronic Drum Programmer ....Sammy Merendino
Music Department Assistant ....Aaron Jodoin
Moving Lighting Programmer ....Aland Henderson
Production/Head Carpenter ....Patrick Shea
Automation Carpenter ....Mike Reininger
Automation Flyman...........................Gabe Harris
Production Electricians ....James J. Fedigan,
Randy Zaibek
Head Electrician ....Michael Brown
Assistant Electrician ....Bradley Brown
Moving Light Technician ....Rocco Williams

Properties Coordinator ....Kathy Fabian/Propstar
Head Properties Supervisor ....Andrew Meeker
Assistant Properties Supervisor ....Jacob White
Production/Head Sound Engineer ....David Patridge
Deck Audio ....Pitsch Karrer
Advance Production Audio ....Kevin Kennedy
Wardrobe Supervisor ....James Hall
Dressers ....Jason Blair, Megan Bowers,
Joshua Burns, Dan Foss,
Ginny Hounsel, Susan Kroeter
Hair Supervisor ....Richard Orton
Assistant Hair Supervisor ....Mitchell Beck
Hair and Wig Stylist ....Sabana Majeed
Makeup Artist ....Guy Smith
Advertising ....SpotCo/
Drew Hodges, Jim Edwards,
Tom Greenwald, Stephen Sosnowski,
Michael Crowley, Tim Falotico
Marketing..SpotCo/
Nick Pramik, Kristen Rathbun
Website & Interactive Marketing ....SpotCo/
Sheila Collins, Marc Mettler,
Callie Goff, Marisa Reo Delmore
Legal Counsel ....Lazarus & Harris LLP/
Scott Lazarus, Esq., Robert C. Harris, Esq.
Accounting ....Marks Paneth & Shron/
Christopher Cacace, Ruthie Skochil
General Management Associates ....Jake Hirzel,
Lane Marsh
General Management Office ....Kaitlin Boland,
Lauren Friedlander, Nina Lutwick,
Mary Catherine McDonald, Jennifer O'Connor
Assistants to Daryl Roth ....Greg Raby, Megan Smith
Assistant to Hal Luftig ....Scott Sinclair
Production Photographer ....Matthew Murphy
Production Assistants ....Derek Michael DiGregorio,
Mitchell Anderson, Shannon Hammonds
Child Guardian ....Bridget Mills
Associate Props Coordinators ....Cassie Dorland,
Carrie Mossman/Propstar
Props Artisans and Shoppers ....Mary Wilson,
Becca Wright, Daniel Moss,
Joshua Hackett, J. Michael Stafford,
Will Barrios, Jasmine Roberts, John Estep
Assistant to Technical Director ....Rhiannon Hansen
Tutoring ....On Location Education
Press Associates ....Sarah Babin, Scott Braun,
Philip Carrubba, Jon Dimond,
Michael Jorgensen, Yufen Kung,
Marie Pace, Pete Sanders, Andy Snyder
Physical Therapy ....Performing Arts Physical Therapy/
Sean Gallagher, PT
Insurance ....Ventura Insurance Brokerage/
Jessica Brown
Banking ....City National Bank/
Erik Piecuch, Anne McSweeney,
Michael Tynan
Payroll ....Checks and Balances Payroll Inc./
Sarah Galbraith, Anthony Walker
Merchandising ....Broadway Merchandising LLC/
Adam S. Gordon, David Eck
Opening Night Coordination ....Serino/Coyne Events/
Suzanne Tobak, Chrissann Gasparro
Shoe Industry Consultant ....Larry Waller,
Walrus Shoe and Leather Co, LLC
Travel ....Road Rebel Travel and Touring Inc.

Theatre Displays ....King Displays

CREDITS AND ACKNOWLEDGEMENTS
Scenery and scenic effects built, painted, electrified and
automated by Showmotion, Inc., Milford, CT. Lighting
equipment from PRG Lighting. Sound equipment by
Masque Sound. Specialty props by Daedalus Design and
Production, Tom Carroll Scenery and MINE metal art.
Costumes by Eric Winterling Inc., Lynne Baccus, Donna
Langman Costumes LLC, Tricorne Inc., Giliberto Inc.,
Pete's Print Shop, Polly Isham Kinney. Millinery by Rodney
Gordon, Inc. Custom fabric painting and printing by Jeff
Fender Studios and Gene Mignola, Inc. Custom shoes and
boots by LaDuca, T.O. Dey and Manolo Blahnik. Onstage
guitars courtesy of Taylor Guitars. Soft goods by iWeiss
Theatrical Solutions. Scenic painting by Scenic Art Studios.
Trucking by Anthony Augliera, Inc.

SPECIAL THANKS
Lisa Barbaris, Sonor Drums, Paiste Cymbals and Roland
USA, Matthew Taylor, Mark Koss, Jessica Colley-Mitchell,
Roselaine Fox, Kate Nowacki, Lindsay McWilliams, Jennifer
Chapman, John Dunnett, Michael Harrell, BraTenders,
Maria Ficalora, Katrina Patterns, Michael Piscitelli, On
Stage Dancewear, Peanut Butter & Co., Mike Dereskewicz,
Morgan Moore, Joanie Schlafer, Jim Waterhouse, Marina
Pulliam. Promotional consideration furnished by Apple,
George Poulios and Suzanne Lindbergh.

Cyndi Lauper wishes to thank her collaborators:
Sammy James Jr., Steve Gaboury,
Rich Morel and Tom Hammer, Stephen Oremus

Makeup provided by
M•A•C Cosmetics

New York Group Sales
Group Sales Box Office/Stephanie Lee
1-800-Broadway ext. 2

Rehearsed at the New 42nd Street Studios

www.KinkyBootsthemusical.com

Kinky Boots

Photos by Brian Mapp

CREW
Lying Down: Ken McGee
Kneeling (L-R): Lois L. Griffing, Bradley Brown, Ray Ranellone, Pitsch Karrer, Michael Brown, Thomas Recktenwald
Standing (L-R): Derek Michael DiGregorio, Tom Burke, Hank Hale, Rocco Williams, Richard Anderson, Stark Sands, Gabe Harris, Joe Mooneyham, Joe Maher, John Blixt, Pat Shea, Andy Meeker, David Patridge, Jake White
On Stairs (L-R): Michele Gutierrez, Mike Reininger

ORCHESTRA
(L-R): Allison Seidner, Will Van Dyke, Brian Usifer, Sammy Merendino, Hiroko Taguchi, Dan Willis, Denise Stillwell, Michael Visceglia, Philip Payton, Michael Aarons

Theatre Operations Associates ....Carrie Jo Brinker, Brian Busby, Michael Composto, Anah Jyoti Klate
Accounting ....Cathy Cerge, Amy Frank, Tariq Hamami, Alexander Parra
Executive Producer, Red Awning ....Nicole Kastrinos
Director of Sales, Givenik.com ....Karen Freidus
Marketing & Operations Assistant,
    Givenik.com ....Taylor Kurpiel
Building Operations Associate ....Erich Bussing
Ticketing and Pricing Associate ....Jonathon Scott
Executive Coordinator ....Ed Lefferson
Executive Assistants ....Clark Mims Tedesco, Beth Given, Julia Kraus
Receptionist ....Lisa Perchinske
Maintenance ....Ralph Santos, Ramon Zapata
Security ....Rasim Hodzic, Terone Richardson
Interns ....Kimille Howard, Amy Larrowe, Christopher Luner, Lana Percival, Steven Rowe

Staff for the Al Hirschfeld Theatre for
Kinky Boots

Theatre Manager ....Albert T. Kim
Associate Theatre Manager ....Carrie Jo Brinker
Treasurer.....................................Carmine LaMendola
Head Carpenter ....Joseph J. Maher, Jr.
Head Propertyperson ....Richard Anderson
Head Electrician ....Michele Gutierrez
Flyman..Gabe Harris
Engineer ....David Neville
Assistant Treasurers ....Vicci Stanton, Gloria Diabo, Jeffrey Nevin, Janette Wernegreen
Carpenters ....Joe Mooneyham, Hank Hale
Propertyperson ....Raymond Ranellone
Electricians ....John Blixt, Tom Burke, Rocco Williams
Head Usher ....Janice Rodriguez
Ticket-Takers ....Tristan Blacer, Lorraine Feeks

Doormen ....Henry E. Menendez, Neil Perez
Front of House Directors ....Julie Burnham, Lawrence Levens, William Meyers
Head Porter ....Jose Nunez
Head Cleaner ....Bethania Alvarez
Ushers ....Clifford Ray Berry, Peter Davino, Heather Gilles, Lisé Greaves, Theresa Lopez, Mark Maciejewski, Mary Marzan, Hollis Miller, Donald Royal, Bart Ryan
Porters ....Tereso Avila, Roberto Ellington
Cleaners...........Michelina Annarumma, Mirjan Aquino

Lobby refreshments by Sweet Hospitality Group.

Security provided by GBA Consulting, Inc.

Kinky Boots

SCRAPBOOK

Correspondent: Tory Ross, "Pat"

Welcome to Price and Son, a once-sleepy shoe factory in Northampton, England that quickly transforms into "The Land of Lola." In this factory, proper British brogues have been replaced by fashion-forward, first-class Kinky Boots sported by fierce, fabulous drags and wonderfully warm and loveable factory workers (except for Trish). I am thrilled to play the pivotal role of Pat Smythe, the assistant (to the) manager at Price and Son and a Lola admirer.

The entire *Kinky Boots* experience, from reading to workshop to Chicago to New York, has been a bit of a dream as the people involved are some of the most wonderfully caring and creative collaborators around. We are truly thrilled to hit the stage each night with the best crew and orchestra on Broadway and share this wonderful and moving story with our incredible audiences.

Coolest Thing About Being in This Show: Besides everyone involved? Definitely speaking in the British dialect 24/7.

Most Exciting Celebrity Visitor: Keith Richards came to the show and had a bit of a meet 'n' greet with Stark and Billy beforehand. During introductions, he shook hands with Stark and leaned in for a hug and kiss with Billy, assuming he was a woman. Wonder what was going through his head during "Land of Lola"? In the inimitable words of Austin Powers, "That's a man, baby!" Also, KATY PERRY.

"Easter Bonnet Sketch: WEWONWEWON THE EASTER BONNET! Should I be the one to take complete credit for winning "Most Fabulous Sketch" at the Easter Bonnet this year? Probably not. But I will. The writing committee (DB, Annaleigh, Eric A, Ellyn, Rusty and I) sat down to re-think our sketch idea after we discovered our "Trannie *Annie*" idea had oddly been done previously (*La Cage*. Really?!). After much open-format-brainstorming, we thought it might be interesting to do a veeeery serious modern dance to Cyndi's "True Colors" using our entire cast of varied shapes and sizes. In full body unitards. Unitards of different colors that would make an actual rainbow at the end. Hours of hand-hemming, a recording session with Harvey (for his Rainbow Connection Beat poetry), fittings, more hemming of unitards, choreo rehearsals with Nathan Peck, debates about streamer cannons and sussing out a wheelchair for our wounded Angel Joey Taranto later, W E W O N W E W O N W E W O N THE EASTER BONNET! I produced it and I bought myself a huge trophy with a rabbit on top to commemorate the joyous occasion.

Who Has Done the Most Shows in Their Career?: I'm gonna eschew any research on this one and just IBDB our Gypsy Robe winner Charlie Sutton. He is sort of a Broadway legend, having appeared in *Kinky Boots, Lysistrata Jones, Catch Me if You Can, How to Succeed..., Women on the Verge..., Addams Family, Cry-Baby, La Cage* and *Wicked*. Now that I'm seeing it in print... TAKE A VACATION, CHARLIE! GIVE YOUR HAMSTRINGS AND YOUR JUMP SPLITS A BREAK!

Special Backstage Rituals: At the places call, we all gather onstage, put our hands in together and after a three-count, say "Oi, Oi, Oi SHOES!" We enact a similar moment at the top of Act Two and chant "Oi, Oi, Oi BOOTS!" It was Eric Anderson who initially introduced the Ois to *Kinky Boots* during an early treadmill rehearsal, and now it's sort of our war-cry.

Favorite Moment During Each Performance: I love how intertwined this group of actors is and how we have now developed traffic patterns at work that bring everyone together. For instance, Marcus Neville, a paragon of virtue in the part of George Moon, is an amazing artist. Every day he scribbles original drawings on bits of scrap paper and presents them during the scene work to Stark Sands, who usually has to answer a question in the moment. George runs off the stage with his "response from Charlie" and shows them to everyone waiting offstage—actors, propsmen, carpenters. I've been keeping and scanning all of them to make a coffee table book to sell for our next Broadway Cares fundraising push.

Favorite In-Theatre Gathering Place: Our fabulous leading lady, Annaleigh Ashford, has a warm and inviting dressing room on the 2nd floor of the Hirschfeld. It seems to be a nice resting spot for the cast on their trek upstairs to their dressing rooms. The character women are on 4, the angels on 4.5 and the character men and children are on 5. It's a 7-flight climb for those guys from the basement at the end of the show! Also, truthfully, she has an automatic candy dispenser her manager gave her on opening night that draws quite a crowd. The Angels host SNOB parties and I also have a full bar, so we congregate wherever people are congregating. We genuinely really like each other.

Favorite Off-Site Hangout: Ssshhhh! Don't tell anyone... but Sundays after our matinee, we typically go to either New York Beer Company or Harley's Smokeshack. Also, our softball team is NAILING IT... so Central Park on Thursdays at 11:30. GO KINKY BATS!

Favorite Snack Foods: Swedish Fish and Sour Patch Kids in the show, Twizzlers and giant Costco containers of Jelly Beans in the rehearsal room (yes Caroline... we do remember when you dropped a whole bucket during a sentimental moment of a run-through), and Schmackary's now that we are camped out at the Hirschfeld.

Mascot: Joey Taranto in a wheelchair wearing a yellow unitard whipping a 9-foot-long rainbow-coloured rhythmic gymnastics ribbon around during our Easter Bonnet sketch. That image pretty much sums up this group.

1. *Yearbook* correspondent Tory Ross at her make-up table in the Hirschfeld Theatre.
2. Gypsy Robe recipient Charlie Sutton (a.k.a. Katie Webber) with nothing to hide.
3. The cast of *Kinky Boots* showing their "True Colors" at the 2013 Easter Bonnet competition, where they took the prize for "Best Presentation."

Kinky Boots
SCRAPBOOK

Favorite Therapy: Olbas, Singers' Secret and FOOT MASSAGES.

Social Media: Ellyn Marie Marsh is an internet presence. She is also our self-appointed social media president. She encouraged us to tweet as our characters after following the lead from Kyle Post (@WiddiBantour). She is also the queen of the #SIP (Saturday Intermission Picture), our liason with our fans (name of said group is currently in callbacks: Kinks, Kinkettes or Sole-Mates?), on Instagram and a maker of the best films ever on Vine. She brought all of her fans from *Priscilla* over to *Kinky Boots* and we are now the proud recipients of cake pops, mini cupcakes, Schmackary's, iPhone cases... you name it. And we love it.

Fastest Costume Change: During our Chicago out-of-town tryout, Lola had a number called "Black Widow" during which she thrust several swords into Antoinette Cookiepuss by way of a magic box. The magic trick was an "axe" metaphor interspersed with all the factory worker firing scenes. When we got to New York, the number was replaced with one called "Bad Girl." Alas, the gigantic box holding the waifish Kevin Smith Kirkwood was cut and with it, the show's fastest costume change. Billy Porter should record both of those cut songs. His vocalises are amazing.

Who Wore the Least?: Look closely at that picture of Gypsy Robe winner Charlie Sutton (previous page, top). Underneath that bikini bottom are "chicken cutlet" hip pads and three pairs of support hose. Sexy!

Catchphrases Only the Company Would Recognize: "Oi, Oi, Oi Shoes/Boots"; "Nailing it, T-DOWN!"; "poon"; "slag"; "You're doin' great, puuunchcaaad, clibbard"; "moooooer"; and "Full Out, Bitches!"

Sweethearts Within the Company: Berger and his e-cigarette, Eric A and his beard, Charlie and his hip pads, Pat and her clibbard, Trish and Don (she wishes), Billy and his Broadway Dreams t-shirts.

Best In-House Parody Lyrics: The recitative-esque top of Charlie's number "Step One," is just BEGGING for parody. Here is today's version: "Lookin' at fairies/I like my sneakers/Sometimes I don't go/into the bath/That makes me smelly/I'm feeling hungry/The trees are spinning/inside my

head." (credit: Jen Perry.) Go ahead and try it yourself!

Memorable Directorial Note: There is a video of Jerry Mitchell doing a reading of "Two and a half feet of irrrrrresistible tuuuuuubular.... SHEX." It's maaaybe one of my most-prized

media possessions.

Company In-Jokes: "Oh, Berger." Also Eric Anderson's "I trust you" trust fall. No one ever catches him.

Nicknames: We like to call Caroline "butterfingers" because she always seems to be dropping things in the bar scene, but I would like to devote this question to our ensemble character names. There's some INCREDIBLE character work happening up on that stage. Paul Canaan is CeeCee Easyflaps. Kyle Taylor Parker is Miss Patti

LeParker. Kyle Post is Widdi Bantour. Kevin Smith Kirkwood is Antoinette Cookiepuss. Charlie Sutton is Katie Webber. Robert Pendilla is Kim CHEE Mora or Ping Pang-Pong, depending upon the role he is covering. Joey Taranto is Terri Dactyl. Danny Sherman is Don Schumaker. Marcus Neville is George Moon. Tory Ross is the pivotal role of Pat Smythe. Andy Kelso is Crispin Gloveless (and Harry). Jen Perry is Trish ("It's just Trish. Don't worry about it"). Adinah Alexander is Marjorie Dawson Coombs. Eric Anderson is Mutt Johnston. Eugene Barry-Hill is Harvey Hitchcock. Stephen Berger is Moeshe (and Mr. Price, Sr.). Caroline Bowman is Maggie Radcliffe. Sandy DeNise is Svetlana (Lana) Boskovich. Eric Leviton is Pacey Hooch Turner. Ellyn Marie Marsh is Gemma Louise Hunter. John Jeffrey Martin is Paddington Crisp. Nathan Peck is Miss Ting in London and Pip Blowfella in Northampton. Lucia Spina is Sally Boules. Timothy Ware is Malachi O'Malley. Stephen Carrasco is Dynah Bottom.

Epic Chicago Moments: I can't end this missive without giving a shout-out to our epic Halloween party in Chicago. Annaleigh and I were sharing a gorgeous two-bedroom that was begging for a huge party, so we spent two weeks decorating with the help of Andy Meeker and Jake White from props, followed by an electrics load-in with the help of Chris Moeller. HISTORY WAS MADE and dried blood was everywhere. We had a bloody bathroom photo booth, a doomsday Fortune Teller in Annaleigh's closet (Really Madame Zandra? Really?), trophies for awards and some wickedly-lethal Jell-o shots. Can't wait for this year's party at Jerry's. We haven't told him yet. Stark came as Archie, which is why Marcus portrays him as such in his cartoons. Anyone who was anyone came to that party. And also the Baton. Remember that night, Trish Bitch?!

1. Before the start of Act I, the cast gathers to chant "Oi, Oi, Oi SHOES!"
2. The "Angels" give songwriter Cyndi Lauper a lift at the opening night party.
3. Halloween during the Chicago run with (L-R): Annaleigh Ashford as Phyllis Diller, Andy Kelso as Prince and Jerry Mitchell as Black Swan.

2012-2013 AWARDS

TONY AWARDS
Best Musical
Best Performance by an Actor
in a Leading Role in a Musical
(Billy Porter)
Best Choreography
(Jerry Mitchell)
Best Original Score (Music and/or Lyrics)
Written for the Theatre
(Cyndi Lauper)

Best Sound Design of a Musical
(John Shivers)
Best Orchestrations
(Stephen Oremus)

DRAMA DESK AWARD
Outstanding Actor in a Musical
(Billy Porter)

DRAMA LEAGUE AWARD
Distinguished Production
of a Musical

OUTER CRITICS CIRCLE AWARDS
Outstanding New Broadway Musical
Outstanding New Score
(Broadway or Off Broadway)
(Cyndi Lauper)
Outstanding Actor in a Musical
(Billy Porter)

CLARENCE DERWENT AWARD
Most Promising Female Performer
(Annaleigh Ashford)

Lewis Black: Running On Empty

Opened: October 9, 2012
Limited Engagement. Closed October 20, 2012 after 8 Performances.

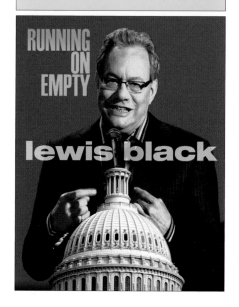

PLAYBILL

The perpetually irked standup comedian and regular on Comedy Central's "The Daily Show" takes to the stage in the last weeks of the Presidential campaign to vent on politics, celebrity and American society in general.

CAST

Lewis Black..............................LEWIS BLACK

RICHARD RODGERS THEATRE

UNDER THE DIRECTION OF JAMES M. NEDERLANDER AND JAMES L. NEDERLANDER

JAMES L. NEDERLANDER   EVA PRICE
JAMES GOSNELL   JO ANNE ASTROW   MARK LONOW

Present

lewis black
RUNNING ON EMPTY

Written and Performed by
LEWIS BLACK

Additional material by John Bowman

Lighting Consultant	Visual Consultant	Sound Consultant
JEFFREY KOGER	SUSAN HILFERTY	PETER FITZGERALD

Technical Supervisor	Tour Manager
NEIL A. MAZZELLA	BEN BREWER

Advertising	Press Representative
SERINO/COYNE	CYBERLAFF INC./ GLENN SCHWARTZ

10/9/12

Photos by Clay McBride

Lewis Black: Running On Empty
SCRABOOK

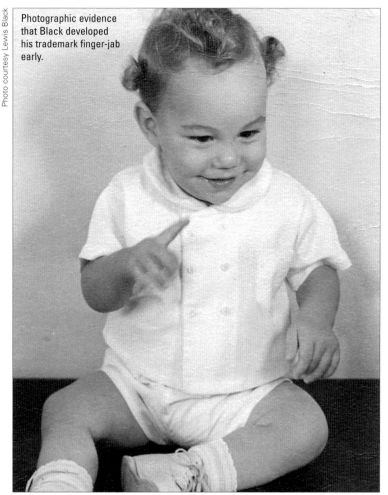

Photo courtesy Lewis Black

Photographic evidence that Black developed his trademark finger-jab early.

Correspondent: Lewis Black

Memorable Opening Night Note: From David Hyde Pierce. He wrote a note: "GO OUT THERE AND MAKE THEM WISH THEY WERE DEAD." I thought that was spectacular.

Memorable Opening Night Gifts: Some extraordinary bottles of wine.

Most Exciting Celebrity Visitors: My parents. Who loved the show. My mother was unusually effusive. Also Whoopi Goldberg, Robin Williams and Michael Moore.

Special Backstage Rituals: A coffee with cream and that's about it. Then I stare at my notes.

Favorite Moment During Each Performance: Whenever I came up with a line for the first time.

Favorite In-Theatre Gathering Place: My dressing room, since it was just me and my tour manager and my opening act, John Bowman.

Off-Site Hangout: The West Bank Cafe.

Favorite Snack Food: Nuts.

Favorite Therapy: After the show…a glass of red wine.

Cell Phone Rings: Hardly any; my audience kind of gets it.

Memorable Press Encounter: CBS *This Morning*. I never get put on network morning shows.

Busiest Day at the Box Office: I think the first few days and when we extended.

Catchphrase Only the Company Would Recognize: I was the company. Hard to have an internal catchphrase. But mine was "Holy shit, I am on Broadway."

Company Legend: Jimmy Nederlander

Sweetheart Within the Company: Me.

Coolest Thing About Being in This Show: Being three blocks from home and finally being on Broadway for a run.

Also: I had a ball.

Special Thanks
Sean Free, Josh Lesnick, David Perry,
Nick Scandalios, Holly Sutton

⊁N⊰
NEDERLANDER

Chairman .... James M. Nederlander
President .... James L. Nederlander

Executive Vice President
Nick Scandalios

Vice President	Senior Vice President
Corporate Development	Labor Relations
Charlene S. Nederlander	**Herschel Waxman**

| Vice President | Chief Financial Officer |
| **Jim Boese** | **Freida Sawyer Belviso** |

HOUSE STAFF FOR
THE RICHARD RODGERS THEATRE

House Manager .... Timothy Pettolina
Box Office Treasurer .... Fred Santore Jr.
Assistant Treasurer .... Corinne Parker-Dorso
Electrician .... Steve Carver
Carpenter .... Kevin Camus
Propertymaster .... Stephen F. DeVerna
Engineer .... Sean Quinn

Lewis Black

James L.
Nederlander
Presenter

Eva Price
Presenter

Jo Anne Astrow
Presenter

Mark Lonow
Presenter

James H. Gosnell
Presenter

Neil A. Mazzella
Hudson Theatrical
Associates
Technical Supervisor

Susan Hilferty
Visual Consultant

The Lion King

First Preview: October 15, 1997. Opened: November 13, 1997.
Still running as of May 31, 2013.

PLAYBILL®

THE LION KING

When the evil lion Scar kills his brother, King Mufasa, and seizes the throne of the African Pridelands, young Prince Simba flees into the wilderness. There he is transformed by some new friends and finally returns to reclaim his crown. Performed by actors in puppetlike costumes designed by director Julie Taymor.

CAST
(in order of appearance)

Rafiki .... TSHIDI MANYE
Mufasa .... ALTON FITZGERALD WHITE
Sarabi .... CHONDRA LA-TEASE PROFIT
Zazu .... JEFF BINDER
Scar .... PATRICK R. BROWN
Young Simba (Wed., Thurs.,
   Sat. Mat., Sun. Mat.) .... DEREK JOHNSON
   (Tue., Fri., Sat. Eve.,
   Sun. Eve.) .... CALEB McLAUGHLIN
Young Nala (Wed., Thurs.,
   Sat. Eve., Sun. Eve.) .... BOBBI BORDLEY
   (Tue., Fri., Sat. Mat.,
   Sun. Mat.) .... ALONIE DOWDEN
Shenzi .... BONITA J. HAMILTON
Banzai .... JAMES BROWN-ORLEANS
Ed .... ENRIQUE SEGURA
Timon .... FRED BERMAN
Pumbaa .... BEN JEFFREY
Simba .... ANDILE GUMBI
Nala .... CHANTEL RILEY
Ensemble Singers .... DERRICK DAVIS,
   LINDIWE DLAMINI, BONGI DUMA,
   JOEL KARIE, RON KUNENE,
   SHERYL McCALLUM, S'BU NGEMA,
   NTELISENG NKHELA, SELLOANE A. NKHELA,

Continued on next page

MINSKOFF THEATRE

UNDER THE DIRECTION OF
JAMES M. NEDERLANDER, JAMES L. NEDERLANDER,
SARA MINSKOFF ALLAN AND THE MINSKOFF FAMILY

Disnep
PRESENTS

THE LION KING

Music & Lyrics by
ELTON JOHN & TIM RICE

Additional Music & Lyrics by
LEBO M, MARK MANCINA, JAY RIFKIN, JULIE TAYMOR, HANS ZIMMER

Book by
ROGER ALLERS & IRENE MECCHI

Starring
PATRICK R. BROWN   ALTON FITZGERALD WHITE   TSHIDI MANYE
JEFF BINDER   BEN JEFFREY   FRED BERMAN
ANDILE GUMBI   CHANTEL RILEY
JAMES BROWN-ORLEANS   BONITA J. HAMILTON   ENRIQUE SEGURA
BOBBI BORDLEY   ALONIE DOWDEN   DEREK JOHNSON   CALEB McLAUGHLIN

LAWRENCE ALEXANDER LaMAR BAYLOR CAMILLE M. BROWN GABRIEL CROOM DERRICK DAVIS
CHARITY DE LOERA LINDIWE DLAMINI BONGI DUMA ANGELICA EDWARDS JIM FERRIS CHRISTOPHER FREEMAN
KEISHA LAREN CLARKE GRAY KENNY INGRAM NICOLE ADELL JOHNSON JOEL KARIE RON KUNENE
LISA LEWIS SHERYL McCALLUM JAYSIN McCOLLUM RAY MERCER S'BU NGEMA NTELISENG NKHELA
SELLOANE A. NKHELA JAMES A. PIERCE III CHONDRA LA-TEASE PROFIT JACQUELINE RENÉ
ARBENDER J. ROBINSON VUSI SONDIYAZI KELLEN STANCIL L. STEVEN TAYLOR ROD THOMAS
NATALIE TURNER DONNA MICHELLE VAUGHN REMA WEBB ALAN WIGGINS CAMILLE WORKMAN

Adapted from the screenplay by
IRENE MECCHI & JONATHAN ROBERTS & LINDA WOOLVERTON

Produced by
PETER SCHNEIDER & THOMAS SCHUMACHER

Scenic Design RICHARD HUDSON	*Costume Design* JULIE TAYMOR	*Lighting Design* DONALD HOLDER	*Mask & Puppet Design* JULIE TAYMOR & MICHAEL CURRY
Sound Design STEVE CANYON KENNEDY	*Hair & Makeup Design* MICHAEL WARD	*Associate Director* JOHN STEFANIUK	*Associate Choreographer* MAREY GRIFFITH
Associate Producer ANNE QUART	*Technical Director* DAVID BENKEN	*Production Stage Manager* RON VODICKA	*Production Supervisor* DOC ZORTHIAN

Music Supervisor CLEMENT ISHMAEL	*Music Director* KARL JURMAN	*Associate Music Producer* ROBERT ELHAI	*Music Coordinator* MICHAEL KELLER	*Orchestrators* ROBERT ELHAI DAVID METZGER BRUCE FOWLER

Music Produced for the *Stage & Additional Score by* MARK MANCINA	*Additional Vocal Score,* *Vocal Arrangements* *& Choral Director* LEBO M	*Casting* BINDER CASTING/ MARK BRANDON, C.S.A.	*Fight Director* RICK SORDELET

©Disney

Choreography by
GARTH FAGAN

Directed by
JULIE TAYMOR

Disnep
on
BROADWAY

10/1/12

Director Julie Taymor with some of the Rafikis from around the world at the 15th Anniversary performance

Photo by Heidi Gutman

205

The Lion King

SCENES AND MUSICAL NUMBERS

ACT I

Scene 1   Pride Rock
      "Circle of Life" with "Nants' Ingonyama" .... Rafiki, Ensemble
Scene 2   Scar's Cave
Scene 3   Rafiki's Tree
Scene 4   The Pridelands
Scene 5   Scar's Cave
Scene 6   The Pridelands
      "I Just Can't Wait to Be King" .... Young Simba, Young Nala, Zazu, Ensemble
Scene 7   Elephant Graveyard
      "Chow Down" .... Shenzi, Banzai, Ed
Scene 8   Under the Stars
      "They Live in You" .... Mufasa, Ensemble
Scene 9   Elephant Graveyard
      "Be Prepared" .... Scar, Shenzi, Banzai, Ed, Ensemble
Scene 10   The Gorge
Scene 11   Pride Rock
      "Be Prepared" (Reprise) .... Scar, Ensemble
      "Nao Tse Tsa" .... Rafiki, Sarabi, Young Nala
Scene 12   Rafiki's Tree
Scene 13   The Desert/The Jungle
      "Hakuna Matata" .... Timon, Pumbaa, Young Simba, Simba, Ensemble

ACT II

Entr'acte   "One by One" .... Ensemble
Scene 1   Scar's Cave
      "The Madness of King Scar" .... Scar, Zazu, Banzai, Shenzi, Ed, Nala
Scene 2   The Pridelands
      "Shadowland" .... Nala, Rafiki, Ensemble
Scene 3   The Jungle
Scene 4   Under the Stars
      "Endless Night" .... Simba, Ensemble
Scene 5   Rafiki's Tree
Scene 6   The Jungle
      "Can You Feel the Love Tonight" .... Timon, Pumbaa, Simba, Nala, Ensemble
      "He Lives in You" (Reprise) .... Rafiki, Simba, Ensemble
Scene 7   Pride Rock
      "King of Pride Rock"/"Circle of Life" (Reprise) .... Ensemble

SONG CREDITS

All songs by Elton John (music) and Tim Rice (lyrics) except as follows:

"**Circle of Life**" by Elton John (music) and Tim Rice (lyrics)
with "**Nants' Ingonyama**" by Hans Zimmer and Lebo M
"**He Lives in You**" ("**They Live in You**"): Music and lyrics by Mark Mancina, Jay Rifkin, and Lebo M
"**Nao Tse Tsa**": Music and lyrics by Jacques Loubelo; "**One by One**": Music and lyrics by Lebo M
"**Shadowland**": Music by Lebo M and Hans Zimmer, lyrics by Mark Mancina and Lebo M
"**Endless Night**": Music by Lebo M, Hans Zimmer, and Jay Rifkin, lyrics by Julie Taymor
"**King of Pride Rock**": Music by Hans Zimmer, lyrics by Lebo M

ADDITIONAL SCORE

Grasslands chant and Lioness chant by Lebo M
Rafiki's chants by Tsidii Le Loka.

CHONDRA LA-TEASE PROFIT,
VUSI SONDIYAZI, L. STEVEN TAYLOR,
REMA WEBB
Ensemble Dancers .....LAWRENCE ALEXANDER,
LaMAR BAYLOR, CAMILLE M. BROWN,
GABRIEL CROOM, CHARITY de LOERA,
CHRISTOPHER FREEMAN,
NICOLE ADELL JOHNSON, LISA LEWIS,
JAYSIN McCOLLUM, RAY MERCER,
DONNA MICHELLE VAUGHN,
CAMILLE WORKMAN

UNDERSTUDIES
Rafiki: ANGELICA EDWARDS,
   SHERYL McCALLUM, NTELISENG NKHELA,
   SELLOANE A. NKHELA, REMA WEBB
Mufasa: DERRICK DAVIS, VUSI SONDIYAZI,
   L. STEVEN TAYLOR
Sarabi: CAMILLE M. BROWN,
   SHERYL McCALLUM, JACQUELINE RENÉ
Zazu: JIM FERRIS, ENRIQUE SEGURA
Scar: JEFF BINDER, L. STEVEN TAYLOR,
   ROD THOMAS
Shenzi: ANGELICA EDWARDS,
   NICOLE ADELL JOHNSON, REMA WEBB
Banzai: KENNY INGRAM, JOEL KARIE
Ed: GABRIEL CROOM, KENNY INGRAM,
   JAYSIN McCOLLUM
Timon: JIM FERRIS, ENRIQUE SEGURA
Pumbaa: JIM FERRIS, ROD THOMAS
Simba: JOEL KARIE, ARBENDER J. ROBINSON,
   ALAN WIGGINS
Nala: NICOLE ADELL JOHNSON,
   SELLOANE A. NKHELA,
   CHONDRA LA-TEASE PROFIT,
   JACQUELINE RENÉ, REMA WEBB

SWINGS
ANGELICA EDWARDS, KEISHA LAREN
CLARKE GRAY, KENNY INGRAM,
JAMES A. PIERCE III, JACQUELINE RENÉ,
ARBENDER J. ROBINSON, KELLEN STANCIL,
NATALIE TURNER, ALAN WIGGINS

DANCE CAPTAINS
KEISHA LAREN CLARKE GRAY,
   KELLEN STANCIL

SPECIALTIES
Circle of Life Vocals: S'BU NGEMA,
   VUSI SONDIYAZI
Mouse Shadow Puppet: JOEL KARIE
Ant Hill Lady: DONNA MICHELLE VAUGHN
Guinea Fowl: LAWRENCE ALEXANDER
Buzzard Pole: CHRISTOPHER FREEMAN
Gazelle Wheel: CHARITY de LOERA
Gazelle: JAYSIN McCOLLUM

Continued on next page

The Lion King

Cast Continued

Lioness Chant Vocal: S'BU NGEMA
Acrobatic Trickster: RAY MERCER
Stilt Giraffe Cross: GABRIEL CROOM
Giraffe Shadow Puppets: JAYSIN McCOLLUM,
    VUSI SONDIYAZI
Cheetah: LISA LEWIS
Scar Shadow Puppets: LAWRENCE ALEXANDER,
    JAYSIN McCOLLUM, VUSI SONDIYAZI
Simba Shadow Puppets: LaMAR BAYLOR,
    CHRISTOPHER FREEMAN, RAY MERCER
One by One Vocal: BONGI DUMA,
    SELLOANE A. NKHELA
One by One Dance: BONGI DUMA,
    RON KUNENE, S'BU NGEMA
Fireflies: CAMILLE M. BROWN
Pumbaa Pole Puppet: VUSI SONDIYAZI
Nala Pole Puppet: LISA LEWIS
Lioness/Hyena Shadow Puppets:
    LINDIWE DLAMINI, RON KUNENE,
    SHERYL McCALLUM,
    NTELISENG NKHELA,
    SELLOANE A. NKHELA

Tshidi Manye, Nteliseng Nkhela and Vusi Sondiyazi
are appearing with the permission of Actors'
Equity Association.

Andile Gumbi is appearing with the permission
of Actors' Equity Association pursuant to an
exchange program.

ORCHESTRA

Conductor: KARL JURMAN
Keyboard Synthesizer/
    Associate Conductor: CHERIE ROSEN
Synthesizers: TED BAKER, PAUL ASCENZO
Wood Flute Soloist/Flute/Piccolo: DAVID WEISS
Concertmaster: FRANCISCA MENDOZA
Violins: KRYSTOF WITEK, AVRIL BROWN
Violin/Viola: RALPH FARRIS
Cellos: ELIANA MENDOZA, BRUCE WANG
Flute/Clarinet/Bass Clarinet: ROBERT DeBELLIS
French Horns: PATRICK MILANDO,
    ALEXANDRA COOK, GREG SMITH
Trombone: ROCK CICCARONE
Bass Trombone/Tuba: MORRIS KAINUMA
Upright and Electric Basses: TOM BARNEY
Drums/Assistant Conductor: TOMMY IGOE
Guitar: KEVIN KUHN
Percussion/Assistant Conductor:
    ROLANDO MORALES-MATOS
Mallets/Percussion: VALERIE DEE NARANJO,
    TOM BRETT
Percussion: JUNIOR "GABU" WEDDERBURN
Music Coordinator: MICHAEL KELLER

Based on the Disney film *The Lion King*
Directed by ROGER ALLERS and ROB MINKOFF;
Produced by DON HAHN
**Special thanks to all the artists and staff of Walt
Disney Feature Animation**

Patrick R. Brown
Scar

Alton Fitzgerald
White
Mufasa

Tshidi Manye
Rafiki

Jeff Binder
Zazu

Ben Jeffrey
Pumbaa

Fred Berman
Timon

Andile Gumbi
Simba

Chantel Riley
Nala

James
Brown-Orleans
Banzai

Bonita J. Hamilton
Shenzi

Enrique Segura
Ed

Bobbi Bordley
*Young Nala
at certain
performances*

Alonie Dowden
*Young Nala
at certain
performances*

Derek Johnson
*Young Simba
at certain
performances*

Caleb McLaughlin
*Young Simba
at certain
performances*

Lawrence Alexander
Ensemble

LaMar Baylor
Ensemble

Camille M. Brown
Ensemble

Gabriel Croom
Ensemble

Derrick Davis
Ensemble

The Lion King

Charity de Loera
Ensemble

Lindiwe Dlamini
Ensemble

Bongi Duma
Ensemble

Angelica Edwards
Swing

Jim Ferris
Standy Zazu, Timon, Pumbaa

Christopher Freeman
Ensemble

Keisha Laren Clarke Gray
Swing, Dance Captain

Kenny Ingram
Swing

Nicole Adell Johnson
Ensemble

Joel Karie
Ensemble

Ron Kunene
Ensemble

Lisa Lewis
Ensemble

Sheryl McCallum
Ensemble

Jaysin McCollum
Ensemble

Ray Mercer
Ensemble

S'bu Ngema
Ensemble

Nteliseng Nkhela
Ensemble

Selloane A. Nkhela
Ensemble

James A. Pierce III
Swing

Chondra La-Tease Profit
Sarabi/Ensemble

Jacqueline René
Swing,

Arbender J. Robinson
Swing

Vusi Sondiyazi
Ensemble

Kellen Stancil
Swing, Dance Captain

L. Steven Taylor
Ensemble

Rod Thomas
Standby Scar, Pumbaa

Natalie Turner
Swing

Donna Michelle Vaughn
Ensemble

Rema Webb
Ensemble

Alan Wiggins
Swing

Camille Workman
Ensemble

Elton John
Music

Tim Rice
Lyrics

Roger Allers
Book

Irene Mecchi
Book

The Lion King

Julie Taymor
Director, Costume Design, Mask/ Puppet Co-Design, Additional Lyrics

Garth Fagan
Choreographer

Lebo M
Additional Music & Lyrics, Additional Vocal Score, Vocal Arrangements, Choral Director

Mark Mancina
Additional Music & Lyrics, Music Produced for the Stage, Additional Score

Hans Zimmer
Additional Music & Lyrics

Jay Rifkin
Additional Music & Lyrics

Richard Hudson
Scenic Design

Donald Holder
Lighting Design

Michael Curry
Mask & Puppet Design

Steve Canyon Kennedy
Sound Design

Michael Ward
Hair & Make-up Design

Mark Brandon, CSA
Binder Casting
Casting

David Benken
Technical Director

John Stefaniuk
Associate Director

Karl Jurman
Music Director/ Conductor

Darren Katz
Resident Director

Ruthlyn Salomons
Resident Dance Supervisor

Robert Elhai
Associate Music Producer, Orchestrator

David Metzger
Orchestrator

Bruce Fowler
Orchestrator

Michael Keller
Music Coordinator

Chris Montan
Executive Music Producer

Thomas Schumacher
Disney Theatrical Productions

Nia Ashleigh
Young Nala

Judah Bellamy
Young Simba

Sant'Gria Bello
Ensemble

Michelle Aguilar Camaya
Ensemble

Alvin Crawford
Ensemble

Garland Days
Swing, Dance Captain

Niles Fitch
Young Simba

Jean Michelle Grier
Sarabi

Zach Law Ingram
Ensemble

Adam Jacobs
Simba

Dennis Johnston
Swing

The Lion King

Charlaine Katsuyoshi
Ensemble

Jennifer Harrison
Newman
Ensemble

Cameron Pow
Zazu

Imani Dia Smith
Young Nala

Torya
*Swing, Dance
Captain*

Phillip W. Turner
Ensemble

Thom Christopher
Warren
*Standby Scar,
Pumbaa, Zazu*

Syndee Winters
Nala

Dashaun Young
Simba

Izell O. Blunt
Swing

Michelle Camaya
Ensemble Dancer

Ian Yuri Gardner
Ensemble Singer

Jaden Jordan
Young Simba

Joshua Landay
Ed

Willia-Noel
Montague
*Swing, Dance
Captain*

Sindisiwe Nxumalo
Ensemble Singer

LaShonda Reese
Ensemble Singer

Derek Smith
Scar

Sophia Stephens
Ensemble Singer

Teshi Thomas
Young Nala

Thom Christopher
Warren
*Standby Scar,
Pumbaa, Zazu*

Buyi Zama
Rafiki

FRONT OF HOUSE
Standing (L): Christopher Quartana
(Associate Theatre Manager)
Standing (R): Victor Irving (Theatre Manager)
First Row (L-R): Jenny Andrea,
Rodolfo Martinez, Jose Guzman
Second Row (L-R): David Eschinger, Steen Feiler
Third Row (L-R): Louis Musano, Jonathan Marcello,
Marion Mooney (Head Usher)
Fourth Row (L-R): Cheryl Budd,
Vicki Thompson, Tim Lueke
Fifth Row (L-R): Rose Ann Corrigan,
Fanny Zhang, Joe Melchior
Sixth Row (L-R): Maria Compton, Magdalena Clavano
Seventh Row (L-R): Joanne Shannon,
Ada Ocasio, Meryl Rosner
Top: Kelvin Bais

Photo by Brian Mapp

The Lion King

Photos by Brian Mapp

CREW
(L-R): Matthew Lavaia (Props),
Douglas Hamilton (Wardrobe),
Walter Weiner (Wardrobe),
Dawn Reynolds (Wardrobe),
Sheila Terrell (Wardrobe),
Karl Jurman (Music Director),
George Zegarsky (Fly Automation),
Stephen Speer (Electrics)

MUSICIANS
Front Row (L-R):
Wilson Torres,
Paul Ascenzo (Assistant Conductor),
Karl Jurman (Music Director),
Bob Bray,
Junior "Gabu" Wedderburn
Back Row (L-R):
Patrick Milando,
George Flynn,
David Weiss,
Carter McLean,
Tom Barney,
Rob DeBellis,
Allen Farnham

CREW/MANAGEMENT
Front Row (L-R):
Don McKennan (Sound Dept),
Pixie Esmonde (Wardrobe),
Thomas Schlenk (Company Manager)
Back Row (L-R):
Ishtar Tamas (Carpenter),
Frank Illo (Head Props),
H. G. Suli (Wardrobe),
Richard McQuail (Flyman),
Aldo "Butch" Servilio
(Deck Automation),
Brenda O'Brien (Makeup)

Staff for THE LION KING Worldwide

Associate Producer ....Anne Quart
Production Supervisor ....Doc Zorthian
Senior Production Manager ....Myriah Perkins
Production Manager ....Thomas Schlenk
Assistant Production Manager ....Michael Height
Associate Director ....John Stefaniuk
Associate Choreographer ....Marey Griffith
Music Supervisor ....Clement Ishmael
Dance Supervisor ....Celise Hicks
Associate Music Supervisor ....Jay Alger
Associate Scenic Designer ....Peter Eastman
Associate Costume
    Designer ....Mary Nemecek Peterson
Associate Mask &
    Puppet Designer ....Louis Troisi
Associate Sound Designer ....John Shivers

Associate Hair & Makeup Designer ....Carole Hancock
Associate Lighting Designer ....Jeanne Koenig
Assistant Lighting Designer ....Marty Vreeland
Assistant Sound Designer ....Shane Cook
Automated Lighting Designer ....Aland Henderson
Production Coordinator ....Kelly Archer
Management Assistant ....Zachary Baer

DISNEY ON BROADWAY PUBLICITY

Senior Publicist ....Dennis Crowley
Associate Publicist ....Ryan Hallett

Staff for THE LION KING New York

Company Manager ....THOMAS SCHLENK
Associate Company Manager ....Christopher A. Recker
Production Stage Manager ....Ron Vodicka
Resident Director ....Darren Katz

Resident Dance Supervisor ....Ruthlyn Salomons
Musical Director/Conductor ....Karl Jurman

Stage Managers ....Carmen I. Abrazado,
            Antonia Gianino, Arabella Powell,
                        Tom Reynolds
Dance Captains ....Keisha Laren Clarke Gray,
                        Kellen Stancil
Fight Captain ....Ray Mercer
Assistant Choreographers ....Norwood J. Pennewell,
                        Natalie Rogers
South African Dialect Coach ....Ron Kunene
Casting Associates ....Jack Bowdan, C.S.A.;
                        Mark Brandon, C.S.A.
Casting Assistant ....Jason Styres
Corporate Counsel ....Michael Rosenfeld
Physical Therapy ....Neuro Tour Physical Therapy/
                        Tarra Taylor

The Lion King

Consulting Orthopedist .... Neil Roth, M.D.
Child Wrangler .... Rick Plaugher
Executive Travel .... Robert Arnao, Patt McRory
Production Travel .... Jill Citron
Web Design Consultant .... Joshua Noah
Advertising .... Serino/Coyne Inc.
Interactive Marketing .... Situation Marketing

Production Carpenter .... Drew Siccardi
Head Carpenter .... Michael Trotto
House Carpenter .... Patrick Sullivan
Assistant Carpenters .... Kirk Bender, Michael Phillips
Automation Carpenters .... Aldo "Butch" Servilio,
George Zegarsky
Carpenters .... Sean Farrugia, Daniel Macormack,
Duane Mirro
Flying Supervision .... Dave Hearn
Production Flymen .... Kraig Bender, Dylan Trotto
House Flyman .... Richard McQuail
Production Electrician .... James Maloney
House Electrician .... Michael Lynch
Board Operator .... Edward Greenberg
House Assistant Electrician .... Stephen Speer
Automated Lighting Technician .... Sean Strohmeyer
Key Spot Operator .... Doug Graf
Assistant Electricians .... William Brennan,
David Holliman, David Lynch,
Joseph P. Lynch
Production Propman .... Victor Amerling
House Propman .... Frank Illo
Props .... Matthew Lavaia, Michael Lavaia,
Robert McCauley
Head Sound .... Alain Van Achte
Sound Assistants .... Donald McKennan, Scott Scheidt
Production Wardrobe Supervisor .... Kjeld Andersen
Assistant Wardrobe Supervisor .... Cynthia Boardman
Puppet Supervisor .... Anne Salt
Puppet Dayworkers .... Islah Abdul-Rahiim,
Ilya Vett
Mask/Puppet Studio .... Jeff Curry
Dressers .... Meredith Chase-Boyd,
Andy Cook, Tom Daniel,
Theresa DiStasi, Donna Doiron,
Pixie Esmonde, Michelle Gore-Butterfield,
Douglas Hamilton, Mark Houston,
Sara Jablon, Mark Lauer, Dawn Reynolds,
Kathryn Rohe, Rita Santi, Sheila Terrell,
Dave Tisue, Walter Weiner
Stitcher .... Janeth Iverson
Production Hair Supervisor .... Jon Jordan
Assistant Hair Supervisor .... Adenike Wright
Production Makeup Supervisor .... Elizabeth Cohen
Assistant Makeup
Supervisor .... Christina Grant
Makeup Artist .... Brenda O'Brien

Music Development .... Nick Glennie-Smith
Music Preparation .... Donald Oliver and Evan Morris/
Chelsea Music Service, Inc.
Synthesizer Programmer .... Ted Baker
Orchestral Synthesizer
Programmer .... Christopher Ward
Electronic Drum Programmer .... Tommy Igoe
Addt'l Percussion Arrangements .... Valerie Dee Naranjo
Music Assistant .... Elizabeth J. Falcone
Personal Assistant to Elton John .... Bob Halley
Assistant to Tim Rice .... Eileen Heinink

Assistant to Mark Mancina .... Chuck Choi

Associate Scenic Designer .... Jonathan Fensom
Assistant Scenic Designer .... Michael Fagin
Lighting Design Assistant .... Karen Spahn
Automated Lighting Tracker .... Lara Bohon
Projection Designer .... Geoff Puckett
Projection Art .... Caterina Bertolotto
Assistant Sound Designer .... Kai Harada
Assistant Costume Designer .... Tracy Dorman
Stunt Consultant .... Peter Moore
Children's Tutoring .... On Location Education
Production Photography .... Joan Marcus,
Marc Bryan-Brown
Associate Producer 1996–1998 .... Donald Frantz
Project Manager 1996–1998 .... Nina Essman
Associate Producer 1998–2002 .... Ken Denison
Associate Producer 2000-2003 .... Pam Young
Associate Producer 2002-2007 .... Todd Lacy
Associate Producer 2003-2008 .... Aubrey Lynch
Original Music Director .... Joseph Church

The Lion King is a proud member of the Broadway Green Alliance.

Disney's *The Lion King* is a registered trademark owned by The Walt Disney Company and used under special license by Disney Theatrical Productions.

HOUSE STAFF FOR THE MINSKOFF THEATRE
House Manager .... Victor Irving
Treasurer .... Nicholas Loiacono
Assistant Treasurer .... Cheryl Loiacono

CREDITS
Scenery built and mechanized by Hudson Scenic Studio, Inc. Additional scenery by Chicago Scenic Studios, Inc.; Edge & Co., Inc.; Michael Hagen, Inc.; Piper Productions, Inc.; Scenic Technologies, Inc.; I. Weiss & Sons, Inc. Lighting by Westsun, vari*lite® automated lighting provided by Vari-Lite, Inc. Props by John Creech Design & Production. Sound equipment by Pro-Mix, Inc. Additional sound equipment by Walt Disney Imagineering. Rehearsal Scenery by Brooklyn Scenic & Theatrical. Costumes executed by Parsons-Meares Ltd., Donna Langman, Eric Winterling, Danielle Gisiger, Suzie Elder. Millinery by Rodney Gordon, Janet Linville, Arnold Levine. Ricola provided by Ricola, Inc. Shibori dyeing by Joan Morris. Custom dyeing and painting by Joni Johns, Mary Macy, Parsons-Meares Ltd., Gene Mignola. Additional Painting by J. Michelle Hill. Knitwear by Maria Ficalora. Footwear by Sharlot Battin, Robert W. Jones, Capezio, Vasilli Shoes. Costume development by Constance Hoffman. Special Projects by Angela M. Kahler. Custom fabrics developed by Gary Graham and Helen Quinn. Puppet Construction by Michael Curry Design, Inc. and Vee Corporation. Shadow puppetry by Steven Kaplan. Pumbaa Puppet Construction by Andrew Benepe. Flying by Foy. Trucking by Clark Transfer. Wigs made at The Wigworkshop by Sam Fletcher. Specialist brushes made by Joseph Begley. Cheetah skins and make-up stamps made by Mike Defeo in the USA. Dry cleaning by Ernest Winzer Cleaners. Marimbas by De Morrow Instruments, Ltd. Latin Percussion by LP Music Group. Drumset by DrumWorkshop. Cymbals by Zildjian. Bass equipment by Eden Electronics. Paper products supplied by Green Forest.

SONG EXCERPTS (used by permission): "Supercalifragilisticexpialidocious" written by Richard M. Sherman and Robert B. Sherman; "Five Foot Two, Eyes of Blue" written by Sam Lewis, Joe Young, and Ray Henderson; "The Lion Sleeps Tonight" written by Hugo Peretti, George David Weiss, Luigi Creatore and Solomon Linda.

NEDERLANDER
Chairman .... **James M. Nederlander**
President .... **James L. Nederlander**

Executive Vice President
Nick Scandalios

Vice President	Senior Vice President
Corporate Development	Labor Relations
Charlene S. Nederlander	**Herschel Waxman**

Vice President	Chief Financial Officer
Jim Boese	**Freida Sawyer Belviso**

DISNEY THEATRICAL PRODUCTIONS
President .... Thomas Schumacher
EVP & Managing Director .... David Schrader
Senior Vice President, International .... Ron Kollen
Vice President, International, Europe .... Fiona Thomas
Vice President, International, Australia .... James Thane
Vice President, Operations .... Dana Amendola
Vice President, Publicity .... Joe Quenqua
Vice President, Domestic .... Jack Eldon
Vice President, Human Resources .... June Heindel
Director, Broadway Mgmt. &
Licensing .... Daniel M. Posener
Director, Domestic Touring .... Michael Buchanan
Director, Worldwide Publicity .... Michael Cohen
Director, Regional Engagements .... Scott A. Hemerling
Director, Regional Engagements .... Kelli Palan
Director, Regional Engagements .... Deborah Warren
Manager, Domestic Touring & Planning .... Liz Botros
Manager, Human Resources .... Jewel Neal
Manager, Human Resources &
Labor Relations .... Valerie Hart
Manager, Publicity .... Lindsay Braverman
Project Manager .... Ryan Pears
Senior Computer Support Analyst .... Kevin A. McGuire
IT/Business Analyst .... William Boudiette
Creative & Production
Executive Music Producer .... Chris Montan
VP, Creative Development .... Ben Famiglietti
VP, Production .... Anne Quart
Director, International Production .... Felipe Gamba
Director, Labor Relations .... Edward Lieber
Associate Director .... Jeff Lee
Production Supervisor .... Clifford Schwartz
Production Manager .... Eduardo Castro
Associate Production Manager .... Kerry McGrath
Associate Production Manager .... Michael Height
Manager, Labor Relations .... Stephanie Cheek
Manager, Physical Production .... Karl Chmielewski
Manager, Creative Development .... Jane Abramson
Manager, Theatrical Licensing .... David R. Scott
Dramaturg & Literary Manager .... Ken Cerniglia
Manager, Education Outreach .... Lisa Mitchell
Marketing
Senior Vice President .... Andrew Flatt

The Lion King
SCRAPBOOK

Correspondent: Patrick R. Brown, "Scar"

Memorable Note, Fax or Fan Letter: After the show one night, I was met at the door by a young (perhaps 20-something) man and his mother. The young man presented me with a placemat from the Disney Cruise Lines "Villains" show in which Scar figured prominently. I thanked him, pasted the gift above my dressing room mirror, and carried on with the business of doing the show. A few months later, Broadway.com was recording a character study of me and happened to pan across my dressing station, a shot which featured the aforementioned gift from the young man. I got a letter from his mother in which she explained that he had seen the video and was so excited that his gift was seen in the shot that he had been going around telling people that he's now famous. The mom called herself a "proud mother of an autistic child" and wanted to share with me because autism can make life challenging and she believes in celebrating the good times. I love to share this story because it reminds me of the impact and effect we can have on people's lives without even knowing it.

Anniversary Parties and/or Gifts: Our star-studded 15th anniversary party at Gotham Hall was lavish and lively, and our engraved iPods were pretty great too.

Most Exciting Celebrity Visitor and What They Did/Said: While we did have a few celebs pass through this year (the gossip rags purport that Justin Beiber broke up with Selena Gomez at our show), our special post-show number at our 15th anniversary performance eventually brought all of the original creative team to the stage, including Julie Taymor, Lebo M and Tim Rice.

Who Wrote This Year's Gypsy of the Year Sketch? What Was It About and Who Was in It?: This year was a huge collaboration led by Ray Mercer with spoken word by L. Steven Taylor, recording by Derrick Davis, music by Bongi Duma and featuring our amazing ensemble dancers: LaMar Baylor, Gabriel Croom, Charity de Loera, Angelica Edwards, Jaysin McCollum, James A. Pierce, Kellen Stancil, Natalie Turner, Donna Michelle Vaughn and Camille Workman. We are proud to say that we won Best Presentation for Gypsy as well as this year's Easter Bonnet.

Which Actor Performed the Most Roles in This Show?: Ensemble member Angelica

1. (L-R): Chondra La-Tease Profit, Lindiwe Dlamini and Alton Fitzgerald White light the Empire State Building yellow to celebrate *The Lion King*'s 15th Anniversary.
2. *The Lion King* wins Best Onstage Performance at the 2012 "Gypsy of the Year" competition.

Edwards covers two principal roles, all of the female ensemble and several puppet "specialties"!

Who Has Done the Most Shows in Their Career?: A totally unscientific study of the more "senior" members of the company reveals that it would have to be me who has that distinction, with almost 30 years in the biz. I win this category only because two of those "senior" members have been with *Lion King* for the past 15 years.

Special Backstage Rituals: Sunday brunch in the female ensemble dressing room.

Favorite Moment During Each Performance: I love the opening number, "Circle of Life." I get to watch it from the wings every show, spying on the audience, watching them react by clapping,

laughing like children or weeping. No matter what mood I'm in, no matter my energy level, even if it's the 10th show of the week, it always lifts and transports me.

Favorite In-Theatre Gathering Place: The female ensemble room, or any place there's cake.

Favorite Off-Site Hangout: Robert Emmett's is a fave stop of cast and crew since it's just at the end of the block and right at a subway entrance. Personally, I love going to The Lambs Club, where you can always get a post-show table and they are genuinely happy to see you. And, on occasion, I take visitors to Bar Centrale just so that they can play "Spot the Celebrity."

Favorite Snack Foods: Our dresser, Theresa, who looks after Zazu and I, keeps a stock of hard boiled eggs in our dressing room fridge which are perfect for a quick pick-up or to stop the hunger pangs in the middle of a show. She also keeps a large supply of her home-made cookies close at hand. (The peanut butter ones rock my world.)

Mascot: For many years, we had a little Chihuahua/Dachshund mix named Zuey. We are now auditioning for the position.

Favorite Therapy: Massage, definitely! But also Bikram yoga is pretty much the only thing that keeps me strong, flexible and energized enough to tackle eight shows a week.

Who Wore the Heaviest/Hottest Costume?: It comes down to Pumbaa vs Scar, but I think the award has to go to Scar since there is a flying harness that eventually gets added to what is already a 50-pound costume.

Catchphrases Only the Company Would Recognize: "Precious Baby," "You're WELCOME!," "Pop the hip, Cassie."

Sweethearts Within the Company: Ensemble members Bongi Duma and Lindiwe Dlamini have been married for 6 years.

Which Orchestra Member Played the Most Instruments and What Were They?: Our five percussionists collectively play upward of 30 different instruments.

Best In-House Parody Lyrics: "Eat your vegetables" ("Giza buyabo"); "Vegetables, my people, vegetables" ("Beso bo my people beso bo").

Coolest Thing About Being in This Show: Gaining a huge network of friends all over the world. Being able to translate the African lyrics for people.

Photo by Joseph Marzullo/WENN

Photo courtesy of the production

Director, Creative Resources ....Victor Adams
Director, Synergy & Partnership ....Kevin Banks
Director, Licensed Brands ....Gary Kane
Director, Media Strategy,
    Planning & Management ....Robin Wyatt
Director, Digital Marketing.....................Kyle Young
Design Manager ....James Anderer
Manager, Media & Strategy ....Jared Comess
Manager, Creative Services ....Lauren Daghini
Manager, Synergy & Partnership ....Sarah Schlesinger
Manager, Consumer Insights ....Craig Trachtenberg
Manager, Digital Marketing.....................Peter Tulba

Sales

Vice President, National Sales................Bryan Dockett
National Sales Manager ....Victoria Cairl
Sr. Manager, Sales & Ticketing ....Nick Falzon
Manager, Group Sales ....Hunter Robertson
Manager, Sales & Ticketing.....................Sarah Bills
Manager, Sales & Ticketing ....Erin Dooley

Business and Legal Affairs

Senior Vice President ....Jonathan Olson
Director..Seth Stuhl
Counsel ....Naila McKenzie
Sr. Paralegal ....Jessica White

Finance

VP, Finance/Business Development ....Mario Iannetta
Director, Finance ....Joe McClafferty
Director, Accounting ....Leena Mathew
Manager, Finance ....Liz Jurist Schwarzwalder
Manager, Accounting ....Adrineh Ghoukassian
Senior Business Analyst ....Sven Rittershaus
Senior Financial Analyst ....Mikhail Medvedev
Senior Business Planner ....Jennifer August
Production Accountant ....Joy Sims Brown
Production Accountant ....Angela DiSanti
Assistant Production Accountant ....Isander Rojas

Administrative Staff

Zachary Baer, Brian Bahr, Elizabeth Boulger, Whitney Britt, Jonelle Brown, Amy Caldamone, Michael Dei Cas, Preston Copley, Cara Epstein, Nicholas Faranda, Phil Grippe, Frankie Harvey, Christina Huschle, Greg Josken, Julie Lavin, Cyntia Leo, Colleen McCormack, Ellen McGowan, Misael Nunez, Brendan Padgett, Matt Quinones, Jillian Robbins, Suzanne Sheptock, Lee Taglin, Anji Taylor

DISNEY THEATRICAL MERCHANDISE

Vice President ....Steven Downing
Merchandise Manager ....Neil Markman
District Manager ....Alyssa Somers
Associate Buyer ....Violet Burlaza
Assistant Manager, Inventory ....Suzanne Jakel
On-Site Retail Manager.........................Jeff Knizer
On-Site Assistant Retail Manager ....Jana Cristiano
Disney Theatrical Productions
guestmail@disneytheatrical.com

Lucky Guy

First Preview: March 1, 2013. Opened: April 1, 2013.
Still running as of May 31, 2013.

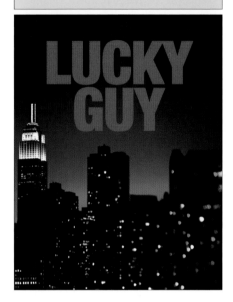

Movie star Tom Hanks makes his Broadway debut playing legendary tabloid columnist Mike McAlary in Nora Ephron's biographical play. The story follows McAlary's rise from the sports desk to star cop reporter at New York papers Newsday, The Daily News and The New York Post, and depicts his delight at working amid the rough, boozy camaraderie of the male-dominated newsrooms of the era. At his peak he confronts mid-career illness, injury and lawsuits, but then rises again to the Pulitzer Prize covering the Abner Louima police brutality story.

CAST

(in order of speaking)

Jim Dwyer	MICHAEL GASTON
Bob Drury	DANNY MASTROGIORGIO
Michael Daly	PETER SCOLARI
Hap Hairston	COURTNEY B. VANCE
Jerry Nachman	RICHARD MASUR
John Cotter	PETER GERETY
Mike McAlary	TOM HANKS
Louise Imerman	DEIRDRE LOVEJOY
Dino Tortorici	DUSTYN GULLEDGE
Alice McAlary	MAURA TIERNEY
Brian O'Regan	BRIAN DYKSTRA
Eddie Hayes	CHRISTOPHER McDONALD
Stanley Joyce	RICHARD MASUR
Debby Krenek	DEIRDRE LOVEJOY
John Miller	DANNY MASTROGIORGIO
Abner Louima	STEPHEN TYRONE WILLIAMS
Reporter	ANDREW HOVELSON

Continued on next page

⊛ BROADHURST THEATRE
235 West 44th Street
A Shubert Organization Theatre

Philip J. Smith, *Chairman*   Robert E. Wankel, *President*

COLIN CALLENDER   ROY FURMAN   ARIELLE TEPPER MADOVER
ROGER & WILLIAM BERLIND   STACEY MINDICH
ROBERT COLE & FREDERICK ZOLLO   DAVID MIRVISH   DARYL ROTH
JAMES D. STERN/DOUGLAS L. MEYER   SCOTT & BRIAN ZEILINGER
IN ASSOCIATION WITH
SONIA FRIEDMAN PRODUCTIONS
AND
THE SHUBERT ORGANIZATION
PRESENT

TOM HANKS
IN

LUCKY GUY

A NEW PLAY BY
NORA EPHRON

ALSO STARRING
CHRISTOPHER McDONALD   PETER GERETY   COURTNEY B. VANCE
PETER SCOLARI   RICHARD MASUR
AND
MAURA TIERNEY
WITH
BRIAN DYKSTRA   MICHAEL GASTON   DUSTYN GULLEDGE   ANDREW HOVELSON
DEIRDRE LOVEJOY   DANNY MASTROGIORGIO   STEPHEN TYRONE WILLIAMS
PAULA JON DEROSE   JOE FORBRICH   THOMAS MICHAEL HAMMOND   MARC DAMON JOHNSON

SCENIC DESIGN	COSTUME DESIGN	SOUND DESIGN	LIGHTING DESIGN
DAVID ROCKWELL	TONI-LESLIE JAMES	SCOTT LEHRER	JULES FISHER & PEGGY EISENHAUER

PROJECTION DESIGN	HAIR & WIG DESIGN	CASTING
BATWIN - ROBIN PRODUCTIONS, INC.	ROBERT-CHARLES VALLANCE	JORDAN THALER / HEIDI GRIFFITHS

PRESS REPRESENTATIVE	ADVERTISING	MARKETING DIRECTOR	TECHNICAL SUPERVISOR
BONEAU/BRYAN-BROWN	SPOTCO	ERIC SCHNALL	PETER FULBRIGHT

PRODUCTION STAGE MANAGER	COMPANY MANAGER	ASSOCIATE PRODUCER	EXECUTIVE PRODUCER
JANE GREY	PENELOPE DAULTON	SENOVVA, INC. SCOTT HUFF	101 PRODUCTIONS, LTD.

DIRECTOR
GEORGE C. WOLFE

4/1/13

Standing (L-R):
Tom Hanks,
Richard Masur,
Andrew Hovelson
Sitting (L-R):
Peter Gerety,
Dustyn Gulledge,
Brian Dykstra

Photo by Joan Marcus

Lucky Guy

The Playbill Broadway Yearbook 2012-2013

Cast Continued

TIME AND PLACE:
New York City 1985-1998

UNDERSTUDIES

For Mike McAlary, Michael Daly, Jim Dwyer:
THOMAS MICHAEL HAMMOND
For Alice McAlary, Louise Imerman/Debby Krenek:
PAULA JON DeROSE
For Bob Drury, Eddie Hayes, Brian O'Regan:
JOE FORBRICH
For Hap Hairston, Abner Louima:
MARC DAMON JOHNSON
For Jerry Nachman/Stanley Joyce, John Cotter:
BRIAN DYKSTRA
For Dino Tortorici:
ANDREW HOVELSON

Production Stage Manager: JANE GREY
Stage Manager: CAMBRA OVEREND

Journalism: A Love Story by Nora Ephron

But for many years I was in love with journalism. I loved the city room. I loved the pack. I loved smoking and drinking scotch and playing dollar poker. I didn't know much about anything, and I was in a profession where you didn't have to. I loved the speed. I loved the deadlines. I loved that you wrapped the fish.

You can't make this stuff up, I used to say.

I'd known since I was a child that I was going to live in New York eventually, and that everything in between would be just an intermission. I'd spent all those years imagining what New York was going to be like. I thought it was going to be the most exciting, magical, fraught-with-possibility place that you could ever live; a place where if you really wanted something you might be able to get it; a place where I'd be surrounded by people I was dying to know; a place where I might be able to become the only thing worth being, a journalist.

And I'd turned out to be right.

Lucky Guy dramatizes key episodes in the life of Mike McAlary. While it is based on extensive research and conversations with many of the people who knew Mike best, it is a dramatization that incorporates fictional elements such as constructed dialog, composite characters and events and adjusted and compressed chronology. The names and logos of the newspapers and other organizations depicted in the play are the property of those organizations, and no assumption should be made that any of the persons, companies or products depicted or mentioned in the play have endorsed this production.

Tom Hanks
Mike McAlary

Maura Tierney
Alice McAlary

Christopher McDonald
Eddie Hayes

Peter Gerety
John Cotter

Courtney B. Vance
Hap Hairston

Peter Scolari
Michael Daly

Richard Masur
Jerry Nachman/ Stanley Joyce

Brian Dykstra
Brian O'Regan

Michael Gaston
Jim Dwyer

Dustyn Gulledge
Dino Tortorici

Andrew Hovelson
Reporter

Deirdre Lovejoy
Louise Imerman/ Debby Krenek

Danny Mastrogiorgio
Bob Drury

Stephen Tyrone Williams
Abner Louima

Paula Jon DeRose
u/s Alice McAlary, Louise Imerman/ Debby Krenek

Joe Forbrich
u/s Eddie Hayes, Bob Drury, Brian O'Regan

Thomas Michael Hammond
u/s Mike McAlary, Michael Daly, Jim Dwyer

Marc Damon Johnson
u/s Hap Hairston, Abner Louima

Nora Ephron
Playwright

George C. Wolfe
Director

David Rockwell
Scenic Design

Lucky Guy

Toni Leslie-James
Costume Design

Scott Lehrer
Sound Design

Jules Fisher and Peggy Eisenhauer
Lighting Designers

Robert-Charles Vallance
Wig and Hair Designer

Jordan Thaler
Casting

Heidi Griffiths
Casting

Jane Grey
Production Stage Manager

Cambra Overend
Stage Manager

Kamilah Forbes
Associate Director

Peter Fulbright
Tech Production Services
Production Manager

Kathy Fabian
Props Supervisor

Stephen Gabis
Dialect Coach

Thomas Schall
Fight Director

Eric Schnall
Marketing Director

Wendy Orshan
101 Productions, Ltd.
Executive Producer

Colin Callender
Producer

Roy Furman
Producer

Arielle Tepper Madover
Producer

Roger Berlind
Producer

Robert Cole
Producer

Frederick Zollo
Producer

David Mirvish
Producer

Daryl Roth
Producer

Douglas L. Meyer
Producer

Scott Zeilinger
Producer

Brian Zeilinger
Producer

Sonia Friedman
Sonia Friedman Productions
Producer

Philip J. Smith
Chairman
The Shubert Organization
Producer

Robert E. Wankel
President
The Shubert Organization
Producer

Photo by Joan Marcus

(L-R): Tom Hanks and Courtney B. Vance

Lucky Guy

Photos by Brian Mapp

STAGE MANAGEMENT
(L-R): Jane Grey (Production Stage Manager), Cambra Overend (Stage Manager), Sara Grady

WARDROBE/HAIR
Top to Bottom: Robert Guy (Wardrobe
Supervisor), Rick Caroto (Hair Supervisor),
Maeve Fiona Butler (Dresser), Sandy Binion
(Mr. Hanks' Dresser), Susan Cook
(Wardrobe Staff), Sara Darneille (Dresser)

FRONT OF HOUSE
Front Row (L-R): Debbie Eng, Damien Palacios (Bartender), Karen Diaz, La'Shone Cleveland, Jennifer Vega
Back Row (L-R): Juan (Tony) Lopez, Hugh Lynch, Nancy Reyes, Danielle Banyai

CREW
(L-R): Charlie DeVerna, Brian McGarity, Christopher Kurtz, David Stollings (Production Sound), Laura Koch, Wilbur Graham, Paul Wimmer

Lucky Guy

(L-R): Tom Hanks and Maura Tierney

Photo by Joan Marcus

Lucky Guy
SCRAPBOOK

Correspondent: Deirdre Lovejoy, "Louise Imerman," "Debby Krenek"

Memorable Opening Night Letter, Fax or Note: A TELEGRAM from my friend, actor Patrick Fabian, and his wife, writer/performer Mandy Steckelberg Fabian. A fantastic typed note from Tom Hanks on Mike McAlary stationery.

Opening Night Gifts: My Valentine (Red) Vintage Typewriter from the Tom Hanks Collection. One of a kind. And so very dear to Tom's typewriter collecting heart! Also, my Custom Dede (my nickname) Bobblehead (a gift from my mother). The Dede Bobblehead is a big hit with my castmates, and on Twitter.

Most Exciting Celebrity Visitor and What They Did/Said: Carol Burnett. I got a photo with her, and Tom [Hanks] photobombed it. It is now my all-time favorite photograph. She said "You were WONDERFUL." I can die happy. Other exciting visitors: Christiane Amanpour, Nancy Pelosi, and Goldie [Hawn] and Kurt [Russell]!

Who Has Done the Most Shows in Their Career: Not sure, but probably Peter Gerety!

Special Backstage Rituals: Our pre-show hands-in "got team" chant (done in a circle onstage at places) where I stage whisper "F*** YOU" and then the guys respond "KISS MY A**!" It is my character Louise's signature line, and a good send-off for the fun we all have doing the show. It is chanted

with great love, in other words.

Favorite Moment During Each Performance: The pre-stage ritual is a favorite. Onstage, I LOVE the opening newsroom sequence. The audience roars and they know they are in for a great ride.

Favorite In-Theatre Gathering Place: Outside Tom's dressing room there is a little hallway—it is a favorite "arriving at the theatre" gathering place for one or many. We like to check in with Mr. Hanks on the way to our dressing rooms.

Favorite Off-Site Hangout: Angus (it's across the street), Joe Allen (for the food and company). Those two (and the occasional Bar Centrale) are my favorites.

Favorite Snack Food: Our producer, Colin Callender, brings in Insomnia Cookies between

shows one day a week usually!

Mascot: Well, I would have to say the Dede Bobblehead, but I am prejudiced!

Favorite Therapy: Ricolas.

Most Memorable Ad-Lib: Courtney going up on a line (he narrates the play A LOT) and saying "I would have said....THIS AND THAT!" in Act Two. Also, one preview saw the video malfunction and Brian Dykstra came to the rescue and said a line from the video content.

Record Number of Cell Phone Rings, Cell Phone Photos or Texting Incidents During a Performance: Lots of rings, but I don't like to give them power or credence by TALKING about them! During BC/EFA collection, Tom told the audience it was okay for them to snap a legal picture—the ENTIRE HOUSE LIT UP WITH FLASHES SIMULTANEOUSLY. It was blinding and it went on for a full few minutes. Ridic! But we make a lot of money, so there's that!

Memorable Press Encounter: I think the press is in shock that there is no dirt to dish on this show. That's memorable!

Memorable Stage Door Fan Encounter: The masses at the stage door EVERY night waiting for Tom. However, the first night (complete with NYPD HORSES for crowd control) was shocking, as it was the harbinger of what was to come. Hundreds and hundreds of fans waiting. But that is a normal thing now!

What Did You Think of the Internet Buzz

on Your Show?: I am just glad we have lived up to and surpassed all the high expectations. It's a fantastic show, with a stellar star performance.

Latest Audience Arrival: There is never an empty seat.

Fastest Costume Change: Tom—ALL THE TIME. He has an entire show filled with QUICK quick changes!!

Busiest Day at the Box Office: EVERY DAY. *WE* CAN'T EVEN GET TICKETS.

Who Wore the Heaviest/Hottest Costume: It's a contemporary show, so it's not too bad. Do my three wigs count?

Who Wore the Least: It's not that kind of show.

Catchphrases Only the Company Would Recognize: "It's good for us, It's good for us" and "F*** you, Kiss my A**!"

Memorable Directorial Note: "There are two pauses in this show, and neither of them are yours."—George C. Wolfe.

Company In-Jokes: That we are getting paid to do this.

Company Legends: Um...Tom Hanks? And will Peter Gerety say his lines? In the right order?

Sweethearts Within the Company: We are all in love with George C. Wolfe.

Ghostly Encounters Backstage: Not yet. Unless you count backstage crossover crashes during tech and previews (it is a fast show).

Coolest Thing About Being in This Show: All of it. It is the hottest show in town and, to top it all off, we've had a BLAST from the first day. We laugh our butts off every day. Never have I had so much fun.

Fan Club Info: Just walk by the stage door after the show...Now THERE's a fan club!

Other Stories: I started the Lucky Girl Blog to tell some of them. You can read it at www.deirdrelovejoy.com. There is a memorable Hanks story or two there!

Some of the actors with their real-life counterparts at the opening night party:
1. Michael Gaston and Jim Dwyer.
2. Christopher McDonald and Eddie Hayes.
3. Danny Mastrogiorgio and Bob Drury.
4. Curtain call on opening night with (L-R): director George C. Wolfe, Maura Tierney, Tom Hanks, Peter Scolari and *Yearbook* correspondent Deirdre Lovejoy.

The Lyons

First Preview: April 5, 2012. Opened: April 23, 2012.
Closed July 1, 2012 after 21 Previews and 80 Performances.

The neurotic Lyons family gathers beside the deathbed of the father, an old curmudgeon who spends his last hours berating his wife and two grown children about how miserable they made his life. But it turns out to be no worse than what they all thought about him—and about each other.

CAST

(in order of speaking)

Rita Lyons .... LINDA LAVIN
Ben Lyons .... DICK LATESSA
Lisa Lyons .... KATE JENNINGS GRANT
Curtis Lyons .... MICHAEL ESPER
Nurse .... BRENDA PRESSLEY
Brian .... GREGORY WOODDELL

ACT I

A hospital room

ACT II

Scene 1: An empty apartment
Scene 2: A hospital room

UNDERSTUDIES

For Ben:
TIM JEROME
For Lisa/Nurse:
EVA KAMINSKY
For Curtis/Brian:
JOHN WERNKE

⊗ CORT THEATRE

138 West 48th Street
A Shubert Organization Theatre

Philip J. Smith, *Chairman*   Robert E. Wankel, *President*

KATHLEEN K. JOHNSON
PRESENTS
THE VINEYARD THEATRE PRODUCTION
OF

LINDA LAVIN

IN

THE LYONS

WRITTEN BY
NICKY SILVER

WITH

MICHAEL ESPER   KATE JENNINGS GRANT
BRENDA PRESSLEY   GREGORY WOODDELL

ALSO STARRING
DICK LATESSA

SCENIC DESIGN	COSTUME DESIGN	LIGHTING DESIGN
ALLEN MOYER	MICHAEL KRASS	DAVID LANDER

ORIGINAL MUSIC & SOUND DESIGN	PRODUCTION MANAGEMENT	FIGHT DIRECTOR
DAVID VAN TIEGHEM	AURORA PRODUCTIONS	THOMAS SCHALL

PRODUCTION STAGE MANAGER	CASTING	ADVERTISING & MARKETING
ROBERT BENNETT	HENRY RUSSELL BERGSTEIN, CSA	aka

GENERAL MANAGER	PRESS REPRESENTATIVE
NIKO COMPANIES, LTD.	SAM RUDY

DIRECTED BY
MARK BROKAW

THE PRODUCER WISHES TO EXPRESS HER APPRECIATION TO THEATRE DEVELOPMENT FUND FOR ITS SUPPORT OF THIS PRODUCTION.

6/4/12

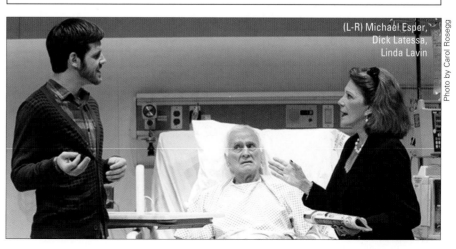

(L-R) Michael Esper, Dick Latessa, Linda Lavin

Photo by Carol Rosegg

The Lyons

Linda Lavin
Rita Lyons

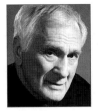
Dick Latessa
Ben Lyons

Michael Esper
Curtis Lyons

Kate Jennings Grant
Lisa Lyons

Brenda Pressley
Nurse

Gregory Wooddell
Brian

Tim Jerome
u/s Ben

Eva Kaminsky
u/s Lisa, Nurse

John Wernke
u/s Curtis, Brian

Nicky Silver
Playwright

Mark Brokaw
Director

Allen Moyer
Set Design

David Lander
Lighting Design

David Van Tieghem
*Original Music and
Sound Design*

Thomas Schall
Fight Director

Gene O'Donovan
Aurora Productions
*Production
Management*

Manny Kladitis
Niko Companies, Ltd
General Manager

Kathleen K. Johnson
Producer

Jonathan Tessero
Associate Producer

Douglas Aibel
*Artistic Director,
Vineyard Theatre
Producer*

Photo by Carol Rosegg
(L-R): Linda Lavin and
Dick Latessa

ALUMNUS

Richard Gallagher
u/s Curtis, Brian

**TRANSFER
STUDENT**

Charlie Hofheimer
Curtis Lyons

The Lyons

(L-R): Kate Jennings Grant and Linda Lavin

(L-R): Dick Latessa and Brenda Pressley

Photos by Carol Rosegg

STAFF FOR *THE LYONS*

GENERAL MANAGEMENT
NIKO COMPANIES, LTD.
Manny Kladitis
Jeffrey Chrzczon   Jason T. Vanderwoude

GENERAL PRESS REPRESENTATIVE
SAM RUDY MEDIA RELATIONS
Sam Rudy   Shane Marshall Brown

ADVERTISING AND MARKETING
aka
Scott A. Moore   Liz Furze
Joshua Lee Poole   Jennifer Sims   Adam Jay
Janette Roush   Sara Rosenzweig

DIGITAL AND INTERACTIVE
aka
Erin Rech   Jen Taylor   Flora Pei

CASTING
Henry Russell Bergstein, CSA

PRODUCTION MANAGEMENT
AURORA PRODUCTIONS, INC.
Gene O'Donovan, Ben Heller
Stephanie Sherline, Anita Shah, Jarid Sumner,
Anthony Jusino, Liza Luxenberg, Steven Dalton,
Eugenio Saenz Flores, Isaac Katzanek
Aneta Feld, Melissa Mazdra

PRODUCTION STAGE MANAGER .....Robert Bennett
Stage Manager ....Lois Griffing
Production Assistant ....Jessica Johnstone
Assistant to the Producer ....Judy Crozier
Assistant Director ....Sam Pinkleton
Assistant Set Designer ....Warren Karp
Assistant Costume Designer ....Brenda Abbandandolo
Assistant Lighting Designer ....Travis McHale

Associate Sound Designer ....David Sanderson
Assistant Sound Designer ....Emma Wilk
Production Carpenter ....Ed Diaz
Flyman ....Brian Hutchinson
Production Electrician ....Scott DeVerna
Production Properties ....Lonnie Gaddy
Advance Properties Supervisor ....Rob Brenner
Sound Board Engineer ....Jim van Bergen
Wardrobe Supervisor ....Eileen Miller
Ms. Lavin's Dresser ....Jessica Moy
Costume Shopper ....Annie Sunai
Property Coordinator ....Tessa Dunning
Legal Counsel ....Levine, Plotkin & Menen/
                                              Loren Plotkin
Accounting ....Rosenberg, Neuwirth & Kuchner/
                                    Mark D'Ambrosi, Sarah Krug
Insurance ....Insurance Office of America/
                                            Carol Bressi-Cilona
Banking................................City National Bank
Production Photographer ....Carol Rosegg
Medical Consultants ....Fidel Lim, Bev Mitchell

VINEYARD THEATRE
Artistic Director ....Douglas Aibel
Executive Producer ....Jennifer Garvey-Blackwell
Co-artistic Director ....Sarah Stern
Managing Director ....Rebecca Habel

CREDITS
Sound equipment provided by Sound Associates. Lighting equipment provided by P.R.G. Scenery by P.R.G. Scenic Technologies. Originally rehearsed at the Davenport Studios.

Linda Lavin's Make-up Design by
J. Roy Helland.

Linda Lavin's Hair Design by
Antonio Soddu.

House Beautiful provided by
Hearst Publications.

Postcard design by Erik Gloege.

SPECIAL THANKS
Michael Guccione, Ann Palmer,
Jeffrey Richards, Jerry Frankel

 THE SHUBERT ORGANIZATION, INC.
Board of Directors

Philip J. Smith	**Robert E. Wankel**
Chairman	President
Wyche Fowler, Jr.	**Diana Phillips**
Lee J. Seidler	**Michael I. Sovern**

Stuart Subotnick

Chief Financial Officer ....Elliot Greene
Sr. Vice President, Ticketing ....David Andrews
Vice President, Finance ....Juan Calvo
Vice President, Human Resources ....Cathy Cozens
Vice President, Facilities ....John Darby
Vice President, Theatre Operations ....Peter Entin
Vice President, Marketing ....Charles Flateman
Vice President, Audit ....Anthony LaMattina
Vice President, Ticket Sales ....Brian Mahoney
Vice President, Creative Projects ........D.S. Moynihan
Vice President, Real Estate ....Julio Peterson

CORT THEATRE
House Manager ....Joseph Traina

222   The Playbill Broadway Yearbook 2012-2013

Macbeth

First Preview: April 7, 2013. Opened: April 21, 2013.
Still running as of May 31, 2013.

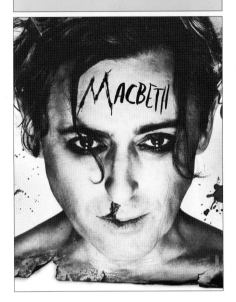

Shakespeare's four-hundred-year-old "tale of sound and fury" is retold here not by an idiot but by a madman, a mental institution inmate played by Scottish actor Alan Cumming who enacts all the major roles himself, either as a therapy or as part of his illness—you decide. A kind of Elizabethan horror movie, the "Scottish Play" charts military general Macbeth's plot to murder his way to the Scottish throne, only to see it all fall apart as his marriage, his friendships, his good name, his crown and finally his life are fed into the fire of his unholy ambition.

CAST

ALAN CUMMING
CHRIS KIPINIAK
JENNY STERLIN
BRENDAN TITLEY

Alan Cumming

Jenny Sterlin

⑤ ETHEL BARRYMORE THEATRE

243 West 47th Street
A Shubert Organization Theatre

Philip J. Smith, *Chairman*   Robert E. Wankel, *President*

KEN DAVENPORT

IN ASSOCIATION WITH

HUNTER ARNOLD

AND

CARL DAIKELER   CODY LASSEN   JOAN RAFFE & JHETT TOLENTINO
JULIA BRODER   LUIGI & ROSE CAIOLA   MICHAEL DESANTIS
NEIL GOODING PRODUCTIONS   JOHN C. HALL   MARGUERITE HOFFMAN   KEN MAHONEY
ELLIOTT MASIE   DEAN ROTH   BELLANCA SMIGEL RUTTER   KAT WHITE

PRESENT

ALAN CUMMING

IN

THE NATIONAL THEATRE OF SCOTLAND'S PRODUCTION OF

BY

WILLIAM SHAKESPEARE

WITH

CHRIS KIPINIAK   JENNY STERLIN   BRENDAN TITLEY

SCENIC & COSTUME DESIGN MERLE HENSEL	LIGHTING DESIGN NATASHA CHIVERS	SOUND DESIGN FERGUS O'HARE	VIDEO DESIGN IAN WILLIAM GALLOWAY
ADDITIONAL CASTING BY CINDY TOLAN		MUSIC BY MAX RICHTER	PRODUCTION STAGE MANAGER KRISTEN HARRIS
PRODUCTION MANAGEMENT JUNIPER STREET PRODUCTIONS, INC.		GENERAL MANAGEMENT BESPOKE THEATRICALS	ASSOCIATE PRODUCER HUNTER CHANCELLOR
PRESS REPRESENTATIVE JEREMY SHAFFER THE PUBLICITY OFFICE		MARKETING & INTERACTIVE DTE AGENCY	ADVERTISING AKA

DIRECTED BY

JOHN TIFFANY & ANDREW GOLDBERG

4/21/13

Alan Cumming in a scene
from *Macbeth*

Photo by Jeremy Daniel

Macbeth

Brendan Titley

Chris Kipiniak

William Shakespeare
Playwright

John Tiffany
Director

Andrew Goldberg
Director

Merle Hensel
Scenic and Costume Design

Natasha Chivers
Lighting Design

Fergus O'Hare
Sound Design

Max Richter
Music

Ana Rose Greene, Guy Kwan,
Joseph DeLuise, Hillary Blanken
Juniper Street Productions
Production Management

Kristen Harris
Production Stage Manager

Maggie Brohn
Bespoke Theatricals
General Management

Amy Jacobs
Bespoke Theatricals
General Management

Devin Keudell
Bespoke Theatricals
General Management

Nina Lannan
Bespoke Theatricals
General Management

Ken Davenport
Producer

Hunter Arnold
Producer

Cody Lassen
Producer

Joan Raffe
Producer

Jhett Tolentino
Producer

Julia Broder
Producer

Luigi & Rose Caiola
Producer

Michael DeSantis
Producer

Neil Gooding
Neil Gooding Productions
Producer

Ken Mahoney
Producer

Elliott Masie
Producer

Dean Roth
Producer

Bellanca Smigel Rutter
Producer

Kat White
Producer

Richard Findlay
Chairman
The National Theatre of Scotland

Allan Burns
Vice Chairman
The National Theatre of Scotland

Photo by Brian Mapp

BOX OFFICE
(L-R): Chuck Loesche, new local member
Alan Cumming (in photo), Karen Winer

Macbeth

Photos by Brian Mapp

FRONT OF HOUSE
Front Row (L-R):
Dan Landon (Manager),
John Barbaretti (Ticket Taker)
Second Row (L-R):
Raya Konyk,
Sherry McIntyre (Head Usher),
Aileen Kilburn
Third Row: Pat Roehrich,
Back Row (L-R):
Nicole McIntyre,
Kate Reiter,
George Nestor

CREW
Front Row (L-R): Jim Wilkinson, Malcolm (the doll),
Christopher Moeller
Back Row (L-R): Julian Andres Arango, Philip Feller,
Kimberly Mark

STAFF FOR *MACBETH*

DAVENPORT THEATRICAL ENTERPRISES
Ken Davenport   Hunter Arnold
Jamie Lynn Ballard   Jody Bell   Jane Caplow
Kayla Greenspan   Michael Karns   Matt Kovich
Jenni Marks   Steven Tartick
Jennifer Ashley Tepper   Jason Wooden

GENERAL MANAGEMENT
BESPOKE THEATRICALS
Devin Keudell   Nina Lannan
Maggie Brohn   Amy Jacobs
Associate General Manager ....Danielle Saks

COMPANY MANAGER
Ryan Conway

GENERAL PRESS REPRESENTATIVES
THE PUBLICITY OFFICE
Jeremy Shaffer
Marc Thibodeau   Michael Borowski

PRODUCTION MANAGEMENT
JUNIPER STREET PRODUCTIONS
Hillary Blanken   Joe DeLuise
Guy Kwan   Ana Rose Greene

ADDITIONAL CASTING BY
Cindy Tolan, CSA   Adam Caldwell, CSA

Production Stage Manager ....**Kristen Harris**
Stage Manager ....Robert Witherow
Dialect Coach ....Stephen Gabis
Movement ....Christine Devaney
Voice...Ross Steen
Video System Engineer ....Salvador Bettencourt Avila
Psychoanalyst Consultant ....Dr. Michael Eigen
Associate Set Designer ....Shoko Kambara
UK Set Associate ....Andy Purves
Associate Lighting Designer ....Dan Walker
Moving Light Programmer ....Marc Polimeni
Associate Video Designer ....Caite Hevner
Associate Sound Designer ....Joanna Lynn Staub
Production Carpenter ....Scott "Gus" Poitras

Advance Flyman ....David M. Cohen
Head Electrician ....Christopher Moeller
Production Electrician ....Randy Zaibek
Production Props ....Mike Pilipski
Head Video ....Greg Peeler
Production Sound ....David Dignazio
Technical Production Assistants ....Jeremy McComish,
Sean Devine
Wardrobe Supervisor ....Julian Andres Arango
Dresser to Mr. Cumming ....Kimberly Mark
Production Assistant ....Oliver Roth
General Management
    Interns ....Valentina Berger Maurett,
Brent Winzek
Advertising ....AKA/
Elizabeth Furze, Scott A. Moore,
Joshua Lee Poole, Pippa Bexon,
Bashan Aquart, Janette Roush,
Jamaal Parham, Adam Jay,
Sarah Borenstein, Tomris Laffly,
Erik Alden, Kara Fleishaker
Marketing & Interactive ....DTE Agency/
Jamie Lynn Ballard, Steven Tartick,
Jennifer Ashley Tepper
Legal Counsel ......Franklin, Weinrib, Reudell & Vassallo/
Daniel M. Wasser
Immigration Legal Counsel ....Kramer, Levin &
Franklin LLP/Mark D. Koestler
Accountant ....FK Partners/Robert Fried
Controller ....Galbraith & Co./Sarah Galbraith
Banking ....City National Bank/Michele Gibbons
Insurance ....Reiff & Associates, LLC/
Regina Newsom
Payroll Services ....Checks and Balances/
Anthony Walker
Travel Agent ....Tzell Travel/The "A" Team,
Andi Henig
Company Physician ....Dr. Karen Thorton
Housing Services ....ABA IDEAL/
Elizabeth Helke
Merchandising ....Marquis Merchandise/
Matt Murphy
Artwork Photography ....Albert Watson
Production Photography
    (Scotland) ....Manuel Harlan

Production Photography
    (Broadway) ....Jeremy Daniel
Executive Assistant
    to Mr. Davenport ....Kayla Greenspan
Assistant to Mr. Cumming ....Sam Morgan

CREDITS
Scenery built by the National Theatre of Scotland. Additional set construction by PRG Scenic Technologies. Lighting by PRG Lighting. Sound equipment by PRG Sound. Video equipment by Worldstage.

Macbeth rehearsed at The Davenport Studios
www.TheDavenportStudios.com

www.MacbethOnBroadway.com

 THE SHUBERT ORGANIZATION, INC.
Board of Directors

Philip J. Smith	**Robert E. Wankel**
Chairman	President
Wyche Fowler, Jr.	**Diana Phillips**
Lee J. Seidler	**Michael I. Sovern**

Stuart Subotnick

Chief Financial Officer ....Elliot Greene
Sr. Vice President, Ticketing ....David Andrews
Vice President, Finance ....Juan Calvo
Vice President, Human Resources ....Cathy Cozens
Vice President, Facilities ....John Darby
Vice President, Theatre Operations ....Peter Entin
Vice President, Marketing ....Charles Flateman
Vice President, Audit ....Anthony LaMattina
Vice President, Ticket Sales ....Brian Mahoney
Vice President, Creative Projects ...........D.S. Moynihan
Vice President, Real Estate ....Julio Peterson

Staff for The Ethel Barrymore
House Manager ....Dan Landon

Mamma Mia!

First Preview: October 5, 2001. Opened: October 18, 2001.
Still running as of May 31, 2013.

As her wedding approaches, Sophie decides to figure out which among three of her free-spirited mother's ex-lovers is her actual father. So she invites all three men to the wedding without telling mom. Set to the hits of the music group ABBA.

CAST

(in order of speaking)

Sophie Sheridan	CHRISTY ALTOMARE
Ali	TRACI VICTORIA
Lisa	THOMASINA E. GROSS
Tanya	FELICIA FINLEY
Rosie	LAUREN COHN
Donna Sheridan	JUDY McLANE
Sky	ZAK RESNICK
Pepper	JACOB PINION
Eddie	ANDREW CHAPPELLE
Harry Bright	GRAHAM ROWAT
Bill Austin	DANIEL COONEY
Sam Carmichael	AARON LAZAR
Father Alexandrios	BRYAN SCOTT JOHNSON

THE ENSEMBLE

DEANNA AGUINAGA, BRENT BLACK,
NATALIE BRADSHAW, ALLYSON CARR,
FELICITY CLAIRE, MARK DANCEWICZ,
STACIA FERNANDEZ,
BRYAN SCOTT JOHNSON,
MONICA KAPOOR, PAUL HEESANG MILLER,
JENNIFER NOTH, GERARD SALVADOR,
SHARONE SAYEGH, VICTOR WALLACE,
LAURIE WELLS, BLAKE WHYTE

Continued on next page

WINTER GARDEN

1634 Broadway

A Shubert Organization Theatre

Philip J. Smith, *Chairman*   Robert E. Wankel, *President*

JUDY CRAYMER, RICHARD EAST AND BJÖRN ULVAEUS
FOR LITTLESTAR IN ASSOCIATION WITH UNIVERSAL

PRESENT

MAMMA MIA!

MUSIC AND LYRICS BY

BENNY ANDERSSON
BJÖRN ULVAEUS

AND SOME SONGS WITH STIG ANDERSON

BOOK BY CATHERINE JOHNSON

PRODUCTION DESIGNED BY
MARK THOMPSON

LIGHTING DESIGNED BY
HOWARD HARRISON

SOUND DESIGNED BY
**ANDREW BRUCE &
BOBBY AITKEN**

MUSICAL SUPERVISOR, ADDITIONAL MATERIAL
& ARRANGEMENTS
MARTIN KOCH

CHOREOGRAPHY
ANTHONY VAN LAAST

DIRECTED BY
PHYLLIDA LLOYD

10/1/12

(L-R): Felicia Finley, Judy McLane and Lauren Cohn

Photo by Joan Marcus

Mamma Mia!

MUSICAL NUMBERS

(in alphabetical order)

CHIQUITITA
DANCING QUEEN
DOES YOUR MOTHER KNOW
GIMME! GIMME! GIMME!
HONEY, HONEY
I DO, I DO, I DO, I DO, I DO
I HAVE A DREAM
KNOWING ME, KNOWING YOU
LAY ALL YOUR LOVE ON ME
MAMMA MIA
MONEY, MONEY, MONEY
ONE OF US
OUR LAST SUMMER
SLIPPING THROUGH MY FINGERS
S.O.S.
SUPER TROUPER
TAKE A CHANCE ON ME
THANK YOU FOR THE MUSIC
THE NAME OF THE GAME
THE WINNER TAKES IT ALL
UNDER ATTACK
VOULEZ-VOUS

Photo by Joan Marcus

Judy McLane
is the
"Dancing Queen"

Cast Continued

UNDERSTUDIES
For Sophie Sheridan:
NATALIE BRADSHAW, FELICITY CLAIRE
For Ali:
NATALIE BRADSHAW,
MONICA KAPOOR, SHARONE SAYEGH
For Lisa:
FELICITY CLAIRE,
MONICA KAPOOR, SHARONE SAYEGH
For Tanya:
STACIA FERNANDEZ, LAURIE WELLS
For Rosie:
STACIA FERNANDEZ, JENNIFER NOTH
For Donna Sheridan:
JENNIFER NOTH, LAURIE WELLS
For Sky:
RYAN SANDER, BLAKE WHYTE
For Pepper:
MARK DANCEWICZ, GERARD SALVADOR
For Eddie:
JON-ERIK GOLDBERG,
PAUL HEESANG MILLER, RYAN SANDER
For Harry Bright:
BRYAN SCOTT JOHNSON,
VICTOR WALLACE
For Bill Austin:
BRENT BLACK, BRYAN SCOTT JOHNSON
For Sam Carmichael:
BRENT BLACK, VICTOR WALLACE
For Father Alexandrios:
BRENT BLACK, VICTOR WALLACE

SWINGS
AJ FISHER, JON-ERIK GOLDBERG,
CHRISTOPHER HUDSON MYERS,
LAUREN SAMBATARO,
RYAN SANDER, LEAH ZEPEL

DANCE CAPTAIN
RYAN SANDER

On a Greek Island, a wedding is about to take place...

PROLOGUE
Three months before the wedding

ACT ONE
The day before the wedding

ACT TWO
The day of the wedding

THE BAND
Music Director/Conductor/Keyboard 1:
WENDY BOBBITT CAVETT
Associate Music Director/Keyboard 2:
ROB PREUSS
Keyboard 3:
STEVE MARZULLO
Keyboard 4:
MYLES CHASE
Guitar 1:
DOUG QUINN
Guitar 2:
JEFF CAMPBELL
Bass:
PAUL ADAMY
Drums:
RAY MARCHICA
Percussion:
DAVID NYBERG
Music Coordinator:
MICHAEL KELLER
Synthesizer Programmer:
NICHOLAS GILPIN

Judy McLane
Donna Sheridan

Christy Altomare
Sophie Sheridan

Lauren Cohn
Rosie

Felicia Finley
Tanya

Aaron Lazar
Sam Carmichael

Daniel Cooney
Bill Austin

Graham Rowat
Harry Bright

Mamma Mia!

Zak Resnick
Sky

Traci Victoria
Ali

Thomasina E. Gross
Lisa

Jacob Pinion
Pepper

Andrew Chappelle
Eddie

Deanna Aguinaga
Ensemble

Brent Black
Ensemble; u/s Bill, Sam, Father Alexandrios

Natalie Bradshaw
Ensemble; u/s Sophie, Ali

Allyson Carr
Ensemble

Felicity Claire
Ensemble; u/s Sophie, Lisa

Mark Dancewicz
Ensemble; u/s Pepper

Stacia Fernandez
Ensemble; u/s Tanya, Rosie

AJ Fisher
Swing

Jon-Erik Goldberg
Swing; u/s Eddie

Bryan Scott Johnson
Father Alexandrios, Ensemble; u/s Bill, Harry

Monica Kapoor
Ensemble; u/s Ali, Lisa

Paul Heesang Miller
Ensemble; u/s Eddie

Christopher Hudson Myers
Swing

Jennifer Noth
Ensemble; u/s Donna, Tanya

Gerard Salvador
Ensemble; u/s Pepper

Lauren Sambataro
Swing

Ryan Sander
Swing, Dance Captain; u/s Sky, Eddie

Sharone Sayegh
Ensemble; u/s Ali, Lisa

Victor Wallace
Ensemble; u/s Sam, Harry, Father Alexandrios

Laurie Wells
Ensemble; u/s Donna, Rosie

Blake Whyte
Ensemble; u/s Sky

Leah Zepel
Swing

Björn Ulvaeus
Music & Lyrics

Benny Andersson
Music & Lyrics

Catherine Johnson
Book

Phyllida Lloyd
Director

Anthony Van Laast, MBE
Choreographer

Mark Thompson
Production Designer

Howard Harrison
Lighting Designer

Andrew Bruce
Sound Designer

Mamma Mia!

Bobby Aitken
Sound Designer

Martin Koch
*Musical Supervisor;
Additional Material;
Arrangements
Musical Supervisor*

David Holcenberg
*Associate Music
Supervisor*

Wendy Bobbitt
Cavett
*Musical Director/
Conductor*

Nichola Treherne
*Associate
Choreographer*

Martha Banta
Resident Director

Janet Rothermel
*Associate
Choreographer*

Tara Rubin
Tara Rubin Casting
Casting

David Grindrod
Casting Consultants

Arthur Siccardi
Arthur Siccardi
Theatrical
Services, Inc.
Production Manager

Judy Craymer
Producer

Richard East
Producer

Maggie Brohn
Bespoke Theatricals
*General
Management*

Amy Jacobs
Bespoke Theatricals
*General
Management*

Devin Keudell
Bespoke Theatricals
*General
Management*

Nina Lannan
Bespoke Theatricals
*General
Management*

Andrew Treagus
*International
Executive Producer*

ALUMNI
2012-2013

Meredith Akins
Swing

Timothy Booth
*Ensemble; u/s Bill,
Harry, Sam, Father
Alexandrios*

Heidi Godt
*Ensemble;
u/s Donna, Rosie*

Tony Gonzalez
*Dance Captain,
Swing; u/s Sky,
Eddie, Father
Alexandrios*

Halle Morse
Lisa

Jennifer Perry
Rosie

Catherine Ricafort
Ensemble; u/s Ali

TRANSFER
STUDENTS
2012-2013

Sydni Beaudoin
Ensemble; u/s Lisa

Timothy Booth
*Ensemble; u/s Sam,
Bill, Father
Alexandrios*

Tony Gonzalez
*Dance Captain,
Swing; u/s Sky,
Eddie, Father
Alexandrios*

Albert Guerzon
Eddie

John Hemphill
*Ensemble;
u/s Sam, Bill,
Father Alexandrios*

Corinne Melançon
*Ensemble;
u/s Donna, Tanya*

Elena Ricardo
Ensemble; u/s Ali

Jennifer Swiderski
*Ensemble; u/s
Donna, Tanya*

Mamma Mia!

WARDROBE & HAIR
Front Row (L-R):
Carey Bertini,
Irene L. Bunis,
Rodd Sovar
Back Row (L-R):
Art Soyk,
Douglas Couture,
Vickey Walker

Photos by Brian Mapp

DOORMAN
Michael Bosch

FRONT OF HOUSE
Bottom Step (L-R):
Dennis Marion, Marc Bonanni
Second Step (L-R):
Chris Gizzi, Rose Ann Cipriano
Third Step (L-R):
Michael Cleary, Craig Dawson,
Mike Lanza
Fourth Step (L-R):
Pep Speed, David Christensen,
Patrick Roberts
Top Step (L-R): Devin Elting,
Elizabeth Reed, James Rees,
unidentified

COMPANY MANAGEMENT/STAGE MANAGEMENT/CREW
Front Row (L-R): Don Lawrence, Reginald Carter, Ryan Conway, Art Soyk, Tony Magner, Michael Maloney
Back Row (L-R): Dean R. Greer, Sherry Cohen, Michael Pule, Stephen Burns, Francis Lofgren, John Maloney

Mamma Mia!

CAST AND CREW

Front: Andy Fenton

Sitting First Row (L-R): Blake Whyte, Deanna Aguinaga, Allyson Carr, Christy Altomare, Sherry Cohen, Sydni Beaudoin, Traci Victoria, Thomasina E. Gross, Elena Ricardo, Tony Gonzalez, Victor Wallace, Felicity Claire, Richard Oser, Aarne Lofgren

Sitting Second Row (L-R): Rene Texeira, Dani Berger, Dennis Marion, Jennifer Noth, Natalie Bradshaw, Judy McLane, Wendy Bobbitt Cavett, Zak Resnick, Lauren Cohn

Standing (L-R): John Maloney, Colin Ahearn, Holly Hanson, Craig Cassidy, Denise DeMirjian, Jennifer Brauer, Michael Cleary, Craig Dawson, Michael Huller, Stacia Fernandez, Albert Guerzon, Reginald Carter, Rodd Sovar, Matt Brauer, Mike Lanza, Don Lawrence, Douglas Couture, Tonya Smith, Paul Heesang Miller, Graham Rowat, Dean R. Greer, Christopher Hudson Myers

Photo by Brian Mapp

LITTLESTAR SERVICES LIMITED

Directors ....Judy Craymer
Richard East
Benny Andersson
Björn Ulvaeus
International Executive Producer ....Andrew Treagus
Business & Finance Director ....Ashley Grisdale
Administrator ....Peter Austin
PA to Judy Craymer ....Katie Wolfryd
Marketing & Communications Manager ....Claire Teare
Head of Accounts ....Jo Reedman
Accountant ....Sheila Egbujie
Administrative Assistant ....Matthew Willis
Receptionist ....Kimberley Wallwork
Legal Services...............................Barry Shaw
Howard Jones at Sheridans
Production Insurance
Services ....W & P Longreach
Business Manager for
Benny Andersson and
Björn Ulvaeus &
Scandinavian Press ....Görel Hanser

ANDREW TREAGUS ASSOCIATES LIMITED

General Manager ....Philip Effemey
International Manager ....Mark Whittemore
PA to Andrew Treagus ....Jacki Harding
International Travel Manager ....Lindsay Jones
Production Coordinator ....Felicity White

EXECUTIVE PRODUCER ....NINA LANNAN

GENERAL MANAGEMENT
BESPOKE THEATRICALS
Devin Keudell
Maggie Brohn   Amy Jacobs   Nina Lannan

COMPANY MANAGER ......J. ANTHONY MAGNER
Assistant Company Manager ....Danielle Saks

PRODUCTION TEAM

ASSOCIATE
CHOREOGRAPHER ....NICHOLA TREHERNE
ASSOCIATE
CHOREOGRAPHER ....JANET ROTHERMEL
RESIDENT DIRECTOR ....MARTHA BANTA
ASSOCIATE
MUSIC SUPERVISOR ......DAVID HOLCENBERG
ASSOCIATE
SCENIC DESIGNER (US) ....NANCY THUN
ASSOCIATE
SCENIC DESIGNER (UK) ....JONATHAN ALLEN
ASSOCIATE
COSTUME DESIGNERS ....LUCY GAIGER
SCOTT TRAUGOTT
ASSOCIATE HAIR DESIGNER ..JOSH MARQUETTE
ASSOCIATE
LIGHTING DESIGNERS ....DAVID HOLMES
ED McCARTHY
ANDREW VOLLER

ASSOCIATE SOUND
DESIGNERS ....BRIAN BUCHANAN
DAVID PATRIDGE
MUSICAL TRANSCRIPTION .....ANDERS NEGLIN
CASTING CONSULTANT ....DAVID GRINDROD

CASTING
TARA RUBIN CASTING
Tara Rubin CSA, Eric Woodall CSA,
Laura Schutzel CSA, Merri Sugarman CSA,
Dale Brown CSA,
Kaitlin Shaw, Lindsay Levine

PRESS REPRESENTATIVE
BONEAU/BRYAN-BROWN
Adrian Bryan-Brown   Joe Perrotta
Kelly Guiod

ADVERTISING AND MARKETING
SERINO COYNE INC.
Nancy Coyne   Greg Corradetti

Advertising ....Kim Hewski, Matt Upshaw,
Lauren Houlberg
Marketing ....Leslie Barrett, Abby Wolbe,
Diana Salameh, Mike Rafael

MUSIC PUBLISHED BY EMI GROVE PARK MUSIC, INC. AND EMI WATERFORD MUSIC, INC.

STAFF FOR *MAMMA MIA!*

PRODUCTION
STAGE MANAGER ....ANDREW FENTON
Stage Managers ....Sherry Cohen, Dean R. Greer

PRODUCTION MANAGER ......ARTHUR SICCARDI

Head Carpenter ....Chris Nass
Assistant Carpenters ....Stephen Burns,
Clark Middleton
Production Electrician ....Rick Baxter
Head Electrician ....Don Lawrence
Assistant Electrician ....Andy Sather
Vari*Lite Programmer ....Andrew Voller
Production Sound ....David Patridge
Head Sound ....Craig Cassidy
Assistant Sound ....Colin Ahearn
Production Properties ....Simon E.R. Evans
Head Properties..........................Gregory Martin
Wardrobe Supervisor ....Irene L. Bunis
Assistant Wardrobe ....Ron Glow
Dressers ....Carey Bertini, Jim Collum,
Lauren Kievit, Douglas Couture,
Jill Heller, Christine Richmond,
Rodd Sovar, I Wang
Hair Supervisor ....Sandy Schlender
Assistant Hair Supervisors ....Colleen Sylvester,
Aaron Kinchen
Assistant Lighting Designer ....Jeffrey Lowney
Assistant Costume Designer ....Robert J. Martin

House Crew ....Richard Carney, Reginald Carter,
Holly Hanson, Mai-Linh Lofgren,
Meredith Kievit, Aarne Lofgren,

Mamma Mia!

SCRAPBOOK

Correspondent: Allyson Carr, Ensemble.

Memorable Note, Fax or Fan Letter: These wonderful kids from Long Island wrote us letters about how much they loved the show and that we made the show an amazing experience for them. Later that week, we received a CD from them singing their favorite *Mamma Mia!* songs. I cried because it meant a lot to me to know how much they enjoyed our show.

Anniversary Parties and/or Gifts: *Mamma Mia!* is the most amazing company to work with when it comes to parties. I have been in the show for six years and every year on our anniversary, they throw us a fun party where we can hang out as a family and think about how far we have come as a company. I had two favorite parties. First was the 10th anniversary party. Not only did we get to dance in the street on Broadway and perform for everyone who came out to see us, but I got a chance to feel what it is like to have an opening night party. Another favorite party is when they rented out the bowling alley and we all played pool, bowled and had a great time hanging out together. These people are not just my friends, they are my family as well.

Most Exciting Celebrity Visitor and What They Did/Said: The most exciting celebrity was probably Miley Cyrus, who came with her family. I was more excited for the children of all the actors and stage crew because they were so happy to see her that it made me feel so warm inside. They were smiling and taking pictures, and just watching them get so excited made me happy.

"Easter Bonnet" Sketch: "Easter Bonnet" this year was by far the best one I have ever been in. Monica Kapoor choreographed our Bollywood

Backstage at "Gypsy of the Year" (L-R): Paul Heesang Miller, *Yearbook* correspondent Allyson Carr, Gerard Salvador.

piece and it was thrilling to perform. Not only has *Mamma Mia!* never done anything like that before, but it was really meaningful to us all.

"Gypsy of the Year" Sketch: "Gypsy" was choreographed and musically done by Stacia Fernandez and Jacob Pinion. It was really great to be onstage with Len Cariou. I also had the privilege to be a lead in the opening number this year that Rommy Sandhu choreographed. It was so fulfilling for me because I have never been the lead on a Broadway stage and I hope that some day that will happen for real. Our skit was about how at *Mamma Mia!* we all have our electronics backstage with us at all times. We asked Bryan Scott Johnson to be the person who feels left out and he doesn't understand why no one talks to each other anymore and, that when we do, it's through text messages. I had a lot of fun working on this piece this year.

Special Backstage Rituals: My backstage rituals are sometimes the same and sometimes totally different. Before a show, I will do a quick warm up at my apartment so that I am ready to sing all my soprano stuff in the show. I tend to roll out and stretch out all my muscles. *Mamma Mia!* isn't very technical, so sometimes room 16 (which is the ladies' ensemble room) likes to have a half hour gathering. We talk about everything that has happened in our lives since we saw each other,

---

Francis Lofgren, John Maloney,
Michael Maloney, Glenn Russo,
Dennis Wiener
Rehearsal Pianist ....Sue Anschutz
Box Office ....Mary Cleary, Lee Cobb,
Steve Cobb, James Drury, Sue Giebler,
Bob McCaffrey, Michael O'Neill,
Ron Schroeder
Associates to Casting Consultant ....Stephen Crockett,
Will Burton
Legal Counsel (U.S.) ....Lazarus & Harris LLP
Scott Lazarus, Esq.
Robert Harris, Esq.
Immigration Counsel ....Mark D. Koestler/
Kramer Levin Naftalis & Frankel LLP
Accounting ....Rosenberg, Neuwirth and Kuchner/
Chris Cacace, In Woo
Interactive Marketing ....Situation Interactive/
Damian Bazadona, John Lanasa,
Maris Smith, Mollie Shapiro
Press Office Staff ....Chris Boneau, Jim Byk,
Jackie Green, Linnae Hodzic,
Jessica Johnson, Amy Kass, Holly Kinney,
Kevin Jones, Emily Meagher,
Aaron Meier, Christine Olver,
Matthew Polk, Heath Schwartz,
Michael Strassheim, Susanne Tighe
Production Photographer ....Joan Marcus
Merchandising ....Max Merchandise, LLC/
Randi Grossman, Meridith Maskara
Merchandising Manager: Marc Bonanni
Theater Displays................................King Display
Insurance ....Dewitt, Stern/
Walton & Parkinson Ltd.
Orthopedic Consultant ....Dr. Philip Baumann

Banking ....City National Bank
Travel Agent ....Tzell Travel
Original Logo Design ....© Littlestar Services Limited

PLAYBILL Edition # 565

CREDITS AND ACKNOWLEDGMENTS

Scenery constructed and painted by Hudson Scenic Studio, Inc. and Hamilton Scenic Specialty. Computer motion control and automation by Feller Precision, Inc. SHOWTRAK computer motion control for scenery and rigging. Sound equipment supplied by Masque Sound. Lighting equipment supplied by Fourth Phase and Vari*Lite, Inc. Soft goods by I. Weiss and Sons. Costumes by Barbara Matera, Ltd., Tricorne New York City and Carelli Costumes, Inc. Additional costume work by Allan Alberts Productions. Millinery by Lynne Mackey. Wet suits by Aquatic Fabricators of South Florida. Custom men's shirts by Cego. Custom knitting by C.C. Wei. Custom fabric printing and dyeing by Dye-namix and Gene Mignola. Shoes by Native Leather, Rilleau Leather and T. O. Dey. Gloves by Cornelia James - London. Hair color by Redken. Properties by Paragon Theme and Prop Fabrication. Cough drops provided by Ricola U.S.A. Physical therapy provided by Sean Gallagher. Drums provided by Pearl. Cymbals provided by Zildjian. Drumsticks provided by Vic Firth. Drum heads provided by Remo.

Mamma Mia! was originally produced in London by LITTLESTAR SERVICES LIMITED on April 6, 1999.

Experience *Mamma Mia!* around the world:
London/Novello Theatre/mamma-mia.com

Broadway/Winter Garden Theatre/telecharge.com
International Tour/mamma-mia.com
For more information on all our
global productions visit: www.mamma-mia.com

Energy-efficient washer/dryer courtesy of
LG Electronics.

 THE SHUBERT ORGANIZATION, INC.
Board of Directors

Philip J. Smith	**Robert E. Wankel**
Chairman	President
Wyche Fowler, Jr.	**Diana Phillips**
Lee J. Seidler	**Michael I. Sovern**

Stuart Subotnick

Chief Financial Officer ....Elliot Greene
Sr. Vice President, Ticketing ....David Andrews
Vice President, Finance ....Juan Calvo
Vice President, Human Resources ....Cathy Cozens
Vice President, Facilities ....John Darby
Vice President, Theatre Operations ....Peter Entin
Vice President, Marketing ....Charles Flateman
Vice President, Audit ....Anthony LaMattina
Vice President, Ticket Sales ....Brian Mahoney
Vice President, Creative Projects ...........D.S. Moynihan
Vice President, Real Estate ....Julio Peterson

House Manager ....Patricia Berry

Mamma Mia!
SCRAPBOOK

which sometimes is only like 10 minutes earlier. At the end of the night I roll out and warm down my voice. One ritual that always happens is a hot bath with Epsom Salts and I ice every night.

Favorite Moment During Each Performance: It's really hard for me to choose my favorite moment. I love when I have my special moments onstage with Judy McLane. She always makes me smile during "Super Trooper." If I had to choose, I'd say it would be the moment I have on stage during "Super Trouper" with Sharone Sayegh. We do this funny skit to each other every night and it makes my show. Even though she just left our show, I will continue to do it because it will always remind me of her.

Favorite In-Theatre Gathering Place: My favorite gathering place is in our ladies ensemble dressing room. We have couches and tons of room to sit around, talk about life, boys, husbands, wedding plans and anything else that we need to discuss with our sisters. We have wine and cheese nights and brunches and holiday parties.

Favorite Off-Site Hangouts: We are either at Emmett's, Lillie's or Natsumi. These three places love us and we give then enough business to stay open!

Favorite Snack Foods: My favorite snack food is either peanut M&Ms or pretzels. If you give me a seltzer water or a ginger ale, I will love you forever.

Favorite Therapy: Favorite therapy for me would either be Ricolas, Emergen-C or a good cup of coffee.

Record Number of Cell Phone Rings, Cell Phone Photos or Texting Incidents During a Performance: Since we are backstage most of the time singing in the booths, we all tend to bring our phones with us. There have been a few times where someone is rushing to get downstairs and they forget to turn off the ringer. So it goes off and we all stick our heads out of the booths to see who claims the phone. One time, our stage manager took the phone away and led the person on a hunt to find it and they did, in the office.

Memorable Stage Door Fan Encounter: I did have a fan come up to me one time and tell me that they have been following my career since I was on the reality show "Fame." I signed her Playbill and also a picture she had of me from my show. For a second I felt like a movie star. My heart felt so warm and fuzzy it totally made my year.

Fastest Costume Change: I guess the fastest costume change I have is after "Mamma Mia" and

I have to come out and do the scene change from the bedroom scene. After that, I run downstairs past the crew and every night I do a weird dance step for them and run to the other side of the stage to get changed into my "Voulez-Vous" costume. It's a fun part of my evening.

Who Wore the Heaviest/Hottest Costume?: The heaviest costumes in the show would have to be the Dynamos and the dads. At the end of the show, they wear shiny spandex tight costumes with these really high platform boots. Aaron Lazar always makes me laugh because he sometimes looks so uncomfortable in it.

Sweethearts Within the Company: A lot of people have met their significant others in *Mamma Mia!*. Right now we have two people dating, but there have been several very successful

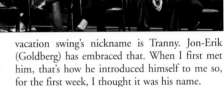
Photo by Monica Simoes

Photo courtesy of Allyson Carr

relationships that are still going strong today.

Company In-Jokes: We are best known for our horrible accents, especially our Indian accents. Monica (Kapoor) is always embarrassed, but it still is funny for everyone to try. Sometimes we just like to play jokes on each other because we are family and sometimes when we get bored, we enjoy making each other laugh.

Tales from the Put-in: Put-ins can be a lot of fun. At times, we dress up in a certain attire so that we make ourselves look as crazy as possible so that the new person going in does not feel too embarrassed that they have to be in costume and we are not. Crazy things have happened where guys play girls, people sing at each other laughing, and are playfully grabbing each others' butts. I love when we get to rehearse together because it's the time that we get to clean up the show, hear each other sing on stage or just get a chance to fool around and have a good time.

Nicknames: Mine is either "Smiley" or "Arena." One of our

vacation swing's nickname is Tranny. Jon-Erik (Goldberg) has embraced that. When I first met him, that's how he introduced himself to me so, for the first week, I thought it was his name.

Embarrassing Moments: I have had a few embarrassing moments. My high school crush came to see me and I got so nervous. When I went to do my jumps in second, I got my shoe caught in my pants and I jumped and fell flat on my butt and slid back. I was caught and couldn't get up so I had to slide on my butt backwards until I could get my shoe out of my pants. Another time, I was in "Voulez-Vous" and I was on with our dance captain Ryan Sander. We were doing our first partner lift and he broke my strap on my shirt. My boob was popping out so he put his hand over it to try and help me fix my shirt. We couldn't, so I just kept going. The entire time I held my shirt up with one hand while trying to do all the partnering work with the other.

Coolest Thing About Being in This Show: The coolest thing about being in *Mamma Mia!* is the fact that no one thought that our show would last. People made fun of it and said it was fluffy, but that is exactly what was needed around 9/11. I feel this is one of the most amazing companies I've ever had the pleasure to work with. Our crew is so down to earth and fun. We play darts and ping pong and they act like my second dads. Our stage management makes our job so fun. They plot out games, Olympic events, door decorating competitions, and they are always there to help us whenever we need them. The band totally rocks. They are incredible and are always willing to help someone rehearse sheet music or record a guitar solo. But the people I get to hang out with at work and outside of work are my amazing cast. We are truly friends. We attend each other's birthday parties, holiday parties, baby showers, bachelor parties, weddings and nights when we just all want to go out and have a few drinks and just be together. I couldn't have asked for a better show to make my Broadway debut in. I now have another family I can count on.

1. At the 2012 "Gypsy of the Year" show (L-R): Paul Heesang Miller, Allyson Carr, Gerard Salvador, Thomasina E. Gross, Sharone Sayegh, Bryan Scott Johnson and Felicity Claire.
2. Tony Gonzalez (front) and Allyson Carr during *Mamma Mia!*'s 10th Anniversary show.
3. Len Cariou (C) surrounded by *Mamma Mia!* cast members (L-R): Felicity Claire, Thomasina E. Gross, Bryan Scott Johnson, Allyson Carr, Sharone Sayegh.

Photo courtesy of Allyson Carr

Manilow on Broadway

First Preview: January 18, 2013. Opened: January 29, 2013.
Limited Engagement. Closed March 2, 2013 after 2 Previews and 25 Performances.

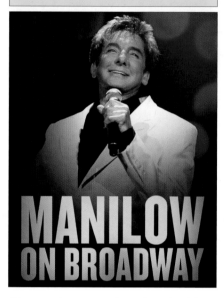

PLAYBILL

The singer/songwriter chats about his life in this concert show featuring his numerous pop hits including "I Write the Songs," "Mandy" and "Looks Like We Made It," plus a song from his long-aborning Broadway musical Harmony.

Executive Producer
RED AWNING

Executive Producer
GARRY C. KIEF

Press Representative
O&M Co.
VARELA MEDIA

Advertising
SPOTCO

General Management
BESPOKE THEATRICALS

General Management
STILETTO ENTERTAINMENT

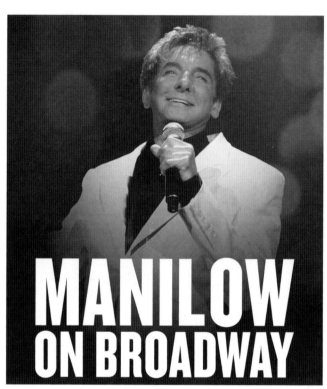

ST. JAMES THEATRE
A JUJAMCYN THEATRE

JORDAN ROTH
President

PAUL LIBIN
Executive Vice President

JACK VIERTEL
Senior Vice President

JUJAMCYN THEATERS AND STILETTO ENTERTAINMENT

PRESENT

1/29/13

Barry Manilow

Kye Brackett
Background Vocals and Choreography

Sharon Hendrix
Background Vocals

Russ McKinnon
Drums

Jordan Roth
President
Jujamcyn Theaters
Producer

Maggie Brohn
Bespoke Theatricals
General Management

Amy Jacobs
Bespoke Theatricals
General Management

Manilow on Broadway

Devin Keudell
Bespoke Theatricals
*General
Management*

Nina Lannan
Bespoke Theatricals
*General
Management*

STAFF FOR MANILOW ON BROADWAY

Executive Producer ....Red Awning/Nicole Kastrinos
Executive Producer ....Garry C. Kief

Production Designer ....Seth Jackson
Sound Design................................Ken Newman
Staging ....Kye Brackett
Special Material ....Larry Amoros
Music Director ....Ron Walters, Jr.
Keyboards ....Joey Melotti
Keyboards ....Ron Pedley
Guitar ....Michael Lent
Drums ....Russ McKinnon
Percussion ....David Rozenblatt
Bass ....Stan Sargeant
Background Vocals..........Kye Brackett, Sharon Hendrix

Production Manager ....Sacha Bambadji
Company Manager ....Adam Kief
Stage Manager ....Amber Jones
Stage Supervisor ....Ken Thomas
NY Technical Supervisor ....Neil A. Mazzella
Band Equipment Techs ....John Bunker,
                                          Gary Zipperman
Lighting Director..........................Jason Workman
Associate Production
    Designers ....Nathan W. Scheuer,
                                          Brent Sandrock
Design Assistant ....Jack Rushen
Spot Light Operators ....Sue Pelkofer, Bob Miller,
                                          Emile LaFargue
Video ....Greg Peeler
Digital Audio Sequencing ....Brian Donovan
Assistant Electrician ....Paul Coltoff
Head Sound Engineer ....Ken Newman
Monitor Engineer ....Will Miller
Band Monitor Engineer/A2 ....Jim Van Bergen
Audio ....Ted Kujawski,
                                     Bernarr Ferebee, JT Burke
Head Tour Carpenter ....Joel Wilson
Flyman ....Ryan McDonough
Wardrobe Master ....Jenny Lind Bryant
New York Wardrobe ....Jo-Ann Bethell Pantuso
Assistant to Mr. Manilow ....Marc Hulett

STILETTO ENTERTAINMENT

Management ....Garry C. Kief
Assistant to Mr. Kief ....Lynn Michelson
Business Management ....Ruth Bryant
Marketing ....John Adams, Kate Guarrieri
Merchandise ....Kyle Novak, Chris Walters
Ticketing ....Kirsten Kief
Fan Club Services ....Tahme Schorr Tartakow,
                                          Vikki Thomas

Talent Agency for
    Mr. Manilow ....Gayle Holcomb, WME
General Management ....Bespoke Theatricals/
                                     Maggie Brohn, Amy Jacobs,
                                     Devin Keudell, Nina Lannan
Company Management ....David Roth
General Press Representative ....O&M Co./
                                     Rick Miramontez, Andy Snyder,
                                     Philip Carrubba, Michael Jorgensen
Public Relations for Mr. Manilow ....Varela Media/
                                          Victoria Varela
Advertising ....SpotCo/
                                     Drew Hodges, Jim Edwards,
                                     Tom Greenwald, Stephen Santore,
                                          Ryan Zatcoff
Marketing..SpotCo/
                                     Nick Pramik, Kristen Rathbun
Legal Counsel ....Donald Dixon, ESQ/
                                     STILETTO Entertainment;
                                     Joe Brenner, Gil Karson/
                                     Grubman, Indursky, Shire & Meiselas PC;
                                     Tucker Cheadle, Tom Ugland/
                                     C. Tucker Cheadle, a Law Corp.
Press Associates ....Sarah Babin, Molly Barnett,
                                     Scott Braun, Jon Dimond,
                                     Yufen Kung, Chelsea Nachman,
                                     Marie Pace, Ryan Ratelle,
                                     Pete Sanders, Elizabeth Wagner
Press Interns ....Valentina Berger, Clio McConnell
Travel Services ....Regency Travel, Inc./
                                     Leigh Sullivan, Nancy Wo

CREDITS

Scenery constructed by Hudson Scenic Studios, Inc. Band risers provided by Robert Achlimbari and All Access Staging and Production. Lighting equipment provided by Michael Golden and Bandit Lites. Video equipment provided by Dave Hyslop, Mark Haney and XL Video. Sound equipment by Tom Arko and Eighth Day Sound Systems, Inc. Radios provided by Jeremy Schilling and Road Radios. Trucking by Chris Gramazio and Stage Call.

To learn more about the production, please visit
www.manilow.com
www.manilowonbroadway.com
www.facebook.com/barrymanilow
www.twitter.com/barrymanilow

SPECIAL THANKS
Yamaha
M•A•C Cosmetics

JUJAMCYN THEATERS

JORDAN ROTH
President
ROCCO LANDESMAN
President, Emeritus

PAUL LIBIN	**JACK VIERTEL**
Executive Vice President	Senior Vice President
MEREDITH VILLATORE	**JENNIFER HERSHEY**
Chief Financial Officer	Vice President, Building Operations

MICAH HOLLINGWORTH   **HAL GOLDBERG**
Vice President,   Vice President,
Company Operations   Theatre Operations

Director of Business Affairs ....Albert Kim
Director of Human Resources ....Michele Louhisdon
Director of Ticketing Services ....Justin Karr
Theatre Operations Managers ....Willa Burke,
                                     Susan Elrod, Emily Hare,
                                     Jeff Hubbard, Albert Kim
Theatre Operations Associates ....Carrie Brinker,
                                     Brian Busby, Michael Composto,
                                          Anah Jyoti Klate
Accounting ....Cathy Cerge, Amy Frank,
                                     Tariq Hamami, Alexander Parra
Executive Producer, Red Awning ....Nicole Kastrinos
Director of Sales, Givenik.com ....Karen Freidus
Marketing & Operations Assistant,
    Givenik.com ....Taylor Kurpiel
Building Operations Associate ....Erich Bussing
Ticketing and Pricing Associate ....Jonathon Scott
Executive Coordinator ....Ed Lefferson
Executive Assistants ....Clark Mims Tedesco,
                                     Beth Given, Julia Kraus
Receptionist ....Lisa Perchinske
Maintenance ....Ralph Santos, Ramon Zapata
Security ....Rasim Hodzic, Terone Richardson
Interns ....Kimille Howard, Amy Larrowe,
                         Christopher Luner, Lana Percival, Steven Rowe

Staff for the St. James Theatre for
Manilow on Broadway

Manager ....Jeff Hubbard
Associate Manager ....Brian Busby
Treasurer ....Vincent Sclafani
Head Carpenter ....Timothy B. McDonough
Head Propertyman ....Timothy M. McDonough
Head Electrician ....Albert Sayers
Flyman ....Ryan McDonough
Engineer ....Zaim Hodzic
Assistant Treasurers ....Carmine Loiacono,
                                     Vincent Siniscalchi
Electricians ....John Bunker, Paul Coltoff,
                                     Brian Donovan, Emile LaFargue,
                                     Bob Miller, Greg Peeler,
                                     Susan Pelkofer, Jim Van Bergen
Head Usher...............................Cynthia Lopiano
Ticket-takers/Directors/Ushers ....Leonard Baron,
                                     Jim Barry, Murray Bradley,
                                     Barbara Carroll, Caroline Choi,
                                     Heather Jewels, Barbara Kagan,
                                     Kristopher Kaye, Andrew Mackay,
                                     Kendra McDuffie, Margaret McElroy,
                                     Leslie Morgenstern, Rebecca Segarra,
                                     Jessica Theisen, Donna Vanderlinden
Doormen ....Russell Buenteo, Adam Hodzic
Head Porter ....Jacobo Medrano
Porters ....Tareq Brown, Francisco Medina,
                                          Donnette Niles
Head Cleaner ....Carmela Tenebruso
Cleaners ....Benita Aliberti, Juana Medrano,
                                          Antonia Moreno

Lobby refreshments by Sweet Concessions.

Security provided by GBA Consulting, Inc.

Manilow on Broadway
SCRAPBOOK

Correspondent: Kye Brackett, Background Vocals and Choreography

Memorable Notes: I'll never forget all the messages of support we got from all the different shows on Broadway when Barry got sick during previews. It wasn't so much the exact things they said; it was more the feeling that we were all part of a community. When we're out touring around, it's just us, so we don't get to have that.

Opening Night Gifts: We're from the pop world, so a lot of traditions and circumstances that normally happen on Broadway don't usually occur for us, and so we forget about the excitement of opening night. Although we didn't do a lot of gifts to each other, our Producers did give us flowers and a Manilow on Broadway cap, which was very cool.

Most Exciting Celebrity Visitors: My favorite was Chita Rivera. She is such a gypsy at heart! She said, "Oh, you (guys) handed them their asses!" I loved her. We also had John Cameron Mitchell, Judith Light, Lesley Gore and Brian d'Arcy James come by. I also loved that Tommy Tune came to visit us. He was the star of my first show, *My One and Only*, in L.A., and it was great of him to come out and see our show at the St. James—which is where *My One and Only* played when it was on Broadway.

Who Has Done the Most Shows: Although this is my Broadway debut, I am definitely the dude with the most production contracts under my belt. As far as done the most shows of OUR show, well…aside from our percussionist, NOONE IN OUR BAND HAS MISSED A SHOW IN 8 YEARS!

Special Backstage Rituals: We meet every day just outside Barry's dressing room and have a fun chat. We talk about what's about to happen, if anything's changing, and it usually ends with Barry saying, "Let's go out there and kick some ass."

After the show, Muffy and I meet up in her dressing room and our AMAZING dresser, Jo-Ann Bethell, has a drink waiting for us, and the three of us toast something special for that night. I love that ritual because it's such an interesting time to reflect while you're still sort of 'in it.'

Favorite Moment During Each Performance: That's got to be "New York City Rhythm." We do a thing we call the Piano Chase in which all the different guys in the band come down and run around the piano, each one showing off his talents when he gets up to the keyboard. The energy of that moment is perfect.

Best In-House Parody Lyric: "Looks like tomatoes…" (for "Looks Like We Made It").

Favorite In-Theatre Gathering Place: The crew room just offstage left. Great coffee and treats…and TV!!!

Favorite Off-Site Hangout: The band generally

Barry Manilow unveils the street sign at 44th Street and Times Square, renaming the block for him during the course of his run. Behind him to the right is producer Jordan Roth.

hangs out at Tir Na Nog, the bar near our hotel, but I think our favorite hang is the Hourglass Tavern.

Favorite Snack Foods: Tea and coffee and anything in the crew room!

Favorite Therapy: Olive oil. We put it in tea or drink it as a shot to lubricate the throat. We got that trick from Debra Byrd. At first we thought, "Ew, gross!" But then after trying it, it's become sort of a beverage for us.

Mascot: Our current mascot is our production manager's 6-year-old. After the show his favorite job is to collect all the paper streamers we shoot out into the audience.

Memorable Ad-Lib: One day people were yelling at the stage while Barry was talking, and he said, "Oh my God, I feel like it's Passover at my house." I loved that!

Technological Interruptions During a Performance: Because we allow the taking of photos and such, this is not really an issue for us. Besides, we're louder than most cell phones, so we don't hear it. However, it *is* annoying when someone gets on the phone and starts talking during a quiet song, which usually happens when someone is calling someone so that they can hear the song over the phone. (Hey!!! Buy your own ticket, pal!)

Memorable Press Encounter: We all came out to see Barry getting his picture hung at Sardi's, which was awesome and the press was also on hand when they [temporarily] renamed 44th Street after him.

Memorable Fan Encounter: We once had a guy during a performance, who was yelling "I love you!" so loudly that we started giggling because he had this really deep voice. Then he started yelling "Daybreak"!, and it started catching on with the audience. (I guess they were too scared NOT to join him). We hadn't done that song in years but because we're the band that knows more of his material than any other he's had, he said (to the band), "Do we know this? And the band started playing. To which Barry said, "I guess we do!" And so we did it, on the spot, unrehearsed.

Catchphrase Only the Company Would Recognize: "Fire in the hole!"

Orchestra Member Who Played the Most Instruments: Our percussionist, David Rozenblatt, plays probably thirty different instruments over the course of the show. He's our one New Yorker (other than Barry), and watching him play all those things is fascinating.

Nicknames: Sharon calls me "Kyelicious" and I call her "Muffalata."

Coolest Things About Being in This Show: Working with a legend and creating history. When most people make history they don't know they're doing it, they're just doing what they do. But I really feel like it's such an amazing experience at this point in my life to be doing this show on Broadway with this pop star, that's very theatrical, even though it's a pop show.

Also, the audience is in such close proximity here on Broadway! Most theatres we play are cavernous and the audience seems so far away. I had an unusual experience in the weeks before our opening just after I found out we were going to Broadway. I thought, "Oh, that will be interesting." But, man, a week or two before we came here, it really started to hit me that, "I'm going to be on Broadway!" By the time we finally got here I almost lost my mind. It's been overwhelming. There are so many subtle things I'm not used to, like: normally when we go home, we come out of a stage door that leads into a parking lot or a casino. But here, we walk out into the middle of the city, into the same crowd (and the energy of those) who just saw our show! Then there's the exuberance and energy of all the other shows on the street as well, and the sensation of walking out into all that is way different than what we normally get to experience after a show. Also, when we got here we received messages from the other shows, welcoming us newcomers. I discovered that there actually is a whole Broadway Community that waits to embrace you; include you. I was very touched by that. That's not something that exists outside Broadway. I always thought Broadway was really cool…but I had no idea what an understatement that'd be.

Mary Poppins

First Preview: October 14, 2006. Opened: November 16, 2006.
Closed March 3, 2013 after 30 Previews and 2619 Performances.

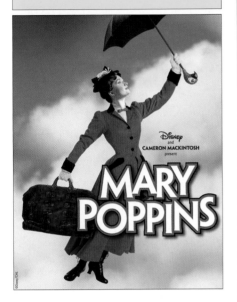

Into the lives of the dysfunctional Banks family of 17 Cherry Tree Lane, London, floats the magical nanny Mary Poppins, who uses her supercalifragilisticexpialidocious powers to escort them on a series of marvelous adventures, accompanied by a friendly chimney sweep named Bert. Along the way she teaches the Bankses the meaning and value of family togetherness. Based on both original P.L. Travers stories and the Disney film musical, with several new songs.

CAST OF CHARACTERS
(in order of appearance)

Bert	GAVIN LEE
George Banks	KARL KENZLER
Winifred Banks	MEGAN OSTERHAUS
Jane Banks	CARLY PAIGE BARON, MAYA JADE FRANK or ELIZABETH TEETER
Michael Banks	AIDAN GEMME, ANTHONY PIERINI or HAYDEN SIGNORETTI
Katie Nanna	KRISTIN CARBONE
Policeman	COREY SKAGGS
Miss Lark	EMILY HARVEY
Admiral Boom	JONATHAN FREEMAN
Mrs. Brill	VALERIE BOYLE
Robertson Ay	DENNIS MOENCH
Mary Poppins	STEFFANIE LEIGH
Park Keeper	JAMES HINDMAN
Neleus	JOSH ASSOR
Queen Victoria	RUTH GOTTSCHALL

Continued on next page

NEW AMSTERDAM THEATRE

Disney
and
CAMERON MACKINTOSH
present

MARY POPPINS

A MUSICAL BASED ON THE STORIES OF P.L. TRAVERS AND THE WALT DISNEY FILM

With

STEFFANIE LEIGH   GAVIN LEE

KARL KENZLER   MEGAN OSTERHAUS

ANN ARVIA   RUTH GOTTSCHALL   DENNIS MOENCH   JONATHAN FREEMAN

and

VALERIE BOYLE

CARLY PAIGE BARON   MAYA JADE FRANK   AIDAN GEMME   ANTHONY PIERINI   HAYDEN SIGNORETTI   ELIZABETH TEETER
JOSH ASSOR   EMILY HARVEY   JAMES HINDMAN   CHUCK REA   JANELLE ANNE ROBINSON   COREY SKAGGS   TOM SOUHRADA

JULIE BARNES   CATHERINE BRUNELL   KATHY CALAHAN   IAN CAMPAYNO   KRISTIN CARBONE   BARRETT DAVIS   ELIZABETH DeROSA
GEOFFREY GOLDBERG   ERIC HATCH   SUZANNE HYLENSKI   KELLY JACOBS   KOH MOCHIZUKI   KATHLEEN NANNI   BRIAN OGILVIE
AMBER OWENS   ROMMY SANDHU   LAURA SCHUTTER   CHRISTOPHER SHIN   JESSE SWIMM   JAMES TABEEK   NIC THOMPSON

Original Music and Lyrics by
RICHARD M. SHERMAN and ROBERT B. SHERMAN

Book by
JULIAN FELLOWES

New Songs and Additional Music and Lyrics by
GEORGE STILES and ANTHONY DREWE

Co-created by
CAMERON MACKINTOSH

Produced for Disney Theatrical Productions by
THOMAS SCHUMACHER

Music Supervisor	Music Director
DAVID CADDICK	ANNBRITT duCHATEAU

Orchestrations by
WILLIAM DAVID BROHN

Broadway Sound Design	Dance and Vocal Arrangements
STEVE CANYON KENNEDY	GEORGE STILES

Associate Choreographer	Associate Director	Associate Producer	Makeup Design
GEOFFREY GARRATT	ANTHONY LYN	ANNE QUART	NAOMI DONNE

Technical Director	Production Stage Manager	Casting
DAVID BENKEN	JIMMIE LEE SMITH	TARA RUBIN CASTING

Co-choreographer	Lighting Design
STEPHEN MEAR	HOWARD HARRISON

Scenic and Costume Design
BOB CROWLEY

Co-direction and Choreography
MATTHEW BOURNE

Directed by
RICHARD EYRE

10/1/12

Gavin Lee as Bert
the Chimney Sweep

Photo by Michael Lee Trench

Mary Poppins

MUSICAL NUMBERS

Mary Poppins takes place in and around the Banks' household somewhere in London at the turn of the last century.

ACT I

"Chim Chim Cher-ee" † ....Bert
"Cherry Tree Lane" (Part 1)* ....George and Winifred Banks, Jane and Michael, Mrs. Brill, and Robertson Ay
"The Perfect Nanny" ....Jane and Michael
"Cherry Tree Lane" (Part 2) ....George and Winifred Banks, Jane, and Michael, Mrs. Brill, and Robertson Ay
"Practically Perfect"* ....Mary Poppins, Jane, and Michael
"Jolly Holiday" † ....Bert, Mary Poppins, Jane, Michael, Neleus, and the Statues
"Cherry Tree Lane" (Reprise),
   "Being Mrs. Banks,"*
   "Jolly Holiday" (Reprise) ....George, Winifred, Jane, and Michael
"A Spoonful of Sugar" ....Mary Poppins, Jane, Michael, Robertson Ay, and Winifred
"Precision and Order"* ....Bank Chairman and the Bank Clerks
"A Man Has Dreams" † ....George Banks
"Feed the Birds" ....Bird Woman and Mary Poppins
"Supercalifragilisticexpialidocious" † ....Mary Poppins, Mrs. Corry, Bert, Jane, Michael, Fannie, Annie, and Customers
"Playing the Game"* ....Mary Poppins, Valentine and other Toys
"Chim Chim Cher-ee" (Reprise) ....Bert and Mary Poppins

ACT II

"Cherry Tree Lane" (Reprise) ....Mrs. Brill, Michael, Jane, Winifred, Robertson Ay, and George
"Brimstone and Treacle" (Part 1)* ....Miss Andrew
"Let's Go Fly a Kite" ....Bert, Park Keeper, Jane, and Michael
"Cherry Tree Lane" (Reprise),
   "Being Mrs. Banks" (Reprise) ....George and Winifred
"Brimstone and Treacle" (Part 2) ....Mary Poppins and Miss Andrew
"Practically Perfect" (Reprise) ....Jane, Michael, and Mary Poppins
"Chim Chim Cher-ee" (Reprise) ....Bert
"Step in Time" † ....Bert, Mary Poppins, Jane, Michael, and the Sweeps
"A Man Has Dreams,"
   "A Spoonful of Sugar" (Reprise) ....George and Bert
"Anything Can Happen"* ....Jane, Michael, Mary Poppins, and the Company
"A Spoonful of Sugar" (Reprise) ....Mary Poppins
"A Shooting Star" † ....Orchestra

* New Songs   † Adapted Songs

SONG CREDITS

"The Perfect Nanny," "A Spoonful of Sugar," "Feed the Birds," "Let's Go Fly a Kite" written by Richard M. Sherman and Robert B. Sherman.

"Chim Chim Cher-ee," "Jolly Holiday," "A Man Has Dreams," "Supercalifragilisticexpialidocious," "Step in Time" written by Richard M. Sherman and Robert B. Sherman, with new material by George Stiles and Anthony Drewe.

"Cherry Tree Lane," "Practically Perfect," "Being Mrs. Banks," "Precision and Order," "Playing the Game," "Brimstone and Treacle," "Anything Can Happen" written by George Stiles and Anthony Drewe.

Cast Continued

Bank Chairman ....JONATHAN FREEMAN
Miss Smythe ....RUTH GOTTSCHALL
Von Hussler ....TOM SOUHRADA
Northbrook ....CHUCK REA
Bird Woman ....ANN ARVIA
Mrs. Corry ....JANELLE ANNE ROBINSON
Fannie ....AMBER OWENS
Annie ....CATHERINE BRUNELL
Valentine ....BARRETT DAVIS
Miss Andrew ....RUTH GOTTSCHALL

ENSEMBLE

JOSH ASSOR, CATHERINE BRUNELL, IAN CAMPAYNO, KRISTIN CARBONE, BARRETT DAVIS, ELIZABETH DeROSA, EMILY HARVEY, ERIC HATCH, JAMES HINDMAN, KELLY JACOBS, KOH MOCHIZUKI, KATHLEEN NANNI, BRIAN OGILVIE, AMBER OWENS, CHUCK REA, JANELLE ANNE ROBINSON, LAURA SCHUTTER, CHRISTOPHER SHIN, COREY SKAGGS, TOM SOUHRADA, NIC THOMPSON

SWINGS

JULIE BARNES, KATHY CALAHAN, GEOFFREY GOLDBERG, SUZANNE HYLENSKI, ROMMY SANDHU, JESSE SWIMM, JAMES TABEEK

Statues, bank clerks, customers, toys, chimney sweeps, lamp lighters and inhabitants of Cherry Tree Lane played by members of the company.

UNDERSTUDIES

Mary Poppins:
CATHERINE BRUNELL, ELIZABETH DeROSA
Bert:
CHUCK REA, JESSE SWIMM
George Banks:
JAMES HINDMAN, COREY SKAGGS, TOM SOUHRADA
Winifred Banks:
KRISTIN CARBONE, EMILY HARVEY, LAURA SCHUTTER
Mrs. Brill:
ANN ARVIA, JULIE BARNES, EMILY HARVEY
Robertson Ay:
BARRETT DAVIS, BRIAN OGILVIE
Bird Woman:
KATHY CALAHAN, KRISTIN CARBONE, JANELLE ANNE ROBINSON
Miss Andrew/Queen Victoria/Miss Smythe:
ANN ARVIA, EMILY HARVEY, JANELLE ANNE ROBINSON

Mary Poppins

Cast Continued

Admiral Boom/Bank Chairman:
JAMES HINDMAN,
COREY SKAGGS, TOM SOUHRADA
Mrs. Corry:
KATHY CALAHAN, KELLY JACOBS
Katie Nanna:
JULIE BARNES, KATHY CALAHAN,
SUZANNE HYLENSKI
Miss Lark:
JULIE BARNES, KATHY CALAHAN,
KELLY JACOBS, LAURA SCHUTTER
Neleus:
BARRETT DAVIS,
GEOFFREY GOLDBERG, JAMES TABEEK
Von Hussler:
KOH MOCHIZUKI,
ROMMY SANDHU, COREY SKAGGS
Northbrook:
GEOFFREY GOLDBERG,
COREY SKAGGS, JESSE SWIMM
Policeman:
GEOFFREY GOLDBERG,
ROMMY SANDHU, TOM SOUHRADA,
JAMES TABEEK
Park Keeper:
CHUCK REA, ROMMY SANDHU,
COREY SKAGGS
Valentine:
GEOFFREY GOLDBERG, BRIAN OGILVIE

DANCE CAPTAINS
BRIAN COLLIER,
GEOFFREY GOLDBERG, KELLY JACOBS

ORCHESTRA
Conductor: ANNBRITT duCHATEAU
Associate Conductor/2nd Keyboard: DALE RIELING
Assistant Conductor/Piano: MILTON GRANGER
Bass: PETER DONOVAN
Drums: DAVE RATAJCZAK
Percussion: DANIEL HASKINS
Guitar/Banjo/E-Bow: NATE BROWN
Horns: RUSSELL RIZNER,
LAWRENCE DiBELLO
Trumpets: JOHN SHEPPARD, JASON COVEY
Trombone/Euphonium: MARC DONATELLE
Bass Trombone/Tuba: JEFF CASWELL
Clarinet: MERYL ABT
Oboe/English Horn: ALEXANDRA KNOLL
Flutes: BRIAN MILLER
Cello: STEPHANIE CUMMINS
Music Contractor: DAVID LAI

Steffanie Leigh
Mary Poppins

Gavin Lee
Bert

Karl Kenzler
George Banks

Megan Osterhaus
Winifred Banks

Valerie Boyle
Mrs. Brill

Ann Arvia
Bird Woman

Ruth Gottschall
*Miss Andrew,
Queen Victoria,
Miss Smythe*

Dennis Moench
Robertson Ay

Jonathan Freeman
*Admiral Boom,
Bank Chairman*

Carly Paige Baron
*Jane Banks
at certain
performances*

Maya Jade Frank
*Jane Banks
at certain
performances*

Aidan Gemme
*Michael Banks
at certain
performances*

Anthony Pierini
*Michael Banks
at certain
performances*

Hayden Signoretti
*Michael Banks
at certain
performances*

Elizabeth Teeter
*Jane Banks
at certain
performances*

Josh Assor
Neleus, Ensemble

Emily Harvey
Miss Lark, Ensemble

James Hindman
*Park Keeper,
Ensemble*

Chuck Rea
*Northbrook,
Ensemble*

Janelle Anne
Robinson
Mrs. Corry

Mary Poppins

Corey Skaggs
Policeman, Ensemble

Tom Souhrada
Von Hussler, Ensemble

Julie Barnes
Swing

Catherine Brunell
Annie, Ensemble

Kathy Calahan
Swing

Ian Campayno
Ensemble

Kristin Carbone
Katie Nanna, Ensemble

Barrett Davis
Valentine, Ensemble

Elizabeth DeRosa
Ensemble

Geoffrey Goldberg
Swing, Dance Captain

Eric Hatch
Ensemble

Suzanne Hylenski
Swing, Dance Captain

Kelly Jacobs
Ensemble, Dance Captain

Koh Mochizuki
Ensemble

Kathleen Nanni
Ensemble

Brian Ogilvie
Ensemble

Amber Owens
Fannie, Ensemble

Rommy Sandhu
Swing

Laura Schutter
Ensemble

Christopher Shin
Ensemble

Jesse Swimm
Swing

James Tabeek
Swing

Nic Thompson
Ensemble

Jimmie Lee Smith
Production Stage Manager

P.L. Travers
Author of Mary Poppins

Thomas Schumacher
Producer and President Disney Theatrical Productions

Cameron Mackintosh
Producer and Co-Creator

Richard M. Sherman
Original Music & Lyrics

Robert B. Sherman
Original Music & Lyrics

Julian Fellowes
Book

George Stiles
New Songs, Additional Music, Dance & Vocal Arrangements

Anthony Drewe
New Songs & Additional Lyrics

Richard Eyre
Director

Matthew Bourne
Co-Director & Choreographer

Bob Crowley
Scenic and Costume Design

Mary Poppins

Stephen Mear
Co-Choreographer

Howard Harrison
Lighting Designer

Steve Canyon
Kennedy
*Broadway Sound
Designer*

William David Brohn
Orchestrations

David Caddick
Music Supervisor

Annbritt duChateau
Musical Director

Naomi Donne
Make-up Designer

Angela Cobbin
Wig Creator

Geoffrey Garratt
*Associate
Choreographer*

Anthony Lyn
Associate Director

David Benken
Technical Director

Tara Rubin
*Tara Rubin Casting
Casting*

ALUMNI
2012-2013

Tia Altinay
Ensemble

Annie Baltic
*Jane Banks
at certain
performances*

Pam Bradley
Swing

Brian Collier
*Swing,
Dance Captain*

Reese Sebastian
Diaz
*Michael Banks
at certain
performances*

Benjamin Howes
*Park Keeper,
Ensemble*

Camille Mancuso
*Jane Banks
at certain
performances*

Noah Marlowe
*Michael Banks
at certain
performances*

Tyler Merna
*Michael Banks
at certain
performances*

Jeff Metzler
Ensemble

Kara Oates
*Jane Banks
at certain
performances*

Chad Seib
*Northbrook,
Ensemble*

TRANSFER
STUDENTS
2012-2013

Tia Altinay
Ensemble

Sarah Bakker
Annie

Brandon Bieber
Ensemble

Nicolas Dromard
Bert

Tiffany Howard
Ensemble

Janet MacEwen
Bird Woman

Jayne Paterson
*Katie Nanna,
Ensemble*

Q. Smith
*Miss Andrew,
Miss Smythe,
Queen Victoria*

Mary Poppins

Photo by Brian Mapp

CREW
Seated (L-R): David Sugarman (Stage Manager), Liza Vest (Assistant Stage Manager)
Kneeling: Jason Trubitt (Assistant Stage Manager)
Standing/Sitting: Jim Horton, Ben Corbett, Alexis Prussack, James Maloney, Dave Hogan, Michael Corbett, Kurt Fischer, David Helck, Gary Matarazzo, Alan Cabrera, Al Manganaro, Gregory Dunkin, Carlos Martinez
On stairs, starting at the top: Gregory Matteis, Bill Romanello, Karen Zabinski, Barbara Hladsky, Chris Lavin, Jimmy Maloney, Victor Amerling, Frank Alter, Andy Catron

THE ORIGINAL FILM SCREENPLAY
FOR WALT DISNEY'S *MARY POPPINS*
BY BILL WALSH * DON DA GRADI
DESIGN CONSULTANT
TONY WALTON

STAFF FOR *MARY POPPINS*

COMPANY MANAGER ....DAVE EHLE
Assistant Company Manager ....Laura Eichholz
Production Stage Manager...............Jimmie Lee Smith
Stage Manager ....David Sugarman
Assistant Stage
    Managers ....Terence Orleans Alexander,
                Jason Trubitt, Liza Vest
Dance Supervisor ....Brian Collier
Dance Captains ....Geoffrey Goldberg,
                Kelly Jacobs
Production Coordinator ....Kerry McGrath

DISNEY ON BROADWAY PUBLICITY
Senior Publicist..............................Dennis Crowley
Associate Publicist ....Ryan Hallett

Associate Scenic Designer ....Bryan Johnson
Scenic Design Associate .... Rosalind Coombes
US Scenic Assistants ....Dan Kuchar,
              Rachel Short Janocko,
              Frank McCullough
UK Scenic Assistants ....Al Turner,
          Charles Quiggin, Adam Wiltshire
Associate Costume Designer ....Christine Rowland
Associate Costume Designer .... Mitchell Bloom
Assistant Costume Designer ....Patrick Wiley
Assistant Costume Designer .... Rick Kelly
Associate Lighting Designer ....Daniel Walker
Assistant Lighting Designer .... Kristina Kloss
Lighting Programmer .... Rob Halliday
Associate Sound Designer .... John Shivers
Wig Creator .... Angela Cobbin
Illusions Designer .... Jim Steinmeyer
Technical Director .... David Benken
Scenic Production Supervisor .... Patrick Eviston
Assistant Technical Supervisor ....Rosemarie Palombo
Production Carpenter ....Drew Siccardi
Production Flyman .... Michael Corbett
Foy Flying Operator ....Raymond King

Automation ....Steve Stackle, David Helck
Carpenters ....Eddie Ackerman, Frank Alter,
             Brett Daley, Tony Goncalves,
             Gary Matarazzo
Production Electrician ....James Maloney
Key Spot Operator .... Joseph P. Garvey
Lighting Console Operator ....Carlos Martinez
Pyro Operator .... Kevin Strohmeyer
Automated Lighting Technician .... Andy Catron
Assistant Electricians .... Gregory Dunkin,
           Al Manganaro, Chris Passalacqua
Production Propman ....Victor Amerling
Assistant Propman .... Tim Abel
Props ....Alan Cabrera, Dave Hogan,
             John Saye, John Taccone
Production Sound Engineer .... Andrew Keister
Sound Engineer .... Kurt Fischer
Sound Engineer.......................... Marie Renee Foucher
Sound Assistant ....Bill Romanello, Karen Zabinski
Production Wardrobe Supervisor ....Helen Toth
Assistant Wardrobe Supervisor ....Abbey Rayburn
Dressers ....Richard Byron, Vivienne Crawford,
           Marjorie Denton, Russell Easley,

Mary Poppins

Steven Epstein, Maya Hardin, Carly Hirschberg, Barbara Hladsky, Larry Kleinstein, Chris Lavin, Janet Netzke, Tom Reiter, Wendy Samland, Gary Seibert

Production Hair Supervisor ....Gary Martori
Hair Dept Assistants ....Chris Calabrese, Paula Schaffer, Cheryl Thomas
Production Makeup Supervisor ....Amy Porter
Child Guardian ....Diane Zelenka
UK Prop Coordinators ....Kathy Anders, Lisa Buckley
UK Wig Shop Assistant ....Beatrix Archer

Music Copyist ....Emily Grishman Music Preparation – Emily Grishman/ Katharine Edmonds
Keyboard Programming ....Stuart Andrews

MUSIC COORDINATOR ....DAVID LAI

DIALECT & VOCAL COACH .....DEBORAH HECHT

Resident Dialect Coach ....Shane Ann Younts
Associate General Manager ....Alan Wasser
Production Co-Counsel ....F. Richard Pappas
Casting Directors ....Tara Rubin, Eric Woodall
Children's Tutoring ....On Location Education, Muriel Kester
Physical Therapy ....Physioarts
Advertising ....Serino Coyne, Inc
Interactive Marketing ....Situation Marketing
Web Design Consultant ....Joshua Noah
Production Photography ....Joan Marcus
Production Travel ....Jill L. Citron
Payroll Managers ....Anthony DeLuca, Cathy Guerra
Corporate Counsel ....Michael Rosenfeld

CREDITS

Scenery by Hudson Scenic, Inc.; Adirondack Studios, Inc.; Proof Productions, Inc.; Scenic Technologies, a division of Production Resource Group, LLC, New Windsor NY. Drops by Scenic Arts. Automation by Hudson Scenic, Inc. Lighting equipment by Hudson Sound & Light, LLC. Lighting truss by Showman Fabricators, Inc. Sound equipment by Masque Sound. Projection equipment by Sound Associates Inc. Magic props by William Kennedy of Magic Effects. Props by The Spoon Group, LLC; Moonboots Productions Inc.; Russell Beck Studio Ltd. Costumes by Barbara Matera Ltd.; Parsons-Meares, Ltd.; Eric Winterling; Werner Russold; Studio Rouge; Seamless Costumes. Millinery by Rodney Gordon, Arnold Levine, Lynne Mackey Studio. Shoes by T.O. Dey. Shirts by Cego. Puppets by Puppet Heap. Flying by Foy. Ricola cough drops courtesy of Ricola USA, Inc. Emergen-C super energy booster provided by Alacer Corp. Makeup provided by M•A•C.

MARY POPPINS rehearsed at the New 42nd Street Studios.

THANKS

Thanks to Marcus Hall Props, Claire Sanderson, James Ince and Sons, Great British Lighting, Bed Bazaar, The Wakefield Brush Company, Heron and Driver, Ivo and Kay Coveney, Mike and Rosi Compton, Bebe Barrett, Charles Quiggin, Nicola Kileen Textiles, Carl Roberts Shaw, David Scotcher

Interiors, Original Club Fenders Ltd., Lauren Pattison, Robert Tatad.

Mary Poppins is a proud member of the Broadway Green Alliance.

FOR CAMERON MACKINTOSH LIMITED

Directors ....Nicholas Allott, Richard Johnston
Deputy Managing Director ....Robert Noble
Executive Producer & Casting Director ....Trevor Jackson
Technical Director ....Nicolas Harris
Financial Controller ....Richard Knibb
Associate Producer ....Darinka Nenadovic
Sales & Marketing Manager ....David Dolman
Head of Musical Development ....Stephen Metcalfe
Production Associate ....Shidan Majidi

DISNEY THEATRICAL PRODUCTIONS

President ....Thomas Schumacher
EVP & Managing Director ....David Schrader
Senior Vice President, International ....Ron Kollen
Vice President, International, Europe ....Fiona Thomas
Vice President, International, Australia ....James Thane
Vice President, Operations ....Dana Amendola
Vice President, Publicity ....Joe Quenqua
Vice President, Domestic ....Jack Eldon
Vice President, Human Resources ....June Heindel
Director, Broadway Mgmt. & Licensing ....Daniel M. Posener
Director, Domestic Touring ....Michael Buchanan
Director, Worldwide Publicity ....Michael Cohen
Director, Regional Engagements ....Scott A. Hemerling
Director, Regional Engagements ....Kelli Palan
Director, Regional Engagements ....Deborah Warren
Manager, Domestic Touring & Planning ....Liz Botros
Manager, Human Resources ....Jewel Neal
Manager, Human Resources & Labor Relations ....Valerie Hart
Manager, Publicity ....Lindsay Braverman
Project Manager ....Ryan Pears
Senior Computer Support Analyst ....Kevin A. McGuire
IT/Business Analyst ....William Boudiette

Creative & Production

Executive Music Producer ....Chris Montan
VP, Creative Development ....Ben Famiglietti
VP, Production ....Anne Quart
Director, International Production ....Felipe Gamba
Director, Labor Relations ....Edward Lieber
Associate Director ....Jeff Lee
Production Supervisor ....Clifford Schwartz
Production Manager ....Eduardo Castro
Manager, Labor Relations ....Stephanie Cheek
Manager, Physical Production ....Karl Chmielewski
Manager, Creative Development ....Jane Abramson
Manager, Theatrical Licensing ....David R. Scott
Dramaturg & Literary Manager ....Ken Cerniglia
Manager, Education Outreach ....Lisa Mitchell

Marketing

Senior Vice President ....Andrew Flatt
Director, Creative Resources ....Victor Adams
Director, Synergy & Partnership ....Kevin Banks
Director, Licensed Brands ....Gary Kane
Director, Media Strategy, Planning & Management ....Robin Wyatt
Director, Digital Marketing....................Kyle Young

Design Manager ....James Anderer
Manager, Media & Strategy ....Jared Comess
Manager, Creative Services ....Lauren Daghini
Manager, Synergy & Partnership ....Sarah Schlesinger
Manager, Consumer Insights ....Craig Trachtenberg
Manager, Digital Marketing......................Peter Tulba

Sales

Vice President, National Sales ....Bryan Dockett
National Sales Manager ....Victoria Cairl
Sr. Manager, Sales & Ticketing ....Nick Falzon
Manager, Group Sales ....Hunter Robertson
Manager, Sales & Ticketing ....Sarah Bills
Manager, Sales & Ticketing ....Erin Dooley

Business and Legal Affairs

Senior Vice President ....Jonathan Olson
Director...................................Seth Stuhl
Counsel ....Naila McKenzie
Sr. Paralegal ....Jessica White

Finance

VP, Finance/Bus. Development ....Mario Iannetta
Director, Finance ....Joe McClafferty
Director, Accounting ....Leena Mathew
Manager, Finance ....Liz Jurist Schwarzwalder
Manager, Accounting ....Adrineh Ghoukassian
Senior Business Analyst ....Sven Rittershaus
Senior Financial Analyst ....Mikhail Medvedev
Senior Business Planner ....Jennifer August
Production Accountant ....Joy Sims Brown
Production Accountant ....Angela DiSanti
Assistant Production Accountant ....Isander Rojas

Administrative Staff

Zachary Baer, Brian Bahr, Elizabeth Boulger, Whitney Britt, Jonelle Brown, Amy Caldamone, Michael Dei Cas, Preston Copley, Cara Epstein, Nicholas Faranda, Phil Grippe, Frankie Harvey, Christina Huschle, Greg Josken, Julie Lavin, Cyntia Leo, Colleen McCormack, Ellen McGowan, Misael Nunez, Brendan Padgett, Matt Quinones, Jillian Robbins, Suzanne Sheptock, Lee Taglin, Anji Taylor.

DISNEY THEATRICAL MERCHANDISE

Vice President ....Steven Downing
Merchandise Manager ....Neil Markman
District Manager ....Alyssa Somers
Associate Buyer ....Violet Burlaza
Assistant Manager, Inventory ....Suzanne Jakel
On-Site Retail Manager ....Scott Koonce
On-Site Assistant Retail Manager ....Thad Wilkes
On-Site Retail Manager.......................Jeff Knizer
On-Site Assistant Retail Manager ....Jana Cristiano

Disney Theatrical Productions
guestmail@disneytheatrical.com

Staff for the New Amsterdam Theatre

Theatre Manager ....John M. Loiacono
Guest Services Manager ....Kenneth Miller
Box Office Treasurer ....Andrew Grennan
Assistant Treasurer ....Anthony Oliva
Chief Engineer ....Frank Gibbons
Engineer ....Dan Milan
Security Manager ....Carl Lembo
Head Usher ....Jeryl Costello
Lobby Refreshments ....Sweet Concessions
Special thanks......................Sgt. Arthur J. Smarsch, Det. Adam D'Amico

Mary Poppins
Scrapbook

Correspondent: Christopher Shin, Ensemble.
Favorite Hangout: The stage left side of the bunker where there is always a stash of carbs and Tea Time in Steffanie and Val's dressing room.
Engaged: Tia Altinay, Katie Nanni and Ian Campayno. Mazel!
Gypsy of the Year Skit: *Misfits!* Written by Tom Souhrada and James Hindman. The skit was about the Land of Misfit musicals including: *GrAnnie, War Whores, Book of Merman* and *Rebecca*.
Carols for a Cure: We recorded a beautiful arrangement of "The Birthday of a King" arranged by the fantastic Richard Rockage.
Memorable Press Encounter: Hearing about our closing notice through Michael Riedel. WAH-WAH.
No So Discreet Audience: There was a show where, during "Jolly Holiday," there was video recording with what looked like a huge old-school VHS video camera with a bright light shining. There are also the amazing people who take pictures/videos with their HUGE iPads.
Flub: Jonathan Freeman, the Bank Chairman, flubbed his line in the second bank scene and offered Mr. Banks a job as "Super Manager."
Falling Apart: During one of the scenes, the prop dog Williby lost his jaw. It fell onto the stage floor and remained there for most of "Supercal."
Autism Show: We had a show where the entire house was filled with autistic kids and their families. We had teched the show just for that audience including a lot of technical/sound changes and a cut scene. The house lights were slightly up through the entire show, so we were VERY aware of the audience. It was really an incredible experience.
Favorite Therapy: Foam roller. Gotta roll out all of those tight muscles from dancing on our deck. Also the amazing therapists at Physioarts who put us back together!
Favorite Snack: Skittles from the skittles pumpkin in C-Pod.
Favorite Quote: "Ain't nobody got time for that."
YouTube Favorites: Purple Diamonds Ramp Kicks and Bang Bang Boom Boom Ladies.
Backstage Ritual: Before "Step in Time" the sweeps all tap their brushes with each other.
Awkward Audience Noises: At the top of the show, as the curtain went up and the overture was ending, in the silence a young child screaming "I don't wanna! I don't wanna! Nooooo!"
Embarrassing Moments: Steffanie Leigh, our Mary, had a moment in "Jolly Holiday" where her bloomers started to fall off, so she ran offstage to take them off before coming back on to finish the number.
Between Show Dinners: Schnipper's, Lazzara's, The Counter.

The Plague: The week before Christmas, our theatre was hit by the plague. Gavin Lee, our Bert, along with his two understudies, were sick. Sam Strasfeld, who had covered the part in the past was brought in for the week to standby and ended up going on for five shows. In that same week, Q. Smith, our Miss Andrew, performed her role as well as the Bird Woman and TORE IT UP.
What Are You Doing?: During a cut show, Janelle Robinson came on during the bush dance in "Jolly Holiday," even though she had been cut. After making her entrance, she ran offstage. Tom Souhrada, our Von Hussler, came on early during the Bank scene. He walked on, walked off, then walked back on.

Backstage with some of the cast of *Mary Poppins*

Photo courtesy of the production

Tales of an Understudy: We had just had a clean up rehearsal and were given a note that during the beginning of "Supercal," we were to sway as if we were following Mary. The sways are choreographed to go to the right and then the left. Our Mary understudy, Catherine Brunell, was on that night and ended up swaying first to the left. After the initial shock, we followed her with the swaying and the entire ensemble made an audible, "OOOOOOOOOOOHHHHHHHH."
Line Please!: In "Playing the Game," after the children wake up, they had both completely dropped their lines. There was an awkward silence and Steffanie Leigh, our Mary, just said "Oh dear," and came right in with next line.
Original Cast Members Who Will Close Out the Show: Janelle Robinson, Katie Nanni, Megan Osterhaus, James Hindman, Nicolas Dromard, Suzanne Hylenski, Rommy Sandhu.
Their Memories and Thoughts Over the Last Six+ Years:
Nicolas Dromard: There's a moment in the show at the end of Act 1 when Bert rides down the roof. As I lay down on the roof and stare at the grid and the lights a few feet from my head, I hear Mary say, "Is that you, Bert?'" and the roof slowly starts to lower. That moment is pure magic for me and can never be duplicated. As the audience is revealed while I'm riding the descending roof, I start singing "Chim Chim Cher-ee." Just the music, the audience and Bert in a very intimate moment.

I will never forget the first time I performed the role of Bert in 2007 in the New Amsterdam, when I was in the ensemble and a Bert understudy. Now I get to close the show playing the role and I get to savor that special moment a few more times. It is such a dream and I will be forever thankful to *Mary Poppins* for the incredible last six and a half years.
James Hindman: As performers, our lives are filled with endless hellos and goodbyes. One show ends, another begins. With *Mary Poppins*, it was a joy and honor to be part of such a wonderful family for such a long time. I will miss that the most. On a lighter note…the funniest thing that ever happened was in previews when one of the sliders skipped its track, cutting off the tail of a dolphin statue and throwing it across stage. An actress waiting to enter screamed thinking it was an actor's head. She wasn't wearing her glasses.
Suzanne Hylenski: I'll always remember sitting at a tech table with my fellow swings and feeling so grateful for the love and support we had for each other. As each of us debuted on stage, we were there cheering each other on. The faces of the swings have changed over the years, but the admiration and respect for each other remain the same. My swing family will always have a special place in my heart.
Katie Nanni: One of my favorite *Mary Poppins* memories was our autism performance for autistic kids and their families. Looking out to the crowd of families who usually were unable to take their children to a Broadway show and seeing and feeling their joy that day puts me at a loss for words. It truly is so hard to put into words how my heart felt that day… Powerful stuff!
Megan Osterhaus: Some of the best moments for me were the shenanigans that went on backstage. There was that strong sense of camaraderie that kept us in touch with our own childlike dispositions. I always knew I would laugh to tears when I walked into that building no matter what kind of day I had.
Janelle Robinson: I'll never forget falling in the trough with Brandon Bieber in "Jolly Holiday" and thinking "I've fallen and I can't get up!" It's also amazing seeing the kids who've played Jane and Michael when they return years later as teenagers…. And story time with Mark Price in the bunker during Act Two.
Rommy Sandhu: Because we (swings) were on so "rarely," each of my kids (all three born during our run) was able to see me perform. During the bows I would wave to them up in their box seats, and I will always cherish hearing them scream "Daddy!!" Then the post-show wonder and joy in their eyes when they finally came onstage afterwards is etched eternally.

Matilda The Musical

First Preview: March 4, 2013. Opened: April 11, 2013.
Still running as of May 31, 2013.

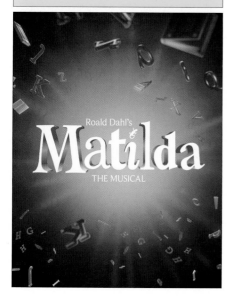

PLAYBILL®

Roald Dahl's
Matilda
THE MUSICAL

Based on Roald Dahl's novelette, this musical tells the story of a little girl genius who refuses to be ground down by parents who despise her or by a cartoonishly evil school headmistress named Miss Trunchbull who is determined to break her spirit. With the help of her kindly schoolteacher Miss Honey, Matilda uses her intelligence, her love of books and a mysterious secret super power to prevail over those who would repress her—and to turn Miss Honey's life around too.

CAST

Party Entertainer	JOHN SANDERS
Doctor	JOHN ARTHUR GREENE
Mrs. Wormwood	LESLI MARGHERITA
Mr. Wormwood	GABRIEL EBERT
Matilda	SOPHIA GENNUSA, OONA LAURENCE, BAILEY RYON, MILLY SHAPIRO
Michael Wormwood	TAYLOR TRENSCH
Mrs. Phelps	KAREN ALDRIDGE
Miss Honey	LAUREN WARD
The Escapologist	BEN THOMPSON
The Acrobat	SAMANTHA STURM
Miss Trunchbull	BERTIE CARVEL
Rudolpho	PHILLIP SPAETH
Sergei	JOHN SANDERS
Other Parts Played By	THAYNE JASPERSON, TAMIKA SONJA LAWRENCE, RYAN STEELE, BETSY STRUXNESS
Bruce	JACK BRODERICK
And on Occasion	JUDAH BELLAMY, LUKE KOLBE MANNIKUS, SAWYER NUNES

Continued on next page

⑧ SAM S. SHUBERT THEATRE
225 West 44th Street
A Shubert Organization Theatre

Philip J. Smith, *Chairman*   **Robert E. Wankel,** *President*

The Royal Shakespeare Company and the Dodgers
present

Roald Dahl's
Matilda
THE MUSICAL

BOOK
Dennis Kelly

MUSIC & LYRICS
Tim Minchin

with

Sophia Gennusa   Oona Laurence   Bailey Ryon   Milly Shapiro

Bertie Carvel   Gabriel Ebert   Lesli Margherita   Lauren Ward

Karen Aldridge, Yurel Echezarreta, John Arthur Greene, Nadine Isenegger, Colin Israel, Thayne Jasperson, Tamika Sonja Lawrence, Celia Mei Rubin, John Sanders, Phillip Spaeth, Ryan Steele, Betsy Struxness, Samantha Sturm, Heather Tepe, Ben Thompson, Clay Thomson, Taylor Trensch

Frenie Acoba, Erica Simone Barnett, Judah Bellamy, Jack Broderick, Ava DeMary, Emma Howard, Luke Kolbe Mannikus, Madilyn Jaz Morrow, Sawyer Nunes, Jared Parker, Beatrice Tulchin, Ted Wilson

ASSOCIATE CHOREOGRAPHERS		ASSOCIATE DIRECTORS	
Ellen Kane Kate Dunn		Thomas Caruso Luke Sheppard Lotte Wakeham	

RSC COMMISSIONING DRAMATURG	CASTING	VOICE DIRECTOR
Jeanie O'Hare	Jim Carnahan C.S.A. Nora Brennan C.S.A.	Andrew Wade

MUSICAL DIRECTOR	MUSIC COORDINATOR	PRODUCTION STAGE MANAGER	COMPANY MANAGER
David Holcenberg	Howard Joines	Kelly A. Martindale	Kimberly Kelley

ADVERTISING/MARKETING	PRESS REPRESENTATIVES	PRODUCTION MANAGEMENT
AKA	Boneau/Bryan-Brown	Aurora Productions

EXECUTIVE PRODUCER	EXECUTIVE PRODUCER	GENERAL MANAGER
Denise Wood	André Ptaszynski	Dodger Management Group

SOUND DESIGN	LIGHTING DESIGN	ILLUSION
Simon Baker	Hugh Vanstone	Paul Kieve

ORCHESTRATIONS & ADDITIONAL MUSIC
Chris Nightingale

SET & COSTUME DESIGN
Rob Howell

CHOREOGRAPHY
Peter Darling

DIRECTOR
Matthew Warchus

Matilda The Musical is profoundly grateful for the support of Patty Baker, Melissa & Daniel Berger, Adam Blanshay, The Broadway Consortium/Stephanie Rosenberg, Gail and Ralph Bryan, Jed & Bronna Canaan, Scott M. Delman, Jerry Frankel, Ronald Frankel, Greenleaf Productions, Dede Harris, Independent Presenters Network, Indigo Arts & Entertainment, Elizabeth McCann, Des McAnuff, Mighty Chippewa Partnership, National Artists Mgt. Co., Michael & Gabrielle Palitz, Pittsburgh CLO, Remarkable Partners, Parag & Usha Saxena, Terry Schnuck, Tom Smedes & Peter Stern, TheatreDreams - North America, Elizabeth Williams, Archana Vats & David Gartside.

Matilda The Musical is a Royal Shakespeare Company Commission. First performed in Stratford-upon-Avon on 9 November 2010.
RSC Artistic Director Gregory Doran, RSC Executive Director Catherine Mallyon
Support for the work of the Royal Shakespeare Company in the United States is led by Royal Shakespeare Company America, Inc.

4/11/13

Photo by Joan Marcus

Lauren Ward (L) as Miss Honey and Bertie Carvel (R) as Miss Trunchbull with the children of *Matilda*

Matilda The Musical

MUSICAL NUMBERS

ACT I

"Miracle"	Company
"Naughty"	Matilda
"School Song"	Company
"Pathetic"	Miss Honey
"The Hammer"	Miss Trunchbull, Miss Honey and Children
"The Chokey Chant"	Company
"Loud"	Mrs. Wormwood and Rudolpho
"This Little Girl"	Miss Honey
"Bruce"	Children

ACT II

"Telly"	Mr. Wormwood and Michael Wormwood
"When I Grow Up"	Company
"I'm Here"	Matilda and The Escapologist
"The Smell of Rebellion"	Miss Trunchbull, Miss Honey and Children
"Quiet"	Matilda
"My House"	Miss Honey
"Revolting Children"	Company

ORCHESTRA

Music Supervisor/Orchestrator:
CHRIS NIGHTINGALE
Music Director/Conductor:
DAVID HOLCENBERG
Children's Music Director/Assistant Conductor:
DEBORAH ABRAMSON
Associate Conductor/Keyboard 1:
MICHAEL GACETTA
Assistant Conductor/Keyboard 2:
SUE ANSCHUTZ
Flute, Clarinet, Alto Sax: STEVE KENYON
Clarinet, Bass Clarinet, Tenor Sax:
HIDEAKI AOMORI
Trumpet 1: MATTHEW PETERSON

Trumpet 2: CJ CAMERIERI
Trombone/Bass Trombone: MIKE BOSCHEN
Drums/Percussion: HOWARD JOINES
Bass: MAT FIELDES
Guitars: ERIC B. DAVIS
Violin/Concertmaster: JONATHAN DINKLAGE
Violin: ELIZABETH LIM-DUTTON
Viola/Violin: WHITNEY LaGRANGE
Cello: JEANNE LeBLANC
Music Technology: PHIJ ADAMS
London Music Preparation: LAURIE PERKINS
New York Music Copyist: Emily Grishman Music
Preparation/EMILY GRISHMAN and
KATHARINE EDMONDS
Music Coordinator: HOWARD JOINES

Cast Continued

Lavender	FRENIE ACOBA
And on Occasion	ERICA SIMONE BARNETT, EMMA HOWARD, HEATHER TEPE
Nigel	JARED PARKER
And on Occasion	LUKE KOLBE MANNIKUS, SAWYER NUNES, HEATHER TEPE, TED WILSON
Amanda	BEATRICE TULCHIN
And on Occasion	ERICA SIMONE BARNETT, AVA DeMARY, HEATHER TEPE
Eric	TED WILSON
And on Occasion	LUKE KOLBE MANNIKUS, SAWYER NUNES, JARED PARKER, HEATHER TEPE
Alice	AVA DeMARY
And on Occasion	MADILYN JAZ MORROW, HEATHER TEPE
Hortensia	EMMA HOWARD
And on Occasion	MADILYN JAZ MORROW
Tommy	JUDAH BELLAMY
And on Occasion	SAWYER NUNES, HEATHER TEPE

UNDERSTUDIES

For Miss Trunchbull: COLIN ISRAEL,
JOHN SANDERS, BEN THOMPSON
For Mrs. Wormwood: TAMIKA SONJA
LAWRENCE, BETSY STRUXNESS
For Mr. Wormwood: JOHN ARTHUR GREENE,
JOHN SANDERS, BEN THOMPSON
For Mrs. Phelps: TAMIKA SONJA LAWRENCE,
CELIA MEI RUBIN, SAMANTHA STURM
For Miss Honey: NADINE ISENEGGER,
SAMANTHA STURM

SWINGS

ERICA SIMONE BARNETT,
YUREL ECHEZARRETA,
NADINE ISENEGGER, COLIN ISRAEL,
LUKE KOLBE MANNIKUS,
MADILYN JAZ MORROW,
SAWYER NUNES, CELIA MEI RUBIN,
HEATHER TEPE, CLAY THOMSON

DANCE CAPTAIN

NADINE ISENEGGER

ASSISTANT/CHILDREN'S DANCE CAPTAIN

CELIA MEI RUBIN

GYM CAPTAIN

CLAY THOMSON

Bertie Carvel and Ted Wilson are appearing with the
permission of Actors' Equity Association.

Photo by Joan Marcus

(L-R): Taylor Trensch, Lesli Margherita and Gabriel Ebert

Matilda The Musical

Sophia Gennusa
Matilda

Oona Laurence
Matilda

Bailey Ryon
Matilda

Milly Shapiro
Matilda

Bertie Carvel
Miss Trunchbull

Gabriel Ebert
Mr. Wormwood

Lesli Margherita
Mrs. Wormwood

Lauren Ward
Miss Honey

Karen Aldridge
Mrs. Phelps

Yurel Echezarreta
Swing

John Arthur Greene
Doctor; u/s Mr. Wormwood

Nadine Isenegger
Swing, Dance Captain; u/s Miss Honey

Colin Israel
Swing; u/s Miss Trunchbull

Thayne Jasperson
Ensemble

Tamika Sonja Lawrence
Ensemble; u/s Mrs. Phelps/ Mrs. Wormwood

Celia Mei Rubin
Swing, Assistant/ Children's Dance Captain; u/s Mrs. Phelps

John Sanders
Party Entertainer/ Sergei; u/s Miss Trunchbull, Mr. Wormwood

Phillip Spaeth
Rudolpho

Ryan Steele
Ensemble

Betsy Struxness
Ensemble; u/s Mrs. Wormwood

Samantha Sturm
The Acrobat; u/s Mrs. Phelps, Miss Honey

Heather Tepe
Swing

Ben Thompson
The Escapologist; u/s Miss Trunchbull, Mr. Wormwood

Clay Thomson
Swing

Taylor Trensch
Michael Wormwood

Frenie Acoba
Lavender

Erica Simone Barnett
Swing

Judah Bellamy
Tommy

Jack Broderick
Bruce

Ava DeMary
Alice

Emma Howard
Hortensia

Jared Parker
Nigel

Luke Kolbe Mannikus
Swing

Madilyn Jaz Morrow
Swing

Sawyer Nunes
Swing

Matilda The Musical

Beatrice Tulchin
Amanda

Ted Wilson
Eric

Roald Dahl
Writer

Dennis Kelly
Book

Tim Minchin
Music and Lyrics

Matthew Warchus
Director

Peter Darling
Choreography

Rob Howell
Set and Costume Design

Chris Nightingale
Orchestrations, Additional Music and Musical Supervision

Simon Baker
Sound Design

Hugh Vanstone
Lighting Design

Paul Kieve
Illusion

Thomas Caruso
Associate Director

Lotte Wakeham
Associate Director

Paul Weimer
Associate Set Designer

Daryl A. Stone
Associate Costume Designer

Joel Shier
Associate Lighting Designer

Jim Carnahan C.S.A.
Casting Director

Nora Brennan C.S.A.
Casting Director

Andrew Wade
Voice Director

David Holcenberg
Musical Director

Howard Joines
Music Coordinator

Deborah Abramson
Children's Music Director

Gene O'Donovan
Aurora Productions
Production Management

Ben Heller
Aurora Productions
Production Management

Gregory Doran
Artistic Director
The Royal Shakespeare Company
Producer

Catherine Mallyon
Executive Director
The Royal Shakespeare Company
Producer

Michael David
The Dodgers
Producer

Edward Strong
The Dodgers
Producer

Rocco Landesman
The Dodgers
Producer

Des McAnuff
The Dodgers
Producer

Photo by Brian Mapp

CHILD GUARDIANS
(L-R): Krystal Rowley, Alissa Zulvergold, Robert Wilson, John Mara, Jr.

248

Matilda The Musical

HAIR DEPARTMENT
(L-R):
Jenna Barrios
(Hair Dresser),
Susan Corrado
(Hair Supervisor)

DOOR PERSONS
(L-R): Rose Alaio,
Léon Mossen

CREW
Front Row (L-R): Gary Fernandez, Mike Cornell (Electrician), Ty Lackey (Sound Board Operator), Brien Brannigan (Electrician Sound),
David L. Bornstein (Head Props), Ronnie Vitelli (House Props), Steve Long (Electrician)
Back Row (L-R): Fran Rapp (Carpenter), Jim Spradling (House Electrician), Kyp Seiferth (Assistant Props), Michael Maher, Jr. (Carpenter),
Ed Jonny (Props), Thomas Manoy (House Carpenter), Joel DeRuyter (Automation Carpenter), Jake Hall (Assistant Sound),
Janet Smith (Electrician Sound), Karen Hyman (Electrician)

ORCHESTRA
Front Row (L-R): Deborah Abramson (Children's Music Director/Assistant Conductor),
Mike Boschen (Trombone/Bass Trombone), David Holcenberg (Music Director)
Back Row (L-R): Michael Gacetta (Associate Conductor), Whitney LaGrange (Viola/Violin),
Elizabeth Lim-Dutton (Violin), Howard Joines (Percussion/Contractor)

COMPANY AND STAGE MANAGEMENT
Front Row (L-R): Michael Altbaum (Assistant Company Manager), Samantha Preiss
(Production Assistant/Sub Stage Manager), Amy Marsico (Assistant Stage Manager),
Deanna Weiner (Production Assistant)
Back Row (L-R): Andrew Gottlieb (Assistant Stage Manager), Kim Kelley (Company
Manager), David Lober (Stage Manager), Kelly A. Martindale (Production Stage Manager)

Matilda The Musical
SCRAPBOOK

Correspondent: John Arthur Greene, "Doctor"; understudy for "Mr. Wormwood"
Memorable Opening Night Gifts: Our set and costume designer Rob Howell gave us a miniature replica of our stage with a scrabble tile letter of our last name.
Most Exciting Celebrity Visitor: Robert DeNiro.
Who Got the Gypsy Robe: Nadine Isenegger.
Special Backstage Rituals: Lots of high-fives.
Favorite Moment During Each Performance: I love watching "When I Grow Up" from the wings! (Still wish I were on a swing.)
Favorite In-Theatre Gathering Place: The Hair Room!
Favorite Off-Site Hangouts: Glass House

Tavern, Becco, Schmackary's.
Favorite Snack Food: Swedish fish, cookies, salted chocolate-covered caramel.
Mascot: The kids won a stuffed gorilla at Dave & Busters and named it Miracle.
Favorite Therapy: We all love Physical Therapy!
What Did You Think of the Web Buzz on Your Show: I think it has all been pretty good. I'm not the best social media junkie.
Memorable Stage Door Fan Encounter: We all got filmed while signing one night and it ended up on YouTube!
Fastest Costume Change: Out of Russians into school kids at the end of the show!
Who Wore the Heaviest/Hottest Costume:

I'm pretty sure that our Trunch, Mr. Bertie Carvel's costume is pretty heavy.
Who Wore the Least: Our Salsa Ladies, Betsy and Samantha.
Which Orchestra Member Played the Most Instruments: Our woodwind section, brass, percussion, and guitar play four or five instruments throughout this show.
Memorable Directorial Note: "Don't spoil the magic."
Embarrassing Moments: Scooters
Superstitions That Turned Out to Be True: Do not say "Macbeth"!
Coolest Thing About Being in This Show: Working on amazing material with an amazing cast!

STAFF FOR *MATILDA THE MUSICAL*

GENERAL MANAGEMENT
DODGER MANAGEMENT GROUP

COMPANY MANAGER
Kimberly Kelley

NATIONAL PRESS REPRESENTATIVES
BONEAU/BRYAN-BROWN

Adrian Bryan-Brown   Jackie Green

Kelly Guiod   Michelle Farabaugh

PRODUCTION MANAGEMENT
AURORA PRODUCTIONS

Gene O'Donovan   Ben Heller

Stephanie Sherline   Liza Luxenberg   Anita Shah

Jarid Sumner   Anthony Jusino   G. Garrett Ellison

Troy Pepicelli   Gayle Riess

Catherine Nelson   Melissa Mazdra

CASTING
JIM CARNAHAN CASTING

Jim Carnahan, CSA

Jillian Cimini: Casting Associate

NORA BRENNAN CASTING

Nora Brennan, CSA

Julia Delehanty

Production Stage Manager	KELLY A. MARTINDALE
Stage Manager	David Lober
Assistant Stage Managers	Andrew C. Gottlieb, Amy Marsico
Assistant Company Manager	Michael Altbaum
Assistant Director	Ryan Emmons
Assistant Choreographer	Leanne Pinder
Associate Scenic Designer	Paul Weimer
Set Model Builders	Evan Adamson, Carl Baldasso
UK Associate Set Designers	Bec Chippendale, Alex Eales
Associate Costume Designer	Daryl A. Stone
Assistant Costume Designer	Rachel Attridge
Costume Design Assistant	Christine Meyers
Associate Lighting Designer	Joel Shier
Assistant Lighting Designer	Craig Stelzenmuller
Lighting Programmer	David Arch
UK Associate Lighting Designer	Tim Lutkin
Media Assoc. & Programmer	Laura Frank
Associate Sound Designer	Tony Smolenski IV

Film Sequence Creation	Peter Glanville, Seonaid Goody/Little Angel Theatre
Puppeteers	Seonaid Goody, Mandy Travis
Production Carpenter	Fran Rapp
Deck Automation Carpenter	Joel DeRuyter
Advance Carpenter	Steve Schroettnig
Production Electricians	Randall Zaibek, James Fedigan
Head Electrician	Michael Cornell
Lead Frontlight Operator	Stephen R. Long
Video Technician	Christopher Kurtz
Production Properties	Emiliano Pares
Head Props	David L. Bornstein
Assistant Props	Kyp Seiferth
Production Sound Engineer	Phil Lojo
Sound Mixer	Ty Lackey
Sound Deck	Jake Hall
Wardrobe Supervisor	Terri Purcell
Assistant Wardrobe Supervisor	Joby Horrigan
Dressers	Margiann Flanagan, Mel Hansen, Peggie Kurz, Marcia McIntosh, Duduzile Mitall, Danny Paul, Jessica Scoblick
Hair and Makeup Supervisor	Susan Corrado
Asst. Hair Supervisor	Monica Costea
Hair Dresser	Jenna Barrios
Head Children's Guardian	Robert Wilson
Guardians	John Mara Jr., Krystal Rowley, Alissa Zulvergold
Associate Dialect Coach	Ben Furey
Assistant Voice Coaches	Ellen Lettrich, Alithea Phillips
Acrobatics Coach	Hector Salazar
Boxing Coach	Jimmy Fusaro
Additional Orchestrations	Laurie Perkins
Music Technology Programming	Phij Adams
Synthesizer Technician	Randy Cohen
Production Assistants	Geoff Maus, Samantha Preiss, Deanna Weiner
Advertising/Marketing/Digital	AKA/ Elizabeth Furze, Scott A. Moore, Bashan Aquart, Elizabeth Findlay, Jennifer Sims, Meghan Bartley, Jamaal Parham, Janette Roush, Adam Jay, Sara Rosenzweig, Sarah Borenstein, Jen Taylor, Flora Pei, Robert Postotnik
Marketing	Dodger Marketing
Web Design/Maintenance	AKA
Merchandising	The Araca Group
Children's Tutoring	On Location Education

Banking	Signature Bank/Barbara von Borstel
Accountants	Schall and Ashenfarb, CPAs
Insurance	AON/Albert G. Ruben
Counsel	Daniel Wasser, Elliot Brown/ Franklin, Weinrib, Rudell & Vassallo, PC
Physical Therapist	Performing Arts PT
Orthopaedist	David S. Weiss M.D., NYU Langone Medical Center
Information Technology Management	ITelagen, Inc.
Production Photographer	Joan Marcus
Theatre Displays	King Displays

Official Website
www.MatildaTheMusical.com

ROYAL SHAKESPEARE COMPANY

Chairman	Nigel Hugill
Deputy Chairman	Lady Sainsbury of Turville CBE
Artistic Director	Gregory Doran
Executive Director	Catherine Mallyon
Originating Artistic Director	Michael Boyd
Originating Executive Director	Vikki Heywood CBE
Executive Producer	André Ptaszynski
Executive Producer	Denise Wood
Director of Commercial Services	Sara Aspley
General Counsel	Caroline Barnett
Marketing Associate	Lydia Cassidy
International Production Coordinator	Georgie Fellows
Head of US Office	Elliot Fishman
Head of Press	Philippa Harland
Director of Sales & Marketing	Chris Hill
Business Affairs Adviser	Jonathan Hull
Technical Director	Simon Marsden
Director of Education	Jacqui O'Hanlon
Press Associate	Ryan Petersen for The Corner Shop PR
Technical Manager, Matilda London	Digby Robinson
Director of Communications	Liz Thompson
Director of Development	Graeme Williamson
Commercial Manager	Kevin Wright

THE DODGERS
Dodger Properties

President	Michael David
Executive Producer	Sally Campbell Morse
Partner Emeritus	Edward Strong
Director of Creative Development	Lauren Mitchell
Director of Business Administration	Pamela Lloyd
Director of Marketing	Jessica Ludwig
Director of Finance	Paula Maldonado

Matilda The Musical

Director, Dodger International ....Dana Sherman
Sr. Assoc. General Manager ....Jennifer F. Vaughan
Production Manager ....Jeff Parvin
Associate General Manager ....Flora Johnstone
Production Management Assistant ....Lyndsey Goode
General Management Assistant ....Lauren Freed
Project Coordinator/Investor Relations ......Andrew Serna
Marketing Manager...........................Jessica Morris
Sales Manager ....Ann E. Van Nostrand
Marketing Assistant ....Tony Lance
Sales Assistant ....Priya Iyer
Senior Finance Associate ....Laurinda Wilson
Finance Associate ....Mariann Fresiello
Finance Assistant ....Daniel Kogan
Executive Assistant to Mr. David ....Ashley Tracey
Seat Manager ....Ben Cohen
Office & Atelier Manager ....Abigail Kornet
Assistant Office & Atelier Manager ....Anne Ezell
Office Assistant ....Scott Dennis
Special Events ....John Haber
Counsel to Dodger Properties ....Nan Bases
CPA to Dodger Properties ....Ira Schall

Dodgers-at-Large

Mark Andrews, Danny Austin, Michael Camp, Sandra Carlson, Dhyana Colony, John Gendron, Richard Hester, West Hyler, Deana Marie Kirsch, James Elliot Love, Jennie Mamary, Ron Melrose, Jason Pelusio, Jean-Michel Quincey, Maureen Rooney, Brandon Smithey, Bridget Stegall, Edward Strong, Tim Sulka, Ellen Szorady, Linda Wright

CREDITS

Scenery built, painted and automated by Hudson Scenic Studio. Additional scenery built and painted by Show Motion Inc., Milford, Connecticut. Sound shop: Sound Associates, Inc. Lighting equipment and special effects by PRG Lighting. Laser effect by Laser Production Services for the Visual Arts. Props provided by BrenBri Props, Prop 'n' Spoon, JCDP. Hair, Wigs and Makeup by Campbell Young Associates. Costumes and shoes provided by Tricorne Costumes, Artur & Tailors, Bra*Tenders, Lynne Mackey Millinery, Rodney Gordon Millinery, Hochi Asiatico, Maria Ficalora Knitwear, T.O. Dey Custom Shoes, La Duca, Gene Mignola Inc., Maggie Dick, Douglas Earl, Giliberto Designs, Beckenstein Custom Shirts, the Royal Shakespeare Company. Scooters provided by Micro Scooters. Harnessed Movement Consultants: Ground Aerial, LLC. Stage manager's database provided by Michael Krug. Rehearsed at the New 42nd Street Studios. Additional rehearsals at the Little Shubert Theatre. Thank you to Sandy Smith Wilson and Leigh Owen Davies.

American Airlines is the official airline of
Matilda The Musical.

The Royal Shakespeare Company would also like to thank everyone who has worked on *Matilda The Musical* in Stratford-upon-Avon and London. Special thanks to all the *Matilda* London production departments who have generously shared their knowledge and experience with the Broadway team. We are especially grateful for the continuing support of the RSC Board, including the generosity of those Board members who supported the development of the show and underwrote the London run. And we thank our senior advisor for America, Ric Wanetik, who also serves as the Executive President of RSC America, for his invaluable counsel on *Matilda*, as well as his ongoing work connecting the RSC to the U.S. Our sincere thanks also to Ronald Daitz, Kimberly Blanchard and Mark Schwed of Weil, Gotshal & Manges LLP for all their pro bono support for the RSC.

RSC, ROYAL SHAKESPEARE COMPANY and the RSC logo are registered trademarks of the Royal Shakespeare Company.

IN MEMORY

It is difficult to imagine producing anything without the presence of beloved Dodger family members James Elliot Love and Jean-Michel Quincey. Friends to everyone they met, James and Jean-Michel stood at the heart of all that is good about the theatrical community. They will be missed, but their spirits abide.

ⓢ THE SHUBERT ORGANIZATION, INC.
Board of Directors

Philip J. Smith
Chairman

Robert E. Wankel
President

Wyche Fowler, Jr.

Diana Phillips

Lee J. Seidler

Michael I. Sovern

Stuart Subotnick

Chief Financial Officer ....Elliot Greene
Sr. Vice President, Ticketing ....David Andrews
Vice President, Finance ....Juan Calvo
Vice President, Human Resources ....Cathy Cozens
Vice President, Facilities ....John Darby
Vice President, Theatre Operations ....Peter Entin
Vice President, Marketing ....Charles Flateman
Vice President, Audit ....Anthony LaMattina
Vice President, Ticket Sales ....Brian Mahoney
Vice President, Creative Projects ............D.S. Moynihan
Vice President, Real Estate ....Julio Peterson

House Manager ....Jonathan Shulman

FRONT OF HOUSE
Front Row (L-R): Martin Cooper, Stephen Ivelja, Maura Gaynor, Erin O'Donnell, Kathryn Tavares, Leonardo Ruiz
Middle Row (L-R): Giovanni LaDuke, Francis Sanabria, Elvis Caban, Jason Weixelman, Paul Rodriguez, Joanne Blessington
Back Row (L-R): Daysha Rodriguez, Brian Gaynair, Pamela Loetterle, Delia Pozo

WARDROBE DEPARTMENT
Front (L-R): Danny Paul (Dresser), Marcia McIntosh (Dresser)
Back (L-R): Melanie Hansen (Dresser), Terri Purcell (Wardrobe Supervisor), Jessica Scoblick (Dresser), Joby Horrigan (Assistant Wardrobe Supervisor), Margiann Flanagan (Dresser) Susan Checklick (Dresser), Daryl A. Stone (Assistant Costume Designer), Peggie Kurz (Dresser)

Memphis

First Preview: September 23, 2009. Opened: October 19, 2009.
Closed August 5, 2012 after 30 Previews and 1,165 Performances.

PLAYBILL®

At the dawn of the rock 'n' roll era a white deejay in Memphis, Tennessee falls in love with "black" music, and then falls in love with a beautiful black singer. The two become pioneers in promoting the new musical sound, and become pioneers in interracial romance in a deeply racist society. When things go better for the music than for the romance, the two have to make some soul-shaking choices.

CAST

(in order of appearance)

White DJ/Mr. Collins/White Father/ Gordon Grant/Ensemble	DAVID McDONALD
Black DJ/Ensemble	KEN ROBINSON
Delray	J. BERNARD CALLOWAY
Gator	DERRICK BASKIN
Bobby	JAMES MONROE IGLEHART
Ensemble/Wailin' Joe/ Reverend Hobson	ANTOINE L. SMITH
Ensemble/ Someday Backup Singer	ERICA DORFLER
Ensemble/Someday Backup Singer/ Double Dutch Girl	LAUREN LIM JACKSON
Ensemble	CARMEN SHAVONE BORDERS
Ensemble/Ethel	MONETTE McKAY
Ensemble/Be Black Trio	DARIUS BARNES
Ensemble/Be Black Trio	SAM J. CAHN
Ensemble/ Be Black Trio	PRESTON W. DUGGER III
Ensemble/Someday Backup Singer	DAN'YELLE WILLIAMSON
Felicia	MONTEGO GLOVER
Huey	ADAM PASCAL

Continued on next page

⑤ SAM S. SHUBERT THEATRE

225 West 44th Street
A Shubert Organization Theatre

Philip J. Smith, *Chairman*   Robert E. Wankel, *President*

JUNKYARD DOG PRODUCTIONS   BARBARA AND BUDDY FREITAG   MARLEEN AND KENNY ALHADEFF
LATITUDE LINK   JIM AND SUSAN BLAIR   DEMOS BIZAR ENTERTAINMENT   LAND LINE PRODUCTIONS
APPLES AND ORANGES PRODUCTIONS   DAVE COPLEY   DANCAP PRODUCTIONS, INC   ALEX AND KATYA LUKIANOV   TONY PONTURO   2 GUYS PRODUCTIONS   RICHARD WINKLER

IN ASSOCIATION WITH
LAUREN DOLL   ERIC AND MARSI GARDINER   LINDA AND BILL POTTER   BROADWAY ACROSS AMERICA   JOCKO PRODUCTIONS   PATTY BAKER   DAN FRISHWASSER
BOB BARTNER/SCOTT AND KAYLIN UNION   LORAINE BOYLE/CHASE MISHKIN   REMMEL T. DICKINSON/MEMPHIS ORPHEUM GROUP   SHADOWCATCHER ENTERTAINMENT/VIJAY AND SITA VASHEE

PRESENT

MEMPHIS

BOOK AND LYRICS BY   MUSIC AND LYRICS BY
JOE DIPIETRO   **DAVID BRYAN**

BASED ON A CONCEPT BY
GEORGE W. GEORGE

STARRING
ADAM PASCAL   **MONTEGO GLOVER**

WITH
DERRICK BASKIN   J. BERNARD CALLOWAY   JAMES MONROE IGLEHART   JOHN JELLISON   NANCY OPEL

DARIUS BARNES   CARMEN SHAVONE BORDERS   ANGELA C. BRYDON   SAM J CAHN   ERICA DORFLER   PRESTON W. DUGGER III
HILLARY ELK   SASHA HUTCHINGS   LAUREN LIM JACKSON   TYRONE JACKSON   ELIZABETH WARD LAND   BRYAN LANGLITZ
KEVIN MASSEY   CANDICE MONET McCALL   DAVID McDONALD   MONETTE McKAY   ANDY MILLS   JUSTIN PATTERSON
JERMAINE R. REMBERT   KEN ROBINSON   JAMISON SCOTT   ANTOINE L. SMITH   CODY WILLIAMS   DAN'YELLE WILLIAMSON

SCENIC DESIGN **DAVID GALLO**	COSTUME DESIGN **PAUL TAZEWELL**	LIGHTING DESIGN **HOWELL BINKLEY**	SOUND DESIGN **KEN TRAVIS**
PROJECTION DESIGN **DAVID GALLO & SHAWN SAGADY**	HAIR & WIG DESIGN **CHARLES G. LaPOINTE**	FIGHT DIRECTOR **STEVE RANKIN**	CASTING **TELSEY + COMPANY RACHEL HOFFMAN, CSA**	ASSOCIATE CHOREOGRAPHER **KELLY DEVINE**
ORCHESTRATIONS **DARYL WATERS & DAVID BRYAN**	MUSICAL DIRECTOR **KENNY J. SEYMOUR**	DANCE ARRANGEMENTS **AUGUST ERIKSMOEN**	MUSIC CONTRACTOR **MICHAEL KELLER**	PRODUCTION STAGE MANAGER **ARTURO E. PORAZZI**
GENERAL MANAGER **ALCHEMY PRODUCTION GROUP CARL PASBJERG & FRANK SCARDINO**	PRODUCTION MANAGEMENT **JUNIPER STREET PRODUCTIONS, INC.**	PRESS AGENT **THE HARTMAN GROUP**	ADVERTISING/MARKETING **aka**

ASSOCIATE PRODUCERS
EMILY AND AARON ALHADEFF   ALISON AND ANDI ALHADEFF   KEN CLAY   JOSEPH CRAIG   RON AND MARJORIE DANZ   CYRENA ESPOSITO   BRUCE AND JOANNE GLANT   MATT MURPHY

MUSIC PRODUCER/MUSIC SUPERVISOR
CHRISTOPHER JAHNKE

CHOREOGRAPHER
SERGIO TRUJILLO

DIRECTOR
CHRISTOPHER ASHLEY

THIS PRODUCTION OF MEMPHIS ORIGINALLY CO-PRODUCED BY LA JOLLA PLAYHOUSE, CHRISTOPHER ASHLEY, ARTISTIC DIRECTOR, MICHAEL S. ROSENBERG, MANAGING DIRECTOR
AND 5TH AVENUE THEATRE, SEATTLE, WA, DAVID ARMSTRONG, PRODUCING ARTISTIC DIRECTOR, BERNADINE GRIFFIN, MANAGING DIRECTOR, AND BILL BERRY, PRODUCING DIRECTOR
ORIGINALLY PRODUCED AS A JOINT WORLD PREMIERE AT NORTH SHORE MUSIC THEATRE, JON KIMBELL, EXECUTIVE PRODUCER
AND THEATREWORKS, ROBERT KELLEY, ARTISTIC DIRECTOR AND PHIL SANTORA, MANAGING DIRECTOR

6/4/12

(Foreground L-R): J. Bernard Calloway, Adam Pascal, Montego Glover and Company

Memphis

MUSICAL NUMBERS

ACT I

"Underground"	Delray, Felicia and Company
"The Music of My Soul"	Huey, Felicia and Company
"Scratch My Itch"	Wailin' Joe and Company
"Ain't Nothin' But a Kiss"	Felicia and Huey
"Hello, My Name Is Huey"	Huey
"Everybody Wants to Be Black on a Saturday Night"	Company
"Make Me Stronger"	Huey, Mama, Felicia and Company
"Colored Woman"	Felicia
"Someday"	Felicia and Company
"She's My Sister"	Delray and Huey
"Radio"	Huey and Company
"Say a Prayer"	Gator and Company

ACT II

"Crazy Little Huey"	Huey and Company
"Big Love"	Bobby
"Love Will Stand When All Else Falls"	Felicia and Company
"Stand Up"	Delray, Felicia, Huey, Gator, Bobby and Company
"Change Don't Come Easy"	Mama, Delray, Gator and Bobby
"Tear Down the House"	Huey and Company
"Love Will Stand/Ain't Nothin' But a Kiss" (Reprise)	Felicia and Huey
"Memphis Lives in Me"	Huey and Company
"Steal Your Rock 'n' Roll"	Huey, Felicia and Company

Adam Pascal
Huey

Montego Glover
Felicia

Derrick Baskin
Gator

J. Bernard Calloway
Delray

James Monroe
Iglehart
Bobby

John Jellison
Mr. Simmons

Nancy Opel
Mama

Darius Barnes
Ensemble; u/s Gator

Carmen Shavone
Borders
Ensemble

Angela C. Brydon
Ensemble

Cast Continued

Mr. Simmons	JOHN JELLISON
Clara/White Mother/	
Ensemble	ELIZABETH WARD LAND
Buck Wiley/Ensemble/	
Martin Holton	JUSTIN PATTERSON
Ensemble/Teenager	HILLARY ELK
Ensemble	KEVIN MASSEY
Ensemble/	
Double Dutch Girl	ANGELA C. BRYDON
Ensemble	CODY WILLIAMS
Ensemble	ANDY MILLS
Perry Como/Ensemble/	
Frank Dryer	JAMISON SCOTT
Ensemble	BRYAN LANGLITZ
Mama	NANCY OPEL

SWINGS

SASHA HUTCHINGS, TYRONE JACKSON,
CANDICE MONET McCALL,
JERMAINE R. REMBERT

UNDERSTUDIES

For Mama: ANGELA C. BRYDON,
  ELIZABETH WARD LAND
For Huey: KEVIN MASSEY,
  JUSTIN PATTERSON
For Felicia: ERICA DORFLER,
  DAN'YELLE WILLIAMSON

For Gator: DARIUS BARNES,
  JERMAINE R. REMBERT,
  ANTOINE L. SMITH
For Bobby: KEN ROBINSON,
  ANTOINE L. SMITH
For Delray: KEN ROBINSON,
  ANTOINE L. SMITH
For Mr. Simmons: DAVID McDONALD,
  JUSTIN PATTERSON

DANCE CAPTAIN

JERMAINE R. REMBERT

TIME

The 1950s

BAND

Conductor: KENNY J. SEYMOUR
Associate Conductor: SHELTON BECTON
Keyboard 1: KENNY J. SEYMOUR
Keyboard 2: SHELTON BECTON
Guitars: JOHN PUTNAM
Bass: GEORGE FARMER
Drums: CLAYTON CRADDOCK
Trumpet: JOHN WALSH
Trombone: BIRCH JOHNSON
Reeds: KEN HITCHCOCK, SCOTT KREITZER
Music Coordinator: MICHAEL KELLER

Memphis

Sam J. Cahn
Ensemble

Erica Dorfler
Ensemble;
u/s Felicia

Preston W.
Dugger, III
Ensemble

Hillary Elk
Ensemble

Sasha Hutchings
Swing

Lauren Lim Jackson
Ensemble

Tyrone Jackson
Swing

Elizabeth Ward Land
Ensemble; u/s Mama

Bryan Langlitz
Ensemble

Kevin Massey
Ensemble; u/s Huey

Candice Monet
McCall
Swing, Assistant
Dance Captain

David McDonald
Ensemble;
u/s Mr. Simmons

Monette McKay
Ensemble

Andy Mills
Ensemble

Justin Patterson
Ensemble; u/s Huey,
Mr. Simmons

Jermaine R. Rembert
Swing, Dance
Captain, Fight
Captain; u/s Gator

Ken Robinson
Ensemble;
u/s Delray

Jamison Scott
Ensemble

Antoine L. Smith
Ensemble; u/s
Delray, Bobby, Gator

Cody Williams
Ensemble

Dan'yelle Williamson
Ensemble; u/s Felicia

Joe DiPietro
Book and Co-Lyrics

David Bryan
Music, Co-Lyrics

Christopher Ashley
Director

Sergio Trujillo
Choreographer

Christopher Jahnke
Music Producer/
Music Supervisor

David Gallo
Set and Co-
Projections Design

Howell Binkley
Lighting Design

Paul Tazewell
Costume Design

Ken Travis
Sound Design

Charles G. LaPointe
Hair and Wig Design

Steve Rankin
Fight Director

Bernard Telsey
Telsey + Company
Casting

Kelly Devine
Associate
Choreographer

Daryl Waters
Co-Orchestrator

Memphis

Kenny J. Seymour
Music Director/Conductor

August Eriksmoen
Dance Arranger

Michael Keller
Music Coordinator

Carl Pasbjerg
Alchemy Production
Group LLC
*General
Management*

Ana Rose Greene, Guy Kwan, Joe DeLuise,
Hillary Blanken
Juniper Street Productions
Production Manager

Beatrice Terry
Associate Director

Edgar Godineaux
*Associate
Choreographer*

Randy Adams
Junkyard Dog
Productions
Producer

Kenny Alhadeff
Junkyard Dog
Productions
Producer

Marleen Alhadeff
Junkyard Dog
Productions
Producer

Sue Frost
Junkyard Dog
Productions
Producer

Barbara Freitag
Producer

Buddy Freitag
Producer

Jim Blair
Producer

Susan Blair
Producer

Nick Demos
Demos Bizar
Entertainment
Producer

Tim Kashani
Apples and Oranges
Productions
Producer

Pamela Winslow
Kashani,
Apples and Oranges
Productions
Producer

Aubrey Dan
Dancap Productions
Inc.
Producer

Alex Lukianov
Producer

Tony Ponturo
Producer

Richard Winkler
Producer

Lauren Doll
Producer

Linda and Bill Potter
Producers

John Gore
CEO
Broadway Across
America
Producer

Thomas B. McGrath
Chairman
Broadway Across
America
Producer

Patty Baker,
Good Productions
Producer

Scott & Kaylin Union
Producers

Loraine Alterman
Boyle
Producer

Chase Mishkin
Producer

Remmel T. Dickinson
Producer

Pat Halloran
Memphis Orpheum
Group
Producer

Memphis

Vijay Vashee
Producer

Sita Vashee
Producer

Ken Clay
Associate Producer

David Armstrong,
Executive Producer/
Artistic Director
The 5th Avenue
Theatre

Bernadine Griffin,
Managing Director,
The 5th Avenue
Theatre

Bill Berry
Producing Director,
The 5th Avenue
Theatre

Christopher Ashley,
Artistic Director
La Jolla Playhouse

Robert Kelley
Artistic Director
TheatreWorks

Phil Santora
Managing Director
TheatreWorks

Betsy Struxness
Ensemble; u/s Mama

STAFF for *MEMPHIS*

GENERAL MANAGEMENT
ALCHEMY PRODUCTION GROUP
Carl Pasbjerg   Frank P. Scardino

COMPANY MANAGER
Jim Brandeberry

PRODUCTION MANAGEMENT
JUNIPER STREET PRODUCTIONS
Hillary Blanken   Guy Kwan
Kevin Broomell   Ana Rose Greene

GENERAL PRESS REPRESENTATIVE
THE HARTMAN GROUP
Michael Hartman
Juliana Hannett   Emily McGill

CASTING
TELSEY + COMPANY
Bernie Telsey CSA, Will Cantler CSA,
David Vaccari CSA, Bethany Knox CSA,
Craig Burns CSA, Tiffany Little Canfield CSA,
Rachel Hoffman CSA, Justin Huff CSA,
Patrick Goodwin CSA, Abbie Brady-Dalton CSA,
David Morris, Cesar A. Rocha, Andrew Femenella,
Karyn Casl, Kristina Bramhall, Jessie Malone

ADVERTISING/MARKETING
aka
Liz Furze   Scott A. Moore   Clint Bond, Jr.
Elizabeth Findlay   Joshua Lee Poole
Adam Jay   Janette Roush
Erik Alden   Meghan Bartley

ASSOCIATE DIRECTOR
Beatrice Terry

ASSOCIATE CHOREOGRAPHER
Edgar Godineaux

Production Stage Manager .... Arturo E. Porazzi
Stage Manager .... Gary Mickelson
Assistant Stage Manager .... Janet Takami
Assistant Stage Manager .... Alexis Shorter
Associate Company Manager .... Michelle H. Tamagawa
Junkyard Dog Associate Producer .... Carolyn D. Miller
Associate to the General Managers .... Amanda Coleman
Dance Captain .... Jermaine R. Rembert
Assistant Dance Captain .... Candice Monet McCall
Assistant Fight Director .... Shad Ramsey
Fight Captain .... Jermaine R. Rembert
Dramaturg .... Gabriel Greene
Dialect Coach .... Stephen Gabis
Make-Up Designer .... Angelina Avallone
Associate Scenic Designer .... Steven C. Kemp
Associate Costume Designer .... Rory Powers
Associate Lighting Designer .... Mark Simpson
Associate Hair Designer .... Leah Loukas
Assistant Costume Designer .... Maria Zamansky
Assistant to the Costume Designer .... Kara Harmon
Assistant to the Lighting Designer .... Amanda Zieve
Assistant Sound Designer .... Alex Hawthorn
Assistant Projection Designer .... Steve Channon
Moving Light Programmer .... David Arch
Projections Programmer .... Florian Mosleh
Production/Head Carpenter .... Hank Hale
Flyman .... Erik Yans
Assistant Carpenter
   (Automation) .... Eric "Speed" Smith
Production Electrician .... James Fedigan
Head Electrician .... Joe Pearson
Production Property Master .... Mike Pilipski
Head Property Master .... John Paull
Assistant Property Master .... Peter Drummond
Production Sound Engineer .... Phillip Lojo
FOH Sound Engineer .... Greg Freedman
Assistant Sound Engineer .... Matthew Lackey
Wardrobe Supervisor .... Rory Powers
Associate Wardrobe Supervisor .... Kyle Wesson

Dressers .... Dora Bonilla, Tasha Cowd,
                        Douglas Earl, Maureen George,
              Betty Gillispie, Billy Hipkins, Lizz Hirons,
                   James Hodun, Kim Kaldenberg
Hair Supervisor .... Michele Rutter
Assistant Hair Supervisor .... Mary Kay Yezerski-Bondoc
Hair Stylists .... Charlene Belmond, Lisa Weiss
Music Copying .... Christopher Deschene
Keyboard Programmer .... Kenny J. Seymour
Music Assistant .... Clare Cooper
Rehearsal Drummer .... Clayton Craddock
Technical Assistant .... Alexandra Paull
Production Assistants .... Megan J. Alvord,
                                       Meg Friedman
Scenic/Projection Studio Manager .... Sarah Zeitler
Production Intern .... Kendra Stockton
Lighting Interns .... Avery Lewis, Jeff Kastenbaum
Scenic Design Interns .... Tiffany Dalian, Caite Hevner
Projection Design Intern .... Wolfram Ott
Sound Interns .... Stephanie Celustka, Cynthia Hannon
Physical Therapy .... Performing Arts Physical Therapy
Digital/Internet Marketing 87AM/
                        Adam Cunningham, Alex Bisker,
              Shai Goller, Brian Sacks, Ariana Sverdlik
Social Media Director .... Carolyn D. Miller
Multicultural Marketing .... Full House Theater Tickets
Production Photographer .... Joan Marcus
Accountant .... Fried & Kowgios LLC
Controller .... Joe Kabula
Legal Counsel .... Beigelman Feldman & Associates PC
Payroll Services .... Castellana Services, Inc.
Banking .... Signature Bank
Insurance .... D.R. Rieff & Associates/Sonny Everett
Hotel Broker .... Road Concierge/Lisa Morris
Air Travel Broker .... Tzell Travel/Andi Hennig
Opening Night
   Coordination .... The Lawrence Company Events
Merchandising .... Marquee Merchandise, LLC/
                                       Matt Murphy
Theatre Displays .... King Displays Inc.

Memphis
SCRAPBOOK

Correspondent: Carolyn D. Miller, Associate Producer and *Memphis* Blogger

Memorable Press Encounter: Oprah Winfrey probably caused the biggest stir. Unfortunately I missed Michelle Obama and her daughters.

—Kevin Massey, Ensemble/ "Huey" understudy

After the one and only Oprah finished graciously taking photos with anyone and everyone who requested, I escorted her, her guests, and security team through what I like to call the 'secret exit' of the Shubert Theatre to her waiting car. As we leisurely walked down the alley behind the rest of her group, she put her arm around my shoulders and said once again how much she enjoyed the show and what terrific performances everyone gave and thanked us for having her. Knowing that this might be a once-in-a-lifetime opportunity, I put my arm around her as well. She also hugged and kissed me before stepping out into the night and into her car. Meeting Oprah and having that short one-on-one time with her was certainly a bucket list moment that I will treasure forever. What an evening!!

—Emily McGill, Memphis Press Rep, The Hartman Group

Favorite Day at *Memphis*: The day of the 2010 Tony Awards. The excitement was palpable and the show and the audience were electric. Then, after the show as we all got ready to perform at the awards, everyone (cast, crew, house staff, producers, artistic) was in such an easy and fun mood. We watched Joe and David and Daryl win their awards on TV in the Stage Manager's

Pitching for the show team in the Broadway Show League

Photo by Monica Simoes

office and J. Bernard almost knocked me into a wall when we won our first Tony!

—Kevin Covert, Original Cast Member

Opening night was amazing. As was closing. It was like rockstar status.

—James M. Iglehart, "Bobby"

Coolest Thing About Being in the Show: The fact that it was "the little show that could." An absolutely original musical not based on a book or a movie, that was ever changing (just wait until the "Unsung *Memphis*" concert). No one knew who or what the hell we were when we opened at The Shubert. I am extremely proud of my time and (hopefully) my contributions at *Memphis*.

—Kevin Covert

Favorite In-Theatre Gathering Place: The stage during warm-up before and after half-hour. It would be the place to catch up on everyone's news, life, family, auditions, shows they saw or classes they took. Old company members would stop through and we'd remember old times. Our amazing producers, stage managers, and company managers would pass through and check in on us and our well being. We had Delray lifts, double-dutch tournaments, spontaneous dance improv, Hidden Talent Sundays! It was everything from sacred time before the show to a block party amongst family.

—Monette McKay, Ensemble

Special Backstage Rituals: There were plenty of ritual backstage shenanigans kept and added-to along the way to keep us laughing, but the one that kept us uplifted and connected was the prayer circle. Every day at places, we'd gather upstage by the drums to take hands, breathe together, and give thanks for being where we were and getting to do what we did. I've been a little late to the spiritual party, so to speak, and when I finally got coaxed into coming to prayer circle, my entire half hour routine changed in order to make sure I got there on time. Over two years, that circle has made me laugh, exalt, cry, and even be moved enough to lead, and this ritual will follow me to every show I'm in from now on. There's no better way to start a show than by saying thank you.

—Betsy Struxness, Ensemble

Catchphrases Only the Company Would Recognize:

"Truh." Short for "trust."

"Miggitty most and liggity least."

"Pop off."

"Thank youuuuuuu."

"And another thing!"

And only my *Memphis* family knows who "Keona and Rokiki" are. ;)

—Monette McKay

Favorite costume: Act II: green silk dress

—Montego Glover, "Felicia Farrell."

Well I have 12 total costume changes in my Wailin' Joe/Rev. Hobson track. I would have to say my favorite costume hands down is Wailin' Joe for obvious reasons. And my least favorite would have to be my "Radio" costume. Because it was the only long-sleeve shirt in the entire scene due to my tattoos. And with my hat it made me look like an old man.

—Antoine L. Smith, "Wailin Joe"/ "Rev. Hobson"/Understudy "Bobby," "Delray," "Gator."

Favorite In-Theatre Snack Food: Delish gummy bears from Duane Reade.

—Montego Glover

CREDITS

Scenery constructed by Showman Fabricators, Inc., Long Island City, NY. Show control and scenic motion control featuring Stage Command® Systems by PRG Scenic Technologies, New Windsor, NY. Additional scenery painted by Scenic Arts Studios, Cornwall, NY. Soft goods built by I. Weiss and Sons, Inc., Long Island City, NY. Lighting equipment provided by PRG Lighting, North Bergen, NJ. Sound equipment provided by Masque Sound, East Rutherford, NJ. Projection equipment provided by Scharff Weisberg Inc., Long Island City, NY. Props built by the Spoon Group, Rahway, NJ. Principal ladies' costumes by Donna Langman. Additional ladies costumes by Euro Co Costumes, Inc.; D. Barak Stribling; Tricorne, Inc.; and Eric Winterling, Inc. Principal men's tailoring by Brian Hemesath. Additional men's tailoring by Jennifer Love Costumes, Inc.; Scafati, Inc.; and D. L. Cerney. Men's finale suits by Top Hat Imagewear. Custom shirts by Cego. Dance shoes by Worldtone Dance. 'Gator' head by Rodney Gordon, Inc. Makeup provided by M•A•C. ©Ernest C. Withers Estate, courtesy Panopticon Gallery, Boston, MA: Dewey Phillips of WHQB, Red Hot and Blue Program, The Hippodrome, Beale Street, Memphis, early 1950s #LV61C. Clarence Gatemouth Brown at Club Handy, Memphis, TN. Count Basie, Ruth Brown, Billy Eckstine, The Hippodrome, 1950s. Percy Mayfield (with drumsticks) and band, The Hippodrome, 1951. Special thanks to Edgar Godineaux, Gabriel Barre, Sarah Nashman, Kent Nicholson, Marilynn Sheldon, TeamTastic, Adam Arian, Mo Brady, Michael Finkle, Debra Hatch, Sue Makkoo, Michael Clark and the many folks that made it happen at NSMT, TheatreWorks, La Jolla Playhouse and the Fifth Avenue Theatre.

Energy-efficient washer/dryer courtesy of LG Electronics.

Memphis
SCRAPBOOK

Memorable Stage Door Encounter: The man who brought me a cheesecake from Junior's every day for three days in a row!
—*Montego Glover*

Memorable Note/Fax/Fan Letters: There are many but I will name a few which come to mind. First Lady Michelle Obama came with her daughters and signed a *Memphis* poster which we framed and hung above the stage door. Ben Vereen saw our show (twice!) and sent a card backstage stating he thought we were the best show on Broadway. Gina Gershon said it looked like we were having so much fun on stage she wished she were doing our show (instead of *Bye Bye Birdie*). Ian McKellen saw our show and sent us a note. I am not sure who was more excited about this—the *X-Men* nerd in me or the *Lord of the Rings* nerd in me. We received cupcakes from Will Smith and Jada Pinkett Smith (something my niece still talks about and remembers fondly), chocolate bars from Whoopi Goldberg, et cetera, et cetera. We also had a group of "superfans" from Hofstra University who repeatedly saw our show and called themselves "The Front Row Crew"—they were there for many milestone performances and they would design a poster or something for us almost every time they attended. We hung these up all over the theatre and they stayed up until we closed. On top of all that there were the countless letters from people who were so moved by our story they could not let the experience end at the curtain call. We received heartfelt letters from people who grew up in the south during this time, or their parents were there during this time, or they themselves were in a mixed race relationship and identified with the story etc. We posted these letters on the callboard or in the office for all to read. We knew we were doing something special when we received one of these letters.
—*Gary Mickelson, Stage Manager*

Most Entertaining Actor: There were many but I would have to say Justin Patterson. He is always willing to ham it up backstage for a good laugh although the same could also be said of Michael McGrath! It was a passing of the torch I suppose.
—*Michele Rutter, Head of Wig Department*
Rhett George: a comic genius. But in his absence it would be Justin Patterson. Did you see the video? It's like that every show no matter how much he denies it.
—*Kevin Massey*
Hmmm. I would have to say James Iglehart, but for purely selfish reasons. Every performance I would come up with an awkward question to ask

him as he exited the stage immediately after Mr. Simmons asked him the awkward question about having a son and his son loving Huey Calhoun. We called it, "Awkward Questions From Your Boss." It started when we were in previews and I had the brilliant/stupid/eventually daunting idea to ask him a different question for every performance. We ran for almost three years and I never repeated a question once and we cracked each other up. On the closing night I still had a bunch of awkward questions for him so I asked him twenty-four questions in rapid succession just before he had to re-enter. Some of my favorites (although we never wrote them down so I am certain I am forgetting some) were: "Hey Bobby...you ever just sit on the toilet eating cheese?" "Hey Bobby...you ever just punch LeVar Burton in the throat at a children's museum?" "Hey Bobby...you ever wake up in the morning, find a dead hobo clown in your bathtub and say to yourself, 'Not again, Lord, NOT AGAIN'?" "Hey Bobby...you ever wake up in a ditch next to Gary Busey with a pistol in your jeans shorts and just think to yourself, 'This feels right'?" "Hey Bobby...would you let me watch you while you eat this soft juicy peach?" Now imagine one thousand one hundred sixty-six similarly awkward questions!
—*Gary Mickelson*

Most Entertaining Crew Member: Betty,

(L-R): Adam Pascal, Montego Glover and Jermaine Rembert at fight rehearsal.

Montego's Dresser. She would sing at the top of her lungs. She was "living" always.
—*Kevin Massey*
For me it would be Betty Ann Gillispie regularly singing the incorrect lyrics slightly off key while doing her version of the choreography. She claimed to be Montego's third cover. Thank God we never needed her!
—*Michele Rutter*
I'm not sure he wants the title "most entertaining" but Head Carpenter Hank Hale gets "most awesome." He truly cared about our

safety, respected our talent, and could give great advice. He was just cool. Not to mention, he had hooks for feet that made all of us dancers squeal with jealousy!
—*Monette McKay*

Trickiest Moment to "Tech": I remember the exits after "Big Love" and after "Stand Up" being a little hairy. Chris and Sergio wanted the show to flow and for the audience to not wait between scenes as scenery was coming onstage/offstage. Almost all our transitions between scenes were just as choreographed as the dances onstage. Liza Gennaro (a choreographer and a teacher) brought about a dozen groups of students over the years to see our show and she always wanted to make sure they saw how intricate these changes were. Anyway, both of the aforementioned transitions after these songs had scenery moving onstage while actors were supposed to be dancing offstage. There were many attempts which made both crew and actors nervous but all the hard work paid off: At one of our many talkbacks, a student asked how (and he mentioned these two scenes specifically) we were able to get the scenery to just magically appear as we transitioned into the next scene. He said something like, "I was watching the end of a scene, people danced off and suddenly we are another place!"
—*Gary Mickelson*

Fastest Wig Change: The entire company changed wigs for the finale!
—*Michele Rutter*

Orchestra Member Who Played the Most Instruments: Ken Hitchcock: Bass Clarinet, Tenor Sax and Baritone Sax.
—*Clayton Craddock, Percussion*

Favorite Part of the Score to Play: Either "Memphis Lives in Me" or "Music of My Soul."
—*Clayton Craddock*

Orchestra Member Who Played the Most Consecutive Performances Without a Sub: Ken Hitchcock.
—*Clayton Craddock*

Most Memorable Ad Lib Onstage: There were many but three of my favorites:
Line as written: "What's shaking brothers and sisters? So glad you found us way up here on the dial. And even though we only reachin' 'bout a mile across downtown Memphis we got us the jumpinest jivinest music in town. And it's Saturday night, meanin' the party's at my favorite Beale Street juke joint... Delllllll-raaaays!" (At this point the set for Delray's Bar rolls onstage and the hardest working ensemble on Broadway performed some sexy choreography as Delray sang "Underground".)
Line as flubbed by Jermaine Rembert: "What's

Memphis
SCRAPBOOK

shaking brothers and sisters... (awkward pause)... we're playing the best music in America...(even longer awkward pause)...we got... Delllll-raaaays!" (At this point the set for Delray's Bar rolls onstage and the hardest working ensemble on Broadway performed some sexy choreography while stifling laughter as Delray sang "Underground" and everyone asked each other, "What the hell was that?")

Line as written: "Hey kids, it's time for Huey Calhoun's after-school television program! And he's letting me be on it!"

Line as flubbed by James Iglehart: "Hey kids, it's time for Huey Calhoun's after-school special... (pause)... right now!"

Lyric as written: "I got my soul and I...got my pride...but I got me...one other thing"

Lyric as flubbed by James Iglehart: "I got my pride...and I...(pause while James loses a pound of nothing but sweat)... ooooooooh, I can sing!"

Then there was the night Chad Kimball got stuck in the DJ Booth. He is supposed to exit the booth and the scene continues as he comes downstage to talk to Mr. Simmons. It was literally impossible to continue the scene with Chad in the booth. He is pulling on the door and panicking and pulling on the door more and panicking more until finally he shouts out, "I'm locked in!" He then remembered there was a secret door to the booth (to facilitate another entrance in a different scene) and he used that door. The audience loved seeing Chad squirm and we had to wait a good long while for the cheers and applause to calm down before we could continue with our story.

—*Gary Mickelson*

Cast Hangouts Outside the Theatre: Some of the favorite cast hangouts include Harlem Tavern. Which, I might add, has an amazing $18 Lobster Dinner every Tuesday night. Chez Lucienne also in Harlem (get the mussels). And Ember Room, which is one of my favorite post-show spots. If you go there you must get the chocolate ribs and calamari. And for a day of relaxation, Spa Castle is the favorite spot amongst the *Memphis* family.

—*Antoine L. Smith*

Cast Nicknames: Ha! Yes. We had the "Tubby club." Carmen Borders and Darius Barnes were called "Tubby," and Elizabeth Ward Land was "Mamma Tubbs," since all three of these folks are anything but. Carmen and I also took to calling each other "Ting Ting" in honor of the iPhone alert that goes ting-ting...If you own the phone, you know

which one I'm talking about. I think it started when she got the phone and didn't turn it on vibrate. I probably got annoyed and then we turned it into a joke.

—*Betsy Struxness*

Understudy Anecdote: Ah, understudying, the cruel lovely joke of theatre. So...I was the understudy for Gladys, Huey's mother, but due to my age and stature, they were forced to make me Huey's sister if I ever went on. Which of course happened. Now, this was a year and a half of my being in the show,

Dan'yelle WIlliamson and Kevin Massey in "Broadway in Bryant Park" in summer 2012.

but two years into the run, so most everyone was dying to see this happen, knowing they'd get a huge laugh out of it. Little did they know. All was going swimmingly until we came to Gladys's big song in the second act, "Change Don't Come Easy." (It's very wordy and if you miss anything you might as well be sunk.) I started off fine and was singing my heart out until I realized I had jumped a verse and gone straight into the chorus, as Derrick Baskin, J. Bernard Calloway, James Monroe Iglehart, and Adam Pascal all looked at me like, "You know you're wrong, right?" Anywho, apparently my Gladys believed SO much in what she was saying that I just repeated the chorus again and got back on track. This sounds very small, but in my head I was going, "Oh no! I'm in the wrong place! What do I do? What am I even saying?" Luckily, I was so convincing that no one in the audience knew, including my agent and friends. Even some of the crew members backstage thought I was changing the words on purpose because I was Huey's sister. So I have lived up to my initials. I'm really good at BS.

—*Betsy Struxness*

Understudy Anecdote: Finding out I was on that evening as "Huey" when I walked by the theatre for half hour and saw my name up in the lobby on the "At This Performance" list, taking almost a half hour rehearsing that pre-

Radio kiss, ha!, getting post show notes with Bea, getting pre and post show notes with Montego (haha, don't put that one in there :), saying something shocking and different every night to the Beale streeters in the huddle before "Tear Down the House," messing with Jay, Derrick and James all throughout the show, hearing through messages or at the stage door how the show and Huey has touched people's lives, and mostly looking at everyone in the cast during "Memphis Lives in Me" during the "wailing section".... I always get choked up there.

—*Kevin Massey*

Understudy Anecdote: My most memorable understudy moment would have to be the first time I went on for "Delray." I had only been in *Memphis* for eleven days in my original track just getting the hang of it all. The Saturday morning of my second week stage management called me and asked if I could go on as Delray (Felicia's brother). Mind you I had zero understudy rehearsals at this time. But my fear was not of going on, but of carrying Felicia up a full flight of stairs. So I came in early, carried Dan'yelle Williamson up the stairs a few times, worked the fight call, and with the complete support of the cast did the show for three straight performances without any hiccups!

—*Antoine L. Smith*

Most Vivid Memory of the Final Performance: Wow. Everything was so heightened and electric, we were just trying to take it all in: the lyrics, the last moments backstage, the applause. I'm going to say, the look on my middle sister's face. It was her first time seeing the show, and the first time all three sisters had been together in over two years: Sheer pride, joy, and love. It didn't get more honest than that. And it just reconfirmed how truly special this show has been for me and everyone it touched.

—*Monette McKay*

"Underground" at the top of the show—all of us were so excited. We knew what it was and we knew what it meant and we were juiced. We were all looking at each other and it was wonderful. "Say a Prayer" was crazy—everyone was trying not to cry and, of course, people falling one by one into crying. The only one who sounded good was Derrick. Emotionally, it was the best ever. Vocally, I have no idea how it sounded, but the audience didn't care.

—*James Monroe Iglehart*

Mike Tyson: Undisputed Truth

First Preview: July 31, 2012. Opened: August 2, 2012.
Limited Engagement. Closed August 12, 2012 after 2 Previews and 10 Performances.

The onetime undisputed world heavyweight boxing champion noted for his brutal fighting style kicks back in this solo show and narrates the story of his triumphs in the ring as well as his sometimes chaotic personal life.

☉ LONGACRE THEATRE

220 West 48th Street
A Shubert Organization Theatre

Philip J. Smith, *Chairman*   **Robert E. Wankel,** *President*

JAMES L. NEDERLANDER, SPIKE LEE & TERRY ALLEN KRAMER

Present

Written By
KIKI TYSON

Directed By
SPIKE LEE

| Scenic Design | Lighting Design | Projection Design | Sound Design |
| TIMOTHY R. MACKABEE | NATASHA KATZ | ERIK PEARSON | RAYMOND SCHILKE |

Technical Supervisor	Production Stage Manager	Dramaturg & Voice Coach
FRED GALLO	GWENDOLYN M. GILLIAM	DE'ADRE AZIZA
GUY KWAN		

| Advertising | Press Representative | General Manager |
| SERINO/COYNE | SUNSHINE SACHS | NIKO COMPANIES, LTD. |

Executive Producers
KIKI TYSON & ADAM STECK

Originally produced at the Hollywood Theatre at MGM Grand by SPI Entertainment, Inc. and Directed by Randy Johnson

8/2/12

Photo by Joseph Marzullo/WENN

Mike Tyson

Photo Courtesy Sunshine Sachs

Mike Tyson: Undisputed Truth

Mike Tyson

Kiki Tyson
Author/Executive Producer

Spike Lee
Director/Producer

Timothy R. Mackabee
Set Design

Natasha Katz
Lighting Design

Erik Pearson
Projection Design

Raymond Schilke
Sound Design

Fred Gallo
Technical Supervisor

Gwendolyn M. Gilliam
Production Stage Manager

De'Adre Aziza
Dramaturg & Voice Coach

Ken Sunshine
Sunshine Sachs
Press Agent

Shawn Sachs
Sunshine Sachs
Press Agent

Manny Kladitis
Niko Companies Ltd.
General Manager

James L. Nederlander
Producer

Terry Allen Kramer
Producer

Adam Steck
Executive/Original Producer

(L-R): Spike Lee, Kanye West, 50 Cent, Mike Tyson, David Maisel

Photo by Joseph Marzullo/WENN

STAFF FOR
MIKE TYSON: UNDISPUTED TRUTH

DJ
DJ CLARK KENT

GENERAL MANAGEMENT
NIKO COMPANIES
Manny Kladitis
Jeffrey Chrzczon   Jason T. Vanderwoude
Walter A. Milani

PRESS REPRESENTATIVE
SUNSHINE SACHS & ASSOCIATES
Ken Sunshine
Emily Fox

PRODUCTION STAGE MANAGER
Gwendolyn M. Gilliam

Production Supervisor ....Fred Gallo, Guy Kwan
Assistant to Mr. Lee ....Kiel Adrian Scott
Assistant to Mr. Tyson ....Reese Robinson
Personal Assistant to Mr. Tyson ....Pashelle Clayton
Voice/Speech Coach ....De'Adre Aziza
Stand-In ....William Wesley
Footage shot by ....Kerwin DeVonish
Assistant Set Designer ....Benson Knight
Associate Lighting Designer.................Aaron Spivey

Assistant Sound Designer ....Kristyn Smith
Asst. Projection Designer ....Jackson Gallagher
Archival Producer ....Mary Recine
Additional Research ....Martha Corcoran
Production Electrician ....Michael Pitzer
Head Electrician ....Michael Hyman
Lighting Programmer ....Sean Beach
Projections Programmer ....Paul Vershbow
Advertising ....Serino/Coyne
    Angelo Desimini, Scott Johnson, Tom Callahan,
        Jeff Carroll, Sarah Marcus
Banking ....JP Morgan Chase/
        Padmini Sivaprakasam
Insurance ....Insurance Office of America/
        Carol Bressi-Cilona
Legal ....Screwvala LLC/
        Erach F. Screwvala, Esq.
Accounting ....Rosenberg, Neuwirth & Kuchner/
        Mark D'Ambrosi, Jana Jevnikar

CREDITS
Sound and lighting equipment provided by PRG Scenic Technologies. Scenery fabrication by PRG Scenic Technologies, a division of Production Resource Group, LLC, New Windsor, NY. Projection equipment provided by WorldStage Scharff Weisberg.

SPECIAL THANKS
Tom Casino

Kenneth Meiselas
Gil Karson

THE SHUBERT ORGANIZATION, INC.
Board of Directors

Philip J. Smith   **Robert E. Wankel**
Chairman   President

Wyche Fowler, Jr.   **Diana Phillips**

Lee J. Seidler   **Michael I. Sovern**

Stuart Subotnick

Chief Financial Officer ....Elliot Greene
Sr. Vice President, Ticketing ....David Andrews
Vice President, Finance ....Juan Calvo
Vice President, Human Resources ....Cathy Cozens
Vice President, Facilities ....John Darby
Vice President, Theatre Operations ....Peter Entin
Vice President, Marketing ....Charles Flateman
Vice President, Audit ....Anthony LaMattina
Vice President, Ticket Sales ....Brian Mahoney
Vice President, Creative Projects ...........D.S. Moynihan
Vice President, Real Estate ....Julio Peterson

---

House Manager ....Bob Reilly

Motown: The Musical

First Preview: March 11, 2013. Opened: April 14, 2013.
Still running as of May 31, 2013.

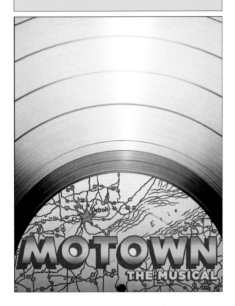

This autobiographical jukebox musical traces the turbulent life and career of Berry Gordy, founder of Motown Records in the early 1960s, which provided an artistic home to two generations of mainly African-American soul, r&b and pop stars including Diana Ross, Marvin Gaye, Smokey Robinson, Gladys Knight, Stevie Wonder and Michael Jackson. The production features faithful recreations of these and many other acts by young performers, many of them chosen by Gordy himself.

CAST

BRANDON VICTOR DIXON ....Berry Gordy
VALISIA LeKAE ....Diana Ross
CHARL BROWN ....Smokey Robinson
BRYAN TERRELL CLARK ....Marvin Gaye
RAYMOND LUKE, JR.,
   JIBREEL MAWRY ...Young Berry/Stevie/Michael

ENSEMBLE

TIMOTHY J. ALEX ....Roger Campbell, Tom Clay,
   Pirate DJ
MICHAEL ARNOLD ......Jackie Wilson Manager,
   Harold Noveck, Studio Head
NICHOLAS CHRISTOPHER ....Four Top,
   Norman Whitfield, Lionel Ritchie
REBECCA E. COVINGTON ....Gwen Gordy,
   Vandella, Gladys Horton, Cindy Birdsong
ARIANA DeBOSE ....Mary Wilson
ANDREA DORA ....Suzanne de Passe
WILKIE FERGUSON III ....Jr. Walker All Star
MARVA HICKS ......Esther Gordy, Lula Hardaway,
   Gladys Knight

Continued on next page

Continued on next page

⇒N⇐ LUNT-FONTANNE THEATRE
UNDER THE DIRECTION OF
JAMES M. NEDERLANDER AND JAMES L. NEDERLANDER

KEVIN McCOLLUM DOUG MORRIS AND BERRY GORDY
Present

MOTOWN
THE MUSICAL

Book by
BERRY GORDY

Music and Lyrics from
THE LEGENDARY MOTOWN CATALOG

BASED UPON THE BOOK *TO BE LOVED:*
THE MUSIC, THE MAGIC, THE MEMORIES
OF MOTOWN BY BERRY GORDY

MUSIC BY ARRANGEMENT WITH
SONY/ATV MUSIC PUBLISHING

Starring

BRANDON VICTOR DIXON
VALISIA LeKAE

CHARL BROWN   BRYAN TERRELL CLARK

TIMOTHY J. ALEX   MICHAEL ARNOLD   NICHOLAS CHRISTOPHER   REBECCA E. COVINGTON   ARIANA DeBOSE
ANDREA DORA   PRESTON W. DUGGER III   WILKIE FERGUSON III   DIONNE FIGGINS   MARVA HICKS   TIFFANY JANENE HOWARD
SASHA HUTCHINGS   LAUREN LIM JACKSON   JAWAN M. JACKSON   MORGAN JAMES   JOHN JELLISON
CRYSTAL JOY   GRASAN KINGSBERRY   JAMIE LaVERDIERE   RAYMOND LUKE, JR.   JIBREEL MAWRY   MARIELYS MOLINA
SYDNEY MORTON   MAURICE MURPHY   JARRAN MUSE   JESSE NAGER   MILTON CRAIG NEALY   N'KENGE   DOMINIC NOLFI
SAYCON SENGBLOH   RYAN SHAW   JAMAL STORY   ERIC LaJUAN SUMMERS   EPHRAIM M. SYKES
JULIUS THOMAS III   DANIEL J. WATTS   DONALD WEBBER, JR.

Scenic Design	Costume Design	Lighting Design	Sound Design	Projection Design
DAVID KORINS	ESOSA	NATASHA KATZ	PETER HYLENSKI	DANIEL BRODIE

Casting	Hair & Wig Design	Associate Director	Assistant Choreographer
TELSEY + COMPANY BETHANY KNOX, CSA	CHARLES G. LaPOINTE	SCHELE WILLIAMS	BRIAN H. BROOKS

Production Stage Manager	Technical Supervisor	General Management	Executive Producer
JULIA P. JONES	DAVID BENKEN	BESPOKE THEATRICALS	NINA LANNAN

Advertising & Marketing	Marketing Outreach	Press Representative	Music Coordinator
SpotCo	MARCIA PENDELTON	BONEAU/BRYAN-BROWN	MICHAEL KELLER

Orchestrations	Music Director/Conductor	Dance Music Arrangements	Additional Arrangements
ETHAN POPP & BRYAN CROOK	JOSEPH JOUBERT	ZANE MARK	BRYAN CROOK

Script Consultants	Creative Consultant
DAVID GOLDSMITH & DICK SCANLAN	CHRISTIE BURTON

Music Supervision & Arrangements by
ETHAN POPP

Choreographed by
PATRICIA WILCOX & WARREN ADAMS

Directed by
CHARLES RANDOLPH-WRIGHT

4/14/13

(L-R): "The Supremes"—
Sydney Morton (Florence Ballard),
Valisia LeKae (Diana Ross),
Ariana DeBose (Mary Wilson)

Photo by Joan Marcus

Motown: The Musical

MUSICAL NUMBERS

Motown music courtesy of Sony/ATV Music Publishing.

"ABC"
"A Breathtaking Guy"
"Ain't No Mountain High Enough"
"Ain't Too Proud to Beg"
"All Night Long"
"Baby I Need Your Lovin'"
"Ball of Confusion"
"Brick House"
"Buttered Popcorn"
"Bye Bye Baby/Two Lovers"
"Can I Close the Door" *
"Cruisin'"
"Dancing in the Street"
"Do You Love Me"
"Get Ready"
"Give It to Me, Baby"
"Good Morning, Heartache"
"Got a Job"
"Happy Birthday"
"Hey Joe (Black Like Me)" *
"I Can't Get Next to You"
"I Can't Help Myself (Sugar Pie, Honey Bunch)"
"I Got the Feeling"
"I Hear a Symphony"
"I Heard It Through the Grapevine"
"(I Know) I'm Losing You"
"I'll Be There"
"It's What's in the Grooves That Counts" *
"I Want You Back"

"Lonely Teardrops"
"Love Is Here and Now You're Gone"
"Mercy, Mercy Me (The Ecology)"
"Money (That's What I Want)"
"My Girl"
"My Guy"
"My Mama Done Told Me"
"Please, Mr. Postman"
"Reach Out (I'll Be There)"
"Reach Out and Touch"
"Reet Petite"
"Remember Me"
"Shop Around"
"Shotgun"
"Sign, Sealed, Delivered"
"Square Biz"
"Stop in the Name of Love"
"Stubborn Kind of Fellow"
"Super Freak"
"The Happening"
"The Love You Save"
"To Be Loved"
"War"
"What's Going On"
"Where Did Our Love Go"
"Who's Loving You"
"You Are You" *
"You're All I Need to Get By"
"You're Nobody 'Til Somebody Loves You"
"You've Really Got a Hold on Me"

* Songs written for this production by Berry Gordy and Michael Lovesmith

ORCHESTRA

Conductor: JOSEPH JOUBERT
Associate Conductor: JASON MICHAEL WEBB
Reeds: TODD GROVES, JACK BASHKOW, ALDEN BANTA
Trumpets: JOHN CHUDOBA, BRIAN PARESCHI
Trombones: BRUCE EIDEM, JASON JACKSON
Violin: SEAN CARNEY
Violin/Viola: ORLANDO WELLS
Cello: AMY RALSKE
Keyboard 1: JASON MICHAEL WEBB
Keyboard 2: ALVIN HOUGH
Guitars: KENNY BRESCIA, BOBBY BAXMEYER
Bass: LUICO HOPPER
Drums: BUDDY WILLIAMS
Percussion: GARY SELIGSON, ROGER SQUITERO

Music Coordinator: MICHAEL KELLER
Keyboard Programmer: RANDY COHEN
Music Preparation: EMILY GRISHMAN MUSIC PREPARATION

(L-R): Brandon Victor Dixon as Berry Gordy and Valisia LeKae as Diana Ross

Photo by Joan Marcus

Cast Continued

TIFFANY JANENE HOWARD ....Anna Gordy, Marvelette
SASHA HUTCHINGS ....Claudette Robinson, Billie Jean Brown, Marvelette
JAWAN M. JACKSON ....Melvin Franklin, Miracle, Commodore
MORGAN JAMES ....Doris Day, Landlady, Teena Marie
JOHN JELLISON ....Ed Sullivan, Shelly Berger, Dudley Buell
GRASAN KINGSBERRY ....Four Top, Stone, Contour, Jackson 5, Georgie Woods
MARIELYS MOLINA ....Marvelette, French Announcer
SYDNEY MORTON ....Florence Ballard
MAURICE MURPHY ....Dennis Edwards, Miracle, Jr. Walker, Commodore
JESSE NAGER ....Temptation, Magnificent Montague, Commodore
MILTON CRAIG NEALY ....Pop Gordy, Commodore, Pip
N'KENGE ....Mary Wells, Mother Gordy, Vandella
DOMINIC NOLFI ....Barney Ales
SAYCON SENGBLOH ....Edna Anderson, Martha Reeves, Chattie Hattie
RYAN SHAW ....Stevie Wonder, Levi Stubbs, Miracle, Pip
JAMAL STORY ....Contour, Hitsville Employee
ERIC LaJUAN SUMMERS ....Jackie Wilson, Four Top, Contour, Brian Holland, Jackson 5, Rick James
EPHRAIM M. SYKES ....Temptation, Robert Gordy, Contour, Jackson 5
JULIUS THOMAS III ....Lamont Dozier, David Ruffin, Jackson 5, Jermaine Jackson, Miller London, Pip
DANIEL J. WATTS ....Contour, Eddie Holland
DONALD WEBBER, JR. ....Temptation, Wiley, Mickey Stevenson, Martin Luther King Jr., Commodore

SWINGS

PRESTON W. DUGGER III,
WILKIE FERGUSON III,
DIONNE FIGGINS, CRYSTAL JOY,
JAMIE LaVERDIERE, JARRAN MUSE

Dance Captain: JAMAL STORY
Assistant Dance Captain: DIONNE FIGGINS

UNDERSTUDIES

For Berry Gordy: JULIUS THOMAS III,
DONALD WEBBER, JR.

Continued on next page

Motown: The Musical

Cast Continued

For Diana Ross:
ARIANA DeBOSE, DIONNE FIGGINS
For Smokey Robinson:
NICHOLAS CHRISTOPHER, JARRAN MUSE
For Marvin Gaye:
MAURICE MURPHY, JARRAN MUSE

SCENES

ACT 1

1983: Pasadena Civic Auditorium,
Berry Gordy's House – Los Angeles
1938: The Gordy Family Home – Detroit,
Urban Street
1957: Auto Assembly Line, Flame Show Bar,
Gwen's House, Jackie Wilson's Manager's
Office, Gordy Home
1959: Hitsville House, WJBK Radio
1962: Motortown Revue, Hitsville Office/
A Payphone in Birmingham
1963: Hitsville Studio A
1964: Caravan Of Stars, Ed Sullivan Theatre Stage
1965: Theater – Manchester, England – Backstage
& Onstage, Paris Hotel, The Copacabana
1968: In and Around Hitsville

ACT 2

1968: Performance Stage
1968: In and Around Hitsville
1969: Hollywood Palace
1970: Frontier Hotel – Outer Lobby & Stage
1971: L.A. Recording Studios, A Resort in the
Bahamas, Smokey's Hotel Room –
Los Angeles, Berry's Office, Sales Dept./
Southern Distributor's Office
1972: Diana's Dressing Room,
Hollywood Movie Set
1975: Motown L.A. Offices
1981: Diana's Dressing Room, Onstage
1983: Berry Gordy's House,
Pasadena Civic Auditorium

A NOTE FROM BERRY GORDY

At Motown, we called ourselves a family and we
were—a big family. While it is impossible to list here
the many people who helped create Motown with
their love and passion, I personally want to thank
them all. Their dedication and talent contributed to
our success, as well as helped to inspire me to bring our
story to Broadway.

Motown was a dream that happened to come true,
and it's because of all of you. Thank you.

Berry Gordy
Founder, Motown

Brandon Victor Dixon
Berry Gordy

Valisia LeKae
Diana Ross

Charl Brown
Smokey Robinson

Bryan Terrell Clark
Marvin Gaye

Timothy J. Alex
Ensemble

Michael Arnold
Ensemble

Nicholas Christopher
Ensemble

**Rebecca E.
Covington**
Ensemble

Ariana DeBose
Ensemble

Andrea Dora
Ensemble

**Preston W.
Dugger III**
Swing

Wilkie Ferguson III
*Ensemble, Partial
Swing*

Dionne Figgins
*Swing, Assistant
Dance Captain*

Marva Hicks
Ensemble

**Tiffany Janene
Howard**
Ensemble

Sasha Hutchings
Ensemble

Lauren Lim Jackson
Ensemble

Jawan M. Jackson
Ensemble

Morgan James
Ensemble

John Jellison
Ensemble

Motown: The Musical

Crystal Joy
Swing

Grasan Kingsberry
Ensemble

Jamie LaVerdiere
Swing

Raymond Luke, Jr.
*Young Berry Gordy,
Michael Jackson,
Stevie Wonder*

Jibreel Mawry
*Young Berry Gordy,
Michael Jackson,
Stevie Wonder*

Marielys Molina
Ensemble

Sydney Morton
Ensemble

Maurice Murphy
Ensemble

Jarran Muse
Swing

Jesse Nager
Ensemble

Milton Craig Nealy
Ensemble

N'Kenge
Ensemble

Dominic Nolfi
Ensemble

Saycon Sengbloh
Ensemble

Ryan Shaw
Ensemble

Jamal Story
*Ensemble,
Dance Captain*

Eric LaJuan
Summers
Ensemble

Ephraim M. Sykes
Ensemble

Julius Thomas III
Ensemble

Daniel J. Watts
Ensemble

Donald Webber, Jr.
Ensemble

Berry Gordy
Book, Producer

Charles
Randolph-Wright
Director

Patricia Wilcox
Choreographer

Warren Adams
Choreographer

David Korins
Scenic Design

ESosa
Costume Design

Natasha Katz
Lighting Design

Peter Hylenski
Sound Design

Daniel Brodie
Projection Design

Ethan Popp
*Music Supervision,
Orchestrations,
Arrangements*

Bryan Crook
*Orchestrations,
Additional
Arrangements*

Zane Mark
*Dance Music
Arrangements*

Joseph Joubert
*Music Director,
Conductor*

Michael Keller
Music Coordinator

Motown: The Musical

Bernard Telsey
Telsey + Company
Casting

Charles G. LaPointe
Hair & Wig Design

J. Jared Janas
Make-up Design

David Goldsmith
Script Consultant

Dick Scanlan
Script Consultant

David Benken
Technical Supervisor

Rod Lemmond
Associate Scenic Designer

Matthew Lacey
Stage Manager

Cody Renard Richard
Assistant Stage Manager

Marcia Pendelton
Walk Tall Girl Productions
Marketing Outreach

Maggie Brohn
Bespoke Theatricals
General Management

Amy Jacobs
Bespoke Theatricals
General Management

Devin Keudell
Bespoke Theatricals
General Management

Nina Lannan
Executive Producer
Bespoke Theatricals
General Management

Kevin McCollum
Producer

Doug Morris
Producer

Darius Kaleb
Young Berry Gordy, Stevie, Michael

Photos by Brian Mapp

BOX OFFICE
Front (L-R): Thomas Waxman, Marc Needleman
Back (L-R): Joe Olcese (Treasurer), Kevin Lynch (Asst. Treasurer)

CREW
Front Row (L-R): Michael L. Shepp, Jr. (Deck Automation), Jeff Zink (Head Carpenter), Teofesta Pusillo (Dresser), Lisa Wellington Swift (Child Guardian), Amanda Duffy (Hair), Brandon Bolton (Assistant Hair Supervisor), Heather Wright (Hair Supervisor), Aughra Moon (Dresser), Jerome Parker (Dresser)
Second Row (L-R): Julia P. Jones (Production Stage Manager), Michael Hyman (Electrician), Anne C. Cline (Dresser), Patti Luther (Dresser), Anna Hoffman (Hair)
Third Row (L-R): Amber Dickerson (Stage Manager), Melissa Joy Crawford (Assistant Wardrobe Supervisor), Sherry Wong (Dresser), Vangeli Kaseluris (Dresser), Amanda Zane (Dresser), Lisa Fraley (Hair), Kathleen Martin (Dresser), Adele Miskie (Dresser), Denise J. Grillo (Props), Savana Leveille (Dresser), Jesse Stevens (Production Sound), Ronald Fleming (Dresser)
Back Row (L-R): Danny Viscardo (House Props), David Grevengoed (Dresser), David Brickman (House Electrician), Cody Renard Richard (Stage Manager), James Hodges (Hair), Kevin Maybee (Hair), Elizabeth Hirons (Dresser), James Roy (Dresser), Eric "Speed" Smith (Assistant Production Props)

Motown: The Musical

BOX OFFICE LOBBY CREW
(L-R): Spencer Cordeiro, Paul Perez, Barry Jenkins (Head Porter),
Tracey Malinowski (House Manager), Leroy Stonekeep

BOX OFFICE/MANAGEMENT
(L-R): Joe Olcese (Treasurer), Nathan Gehan (Company
Manager), Kevin Lynch (Assistant Treasurer)

Photos by Brian Mapp

FRONT OF HOUSE
Front Row (L-R): Kirstin DeCicco, Raymond Luke, Jr. (actor), Raymond Luke, Sr., Tracey Malinowski (House Manager)
Second Row (L-R): Stephanie Colon, Evelyn Fernandez, Brenden Imperato, Lauren Banyai
Third Row (L-R): Angalic Cortes, Stephanie Martinez
Fourth Row (L-R): Madeline Flores, Melissa Ocasio, Philip Zhang, Jessica Gonzalez (Chief Usher), Roberto Calderon (standing)
Fifth Row (L-R): Joanne DeCicco, Carmela Cambio
Sixth Row (L-R): Sheron Richardson, Sharon Grant, Charles Thompson, Richard Darbasie
Back Row (L-R): Kayla Christie, Anthony Marcello, Bryant Reeves

Motown: The Musical

STAFF FOR *MOTOWN*

GENERAL MANAGEMENT
BESPOKE THEATRICALS
Maggie Brohn
Amy Jacobs   Devin Keudell   Nina Lannan
Associate General Manager ....David Roth

Company Manager
Nathan Gehan
Associate Company Manager
Michelle H. Tamagawa

PRODUCTION MANAGEMENT
David Benken   Rose Palombo

GENERAL PRESS REPRESENTATIVE
BONEAU/BRYAN-BROWN
Adrian Bryan-Brown
Joe Perrotta   Michael Strassheim

WEST GRAND MEDIA PRODUCTIONS
Michael Lovesmith, President
Brenda Boyce, Director of Creative Services/Archivist

CASTING
TELSEY + COMPANY
Bernie Telsey CSA, Will Cantler CSA,
David Vaccari CSA,
Bethany Knox CSA, Craig Burns CSA,
Tiffany Little Canfield CSA,
Rachel Hoffman CSA,
Justin Huff CSA, Patrick Goodwin CSA,
Abbie Brady-Dalton CSA,
David Morris, Cesar A. Rocha CSA,
Andrew Femenella, Karyn Casl CSA,
Kristina Bramhall, Jessie Malone, Conrad Woolfe

MARKETING SERVICES
SPOTCO
Nick Pramik   Kristen Rathbun   Julie Wechsler

PRODUCTION
STAGE MANAGER ....**Julia P. Jones**
Stage Manager ....Matthew Lacey
Assistant Stage Manager ....Amber Dickerson
Assistant Stage Manager ....Cody Renard Richard
Dance Captain ....Jamal Story
Assistant Dance Captain ....Dionne Figgins
Associate Scenic Designer ....Rod Lemmond
Assistant Scenic Designer ....Amanda Stephens
Assistants to Scenic Designer ....Stephen Edwards,
Miriam Grill, Emily Inglis,
Sarah Wreede
Associate Costume Designer ....Cathy Parrott
Assistant Costume Designers ....Sarah Sophia Lidz,
Robert J. Martin, Aileen Abercrombie
Assistant to Costume Designer ....Will Lowry
Associate Lighting Designer ....Aaron Spivey
Assistant Lighting Designer ....Ken Elliott
Moving Light Programmer ....Sean Beach
Projection Programmer ....Patrick Southern
Assistant
Projection Designer ....Hannelore Williams

Lead Projections Animation ....Gabriel Aronson
Interactive Projection Programmer ....Michael Kohler
Assistant
Projections Animation ....Allison Pottasch
Projections Intern ....Stormy Pyeatte
Associate Sound Designer ....Keith Caggiano
Associate to the
Hair Designer ....Leah Loukas
Assistant to the
Hair Designer ....Gretchen Androsavich

Makeup Designer ....J. Jared Janas

Associate Makeup Designer ....Elias Aguirre
Production Carpenter ....Patrick Eviston
Head Carpenter ....Jeff Zink
Deck Automation ....Michael L. Shepp, Jr.
Fly Automation ....John McPherson
Production Electrician ....Michael Pitzer
Advance Electrician ....Jeremy Wahlers
Head Electrician ....Michael Hyman
Production Sound ....Phil Lojo
Advance Sound ....Darren Shaw
Head Sound ....Jesse Stevens
Production/Head Properties ....Denise J. Grillo
Assistant Props ....Eric Speed Smith
Props Shopper ....Keen Gat
Technical Production Assistant ....Lisa Jaeger
Wardrobe Supervisor ....Christina M. Ainge
Assistant
Wardrobe Supervisor ....Melissa Joy Crawford
Dressers ....Ron Fleming,
David Grevengoed, Richard Gross,
Elizabeth Hirons, Vangeli Kaseluris,
Savana Leveille, Patti Luther,
Kat Martin, Adele Miskie,
Pinky Pusillo, Erin Roth,
James Roy, Sherry Wong
Seamstress....................................Aughra Moon
Hair/Wig Supervisor ....Heather Wright
Hair Assistants ....Brandon Bolton,
Amanda Duffy, Lisa Fraley,
James Hodges, Anna Hoffman,
Kevin Maybee
Production Music Associate ....Darren Ledbetter
Chromatic Harmonica ....Rob Paparozzi
Associate Keyboard Programmer ....Tim Crook
Tutoring ....On Location Education
Children's Guardian ....Lisa Wellington Swift
Costume Shopper ....Isabelle Simone
Costume Interns ....Emma Bonoli, Amy Price
Production Assistants ....Kayliane Burns,
Chris Crowthers, Lizzy Lee,
Anne McPherson, Michael Ulreich
Assistant to Mr. Gordy ....Mario Escobar
Assistant to Mr. Morris ....Jane Ellis
Assistant to Mr. McCollum ....Lucas McMahon
Assistant to
Mr. Randolph-Wright ....Rashad Anthony
Orthopedist ....David S. Weiss, MD/
NYU Langone Medical Center
Physical Therapy ....Encore Physical Therapy/
Mark Hunter Hall
Production Photographer ....Joan Marcus

Advertising ....SpotCo/Drew Hodges,
Jim Edwards, Tom Greenwald,
Ilene Rosen, Beth Watson,
Corey Schwitz, Laura Fraenkel,
Mary Rose Curry
Online/Digital Interactive ....SpotCo/
Kristen Bardwil, Amanda Baker,
Sheila Collins, Callie Goff,
Rebecca Cohen, Marisa Delmore,
Shelby Ladd, Marc Mettler
Accountant ....Robert Fried CPA/
Fried & Kowgios CPAS LLP
Comptroller ....Galbraith & Company/
Tabitha Falcone
General Management Associates ....Danielle Saks,
Jimmy Wilson
General Management
Interns ....Valentina Berger Maurett,
Brent Winzek
Insurance ....AON Albert G. Ruben
Insurance Services, Inc./Claudia Kaufman
Banking ....Signature Bank/Margaret Monigan
Payroll ....Checks and Balances Payroll Inc.
Travel Agent ....Tzell Travel/The "A" Team,
Andi Henig
Legal Counsel ....Levine Plotkin & Menin, LLP
Legal Counsel ....Franklin, Weinrib,
Rudell & Vassallo, P.C.
Merchandising ....Bravado
Opening Night
Coordination ....STAMP Event Management

CREDITS

Scenery and automation constructed by Hudson Scenic Studios. Scenery and props constructed by Proof Productions, Inc. and Daedalus Design and Production Inc. Costumes by Artur & Tailors; Beckenstein's Men's Fabric Czar; Cygnet Studio, Inc.; Giliberto Designs Inc.; Katrina Patterns; Maggie Dick; Timberlake Studio; Scafati; Tricorne, Inc.; Fur and Furgery, Arel Studios. Lighting equipment by PRG Lighting, Inc. Sound equipment by PRG Sound, Inc. Video projection system is provided by WorldStage Inc. Custom shoes by T.O. Dey and Worldtone. Custom beading by Tricorne, Inc. Millinery by Arnold Levine and JJ Hat Center. Custom painting by Hochi Asiatico. Gloves by LaCrasia. Military and security uniforms supplied by Jim Korn and KSI NYC. Props by Paragon Theme and Prop Fabrication, Craig Gregg and Zoe Morsette. Cosmetics sponsor: IMAN Cosmetics. Onstage guitars compliments of Gibson Guitars USA. Special thanks to Bra*Tenders, Brooks Brothers and Michael Santulli.

The producers wish to thank and acknowledge
Marty Bandier for his support of this production.

SPONSORS
American Airlines
Chrysler
Swarovski Crystal

Motown: The Musical rehearsed at the
New 42nd Street Studios

Motown: The Musical

The official home of Hitsville U.S.A.
MOTOWN MUSEUM
www.motownmuseum.org

www.motownthemusical.com

MUSIC CREDITS

"**ABC**" by Mizell, Alphonso J./Perren, Freddie/Richards, Deke/Gordy, Berry Jr./Jobete Music Co. Inc. (ASCAP). "**A Breathtaking Guy**" by Robinson, Smokey/Jobete Music Co. Inc. (ASCAP). "**Ain't No Mountain High Enough**" by Simpson, Valerie/Ashford, Nickolas/Jobete Music Co. Inc. (ASCAP). "**Ain't Too Proud to Beg**" by Whitfield, Norman J./Holland, Edward, Jr./Stone Agate Music (BMI). "**All Night Long**" by Richie, Lionel, Brenda Richie Publishing, Brockman Music (ASCAP). "**Baby I Need Your Loving**" by Holland, Brian/Holland, Edward, Jr./Dozier, Lamont Herbert/Stone Agate Music (BMI. "**Baby Love**" by Holland, Brian/Holland, Edward, Jr./ Dozier, Lamont Herbert/Stone Agate Music (BMI). "**Ball of Confusion (That's What the World Is Today)**" by Whitfield, Norman J./Strong, Barrett/Stone Agate Music (BMI). "**Brick House**" by Richie, Lionel/Lapread, Ronald/Orange, Walter/Williams, Milan/McClary, Thomas/King, William/Jobete Music Co. Inc. OBO itself and Cambrae Music/Hanna Music/Libren Music/Macawrite Music/Old Fashion Publishing/Walter Orange Music (ASCAP). "**Buttered Popcorn**" by Gordy, Berry Jr./Ales, Barney/Jobete Music Co. Inc. (ASCAP)/Stone Agate Music (BMI). "**Bye Bye Baby**" by Wells, Mary/Stone Agate Music (BMI). "**Can I Close the Door**" Written by Berry Gordy and Michael Lovesmith. "**Cruisin'**" by Robinson, Smokey/Tarplin, Marvin/Jobete Music Co. Inc. OBO Bertam Music Company (ASCAP). "**Dancing in the Street**" by Gaye, Marvin P./Hunter, Ivy Jo/Stevenson, William/Stone Agate Music (BMI)/Jobete Music Co. Inc. OBO itself and MGIII Music, NMG Music and FCG Music (ASCAP). "**Do You Love Me**" by Gordy, Berry Jr./Jobete Music Co. Inc. (ASCAP). "**Get Ready**" by Robinson, Smokey/Jobete Music Co. Inc. (ASCAP). "**Give It to Me Baby**" by James, Rick/Jobete Music Co. Inc. (ASCAP). "**Good Morning Heartache**" by Drake, Ervin M./Fisher, Dan/Higginbotham, Irene/Lindabet Music Corporation, Microhits Music Corp., Sony/ATV Tunes, LLC. (ASCAP). "**Got a Job**" by Robinson, Smokey/Gordy, Berry Jr./Carlo, Tyran/Jobete Music Co. Inc. obo itself and Taj Mahal Music/Third Above Music Inc. (ASCAP). "**Happy Birthday**" by Wonder, Stevie/Jobete Music Co. Inc. and Black Bull Music c/o EMI April Music Inc. (ASCAP). "**Hey Joe (Black Like Me)**" Written by Berry Gordy and Michael Lovesmith. "**I Can't Get Next to You**" by Whitfield, Norman J./Strong, Barrett/Stone Agate Music (BMI). "**I Can't Help Myself (Sugar Pie Honey Bunch)**" by Holland, Brian/Dozier, Lamont Herbert/Holland, Edward, Jr./Stone Agate Music (BMI). "**I Hear a Symphony**" by Holland, Brian/Dozier, Lamont Herbert/ Holland, Edward, Jr./Stone Agate Music (BMI). "**I Heard It Through the Grapevine**" by Whitfield, Norman J./Strong, Barrett/Stone Agate Music (BMI). "**(I Know) I'm Losing You**" by Whitfield, Norman J./Holland, Edward, Jr./Grant, Cornelius/Stone Agate Music (BMI). "**I'll Be There**" by Davis, Hal/Gordy, Berry Jr./West, Bob/Hutch, Willie/Jobete Music Co. Inc. (ASCAP). "**Inner City Blues (Make Me Wanna Holler)**" by Gaye, Marvin P./Nyx, James/Jobete Music Co. Inc. obo itself and MGIII Music, NMG Music and FCG Music (ASCAP). "**It's What's in the Grooves That Counts**" Written by Berry Gordy and Michael Lovesmith. "**Itsy Bitsy Teeny Weeny Yellow Polka Dot Bikini**" by Pockriss, Lee J./Vance, Paul/Emily Music Corp, Music Sales Corp (ASCAP). "**I Want You Back**" by Perren, Freddie/Mizell, Alphonso J./Gordy, Berry Jr./Richards, Deke/Jobete Music Co. Inc. (ASCAP). "**Lonely Teardrops**" by Gordy, Berry Jr./Fuqua, Gwendolyn Gordy/Carlo, Tyran/Jobete Music Co. Inc. obo Old Brompton Road Music. (ASCAP)/Third Above Music Inc. (ASCAP). "**Love Is Here and Now You're Gone**" by Holland, Brian/Dozier, Lamont Herbert/Holland, Edward, Jr./Stone Agate Music (BMI). "**Mama Done Told Me (My)**" by Robinson, Smokey/Gordy, Berry Jr./Carlo, Tyran/Jobete Music Co. Inc. (ASCAP). "**Mercy Mercy Me (The Ecology)**" by Gaye, Marvin P./Jobete Music Co. Inc. obo itself and MGIII Music, NMG Music and FCG Music (ASCAP). "**Money (That's What I Want)**" by Gordy, Berry Jr./Bradford, Janie/Jobete Music Co. Inc. (ASCAP)/Stone Agate Music (BMI). "**My Girl**" by White, Ronald/Robinson, Smokey/Jobete Music Co. Inc. (ASCAP). "**My Guy**" by Robinson, Smokey/Jobete Music Co. Inc. (ASCAP). "**Papa Was a Rollin' Stone**" by Whitfield, Norman J./Strong, Barrett/Stone Diamond Music Corp. (BMI). "**Please, Mr. Postman**" by Garrett, William/Dobbins, Georgia/Holland, Brian/Gorman, Freddie/Bateman, Robert/Jobete Music Co. Inc. (ASCAP)/Stone Diamond Music Corp. (BMI)/EMI Blackwood Music Inc. (BMI). "**Reach Out and Touch (Somebody's Hand)**" by Ashford, Nickolas/Simpson, Valerie/Jobete Music Co. Inc. (ASCAP). "**Reach Out I'll Be There**" by Holland, Brian/Dozier, Lamont Herbert/Holland, Edward, Jr./Stone Agate Music (BMI). "**Reet Petite (The Sweetest Girl in Town)**" by Gordy, Berry Jr./Carlo, Tyran/Jobete Music Co. Inc. (ASCAP)/Third Above Music Inc. (ASCAP). "**Remember Me**" by Ashford, Nickolas/Simpson, Valerie/Jobete Music Co. Inc. (ASCAP). "**Shop Around**" by Robinson, Smokey/Gordy, Berry Jr./Jobete Music Co. Inc. (ASCAP). "**Shotgun**" by Dewalt, Autry/Stone Agate Music (BMI). "**Signed Sealed Delivered I'm Yours**" by Wonder, Stevie/Wright, Syreeta/Garrett, Lee/Hardaway, Lula Mae/Jobete Music Co. Inc. and Black Bull Music c/o EMI April Music Inc. (ASCAP)/Swandi Music (BMI) c/o EMI Blackwood Music Inc. (BMI). "**Square Biz**" by Brockert, Mary C./MC Grier, Allen, Henry/Jobete Music Co. Inc. obo itself and McNella Music (ASCAP). "**Stop in the Name of Love**" by Holland, Brian/Dozier, Lamont Herbert/Holland, Edward, Jr./Stone Agate Music (BMI). "**Stubborn Kind of Fellow**" by Gaye, Marvin P./Gordy, George/Stevenson, William Stone Agate Music (BMI)/Jobete Music Co. Inc. obo itself aAnd MGIII Music, NMG Music and FCG Music (ASCAP). "**Super Freak**" by James, Rick/Miller, Alonzo Jobete Music Co. Inc. (ASCAP)/Stone Diamond Music Corp. (BMI). "**The Happening**" by Dozier, Lamont Herbert/Holland, Edward, Jr./Holland, Brian/De Vol, Frank/Jobete Music Co. Inc. (ASCAP)/Stone Agate Music (BMI. "**The Love You Save**" by Perren, Freddie/Mizell, Alphonso J./Gordy, Berry Jr./Richards, Deke/Jobete Music Co. Inc. (ASCAP). "**Theme From Mahogany 'Do You Know Where You're Going To'**" by Goffin, Gerry/Masser, Michael/Jobete Music Co. Inc. (ASCAP)/Screen Gems-EMI Music Inc. (BMI). "**To Be Loved**" by Gordy, Berry Jr./Fuqua, Gwendolyn Gordy/Carlo, Tyran/Jobete Music Co. Inc. obo Old Brompton Road Music. (ASCAP)/Third Above Music Inc. (ASCAP). "**Two Lovers**" by Robinson, Smokey/Jobete Music Co. Inc. (ASCAP). "**War**" by Whitfield, Norman J./Strong, Barrett/Stone Agate Music (BMI). "**What Christmas Means to Me**" by Gordy, George/Story, Allen/Gaye, Anna Gordy/Jobete Music Co. Inc. (ASCAP)/Stone Agate Music (BMI). "**What's Going On**" by Benson, Renaldo/Cleveland, Alfred W./Gaye, Marvin P./Stone Agate Music (BMI)/Jobete Music Co. Inc. obo itself and MGIII Music, NMG Music and FCG Music (ASCAP). "**Where Did Our Love Go**" by Holland, Edward, Jr./Holland, Brian/Dozier, Lamont Herbert/Stone Agate Music (BMI). "**Who's Lovin' You**" by Robinson, Smokey/Jobete Music Co. Inc. (ASCAP). "**You Are the Sunshine of My Life**" by Wonder, Stevie/Jobete Music Co. Inc. and Black Bull Music c/o EMI April Music Inc. (ASCAP). "**You Are You**" Written by Berry Gordy and Michael Lovesmith. "**You Can't Hurry Love**" by Holland, Edward, Jr./Holland, Brian/Dozier, Lamont Herbert/Stone Agate Music (BMI). "**You're All I Need to Get By**" by Ashford, Nickolas/Simpson, Valerie/Jobete Music Co. Inc. (ASCAP). "**You're Nobody 'Til Somebody Loves You**" by Cavanaugh, James/Morgan, Russ/Stock, Larry/Larry Stock Music Co.; Shapiro Bernstein & Co., Inc.; Southern Music Publishing Co., Inc. (ASCAP). "**You've Really Got a Hold on Me**" by Robinson, Smokey/Jobete Music Co. Inc. (ASCAP).

NEDERLANDER

Chairman	James M. Nederlander
President	James L. Nederlander

Executive Vice President
Nick Scandalios

Vice President	Senior Vice President
Corporate Development	Labor Relations
Charlene S. Nederlander	**Herschel Waxman**

Vice President	Chief Financial Officer
Jim Boese	**Freida Sawyer Belviso**

STAFF FOR THE LUNT-FONTANNE

House Manager	Tracey Malinowski
Treasurer	Joe Olcese
Assistant Treasurer	Kevin Lynch
House Carpenter	Terry Taylor
House Electrician	Dennis Boyle
House Propertyman	Andrew Bentz
House Flyman	Matt Walters
House Engineers	Robert MacMahon, Joseph Riccio III

2012-2013 AWARDS

THEATRE WORLD AWARD
For Outstanding Broadway
or Off-Broadway Debut
(Valisia LeKae)

FRED AND ADELE ASTAIRE AWARDS
Outstanding Choreography
of a Broadway Show
(Patricia Wilcox & Warren Adams)
Outstanding Male Dancer in a Broadway Show
(Eric LaJuan Summers)

The Mystery of Edwin Drood

First Preview: October 19, 2012. Opened: November 13, 2012.
Limited Engagement. Closed March 10, 2013 after 28 Previews and 136 Performances.

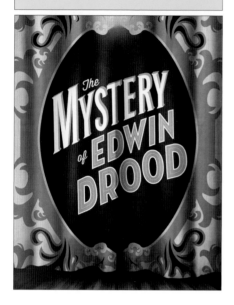

PLAYBILL

Revival of the 1985 Tony-winning musical based on a murder mystery novel that author Charles Dickens left incomplete upon his death. In rural Cloisterham, young man Edwin Drood vanishes on Christmas Eve, leaving an abundance of possible killers. The story is framed as a presentation at a Victorian English music hall, and is notable for having multiple endings. Given the clues, the audience votes to determine which ending will be played at that performance.

CAST

(in order of appearance)

Chairman/Mr. William Cartwright ..JIM NORTON
Stage Manager and Barkeep/
   Mr. James Throttle ....NICK CORLEY
John Jasper/Mr. Clive Paget ....WILL CHASE
Edwin Drood/
   Miss Alice Nutting ......STEPHANIE J. BLOCK
Rosa Bud/Miss Deirdre Peregrine ...BETSY WOLFE
Beatrice/Miss Violet Balfour .....ALISON CIMMET
Wendy/Miss Isabel Yearsley ....JANINE DiVITA
Helena Landless/
   Miss Janet Conover ....JESSIE MUELLER
The Reverend Mr. Crisparkle/
   Mr. Cedric Moncrieffe ......GREGG EDELMAN
Neville Landless/
   Mr. Victor Grinstead ....ANDY KARL
The Princess Puffer/
   Miss Angela Prysock ....CHITA RIVERA
Durdles/
   Mr. Nick Cricker ....ROBERT CREIGHTON

Continued on next page

STUDIO 54

ROUNDABOUT THEATRE COMPANY

Todd Haimes, Artistic Director
Harold Wolpert, Managing Director
Julia C. Levy, Executive Director

Presents

Stephanie J. Block   Will Chase   Gregg Edelman   Jim Norton

and

Chita Rivera

in

The MYSTERY of EDWIN DROOD

Book, Music, and Lyrics by
Rupert Holmes

with

Andy Karl   Jessie Mueller   Betsy Wolfe

Nicholas Barasch   Peter Benson   Robert Creighton

Alison Cimmet   Kyle Coffman   Nick Corley   Janine DiVita   Jenifer Foote   Justin Greer
Shannon Lewis   Spencer Plachy   Kiira Schmidt   Eric Sciotto   Jim Walton

Set Design	*Costume Design*	*Lighting Design*	*Sound Design*
Anna Louizos	William Ivey Long	Brian Nason	Tony Meola

Orchestrations	*Dance Arrangements*	*Hair & Wig Design*	*Make-up Design*	*Dialect Coach*
Rupert Holmes	Sam Davis	Paul Huntley	Angelina Avallone	Kate Wilson

Production Stage Manager	*Casting*	*Associate Director*	*Associate Choreographer*	*Technical Supervisor*
Lori M. Doyle	Jim Carnahan, C.S.A. Carrie Gardner, C.S.A. Stephen Kopel, C.S.A.	Dave Solomon	Angie Canuel	Steve Beers

Associate Managing Director	*Director of Marketing & Audience Development*	*Director of Development*	*Press Representative*
Greg Backstrom	Tom O'Connor	Lynne Gugenheim Gregory	Boneau/Bryan-Brown

Founding Director	*Adams Associate Artistic Director**
Gene Feist	Scott Ellis

Executive Producer
Sydney Beers

Musical Direction by
Paul Gemignani

Choreography by
Warren Carlyle

Directed by
Scott Ellis

The Mystery of Edwin Drood is suggested by the unfinished novel by Charles Dickens.
Major support for *The Mystery of Edwin Drood* provided by The Blanche and Irving Laurie Foundation.
The Mystery of Edwin Drood benefits from Roundabout's Musical Theatre Fund, with gifts from
Marty and Perry Granoff, HRH Foundation, Peter and Leni May, and Tom and Diane Tuft.
*Generously underwritten by Margot Adams, in memory of Mason Adams.
Roundabout Theatre Company is a member of the League of Resident Theatres.
www.roundabouttheatre.org

11/13/12

(L-R): WIll Chase and Stephanie J. Block

Photo by Joan Marcus

The Mystery of Edwin Drood

MUSICAL SYNOPSIS

SETTING
London's Music Hall Royale, 1895

ACT I

"THERE YOU ARE"	Chairman & Company
"A MAN COULD GO QUITE MAD"	Jasper
"TWO KINSMEN"	Drood & Jasper
"MOONFALL"	Rosa
"MOONFALL QUARTET"	Helena, Rosa, Wendy, Beatrice
"THE WAGES OF SIN"	Puffer, with Company
"JASPER'S VISION/SMOKE BALLET"	
"CEYLON/A BRITISH SUBJECT"	Helena, Neville, Drood, Rosa, Crisparkle, with Company
"BOTH SIDES OF THE COIN"	Jasper & Chairman, with Company
"PERFECT STRANGERS"	Drood & Rosa
"NO GOOD CAN COME FROM BAD"	Neville, Rosa, Helena, Drood, Crisparkle, Jasper & Waiters, with Ensemble
"NEVER THE LUCK"	Bazzard, with Company
"OFF TO THE RACES"	Chairman, Durdles & Deputy, with Company

ACT II

"AN ENGLISH MUSIC HALL"	Chairman & Company
"SETTLING UP THE SCORE"	Datchery & Puffer, with Company
"THE NAME OF LOVE/MOONFALL (REPRISE)"	Rosa & Jasper, with Company
"DON'T QUIT WHILE YOU'RE AHEAD"	Puffer & Company
"THE SOLUTION"	Company

ORCHESTRA
Conductor: PAUL GEMIGNANI
Associate Conductor: MARK MITCHELL
Assistant Conductor: TONY GERALIS
Strings: SYLVIA D'AVANZO, LOUISE OWEN, MARY WHITAKER, ROGER SHELL
Woodwinds: ERIC WEIDMAN, JULIE FERRARA, DON McGEEN
Brass: DOMINIC DERASSE, MICHAEL ATKINSON, BRUCE EIDEM, DEAN PLANK

Rhythm Section: MARK MITCHELL, TONY GERALIS, JOHN BEAL, PAUL PIZZUTI
Synthesizer Programmer: RANDY COHEN

Music Copying: Emily Grishman Music Preparation—KATHARINE EDMONDS/ EMILY GRISHMAN

Cast Continued

Deputy/
Master Nick Cricker ....NICHOLAS BARASCH
Bazzard/Mr. Phillip Bax ....PETER BENSON
The Citizens of Cloisterham:
Miss Violet Balfour ....ALISON CIMMET
Mr. Christopher Lyon ....KYLE COFFMAN
Mr. James Throttle ....NICK CORLEY
Miss Isabel Yearsley ....JANINE DiVITA
Miss Florence Gill ....SHANNON LEWIS
Mr. Harry Sayle ....SPENCER PLACHY
Miss Gwendolen Pynn ....KIIRA SCHMIDT
Mr. Alan Eliot ....ERIC SCIOTTO
Mr. Montague Pruitt ....JIM WALTON

SWINGS
JENIFER FOOTE, JUSTIN GREER

UNDERSTUDIES
For Deputy:
KYLE COFFMAN
For Bazzard, Durdles, Rev. Mr. Crisparkle:
NICK CORLEY
For Edwin Drood, Rosa Bud:
JANINE DiVITA
For John Jasper, Neville Landless:
SPENCER PLACHY, ERIC SCIOTTO
For Helena Landless, Princess Puffer:
ALISON CIMMET
For Rev. Mr. Crisparkle, Chairman:
JIM WALTON

Production Stage Manager ....LORI M. DOYLE
Stage Manager ......SCOTT TAYLOR ROLLISON
Dance Captain ....JUSTIN GREER

Stephanie J. Block
Alice Nutting/ Edwin Drood

Will Chase
John Jasper/ Mr. Clive Paget

Gregg Edelman
Reverend Mr. Crisparkle/Mr. Cedric Moncrieffe

Jim Norton
Chairman/ Mr. William Cartwright

Chita Rivera
The Princess Puffer/Miss Angela Prysock

Andy Karl
Neville Landless/ Mr. Victor Grinstead

Jessie Mueller
Helena Landless/ Miss Janet Conover

The Mystery of Edwin Drood

Betsy Wolfe
Rosa Bud/Miss Deirdre Peregrine

Nicholas Barasch
Deputy/Master Nick Cricker

Peter Benson
Bazzard/ Mr. Phillip Bax

Robert Creighton
Durdles/ Mr. Nick Cricker

Alison Cimmet
Beatrice/Miss Violet Balfour, u/s Helena Landless, Princess Puffer

Kyle Coffman
Mr. Christopher Lyon, u/s Deputy

Nick Corley
Stage Manager and Barkeep/Mr. James Throttle, u/s Bazzard, Durdles, Rev. Mr. Crisparkle

Janine DiVita
Wendy/Miss Isabel Yearsley, u/s Edwin Drood, Rosa Bud

Jenifer Foote
Swing

Justin Greer
Swing

Shannon Lewis
Miss Florence Gill

Spencer Plachy
Mr. Harry Sayle, u/s John Jasper, Neville Landless

Kiira Schmidt
Miss Gwendolen Pynn

Eric Sciotto
Mr. Alan Eliot, u/s John Jasper, Neville Landless

Jim Walton
Mr. Montague Pruitt, u/s Rev. Mr. Crisparkle, Chairman

Rupert Holmes
Book, Music, Lyrics & Orchestrations

Scott Ellis
Director

Warren Carlyle
Choreographer

Paul Gemignani
Music Direction

Anna Louizos
Set Design

William Ivey Long
Costume Design

Brian Nason
Lighting Design

Tony Meola
Sound Design

Sam Davis
Dance Arrangements

Paul Huntley
Hair and Wig Design

Angelina Avallone
Make-up Design

Dave Solomon
Associate Director

Angie Canuel
Associate Choreographer

Kate Wilson
Dialect Coach

Teressa Jennings
Associate to Rupert Holmes

Jim Carnahan
Casting

Stephen Kopel
Casting

Carrie Gardner
Casting

Gene Feist
Founding Director Roundabout Theatre Company

Todd Haimes
Artistic Director Roundabout Theatre Company

The Mystery of Edwin Drood

Erin Davie
Rosa Bud/Miss Deirdre Peregrine

Andrew Samonsky
Neville Landless/ Mr. Victor Grinstead

Photos by Brian Mapp

MUSICIANS
(L-R): Julie Ferrara, Mark Mitchell, Dean Plank, Don McGeen

2012-2013 AWARD

DRAMA DESK AWARD
Outstanding Sound Design
in a Musical
(Tony Meola)

WARDROBE AND HAIR
Front Row (L-R):
Carrie Rohm, Sam Brooks,
Jessica Selig,
Joe Hickey,
Mikey Goodmark
Back Row (L-R):
Stacy Sarmiento,
Ashley Leitzel, Kelly Reed,
Katherine Sorg,
Jessica Scoblick,
Rosemary Bentinck

STAGE MANAGEMENT
(L-R): Scott Taylor Rollison (Stage Manager), James Lawson
(Company Manager),Lori M. Doyle (Production Stage Manager),
Zac Chandler (Assistant Stage Manager)

BOX OFFICE
(L-R): Joe Clark,
Laura Marshall,
Carlos Morris

FRONT OF HOUSE
Front (L-R): Victor Rosa, Justin Brown, LaConya Robinson
On Stairs from top: Essence Mason, Linda Gjonbalaj, Samantha Rivera, John Acosta,
Aaron Netsky, Shirelle Ruddock

CREW
Front Row (L-R): Lawrence Jennino, Erin Delaney, Peter Malbuisson, Erika Warmbrunn, Francis Elers, Dorion Fuchs, Josh Maszle
Back Row (L-R): Julie Sandy, Dan Mendeloff, Thomas Goehring, Dan Hoffman, Steve Jones, John Wooding, Craig Van Tassel, Jessica Morton

The Mystery of Edwin Drood

ROUNDABOUT THEATRE COMPANY STAFF
ARTISTIC DIRECTOR ....**TODD HAIMES**
MANAGING DIRECTOR ....**HAROLD WOLPERT**
EXECUTIVE DIRECTOR ....**JULIA C. LEVY**
ADAMS ASSOCIATE
   ARTISTIC DIRECTOR ....**SCOTT ELLIS**

ARTISTIC STAFF

DIRECTOR OF ARTISTIC DEVELOPMENT/
  DIRECTOR OF CASTING ....Jim Carnahan
Artistic Consultant ....Robyn Goodman
Resident Directors ....Doug Hughes, Sam Gold
Associate Artists ....Mark Brokaw, Scott Elliott,
           Bill Irwin, Joe Mantello,
        Kathleen Marshall, Theresa Rebeck
Literary Manager ....Jill Rafson
Senior Casting Director ....Carrie Gardner
Casting Director ....Stephen Kopel
Casting Associate ....Jillian Cimini
Casting Assistants ....Lain Kunin, Rachel Reichblum
Artistic Associate ....Amy Ashton
Literary Associate ....Josh Fiedler
The Blanche and Irving Laurie Foundation
  Theatre Visions Fund
    Commissions ....David West Read
Educational Foundation of
  America Commissions ....Bekah Brunstetter,
        Lydia Diamond, Diana Fithian,
          Julie Marie Myatt
Roundabout Commissions.............Helen Edmundson,
      Andrew Hinderaker, Stephen Karam,
      Steven Levenson, Matthew Lopez,
          Kim Rosenstock
Casting Interns ....Eric Byrd, Cat Gagliotti,
        Rebecca Henin, Krystal Rowley
Script Readers ....Shannon Deep, Ben Izzo,
         Liz Malta, Alexis Roblan
Artistic Apprentice ....Nikki DiLoreto

EDUCATION STAFF

EDUCATION DIRECTOR ....Greg McCaslin
Associate Education Director ....Jennifer DiBella
Education Program Manager ....Aliza Greenberg
Education Program Associate ....Sarah Malone
Education Assistant ....Lou-Lou Igbokwe
Education Dramaturg ....Ted Sod
Teaching Artists ....Josh Allen, Cynthia Babak,
        Victor Barbella, LaTonya Borsay,
     Mark Bruckner, Chloe Chapin, Joe Doran,
    Elizabeth Dunn-Ruiz, Carrie Ellman-Larsen,
     Theresa Flanagan, Deanna Frieman,
    Sheri Graubert, Adam Gwon, Devin Haqq,
    Carrie Heitman, Karla Hendrick, Jason Jacobs,
   Alana Jacoby, Lisa Renee Jordan, Jamie Kalama,
    Alvin Keith, Erin McCready, James Miles,
   Nick Moore, Meghan O'Neil, Drew Peterson,
    Nicole Press, Leah Reddy, Amanda Rehbein,
   Nick Simone, Heidi Stallings, Daniel Sullivan,
   Carl Tallent, Vickie Tanner, Larine Towler,
    Jennifer Varbalow, Kathryn Veillette,
    Leese Walker, Gail Winar, Chad Yarborough
Teaching Artist Emeritus ....Reneé Flemings
Education Apprentice ....Maia Collier

EXECUTIVE ADMINISTRATIVE STAFF

ASSOCIATE MANAGING
  DIRECTOR....................Greg Backstrom
Assistant Managing Director ....Katharine Croke
Assistant to the Managing Director .....Christina Pezzello
Assistant to the Executive Director ....Nicole Tingir

MANAGEMENT/ADMINISTRATIVE STAFF

GENERAL MANAGER ....Sydney Beers
General Manager,
  American Airlines Theatre ....Denise Cooper
General Manager,
  Steinberg Center ....Nicholas J. Caccavo
Human Resources Director ....Stephen Deutsch
Operations Manager ....Valerie D. Simmons
Associate General Manager ....Maggie Cantrick
Office Manager ....Scott Kelly
Archivist ....Tiffany Nixon
Receptionists ....Dee Beider, Emily Frohnhoefer,
        Elisa Papa, Allison Patrick
Messenger ....Darnell Franklin
Management Apprentice ....Holli Campbell

FINANCE STAFF

DIRECTOR OF FINANCE................Susan Neiman
Payroll Director ....John LaBarbera
Accounts Payable Manager ....Frank Surdi
Payroll Benefits Administrator ....Yonit Kafka
Manager Financial Reporting ....Joshua Cohen
Business Office Assistant....................Jackie Verbitski
Business Office Apprentice ....Mara Abeleda

DEVELOPMENT STAFF

DIRECTOR OF
  DEVELOPMENT ....Lynne Gugenheim Gregory
Assistant to the Director of Development ....Liz Malta
Director, Institutional Giving ....Liz S. Alsina
Director, Special Events.......................Lane Hosmer
Director, Individual Giving ....Christopher Nave
Associate Director, Individual Giving ....Tyler Ennis
Manager, Telefundraising ....Gavin Brown
Manager, Special Events ....Natalie Corr
Manager, Friends of Roundabout ....Marisa Perry
Manager, Donor Information Systems ....Lise Speidel
Institutional Giving Officer,
  Solicitations and Special Projects ....Brett Barbour
Individual Giving Officer ....Toni Rosenbaum
Institutional Giving Officer,
  Stewardship and Prospect
  Development ....Kimberly Sidey
Special Events Assistant ....Genevieve Carroll
Development Assistant ....Martin Giannini
Special Events Apprentice ....Alayna George
Development Apprentice ....Haley Tanenbaum

INFORMATION TECHNOLOGY STAFF

DIRECTOR OF
  INFORMATION TECHNOLOGY ..Daniel V. Gomez
System Administrator.............................Jim Roma
DBA/Developer ....Rajan Eddy
Web Administrator ....Robert Parmelee
IT Associate ....Cary Kim

MARKETING STAFF

DIRECTOR OF MARKETING &
  AUDIENCE DEVELOPMENT ....Tom O'Connor

Senior Marketing Manager ....Rani Haywood
Manager, Design & Production ....Eric Emch
Digital Content Producer ....Mark Cajigao
Marketing Associate,
  Events & Promotions...............Rachel LeFevre-Snee
Marketing Associate, Digital ....Alex Barber
Marketing Assistant ....Dayna Johnson
Director of Telesales
  Special Promotions ....Marco Frezza
Telesales Manager ....Patrick Pastor
Telesales Office Coordinator ....Adam Unze
Marketing Apprentices ....Tyler Beddoe,
           Maureen Keleher
Digital Marketing Apprentice ....Laura Abbott

AUDIENCE SERVICES STAFF

DIRECTOR OF AUDIENCE
  SERVICES ....Wendy Hutton
Associate Director of Audience Services.........Bill Klemm
Box Office Managers ....Edward P. Osborne,
      Jaime Perlman, Krystin MacRitchie,
          Nicole Nicholson
Group Sales Manager ....Jeff Monteith
Assistant Box Office Managers ....Robert Morgan,
      Joseph Clark, Andrew Clements,
        Catherine Fitzpatrick
Assistant Audience Services Managers ....Robert Kane,
        Lindsay Ericson,
        Jessica Pruett-Barnett,
        Kaia Lay Rafoss
Customer Services Coordinator ....Thomas Walsh
Audience Services ....Jennifer Almgreen,
      Solangel Bido, Jay Bush,
    Lauren Cartelli, Adam Elsberry,
    Joe Gallina, Ashley Gezana,
   Alanna Harms, Kara Harrington,
    Nicki Ishmael, Kiah Johnson,
    Rebecca Lewis-Whitson,
   Kate Longosky, Michelle Maccarone,
   Mead Margulies, Laura Marshall,
   Chuck Migliaccio, Carlos Morris,
   Katie Mueller, Sarah Olsen, Josh Rozett,
    Heather Seibert, Nalane Singh,
    Ron Tobia, Hannah Weitzman
Audience Services Apprentice ....Blair Laurie

SERVICES

Counsel ....Paul, Weiss,
    Rifkind, Wharton and Garrison LLP,
  Charles H. Googe Jr., Carol M. Kaplan
Counsel ....Rosenberg & Estis
Counsel ....Andrew Lance,
    Gibson, Dunn, & Crutcher, LLP
Counsel ....Harry H. Weintraub,
    Glick and Weintraub, P.C.
Counsel ....Stroock & Stroock & Lavan LLP
Counsel ....Daniel S. Dokos,
    Weil, Gotshal & Manges LLP
Counsel ....Claudia Wagner/
    Manatt, Phelps & Phillips, LLP
Immigration Counsel ....Mark D. Koestler and
         Theodore Ruthizer
House Physicians ....Dr. Theodore Tyberg,
        Dr. Lawrence Katz
House Dentist ....Neil Kanner, D.M.D.
Insurance ....DeWitt Stern Group, Inc.

The Mystery of Edwin Drood

(L-R): Chita Rivera, Stephanie J. Block, WIll Chase

Accountant ....Lutz & Carr CPAs, LLP
Advertising ....Spotco/
Drew Hodges, Jim Edwards,
Tom Greenwald, Ilene Rosen, Josh Fraenkel
Interactive Marketing.................Situation Interactive/
Damian Bazadona, John Lanasa,
Eric Bornemann, Mollie Shapiro,
Danielle Migliaccio
Events Photography................Anita and Steve Shevett
Production Photographer ....Joan Marcus
Theatre Displays.............King Displays, Wayne Sapper
Lobby Refreshments.....................Sweet Concessions
Merchandising ....Spotco Merch/
James Decker

MANAGING DIRECTOR
EMERITUS ....Ellen Richard

Roundabout Theatre Company
231 West 39th Street, New York, NY 10018
(212) 719-9393.

GENERAL PRESS REPRESENTATIVE
BONEAU/BRYAN-BROWN
Adrian Bryan-Brown
Matt Polk   Jessica Johnson   Amy Kass

CREDITS FOR *THE MYSTERY OF EDWIN DROOD*
Company Manager ....**James Lawson**
Production Stage Manager ....Lori M. Doyle
Stage Manager ....Scott Taylor Rollison
Dance Captain..................................Justin Greer
Fight Captain ....Kyle Coffman
Associate Scenic Designer ....Jeremy W. Foil
Assistant Scenic Designer ....Aimee Dombo
Assistants to the
Scenic Designer ....Deborah Wheatley,
Aaron Sheckler
Associate Costume Designer ....Tom Beall
Assistant to the Costume Designer ....Jennifer Raskopf
Costume Intern ....Amanda Dobrzeniecki

WIL Studio Director ....Donald Sanders
Assistant Lighting Designer ....Ken Elliott
Assistant to the
Lighting Designer ....Luamar Cervejeira
Assistant Sound Designers ....David Gotwald,
Adair Mallory, Reece Nunez
Sound Design Intern ....Kymberly Donowski
Associate Wig/Hair Designer ....Giovanna Calabretta
Assistant Wig/Hair Designer ....Carrie Rohm
Assistant Make-up Designer ....Robert Amodeo
Associate to Rupert Holmes ....Teressa Jennings
Personal Assistant to
Chita Rivera ....Rosemary Bentinck
Orchestration Associate ....Ben Krauss
Script Supervisor ....Alicia Rachel Becker
Rehearsal Pianists ....Mark Mitchell, Tony Geralis
Rehearsal Drummer ....Paul Pizzuti
Production Properties Supervisor ....Timothy M. Abel
Assistant Production Props ....Meghan Abel
Production Carpenter ....Dan Hoffman
Production Electrician ....John Wooding
Running Properties ....Lawrence Jennino
Flyman ....Steve Jones
Automation Operator ....Peter Malbuisson
Local One Apprentice ....Thomas Goehring
Follow Spots ....Erika Warmbrunn, Dorion Fuchs
Deck Electrician ....Jessica Morton
Properties ....Erin Delaney, Dan Mendeloff,
Julie Sandy
Sound Operator ....Josh Maszle
Deck Sound ....Craig Van Tassel
Moving Light Programmer ....Alex Fogel
Wardrobe Supervisor ....Stacy Sarmiento
Dressers ....Sam Brooks, Mikey Goodmark,
Joe Hickey, Jessica Selig,
Katherine Sorg, Jessica Scoblick
Hair and Wig Supervisor ....Carrie Rohm
Hair Dresser ....Kelly Reed
Production Assistant ....Zac Chandler
Rehearsal Production Assistants ....Kendall Booher,
David S. Cohen

Tutoring ....On Location Education
Tutors ....Onsy Elshamy, Janet Wallen,
Patricia Mueller
Child Guardians ....Felicia Velasco, Natasha Harper
Physical Therapists ....PhysioArts
Directorial Observer ....Christina Coleburn

Fight Director ....**Rick Sordelet**

CREDITS

Scenery built, painted, automated and electrified by Showmotion, Inc., Milford, CT. Automation and show control by Showmotion, Inc. Milford, CT using the AC2 computerized motion control system. Scenery by Showman Fabricators. Soft goods provided by I. Weiss, Rosebrand. Lighting equipment by PRG Lighting. Audio equipment by PRG Audio. Costumes by Jennifer Love Costumes, EuroCo Costumes, Tricorne Costumes. Millinery by Rodney Gordon. Shoes by JC Theatrical and La Duca Shoes. Undergarments & hosiery by Bra*Tenders. Props by Joe Props Shop, Costume Armour, Prop N Spoon.

Mr. Holmes' orchestrations written in
Finale 2012 software.

STUDIO 54 THEATRE STAFF

Operations Manager ....Valerie D. Simmons
House Manager ....LaConya Robinson
Associate House Manager ....Jack Watanachaiyot
Head Treasurer ....Krystin MacRitchie
Associate Treasurer ....Joe Clark
Assistant Treasurers ....Kara Harrington,
Laura Marshall
House Carpenter ....Dan Hoffman
House Electrician ....John Wooding
House Properties ....Lawrence Jennino
Security ....Gotham Security
Maintenance ....Reliable Cleaning/
Jason Battle, Ralph Mohan
Lobby Refreshments by .... Sweet Concessions

The Mystery of Edwin Drood
Scrapbook

Correspondent: Robert Creighton, "Durdles/ Mr. Nick Cricker"

Opening Night Gifts: One of the most significant and classiest opening night gifts I have ever received came from our author, Rupert Holmes. He purchased a complete set of Dickens' works, published in 1892, and gave each person in the cast one of the volumes from the set. I got "Dombey & Son," which I had never read before. "The Mystery of Edwin Drood" went to our Drood, Stephanie J. Block. Rupert signed each one. Mine says, "To Durdles, Nick Cricker and Robert," followed by a lovely personal note. Included for each of us, was an hilarious and touching letter printed on embossed paper outlining the acquisition of the set and the significance in dividing it amongst the cast and creative team of our show. It was brilliant, as Rupert is wont to be.

The other gift was a small crystal mouse given to us by director Scott Ellis. On the first day of rehearsals he told a story about being in the chorus of the original *The Rink*. He pulled out the crystal mouse that Chita Rivera, who was the leading lady of that show, gave him on opening night. On our opening night of *Drood* he gave each of us our own crystal mouse, which was very cool.

Most Exciting Celebrity Visitors: We've had quite a few celebrities visiting the show. They can usually be found visiting our resident theatre royalty, Chita, in her dressing room. If she catches you passing by she will often pull you in and make an introduction. Composer John Kander was in attendance opening night. Afterward he said to me of Chita, "You know, you were chosen to be the lover tonight opposite my best friend!"

Who Got the Gypsy Robe: Eric Sciotto. This is his eleventh Broadway show! It was brought over by Merwin Foard from *Annie* and presented in the always-inspiring way that it is. We have several cast members who had won the robe before, including Chita, and they all listed the shows for which they had won. There were a lot! Also called forward was Spencer Plachy, who was the only member of the cast making a Broadway debut. Everyone gave him a rousing cheer!

"Carols for a Cure" Carol: We recorded a version of "Good King Wenceslas."

Actor Who Performed the Most Roles in This Show: Everyone in this show plays two roles: their Music Hall character and their *Edwin Drood* character. But Stephanie J. Block does come back disguised as Dick Datchery, so I guess that's one extra for her.

Actor Who Has Done the Most Shows in Their Career: I can't imagine it's anyone but Chita. But if you include West End shows, Jim Norton is right up there.

Special Backstage Rituals: I get a hug in the same spot each night from Jessie Mueller; and Chita and I do a double kiss on the cheeks before each performance. In the play, Durdles is a happy drunk, so before each performance our

1. Hanging out at the cast album recording session waiting to record our "confessions" (L-R): Andy Karl, Betsy Wolfe, Peter Benson, Jessie Mueller, *Yearbook* correspondent Robert Creighton and Stephanie J. Block.
2. Robert Creighton contrasts teeth with Kiira Schmidt.
3. (L-R): Andy Karl and Peter Benson warm up with some disco in their shared dressing room.

bartender Jake pours me just enough Johnnie Walker Black to cover the bottom of a glass. I swish it around in my mouth so that when I'm out in the audience talking to people they can smell it on my breath. Feels a little naughty and fun.

Before each show we all mingle with the audience in character and pretend to be Music Hall people. Will Chase often goes right out to the box office in character and in costume and helps people get their tickets. He also has been known to go out on the street outside the theatre and help people out of their taxis or greet people as they arrive. On opening night he was photographed on the red carpet in costume and in character.

Peter Benson and Andy Karl share a dressing room and they love to amuse Jessie Mueller and Betsy Wolfe, who have a dressing room directly across from theirs. They make up songs, play guitar, rap, dance—you name it. They come up with something new and entertaining every day. They are genuinely hysterical. We recorded a YouTube video that Andy Karl wrote and directed. He got Roundabout to let us use the

theatre and the costumes and he had it planned down to the last detail. The whole cast was into it, and we shot it in one long Friday afternoon. It's a hip-hop tune called "Bustle-Fluffah," and you have to see it to understand it. http://www.youtube.com/watch?v=TzNcryo 2Rg4

Favorite Moments During Each Performance: I have two. I love doing the opening scene with Jim Norton. It's filled with old Music Hall-style jokes, and the audience has fun with it. I literally can't wait to do that every day. I also love when Stephanie hits the last note of the show in the song "The Writing on the Wall." She belts it and we sing under it, and I get choked up. It's a very powerful ending and she sings it so incredibly. During the run of our show hurricane Sandy struck the northeast and the tragedy in Newtown, Connecticut happened. Both times that song's lyrics about "living" and "survival" took on much deeper meaning and we were all very emotional getting through it.

Favorite In-Theatre Gathering Places: There is a big wide hallway downstairs beneath the

The Mystery of Edwin Drood
SCRAPBOOK

stage that serves as our greenroom. That's the main spot. Every Sunday night, after our weekend shows are done, the bar opens in Chita's dressing room and anyone is welcome to stop by and have a drink. One Sunday, she and I sat on the couch and talked about life for half an hour. I can tell you that more important than the fact that she's a legend she is the most down-to-earth, warm, caring person you could imagine.

Favorite Snack Food: Betsy Wolfe is a baker and often comes in with baked goods that are out of this world. During rehearsal she would bring us coffee cake. We've now gotten into frosted ginger snaps. There is a big bowl of candy stage left near the wings. It got filled during Tech rehearsals and has stayed filled since. I have no idea who fills it up, but they do!

Mascot: Stephanie J. Block's dog, Macaco, who appears with her briefly on stage. Macaco now also has an understudy, Meatshelf, who has his own Twitter account, no less.

Favorite Therapies: We have great physical therapists who come in here. The sign-up sheets are always full so I know people are availing themselves of that. Quite a few dressing rooms also have quite a full bar setup. That's a good therapy and very "music hall."

Most Memorable Ad-Libs: There have been quite a few, especially in the section near the end of the show where the audience picks who will be the Lovers. We have set lines, but we also often ad-lib a reaction, which gives the audience a big laugh. Chita is especially fun with this. When she has to do the Lovers section with "Deputy," the 14-year-old character, she looks at the audience, crosses herself, and sighs "Oh, boy!" Which cracks everybody up.

Cell Phone Incidents During a Performance: Our show is set in 1895 and every night we go out into the house to warm up the audience in character. I've had a lot of occasions when people would pull out their phones and want to take a picture. I act confused, like someone in the 1890's would be. They usually laugh…and put it away.

Web Buzz on the Show: A lot of people who have such fondness for the show are pleased to see such a first-class production. People seem relieved that it's being handled so well. A lot of others had no clue about the show at all, but had a great time when they saw it. They go online asking what it was like when someone else won.

Memorable Press Encounter: The principals had a very fun, very long day doing the photo

1. Gregg Edelman and Robert Creighton with their opening night gifts, crystal mice.
2. Chita Rivera (R) getting into costume in her dressing room with her personal assistant Rosemary Bentinck.
3. Jessie Mueller: Will Helena be the Murderer tonight? Waiting backstage for the audience's choice.

shoot for the show-poster at a studio in Tribeca. Very bonding. The entire cast did interviews in character one day for press purposes. It was all about who the public should vote for. Very fun.

Memorable Stage Door Fan Encounter: I've had a couple of times when someone tells me they've played Durdles, and wants to chat all about the voting for Durdles and the character, etc. This is a very gracious cast when it comes to the fans at the stage door. Everybody takes the time to sign people's programs.

Fastest Costume Change: Well SJB does a quick change from Detective Dick Datchery into her bloomers right on stage! Even though the audience knows it's coming they get a kick out of her pulling her undergarments just off

the shoulder accompanied by a cymbal crash! It's a nice move!

Heaviest/Hottest Costume: There are a lot of heavy, wooly, Dickens-style-Victorian clothes on that stage. Everybody is hot at some point.

Who Wore the Least: We have the Opium Den dream sequence where all the ladies dance in Jasper's hallucination. They have lovely sort of antique lingerie on. They are all so beautiful, and Warren Carlyle choreographed a super sexy sequence here in what we call "the smoke ballet." It is a little gift to the audience!

Orchestra Member Who Played the Most Instruments: On the day we recorded our cast album, I heard one of the woodwind players say she plays ten instruments in the show.

Best In-House Parody Lyrics: From my dressing room I can hear Will Chase, Andy Karl, and Peter Benson and there are new parody lyrics every other day. My favorite consistent one is when Will is on his way down the stairs for an entrance and is singing along with Reverend Crisparkle. "There are two subjects we don't discuss. One is our Monarch, the other's Russsssss"—instead of "us." Probably not funny in writing but funny every time I hear it in the hall.

Memorable Directorial Note: Well…let's just say Scott Ellis is big on "pace."

Understudy Anecdote: There have been very few days when anyone misses a show. One wild one was when our Nicholas Barasch had to leave mid-show when he became ill. Kyle Coffman stepped in for the first time as young Nick Cricker just before the first act finale. No one even knew it was happening, so it was pretty funny. He then was chosen as the lover and got to sing it with Chita. Nailed it.

Embarrassing Moments: Because the show is sort of stylized and we have a very fun-loving cast, there may or may not have been a couple of moments where controlling one's laughter on stage has been a challenge.

Coolest Thing About Being in This Show: For starters: the voices! And, I think for everyone the coolest thing is feeling like we are in the company of a remarkable cast across the board. Anyone in the ensemble could step into a principal role at any moment. Plus, the ending can change every night and no matter whose hands the confession or the love scene or the detective is in, it is always fun for us to watch. Also, Chita…nothing else needs to be said.

Photos courtesy Robert Creighton

The Nance

First Preview: March 21, 2013. Opened: April 15, 2013.
Still running as of May 31, 2013.

Set in the strippers-and-comics world of late 1930s New York Burlesque, Douglas Carter Beane's new play tells the story of Chauncey Miles, a comedian known as a "nance"—one who adopts a stereotyped gay persona. The star act of the Irving Place Theatre, he lives his offstage life in the shadows because he is actually gay himself in a deeply homophobic society. Self-loathing and promiscuous, he finds himself battling his ambivalence toward a budding relationship with a sweet young man, even as crusading politicians move to close down all Burlesque theatres. This production is notable for its detailed recreation of some classic Burlesque songs, dances and comedy skits.

CAST

(in order of appearance)

Chauncey ....NATHAN LANE
Ned.......................................JONNY ORSINI
Efram ....LEWIS J. STADLEN
Sylvie ....CADY HUFFMAN
Joan ....JENNI BARBER
Carmen ....ANDRÉA BURNS
Rose, the Wardrobe Mistress ......MYLINDA HULL
Charlie, a Stagehand.............GEOFFREY ALLEN
MURPHY

TIME AND PLACE

1937, The Irving Place Theatre, an automat,
a courthouse, Chauncey's apartment.

Assistant Stage Manager ..ANDREA O. SARAFFIAN
Dance Captain ....MEGAN SIKORA

Continued on next page

⊛ LYCEUM THEATRE

149 West 45th Street
A Shubert Organization Theatre

Philip J. Smith, *Chairman*   Robert E. Wankel, *President*

LINCOLN CENTER THEATER

under the direction of
André Bishop and Bernard Gersten

presents

THE NANCE

a new play by
Douglas Carter Beane

with (in alphabetical order)

Jenni Barber   Andréa Burns   Cady Huffman
Mylinda Hull   Nathan Lane   Geoffrey Allen Murphy
Jonny Orsini   Lewis J. Stadlen

Sets	Costumes	Lighting
John Lee Beatty	Ann Roth	Japhy Weideman

Sound	Original Music	Orchestrations	Conductor
Leon Rothenberg	Glen Kelly	Larry Blank	David Gursky

Stage Manager	Hair/Wigs	Casting
Rolt Smith	David Brian Brown	Daniel Swee

Executive Director of Development & Planning	Director of Marketing	General Press Agent
Hattie K. Jutagir	Linda Mason Ross	Philip Rinaldi

Managing Director	Production Manager
Adam Siegel	Jeff Hamlin

Choreography
Joey Pizzi

Directed by
Jack O'Brien

Special thanks to The Harold and Mimi Steinberg Charitable Trust
for supporting new American plays at LCT.
American Airlines is the Official Airline of Lincoln Center Theater.

4/15/13

(L-R): Jonny Orsini
and Nathan Lane

Photo by Joan Marcus

The Nance

(L-R): Lewis J. Stadlen, Cady Huffman, Nathan Lane and Jonny Orsini

Cast Continued

UNDERSTUDIES
For Chauncey: STEPHEN DeROSA
For Ned, Charlie: MATTHEW GOODRICH
For Efram: MICHAEL KOSTROFF
For Sylvie, Carmen: MYLINDA HULL
For Joan, Carmen, Rose: MEGAN SIKORA

THE BAND
Conductor/Piano: DAVID GURSKY
Woodwinds: JAMES ERCOLE
Trumpet: CRAIG JOHNSON
Bass: JOHN BEAL
Drums/Percussion: BRUCE DOCTOR
Music Coordinator: BRUCE DOCTOR

Jenni Barber
Joan

Andréa Burns
Carmen

Cady Huffman
Sylvie

Mylinda Hull
Rose

Nathan Lane
Chauncey

Geoffrey Allen Murphy
Charlie

Jonny Orsini
Ned

Lewis J. Stadlen
Efram

Stephen DeRosa
Understudy

Matthew Goodrich
Understudy

Michael Kostroff
Understudy

Megan Sikora
Understudy

Douglas Carter Beane
Playwright

Jack O'Brien
Director

John Lee Beatty
Sets

Ann Roth
Costumes

Japhy Weideman
Lighting

Leon Rothenberg
Sound

Glen Kelly
Original Music

Larry Blank
Orchestrations

David Gursky
Conductor

The Nance

David Brian Brown
Hair/Wigs

Bruce Doctor
Music Coordinator

André Bishop
*Artistic Director
Lincoln Center
Theater*

Bernard Gersten
*Executive Producer
Lincoln Center
Theater*

STAGE MANAGEMENT
(L-R): Andrea O. Saraffian
(Assistant Stage Manager),
Rolt Smith (Stage Manager),
Holly Coombs

WARDROBE
(L-R): Maria Goya, Andrea Gonzalez,
Linda Lee, Kenneth R. Brown,
Shonté Walker, Kimberly Butler,
Erick Medinilla, Mark Jones

BOX OFFICE
(L-R): Michael Taustine, Shari Teitelbaum
Not Pictured: Melissa Traina, Rianna Bryceland

BAND
(L-R): James Ercole (Woodwinds), David Gursky (Conductor/Piano), John Beal (Bass),
Craig Johnson (Trumpet), Bruce Doctor (Drums/Percussion/Music Coordinator)

FRONT OF HOUSE
Front Row (L-R): Janice Jenkins (Usher), Chris Santiago (Usher), Gerry Belitsis (Usher), Robert Lugo (Usher),
Elsie Grosvenor (Usher)
Back Row (L-R): Stephanie Wallis (House Manager), Joseph Pittman (Ticket Taker), Carmen Sanchez (Porter),
Kevin Pinzon (Usher)

HAIR DEPARTMENT
(L-R): Cheryl Thomas (Hair Assistant),
Gary Martori (Hair Supervisor)

STAGE DOOR
Elena Bennett

The Nance

Photo by Brian Mapp

CREW
Sitting (L-R): Marc Salzberg, Rob Presley, Liz Coleman, George Meagher
Standing (L-R): Paul Brydon, John Lofgren, Greg Cushna, Mark Diaz, Ray Chan, Dave Karlson, Bob Miller, Shannon January, Michael Pitzer
Back Center: Leah Nelson

LINCOLN CENTER THEATER

ANDRÉ BISHOP   BERNARD GERSTEN
ARTISTIC DIRECTOR EXECUTIVE PRODUCER

ADMINISTRATIVE STAFF

MANAGING DIRECTOR ....ADAM SIEGEL
General Manager ....Jessica Niebanck
Associate General Manager ....Meghan Lantzy
General Management Assistant ....Laura Stuart
Facilities Manager ....Alex Mustelier
Associate Facilities Manager ....Michael Assalone
GENERAL PRESS AGENT ....PHILIP RINALDI
Press Associates ....Amanda Dekker Kaus,
Ryan Hallett
Press Assistant .... Zoe Tarmy
PRODUCTION MANAGER ....JEFF HAMLIN
Associate Production Manager ....Paul Smithyman
EXECUTIVE DIRECTOR OF
DEVELOPMENT AND
PLANNING ....HATTIE K. JUTAGIR
Associate Director of Development .....Rachel Norton

Manager of Special Events and Advisor,
LCT Young Angels ....Karin Schall
Grants Writer ....Neal Brilliant
Manager, Patron Program ....Sheilaja Rao
Assistant to the Executive Director of
Development and
Planning ....Raelyn R. Lagerstrom
Development Associate/
LCT Young Angels &
Special Events ....Jenny Rosenbluth-Stoll
Development Assistant/
Patron Program ....Sydney Rais-Sherman
DIRECTOR OF FINANCE..........DAVID S. BROWN
Controller ....Susan Knox
Finance Assistant ....Kristen Parker
Systems Manager ....Stacy Valentine
IT Support Assistant ....Allotey Peacock
DIRECTOR OF MARKETING ..LINDA MASON ROSS
Associate Director of Marketing ....Ashley Dunn
Digital Marketing Associate.............Rebecca Leshin
Marketing Assistant ....David Cannon

DIRECTOR OF EDUCATION ....KATI KOERNER
Associate Director of Education ....Alexandra Lopez
Education Assistant ....Jennifer Wintzer
Assistant to the
Executive Producer ....Barbara Hourigan
Office Manager ....Brian Hashimoto
Messenger ....Esau Burgess
Reception ....Anna Strasser, Michelle Metcalf

ARTISTIC STAFF

ASSOCIATE DIRECTORS ......GRACIELA DANIELE,
NICHOLAS HYTNER,
JACK O'BRIEN,
SUSAN STROMAN,
DANIEL SULLIVAN
RESIDENT DIRECTOR .... BARTLETT SHER
DRAMATURG and DIRECTOR,
LCT DIRECTORS LAB.........ANNE CATTANEO
CASTING DIRECTOR ....DANIEL SWEE, CSA
MUSICAL THEATER
ASSOCIATE PRODUCER ....IRA WEITZMAN

The Nance
SCRAPBOOK

Correspondent: Jonny Orsini, "Ned"

Memorable Opening Night Letter, Fax or Note: If you need a fluffer, here's my number.

Most Exciting Celebrity Visitor and What They Did/Said: Jerry Lewis: "There should be more girls in this show." (Three strippers ain't enough for Jerry!)

Special Backstage Rituals: Andréa Burns has the most harmoniously gorgeous vocal warm-up I have ever heard.

Favorite Moment During Each Performance: When the characters in our show come together in the "eggs scene" for a dinner party. So much love and it reflects our real cast dynamic.

Favorite In-Theatre Gathering Place: Nathan's room on the boys' floor. He is a very gracious host.

Favorite Snack Food: Anything in the bowl of snacks provided at the stage door by Elena [Bennett]. She is a smiling gift every day walking in that door!

Mascot: "Fat Burt."

Favorite Therapy: Having a good laugh backstage.

Most Memorable Ad-Lib: "I show my titties to the committee" (followed by question mark facial expression)—Cady Huffman as "Sylvie."

Record Number of Cell Phone Rings, Cell Phone Photos or Texting Incidents During a Performance: More than zero is too many. Don't leave out the discussions about whose hearing aid is causing the feedback. Certainly adds new colors to the scene.

What Did You Think of the Internet Buzz On Your Show?: All that positive stuff was spot on, obviously.

Fastest Costume Change: Probably getting Nathan into drag for his incredible "Hortense" monologue. Ken [Brown] is a real pro!

Catchphrases Only the Company Would Recognize: "Meet ya round the corner...."

Memorable Directorial Note: "More tits!" Just kidding. That never happened. Jack is a classy director.

Company Legends: Nathan Lane. Lewis J. Stadlen. Jack O'Brien. Ann Roth. John Lee Beatty... I don't know if that was the question, but, let's be real. This company is incredible.

Sweethearts Within the Company: Jenni Barber, Megan Sikora. Can I cuddle them both right now please?

Superstitions That Turned Out to Be True: During previews, someone said the name of the Scottish play one afternoon in the theatre and that night, the fire alarm went off and all kinds of wonky things. Believe!

Coolest Thing About Being in This Show: Please See: Legendary Company. Also, Jack O'Brien has such a huge heart and really assembled a true family. And Doug's play alternately makes you laugh out loud and rips your heart out. What more could a person ask for? Honestly?

ARTISTIC DIRECTOR/LCT3	PAIGE EVANS
Artistic Administrator	Julia Judge
Casting Associate	Camille Hickman
LCT3 Associate	Natasha Sinha
Lab Assistant	Kate Marvin

SPECIAL SERVICES

Advertising	Serino/Coyne: Jim Russek, Roger Micone, Nick Nolte, Nathaniel Hill
Marketing Promotion	Serino/Coyne: Leslie Barrett, Diana Salameh
Digital Outreach	Serino/Coyne: Jim Glaub, Ian Weiss, Whitney Creighton, Crystal Chase, Isabel Hittleman
Principal Poster Artist	James McMullan
Counsel	Charles H. Googe, Esq.; Carol Kaplan, Esq. and Caroline Barnard, Esq. of Paul, Weiss, Rifkind, Wharton & Garrison
Immigration Counsel	Theodore Ruthizer, Esq.; Mark D. Koestler, Esq. of Kramer, Levin, Naftalis & Frankel, LLP
Labor Counsel	Michael F. McGahan, Esq. of Epstein, Becker & Green, P.C.
Auditor	Frederick Martens, C.P.A. Lutz & Carr, L.L.P.
Insurance	Jennifer Brown of DeWitt Stern Group
Production Photographer	Joan Marcus
Video Services	Fresh Produce Productions/ Frank Basile
Consulting Architect	Hugh Hardy, H3 Hardy Collaboration Architecture
Construction Manager	Yorke Construction
Payroll Service	Castellana Services, Inc.
Merchandising	Marquee Merchandise,LLC/ Matt Murphy

STAFF FOR *THE NANCE*

COMPANY MANAGER	MATTHEW MARKOFF
Assistant Director	Seth Sikes
Associate Choreographer	Jim Borstelmann
Assistant Set Designer	Kacie Hultgren
Associate Costume Designer	Matthew Pachtman
Assistant Costume Designer	Jessica Pabst
Associate Lighting Designer	Justin Partier
Assistant Lighting Designer	Weston Wetzel
Associate Sound Designer	Danny Erdberg
Props Supervisor	Buist Bickley
Props Shopper	Susan Barras
Production Carpenter	John Weingart
Production Electrician	David Karlson
Production Propertyman	John Ross
Production Soundman	Marc Salzberg
Lighting Programmer	Victor Seastone
Hair Supervisor	Gary Martori
Hair Assistant	Cheryl Thomas
Wardrobe Supervisor	Linda Lee
Dressers	Kenneth R. Brown, Kimberly Butler, Andrea Gonzalez, Erick Medinilla, Shonté Walker
Music Copyist	Anixter Rice Music Services
Burlesque Drum Arrangements	Bruce Doctor
Synthesizer Programmer	Randy Cohen
Production Assistants	Holly Coombs, Christopher Munnell, Tori Sheehan
Assistant to Douglas Carter Beane	Michael Bradshaw Flynn
Make-up Designer	Allen Weisinger

Technical supervision by
William Nagle and Patrick Merryman

CREDITS

Scenery and scenic effects built, painted, electrified and automated by Show Motion, Inc., Milford, CT. Costumes by Eric Winterling, Inc., Giliberto Designs, Inc. Millinery by Rodney Gordon, Inc. Fabric painting and dyeing by Jeff Fender Studios. Lighting equipment from Hudson Sound and Light, LLC. Sound equipment by Masque Sound. Makeup provided by M•A•C.

The Author thanks the Sundance Institute Playwright's Retreat at the Ucross Foundation for the time and place to create this play.

Visit www.lct.org
For groups of 20 or more:
Caryl Goldsmith Group Sales
(212) 889-4300

 THE SHUBERT ORGANIZATION, INC.
Board of Directors

Philip J. Smith	**Robert E. Wankel**
Chairman	President
Wyche Fowler, Jr.	**Diana Phillips**
Lee J. Seidler	**Michael I. Sovern**

Stuart Subotnick

Chief Financial Officer	Elliot Greene
Sr. Vice President, Ticketing	David Andrews
Vice President, Finance	Juan Calvo
Vice President, Human Resources	Cathy Cozens
Vice President, Facilities	John Darby
Vice President, Theatre Operations	Peter Entin
Vice President, Marketing	Charles Flateman
Vice President, Audit	Anthony LaMattina
Vice President, Ticket Sales	Brian Mahoney
Vice President, Creative Projects	D.S. Moynihan
Vice President, Real Estate	Julio Peterson

House Manager	Thia Calloway

Newsies

First Preview: March 15, 2012. Opened: March 29, 2012.
Still running as of May 31, 2013.

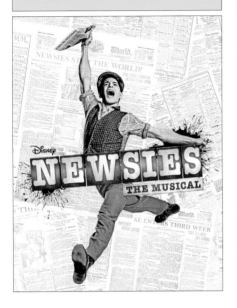

PLAYBILL®

A musical based on the cult 1992 Disney film about the real-life 1899 New York City newsboy strike. Street-wise "newsie" Jack Kelly reaches his limit when wealthy publisher Joseph Pulitzer tries to squeeze a few more precious pennies out of the hardworking street-hawkers. With help from a crusading journalist, the plucky Jack organizes the newsboys of all the papers in all the boroughs into a union, and manages—despite a series of setbacks—to push the city's publishers into an unexpected corner. But what about Jack's dream to chuck it all and move to a better life in Santa Fe?

CAST
(in order of appearance)

Jack Kelly	COREY COTT
Crutchie	ANDREW KEENAN-BOLGER
Race	RYAN BRESLIN
Albert	GARETT HAWE
Specs	RYAN STEELE
Henry	IAIN YOUNG
Finch	AARON J. ALBANO
Elmer	EVAN KASPRZAK
Romeo	ANDY RICHARDSON
Mush	DAVID GUZMAN
Katherine	KARA LINDSAY
Darcy	THAYNE JASPERSON
Nuns	LaVON FISHER-WILSON, JULIE FOLDESI, LAURIE VELDHEER
Morris Delancey	MIKE FAIST
Oscar Delancey	BRENDON STIMSON
Wiesel	JOHN E. BRADY

Continued on next page

⇒N⇐ NEDERLANDER THEATRE

UNDER THE DIRECTION OF
JAMES M. NEDERLANDER AND JAMES L. NEDERLANDER

Disney Theatrical Productions
under the direction of
Thomas Schumacher

Presents

DISNEY
NEWSIES
THE MUSICAL

Music by	Lyrics by	Book by
ALAN MENKEN	**JACK FELDMAN**	**HARVEY FIERSTEIN**

Based on the Disney film written by BOB TZUDIKER and NONI WHITE

Starring
COREY COTT

JOHN DOSSETT   KARA LINDSAY   LaVON FISHER-WILSON   BEN FANKHAUSER
ANDREW KEENAN-BOLGER   NICHOLAS LAMPIASI   JAKE LUCAS

AARON J. ALBANO   MARK ALDRICH   TOMMY BRACCO   JOHN E. BRADY   RYAN BRESLIN
CAITLYN CAUGHELL   JULIAN DeGUZMAN   MIKE FAIST   MICHAEL FATICA   JULIE FOLDESI
DAVID GUZMAN   JACOB GUZMAN   GARETT HAWE   THAYNE JASPERSON   EVAN KASPRZAK   JESS LePROTTO
STUART MARLAND   ANDY RICHARDSON   TOM ALAN ROBBINS   JACK SCOTT   RYAN STEELE   BRENDON STIMSON
NICK SULLIVAN   LAURIE VELDHEER   IAIN YOUNG   STUART ZAGNIT

Scenic Design	Costume Design	Lighting Design	Sound Design
TOBIN OST	**JESS GOLDSTEIN**	**JEFF CROITER**	**KEN TRAVIS**

Projection Design	Hair & Wig Design	Fight Direction	Casting
SVEN ORTEL	**CHARLES G. LAPOINTE**	**J. ALLEN SUDDETH**	**TELSEY + COMPANY JUSTIN HUFF, CSA**

Associate Producer	Technical Supervision	Production Manager	Production Stage Manager
ANNE QUART	**NEIL MAZZELLA & GEOFFREY QUART**	**EDUARDO CASTRO**	**THOMAS J. GATES**

Music Director/ Dance Music Arrangements	Music Coordinator	Associate Director	Associate Choreographer
MARK HUMMEL	**JOHN MILLER**	**RICHARD J. HINDS**	**LOU CASTRO**

Orchestrations by
DANNY TROOB

Music Supervision
Incidental Music &
Vocal Arrangements by
MICHAEL KOSARIN

Choreographed by
CHRISTOPHER GATTELLI

Directed by
JEFF CALHOUN

World Premiere, Paper Mill Playhouse, in Millburn, New Jersey on September 25, 2011.   Mark S. Hoebee, Producing Artistic Director, Todd Schmidt, Managing Director

10/1/12

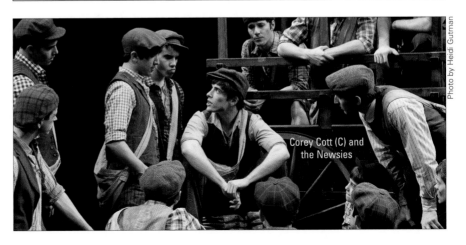

Corey Cott (C) and the Newsies

Photo by Heidi Gutman

Newsies

MUSICAL NUMBERS

ACT I

Prologue: Rooftop, Dawn
"Santa Fe" (Prologue) .... Jack, Crutchie
Scene 1: Newsie Square
"Carrying the Banner" .... Jack, Newsies
Scene 2: Pulitzer's Office, Afternoon
"The Bottom Line" .... Pulitzer, Seitz, Bunsen, Hannah
Scene 3: A Street Corner
Scene 4: Medda's Theater
"That's Rich" .... Medda
"I Never Planned on You/Don't Come a-Knocking" .... Jack, Bowery Beauties
Scene 5: Newsie Square, Next Morning
"The World Will Know" .... Jack, Davey, Les, Newsies
Scene 6: Jacobi's Deli and Street, Afternoon
"The World Will Know" (Reprise) .... Newsies
Scene 7: Katherine's Office
"Watch What Happens" .... Katherine
Scene 8: Newsie Square, Next Morning
"Seize the Day" .... Davey, Jack, Newsies
Scene 9: Rooftop
"Santa Fe" .... Jack

ACT II

Entre'acte
Scene 1: Jacobi's Deli, Next Morning
"King of New York" .... Davey, Katherine, Les, Newsies
Scene 2: Medda's Theater
"Watch What Happens" (Reprise) .... Davey, Jack, Katherine, Les
Scene 3: Pulitzer's Office and Cellar, Afternoon
"The Bottom Line" (Reprise) .... Pulitzer, Seitz and Mayor
Scene 4: Brooklyn Bridge and Medda's Theater
"Brooklyn's Here" .... Spot Conlon and Newsies
Scene 5: Rooftop
"Something to Believe In" .... Katherine, Jack
Scene 6: Pulitzer's Cellar
"Seize the Day" (Reprise) .... Newsies
"Once and for All" .... Jack, Davey, Katherine, Newsies
Scene 7: Pulitzer's Office, Next Morning
"Seize the Day" (Reprise) .... Newsies
Scene 8: Newsie Square
"Finale" .... Jack, Newsies

(L-R): Kara Lindsay and Corey Cott

Photo by Heidi Gutman

Newsies

Cast Continued

Pulitzer:
JOHN E. BRADY, STUART MARLAND
Roosevelt:
MARK ALDRICH, STUART ZAGNIT
Seitz/Bunsen:
EVAN KASPRZAK, STUART ZAGNIT
Snyder:
NICK SULLIVAN, STUART ZAGNIT
Wiesel/Stage Manager/Jacobi/Mayor:
NICK SULLIVAN, STUART ZAGNIT
Hannah:
CAITLYN CAUGHELL, JULIE FOLDESI

PLACE:

Lower Manhattan

TIME:

Summer, 1899

ORCHESTRA

Conductor:
MARK HUMMEL
Associate Conductor:
STEVEN MALONE
Assistant Conductor:
MAT EISENSTEIN
Woodwinds:
TOM MURRAY, MARK THRASHER
Trumpet/Flugel:
TREVOR D. NEUMANN
Trombone:
DAN LEVINE
Guitar:
BRIAN KOONIN
Bass:
RAY KILDAY
Drums:
PAUL DAVIS
Percussion:
ED SHEA
Keyboards:
MAT EISENSTEIN, STEVEN MALONE
Violin:
MARY ROWELL
Cello:
DEBORAH ASSAEL-MIGLIORE

Electronic Music Programmer:
JEFF MARDER
Music Coordinator:
JOHN MILLER

Corey Cott
Jack Kelly

John Dossett
Joseph Pulitzer

Kara Lindsay
Katherine

LaVon Fisher-Wilson
Medda

Ben Fankhauser
Davey

Andrew Keenan-Bolger
Crutchie

Nicholas Lampiasi
Les

Jake Lucas
Les

Aaron J. Albano
Finch, Ensemble

Mark Aldrich
Seitz, Ensemble

Tommy Bracco
Spot Conlon, Scab, Ensemble

John E. Brady
Wiesel, Stage Manager, Mr. Jacobi, Mayor, Ensemble

Ryan Breslin
Race, Ensemble

Caitlyn Caughell
Swing

Julian DeGuzman
Swing

Mike Faist
Morris Delancey, Ensemble

Michael Fatica
Swing

Julie Foldesi
Nun, Ensemble

David Guzman
Mush, Ensemble

Jacob Guzman
Sniper, Scab, Ensemble

Newsies

Garett Hawe
Albert, Bill, Ensemble

Thayne Jasperson
Darcy, Ensemble

Evan Kasprzak
Elmer, Ensemble

Jess LeProtto
Buttons, Scab, Ensemble

Stuart Marland
Snyder, Ensemble

Andy Richardson
Romeo, Ensemble

Tom Alan Robbins
Roosevelt, Ensemble

Jack Scott
Swing

Ryan Steele
Specs, Ensemble, Dance Captain

Brendon Stimson
Oscar Delancey, Ensemble

Nick Sullivan
Bunsen, Ensemble

Laurie Veldheer
Hannah, Ensemble

Iain Young
Henry, Ensemble

Stuart Zagnit
Swing

Alan Menken
Composer

Jack Feldman
Lyrics

Harvey Fierstein
Book

Bob Tzudiker
Original Screenplay

Noni White
Original Screenplay

Jeff Calhoun
Director

Christopher Gattelli
Choreographer

Tobin Ost
Scenic Design

Jess Goldstein
Costume Design

Jeff Croiter
Lighting Design

Ken Travis
Sound Design

Sven Ortel
Projection Design

Michael Kosarin
Music Supervisor, Vocal and Incidental Music Arrangements

Danny Troob
Orchestrations

Mark Hummel
Music Director, Dance Music Arrangements

John Miller
Music Coordinator

Charles G. LaPointe
Hair & Wig Design

J. Allen Suddeth
Fight Director

Bernard Telsey
Telsey + Company Casting

Richard J. Hinds
Associate Director

Lou Castro
Associate Choreographer

Newsies

Neil A. Mazzella
Technical Supervisor

Geoffrey Quart
Technical Supervisor

Thomas Schumacher
Disney Theatrical
Productions
Producer

Kevin Carolan
*Roosevelt, Fight
Captain, Ensemble*

Kyle Coffman
Henry, Ensemble

JP Ferreri
Scab, Ensemble

Lewis Grosso
Les

Capathia Jenkins
Medda Larkin

Jeremy Jordan
Jack Kelly

Matthew J.
Schechter
Les

Ephraim Sykes
Mush, Ensemble

Alex Wong
Scab, Ensemble

Kevin Carolan
Ensemble

Joshua Colley
Les

JP Ferreri
Swing

John Michael
Fiumara
Specs, Ensemble

Hogan Fulton
Romeo, Ensemble

Liana Hunt
*Hannah, Ensemble,
Nun*

Adam Kaplan
*Morris Delancey,
Ensemble*

Tommy Martinez
Romeo, Ensemble

Ron Raines
Joseph Pulitzer

Clay Thomson
Spot Conlon, Scab

STAFF FOR *NEWSIES*

COMPANY MANAGER ....EDUARDO CASTRO
Production Stage Manager ....Thomas J. Gates
Assistant Company Manager ....Emily Powell
Stage Manager ....Timothy Eaker
Assistant Stage Manager ....Becky Fleming
Production Coordinator ....Kerry McGrath
Dance Captain ....Ryan Steele
Assistant Dance Captain ....Michael Fatica
Fight Captain ....Mark Aldrich
Production Assistants ....Bryan Bradford, Patrick Egan,
Aaron Elgart, Mark A. Stys, Amanda Tamny

DISNEY ON BROADWAY PUBLICITY
Senior Publicist ....Dennis Crowley
Associate Publicist ....Ryan Hallett

Associate Scenic Designer ....Christine Peters
Assistant Scenic Designer ....Jerome Martin
Assistant Set Designer ....John Raley
Associate Costume Designer ....Mike Floyd
Associate Costume Designer ....China Lee
Associate Lighting Designer ....Cory Pattak
Assistant Lighting Designer ....Wilburn Bonnell
Associate Sound Designer ....Alex Hawthorn
Moving Light Programmer ....Victor Seastone

Assistant Projection Designer ....Lucy Mackinnon
Assistant to the
Projection Designer ....Gabe Rives-Corbett
Projection Programmer ....Florian Mosleh
Assistant Hair and Wig Designer ....Leah Loukas
Assistant Fight Director ....Ted Sharon
Technical Supervision ....Neil A. Mazzella
Technical Supervision ....Troika Entertainment
Technical Associates ....Irene Wang, Sam Ellis
Technical Production Assistant ....Canara Price
Advance Carpenter ....Sam Mahan
Head Carpenter ....Eddie Bash
Automation ....Karl Schuberth

Newsies

COMPANY MANAGEMENT
Emily Powell, Eduardo Castro

HAIR DEPARTMENT
Amanda Duffy

CREW
Danny Braddish, Gerald Urciuoli

Carpenter ....Michael Allen
Production Electrician ....James Maloney
Associate Production Electrician ....Brad Robertson
Production Properties ....Emiliano Pares
Head Properties ....Brian Schweppe
Assistant Properties ....Michael Critchlow
Production Sound ....Phil Lojo, Paul DelCioppo
Head Sound ....Cassy Givens
Sound Assistant ....Gabe Wood
Wardrobe Supervisor ....Rick Kelly
Dressers ....Jenny Barnes, Gary Biangone,
　　　　　Franklin Hollenbeck, Phillip Rolfe,
　　　　　Keith Shaw, Franc Weinperl
Hair Supervisor ....Frederick Waggoner
Hairdresser ....Amanda Duffy
Associate Music Director ....Steven Malone
Additional Orchestrations ....Steve Margoshes,
　　　　　Dave Siegel
Music Preparation ....Anixter Rice Music Services
Electronic Music Programming ....Jeff Marder
Associate to Mr. Menken ....Rick Kunis
Assistant to John Miller ....Jennifer Coolbaugh
Rehearsal Musicians ....Paul Davis, Mat Eisenstein
Music Production Assistant ....Brendan Whiting
Dialect & Vocal Coach ....Shane Ann Younts
Assistant to Mr. Calhoun ....Derek Hersey
Children's Guardian ....Vanessa Brown
Children's Tutoring ....On Location Education/
　　　　　Nancy Van Ness, Beverly Brennan
Physical Therapy ....PhysioArts

CASTING
TELSEY + COMPANY
Bernie Telsey CSA, Will Cantler CSA,
David Vaccari CSA, Bethany Knox CSA,
Craig Burns CSA, Tiffany Little Canfield CSA,
Rachel Hoffman CSA, Justin Huff CSA,
Patrick Goodwin CSA, Abbie Brady-Dalton CSA,
David Morris, Cesar A. Rocha, Andrew Femenella,
Karyn Casl, Kristina Bramhall, Jessie Malone

Advertising ....Serino Coyne, Inc.
Production Photography ....Deen Van Meer
Production Travel .... Jill L. Citron
Payroll Managers .... Anthony DeLuca, Cathy Guerra
Counsel–Immigration ....Michael Rosenfeld

CREDITS
Custom scenery and automation by Hudson Scenic Studio, Inc. Lighting equipment by Production Resource Group, LLC. Sound equipment by Masque Sound. Video projection system provided by Scharff Weisberg, Inc. Soft goods by iWeiss. Costumes by Carelli Costumes, Jennifer Love Studios, Claudia Diaz Costumes. Millinery by Rodney Gordon. Shoes by JC Theatrical & Custom Footwear Inc.; T.O. Dey; Capezio. Rehearsal sets by Proof Productions, Inc. Smoke effect by Jauchem & Meeh, NYC. Dry cleaning by Ernest Winzer Cleaners. Special thanks to Bra*Tenders for undergarments and hosiery. Ricola cough drops courtesy of Ricola USA, Inc. Fabric painting and distressing by Jeff Fender Studios.

NEWSIES rehearsed at the
New 42nd Street Studios & Ripley Grier Studios

THANKS
Thanks to the TDF Costume Collection; Paper Mill Playhouse; Prop N Spoon; Jake Zerrer

NEDERLANDER
Chairman ....**James M. Nederlander**
President ....**James L. Nederlander**

Executive Vice President
Nick Scandalios

Vice President
Corporate Development
Charlene S. Nederlander

Senior Vice President
Labor Relations
Herschel Waxman

Vice President
Jim Boese

Chief Financial Officer
Freida Sawyer Belviso

STAFF FOR THE NEDERLANDER THEATRE
House Manager ....Jesse White
Treasurer ....Anthony Giannone
Assistant Treasurer ....Richard Loiacono
House Carpenter ....Joseph Ferreri Sr.
Flyman.......................................Joseph Ferreri Jr.
House Electrician ....Rick Poulin
House Properties ....William Wright
Head Usher ....Trish Ryan

DISNEY THEATRICAL PRODUCTIONS
President ....Thomas Schumacher
EVP & Managing Director ....David Schrader
Senior Vice President, International ....Ron Kollen
Vice President, International,
　Europe ....Fiona Thomas
Vice President, International,
　Australia ....James Thane
Vice President, Operations ....Dana Amendola
Vice President, Publicity ....Joe Quenqua
Vice President, Domestic ....Jack Eldon
Vice President, Human Resources ....June Heindel
Director, Broadway Mgmt. &
　Licensing ....Daniel M. Posener
Director, Domestic Touring..............Michael Buchanan
Director, Worldwide Publicity ....Michael Cohen
Director, Regional Engagements ....Scott A. Hemerling

MERCHANDISE
(L-R): James Thad Wilkes, Sai Fogle, Chris Gibson, Brett Warnke

BOX OFFICE
(L-R): Ian Washam, Richard Loiacono, Brooke Heller, Chris Montague

Newsies

Director, Regional Engagements ....Kelli Palan
Director, Regional Engagements ....Deborah Warren
Manager, Domestic Touring & Planning ....Liz Botros
Manager, Human Resources ....Jewel Neal
Manager, Human Resources &
    Labor Relations ....Valerie Hart
Manager, Publicity ....Lindsay Braverman
Project Manager ....Ryan Pears
Senior Computer Support Analyst ....Kevin A. McGuire
IT/Business Analyst ....William Boudiette

Creative & Production
Executive Music Producer ....Chris Montan
VP, Creative Development ....Ben Famiglietti
VP, Production ....Anne Quart
Director, International Production ....Felipe Gamba
Director, Labor Relations....................Edward Lieber
Associate Director ....Jeff Lee
Production Supervisor ....Clifford Schwartz
Production Manager ....Eduardo Castro
Manager, Labor Relations ....Stephanie Cheek
Manager, Physical Production ....Karl Chmielewski
Manager, Creative Development ....Jane Abramson
Manager, Theatrical Licensing ....David R. Scott
Dramaturg & Literary Manager ....Ken Cerniglia
Manager, Education & Outreach ....Lisa Mitchell

Marketing
Senior Vice President..........................Andrew Flatt
Director, Creative Resources ....Victor Adams
Director, Synergy & Partnership ....Kevin Banks
Director, Licensed Brands ....Gary Kane
Director, Media Strategy,
    Planning & Management ....Robin Wyatt
Director, Digital Marketing....................Kyle Young
Design Manager ....James Anderer
Manager, Media & Strategy ....Jared Comess
Manager, Creative Services ....Lauren Daghini
Manager, Synergy & Partnership ....Sarah Schlesinger
Manager, Consumer Insights ....Craig Trachtenberg
Manager, Digital Marketing ....Peter Tulba

Sales
Vice President, National Sales...............Bryan Dockett
National Sales Manager ....Victoria Cairl
Sr. Manager, Sales & Ticketing ....Nick Falzon
Manager, Group Sales ....Hunter Robertson
Manager, Sales & Ticketing ....Sarah Bills
Manager, Sales & Ticketing ....Erin Dooley

Business and Legal Affairs
Senior Vice President ....Jonathan Olson
Director..Seth Stuhl
Counsel ....Naila McKenzie
Sr. Paralegal ....Jessica White

Finance
VP, Finance/Business Development ....Mario Iannetta
Director, Finance ....Joe McClafferty
Director, Accounting ....Leena Mathew
Manager, Finance ....Liz Jurist Schwarzwalder
Manager, Accounting ....Adrineh Ghoukassian
Senior Business Analyst ....Sven Rittershaus
Senior Financial Analyst ....Mikhail Medvedev
Senior Business Planner ....Jennifer August
Production Accountant ....Joy Sims Brown
Production Accountant ....Angela DiSanti
Assistant Production Accountant ....Isander Rojas

Administrative Staff
Kelly Archer, Zachary Baer, Brian Bahr, Elizabeth Boulger, Whitney Britt, Jonelle Brown, Amy Caldamone, Michael DeiCas, Preston Copley, Cara Epstein, Nicholas Faranda, Phil Grippe, Frankie Harvey, Christina Huschle, Greg Josken, Julie Lavin, Cyntia Leo, Colleen McCormack, Ellen McGowan, Kerry McGrath, Misael Nunez, Brendan Padgett, Matt Quinones, Jillian Robbins, Suzanne Sheptock, Lee Taglin, Anji Taylor

DISNEY THEATRICAL MERCHANDISE
Vice President ....Steven Downing
District Manager ....Alyssa Somers
Merchandise Manager ....Neil Markman
Associate Buyer ....Violet Burlaza
Assistant Manager, Inventory ....Suzanne Jakel
On-Site Retail Manager ....James Thad Wilkes
Senior Lead Sales Associates ....Georgia Nikki Dillon,
                                            Anna Lewgood

Disney Theatrical Productions
guestmail@disneytheatrical.com

Photos by Brian Mapp

CREW
Upper Level (L-R): Jason LaPenna, Matt Maloney, Brad Robertson, Michael Allen
Lower Level (L-R): Rick Poulin, Eddie Bash, Joe Ferreri, Jr., Billy Wright Sr., Karl Schuberth, Billy Wright Jr., Mike Critchlow, Chris Riggins, Michael "Jersey" Van Nest
In Front: Kyp Seiferth

BARTENDERS
(L-R): Jonathan Butler, Dyann Griego, Norman Spiller

SOUND DEPARTMENT
(L-R): Cassy Givens, Aaron Straus, Gabe Wood

Newsies

DOORMAN
Joaquin Quintana

FRONT OF HOUSE
Front Row (R):
Charlene Grant
Middle Row (L-R):
Rey Rosaly,
Dana Diaz,
Joseph Candelaria
Top Row (L-R):
Jesse White
(House Manager),
Angel Diaz,
Hugh Stumpp,
Derrick Henriquez

ORCHESTRA
Front Row (L-R): Ed Shea, Brian Koonin, Deborah Assael, Mark Hummel, Mark Thrasher, Dan Levine, Paul Davis
Back Row (L-R): Ray Kilday, Steven Malone, Tom Murray, Mary L. Rowell, Mat Eisenstein

STAGE MANAGEMENT
(L-R): Timothy Eaker,
Becky Fleming,
Thomas J. Gates

WARDROBE
Top Level (L-R):
Franc Weinperl,
Keith Shaw
Middle Level (L-R):
Phillip Rolfe,
Franklin Hollenbeck
Lower Level (L-R):
Jenny Barnes,
Rick Kelly

Photos by Brian Mapp

Newsies
SCRAPBOOK

Correspondent: Tim Eaker, Stage Manager
Memorable Fan Gift: Tommy Bracco received a giant wheel of Swiss cheese. There was no return address. We still don't know who it was from.
Anniversary Party: We celebrated six months with a bowling party. Thanks Jack, Harvey & Alan!
Most Exciting Celebrity Visitor: Olympic Gold Medalist Gabby Douglas came backstage after seeing the show and had a handstand competition with some of the boys on our stage. She won.
Actor Who Performed the Most Roles: Michael Fatica, Newsie Swing. All of our swings are crazy super amazing.
Who Has Done the Most Shows: Aaron Albano—a.k.a. 'Grandpa Newsie' (six Broadway shows and recipient of the Gypsy Robe).
Special Backstage Rituals: Prayer/energy/focus circle before every show at the five-minute call for anyone who wants to participate.
John Dossett wishes "good show" to everyone in the cast, crew and orchestra before each performance and hands out a Lifesaver mint. You can set your watch by it.
Following the first Pulitzer scene, the "Oldsies" [adult cast members] hide Nick Sullivan's Ledger Book prop so that he has to find it before the next time he needs it. Sometimes the crew joins in to hand it off to him the second he's walking onstage.
Several of the boys, and stage management, raise their arms and serenade Katherine, Medda and Roosevelt as they exit into the wings.
Favorite Moments During Each Performance: Watching the boys "kill it" every day during "Seize the Day"! Also Ryan Steele's paper spin.
Favorite In-Theatre Gathering Places: "The Chicken Coop" a.k.a. the Newsies' dressing room. The Third Floor food table. The Girlsies' Dressing Room. They have a special visitor's bench.
Favorite Off-Site Hangouts: Schnipper's, Starbucks, Schmackary's, Patron, New York Beer Company, The Beer Authority.
Favorite Snack Foods: Flamin' Hot Cheetos— AKB. Cookie Cake, especially by Mike Faist. Pretty much any dessert under the sun.
Mascot: Bandit, Aaron Albano's beagle.
"Gypsy of the Year" Skit: "Dance Like the Newsies" by Kevin Carolan, JP Ferreri and Vanessa Brown. Music by Robert Lopez and Jeff

Top (L-R): Librettist Harvey Fierstein, producer Thomas Schumacher, lyricist Jack Feldman, composer Alan Menken, director Jeff Calhoun and choreographer Christopher Gattelli with (bottom) dancers from the cast of *Newsies* (L-R): Ryan Breslin, Garett Hawe, Brendon Stimson, Tommy Bracco, Aaron J. Albano, and Evan Kasprzak, celebrating the show's first anniversary.

Marx. Choreographed by JP Ferreri. It starred Kevin Carolan, Stuart Zagnit, Jake Lucas, Nick Lampiasi, Caitlyn Caughell, Laurie Veldheer, JP Ferreri, Evan Kasprzak, Jacob Guzman & David Guzman.
"Carols for a Cure" Carol: "God Rest Ye Merry Gentlemen."
Favorite Therapies: PT, PT, lots of foam roller time and PT.
Memorable Ad-Libs: Ron Raines: "You're getting hungry" instead of "You're getting warmer." Jeremy Jordan: "Well…TOO BAD!" instead of "Well it ain't right!"
John Brady as the Mayor: "Mr. Mayor! … err … Pulitzer … Governor's here…" instead of "Good morning Mr. Pulitzer, I believe you know the Governor."
Stuart Zagnit after creating the word 'rescue' (instead of refuge) "And you, Jack, your abuses of Mr. Snyder will be thoroughly investigated…"
Technological Interruptions: It's amazing how many people take videos and photos in the front row!
Memorable Stage Door Fan Encounter: One

Fansie handmade her own Bowery Beauty costume for Halloween (remarkably similar) and wore it to the show.
Web Buzz on the Show: It's unreal. Our Fansies are mostly young and very involved with Twitter, et cetera. Our gifts from them are surprisingly specific to our interests and personalities.
Most Unwieldy Costume: Medda's hat is quite immense. She nearly has to tilt her head to get through doorways.
Who Wore the Least: The shirtless Newsies: Ryan Steele, Kyle Coffman.
Catchphrases Only the Company Would Recognize: "Gorg." "Hai." "Like." "That's Rich." "You must be joking." "See you later."
Orchestra Member Who Played the Most Instruments: Ed Shea, percussionist, in a feat of brilliantly choreographed musicality, plays Bells, Xylophone, Chimes, Congas, Bongos, Snare & Field Drum, Bass Drum, Timpani, Triangle, Tambourine, Canasta, Shaker, 2 Cowbells, 2 Tambourines, Castanets, Vibra Slap, 2 Wood Blocks, Gong, Wind Whistle & Ratchit. Ed has also been the percussionist for Johnny Mathis since 1977.
Orchestra Member Who Played the Most Consecutive Performances Without a Sub: Steven Malone, keyboardist and associate conductor played 15 weeks without missing a performance.
Best In-House Parody Lyric: Nick Sullivan in his character of Bunsen sings "Bunsen for All" in place of "Once and For All."
Memorable Directorial Notes: "Best idea wins." "Enjoy these times because these are the good times." Any time he took the time to point out someone's excellence. (No one went unnoticed.)
Company In-Joke: Clothing optional fight-call.
Nicknames: The Oldsies: "Fidildo Francese," "Bruce Loosenoosky," "Mac Bunsenski," "Willie Conklin."
The Girlsies: "Jack Scott Kelly."
"Talls" (when understudy Caitlyn goes on as Smalls).
Embarrassing Moments: Roosevelt's mustache only half-on during the penultimate scene with no one able to keep a straight face except for Kevin Carolan (Roosevelt) himself. Jeremy Jordan fell flat on his face while running onstage for his bow…twice.
Caitlyn Caughell on for her Broadway debut as 'Smalls' missed getting onto the wagon for her solo during "Brooklyn's Here." The light came up on her spot for her line as she yells "So's the Bronx!" from somewhere hidden in the towers. It has since become known as "Where's the Bronx?"
Superstition That Turned Out To Be True: When a Newsie swing brags about not having to shave…they usually end up going on.
Also: Michael Fatica likes to hide in the Girlsies' dressing room and scare Julie Foldesi when she comes in.

The chorus and creators of *Newsies* win the sixth annual Actors' Equity Association's Advisory Committee on Chorus Affairs Award for Outstanding Broadway Chorus.

Nice Work If You Can Get It

First Preview: March 29, 2012. Opened: April 24, 2012.
Still running as of May 31, 2013.

PLAYBILL

Traditional-style screwball Broadway musical comedy loosely based on the 1926 show Oh, Kay! *with a completely new libretto, drawing liberally on the Gershwin songbook. Three bootleggers, including the pretty Billie Bendix, hide their illegal booze in the basement of a Long Island summer house owned by wealthy playboy Jimmy Winter, who is about to marry for the fourth time. But the nuptials are complicated when the wedding party arrives at the house and Jimmy falls for Billie instead.*

CAST

(in order of appearance)

Jeannie Muldoon	ROBYN HURDER
Jimmy Winter	MATTHEW BRODERICK
Billie Bendix	KELLI O'HARA
Duke Mahoney	CHRIS SULLIVAN
Cookie McGee	MICHAEL McGRATH
Chief Berry	STANLEY WAYNE MATHIS
Senator Max Evergreen	TERRY BEAVER
Duchess Estonia Dulworth	JUDY KAYE
Eileen Evergreen	JENNIFER LAURA THOMPSON
Millicent Winter	ESTELLE PARSONS

The Chorus Girls

Olive	CAMERON ADAMS
Dottie	KIMBERLY FAURÉ
Midge	STEPHANIE MARTIGNETTI
Alice	SAMANTHA STURM
Rosie	KRISTEN BETH WILLIAMS
Flo	CANDICE MARIE WOODS

Continued on next page

---

⑤ IMPERIAL THEATRE

249 West 45th Street
A Shubert Organization Theatre

Philip J. Smith, *Chairman*   **Robert E. Wankel,** *President*

Scott Landis, Roger Berlind, Sonia Friedman Productions, Roy Furman,
Standing CO Vation, Candy Spelling, Freddy DeMann, Ronald Frankel, Harold Newman, Jon B. Platt,
Raise the Roof 8, Takonkiet Viravan, William Berlind/Ed Burke, Carole L. Haber/Susan Carusi,
Buddy and Barbara Freitag/Sanford Robertson, Jim Herbert/Under the Wire,
Emanuel Azenberg, The Shubert Organization

PRESENT

**Matthew   Kelli
Broderick   O'Hara**

STARRING IN

NICE WORK
If You Can Get It
A New Musical Comedy

MUSIC & LYRICS BY
George Gershwin and Ira Gershwin

BOOK BY
Joe DiPietro
Inspired by material by Guy Bolton and P.G. Wodehouse

ALSO STARRING
**Michael McGrath   Jennifer Laura Thompson   Chris Sullivan
Robyn Hurder   Stanley Wayne Mathis   Terry Beaver**

WITH
Judy Kaye
AND
Estelle Parsons

Cameron Adams   Clyde Alves   Kaitlyn Davidson   Jason DePinto   Kimberly Fauré   Robert Hartwell
Grasan Kingsberry   Stephanie Martignetti   Barrett Martin   Michael X. Martin   Shina Ann Morris   Adam Perry
Jeffrey Schecter   Jennifer Smith   Joey Sorge   Samantha Sturm   Kristen Beth Williams   Candice Marie Woods

SCENIC DESIGN	COSTUME DESIGN	LIGHTING DESIGN	SOUND DESIGN
Derek McLane	Martin Pakledinaz	Peter Kaczorowski	Brian Ronan

HAIR & WIG DESIGN	MAKE-UP DESIGN	PROJECTION DESIGN	CASTING BY
Paul Huntley	Angelina Avallone	Alexander V. Nichols	Binder Casting
Jay Binder/Jack Bowdan

ORCHESTRATOR	MUSIC DIRECTOR	MUSIC COORDINATOR	ASSOCIATE DIRECTOR	ASSOCIATE CHOREOGRAPHER
Bill Elliott	Tom Murray	Seymour Red Press	Marc Bruni	David Eggers

PRESS REPRESENTATIVE	ADVERTISING & MARKETING	TECHNICAL DIRECTOR	PRODUCTION STAGE MANAGER	GENERAL MANAGEMENT
Boneau/Bryan-Brown	Serino/Coyne	Neil Mazzella	Bonnie L. Becker	101 Productions, Ltd.

MUSIC SUPERVISION AND ARRANGEMENTS
David Chase

DIRECTED AND CHOREOGRAPHED BY
Kathleen Marshall

This production is dedicated to the memory of Martin Pakledinaz.
1953-2012

The worldwide copyrights in the works of George Gershwin and Ira
Gershwin for this presentation are licensed by the Gershwin Family.

Original cast recording available on Shout Factory.

10/1/12

Kelli O'Hara and Matthew Broderick

Photo by Joan Marcus

Nice Work If You Can Get It

SCENES AND MUSICAL NUMBERS

ACT I

Overture ....Orchestra

SCENE 1: A Speakeasy
"Sweet and Lowdown"............................Jimmy, Jeannie, Chorus Girls, Society Guys

SCENE 2: Outside the Speakeasy, a Dimly Lit Dock
"Nice Work If You Can Get It" ....Jimmy, Billie
"Nice Work If You Can Get It" (Reprise) ....Billie
"Demon Rum" ....Duchess, Chief Berry, Senator, Vice Squad

SCENE 3: The Ritzy Front Lawn of Jimmy's Beach House
"Someone to Watch Over Me" ....Billie

SCENE 4: The Ritzy Bathroom
"Delishious" ....Eileen, Bubble Girls & Boys

SCENE 5: The Ritzy Living Room
"I've Got to Be There" ....Jimmy, Jeannie, Chorus Girls
"I've Got to Be There" (Reprise) ....Jeannie, Chorus Girls

SCENE 6: Jimmy's Ritzy Bedroom
"Treat Me Rough" ....Billie
"Let's Call the Whole Thing Off" ....Jimmy, Billie, Chief Berry

SCENE 7: The Ritzy Front Lawn
"Do It Again"* ....Jeannie, Duke

SCENE 8: The Ritzy Living Room
"'S Wonderful" ....Jimmy, Billie
"Fascinating Rhythm" ....Jimmy, Cookie & Company

ACT II

SCENE 1: The Ritzy Veranda
"Lady Be Good" ....Orchestra
"But Not for Me" ....Billie
"By Strauss" ....Duchess
"Sweet and Lowdown" (Reprise) ....Cookie

SCENE 2: The Ritzy Dining Room
"Do, Do, Do" ....Jimmy, Elliot, Vic, Floyd
"Hangin' Around With You" ....Billie
"Looking for a Boy" ....Duchess, Cookie
"Blah, Blah, Blah" ....Duke, Jeannie

SCENE 3: Jimmy's Ritzy Bedroom
"Let's Call the Whole Thing Off" (Reprise) ....Billie, Jimmy
"Will You Remember Me?" ....Billie, Jimmy

SCENE 4: The Ritzy Living Room
"I've Got to Be There" (Reprise) ....Chorus Girls, Vice Squad
"I've Got a Crush on You" ....Eileen, Chorus Girls, Vice Squad
"Blah, Blah, Blah" (Reprise) ....Jeannie, Duke
"Looking for a Boy" (Reprise) ....Cookie, Duchess
"Delishious" (Reprise) ....Chief Berry, Eileen

SCENE 5: The Boat House
"Someone to Watch Over Me" (Reprise) ....Jimmy, Billie

SCENE 6: The Ritzy Veranda
Finale ....Full Company

*"Do It Again," music by George Gershwin, lyrics by Buddy DeSylva
GERSHWIN INSTRUMENTAL COMPOSITIONS
Excerpts from *Rialto Ripples* (1916), *Novelette in Fourths* (ca. 1919), *Rhapsody in Blue* (1924),
Impromptu in Two Keys (ca. 1924), Prelude I (1926), *Prelude II: Blue Lullaby* (1926),
Prelude III: Spanish Prelude (1926), *The Three Note Waltz* (ca. 1926),
Prelude: Sleepless Night (ca. 1926), *Concerto in F* (1927), *Second Rhapsody* (1932),
Cuban Overture (1933), *Promenade (Walking the Dog)* (1937).

Cast Continued

The Vice Squad
Elliot ....CLYDE ALVES
Slim ....ROBERT HARTWELL
Fletcher ....BARRETT MARTIN
Edgar ....ADAM PERRY
Floyd ....JEFFREY SCHECTER
Vic ....JOEY SORGE

SWINGS
KAITLYN DAVIDSON, JASON DePINTO,
GRASAN KINGSBERRY, SHINA ANN MORRIS

UNDERSTUDIES
Standby For Duke, Cookie, Chief Berry, Senator:
MICHAEL X. MARTIN
Standby For Duchess, Millicent:
JENNIFER SMITH
For Jeannie:
KIMBERLY FAURÉ,
KRISTEN BETH WILLIAMS
For Jimmy
CLYDE ALVES, JOEY SORGE
For Billie
CAMERON ADAMS,
STEPHANIE MARTIGNETTI
For Duke:
BARRETT MARTIN
For Cookie and Chief Berry:
JEFFREY SCHECTER
For Duchess:
KRISTEN BETH WILLIAMS
For Eileen
KIMBERLY FAURÉ,
KRISTEN BETH WILLIAMS

DANCE CAPTAIN
JASON DePINTO

ASSISTANT DANCE CAPTAIN
KAITLYN DAVIDSON

TIME
July, 1927

PLACE
Long Island, New York

ORCHESTRA
Conductor:
TOM MURRAY
Associate Conductor:
SHAWN GOUGH
Assistant Conductor:
JOSEPH JOUBERT
Music Coordinator:
SEYMOUR RED PRESS

Continued on next page

Nice Work If You Can Get It

Matthew Broderick
Jimmy Winter

Kelli O'Hara
Billie Bendix

Estelle Parsons
Millicent Winter

Judy Kaye
Duchess Estonia Dulworth

Michael McGrath
Cookie McGee

Jennifer Laura Thompson
Eileen Evergreen

Chris Sullivan
Duke Mahoney

Robyn Hurder
Jeannie Muldoon

Stanley Wayne Mathis
Chief Berry

Terry Beaver
Senator Max Evergreen

Cameron Adams
Olive

Clyde Alves
Elliot

Kaitlyn Davidson
Swing, Asst. Dance Captain

Jason DePinto
Swing, Dance Captain

Violin:
PAUL WOODIEL
Woodwinds:
RALPH OLSEN, TODD GROVES,
RICHARD HECKMAN, JAY BRANDFORD
Trumpets:
ROBERT MILLIKAN,
BRIAN PARESHI, SHAWN EDMONDS
Trombones:
CLINT SHARMAN,
JASON JACKSON, JACK SCHATZ
Piano/Accordion:
SHAWN GOUGH
Piano/Keyboards:
JOSEPH JOUBERT
Drums:
JOHN REDSECKER
Percussion:
ANDREW BLANCO
Guitar:
JAMES HERSHMAN
Bass:
RICHARD SARPOLA

Kimberly Fauré
Dottie

Robert Hartwell
Slim

Grasan Kingsberry
Swing

Stephanie Martignetti
Midge

Barrett Martin
Fletcher

Michael X. Martin
Standby

Shina Ann Morris
Swing

Adam Perry
Edgar

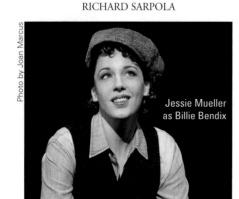

Photo by Joan Marcus

Jessie Mueller as Billie Bendix

Jeffrey Schecter
Floyd

Jennifer Smith
Standby

Joey Sorge
Vic

Samantha Sturm
Alice

Nice Work If You Can Get It

Kristen Beth
Williams
Rosie

Candice Marie
Woods
Flo

George Gershwin
Composer

Ira Gershwin
Lyricist

Joe DiPietro
Book

Guy Bolton
Source Material

P.G. Wodehouse
Source Material

Kathleen Marshall
*Director &
Choreographer*

David Chase
*Music Supervision
and Arrangements*

Derek McLane
Scenic Design

Martin Pakledinaz
Costume Design

Peter Kaczorowski
Lighting Design

Brian Ronan
Sound Design

Paul Huntley
Hair & Wig Design

Alexander V. Nichols
Projection Design

Kathy Fabian
Propstar
*Properties
Coordinator*

Angelina Avallone
Makeup Design

Tom Murray
Music Director

Bill Elliott
Orchestrations

Shawn Gough
Associate Conductor

Seymour Red Press
Music Coordinator

Marc Bruni
Associate Director

David Eggers
*Associate
Choreographer*

Jay Binder
Binder Casting
Casting

Jack Bowdan
Binder Casting
Casting

Mark Brandon
Binder Casting
Casting

Wendy Orshan
101 Productions, Ltd.
*General
Management*

Scott Landis
Producer

Roger Berlind
Producer

Sonia Friedman
Sonia Friedman
Productions
Producer

Roy Furman
Producer

Chris Bensinger
Standing Co Vation
Producer

Richard Winkler
Standing Co Vation
Producer

Jamie deRoy
Standing Co Vation
Producer

Michael Filerman
Standing Co Vation
Producer

Nice Work If You Can Get It

Photo by Brian Mapp

CREW
Front Row, Seated (L-R): Chris Noke, Charles Underhill, Heidi Brown, Bonnie L. Becker, Katrina Elliott, Susan Checklick, Lauren Gallitelli, Ginny Hounsel
Back Row, Seated (L-R): Majid Younis, Tom Lawrey, Jason Wilcozs, Karen L. Eifert, Tina Clifton
Standing (L-R): Mike Caffrey, John Tutalo, Chris Devany, Scott Rowen, Neil Rosenberg, Louis Igoe, Justin Sanok, Erik Lofgren, Richard Fullum, William K. Rowland II, Paul Wimmer, Paul Ludick, Sam Brooks

Dennis Grimaldi
Standing Co Vation
Producer

Remmel T. Dickinson
Standing Co Vation
Producer

Bruce Robert Harris
Standing Co Vation
Producer

Jack W. Batman
Standing Co Vation
Producer

Candy Spelling
Producer

Freddy DeMann
Producer

Jon B. Platt
Producer

Jennifer
Manocherian
Raise The Roof 8
Producer

Elaine Krauss
Raise The Roof 8
Producer

Jean Doumanian
Raise The Roof 8
Producer

Harriet Newman
Leve
Raise The Roof 8
Producer

Carole L. Haber
Producer

Buddy Freitag
Producer

Barbara Freitag
Producer

Sanford Robertson
Producer

Jacki Barlia Florin
Under the Wire
Producer

Douglas Denoff
Under the Wire
Producer

Margot Astrachan
Under the Wire
Producer

Emanuel Azenberg
Producer

Philip J. Smith
Chairman
The Shubert
Organization
Producer

Robert E. Wankel
President
The Shubert
Organization
Producer

Nice Work If You Can Get It

Andrew Cao
Swing

Will Chase
Jimmy Winter

Erin Dilly
Billie Bendix

Donna English
Standby for Millicent

Richard Poe
Standby for Senator

Andrew Cao
Swing

Blythe Danner
Millicent Winter

John Treacy Egan
Chief Berry

Donna English
*Standby for
Duchess, Millicent*

Paloma Garcia-Lee
Alice

Kaitlin Mesh
Swing

Jessie Mueller
Billie Bendix

Brad Oscar
Cookie McGee

Conrad John Schuck
*Senator Max
Evergreen*

Emily Tyra
Rosie

Correy West
Slim

Photo by Brian Mapp

FRONT OF HOUSE
Seated (L-R): Michael Knowles, Frances Barberetti, Marilyn Wassbotten, Judy Gilburt
Standing (L-R): Ed Phillins, Dennis Norwood, Ron Albanese, Joan Seymour, Lois Fernandez,
Janet Kay, Larry Scheraldi

Nice Work If You Can Get It

STAFF FOR *NICE WORK IF YOU CAN GET IT*

GENERAL MANAGEMENT
101 PRODUCTIONS, LTD.
Wendy Orshan   Jeffrey M. Wilson
Elie Landau
Ron Gubin   Chris Morey

COMPANY MANAGER
Katrina Elliott

GENERAL PRESS REPRESENTATIVE
BONEAU / BRYAN-BROWN
Chris Boneau   Heath Schwartz   Michael Strassheim

CASTING
JAY BINDER CASTING
Jay Binder CSA
Jack Bowdan CSA, Mark Brandon
Assistant: Jason Styres

TECHNICAL SUPERVISION
HUDSON THEATRICAL ASSOCIATES
Neil A. Mazzella

TECH PRODUCTION SERVICES
Peter Fulbright
Mary Duffe   James Kolpin

Production Stage Manager	Bonnie L. Becker
Stage Manager	Charles Underhill
Assistant Stage Manager	Scott Rowen
Associate Company Manager	Michelle Tamagawa
Associate Director	Marc Bruni
Associate Choreographer	David Eggers
Dance Captain	Jason DePinto
Assistant Dance Captain	Kaitlyn Davidson
SDC Observer	Lorna Ventura
Associate Tech Supervisors	Sheena Crespo, Irene Wang
Associate Scenic Designer	Shoko Kambara
Assistant Scenic Designer	Erica Hemminger
Associate Costume Designer	Amy Clark
Assistant Costume Designers	Leon Dobkowski, Justin Hall, Heather Lockard, Amanda Seymour
Associate Lighting Designer	Paul Toben
Assistant Lighting Designer	Sarah Jakubasz
Associate Sound Designer	Cody Spencer
Assistant Sound Designer	Jessica Weeks
Assistant Makeup Designer	Jorge Vargas
Props Coordinator	Kathy Fabian/Propstar
Assistant Props Coordinators	Carrie Mossman, Mike Billings
Production Carpenter	Paul Wimmer
Assistant Carpenter/Automation	Richard Force
House Carpenter	Walter Bullard
Production Electrician	Jimmy Maloney, Jr.
Associate Production Electrician	Tom Lawrey
Head Electrician	Jason Wilcozs
Moving Light Programmer	Josh Weitzman
House Electrician	Paul Dean
Video Programmer	Alexander V. Nichols
Assistant Video Programmer	Christian DeAngelis
Production Props Supervisor	Neil Rosenberg
Head Props	John Tutalo
House Props	Heidi Brown

Blythe Danner as
Millicent Winter

Photo by Joan Marcus

Advance Sound	Chris Sloan
Sound Operator	Louis Igoe
Sound Assistant	Chris Devany
Wardrobe Supervisor	Karen L. Eifert
Assistant Wardrobe Supervisor	Gayle Palmieri
Dressers	Dani Berger, Susan Checklick, Fran Curry, Suzanne Delahunt, Lauren Gallitelli, Paul Ludick, Geoffrey Polischuck, Mark Trezza
Hair/Make-up Supervisor	Nathaniel Hathaway
Hair/Make-up Assistants	Charlene Belmond, Heather Wright
Assistant to the Costume Designer	Valerie Marcus Ramshur
Music Copying	Emily Grishman Music Preparation/ Katharine Edmonds, Emily Grishman
Music Coordinator	Seymour Red Press
Music Department Production Asst	James Ballard
Physical Therapist	Neurosport NYC, LLC/ Natalie Kinghorn, MPT
Medical Director	Dr. Neil S. Roth
Keyboard Programmer	Randy Cohen
Scenic Studio Assistant	Paul DePoo
Production Assistants	Julie DeVore, Lauren Hirsh, Johnny Milani
Legal Counsel	Lazarus & Harris LLP/ Scott Lazarus, Esq.; Robert C. Harris, Esq.
Accountant	FK Partners, Robert Fried
Comptroller	Galbraith & Co./Kenny Noth
Advertising	Serino/Coyne/ Angelo Desimini, Sandy Block, Matt Upshaw, Peter Gunther, Lauren Houlberg, Christina Hernandez
Marketing	Serino/Coyne/ Leslie Barrett, Abby Wolbe
Marketing	Leanne Schanzer Promotions, Inc./ Leanne Schanzer, Justin Schanzer, Kara Laviola, Nicole Conter, Kim Gordon; Production: Michael Schanzer
Digital Outreach & Website	Serino/Coyne/ Jim Glaub, Chip Meyrelles, Laurie Connor, Kevin Keating, Mark Seeley
101 Productions, Ltd. Staff	Beth Blitzer, Christina Boursiquot, Kathy Kim, Mike McLinden, Michael Rudd
101 Productions, Ltd. Interns	Simon Pincus, Sarah Springborn
Banking	City National Bank/Anne McSweeney
Insurance	Dewitt Stern Group, Inc.
Opening Night Coordinator	Michael Lawrence

Merchandising	Encore Merchandising
Production Photographer	Joan Marcus
Payroll Services	Castellana Services, Inc.
Group Sales	Telecharge.com Group Sales

www.NiceWorkOnBroadway.com

The *Nice Work If You Can Get It* original cast recording is now available on Shout! Factory Records distributed by Sony.

CREDITS
Scenery constructed by Hudson Scenic Studio, Global Scenic Services. Lighting by PRG. Sound by Masque Sound. Costumes constructed by Parsons-Mears Ltd., Tricorne Inc., Eric Winterling, Inc., Artur Tailors, Arel Studios, Maryanne Krostyne, Paul Chang, Cego custom shirts, Christine Szczepanski, Vogue Too, Maria Ficalora, Lynne Mackey Studio, Arnold S. Levine Inc., Rodney Gordon, Fritz Masten, custom dance shoes by LaDuca, T.O. Dey custom shoes. Pianos by Yamaha. Makeup provided by M•A•C Cosmetics. Ukuleles provided by Martin & Co. Prop Artisans: Mary Wilson, John Estep, Holly Griffin, Jessica Provenzale, Sarah Bird, Laura Gravenstine, Tom Carroll Scenery, Costume Armour, Aardvark Interiors. Upholstery by Mimi Sason. Special thanks to Bra*Tenders for hosiery and undergarments.

Al Hirschfeld image reproduced by arrangement with Hirschfeld's exclusive representative, the Margo Feiden Galleries Ltd., New York.

SPECIAL THANKS
The George & Ira Gershwin Family, Ira Pittelman, Tom Hulce, Michael Sukin, Elliot Brown, Roberta Korus, Adina Schecter, Andrew Fishman, Dave Auster, Todd Haimes, Michael Hartman, Rob Fisher, Rob Berman, Abbie Strassler, Giulia, Early Halloween, Too the Moon Alice, NY Vintage, JJ Hat Center.

THE SHUBERT ORGANIZATION, INC.
Board of Directors

Philip J. Smith	**Robert E. Wankel**
Chairman	President
Wyche Fowler, Jr.	**Diana Phillips**
Lee J. Seidler	**Michael I. Sovern**

Stuart Subotnick

Chief Financial Officer	Elliot Greene
Sr. Vice President, Ticketing	David Andrews
Vice President, Finance	Juan Calvo
Vice President, Human Resources	Cathy Cozens
Vice President, Facilities	John Darby
Vice President, Theatre Operations	Peter Entin
Vice President, Marketing	Charles Flateman
Vice President, Audit	Anthony LaMattina
Vice President, Ticket Sales	Brian Mahoney
Vice President, Creative Projects	D.S. Moynihan
Vice President, Real Estate	Julio Peterson

House Manager	Joann Swanson

Once

First Preview: February 28, 2012. Opened: March 18, 2012.
Still running as of May 31, 2013.

A bittersweet romantic musical based on the 2006 Oscar-winning film of the same title, about an Irish street musician who gains new inspiration when he meets a Czech woman who reawakens his musical muse—and his heart. Staged with a company of actors who also function as the onstage orchestra.

CAST

(in alphabetical order)

Eamon	DAVID ABELES
	Guitar, Piano, Melodica, Harmonica
Andrej	WILL CONNOLLY
	Electric Bass, Ukulele, Tambourine, Cajon, Guitar
Réza	ELIZABETH A. DAVIS
	Violin
Guy	STEVE KAZEE
	Guitar
Da	DAVID PATRICK KELLY
	Mandolin
* Ivanka	ELIZA HOLLAND MADORE
Girl	CRISTIN MILIOTI
	Piano
Baruška	Anne L. Nathan
	Piano, Accordion, Tambourine, Melodica
Švec	LUCAS PAPAELIAS
	Banjo, Guitar, Mandolin, Drum Set
* Ivanka	RIPLEY SOBO
Bank Manager	ANDY TAYLOR
	Violin, Accordion, Cello, Guitar, Mandolin
Ex-Girlfriend	ERIKKA WALSH
	Violin

Continued on next page

---

⑤ BERNARD B. JACOBS THEATRE

242 West 45th Street
A Shubert Organization Theatre

Philip J. Smith, *Chairman*   **Robert E. Wankel,** *President*

BARBARA BROCCOLI   JOHN N. HART JR.   PATRICK MILLING SMITH   FREDERICK ZOLLO
BRIAN CARMODY   MICHAEL G. WILSON   ORIN WOLF PRODUCTIONS   THE SHUBERT ORGANIZATION
ROBERT COLE, EXECUTIVE PRODUCER

in association with

NEW YORK THEATRE WORKSHOP

present

Once

book
ENDA WALSH

music and lyrics
GLEN HANSARD & MARKÉTA IRGLOVÁ

based on the motion picture written and directed by
JOHN CARNEY

starring

STEVE KAZEE   **CRISTIN MILIOTI**

DAVID ABELES   WILL CONNOLLY   ELIZABETH A. DAVIS   DAVID PATRICK KELLY
ELIZA HOLLAND MADORE   ANNE L. NATHAN   LUCAS PAPAELIAS   RIPLEY SOBO
ANDY TAYLOR   ERIKKA WALSH   PAUL WHITTY   J. MICHAEL ZYGO

scenic and costume design
BOB CROWLEY

lighting design
NATASHA KATZ

sound design
CLIVE GOODWIN

dialect coach
STEPHEN GABIS

casting
JIM CARNAHAN, CSA/STEPHEN KOPEL

production stage manager
BESS MARIE GLORIOSO

production manager
AURORA PRODUCTIONS

press representative
BONEAU/BRYAN-BROWN

company manager
LISA M. POYER

music supervisor and orchestrations
MARTIN LOWE

movement by
STEVEN HOGGETT

directed by
JOHN TIFFANY

Once was originally developed at the American Repertory Theater, Cambridge, Massachusetts, in April 2011,
Diane Paulus, Artistic Director, Diane Borger, Producer
The producers wish to express their appreciation to Theatre Development Fund for its support of this production.

10/1/12

Arthur Darvill and Joanna Christie

Photo by Joan Marcus

Once

MUSICAL NUMBERS

ACT I

"Leave" .... Guy
"Falling Slowly" .... Guy & Girl
"North Strand" .... Ensemble
"The Moon" .... Andrej (as Ensemble)
"Ej, Pada, Pada, Rosicka" .... Ensemble
"If You Want Me" .... Guy, Girl, Ensemble
"Broken Hearted Hoover Fixer Sucker Guy" .... Guy
"Say It to Me Now" .... Guy
"Abandoned in Bandon" .... Bank Manager
"Gold" .... Guy & Ensemble

ACT II

"Sleeping" .... Guy
"When Your Mind's Made Up" .... Guy, Girl, Ensemble
"The Hill" .... Girl
"Gold" (A capella) .... Company
"The Moon" .... Company
"Falling Slowly" (Reprise) .... Guy, Girl, Ensemble

Photo by Joan Marcus

Paul Whitty and
Elizabeth A. Davis

Cast Continued

Billy .... PAUL WHITTY
    Guitar, Ukulele, Cajon, Snare Drum
Emcee .... J. MICHAEL ZYGO
    Guitar

* Eliza Holland Madore and Ripley Sobo alternate in
the role of Ivanka.

Dance Captain: J. MICHAEL ZYGO
Music Captain: DAVID ABELES

UNDERSTUDIES

For Eamon: JOE CARROLL, SAMUEL COHEN,
    BRANDON ELLIS
For Andrej: JOE CARROLL, BRANDON ELLIS,
    BEN HOPE
For Réza: ANDREA GOSS, ERIKKA WALSH
For Guy: J. MICHAEL ZYGO
For Da: SAMUEL COHEN
For Girl: ANDREA GOSS, ERIKKA WALSH
For Baruška: JOANNE BORTS
For Švec: JOE CARROLL, BRANDON ELLIS,
    BEN HOPE
For Bank Manager: BRANDON ELLIS
For Ex-Girlfriend: ANDREA GOSS
For Billy: BRANDON ELLIS, J. MICHAEL ZYGO
For Emcee: JOE CARROLL, SAMUEL COHEN,
    BEN HOPE

STANDBYS

For Girl: LAURA DREYFUSS
For Guy: BEN HOPE

2012-2013 AWARD

GRAMMY AWARD
Best Musical Theater Album

Steve Kazee
Guy

Cristin Milioti
Girl

David Abeles
Eamon,
Music Captain

Will Connolly
Andrej

Elizabeth A. Davis
Réza

David Patrick Kelly
Da

Eliza Holland Madore
Ivanka

Once

Anne L. Nathan
Baruška

Lucas Papaelias
Švec

Ripley Sobo
Ivanka

Andy Taylor
Bank Manager

Erikka Walsh
*Ex-Girlfriend,
u/s Girl, Réza*

Paul Whitty
Billy

J. Michael Zygo
*Emcee, u/s Guy, Billy,
Dance Captain*

Joanne Borts
u/s Baruška

Joe Carroll
*u/s Eamon, Andrej,
Švec, Emcee*

Samuel Cohen
*u/s Da, Eamon,
Emcee*

Laura Dreyfuss
Standby

Brandon Ellis
*u/s Bank Manager,
Billy, Andrej, Švec,
Eamon*

Andrea Goss
*u/s Girl, Réza,
Ex-Girlfriend*

Ben Hope
*u/s Guy, Andrej,
Švec, Emcee*

Enda Walsh
Playwright

Glen Hansard
Music and Lyrics

Markéta Irglová
Music and Lyrics

John Carney
*Writer and Director
of the Film, Once*

John Tiffany
Director

Steven Hoggett
Movement

Martin Lowe
*Musical Supervisor,
Orchestrations, and
Additional Material*

Bob Crowley
*Scenic and Costume
Design*

Natasha Katz
Lighting Design

Clive Goodwin
Sound Design

Stephen Gabis
Dialect Coach

Liz Caplan
Liz Caplan Vocal
Studios, LLC
Vocal Supervisor

Jim Carnahan
Casting

Gene O'Donovan
Aurora Productions
*Production
Management*

Ben Heller
Aurora Productions
*Production
Management*

Barbara Broccoli
Producer

John N. Hart, Jr.
Producer

Patrick Milling Smith
Producer

Frederick Zollo
Producer

Brian Carmody
Producer

Michael G. Wilson
Producer

Once

Orin Wolf
Orin Wolf
Productions
Producer

Philip J. Smith
The Shubert
Organization
Producer

Robert E. Wankel
The Shubert
Organization
Producer

Robert Cole
Executive Producer

James C. Nicola
Artistic Director
NYTW
Producer

Diane Paulus
Artistic Director
A.R.T.
Workshop Producer

Charles Stone
Associate Producer

Mckayla Twiggs
Ivanka

Joanna Christie
Girl

Arthur Darvill
Guy

Jillian Lebling
Ivanka

Katrina Lenk
Réza

Don Noble
*u/s Da, Eamon,
Emcee*

Erica Swindell
*u/s Girl, Réza,
Ex-Girlfriend*

Carlos Valdes
Andrej

Claire Wellin
Réza

Photos by Brian Mapp

BOX OFFICE
(L-R): Marshall Kolbrenner, Karen Coscia, Michael Kolbrenner

STAGE MANAGEMENT
(L-R): Ana M. Garcia, Bess Marie Glorioso, Katherine Shea

WARDROBE
(L-R): Cailin Anderson, Kate Chihaby, Kathleen Gallagher

Once

CREW
(L-R): Fred Ricci, Reid Hall, Reg Vessey, Jason Choquette (sitting), Jonathan Cohen, Wally Flores, Martin Perrin

FRONT OF HOUSE
Standing: Billy Mitchell (House Manager)
Front: Kair Martin
Second Row (L-R): Eva Frances Laskow (Head Usher), Holly Madison, Joy Mayweather
Third Row: Rosa Pesante
Fourth Row (L-R): Gerry Bellitus, John Seid, Leo Ruiz
Top: Sean Cutler (Ticket Taker)

Photos by Brian Mapp

Once

Company Manager ....Lisa M. Poyer
Associate Company Manager ....Susan Keappock
Assistant Company Manager ....Katie Pope

Production Stage Manager ....Bess Marie Glorioso
Stage Manager ....Ana M. Garcia
Assistant Stage Manager ....Katherine Shea

Associate Producer ....Charles Stone
Associate Producer ....Ben Limberg
Resident Director ....Shaun Peknic
Movement Associate ....Yasmine Lee
Associate Music Supervisor ....Rob Preuss
Vocal Supervisor ....Liz Caplan Vocal Studios, LLC
Associate Scenic Designer ....Frank McCullough
Assistant Lighting Designers ....Peter Hoerburger,
Yael Lubetzky
Assistant Sound Designer/
Advance Audio ....Brian Walters
Czech Diction and Translation ....Suzanna Halsey

Assistant to John N. Hart, Jr. ....Maximillian Traber
Assistant to Patrick Milling Smith ....Catherine Waage
Assistant to Robert Cole &
Frederick Zollo ....Gabriel Schicchi

Production Carpenter ....Rebecca O'Neill
Production Electrician ....Michael Pitzer
Production Props ....Reg Vessey
Production Sound Engineer ....Phillip Lojo/
Paul Delcioppo
Head Electrician ....Eric Norris
Sound Engineer ....Dan Hochstine
Instrument Technician ....Reid Hall
Props Supervisor ....Matt Hodges
UK Props ....Lisa Buckley
Moving Light Programmer ....Sean Beach
Advance Production Sound ....Jason Choquette
NYTW Costume Liaison ....Jeffrey Wallach
Wardrobe Supervisor ....Kathleen Gallagher
Dressers ....Cailin Anderson, Katie Chihaby
Child Actor Guardian ....Lisa Schwartz
Tutoring ....On Location Education/Muriel Kester

Production Assistants ....Brandon Bart, Dale Ducko,
Melanie Ganim, Eric Love,
Ryan McCurdy, Danese C. Smalls,
Katie Summerfield

Advertising ....SpotCo/
Drew Hodges, Jim Edwards,
Tom Greenwald, Y. Darius Suyama, Laura Ellis
Website and Online Marketing ....SpotCo/
Sara Fitzpatrick, Marc Mettler,
Michael Crowley, Caraline Sogliuzzo
Marketing and Promotions ....SpotCo/
Nick Pramik, Kristen Rathbun,
Julie Wechsler, Caroline Newhouse
Legal
Counsel .....Franklin, Weinrib, Rudell & Vassallo, P.C./
Jonathan Lonner, Heather Reid
Additional Legal
Counsel ....Frankfurt, Kurnit, Klein & Selz, P.C./
Mark Merriman
Immigration Counsel ....Shannon K. Such
Accountant ....Fried & Kowgios CPAs LLP/
Robert Fried, CPA
Comptroller ....Anne Stewart FitzRoy, CPA
Orthopaedist ....David S. Weiss, M.D.
Banking ....City National Bank/
Anne McSweeney, Michael Tynan
Insurance ....Dewitt Stern Group/
Peter Shoemaker, Rebecca LaFazia
Payroll Service ....Castellana Payroll Services, Inc./
Lance Castellana, James Castellana,
Norman Sewell
Travel ....Kristine Ljungdahl, Manifest Travel
Production Photographer ....Joan Marcus
Opening Night
Coordination ....The Lawrence Company Events, Inc./
Michael P. Lawrence
Theatre Displays ....King Displays, Inc.
Group Sales ....Telecharge.com Group Sales/
212-239-6262, 1-800-432-7780,
www.telecharge.com/groups

(L-R): Katrina Lenk and Erikka Walsh

Photo by Joan Marcus

One Man, Two Guvnors

First Preview: April 6, 2012. Opened: April 18, 2012.
Limited Engagement. Closed September 2, 2012 after 13 Previews and 159 Performances.

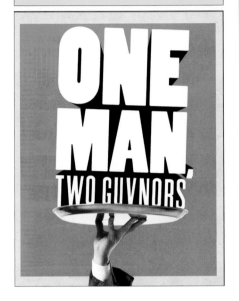

British farce (based on Carlo Goldoni's commedia dell'arte masterpiece The Servant of Two Masters*) about a man who finds himself in the employ of two tough characters on the run from the law. His efforts to serve them both simultaneously without one finding out about the other (and without any of them winding up in the hands of the constabulary) provides the ever-escalating action. The production's centerpiece is James Corden's manic performance as the overworked and underfed employee, Francis Henshall.*

CAST

(in order of appearance)

Harry Dangle	MARTYN ELLIS
Dolly	SUZIE TOASE
Lloyd Boateng	TREVOR LAIRD
Charlie "The Duck" Clench	FRED RIDGEWAY
Pauline Clench	CLAIRE LAMS
Alan Dangle	DANIEL RIGBY
Francis Henshall	JAMES CORDEN
Rachel Crabbe	JEMIMA ROOPER
Stanley Stubbers	OLIVER CHRIS
Gareth	BEN LIVINGSTON
Alfie	TOM EDDEN

Ensemble ....ELI JAMES, BEN LIVINGSTON,
SARAH MANTON, STEPHEN PILKINGTON,
DAVID RYAN SMITH, NATALIE SMITH

Continued on next page

☺ THE MUSIC BOX

239 W. 45th Street
A Shubert Organization Theatre

Philip J. Smith, *Chairman*   **Robert E. Wankel,** *President*

NATIONAL THEATRE OF GREAT BRITAIN
under the direction of
NICHOLAS HYTNER and NICK STARR
and
BOB BOYETT

NATIONAL ANGELS   CHRIS HARPER   TIM LEVY

SCOTT RUDIN   ROGER BERLIND   HARRIET NEWMAN LEVE   STEPHANIE P. McCLELLAND
BROADWAY ACROSS AMERICA   JAM THEATRICALS   DARYL ROTH
SONIA FRIEDMAN   HARRIS KARMA PRODUCTIONS   DEBORAH TAYLOR   RICHARD WILLIS

Present

JAMES CORDEN

In

ONE MAN, TWO GUVNORS

By **RICHARD BEAN**

Based on *THE SERVANT OF TWO MASTERS* by CARLO GOLDONI

With songs by **GRANT OLDING**

With

OLIVER CHRIS   JEMIMA ROOPER

TOM EDDEN   MARTYN ELLIS   TREVOR LAIRD   CLAIRE LAMS
FRED RIDGEWAY   DANIEL RIGBY   SUZIE TOASE
BRIAN GONZALES   ELI JAMES   BEN LIVINGSTON   SARAH MANTON
STEPHEN PILKINGTON   DAVID RYAN SMITH   NATALIE SMITH
JACOB COLIN COHEN   AUSTIN MOORHEAD   JASON RABINOWITZ   CHARLIE ROSEN

Director **NICHOLAS HYTNER**

Physical Comedy Director **CAL McCRYSTAL**

Designer **MARK THOMPSON**

Lighting Designer **MARK HENDERSON**

Sound Designer **PAUL ARDITTI**

Associate Director and Choreographer	Original UK Casting	US Casting	Music Director
ADAM PENFORD	**ALASTAIR COOMER CDG**	**TARA RUBIN CASTNG, CSA**	**CHARLIE ROSEN**

Production Stage Manager	Technical Supervisor	NT Technical Producer	NT Administrative Producer
WILLIAM JOSEPH BARNES	**DAVID BENKEN**	**KATRINA GILROY**	**ROBIN HAWKES**

Press Representative	Advertising & Marketing	General Management
BONEAU/BRYAN-BROWN	**SPOTCO**	**JAMES TRINER**

National Theatre is supported by Arts Council England
The Producers wish to express their appreciation to Theatre Development Fund for its support of this production.

6/4/12

(L-R): Suzie Toase, Oliver Chris, James Corden, Jemima Rooper

Photo by Joan Marcus

One Man, Two Guvnors

Cast Continued

THE CRAZE

JASON RABINOWITZ (Lead Vocals)
AUSTIN MOORHEAD (Lead Guitar)
CHARLIE ROSEN (Music Director/Bass)
JACOB COLIN COHEN (Drums/Percussion)

UNDERSTUDIES

For Francis:
BRIAN GONZALES
For Stanley:
ELI JAMES
For Rachel:
NATALIE SMITH
For Charlie:
MARTYN ELLIS, BEN LIVINGSTON
For Harry:
BEN LIVINGSTON
For Dolly, Pauline:
SARAH MANTON
For Alan, Alfie:
STEPHEN PILKINGTON
For Lloyd, Gareth:
DAVID RYAN SMITH
For Female Ensemble:
LIZ BALTES
For Lead Guitar, Drums, Lead Singer:
CHARLIE ROSEN
For Bass, Lead Singer:
MATT CUSACK
For Lead Singer, Drums:
ZACH JONES

DANCE CAPTAIN/FIGHT CAPTAIN

DAVID RYAN SMITH

James Corden is appearing with the permission of Actors' Equity Association. Oliver Chris, Jemima Rooper, Tom Edden, Martyn Ellis, Trevor Laird, Claire Lams, Fred Ridgeway, Daniel Rigby and Suzie Toase are appearing with the support of Actors' Equity Association pursuant to an exchange program between American Equity and UK Equity.

James Corden
Francis Henshall

Oliver Chris
Stanley Stubbers

Jemima Rooper
Rachel Crabbe

Tom Edden
Alfie

Martyn Ellis
Harry Dangle

Trevor Laird
Lloyd Boateng

Claire Lams
Pauline Clench

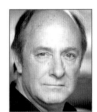
Fred Ridgeway
Charlie Clench

Daniel Rigby
Alan

Suzie Toase
Dolly

Brian Gonzales
Ensemble

Eli James
Ensemble

Ben Livingston
Gareth/Ensemble

Sarah Manton
Ensemble

Stephen Pilkington
Ensemble

David Ryan Smith
Ensemble

Natalie Smith
Ensemble

Jacob Colin Cohen
Drums/Percussion

Austin Moorhead
Lead Guitar

Jason Rabinowitz
Lead Vocals

Charlie Rosen
Music Director/Bass

Matt Cusack
u/s Bass, Lead Singer

Zach Jones
u/s Lead Singer, Percussion

One Man, Two Guvnors

Liz Baltes
Assistant Stage Manager; Understudy

Richard Bean
Author

Nicholas Hytner
Director

Cal McCrystal
Physical Comedy Director

Mark Thompson
Set and Costume Design

Mark Henderson
Lighting Design

Paul Arditti
Sound Design

Grant Olding
Composer

Adam Penford
Associate Director/ Choreographer

Tara Rubin Casting
US Casting

David Benken
Technical Supervisor

James Triner
General Manager

Bob Boyett
Producer

Roger Berlind
Producer

Harriet Newman Leve
Producer

Stephanie P. McClelland
Producer

John Gore
*CEO
Broadway Across America
Producer*

Thomas B. McGrath
*Chairman
Broadway Across America
Producer*

Arny Granat
*Jam Theatricals
Producer*

Steve Traxler
*Jam Theatricals
Producer*

Daryl Roth
Producer

Sonia Friedman Productions
Producer

Dede Harris
Producer

Sharon Karmazin
Producer

Deborah Taylor
Producer

Richard Willis
Producer

STAFF FOR *ONE MAN, TWO GUVNORS*

GENERAL MANAGEMENT
James Triner

PRESS REPRESENTATIVE
BONEAU/BRYAN-BROWN
Adrian Bryan-Brown
Jessica Johnson   Christine Olver

CASTING
TARA RUBIN CASTING
Tara Rubin, CSA; Lindsay Levine;
Eric Woodall, CSA; Merri Sugarman, CSA;

Dale Brown, CSA; Stephanie Yankwitt, CSA;
Kaitlin Shaw

PRODUCTION MANAGEMENT
David Benken   Rose Palombo

COMPANY MANAGER
Elizabeth M. Talmadge

Production Stage Manager ....William Joseph Barnes
Stage Manager ....Chris Zaccardi
Assistant Stage Manager ....Liz Baltes
Music Director ....Charlie Rosen
UK Production Manager ....Anna Anderson
Associate Scenic Designer ....Peter Eastman

Associate Costume Designer ....Daryl Stone
UK Associate Lighting Designer ....Tom Snell
US Associate Lighting Designer ....Michael Jones
Moving Light Programmer ....Marc Polimeni
UK Associate Sound Designer ....John Owens
US Associate Sound Designer ....Drew Levy
Hair Coordinator ....Campbell Young Associates
Head Carpenter ....John McPherson
Advance Rigger ....Michael Shepp
Production Electrician ....Jon Lawson
Head Electrician ....Michael W. Brown
Head Sound Engineer ....Lucas Indelicato
Production Properties Coordinator ....Denise J. Grillo
Assistant Props ....Kevin Crawford
Wardrobe Supervisor ....Raymond Panelli

One Man, Two Guvnors
SCRAPBOOK

Correspondent: Tom Edden "Alfie"

Memories of the Last Week of the Run: Our final performance was a Sunday matinee, and it's traditional on the last matinee that cast members will prank each other while they're on stage. Someone brought the company manager's dog on stage and all hell broke loose. For the bit where James supposedly drinks a glass of wine, Ollie [Oliver Chris] filled it with real wine and James had to drink this pretty generous glass of wine. Just before the bit where James brings a woman up from the audience and later empties a fire extinguisher in her face, James threw a jug of water on Ollie in retaliation for the wine incident.

These pranks were very much enjoyed by the audience and in our show the audience got in on the pranks. In the audience-participation scene when James Corden asks if anyone has a sandwich, ten or twelve people lined up at the stage with strange offerings: a box of fries, a serving of fish and chips, things like that.

I'll never forget the look on Fred Ridgeway's face when Jemima delivers her line, "My body." She has been disguised as a man the whole show and finally reveals that she's a woman by turning upstage, opening her shirt and showing James and Fred that she has breasts. Of course, usually they are covered up and Fred and James react as if they are not. But on the last night she decided to give them the Full Monty. The audience couldn't see what Fred and James (and those of us backstage) were seeing, but they understood immediately what was happening, and it brought the house down. It felt like an eternity of laughter. It stopped the show and Fred forgot his lines. For one special moment there was almost no division between us huddled in the wings laughing and the audience sitting in their seats laughing. It was very, very special; something everyone will remember.

The producers knew we were going to have a busy final weekend so they threw a farewell party the previous Thursday night at a hotel with a rooftop restaurant. There were flowers and food and drinks and gifts and we stayed until we were kicked out. But even so, we cried for the next four nights in a row, bereft and bereaved, and were a bit of a mess after the bows at the final performance.

For our last bows I decided to wear one of those trashy "I Love NY" t-shirts. When I came out for my bow, in a kind of diva-ish moment, I kissed the stage. The audience just went crazy. But they also applauded me when I made my first entrance. It was a very affectionate audience. It was the perfect end to my journey here in New York. There are awards in London but I had never come close to winning one. Here, I won the Drama Desk Award as Outstanding Featured Actor in a Play, and was nominated for a Tony Award.

James had recalled for us how emotional the curtain call had been when he appeared here in *History Boys* some years back. So there was no curtain speech for *One Man, Two Guvnors*. But the audience was really exultant and didn't want to let him go. I've never experienced anything like that.

It was very tough saying goodbye to each other, and to the show, and to New York. The peculiarity of the business is that you go through an intense period of close relationships when you work on a show. The theatre itself becomes like a pressure cooker. Even the people you don't necessarily get on with get under your skin. Then, suddenly, it's all over. We all became a little family and it's tough to leave your family. And that includes our great friends at the Music Box Theatre. The staff there is so wonderful! The permanent staff and the floating staff were so wonderfully welcoming and warm and such fun: the wig people and the costume people and the crew—they really made the experience wonderful for us. The theatre was built by Irving Berlin and the house manager's office is Irving Berlin's old office. He showed us a secret cubby hole in a corner of the office that had a treasure trove of old material from back then.

Two or three weeks before the end the production company announced that we had recouped. I think we did quite well, coming into Broadway as a straight play with no star—though James is certainly a star now. We played out the whole planned run and didn't have to close early. During the final week, while we were taking our bows, a chap in the front row held up a sign saying "Please continue." But we were planned as a limited run and James has gotten so busy we couldn't have stayed if we wanted to. It was nice to know that someone felt that way, but I think there is something to be said for quitting while you're ahead. I'm pleased that we didn't dribble out; we went out with a bang.

Assistant Wardrobe Supervisor	Suzan Cerceo
Dressers	Karen Gilbert, Jean Steinlein, Chip White
Stitcher/Laundry	Kathryn Guida, Scott Tucker
Hair Supervisor	Carmel Vargyas
Hairdresser	Kevin R. Maybee
Production Assistants	Morgan Holbrook, Katie McKee, James C. Steele, Michael Tosto
General Management Assistant	Amanda Hutt
Banking	JPMorgan/Chase
Payroll	Castellana Services, Inc.
Production Accountant	Rosenberg, Neuwirth & Kuchner/ Chris Cacace
Insurance	DeWitt Stern Group
Legal Counsel	Lazarus & Harris LLP/ Scott Lazarus, Esq., Robert C. Harris, Esq.
Merchandising	Encore Merchandising
Advertising	SPOTCO/ Drew Hodges, Jim Edwards, Tom Greenwald, Jim Aquino, Laura Ellis
Website Design	SPOTCO/ Sara Fitzpatrick, Marc Mettler, Kristen Bardwil, Michelle Haines, Cory Spinney
Marketing	SPOTCO/ Nick Pramik, Kristen Rathbun, Julie Wechsler, Caroline Newhouse
Theatre Displays	BAM Signs/Adam Miller
Group Sales	Shubert Group Sales
Housing Accommodations	Gregory Diaz/ Premier Furnished Solutions
Flight/Hotel Arrangements	Andi Henig/Tzell Travel

FOR BOYETT THEATRICALS

Executive Assistant	Diane Murphy
Office Assistants	Michael Mandell, Kiefer Mansfield

FOR THE NATIONAL THEATRE OF GREAT BRITAIN

Chairman of the NT Board	John Makinson
Director of the National Theatre	Nicholas Hytner
Executive Director	Nick Starr
Chief Operating Officer	Lisa Burger
NT Associate Producer	Pádraig Cusack
Producer	Chris Harper
Technical Producer	Katrina Gilroy
Administrative Producer	Robin Hawkes
Assistant Producer	Marianne Dicker
Producing Assistant	Hetty Wooding
Head of Music	Matthew Scott
Casting	Alastair Coomer
Production Accountant	Michelle Woods
Assistant Production Accountant	Akos Koranteng
General Counsel	Peter Taylor

Mark Henderson's lighting design re-created by Tom Snell, National Theatre.

CREDITS

Scenery constructed by the National Theatre Carpentry and Paintframe Departments, and Hudson Scenic Studio, Inc. Technical drawings by the National Theatre Digital Design and Drawing Department. Properties constructed by the National Theatre Props Department. Costumes constructed by the National Theatre Costume Department. Lighting equipment from PRG Lighting. Sound equipment from Sound Associates, Inc. Special thanks to Bra*Tenders for hosiery and undergarments.

Rehearsed at the New 42nd Street Studios

SPECIAL THANKS

Special thanks to the National Theatre's Digital, Finance, Graphics, Marketing and Press Departments; the West End team of *One Man, Two Guvnors*.

 THE SHUBERT ORGANIZATION, INC.
Board of Directors

Philip J. Smith	**Robert E. Wankel**
Chairman	President
Wyche Fowler, Jr.	**Diana Phillips**
Lee J. Seidler	**Michael I. Sovern**

Stuart Subotnick

Chief Financial Officer	Elliot Greene
Sr. Vice President, Ticketing	David Andrews
Vice President, Finance	Juan Calvo
Vice President, Human Resources	Cathy Cozens
Vice President, Facilities	John Darby
Vice President, Theatre Operations	Peter Entin
Vice President, Marketing	Charles Flateman
Vice President, Audit	Anthony LaMattina
Vice President, Ticket Sales	Brian Mahoney
Vice President, Creative Projects	D.S. Moynihan
Vice President, Real Estate	Julio Peterson

House Manager	Jonathan Shulman

Orphans

First Preview: March 26, 2013. Opened: April 18, 2013.
Limited Engagement. Closed May 19, 2013 after 27 Previews and 37 Performances.

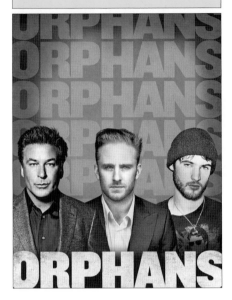

PLAYBILL

Two orphaned young men living off small-time thievery in a run-down Philadelphia row house get more than they bargained for when they kidnap a wealthy businessman and hold him for ransom. The businessman, who was raised in an orphanage, sets himself up as their father figure and tries to steer them on the right path in life before his own dark past catches up with him. Broadway debut of a 1983 play that was a hit Off-Broadway, in Chicago and in London.

CAST
(in order of appearance)

Phillip .... TOM STURRIDGE
Treat .... BEN FOSTER
Harold .... ALEC BALDWIN

North Philadelphia
Sometime in the not-too-distant past

Stage Manager .... TRISHA HENSON

Tom Sturridge is appearing with the support of Actors' Equity Association pursuant to an exchange program between American Equity and UK Equity.

UNDERSTUDIES
For Phillip: JONATHAN GORDON
For Harold: BRUCE McCARTY
For Treat: JEFF WARD

---

⑤ GERALD SCHOENFELD THEATRE
236 West 45th Street
A Shubert Organization Theatre

Philip J. Smith, *Chairman*   Robert E. Wankel, *President*

FREDERICK ZOLLO   ROBERT COLE
THE SHUBERT ORGANIZATION   ORIN WOLF
LUCKY VIII   SCOTT M. DELMAN   JAMES P. MACGILVRAY   STYLESFOUR PRODUCTIONS

present

ALEC BALDWIN
BEN FOSTER   TOM STURRIDGE

in

ORPHANS

by

LYLE KESSLER

SCENIC DESIGN BY	COSTUME DESIGN BY	LIGHTING DESIGN BY
JOHN LEE BEATTY	JESS GOLDSTEIN	PAT COLLINS

SOUND DESIGN BY	ORIGINAL MUSIC COMPOSED BY	FIGHT DIRECTION
PETER FITZGERALD	TOM KITT	THOMAS SCHALL

PRODUCTION MANAGEMENT	DIALECT COACH	CASTING	PRODUCTION STAGE MANAGER
AURORA PRODUCTIONS	DEBORAH HECHT	CAPARELLIOTIS CASTING	ROY HARRIS

PRESS REPRESENTATIVE	ADVERTISING & MARKETING	COMPANY MANAGER	GENERAL MANAGER
BONEAU/BRYAN-BROWN	SERINO/COYNE	BRUCE KLINGER	LISA M. POYER

DIRECTED BY
DANIEL SULLIVAN

The producers wish to express their appreciation to Theatre Development Fund for its support of this production.

4/18/13

(L-R): Tom Sturridge, Alec Baldwin and Ben Foster

Photo by Joan Marcus

Orphans

Alec Baldwin
Harold

Ben Foster
Treat

Tom Sturridge
Phillip

Jonathan Gordon
u/s Phillip

Bruce McCarty
u/s Harold

Jeff Ward
u/s Treat

Lyle Kessler
Playwright

Daniel Sullivan
Director

John Lee Beatty
Scenic Design

Jess Goldstein
Costume Design

Pat Collins
Lighting Design

Tom Kitt
Composer

Deborah Hecht
Dialect Coach

Thomas Schall
Fight Director

David Caparelliotis
Caparelliotis Casting
Casting

Gene O'Donovan
Aurora Productions
Production Management

Ben Heller
Aurora Productions
Production Management

Frederick Zollo
Producer

Robert Cole
Producer

Philip J. Smith
The Shubert Organization
Producer

Robert E. Wankel
The Shubert Organization
Producer

Orin Wolf
Producer

Wendy Federman
Lucky VIII
Producer

Carl Moellenberg
Lucky VIII
Producer

Scott M. Delman
Producer

John Styles
StylesFour Productions
Producer

Dave Clemmons
StylesFour Productions
Producer

2012-2013 AWARDS

OUTER CRITICS CIRCLE AWARD
Outstanding Featured Actor in a Play
(Tom Sturridge)

THEATRE WORLD AWARD
For Outstanding Broadway
or Off-Broadway Debut
(Tom Sturridge)

DRESSERS
(L-R): Emily Merriweather, Derek Moreno

Orphans

FRONT OF HOUSE
Front Row (L-R):
Francine Kramer (Chief Usher),
David Conte (House Manager)
Back Row (L-R):
Kamani Lall (Usher),
Alexandra Zavilowicz (Usher)
Paul Brown (Headsets)

STAFF FOR *ORPHANS*

GENERAL MANAGEMENT
ROBERT COLE PRODUCTIONS, LLC
Lisa M. Poyer

GENERAL PRESS REPRESENTATIVE
BONEAU/BRYAN-BROWN
Chris Boneau Jackie Green Emily Meagher

PRODUCTION MANAGEMENT
AURORA PRODUCTIONS
Gene O'Donovan   Ben Heller
Stephanie Sherline, Anita Shah, Jarid Sumner,
Anthony Jusino, Liza Luxenberg,
G. Garrett Ellison, Troy Pepicelli, Gayle Riess,
Catherine Nelson, Melissa Mazdra

CASTING
CAPARELLIOTIS CASTING

Company Manager ....Bruce Klinger
Production Stage Manager ....Roy Harris
Stage Manager ....Trisha Henson
Assistant Director ....Jonathan Sullivan
Assistant Scenic Designer ....Kacie Hultgren
Associate Costume Designer ....China Lee
Associate Lighting Designers ....Stephen T. Sorenson,
Michael Gottlieb
Assistant Sound Designer ....Kate Foretek
Production Carpenter ....Jason Clark
Production Electrician ....Brendan Quigley
Head Electrician ....Keith Buchanan
Production Sound ....Brad Gyorgak
Production Props ....Chris Pantuso
Wardrobe Supervisor ....Patrick Bevilacqua
Dressers ....Emily Merriweather, Derek Moreno
Production Assistant ....Alex Mark
Assistant to Messrs. Zollo & Cole ....Jennifer Kim
Assistant to the General Manager ....Amanda Hutt
Assistant to Mr. Baldwin ....Monica Hopkins

Advertising ....Serino/Coyne/
Greg Corradetti, Robert Jones,
Carolyn London, Vanessa Javier,
Ben Skinner
Digital Outreach and Website ....Serino/Coyne/
Jim Glaub, Chip Meyrelles,
Laurie Connor, Kevin Keating,
Whitney Manalio Creighton,
Jenna Lauren Freed, Emily Genduso
Marketing ....Serino/Coyne/
Leslie Barrett, Abby Wolbe
Legal Counsel ....Fitelson, Lasky, Aslan,
Couture & Garmise LLP/
Richard Garmise, Esq.
Immigration Counsel ....Fragomen, Del Rey,
Bernsen & Loewy, LLP/
Freddi M. Weintraub, Susanah Wade
Accountant ....Fried & Kowgios, CPAs LLP/
Robert Fried, CPA
Comptroller ....Anne Stewart FitzRoy, CPA
Banking ....City National Bank/
Anne McSweeney, Michael Tynan
Insurance ....DeWitt Stern Group Inc./
Peter Shoemaker, Rebecca LaFazia
Payroll Service ....Castellana Payroll Services, Inc./
Lance Castellana, James Castellana,
Norman Sewell
Production Photographer ....Joan Marcus
Opening Night
Coordination ....The Lawrence Company Events, Inc./
Michael P. Lawrence
Group Sales ....Telecharge.com Group Sales/
212-239-6262, 1-800-432-7780

www.telecharge.com/groups

CREDITS
Scenery constructed and automated by Hudson Scenic
Studio, Inc. Lighting equipment from PRG Lighting. Sound
equipment from Sound Associates. Custom tailoring by
Saint Laurie Merchant Tailors, New York. *Orphans* was

originally produced in 1983 by The Matrix Theatre, Los
Angeles, California; Joseph Stern, Artistic Director.
Headshot for Alec Baldwin: Mary Ellen Matthews.
Headshot for Tom Sturridge: Julian Broad Contour by
Getty Images.

Rehearsed at the New 42nd Street Studios

SPECIAL THANKS
Dr. Glenn Saxe, Daniel Otti, New York Parkour

www.OrphansOnBroadway.com

 THE SHUBERT ORGANIZATION, INC.
Board of Directors

Philip J. Smith	Robert E. Wankel
Chairman	President
Wyche Fowler, Jr.	**Diana Phillips**
Lee J. Seidler	**Michael I. Sovern**

Stuart Subotnick

Chief Financial Officer ....Elliot Greene
Sr. Vice President, Ticketing ....David Andrews
Vice President, Finance ....Juan Calvo
Vice President, Human Resources ....Cathy Cozens
Vice President, Facilities ....John Darby
Vice President, Theatre Operations ....Peter Entin
Vice President, Marketing ....Charles Flateman
Vice President, Audit ....Anthony LaMattina
Vice President, Ticket Sales ....Brian Mahoney
Vice President, Creative Projects ...........D.S. Moynihan
Vice President, Real Estate ....Julio Peterson

Theatre Manager ....David M. Conte

Orphans
SCRAPBOOK

Correspondent: Roy Harris, Production Stage Manager

Once we got past the first ten days of rehearsal—in which one actor left the show amid many emails, tweets, and an angry media clamoring for information that was none of their business—Ben Foster replaced the original Treat and joined us with Alec Baldwin as Harold and Tom Sturridge as Phillip. Daniel Sullivan was at the helm, and we all knew it was going to be quite a ride. *Orphans* by Lyle Kessler was originally done Off-Broadway in 1985 in an acclaimed production from Steppenwolf Theatre Company. We were so happy to be part of the first Broadway incarnation. Rehearsals were fast and furious on the sixth floor of New 42nd Street Studios.

Treat, a petty thief, lives in North Philly with his troubled, younger brother Phillip, who hasn't left the house in a decade. One night, Treat brings home a Chicago gangster, and things begin to change. Because there is a lot of violent behavior in the play, fight director Tom Schall was on hand at many rehearsals. One actor hits another over the head with the handle of a gun, two actors race up and down a cramped stairwell doing all kinds of leaps and bounds, the two brothers have a major fight in the final scene. And another tears up closets and furniture. Once in the theatre, we did a fight call before each show, so there would be no injuries. Fight call was especially entertaining because Alec, who is a great raconteur, would regale us all with great theatre stories and spot-on impressions of Richard Burton, John Guare, our playwright Lyle Kessler, and an extraordinarily uncanny one of Al Pacino.

Tech was pretty straightforward, and it turned out to be mostly about finally working with the real props, stairs, et cetera. It's a very physical play, but even more so because Tom Sturridge chose an unusual approach to his character. He felt, since Phillip hasn't been out of the house in a long time (and is basically unsocialized), that his feet wouldn't hit the floor very often. So Tom jumped, leapt, and swung around from one piece of furniture to another: from a credenza to the dining-room table to an easy chair in the living room to a sofa and then to a window seat from which he watched passersby. Once we were ensconced in the Schoenfeld, Tom and Ben got physical therapy once a week, to keep them in as good shape as possible to fulfill the demands of their roles.

From our first preview on, audiences were galvanized by the complex relationship of the two brothers and watched with rapt attention as Harold takes over the house and, in various ways, becomes a father to both boys. We opened on Thursday, April 18, after three weeks of previews, to mostly good reviews, but a particularly vitriolic one from the *New York Times*. Two weeks later, we got Tony nominations for best revival and best performance by an actor in a leading role, Tom Sturridge. Tom also got a Theatre World Award for a particularly accomplished Broadway debut.

We were all saddened when we had to close the show six weeks early, despite those two Tony nominations. The people who go to the theatre these days look to the *Times'* critic's opinion, and his dismissal of our show made it impossible to sell seats.

Photos by Brian Mapp

CREW
Front Row (L-R):
Jason Clark (Production Carpenter), Brad Gyorgak (Production Sound), Chris Pantuso (Production Props)
Back Row (L-R):
Tim McWilliams (House Carpenter), Leslie Ann Kilian (House Electrician) Keith Buchanan (Production Lights) Steve McDonald (House Props)

MANAGEMENT
(L-R): Roy Harris (Production Stage Manager and *Yearbook* correspondent), Trisha Henson (Stage Manager), Alex Mark (Production Assistant), Bruce Klinger (Company Manager)

The Other Place

First Preview: December 11, 2012. Opened: January 10, 2013.
Limited Engagement. Closed March 3, 2013 after 34 Previews and 61 Performances.

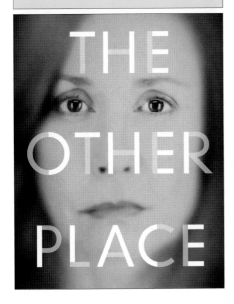

A brilliant female scientist seems to have a strong grasp on her life and relationships. But over the course of this eighty-minute drama we see her gradually lose her grip as dementia weakens her once-acute mind. The progress of her malady is reflected in imaginary scenes on the phone with her long-lost runaway daughter. To reunite with the daughter, the scientist believes she must return to the summer house where they were last together, a cottage known as "The Other Place."

CAST
(in order of appearance)

Juliana ....LAURIE METCALF
The Woman ....ZOE PERRY
Ian ....DANIEL STERN
The Man ....JOHN SCHIAPPA

TIME AND PLACE:

Boston, the Present
Cape Cod, Ten Years Ago and the Present

Stage Manager ....KELLY BEAULIEU

UNDERSTUDIES

For Ian, The Man:
TONY CARLIN
For Juliana:
HENNY RUSSELL
For the Woman:
DANIELLE SLAVICK

MANHATTAN THEATRE CLUB
SAMUEL J. FRIEDMAN THEATRE

ARTISTIC DIRECTOR
LYNNE MEADOW

EXECUTIVE PRODUCER
BARRY GROVE

BY SPECIAL ARRANGEMENT WITH
MCC THEATER

PRESENTS

THE OTHER PLACE

BY
SHARR WHITE

WITH

**LAURIE METCALF   DANIEL STERN
ZOE PERRY   JOHN SCHIAPPA**

SCENIC DESIGN
**EUGENE LEE
& EDWARD PIERCE**

COSTUME DESIGN
DAVID ZINN

LIGHTING DESIGN
JUSTIN TOWNSEND

ORIGINAL MUSIC & SOUND DESIGN
FITZ PATTON

VIDEO & PROJECTION DESIGN
WILLIAM CUSICK

CASTING
**CAPARELLIOTIS CASTING
& TELSEY + COMPANY**

PRODUCTION STAGE MANAGER
BARCLAY STIFF

DIRECTED BY
JOE MANTELLO

ARTISTIC PRODUCER
MANDY GREENFIELD

GENERAL MANAGER
FLORIE SEERY

DIRECTOR OF ARTISTIC DEVELOPMENT
JERRY PATCH

DIRECTOR OF MARKETING
DEBRA WAXMAN-PILLA

PRESS REPRESENTATIVE
BONEAU/BRYAN-BROWN

PRODUCTION MANAGER
JOSHUA HELMAN

DIRECTOR OF CASTING
NANCY PICCIONE

ARTISTIC LINE PRODUCER
LISA McNULTY

DIRECTOR OF DEVELOPMENT
LYNNE RANDALL

WORLD PREMIERE AT MCC THEATER MARCH 11, 2011.
ARTISTIC DIRECTORS: ROBERT LUPONE, BERNARD TELSEY, AND WILLIAM CANTLER; EXECUTIVE DIRECTOR: BLAKE WEST.
PRODUCTION SUPPORT PROVIDED BY THE ALFRED P. SLOAN FOUNDATION AS PART OF THE MTC/SLOAN SCIENCE THEATRE INITIATIVE.
ADDITIONAL SUPPORT FOR *THE OTHER PLACE* IS PROVIDED BY THE BLANCHE AND IRVING LAURIE FOUNDATION.
MANHATTAN THEATRE CLUB WISHES TO EXPRESS ITS APPRECIATION TO THEATRE DEVELOPMENT FUND FOR ITS SUPPORT OF THIS PRODUCTION.
THE OTHER PLACE WAS INITIALLY DEVELOPED IN ASSOCIATION WITH MATT OLIN.

1/10/13

(L-R): Laurie Metcalf and Zoe Perry

Photo by Joan Marcus

The Other Place

Laurie Metcalf
Juliana

Zoe Perry
The Woman

Daniel Stern
Ian

John Schiappa
The Man

Tony Carlin
u/s Ian, The Man

Henny Russell
u/s Juliana

Danielle Slavick
u/s The Woman

Sharr White
Playwright

Joe Mantello
Director

Eugene Lee
Scenic Design

Edward Pierce
Scenic Design

David Zinn
Costume Design

Justin Townsend
Lighting Design

Fitz Patton
*Original Music
& Sound Design*

William Cusick
*Video & Projection
Design*

Barclay Stiff
*Production Stage
Manager*

Kelly Beaulieu
Stage Manager

David Caparelliotis
*Caparelliotis Casting
Casting*

Bernard Telsey
*Telsey + Company
Casting*

Lynne Meadow
*Artistic Director
Manhattan Theatre
Club, Inc.*

Barry Grove
*Executive Producer
Manhattan Theatre
Club, Inc.*

Bill Pullman
Ian

FRONT OF HOUSE
Sitting (L-R): Tim Gonzalez, Lyanna Alvarado, Wendy Wright, Richard Ponce, Danielle Doherty
Standing (L-R): Dinah Glorioso, Ed Brashear, Christine Snyder, Josh Diaz, Jim Joseph, Jackson Ero

BOX OFFICE
(L-R): Rachel James, Geoffrey Nixon
Not pictured: David Dillon (Treasurer)

Photos by Brian Mapp

The Other Place

(L-R): Laurie Metcalf and Daniel Stern

Photo by Joan Marcus

The Other Place
SCRAPBOOK

Correspondent: Zoe Perry, "The Woman"

Special Backstage Rituals: We all gather around our stage manager, Barclay Stiff, post curtain call to confirm the run time and joke about any unexpected hiccups.

Favorite Moment During Each Performance: Listening to the close of the play featuring my three favorite actors, Danny, Laurie and John.

Favorite In-Theatre Gathering Place: Laurie's dressing room is a good spot to harass all those who pass by.

Favorite Off-Site Hangout: Feeding off of the comfort food from Rotisserie has become a staple.

Record Number of Cell Phone Rings During a Performance: Not a record, but a memorable cell phone ring came during one of the quietest moments towards the end of the play, on opening night.

What the Cast Thought of the Internet Buzz on the Show: Laurie's the only one brave enough to read tweets, but she's reported back that they're positive.

Fastest Costume Change: I've got a pretty quick turnaround from pajamas into a doctor's outfit.

Catchphrases Only the Company Would Recognize: "Hold the Powdered Sugar," "And a banana."

Fan Club Info: A fan of Laurie's and Danny's is very interested to know if they have a bobo.

1. Daughter and mother (in life and on stage), Zoe Perry (L) and Laurie Metcalf after opening night.
2. Arriving for opening night, Lynne Meadow, Artistic Director, and Barry Grove, Executive Producer, of the Manhattan Theatre Club.
3. Curtain call, opening night: (L-R): John Schiappa, playwright Sharr White, Daniel Stern, Laurie Metcalf and Zoe Perry.
4. Evelyn White, with husband and playwright Sharr White, heading into the opening night performance of his play.

CREW
Front Row (L-R): Erin Moeller, Andrew Braggs, Skye Bennett, Natasha Steinhagen, Jeremy Von Deck
Back Row (L-R): Vaughn Preston, Louis Shapiro, Leah Redmond, Chris Wiggins, Jane Masterson, Gerry Pavon, Timothy Walters, Catherine Lynch

The Performers

First Preview: October 23, 2012. Opened: November 14, 2012.
Closed November 18, 2012 after 24 Previews and 6 Performances.

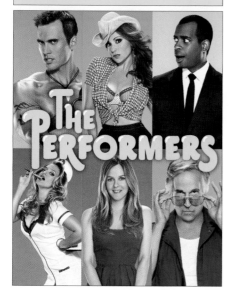

PLAYBILL

A blue comedy involving a New York Post reporter sent to cover the denizens of California's pornographic film community as they prepare for their annual awards ceremony. The reporter and his mousy wife begin to question their own relationship as they observe the unusual stresses in the marriage of porn stars Mandrew and Peeps that arise when Mandrew kisses a pneumatically-enhanced co-star off-screen. A well-endowed elder statesman of porn helps them all get their romances back on track.

CAST
(in order of appearance)

Mandrew	CHEYENNE JACKSON
Lee	DANIEL BREAKER
Peeps	ARI GRAYNOR
Sara	ALICIA SILVERSTONE
Chuck Wood	HENRY WINKLER
Sundown LeMay	JENNI BARBER

Place:
A hotel in Las Vegas, Nevada

Time:
The present

UNDERSTUDIES

For Mandrew/Lee: MARK JUNEK
For Peeps/Sundown LeMay: ARIANA SHORE
For Sara/Sundown LeMay: KAILY SMITH
For Chuck Wood: WILLIAM HILL

---

⑤ LONGACRE THEATRE
220 West 48th Street
A Shubert Organization Theatre

Philip J. Smith, *Chairman*   Robert E. Wankel, *President*

ROBYN GOODMAN   AMANDA LIPITZ   SCOTT M. DELMAN

CYNTHIA STROUM   PLAYING PRETEND PRODUCTIONS
KEVIN KINSELLA   BRUCE BENDELL/SCOTT PRISAND
MORRIS BERCHARD   RICHARD VAGUE   KAREN SEGAL   RUSSELL J. NOTIDES
BURNT UMBER/REBECCA GOLD   DEBBIE BUSLIK/JAMIE BENDELL
KEVIN McCOLLUM

PRESENT

CHEYENNE JACKSON   ARI GRAYNOR
DANIEL BREAKER   JENNI BARBER

WITH

ALICIA SILVERSTONE

AND

HENRY WINKLER

IN

The Performers

BY

DAVID WEST READ

SET DESIGNER ANNA LOUIZOS	COSTUME DESIGNER JESSICA WEGENER SHAY	LIGHTING DESIGNER JEFF CROITER	SOUND DESIGNER NEVIN STEINBERG
PROJECTION DESIGNER RICHARD DiBELLA	HAIR AND WIG DESIGNER CHARLES G. LaPOINTE		COMPOSER JULIAN FLEISHER
PRODUCTION STAGE MANAGER CHARLES M. TURNER III	CASTING CINDY TOLAN		PRESS REPRESENTATIVE SAM RUDY MEDIA RELATIONS
PRODUCTION MANAGEMENT THEATRETECH, INC./ BRIAN LYNCH & CHRIS KLUTH	ASSOCIATE PRODUCER JOSH FIEDLER		GENERAL MANAGEMENT LIZBETH CONE STEPHEN KOCIS

DIRECTED BY

EVAN CABNET

ORIGINALLY COMMISSIONED BY SOUTH COAST REPERTORY.
THE PRODUCERS WISH TO EXPRESS THEIR APPRECIATION TO THE THEATRE DEVELOPMENT FUND FOR ITS SUPPORT OF THIS PRODUCTION.

11/14/12

(Clockwise from top left): Henry Winkler, Jenni Barber, Ari Graynor, Cheyenne Jackson, Alicia Silverstone and Daniel Breaker

Photo by Carol Rosegg

The Performers

Cheyenne Jackson
Mandrew

Ari Graynor
Peeps

Daniel Breaker
Lee

Jenni Barber
Sundown LeMay

Alicia Silverstone
Sara

Henry Winkler
Chuck Wood

William Hill
u/s Chuck Wood

Mark Junek
u/s Mandrew, Lee

Ariana Shore
u/s Peeps, Sundown LeMay

Kaily Smith
u/s Sara, Sundown LeMay

David West Read
Playwright

Evan Cabnet
Director

Anna Louizos
Set Design

Jessica Wegener Shay
Costume Design

Jeff Croiter
Lighting Design

Charles G. LaPointe
Hair and Wig Design

Brian Lynch
Theatretech, Inc.
Production Management

Charles M. Turner, III
Production Stage Manager

Robyn Goodman
Producer

Amanda Lipitz
Producer

Scott M. Delman
Producer

Cynthia Stroum
Producer

Kevin Kinsella
Producer

Scott Prisand
Producer

Morris Berchard
Producer

Judi Krupp
Burnt Umber Productions
Producer

Bill Gerber
Burnt Umber Productions
Producer

Rebecca Gold
Producer

Kevin McCollum
Producer

PRODUCTION STAFF FOR *THE PERFORMERS*

GENERAL MANAGEMENT
AGED IN WOOD MANAGEMENT, INC.
Stephen Kocis   Lizbeth Cone

EXECUTIVE CONSULTANT
Emanuel Azenberg

GENERAL PRESS REPRESENTATIVE
Sam Rudy Media Relations
Sam Rudy   Shane Marshall Brown   Bill Coyle

CASTING
Cindy Tolan
Casting Associate ....Adam Caldwell

PRODUCTION MANAGEMENT
THEATRETECH, INC.
Brian Lynch   Chris Kluth

COMPANY MANAGER
Elizabeth M. Talmadge

Production Stage Manager ....**Charles M. Turner III**
Stage Manager ....Matt Schreiber
Assistant Director ....Lee Kasper
Associate Scenic Designer ....Aimee B. Dombo

The Performers
SCRAPBOOK

(L-R): Jenni Barber, Cheyenne Jackson, Ari Graynor, Henry Winkler, Alicia Silverstone and Daniel Breaker take bows on opening night.

Associate Costume Designer ....Sarah Laux
Costume Shopper ....Kristina Makowski
Associate Sound Designer ....David Thomas
Moving Light Programmer ....Evan Purcell
Associate Lighting Designer ....Jake DeGroot
Assistant Lighting Designer ....Wilburn Bonnell
Associate Sound Designer ....Jason Crystal
Assistant Sound Designer ....David Thomas
Video Programmer ....Joshua Kohler
Fight Director ....Ron Piretti
Prosthetics/Make-Up Designer ....Adam Bailey
Make-Up Designer ....Ashley Ryan
Advance Sound Engineer ....Jason Crystal
Production Carpenter ....Chris Kluth
Production Electrician ....Keith Buchanan
Production Sound Engineer ....Darin Stillman
Production Props Supervisor ....George Wagner
Wardrobe Supervisor ....Susan Checklick
Dresser ....Melanie Hansen
Hair Supervisor ....Pat Marcus
Production Assistants ....Courtney James,
Lily Lamb-Atkinson
Legal Counsel ....Farber Law, LLC/
Andrew Farber, Esq.
Legal Intern ....Travis Triano
Comptroller ....Galbraith & Company/
Sarah Galbraith, Heather Allen
Banking ....Signature Bank/
Barbara Von Borstel, Tom Kasulka,
Mary Ann Fanelli
Accountant ....Fried & Kowgios Partners/Robert Fried
Insurance ....Reiff & Associates, LLC/
Dennis R. Reiff, Regina Newsom
On-Stage Merchandising ....George Fenmore/
More Merchandising International
Merchandise ....Creative Goods/Peter Milano
Advertising ....SPOTCO/
Drew Hodges, Jim Edwards,
Tom Greenwald, Beth Watson,
Corey Schwitz
Online Marketing ....Situation Interactive/
Damian Bazadona, Joaquin Esteva,
John Lanasa, Nicole Merchant,
Chris Powers, Chris Hawthorne

Marketing ....DTE Marketing/
Ken Davenport, Steven Tartick,
Jennifer Ashley Tepper,
Jamie Lynn Ballard
Payroll Services ....Checks & Balances/
Anthony Walker
Production Photography ....Carol Rosegg
Cover Art Photography ....Matt Hoyle
Theatre Displays ....King Displays, Inc.
Sponsorship ....Uber

AGED IN WOOD, LLC

Producer ....Robyn Goodman
Producer ....Stephen Kocis
Director of Creative Development ....Josh Fiedler
Associate ....Dana Everitt

AMANDA LIPITZ PRODUCTIONS

Associate Producer ....Rachel Routh
Assistant ....Brandon Piper

CREDITS

Automation and show control by Show Motion Inc., Milford CT, using the AC2 computerized motion control system. Lighting equipment from PRG Lighting. Sound equipment from PRG Audio. Video equipment from PRG Video. Costumes executed by John Kristiansen New York Inc. Make-up provided by M•A•C Cosmetics. Melitta coffee machines courtesy of CoffeeForLess.com. GE microwave ovens courtesy of General Electric. Props by Spoon Group. Custom ottoman cover and certain other props provided by Prop N Spoon. Custom bedding, ottoman and furniture upholstery provided by Martin Albert Interiors, Inc., NYC. Custom AFA Award trophy built by John Creech Design and Production, Brooklyn, NY.

MUSIC CREDITS

"Can't Smile Without You" written by Chris Arnold, David Martin, Geoff Morrow. All rights owned or administered by Universal-Songs of Polygram International, Inc. on behalf of Universal/Dick James Music Ltd. ©1975/[BMI]. Used by permission.

The Performers
was rehearsed at the Snapple Theater Center.

SPECIAL THANKS
Scott Aiello, Amy Ashton, Lindsay Nicole Chambers, Matt Dellapina, Cary Donaldson, Stephanie Janssen, Greta Lee, Jessica Love, Kate MacCluggage, Mackenzie Meehan, Jill Rafson, David Ross, Julie Sharbutt, The Shubert Organization, Paige Evans, Daniel Swee.

www.ThePerformersOnBroadway.com

Follow *The Performers* on Facebook and Twitter:
http://www.facebook.com/
ThePerformersOnBroadway.com
www.twittter.com/performersbway @performersbway

 THE SHUBERT ORGANIZATION, INC.
Board of Directors

Philip J. Smith	**Robert E. Wankel**
Chairman	President
Wyche Fowler, Jr.	**Diana Phillips**
Lee J. Seidler	**Michael I. Sovern**

Stuart Subotnick

Chief Financial Officer ....Elliot Greene
Sr. Vice President, Ticketing ....David Andrews
Vice President, Finance ....Juan Calvo
Vice President, Human Resources ....Cathy Cozens
Vice President, Facilities ....John Darby
Vice President, Theatre Operations ....Peter Entin
Vice President, Marketing ....Charles Flateman
Vice President, Audit ....Anthony LaMattina
Vice President, Ticket Sales ....Brian Mahoney
Vice President, Creative Projects ...........D.S. Moynihan
Vice President, Real Estate ....Julio Peterson

House Manager ....Bob Reilly

Peter and the Starcatcher

First Preview: March 28, 2012. Opened: April 15, 2012.
Closed January 20, 2013 after 18 Previews and 319 Performances. (Transferred to Off-Broadway.)

Rick Elice's adaptation of the book by syndicated humor columnist Dave Barry and novelist Ridley Pearson, which offers a swashbuckling prequel to Peter Pan. It explains not only how Pan, Tinkerbell, Captain Hook and the Lost Boys came to Neverland, but reveals the origin of magic itself in the precious extraterrestrial substance known as "Starstuff" (a.k.a. Fairy Dust) and the organization (the Starcatchers) that has formed to gather it as it falls from the heavens. A distinctive feature of this production is Roger Rees' and Alex Timbers' staging, which makes innovative use of lowest-tech traditional stagecraft to stimulate the imagination.

CAST

(in alphabetical order)

Fighting Prawn	TEDDY BERGMAN
Mrs. Bumbrake	ARNIE BURTON
Boy	ADAM CHANLER-BERAT
Slank/Hawking Clam	MATT D'AMICO
Smee	KEVIN DEL AGUILA
Prentiss	CARSON ELROD
Alf	GREG HILDRETH
Lord Aster	RICK HOLMES
Captain Scott	ISAIAH JOHNSON
Molly	CELIA KEENAN-BOLGER
Ted	ERIC PETERSEN
Black Stache	MATTHEW SALDÍVAR

Continued on next page

⇥N⇤ BROOKS ATKINSON THEATRE
UNDER THE DIRECTION OF JAMES M. NEDERLANDER AND JAMES L. NEDERLANDER

Nancy Nagel Gibbs   Greg Schaffert   Eva Price   Tom Smedes   Disney Theatrical Productions

Suzan & Ken Wirth/DeBartolo Miggs   Catherine Schreiber   Daveed Frazier & Mark Thompson
Jack Lane   Jane Dubin   Allan S. Gordon/Adam S. Gordon   Baer & Casserly/Nathan Vernon
Rich Affannato/Peter Stern   Brunish & Trinchero/Laura Little Productions   Larry Hirschhorn/Hummel & Greene
Jamie deRoy & Probo Prods./Radio Mouse Ent.   Hugh Hysell/Freedberg & Dale

New York Theatre Workshop

Present

PETER AND THE STARCATCHER

A New Play By

Rick Elice

Based Upon the Novel by Dave Barry and Ridley Pearson

Starring

Adam Chanler-Berat   Celia Keenan-Bolger   Matthew Saldívar

Teddy Bergman   Arnie Burton   Matt D'Amico
Kevin Del Aguila   Carson Elrod   Greg Hildreth
Rick Holmes   Isaiah Johnson   Eric Petersen

Betsy Hogg   Orville Mendoza   Jason Ralph   John Sanders

Scenic Design	Costume Design	Lighting Design	Sound Design
Donyale Werle	Paloma Young	Jeff Croiter	Darron L West

Music Direction	Technical Supervisor	Production Stage Manager
Marco Paguia	David Benken	Kristen Harris

Casting	Press	General Management
Jim Carnahan, CSA	O&M Co.	321 Theatrical Management
Jack Doulin, CSA		
Tara Rubin, CSA		

Music By

Wayne Barker

Movement

Steven Hoggett

Directed By

Roger Rees and Alex Timbers

Originally Presented as a "Page to Stage" Workshop Production by La Jolla Playhouse, 2009
Christopher Ashley, Artistic Director & Michael S. Rosenberg, Managing Director

We wish to express our appreciation to Theatre Development Fund for its support of this production.

10/1/12

(L-R): Matthew Saldívar as Black Stache and Kevin Del Aguila as Smee

Photo by Joan Marcus

Peter and the Starcatcher

Adam Chanler-Berat and Celia Keenan-Bolger

Photo by Joan Marcus

UNDERSTUDIES

Understudy for Molly/Ted/Mrs. Bumbrake:
BETSY HOGG
For Smee/Alf/Fighting Prawn/Slank/Hawking
Clam/Mrs. Bumbrake:
ORVILLE MENDOZA
For Boy/Prentiss/Ted/Fighting Prawn/Captain Scott:
JASON RALPH
For Black Stache/Lord Aster/Captain Scott/
Mrs. Bumbrake/Smee:
JOHN SANDERS
For Black Stache:
CARSON ELROD
For Lord Aster/Slank/Hawking Clam/Alf:
ISAIAH JOHNSON

Movement Captain/Fight Captain:
TEDDY BERGMAN

MUSICIANS

Conductor: MARCO PAGUIA
Drums/Percussion: DEANE PROUTY
Keyboard and Electronic
    Percussion Programmer: RANDY COHEN
Arrangements by: WAYNE BARKER
Additional Arrangements by: MARCO PAGUIA

Adam Chanler-Berat *Boy*	**Celia Keenan-Bolger** *Molly*	**Matthew Saldívar** *Black Stache*	**Teddy Bergman** *Fighting Prawn*	**Arnie Burton** *Mrs. Bumbrake*	**Matt D'Amico** *Slank/Hawking Clam*	**Kevin Del Aguila** *Smee*

Carson Elrod *Prentiss*	**Greg Hildreth** *Alf*	**Rick Holmes** *Lord Aster*	**Isaiah Johnson** *Captain Scott*	**Eric Petersen** *Ted*	**Betsy Hogg** *u/s Molly/Ted/ Mrs. Bumbrake*	**Orville Mendoza** *u/s Smee/Alf/ Fighting Prawn/ Slank/Mrs. Bumbrake*

Jason Ralph *u/s Boy/Prentiss/ Ted/Fighting Prawn/Captain Scott*	**John Sanders** *u/s Black Stache/ Lord Aster/ Captain Scott/ Mrs. Bumbrake*	**Rick Elice** *Playwright*	**Roger Rees** *Director*	**Alex Timbers** *Director*	**Wayne Barker** *Composer*	**Steven Hoggett** *Movement*

Peter and the Starcatcher

Donyale Werle
Set Designer

Paloma H. Young
Costume Designer

Jeff Croiter
Lighting Design

Darron L. West
Sound Designer

Marco Paguia
Musical Director

Marcia Goldberg
321 Theatrical
Management
*General
Management*

Nancy Nagel Gibbs
321 Theatrical
Management
*General
Management*

Nina Essman
321 Theatrical
Management
*General
Management*

David Benken
Technical Supervisor

Dave Barry
Original Novel

Ridley Pearson
Original Novel

Nancy Nagel Gibbs
Producer

Greg Schaffert
Producer

Eva Price
Producer

Tom Smedes
Producer

Suzan Wirth
Co-Producer

Ken Wirth
Co-Producer

Lisa DeBartolo
DeBartolo Miggs
Co-Producer

Don Miggs
DeBartolo Miggs
Co-Producer

Catherine Schreiber
Co-Producer

Daveed Frazier
Co-Producer

Mark Thompson
Co-Producer

Jack Lane
Co-Producer

Jane Dubin
Co-Producer

Allan S. Gordon
Co-Producer

Adam S. Gordon
Co-Producer

Zachary Baer
Baer & Casserly/
Nathan Vernon
Co-Producer

Tom Casserly
Baer & Casserly/
Nathan Vernon
Co-Producer

Nathan Vernon
Baer & Casserly/
Nathan Vernon
Co-Producer

Rich Affannato
Co-Producer

Peter Stern
Co-Producer

Corey Brunish
Brunish & Trinchero/
Laura Little
Productions
Co-Producer

Brisa Trinchero
Brunish & Trinchero/
Laura Little
Productions
Co-Producer

Laura Little
Brunish & Trinchero/
Laura Littlr
Productions
Co-Producer

Larry Hirschhorn
Larry Hirschhorn/
Hummel & Greene
Co-Producer

Peter and the Starcatcher

Martin Hummel
Larry Hirschhorn/
Hummel & Greene
Co-Producer

R.K. Greene
Larry Hirschhorn/
Hummel & Greene
Co-Producer

Jamie deRoy
deRoy/Probo
Prods/Radio Mouse
Co-Producer

M. Kilburg Reedy
deRoy/Probo
Prods/Radio Mouse
Co-Producer

Jason E. Grossman
deRoy/Probo
Prods/Radio Mouse
Co-Producer

Hugh Hysell
Hugh Hysell/
Freedberg & Dale
Co-Producer

Avram Freedberg
Hugh Hysell/
Freedberg & Dale
Co-Producer

Marybeth Dale
Hugh Hysell/
Freedberg & Dale
Co-Producer

James C. Nicola
Artistic Director
New York Theatre
Workshop
Producer

Christopher Ashley
Artistic Director
La Jolla Playhouse
Producer

Michael S.
Rosenberg
Managing Director
La Jolla Playhouse
Producer

Christian Borle
Black Stache

David Rossmer
Ted

Evan Harrington
Alf

Emily Walton
u/s Molly/Ted/
Mrs. Bumbrake

COMPANY AND STAGE MANAGEMENT
(L-R): Brent McCreary (Company Management), Tracy Geltman (Company Management),
McKenzie Murphy, Clifford Schwartz, Kristen Harris, Katherine Wallace (All Stage Management)

FRONT OF HOUSE
Front Row (L-R): Ilona Figueroa, Megan Frazier, Tara McCormack,
Marie Gonzalez, Kaitlin Dato, Marion Danton
Back Row (L-R): Austin Branda, Hector Aguilar, Sam Figert,
James Holley, Roberto Rivera, Kimberlee Imperato

BOX OFFICE
(L-R): Richard Aubrey, William O'Brien

Peter and the Starcatcher

CREW

Front Row (L-R): Jerry Marshall (Production Props), Tommy Grasso (Sound), Bill Smith (Engineer), Jamie Englehart (Wardrobe), Jessica Dermody (Wardrobe), Marc Schmittroth (Spot Operator), Joe Maher (House Flyman), Joe DePaulo (House Props)

Back Row (L-R): Rob Bass (Production Sound), Patrick Eviston (Production Carpenter), Manny Becker (House Electrician), Tommy Lavaia (House Carpenter), Mike Attianese (Flyman), Bill Staples (Spot Operator), Brian McGarity (House Electrician), John Senter (Sound). Not pictured: Eric Smith (Head Carpenter)

STAFF FOR *PETER AND THE STARCATCHER*

GENERAL MANAGEMENT
321 THEATRICAL MANAGEMENT
Nina Essman   Marcia Goldberg

CASTING
Jim Carnahan, CSA   Jillian Cimini
Carrie Gardner, CSA   Stephen Kopel
Michael Morlani   Rachel Reichblum

GENERAL PRESS REPRESENTATIVE
O&M CO.
Rick Miramontez   Molly Barnett
Ryan Ratelle   Chelsea Nachman

PRODUCTION MANAGEMENT
David Benken   Rose Palombo

COMPANY MANAGER
Tracy Geltman

PRODUCTION STAGE MANAGER ......Kristen Harris
Assistant Stage Manager ....Katherine Wallace
Assistant Company Manager ....Brent McCreary
Dramaturg ....Ken Cerniglia
For Disney Theatrical ....Daniel Posener
Assistant Director ....Jess Chayes
Movement Associate ....Stephen Brotebeck
Associate Scenic Designer ....Michael Carnahan
Assistant to Prop Sculptor ....Craig Napoliello
Assistant to Scenic Designer ....Stephen Dobay
Rendering Painter ....Hannah Davis
Associate Costume Designer ....Matthew Pachtman
Assistant to Costumer Designer ....David Mendizabal
Associate Lighting Designer ....Joel Silver
Assistant Lighting Designer ......Cory Pattak, Andy Fritsch
Assistant to Lighting Designer ....Grant Yeager
Associate Sound Designer ....Charles Coes
Fight Director ....Jacob Grigolia-Rosenbaum
Production Carpenter ....Eric Smith
Advance Carpenter ....Michael Muery
Production Electrician ....Brian GF McGarity
Production Props ....Stuart Metcalf

Sound Engineer ....Rob Bass
Vari Light Programmer ....Timothy Rogers
Wardrobe Supervisor ....Jessica Dermody
Dressers ....Jamie Englehart, Timothy Greer
Hair Stylist ....Brandon Dailey
Hair Consultant ....J. Jared Janas
Production Assistants ....Morgan Holbrook,
                 McKenzie Murphy, Samantha Preiss
Advertising ....Serino/Coyne/
                 Greg Corradetti, Robert Jones,
         Ryan Cunningham, Vanessa Javier, David Barrineau
Digital Outreach & Website ....Serino/Coyne/
                 Jim Glaub, Chip Meyrelles,
                 Laurie Connor, Kevin Keating,
                 Whitney Creighton, Crystal Chase
Marketing..............Leanne Schanzer Promotions, Inc./
                 Leanne Schanzer, Justin Schanzer,
                 Kara Laviola, Ekaterina Zaitseva,
                 Chelsey Berger;
                 Production: Michael Schanzer
Merchandise ....Broadway Merchandising, Inc.
Special Promotions ....Jeffrey Solis
Group Sales ....Nathan Vernon (877-321-0020)
Banking ....City National Bank/Michele Gibbons
Payroll ....Checks and Balances
Director of Finance ....John DiMeglio
Accountant ....FK Partners CPAs LLP/Robert Fried
Insurance ....AON/Albert G. Ruben Insurance
Legal Counsel ....Brooks & Distler/Tom Distler, Esq.

321 THEATRICAL MANAGEMENT
Michael Bolgar, Bob Brinkerhoff, Mattea Cogliano-Benedict, Tara Geesaman, Andrew Hartman, Amy Merlino, Alex Owen, Rebecca Peterson, Ken Silverman, Tammie Ward, Haley Ward

www.peterandthestarcatcher.com

SPECIAL THANKS
Michael Keller, Wendy Lefkon, Kaitlin Conci, Aaron Glick, Broadway Green Alliance, Kids Night on Broadway, Build it Green, Recycle-a-Bicycle, Salvation Army, Housing Works, Paper Mache Monkey, Paul Jepson, Chris Ashley, Dana Harrel, Gabriel Greene, Jim Nicola, Bill Darger, Kris Kukul,

Amanda Charlton, Williamstown Theatre Festival, Michele Steckler, Neil Patel, Joe Huppert, Eric Stahlhammer, Kelly Devine, Adrienne Campbell-Holt, Amy Groeschel, Steve Rosen, Eric Love, Adam Green, Danny Deferarri, Rob O'Hare, all the actors who helped us along the way.

CREDITS
Computer motion control and automation of scenery and rigging by Showman Fabricators, Inc. Sound by Masque Sound. Lighting by PRG Lighting. Costumes by Artur & Tailors, Inc., Giliberto Designs, Inc., Katrina Patterns, Marie Stair, Melissa Crawford. Custom leatherwear by David Menkes. Custom knitwear by Knit Illustrated. Millinery by Jeffrey Wallach and Rodney Gordon, Inc. Fabric dyeing and painting by Jeff Fender Studios and Juliann Kroboth. Custom tattoos by TEMPTU. Props by Kathy Fabian and Jerard Studios.

✕N✕ NEDERLANDER

Chairman ....**James M. Nederlander**
President ....**James L. Nederlander**

Executive Vice President
Nick Scandalios

Vice President	Senior Vice President
Corporate Development	Labor Relations
Charlene S. Nederlander	**Herschel Waxman**

Vice President	Chief Financial Officer
Jim Boese	**Freida Sawyer Belviso**

STAFF FOR THE BROOKS ATKINSON THEATRE
Theatre Manager .... Susan Martin
Treasurer .... Peter Attanasio
Associate Treasurer .... Elaine Amplo
House Carpenter .... Thomas Lavaia
Flyman .... Joe Maher
House Electrician .... Manuel Becker
House Propman .... Joseph P. DePaulo
House Engineer .... Reynold Barriteau

Peter and the Starcatcher
SCRAPBOOK

Correspondent: Teddy Bergman, "Fighting Prawn"

Memorable Milestone Parties: Duane Reade the clown performed at opening. He's the worst in New York.

Most Exciting Celebrity Visitor: Joan Rivers told us we didn't suck.

Actor Who Performed the Most Roles: Teddy Bergman: Grempkin, Mack, Sanchez, Fighting Prawn, sailor, pirate, door, wall, ocean, jungle, devout passenger, gambler, half ship—13.

Who Has Done the Most Shows: Arnie Burton only missed a single show.

Special Backstage Ritual: Greg Hildreth's costume surprise for Celia Keenan-Bolger.

Favorite Moment: Off-stage at the top of the jungle scene, Rick Holmes and Matt D'Amico show us the meaning of love every night.

Favorite In-Theatre Gathering Place: Stage management office.

Off-Site Hangout: Glass House Tavern.

Favorite Snack Foods: Pretzel sticks.

Mascot: Felix Del Aguila.

Favorite Therapy: Carolyn's sweet, tender hands.

Memorable Ad-Lib: "It's awfully noisy on this deck." Celia Keenan-Bolger after Rick Holmes fell off the onstage raft during what is supposed to be a very quiet scene.

Record Number of Cell Phone Rings: Four: It was an alarm and Celia Keenan-Bolger (again) stopped the show and ad-libbed: "We ask you now to imagine a cell phone has gone off four times."

Memorable Stage Door Fan Encounter: A psychic gave us all her cards and then told me we'd write about it. She's good.

What Did You Think of the Web Buzz on Your Show: Arousing.

Fastest Costume Change: Kevin Del Aguila's de-mermaiding in the last scene.

Who Wore the Least: All us sexy mermaids.

Catchphrases Only the Company Would Recognize: In response to any dramaturgical question: "Great question...can you grab a rope for me?"

Sweethearts Within the Company: Rick Holmes and his mirror

Best In-House Parody Lyrics: "And as the sea was gently glitt'ring from the deck, for a sec, you can see my lovely...."

Memorable Directorial Note: Being accused of acting like a performance artist from the Castro.

Company In-Joke: Titoooooooooooooooooos.

Company Legends: The one mistake Christian Borle ever made, and what happened after.

Understudy Anecdote: Sliding off the front of the stage into the first row of the audience mid performance. JR, you got right back on the horse.

1. The cast cheers a Mayoral Proclamation upon the show's 100th performance July 11, 2012.
2. Celia Keenan-Bolger (L) and Kevin Del Aguila (R) bid farewell to Christian Borle on his final performance June 30, 2012.
3. Members of the cast and creative team display a cake marking the show's 100th performance.

The Phantom of the Opera

First Preview: January 9, 1988. Opened: January 26, 1988.
Still running as of May 31, 2013.

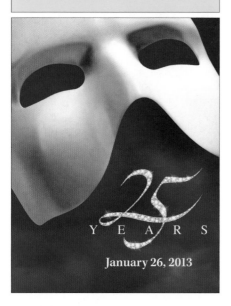

PLAYBILL®

25 YEARS

January 26, 2013

The dashing Raoul is in love with Christine Daaé, a pretty soprano in the chorus of the Paris Opera. But Raoul discovers that she is under the spell of the legendary Phantom of the Opera, a disfigured musical genius who haunts the endless grottos beneath the ancient opera house. The obsessed Phantom demands that Christine be elevated to star and that the company produce an unplayable opera he has written. When his commands are not obeyed the Phantom becomes violent, even murderous. Raoul strives ever more desperately to free Christine from his clutches. As a torch-wielding mob closes in on his lair, the Phantom makes one last bid for Christine's love.

CAST

The Phantom of the Opera	HUGH PANARO
Christine Daaé	SIERRA BOGGESS
Christine Daaé (Wed. & Thurs. Mat. Performances)	SAMANTHA HILL
Raoul, Vicomte de Chagny	KYLE BARISICH
Carlotta Giudicelli	MICHELE McCONNELL
Monsieur André	JIM WEITZER
Monsieur Firmin	TIM JEROME
Madame Giry	ELLEN HARVEY
Ubaldo Piangi	CHRISTIAN ŠEBEK
Meg Giry	KARA KLEIN
Auctioneer/Monsieur Reyer/Hairdresser ("Il Muto")	CARRINGTON VILMONT
Don Attilio ("Il Muto")	DAVID MICHAEL GARRY
Jeweler ("Il Muto")	NATHAN PATRICK MORGAN
Monsieur Lefèvre/Firechief	KENNETH KANTOR
Joseph Buquet	RICHARD POOLE

25TH ANNIVERSARY PERFORMANCE, SATURDAY, JANUARY 26, 2013

ⓢ MAJESTIC THEATRE

247 West 44th Street
A Shubert Organization Theatre
Philip J. Smith, *Chairman*   **Robert E. Wankel,** *President*

CAMERON MACKINTOSH and
THE REALLY USEFUL THEATRE COMPANY, INC.

present

THE PHANTOM OF THE OPERA.

Starring

HUGH PANARO
SIERRA BOGGESS
KYLE BARISICH

JIM WEITZER   TIM JEROME   MICHELE McCONNELL
ELLEN HARVEY   CHRISTIAN ŠEBEK   KARA KLEIN

At certain performances
SAMANTHA HILL
plays the role of "Christine"

Music by

ANDREW LLOYD WEBBER

Lyrics by **CHARLES HART**

Additional Lyrics by **RICHARD STILGOE**

Book by **RICHARD STILGOE & ANDREW LLOYD WEBBER**

Based on the novel "Le Fantôme de L'Opéra" by **GASTON LEROUX**

Production Design by **MARIA BJÖRNSON**   Lighting by **ANDREW BRIDGE**

Sound Design by **MICK POTTER**   Original Sound Design by **MARTIN LEVAN**

Musical Supervision & Direction **DAVID CADDICK**   Musical Director **KRISTEN BLODGETTE**

Production Supervisor **SETH SKLAR-HEYN**   Associate Choreographer **DENNY BERRY**

Orchestrations by **DAVID CULLEN & ANDREW LLOYD WEBBER**

Casting by **TARA RUBIN CASTING**   Original Casting by **JOHNSON-LIFF ASSOCIATES**

General Management **ALAN WASSER ASSOCIATES**

Musical Staging & Choreography by **GILLIAN LYNNE**

Directed by **HAROLD PRINCE**

1/21/13

Sierra Boggess
and Hugh Panaro

The Phantom of the Opera

MUSICAL NUMBERS

PROLOGUE
The stage of the Paris Opéra House, 1911

OVERTURE

ACT I — PARIS, LATE NINETEENTH CENTURY

Scene 1—The dress rehearsal of "Hannibal"
"Think of Me" ....Carlotta, Christine, Raoul
Scene 2—After the Gala
"Angel of Music" ....Christine and Meg
Scene 3—Christine's dressing room
"Little Lotte/The Mirror" (Angel of Music) ....Raoul, Christine, Phantom
Scene 4—The Labyrinth underground
"The Phantom of the Opera" ....Phantom and Christine
Scene 5—Beyond the lake
"The Music of the Night" ....Phantom
Scene 6—Beyond the lake, the next morning
"I Remember/Stranger Than You Dreamt It" ....Christine and Phantom
Scene 7—Backstage
"Magical Lasso" ....Buquet, Meg, Madame Giry and Ballet Girls
Scene 8—The Managers' office
"Notes/Prima Donna" ....Firmin, André, Raoul, Carlotta, Giry, Meg,
Piangi and Phantom
Scene 9—A performance of "Il Muto"
"Poor Fool, He Makes Me Laugh" ....Carlotta and Company
Scene 10—The roof of the Opéra House
"Why Have You Brought Me Here/Raoul, I've Been There" ....Raoul and Christine
"All I Ask of You" ....Raoul and Christine
"All I Ask of You" (Reprise) ....Phantom

ENTR'ACTE

ACT II — SIX MONTHS LATER

Scene 1—The staircase of the Opéra House, New Year's Eve
"Masquerade/Why So Silent" ....Full Company
Scene 2—Backstage
Scene 3—The Managers' office
"Notes/Twisted Every Way" ....André, Firmin, Carlotta, Piangi, Raoul,
Christine, Giry and Phantom
Scene 4—A rehearsal for "Don Juan Triumphant"
Scene 5—A graveyard in Perros
"Wishing You Were Somehow Here Again" ....Christine
"Wandering Child/Bravo, Bravo" ....Phantom, Christine and Raoul
Scene 6—The Opéra House stage before the Premiere
Scene 7—"Don Juan Triumphant"
"The Point of No Return" ....Phantom and Christine
Scene 8—The Labyrinth underground
"Down Once More/Track Down This Murderer" ....Full Company
Scene 9—Beyond the lake

Cast Continued

Passarino
("Don Juan Triumphant") .....JEREMY STOLLE
Slave Master ("Hannibal") ....JUSTIN PECK
Solo Dancer ("Il Muto") ....KFIR
Page ("Don Juan
Triumphant") ....KELLY JEANNE GRANT
Porter/Fireman ....ANDREW DROST
Spanish Lady
("Don Juan Triumphant") ....LYNNE ABELES
Wardrobe Mistress/
Confidante ("Il Muto") ...SATOMI HOFMANN
Princess ("Hannibal") ....ELIZABETH WELCH
Madame Firmin ....SUSAN OWEN
Innkeeper's Wife
("Don Juan Triumphant") ......HEATHER HILL
Marksman ....PAUL A. SCHAEFER
The Ballet Chorus of the
Opéra Populaire ....AMANDA EDGE,
JESSY HENDRICKSON,
GIANNA LOUNGWAY, MABEL MODRONO,
AUBREY MORGAN, JESSICA RADETSKY
Ballet Swing ....LAURIE V. LANGDON
Swings ....SCOTT MIKITA,
GREG MILLS, JANET SAIA

UNDERSTUDIES

For the Phantom: GREG MILLS,
PAUL A. SCHAEFER, JEREMY STOLLE
For Christine: SUSAN OWEN,
ELIZABETH WELCH
For Raoul: GREG MILLS, PAUL A. SCHAEFER,
JEREMY STOLLE
For Firmin: KENNETH KANTOR,
SCOTT MIKITA, CARRINGTON VILMONT
For André: SCOTT MIKITA, GREG MILLS,
RICHARD POOLE
For Carlotta: LYNNE ABELES,
SATOMI HOFMANN, JANET SAIA
For Mme. Giry: KELLY JEANNE GRANT,
SATOMI HOFMANN, JANET SAIA
For Piangi: ANDREW DROST,
NATHAN PATRICK MORGAN,
JEREMY STOLLE
For Meg Giry: AMANDA EDGE
Dance Captain: LAURIE V. LANGDON

ORCHESTRA

Conductors: DAVID CADDICK,
KRISTEN BLODGETTE, DAVID LAI,
TIM STELLA, NORMAN WEISS

The Phantom of the Opera

Violins: JOYCE HAMMANN (Concert Master),
   CLAIRE CHAN, KURT COBLE,
   JAN MULLEN, KAREN MILNE,
   SUZANNE GILMAN
Violas: VERONICA SALAS,
   DEBRA SHUFELT-DINE
Cellos: TED ACKERMAN, KARL BENNION
Bass: MELISSA SLOCUM
Harp: HENRY FANELLI
Flute: SHERYL HENZE
Flute/Clarinet: ED MATTHEW
Oboe: MELANIE FELD
Clarinet: MATTHEW GOODMAN
Bassoon: ATSUKO SATO
Trumpets: LOWELL HERSHEY,
   FRANCIS BONNY
Bass Trombone: WILLIAM WHITAKER
French Horns: DANIEL CULPEPPER,
   PETER REIT, DAVID SMITH
Percussion: ERIC COHEN, JAN HAGIWARA
Keyboards: TIM STELLA, NORMAN WEISS

Hugh Panaro
*The Phantom
of the Opera*

Sierra Boggess
Christine Daaé

Kyle Barisich
*Raoul, Vicomte
de Chagny*

Jim Weitzer
Monsieur André

Tim Jerome
Monsieur Firmin

Michele McConnell
Carlotta Giudicelli

Ellen Harvey
Madame Giry

Christian Šebek
Ubaldo Piangi

Kara Klein
Meg Giry

Samantha Hill
*Christine Daaé
at certain
performances*

Lynne Abeles
Spanish Lady

Andrew Drost
Porter/Fireman

Amanda Edge
Ballet Chorus

David Michael Garry
Don Attilio

Kelly Jeanne Grant
Page

Jessy Hendrickson
Ballet Chorus

Heather Hill
Innkeeper's Wife

Satomi Hofmann
*Wardrobe Mistress/
Confidante*

Kenneth Kantor
*Monsieur Lefèvre/
Firechief*

Kfir
Solo Dancer

Laurie V. Langdon
*Dance Captain/
Ballet Swing*

Gianna Loungway
Ballet Chorus

Scott Mikita
Swing

Greg Mills
Swing

Mabel Modrono
Ballet Chorus

Aubrey Morgan
Ballet Chorus

Nathan Patrick
Morgan
Jeweler

Susan Owen
Madame Firmin

Justin Peck
Slave Master

The Phantom of the Opera

Richard Poole
Joseph Buquet

Jessica Radetsky
Ballet Chorus

Janet Saia
Swing

Paul A. Schaefer
Marksman

Jeremy Stolle
Passarino

Carrington Vilmont
*Auctioneer/
Monsieur Reyer/
Hairdresser*

Elizabeth Welch
Princess

Andrew Lloyd
Webber
*Composer/Book/
Co-Orchestrator*

Harold Prince
Director

Charles Hart
Lyrics

Richard Stilgoe
*Book and Additional
Lyrics*

Gillian Lynne
*Musical Staging
and Choreography*

Maria Björnson
Production Design

Andrew Bridge
Lighting Designer

Mick Potter
Sound Designer

Martin Levan
*Original Sound
Designer*

David Cullen
Co-Orchestrator

David Caddick
*Musical Supervisor
and Direction*

Kristen Blodgette
*Associate Musical
Supervisor*

Seth Sklar-Heyn
*Production
Supervisor*

Denny Berry
*Production
Dance Supervisor/
Associate
Choreographer*

Jake Bell
*Technical
Production
Manager*

David Lai
Conductor

Tara Rubin
Tara Rubin Casting
Casting

Alan Wasser
General Manager

Cameron Mackintosh
Producer

Dara Adler
Ballet Chorus

Polly Baird
Ballet Chorus

Kimilee Bryant
Spanish Lady

Nicholas
Cunningham
Slave Master

Aaron
Galligan-Stierle
Monsieur André

Paloma Garcia-Lee
Ballet Chorus

Joelle Gates
Ballet Chorus

Arlo Hill
*Passarino/Monsieur
Reyer/Hairdresser*

The Phantom of the Opera

Cristin J. Hubbard
Madame Giry

Mary Illes
Innkeeper's Wife

Kris Koop
Madame Firmin

John Kuether
Auctioneer/Don Attilio

Gina Lamparella
Page

Dustin Layton
Solo Dancer

Kevin Ligon
Monsieur Firmin

Frank Mastrone
Jeweler

Heather McFadden
Meg Giry

Trista Moldovan
Christine Daaé

Marni Raab
Christine Daaé

Rebecca Robbins
Wardrobe Mistress/ Confidante

James Romick
Swing

Julie Schmidt
Swing

Carly Blake Sebouhian
Ballet Chorus

James Zander
Slave Master

25 Years Transfer Students 2012-2013

Polly Baird
Ballet Chorus

Sarah Bakker
Madame Firmin

Courtney Combs
Ballet Chorus

Arlo Hill
Swing

Peter Jöback
The Phantom of the Opera

Dustin Layton
Solo Dancer

Marni Raab
Christine Daaé at certain performances

Rebecca Robbins
Page

Julie Schmidt
Swing

Carly Blake Sebouhian
Ballet Chorus

ORCHESTRA
Front Row (L-R): Lowell Hershey, Garry Ianco, Pattee Cohen, Francis Bonny, Laura Covey, Karl Bennion
Back Row (L-R): Norman Weiss, Matthew Goodman, Martha Hyde, Daniel Culpepper, Peter Reit, Bill Whitaker
Not pictured: Ted Ackerman, Kristen Blodgette, David Caddick, Claire Chan, Kurt Coble, Eric Cohen, Henry Fanelli, Melanie Feld, Suzanne Gilman, Jan Hagiwara, Sheryl Henze, David Lai, Ed Matthew, Karen Milne, Jan Mullen, Veronica Salas, Atsuko Sato, Debra Shufelt-Dine, Melissa Slocum, Tim Stella

Photo by Brian Mapp

The Phantom of the Opera

CREW
Front: Rob Wallace
Middle Row (L-R):Joe Grillman, Giancarlo Cottignoli, Santos Sanchez, Matthew Mezick
Back Row (L-R): Bill Kazdan, George Dummitt, Matt Maloney, Frank Dwyer, Steve Clem, Jack Farmer
Not pictured: Innumerable and all working!

MANAGEMENT
Front Row (L-R): Seth Sklar-Heyn (Production Supervisor),
Gregory Livoti (Stage Manager), Steve Greer (Company Manager),
Katherine McNamee (Asstistant Company Manager),
Craig Jacobs (Production Stage Manager)
Center Left: Laurie V. Langdon (Dance Captain)
From top of Stairs (L-R): Bethe Ward (Stage Manager since opening),
Andrew Glant-Linden, Michael Borowski (Press Rep)

WARDROBE/HAIR/MAKE-UP
Front Row (L-R): Ron Blakely, Pearleta Price, Robert Strong Miller,
Thelma Pollard, Julie Ratcliffe
Middle Row (L-R): Jennifer Caruso, Mary Lou Rios, Emma Atherton
Sarah Snider, Victoria Tinsman, Tyrel Limb
Back Row (L-R): George Sheer, Michael Jacobs, Jennifer Arnold,
Victoria Tjoelker, Annette Lovece

FRONT OF HOUSE
Front Row (L-R): Lawrence Darden, Bob Reilly, Sylvia Bailey, Virginia Kinard, Dorothy Curich, Theresa Aceves, Cynthia Carlin, Peter Kulok (House Manager)
Middle Row (L-R): Ken Costigan, Gwen Coley, Joan Thorn, Perry Dell'Aquila, Donald Farr, Debbie Vogel, Diona Woodward, Lisa Bruno, Rose Anna Mineo, Ji-Ming Zhu
Back Row (L-R): Lucia Cappelletti, Tony Stavick, Topher McLean, Wade Walton, Phillip Varricchio, Matt Wagner, Cameron Perry, Andre Campbell, Margot Welch

The Phantom of the Opera

STAFF FOR *THE PHANTOM OF THE OPERA*

General Manager
ALAN WASSER ASSOCIATES
Alan Wasser   Allan Williams

General Press Representative
THE PUBLICITY OFFICE
Marc Thibodeau   Michael S. Borowski
Jeremy Shaffer

Assistant to Mr. Prince
RUTH MITCHELL

Production Supervisor
SETH SKLAR-HEYN

Production Dance Supervisor
DENNY BERRY

Associate Musical Supervisor
KRISTEN BLODGETTE

Casting
TARA RUBIN CASTING

Technical Production Manager .... JAKE BELL
Company Manager ....STEVE GREER
Production Stage Manager .... CRAIG JACOBS
Stage Managers .... Bethe Ward, Gregory T. Livoti
Assistant Company Manager .... Katherine McNamee

U.S. Design Staff
Associate Scenic Designer .... DANA KENN
Associate Costume Designer .... SAM FLEMING
Associate Lighting Designer .... VIVIEN LEONE
Associate Sound Designer .... PAUL GATEHOUSE
Sculptures Consultant .... Stephen Pyle
Pro Tools Programmer .... Lee McCutcheon

Casting Associates .... Eric Woodall, CSA;
Merri Sugarman, CSA
Casting Assistants .... Kaitlin Shaw, Lindsay Levine
Dance Captain .... Laurie V. Langdon
Production Carpenter .... Joseph Patria
Production Electrician .... Robert Fehribach
Production Propertyman .... Timothy Abel
Production Sound Engineer .... Garth Helm
Production Wig Supervisor .... Leone Gagliardi
Production Make-up
Supervisor .... Thelma Pollard
Assistant Make-up Supervisors ...... Magdalena Kolodziej,
Pearleta N. Price, Shazia J. Saleem
Head Carpenter .... Russell Tiberio III
Automation Carpenters .... Santos Sanchez,
Michael Girman
Assistant Carpenter .... Giancarlo Cottignoli
Flyman .... Daryl Miller
Head Electrician .... Alan Lampel
Assistant Electrician .... JR Beket
Head Props .... Matthew Mezick
Asst. Props./Boat Captain .... Joe Caruso
Sound Operator .... Paul Verity
Asst. Sound Operator .... Rafe Carlotto
Wardrobe Supervisor .... Julie Ratcliffe
Assistant Wardrobe Supervisor .... Robert Strong Miller

Wardrobe Staff .... Jennifer Arnold, Ron Blakely,
Aaron Carlson, Jennifer Caruso,
Eileen Casey, Erna Dias, Terence Doherty,
Michael Jacobs, Annette Lovece,
Margie Marchionni, Ann McDaniel,
Peter McIver, Andrew Nelson,
Elena Pellicciaro, Mary Lou Rios,
George Sheer, Rosemary Taylor
Hair Supervisor .... Leone Gagliardi
Hairdressers .... Tiffany Bolick, Charise Champion,
Karen Dickenson, Victoria Tinsman

Conductor .... David Lai
Associate Conductor .... Tim Stella
Assistant Conductor .... Norman Weiss
Musical Preparation
Supervisor (U.S.) .... Chelsea Music Service, Inc
Synthesizer Consultant .... Stuart Andrews

Assistants to the Gen. Mgr. .... Lauren Friedlander,
Jake Hirzel, Jennifer O'Connor

Legal Counsel .... F. Richard Pappas
Accounting .... Rosenberg, Neuwirth and Kutchner
Christopher A. Cacace
Logo Design and Graphics .... Dewynters Plc
London
Merchandising .... Dewynters Advertising Inc.
Advertising .... Serino Coyne Inc.,
Greg Corradetti, Marci Kaufman
Marketing Direction .... Type A Marketing
Anne Rippey
Displays .... King Displays, Wayne Sapper
Insurance (U.S.) .... DeWitt Stern Group
Peter K. Shoemaker
Insurance (U.K.) .... Walton & Parkinson Limited
Richard Walton
Banking .... Signature Bank/
Barbara von Borstel
Payroll Service .... Castellana Services, Inc.

Original Production Photographer .... Clive Barda
Additional Photography .... Joan Marcus,
Bob Marshak, Peter Cunningham
House Manager .... Peter Kulok

CREDITS AND ACKNOWLEDGMENTS
Scenic construction and boat automation by
Hudson Scenic Studios.
Scenery automation by Jeremiah J. Harris Associates,
Inc./East Coast Theatre Supply, Inc. Scenery painted by
Nolan Scenery Studios. Set and hand properties by McHugh
Rollins Associates, Inc. Sculptural elements by Costume
Armour. "Opera Ball" newell post statues and elephant by
Nino Novellino of Costume Armour. Proscenium sculptures
by Stephen Pyle. Draperies by I. Weiss and Sons, Inc. Soft
goods provided by Quartet Theatrical Draperies. Safety
systems by Foy Lighting equipment and special lighting
effects by Four Star Lighting, Inc. Sound equipment and
technical service provided by Masque Sound and Recording
Corp. Special effects designed and executed by Theatre
Magic, Inc., Richard Huggins, President. Costumes
executed by Barbara Matera, Ltd. Costumes for "Hannibal"
and "Masquerade" executed by Parsons/Meares, Ltd. Men's
costumes by Vincent Costumes, Inc. Costume crafts for
"Hannibal" and "Masquerade" by Janet Harper and
Frederick Nihda. Fabric painting by Mary Macy. Additional

costumes by Carelli Costumes, Inc. Costume accessories by
Barak Stribling. Hats by Woody Shelp. Millinery and masks
by Rodney Gordon. Footwear by Sharlot Battin of Montana
Leatherworks, Ltd. Shoes by JC Theatrical and Costume
Footwear and Taffy's N.Y. Jewelry by Miriam Haskell
Jewels. Eyeglasses by H.L. Purdy. Wigs by The Wig Party.
Garcia y Vega cigars used. Makeup consultant Kris Evans.
Emer'gen-C super energy booster provided by Alacer Corp.

Champagne courtesy of
Champagne G.H. Mumm

Furs by Christie Bros.

Shoes supplied by Peter Fox Limlted

"The Phantom" character make-up created and
designed by Christopher Tucker
Magic Consultant—Paul Daniels

CAMERON MACKINTOSH, INC.
Managing Director .... Nicholas Allott
Production Associate .... Shidan Majidi

THE REALLY USEFUL GROUP LTD.
Directors
Andrew Lloyd Webber   Madeleine Lloyd Webber
Mark Wordsworth   Barney Wragg
Jonathan Hull   Bishu Chakraborty

Performance rights to *The Phantom of the Opera*
are licensed by R&H Theatricals:
www.rnhtheatricals.com

To learn more about the production,
please visit
www.PhantomBroadway.com
Find us on Facebook: PhantomBroadway
and Twitter: TheOperaGhosts

Energy-efficient washer/dryer courtesy of
LG Electronics.

 THE SHUBERT ORGANIZATION, INC.
Board of Directors

The Phantom of the Opera
Scrapbook

Correspondents: Kris Koop Ouellette (*Phantom* graduate, Class of 2012); Kelly Jeanne Grant "Page"; Ellen Harvey "Madame Giry"; Satomi Hofmann "Wardrobe Mistress"/"Confidante"; Alexi Melvin, *Phantom* Merchandise and former *Phantom* Walk-On.

Most Exciting Celebrity Visitor: I really enjoyed hearing Ramin Karimloo perform at the finale of the 25th Anniversary Performance. It was wonderful to meet him. What a sweetheart!!
— *Kelly Jeanne Grant*
Sarah Brightman at the 25th. — *Ellen Harvey*
Suri Cruise came in with mom, Katie, and a couple of her friends...ADORABLE child!
— *Satomi Hofmann*

Memorable Directorial Notes: Hal Prince Note Session: August 2, 2012.
Opening Line to Address the Company: "I've got a lot of notes and they aren't all on the same point, but one important thing is: WHAT IS TRUTH?" "In the effort to humiliate someone, which is always a good way to start a rehearsal. Who? YOU. You know what happened—the pig's ass was facing front."
To Kyle Barisich (Raoul): "After the Dressing Room Scene…Coming down the stairs to look for someone to help you open the door is fantastic."
Kyle: "Seth [our new, young Production Supervisor] gave me that one."
Hal to Seth: "That's ONE…" (Howling, loving laughter from the entire room.)
Directing Mme. Giry's subtext on her actual line, "And YOU. You were a disgrace." (SUBTEXT): "And YOU, you were...FAT." (Woof. Talking to a group of ballerinas? That's just COLD!!!!)

Actor Who Performs the Most Roles in This Show: Greg Mills! He covers every male role in the show except Firmin, and he is brilliant!!
— *Kelly Jeanne Grant*

Who Has Done the Most Broadway Shows in Their Career?: Probably Ken Kantor? If he hasn't been in it, he still knows it backward and forward.
— *Satomi Hofmann*

Special Backstage Rituals: Fist bumps with Hugh Panaro on his way to his first "Phantom" entrance. It is his way of saying "hello" to the ensemble.
— *Kelly Jeanne Grant*
Hand-slaps after Meg's screaming exit during the Don Juan Panic. — *Satomi Hofmann*

Favorite Moment During Each Performance: Being on the stairs and singing the key change of "Masquerade." It is a MAGICAL feeling when we are all singing together as one voice.
— *Kelly Jeanne Grant*
Getting my "Giry" wig on. I know it sounds crazy, but I love it so much. And Tiffany, my hair person, does such an amazing job with it.
— *Ellen Harvey*

Favorite In-Theatre Gathering Place: The Green Room!! — *Kelly Jeanne Grant*
Hugh's dressing room when Soot (the dog) is in the house! — *Ellen Harvey*

Favorite Off-Site Hangouts: Schmackary's for cookies before the second show, and Angus McIndoe's across the street for drinks after the show. — *Kelly Jeanne Grant*
I was very sad to see Rio & You close. Was

Hugh's and my favorite! — *Satomi Hofmann*
Virgil's Real BBQ right down the street from the Majestic. It was the perfect setting for my "BEER, BBQ and BYE-BYE" celebration. Only the farewell hugs were tastier than the food and drink!
— *Kris Koop Ouellette*

Favorite Snackie Treats: Norman Weiss' blondies for Saturday matinee intermission. They are AMAZING!!" — *Kelly Jeanne Grant*

Phantom Mascots: Fun new "mini me" dolls made by a very sweet "Phan" named Amanda. I have grown very attached to my little "Pocket Giry" doll! — *Kelly Jeanne Grant*

Favorite Therapy: Janet Saia's Hot Yoga class between shows on Wednesday."
— *Kelly Jeanne Grant*

Fastest Costume Changes: In the show? Carlotta's "Il Muto" change behind the bed, or Meg's "Il Muto" change… My fastest change? From my auction cape into my Hannibal Jug Princess (that's her real name…) during the overture."
— *Kelly Jeanne Grant*

For the character who NEVER changes clothes in the show (which I absolutely love), I have 15 seconds to remove my "Masquerade" cape and hat with the help of a dresser, then grab my cane before I have to come back on stage." — *Ellen Harvey*
My intermission change! OUT OF white "Confidante" paint (which covers my face and neck and chest), wig, and huge costume INTO full makeup, wig change, boots and into another HUGE costume for "Masquerade." In other words —INTERMISSION? What intermission?!" (NO TIME TO PEE!!!!) — *Satomi Hofmann*

Heaviest/Hottest Costumes: Carlotta's Hannibal dress... Yikes!! My Sitzprobe dress. Built out of carpet-like fabric and has a giant lobster cage on my bum! — *Kelly Jeanne Grant*

My Wardrobe Mistress costume: long sleeves, floor-length skirt, turtleneck. TURTLENECK. It's like a sauna in there!" — *Satomi Hofmann*

Who Wears the Least?: Any of our beautiful ballerinas in "Hannibal." — *Kelly Jeanne Grant*
Probably the ballerinas. Damn them.
— *Satomi Hofmann*
Everyone on the evening of my last performance. EVERYONE. I am a very lucky, lucky lady!!!!!
— *Kris Koop Ouellette*

Easiest Costume: Madame Giry. No changes. (How easy is that?) — *Kelly Jeanne Grant*

Catchphrases Only the Company Would Recognize: "Oh God... The STAIRS!!" (Up and down to our dressing rooms.) (By the way, in a two-show day, I climb exactly 1,443 steps per show.)
— *Kelly Jeanne Grant*

Cell Phone Issues, Onstage and Off: The ever-popular loud rock-tune cell phone ring during our very silent auction scene that starts the show... Charming! — *Kelly Jeanne Grant*

Embarrassing Moments On Stage and Off: As Christine on tour, I tried to throw the "wedding bouquet" off stage during final lair scene, and it stuck in the armpit of one of the angel candelabras and vibrated loudly like an arrow stuck to a target. (I couldn't make that happen again if I tried.) It was so embarrassing, Raoul (Shawn McLaughlin) and I could hardly keep from laughing on stage.
— *Kelly Jeanne Grant*
Being stuck center stage because Ken Kantor is standing on my skirt! I couldn't move because I was laughing so hard and didn't want the audience to see! But I got my revenge. I threw him a look during the second show and he completely went up on his line! The right line: "I don't think there's much more I can do to assist you gentlemen. Good luck. If you need me, I shall be in Frankfurt." What came out: "Uh.. forgive me... I apologize, but it appears I don't have a reason to be here anymore. If you need me, I shall be in Frankfurt."
— *Satomi Hofmann*

Company Sweethearts: Paul Schaefer and Paloma Garcia-Lee or Trista Moldovan and Stephen Tewksbury (both couples are so cute!!)

Coolest Thing About Being in This Show: Getting to take a bow eight shows a week on Broadway with the sweetest, greatest cast and crew ever. I am so proud of our show and our *Phantom* "Phamily"!! — *Kelly Jeanne Grant*
I have performed in other Broadway shows, but to my relatives and friends overseas I have finally "made it" as an actor! And, of course, being a part of theatrical history is pretty awesome.
— *Ellen Harvey*
Being a part of the 25th Anniversary...amazing!
— *Satomi Hofmann*

1. The great Erna Dias, a dresser for Christine, who has been at *Phantom* since the beginning, doing her thing with Trista Moldovan.
2. Masqueraders (L-R): Satomi Hofmann, Heather Hill, Lynne Abeles, Ken Kantor, Greg Mills.

Photos courtesy of Kris Koop Ouellette

The Phantom of the Opera
SCRAPBOOK

Phantom Celebrates 25 Years on Broadway with an Unforgettable Gala Performance

The scene outside of the Majestic Theatre on January 26, 2013 just before the doors were opened was not unusual. Excitement and anticipation to see Broadway's beloved *The Phantom of the Opera* filled the air as it did every night.

Specially invited patrons began to file into the theatre, passing through the festive doors that read "25 Years" in elegant, white lettering. Each and every one of them was there to celebrate his/her own history with the production.

One of *Phantom*'s advertising slogans, seen plastered on billboards in Times Square and on the side of New York City buses, is "Remember your first time?" These collective "firsts" were on the minds of the audience as they settled into their seats. Whether they were reflecting back on their first time seeing the show, performing onstage in the show, working behind the scenes, or a combination, everyone gathered on that night to do exactly that, to remember.

A giant projection screen floated above the stage showcasing the 25th Anniversary logo, which was soon replaced by an awe-inspiring video—outlining the history and epic success of this musical. There was no shortage of smiles, gasps, giggles, applause, and even a few tears among those who were fortunate enough to be watching.

If you've seen *Phantom* even once, there's no doubt that you left the theatre with the image branded in your mind of the haunting and monumental chandelier rising above your head. With that powerful blast of the organ, the chandelier rose once more—the electricity in the room more powerful than ever before on the night of *Phantom*'s 25th anniversary on Broadway.

Throughout the epic performance there were sporadic bursts of laughter and acknowledgement at unexpected moments. At intermission, the woman next to me asked her friend, who was a former crew member, why this was. "They're thinking back to when that was them up there," he informed her. "Everyone had their favorite moments to perform."

To date, 34 Christine Daaés and 31 Phantoms (including understudies) have performed on the stage of the Majestic. I have seen a good majority of these performers in my years as a *Phantom* enthusiast, starting with the dynamic original couple Michael Crawford and Sarah Brightman, but I have never seen anything like the chemistry between Hugh Panaro and Sierra Boggess. I could think of no pair better to have taken on the roles for the historic performance.

Ms. Boggess' lovely and haunting rendition of "Wishing You Were Somehow Here Again" earned her possibly one of the lengthiest and most enthusiastic "Wishing" applauses in *Phantom* history. After playing Christine for the 25th Anniversary in London at the Royal Albert Hall as well as in the Las Vegas cast, Boggess possessed a crystal-clear understanding of the character, making her performance unforgettable. Those exquisite vocal cords didn't hurt either.

Mr. Panaro is one of Broadway's most beloved Phantoms, having played the role on and off since 1999. He gave one of his most memorable and passionate performances to date, wooing not only his beautiful onstage Christine, but also the many, many Christine alumni sitting in the audience, including Rebecca Luker, Sandra Joseph, Rebecca Pitcher, Jennifer Hope Wills, Marni Raab, Julie Hanson, Sara Jean Ford, just to name a few!

Immediately following the curtain call, which was received with thunderous applause, the company took one giant step back to make way for none other than acclaimed producer Cameron Mackintosh and beloved director Hal Prince. The two shared their words of pride and delight before introducing a video of none other than Lord Andrew Lloyd Webber, who sadly could not attend the event due to back surgery.

Lord Lloyd Webber also appeared in a video with his ex-wife Sarah Brightman. They shared an endearing rapport as they reflected back on their time with the original London and Broadway companies of *Phantom*. As the video ended, the audience was instantly on its feet for Broadway's first Christine, Ms. Brightman. She made a lovely, humble speech that illustrated her gratitude.

Ms. Boggess, even though outnumbered by a quartet of Phantoms, sang a haunting and powerful rendition of "The Phantom of the Opera" with Mr. Panaro, John Owen-Jones (UK Anniversary Tour), Ramin Karimloo (*Love Never Dies*, London), and Peter Jöback (London). The Phantoms also shared in a beautiful "Music of the Night" serenade, eventually being joined by the hundreds of *Phantom* alumni in the audience, who all rose from their seats as they sang. It was a truly goose bump-inducing moment that will not soon be forgotten. Equally unforgettable was the more-than-deserved standing ovation that the backstage crew—some of whom have been with the production for the entire 25 years—received as they took the stage with the cast.

After the chandelier expelled an unexpected heap of confetti upon the audience, the party really began. The New York Public Library underwent a *Phantom* makeover, emulating the true essence of the show from the exterior staircase covered in candles and a glowing mask on the façade, to the long, dark and haunting hallways and decorative mannequins fit for a masquerade in the interior. Food and drinks were served as *Phantom* folk mingled, taking up every inch of the two grand levels of the building.

We all stood together sharing a palpable sense of wonder and awe, grateful to be some part of the most important moment in *Phantom* history to date. A milestone that might never be surpassed by any other Broadway Musical, and an evening shared by the people who helped create "The Music of the Night."

— *Alexi Melvin*

Photos by Monica Simoes

1. The exterior of the New York Public Library, site of the 25th Anniversary celebration.
2. Curtain call at the Majestic Theatre on January 26, 2013 (L-R): John Owen-Jones, Hal Prince, Hugh Panaro, Sierra Boggess, Cameron Mackintosh, Ramin Karimloo, Peter Jöback, and Sir Andrew Lloyd Webber on screen .
3. (L-R): Cameron Mackintosh, Sarah Brightman and Harold Prince with Katherine Oliver, the Commissioner of the New York City Mayor's Office of Media and Entertainment declaring Jan. 26, 2013 as "*Phantom of the Opera* Day."

Picnic

First Preview: December 14, 2012. Opened: January 13, 2013.
Limited Engagement. Closed February 24, 2013 after 36 Previews and 49 Performances.

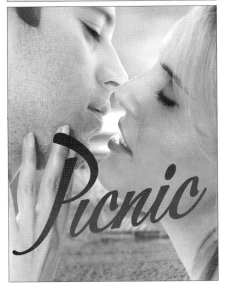

PLAYBILL®

In a small Kansas town, the lives of a group of women are thrown into confusion with the sudden arrival of a hunky young drifter in their midst. Repressed longings rise to the surface of even the youngest and oldest among them. As everyone prepares for the annual community picnic, some longstanding relationships are destroyed while others are nudged to fulfillment.

CAST

(in order of appearance)

Mrs. Helen Potts	ELLEN BURSTYN
Hal Carter	SEBASTIAN STAN
Millie Owens	MADELEINE MARTIN
Bomber Gutzel	CHRIS PERFETTI
Madge Owens	MAGGIE GRACE
Flo Owens	MARE WINNINGHAM
Rosemary Sydney	ELIZABETH MARVEL
Mrs. Potts' Mother	LIZBETH MACKAY
Alan Seymour	BEN RAPPAPORT
Irma Kronkite	MADDIE CORMAN
Christine Schoenwalder	CASSIE BECK
Howard Bevans	REED BIRNEY

Continued on next page

AMERICAN AIRLINES THEATRE

ROUNDABOUTTHEATRECOMPANY

Todd Haimes, Artistic Director
Harold Wolpert, Managing Director
Julia C. Levy, Executive Director
In association with
Darren Bagert and Martin Massman
Present

Reed Birney   Maggie Grace   Elizabeth Marvel   Sebastian Stan   Mare Winningham
and
Ellen Burstyn
in

Picnic

By
William Inge

with

Madeleine Martin   Ben Rappaport

Cassie Beck   Maddie Corman   Lizbeth Mackay   Chris Perfetti

Set Design Andrew Lieberman	*Costume Design* David Zinn	*Lighting Design* Jane Cox	*Sound Design* Jill BC Du Boff
Hair & Wig Design Tom Watson	*Choreography* Chase Brock	*Fight Director* Christian Kelly-Sordelet	*Dialect Coach* Kate Wilson

Production Stage Manager Jill Cordle	*Production Management* Aurora Productions	*Casting* Jim Carnahan, C.S.A. & Carrie Gardner, C.S.A.	*Picnic General Manager* Denise Cooper	*Press Representative* Boneau/Bryan-Brown

Associate Managing Director Greg Backstrom	*Director of Marketing & Audience Development* Tom O'Connor	*Director of Development* Lynne Gugenheim Gregory

General Manager Sydney Beers	*Founding Director* Gene Feist	*Adams Associate Artistic Director** Scott Ellis

Directed by
Sam Gold

*Generously underwritten by Margot Adams, in memory of Mason Adams.
Roundabout Theatre Company is a member of the League of Resident Theatres.
www.roundabouttheatre.org

1/13/13

(L-R): Ellen Burstyn, Sebastian Stan and Maggie Grace

Photo by Joan Marcus

Picnic

SCENE

The action of the play takes place in a small Kansas town in the yard shared by Flo Owens and Helen Potts.

Act I

Labor Day, early morning

Act II

Same day, just before sunset

Act III

Scene 1: Early next morning, before daylight
Scene 2: Later the same morning, after sunrise

UNDERSTUDIES

For Rosemary Sydney: CASSIE BECK
For Howard Bevans: PETER BRADBURY
For Madge Owens, Millie Owens,
  Christine Schoenwalder,
  Mrs. Potts' Mother: DANI DE WAAL
For Hal Carter, Alan Seymour,
  Bomber Gutzel: MATTHEW GOODRICH
For Mrs. Potts, Flo Owens,
  Irma Kronkite: LIZBETH MACKAY

Production Stage Manager: JILL CORDLE
Stage Manager: MORGAN R. HOLBROOK

(L-R): Ellen Burstyn, Ben Rappaport, and Maggie Grace

Photo by Joan Marcus

Reed Birney
Howard Bevans

Maggie Grace
Madge Owens

Elizabeth Marvel
Rosemary Sydney

Sebastian Stan
Hal Carter

Mare Winningham
Flo Owens

Ellen Burstyn
Mrs. Helen Potts

Madeleine Martin
Millie Owens

Ben Rappaport
Alan Seymour

Cassie Beck
Christine Schoenwalder

Maddie Corman
Irma Kronkite

Lizbeth Mackay
*Mrs. Potts' Mother;
u/s Mrs. Potts,
Flo Owens, Irma
Kronkite*

Chris Perfetti
Bomber Gutzel

Peter Bradbury
u/s Howard

Dani De Waal
*u/s Millie,
Madge, Christine,
Mrs. Potts' Mother*

Picnic

Matthew Goodrich
u/s Hal, Bomber, Alan

William Inge
Playwright

Sam Gold
Director

Andrew Lieberman
Set Design

David Zinn
Costume Design

Jane Cox
Lighting Designer

Jill BC Du Boff
Sound Design

Chase Brock
Choreography

Christian
Kelly-Sordelet
Fight Director

Matthew Hodges
*Properties
Supervisor*

Kate Wilson
Dialect Coach

Randall Poster
Music Supervisor

Jim Carnahan, CSA
Casting

Carrie Gardner, CSA
Casting

Darren Bagert

Martin Massman

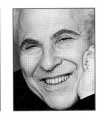

Gene Feist
*Founding Director
Roundabout Theatre
Company*

Todd Haimes
*Artistic Director
Roundabout Theatre
Company*

Photo by Brian Mapp

CREW
Front: Dale Carman
Second Row (L-R): Susan Fallon, Bobbi Morse, Manuela LaPorte, Hannah Overton, Robert Dowling II
Third Row (L-R): Pamela Short, Elizabeth Coleman, Carly DiFulvio (Company Manager)
Back Row (L-R): Brian Maiuri, Glenn Merwede, Jill Cordle (Production Stage Manager), Morgan R. Holbrook (Stage Manager)

Picnic

SECURITY
Adolf Torres

BOX OFFICE
(L-R): Solangel Bido, Robert Morgan

FRONT OF HOUSE
(L-R): Zipporah Aguasvivas, James Miller, Crystal Suarez

ROUNDABOUT THEATRE COMPANY STAFF
ARTISTIC DIRECTOR ....**TODD HAIMES**
MANAGING DIRECTOR ....**HAROLD WOLPERT**
EXECUTIVE DIRECTOR ....**JULIA C. LEVY**
ADAMS ASSOCIATE
   ARTISTIC DIRECTOR ....**SCOTT ELLIS**

ARTISTIC STAFF
DIRECTOR OF ARTISTIC DEVELOPMENT/
   DIRECTOR OF CASTING ....Jim Carnahan
Artistic Consultant ....Robyn Goodman
Resident Directors ....Doug Hughes, Sam Gold
Associate Artists ....Mark Brokaw, Scott Elliott,
                    Bill Irwin, Joe Mantello,
          Kathleen Marshall, Theresa Rebeck
Literary Manager ....Jill Rafson
Senior Casting Director ....Carrie Gardner
Casting Director ....Stephen Kopel
Casting Associate ....Jillian Cimini
Casting Assistants ....Lain Kunin, Logan Reid
Artistic Associate ....Amy Ashton
Literary Associate ....Josh Fiedler
The Blanche and Irving Laurie Foundation
   Theatre Visions Fund
     Commissions ....David West Read
Educational Foundation of
   America Commissions ....Bekah Brunstetter,
          Lydia Diamond, Diana Fithian,
                 Julie Marie Myatt
Roundabout Commissions.............Helen Edmundson,
          Andrew Hinderaker, Stephen Karam,
          Steven Levenson, Matthew Lopez,
                 Kim Rosenstock
Casting Interns ....Eric Byrd, Cat Gagliotti,
          Rebecca Henin, Krystal Rowley
Script Readers ....Shannon Deep, Liz Malta,
          Michael Perlman, Alexis Roblan
Artistic Apprentice ....Nikki DiLoreto

EDUCATION STAFF
EDUCATION DIRECTOR ....Greg McCaslin
Associate Education Director ....Jennifer DiBella
Education Program Manager ....Aliza Greenberg
Education Program Associate ....Sarah Malone
Education Assistant ....Lou-Lou Igbokwe
Education Dramaturg ....Ted Sod
Teaching Artists ....Josh Allen, Cynthia Babak,
          Victor Barbella, LaTonya Borsay,

Mark Bruckner, Chloe Chapin, Joe Doran,
Elizabeth Dunn-Ruiz, Carrie Ellman-Larsen,
Theresa Flanagan, Deanna Frieman,
Sheri Graubert, Adam Gwon, Devin Haqq,
Carrie Heitman, Karla Hendrick, Jason Jacobs,
Alana Jacoby, Lisa Renee Jordan, Jamie Kalama,
Erin McCready, James Miles, Nick Moore,
Meghan O'Neil, Drew Peterson, Nicole Press,
Leah Reddy, Amanda Rehbein, Nick Simone,
Heidi Stallings, Daniel Sullivan, Carl Tallent,
Vickie Tanner, Larine Towler, Jennifer Varbalow,
Kathryn Veillette, Leese Walker,
Gail Winar, Chad Yarborough
Teaching Artist Emeritus ....Renee Flemings
Education Apprentices ....Paul Brewster, Maia Collier

EXECUTIVE ADMINISTRATIVE STAFF
ASSOCIATE MANAGING
   DIRECTOR............................Greg Backstrom
Assistant Managing Director ....Katharine Croke
Assistant to the Managing Director ......Christina Pezzello
Assistant to the Executive Director ....Nicole Tingir

MANAGEMENT/ADMINISTRATIVE STAFF
GENERAL MANAGER ....Sydney Beers
General Manager,
   American Airlines Theatre ....Denise Cooper
General Manager,
   Steinberg Center ....Nicholas J. Caccavo
Human Resources Director ....Stephen Deutsch
Operations Manager ....Valerie D. Simmons
Associate General Manager ....Maggie Cantrick
Office Manager ....Scott Kelly
Archivist ....Tiffany Nixon
Receptionists ....Dee Beider, Emily Frohnhoefer,
                Elisa Papa, Allison Patrick
Messenger ....Darnell Franklin
Management Apprentice ....Holli Campbell

FINANCE STAFF
DIRECTOR OF FINANCE.................Susan Neiman
Payroll Director ....John LaBarbera
Accounts Payable Manager ....Frank Surdi
Payroll Benefits Administrator ....Yonit Kafka
Manager Financial Reporting ....Joshua Cohen
Business Office Assistant ....Jackie Verbitski
Business Office Apprentice ....Mara Abeleda

DEVELOPMENT STAFF
DIRECTOR OF
   DEVELOPMENT ....Lynne Gugenheim Gregory
Assistant to the Director of Development ....Liz Malta
Director, Institutional Giving ....Liz S. Alsina
Director, Special Events ....Lane Hosmer
Director, Individual Giving ....Christopher Nave
Associate Director, Individual Giving ....Tyler Ennis
Manager, Telefundraising ....Gavin Brown
Manager, Special Events ....Natalie Corr
Manager, Friends of Roundabout ....Marisa Perry
Manager, Donor Information Systems ....Lise Speidel
Institutional Giving Officer,
   Solicitations and Special Projects ....Brett Barbour
Individual Giving Officer ....Jordan Frausto
Individual Giving Officer ....Toni Rosenbaum
Institutional Giving Officer,
   Stewardship and Prospect
   Development ....Kimberly Sidey
Special Events Assistant ....Genevieve Carroll
Development Assistant ....Martin Giannini
Special Events Apprentice ....Alayna George
Development Apprentice ....Haley Tanenbaum

INFORMATION TECHNOLOGY STAFF
DIRECTOR OF
   INFORMATION TECHNOLOGY ..Daniel V. Gomez
Systems Administrator ....Jim Roma
Tessitura &
   Applications Administrator ....Yelena Ingberg
Database Administrator/Developer ....Rajan Eddy
Web Administrator ....Robert Parmelee
IT Associate ....Cary Kim

MARKETING STAFF
DIRECTOR OF MARKETING &
   AUDIENCE DEVELOPMENT ....Tom O'Connor
Senior Marketing Manager ....Rani Haywood
Manager, Design & Production ....Eric Emch
Digital Content Producer ....Mark Cajigao
Marketing Associate,
   Events & Promotions...............Rachel LeFevre-Snee
Marketing Associate, Digital ....Alex Barber
Marketing Assistant ....Dayna Johnson
Director of Telesales
   Special Promotions ....Marco Frezza
Telesales Manager ....Patrick Pastor
Telesales Office Coordinator ....Adam Unze

Picnic
SCRAPBOOK

Correspondent: Jill Cordle, PSM.
Opening Night Gifts: Mini picnic baskets, ceramic "hand."
Most Exciting Celebrity Visitor: Liam Neeson.
Who Has Done the Most Shows in Their Career: Ellen Burstyn.
Special Backstage Rituals: Gratitude circle before every show. Playing our two-show *Picnic* trivia game and winning crowns!

Favorite Moment During Each Performance: Picnic basket hand-off from props person to actor.
Favorite In-Theatre Gathering Place: Trap room for brunch.
Favorite Snack Food: Bacon and sausage made by the crew at brunch.
Most Memorable Ad-Lib: "Collard greens."

(L-R): Elizabeth Marvel, Ellen Burstyn and Reed Birney take a photo break at rehearsal.

Marketing Apprentices ....Tyler Beddoe, Maureen Keleher
Digital Marketing Apprentice ....Laura Abbott

AUDIENCE SERVICES STAFF
DIRECTOR OF AUDIENCE
   SERVICES ....Wendy Hutton
Associate Director of Audience Services ....Bill Klemm
Box Office Managers ....Edward P. Osborne, Jaime Perlman, Krystin MacRitchie, Catherine Fitzpatrick
Group Sales Manager ....Jeff Monteith
Assistant Box Office Managers ....Robert Morgan, Joseph Clark, Andrew Clements, Nicki Ishmael
Assistant Audience Services Managers ....Robert Kane, Lindsay Ericson, Jessica Pruett-Barnett, Kaia Lay Rafoss
Customer Services Coordinator ....Thomas Walsh
Audience Services ....Jennifer Almgreen, Solangel Bido, Jay Bush, Lauren Cartelli, Adam Elsberry, Joe Gallina, Ashley Gezana, Alanna Harms, Kara Harrington, Kiah Johnson, Mark Lavey, Rebecca Lewis-Whitson, Michelle Maccarone, Mead Margulies, Laura Marshall, Chuck Migliaccio, Carlos Morris, Katie Mueller, Sarah Olsen, Tom Protulipac, Josh Rozett, Heather Seibert, Nalane Singh, Ron Tobia, Hannah Weitzman
Audience Services Apprentice ....Blair Laurie

SERVICES
Counsel ....Paul, Weiss, Rifkind, Wharton and Garrison LLP, Charles H. Googe Jr., Carol M. Kaplan
Counsel ....Rosenberg & Estis
Counsel ....Andrew Lance, Gibson, Dunn, & Crutcher, LLP
Counsel ....Harry H. Weintraub, Glick and Weintraub, P.C.
Counsel ....Stroock & Stroock & Lavan LLP
Counsel ....Daniel S. Dokos, Weil, Gotshal & Manges LLP
Counsel ....Claudia Wagner/ Manatt, Phelps & Phillips, LLP
Immigration Counsel ....Mark D. Koestler and Theodore Ruthizer
House Physicians ....Dr. Theodore Tyberg, Dr. Lawrence Katz
House Dentist ....Neil Kanner, D.M.D.
Insurance ....DeWitt Stern Group, Inc.
Accountant ....Lutz & Carr CPAs, LLP
Advertising ....Spotco/ Drew Hodges, Jim Edwards, Tom Greenwald, Ilene Rosen, Josh Fraenkel

Interactive Marketing ....Situation Interactive/ Damian Bazadona, John Lanasa, Elizabeth Kandel, Mollie Shapiro, Danielle Migliaccio
Events Photography ....Anita and Steve Shevett
Production Photographer ....Joan Marcus
Theatre Displays ....King Displays, Wayne Sapper
Lobby Refreshments ....Sweet Concessions
Merchandising ....Spotco Merch/ James Decker

MANAGING DIRECTOR
   EMERITUS ....Ellen Richard

Roundabout Theatre Company
231 West 39th Street, New York, NY 10018
(212) 719-9393.

GENERAL PRESS REPRESENTATIVE
BONEAU/BRYAN-BROWN
Adrian Bryan-Brown
Matt Polk   Jessica Johnson   Amy Kass

CREDITS FOR *PICNIC*
Company Manager ....Carly DiFulvio
Production Stage Manager ....Jill Cordle
Stage Manager ....Morgan R. Holbrook
Production Management by ......Aurora Productions Inc./ Gene O'Donovan, Ben Heller, Stephanie Sherline, Jarid Sumner, Anthony Jusino, Anita Shah, Liza Luxenberg, Garrett Ellison, Troy Pepicelli, Gayle Riess, Cat Nelson, Melissa Mazdra
Assistant Director ....Osheen Jones
Assistant Scenic Designer ....Christopher Morris
Associate Costume Designer ....Jacob A. Climer
Assistant to the Costume Designer ....Sarah Laux
Associate Lighting Designer ....Bradley King
Assistant to the Lighting Designer ....Alexandra Mannix
Associate Sound Designer ....David Sanderson
Make-Up Designer ....Ashley Ryan
Production Properties Supervisor ....Matthew Hodges
Music Supervisor ....Randall Poster
Music Coordinator ....Meghan Currier
Assistant to the Choreographer ....Marlo Hunter
Fight Directors ....Christian Kelly-Sordelet, Rick Sordelet
Production Carpenter ....Glenn Merwede
Production Electrician ....Brian Maiuri
Running Properties ....Robert W. Dowling II
Sound Operator ....Dann Wojnar
Wardrobe Supervisor ....Susan Fallon
Dressers ....Dale Carman, Pamela Short

Wardrobe Dayworker ....Barbara Morse
Hair and Wig Supervisor ....Manuela LaPorte
Production Assistant ....Shelley Miles
SDV Foundation Observer ....Jenna Worsham
Assistant to Darren Bagert ....Matthew Masten

CREDITS
Scenery constructed by Showman Fabricators Inc., Long Island City, NY. Lighting equipment by PRG Lighting. Sound equipment by Sound Associates. Custom costumes constructed by Tricorne Inc., Donna Langman and Bobby Tilley. Additional costumes by Helen Uffner Vintage Clothing, LLC, and the TDF Costume Collection. Custom properties fabricated by Sarah Bird, Gloria Sun and Cairo Studios. Special thanks to Bra*Tenders for hosiery and undergarments.

MUSIC CREDITS
"**Barbara Lee**" and "**I Need You Baby**" by Deborah Chessler, courtesy of Edwin H. Morris & Company, a division of MPL Music Publishing, Inc. (ASCAP). "**It Ain't Gonna Be Like That**" by Frankie Laine, Melvin H. Torme. Publisher: Marmor Music Co. "**Good Rockin Tonight**" by Roy Brown. Publisher: Brown Angel Music Publishing (BMI). "**I'd Rather Have You Under the Moon**" by Fay Whitman Manus (words), Helen Miller (music). Publisher: Brightview Music. "**Tell Me So**" by Deborah Chessler, courtesy of Edwin H. Morris & Company, a division of MPL Music Publishing, Inc. (ASCAP). Used by permission.

Makeup provided by M•A•C Cosmetics.

AMERICAN AIRLINES THEATRE STAFF
Company Manager ....Carly DiFulvio
House Carpenter ....Glenn Merwede
House Electrician ....Brian Maiuri
House Properties ....Robert W. Dowling II
House Sound ....Dann Wojnar
IA Apprentice ....Hannah Overton
Wardrobe Supervisor ....Susan J. Fallon
Box Office Manager ....Ted Osborne
Assistant Box Office Manager ....Robert Morgan
House Manager ....Stephen Ryan
Associate House Manager ....Zipporah Aguasvivas
Head Usher ....Crystal Suarez
House Staff ....Christopher Busch, Oscar Castillo, Anne Ezell, Saira Flores, Denise Furbert, Rebecca Knell, James Miller, Enrika Nicholas, Jazmine Perez, CharDia Reynolds, Celia Torres, Dominga Veloz Rivera
Security ....Julious Russell

Pippin

First Preview: March 23, 2013. Opened: April 25, 2013.
Still running as of May 31, 2013.

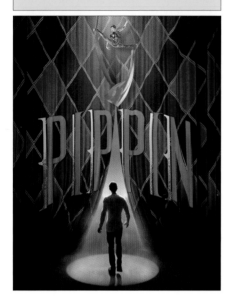

Revival of the 1972 musical about medieval emperor Charlemagne's heir-apparent who wants to do something wonderful and unique with his life—but isn't quite sure exactly what that might be. Egged on by the mysterious Leading Player and her minions, Pippin tries war, sex, politics, et cetera, before discovering the one thing that has the best chance of leading to his heart's content. This production is notable for director Diane Paulus' circus-style staging.

CAST
(in order of appearance)

Leading Player	PATINA MILLER
Fastrada	CHARLOTTE d'AMBOISE
Berthe	ANDREA MARTIN
Lewis	ERIK ALTEMUS
Charles	TERRENCE MANN
Pippin	MATTHEW JAMES THOMAS
Catherine	RACHEL BAY JONES
Theo	ANDREW CEKALA, ASHTON WOERZ
The Players	GRÉGORY ARSENAL,

LOLITA COSTET, COLIN CUNLIFFE,
ANDREW FITCH, ORION GRIFFITHS,
VIKTORIA GRIMMY, OLGA KARMANSKY,
BETHANY MOORE, STEPHANIE POPE,
PHILIP ROSENBERG, YANNICK THOMAS,
MOLLY TYNES, ANTHONY WAYNE

ADDITIONAL PARTS AND SPECIALTIES

Noble: STEPHANIE POPE
Peasant: ANDREW FITCH

Continued on next page

☻ THE MUSIC BOX
239 W. 45th Street
A Shubert Organization Theatre

Philip J. Smith, *Chairman*   **Robert E. Wankel,** *President*

Barry and Fran Weissler   Howard and Janet Kagan

Lisa Matlin   Kyodo Tokyo   A&A Gordon/Brunish Trinchero   Tom Smedes/Peter Stern
Broadway Across America   Independent Presenters Network   Norton Herrick   Allen Spivak   Rebecca Gold
Joshua Goodman   Stephen E. McManus   David Robbins/Bryan S. Weingarten   Philip Hagemann/Murray Rosenthal
Jim Kierstead/Carlos Arana/Myla Lerner   Hugh Hayes/Jamie Cesa/Jonathan Reinis

Sharon A. Carr/Patricia R. Klausner   Ben Feldman   Square 1 Theatrics   Wendy Federman/Carl Moellenberg
Bruce Robert Harris/Jack W. Batman   Infinity Theatre Company/Michael Rubenstein   Michael A. Alden/Dale Badway/Ken Mahoney

PRESENT

The American Repertory Theater production of

PIPPIN

BOOK BY	MUSIC & LYRICS BY
Roger O. Hirson	**Stephen Schwartz**

STARRING

Matthew James Thomas   **Patina Miller**

Terrence Mann   **Charlotte d'Amboise**   **Rachel Bay Jones**

AND

Andrea Martin

Erik Altemus   Grégory Arsenal   Andrew Cekala   Lolita Costet   Colin Cunliffe   Andrew Fitch
Orion Griffiths   Viktoria Grimmy   Sabrina Harper   Olga Karmansky   Bethany Moore   Brad Musgrove
Stephanie Pope   Philip Rosenberg   Yannick Thomas   Molly Tynes   Anthony Wayne   Ashton Woerz

SCENIC DESIGN BY	LIGHTING DESIGN BY	COSTUME DESIGN BY	SOUND DESIGN BY
Scott Pask	**Kenneth Posner**	**Dominique Lemieux**	**Jonathan Deans & Garth Helm**

ILLUSIONS BY	FIRE EFFECTS BY	FLYING EFFECTS BY
Paul Kieve	**Chic Silber**	**ZFX, Inc.**

TECHNICAL SUPERVISOR	DESIGN SUPERVISOR	ADVERTISING	PRESS REPRESENTATIVE
Jake Bell	**Edward Pierce**	**SpotCo**	**Boneau/Bryan-Brown**

MUSIC DIRECTOR	MUSIC COORDINATOR	CASTING	ASSOCIATE PRODUCER
Charlie Alterman	**John Miller**	**Duncan Stewart/Benton Whitley**	**James L. Simon**

ASSOCIATE DIRECTOR/PRODUCTION STAGE MANAGER	ASSISTANT CHOREOGRAPHER	COMPANY MANAGER
Nancy Harrington	**Brad Musgrove**	**Jeff Klein**

EXECUTIVE PRODUCER	GENERAL MANAGER
Alecia Parker	**B.J. Holt**

ORCHESTRATIONS BY

Larry Hochman

MUSIC SUPERVISION AND ARRANGEMENTS BY

Nadia DiGiallonardo

CIRCUS CREATION BY

Gypsy Snider

of Les 7 doigts de la main

CHOREOGRAPHY BY

Chet Walker

in the style of Bob Fosse

DIRECTED BY

Diane Paulus

Special thanks to American Repertory Theater at Harvard University and Les 7 doigts de la main for their help in developing this production.
A.R.T. Artistic Director, Diane Paulus and Producer, Diane Borger, Les 7 doigts de la main Directeur General, Nassib el Husseini

4/25/13

(L-R): Patina Miller and Matthew James Thomas

Pippin

MUSICAL NUMBERS

ACT I

Scene 1: THE OPENING
"Magic to Do" ....The Players
"Corner of the Sky" ....Pippin
Scene 2: HOME ....Leading Player, Charles, Pippin, Lewis and Fastrada
Scene 3: GLORY
"War Is a Science" ....Charles and The Players
"Glory" ....Leading Player and The Players
Scene 4: THE FLESH
"Simple Joys" ....Leading Player and The Players
"No Time at All" ....Berthe and The Players
"With You" ....Pippin and The Players
Scene 5: REVOLUTION
"Spread a Little Sunshine" ....Fastrada
"Morning Glow" ....Pippin and The Players

ACT II

"Entr'acte"
Scene 1: POLITICS
Scene 2: ENCOURAGEMENT
"On the Right Track" ....Leading Player and Pippin
Scene 3: ORDINARY LIFE
"Kind of Woman" ....Catherine
"Extraordinary" ....Pippin and The Players
"Love Song" ....Pippin and Catherine
Scene 4: THE FINALE ....Leading Player, Pippin and The Players

ORCHESTRA

Conductor/Keyboard: CHARLIE ALTERMAN
Associate Conductor/Keyboard:
SONNY PALADINO
Reeds: EDWARD JOFFE, RICK HECKMAN
Trumpet: DAVE TRIGG
Trombone: MICHAEL DAVIS
Violin/Viola: RICK DOLAN
Cello: PETER SACHON
Guitar: LARRY SALTZMAN

Bass: STEVE MILLHOUSE
Drums: JARED SCHONIG
Percussion: SEAN RITENAUER

Music Coordinator: JOHN MILLER
Music Preparation:
DONALD OLIVER & PAUL
HOLDERBAUM/Chelsea Music, Inc.
Keyboard Programmer: RANDY COHEN

The Manson Trio:
ANDREW FITCH, ANTHONY WAYNE
Head: COLIN CUNLIFFE
"With You" Hand Balancing:
GRÉGORY ARSENAL, PHILIP ROSENBERG
Rolla Bolla: ORION GRIFFITHS
Bolero: YANNICK THOMAS, LOLITA COSTET

UNDERSTUDIES

For Pippin: ERIK ALTEMUS
For Lewis: COLIN CUNLIFFE
For Berthe: SABRINA HARPER
For Leading Player:
STEPHANIE POPE, MOLLY TYNES
For Catherine:
BETHANY MOORE, MOLLY TYNES
For Fastrada:
SABRINA HARPER, MOLLY TYNES
For Charles:
COLIN CUNLIFFE, ANDREW FITCH

SWINGS

SABRINA HARPER, BRAD MUSGROVE
Dance Captain: BRAD MUSGROVE
Assistant Dance Captain: PHILIP ROSENBERG

Original choreography for "Manson Trio"
by BOB FOSSE.
"Spread a Little Sunshine" dance arrangement
by ZANE MARK.
Special trapeze routine performed with
YANNICK THOMAS.

Matthew James Thomas is sppearing with the
permission of Actors' Equity Association pursuant
to an exchange program between
American Equity and UK Equity.

2012-2013 AWARDS

TONY AWARDS
Best Revival of a Musical
Best Direction of a Musical
(Diane Paulus)
Best Performance by an Actress
in a Leading Role in a Musical
(Patina Miller)
Best Performance by an Actress
in a Featured Role in a Musical
(Andrea Martin)

DRAMA DESK AWARDS
Outstanding Revival of a Musical
Outstanding Featured Actress in a Musical
(Andrea Martin)
Outstanding Director of a Musical
(Diane Paulus)
Outstanding Choreography
(Chet Walker and Gypsy Snider)

Photos by Joan Marcus

Patina Miller   Andrea Martin

FRED AND ADELE ASTAIRE AWARDS
Outstanding Choreography
of a Broadway Show
(Chet Walker)
Outstanding Female Dancer
in a Broadway Show
(Charlotte d'Amboise)

OUTER CRITICS CIRCLE AWARDS
Outstanding Revival of a Musical
Outstanding Director of a Musical
(Diane Paulus)
Outstanding Choreographer
(Chet Walker)
Outstanding Lighting Design (Play or Musical)
(Kenneth Posner)
Outstanding Actress in a Musical
(Patina Miller)
Outstanding Featured Actor in a Musical
(Terrence Mann)
Outstanding Featured Actress in a Musical
(Andrea Martin)

THE DRAMA LEAGUE AWARD
Distinguished Revival of a Musical

Pippin

Matthew James
Thomas
Pippin

Patina Miller
Leading Player

Terrence Mann
Charles

Charlotte d'Amboise
Fastrada

Rachel Bay Jones
Catherine

Andrea Martin
Berthe

Andrew Cekala
Theo

Ashton Woerz
Theo

Erik Altemus
Lewis; u/s Pippin

Grégory Arsenal
Player

Lolita Costet
Player

Colin Cunliffe
*Player; u/s Lewis,
Charles*

Andrew Fitch
Player; u/s Charles

Orion Griffiths
Player

Viktoria Grimmy
Player

Sabrina Harper
*Player, Swing;
u/s Berthe, Fastrada*

Olga Karmansky
Player

Bethany Moore
Player; u/s Catherine

Brad Musgrove
*Swing, Assistant
Choreographer*

Stephanie Pope
*Player; u/s Leading
Player*

Philip Rosenberg
*Player, Assistant
Dance Captain*

Yannick Thomas
Player

Molly Tynes
*Player; u/s Leading
Player, Catherine,
Fastrada*

Anthony Wayne
Player

Stephen Schwartz
Music & Lyrics

Diane Paulus
Director

Chet Walker
Choreographer

Gypsy Snider
Circus Creation

Nadia DiGiallonardo
*Music Supervisor
and Arrangements*

Larry Hochman
Orchestrations

Scott Pask
Scenic Design

Kenneth Posner
Lighting Design

Dominique Lemieux
Costume Design

Jonathan Deans
Sound Designer

Garth Helm
Sound Designer

Pippin

Paul Kieve
Illusions

Jake Bell
Technical Supervisor

Edward Pierce
Design Supervisor

John Miller
Music Coordinator

Charlie Alterman
Music Director

Nancy Harrington
*Associate Director/
Production Stage
Manager*

Duncan Stewart
Casting

Benton Whitley
Casting

Mia Walker
Assistant Director

Fran & Barry Weissler
Producer

Howard & Janet Kagan
Producer

Lisa Matlin
Producer

Allan Gordon
Producer

Adam Gordon
Producer

Corey Brunish
Producer

Brisa Trinchero
Producer

Tom Smedes
Producer

Peter Stern
Producer

John Gore
Broadway Across
America
Producer

Norton Herrick
Producer

Allen Spivak
Producer

Rebecca Gold
Producer

Joshua Goodman
Producer

Bryan Weingarten
Producer

Philip Hagemann
Producer

Murray Rosenthal
Producer

Jim Kierstead
Producer

Carlos Arana
Producer

Myla Lerner
Producer

Hugh Hayes
Producer

Jamie Cesa
Producer

Jonathan Reinis
Producer

Ben Feldman
Producer

Pippin

Sharon A. Carr
Producer

Patricia R. Klausner
Producer

Jay Leland Krottinger
Square 1 Theatrics
Producer

Ryan Tanner
Square 1 Theatrics
Producer

Wendy Federman
Producer

Carl Moellenberg
Producer

Bruce Robert Harris
Producer

Jack W. Batman
Producer

Anna & Alan Ostroff
Infinity Theatre Co.
Producers

Michael Rubenstein
Producer

Michael A. Alden
Producer

Dale Badway
Producer

Ken Mahoney
Producer

James L. Simon
Associate Producer

Alecia Parker
Executive Producer

MANAGEMENT
(L-R): Brad Musgrove
(Dance Captain),
Nancy Harrington
(Production Stage Manager),
Stephen Gruse
(Assistant Stage Manager),
Julie Baldauff
(Stage Manager)

CREW
Front Row (L-R): Reece Nunez, Chris Pravata, John Carlotto, Alan Schuster, William Rowland II, William K. Rowland, Kevin Strohmeyer, Marjorie Denton, Michael Cecchini, Dennis Maher
Under the Stairs: Joseph "Dana" Gracey
Back Row (L-R): Kyle Garnett, Michael Sancineto, Worth Strecker
Stairs (From Top): Sandy Paradise, Thomas Sharkey, Kim Garnett

WARDROBE
Front (L-R): Michael Sancineto, Marjorie Denton, Thomas Sharkey, Meghan Carsella
Stairs (From Top): David Thompson, Sara Foster, Emily Ockenfels

Photos by Brian Mapp

Pippin

MUSICIANS
Front (L-R): Charlie Alterman (Music Director/Conductor), Rick Dolan
Back (L-R): Michael Davis, Larry Saltzman, Sean Ritenauer, Jared Schonig

BOX OFFICE
(L-R): Tim Moran, Brian Cobb, Brendan Berberich

MARKETING STRATEGY
Clint Bond, Jr.   Ken Sperr

GENERAL PRESS REPRESENTATIVE
BONEAU/BRYAN-BROWN
Adrian Bryan-Brown   Heath Schwartz   Amy Kass

Production Stage Manager	Nancy Harrington
Stage Manager	Julie Baldauff
Assistant Stage Manager	Stephen R. Gruse
Management Assistant	Tyler Forrest
Casting Associate	Andrea Zee
Assistant Director	Mia Walker
Assistant to Gypsy Snider	Jeslyn Kelly
Drama League Ass't Director	Christopher Windom
SDC Observer	Patrick Boyd
Associate Scenic Designer	Jeff Hinchee
Assistant Scenic Designers	Nick Francone, Jennifer Price-Fick
Apprentice Scenic Designer	Stephen Davan
Assistant Costume Designer	Jessica Worsnop
Costume Design Assistant	Jason Bishop
"Fastrada" Costume Specialty	Viktoria Grimmy
Associate Lighting Designer	Anthony Pearson
Assistant Lighting Designer	Jonathan Spencer
Production Carpenter	Todd Frank
Assistant Carpenter	Michael Cecchini
Production Electrician	James Fedigan
Head Electrician	Patrick Ainge
Production Props Coordinator	Worth Strecker
Illusion Props	Ron Bin Ion, Bill Smith
Props Artisan	Bob Flanagan
Associate Sound Designer	Drew Levy
Production Sound	Nick Borisjuk
Sound Engineer	Steve Henshaw
Sound Programmer	Will Pickens
Deck Sound	Reece Nunez
Automated Lighting Programmer	Timothy F. Rogers
Wardrobe Supervisor	Meghan Carsella
Dressers	Marjorie Denton, David Thompson, Sara Foster, Thomas Roger Sharkey, Laura Horner, Michael Sancineto
Hair/Make-up Supervisor	Katie Beatty
Assistant Hair/Make-up	Jonathan Sharpless
Make-up Artisan	Hagen Linss
Assistant Keyboard Programmer	Tim Crook

Dialect Coach	Nancy Houfek
Associate Fire Specialist	Aaron Waitz
Production Assistant	Sharika Niles
Assistant to John Miller	Nichole Jennino
Music Assistant	Ben Rauhala
Music Intern	Peter Hodgson
Legal Counsel	Seth Gelblum/Loeb & Loeb
Accountant	Marks Paneth & Shron LLP/ Mark D'Ambrosi, Marina Flom
Advertising	SpotCo/ Drew Hodges, Ilene Rosen, Tom Greenwald, Stephen Sosnowski, Michelle Haines, Timothy Falotico, Marc Mettler, Kristen Bardwil
Website Design	ArtHouse Interactive/ Sara Fitzpatrick
Production Photography	Joan Marcus
Children's Supervisor	Thomas Bradfield
Children's Teachers	On Location Education
Banking	City National Bank/ Stephanie Dalton, Michele Gibbons
Insurance	Aon/ Albert G. Ruben Insurance Services, Inc.
Sports Medicine Physician	Jordan D. Metzl, MD/ Hospital for Special Surgery
Opening Night	Foresight Events/ Jennifer O'Connor, Connie Wilkin
Merchandising	Broadway Merchandising, LLC
Payroll Services	Castellana Services, Inc.
Theatre Displays	BAM Signs, Inc.
Group Sales	Group Sales Box Office Broadway.com/Groups

NATIONAL ARTISTS MANAGEMENT CO.

Chief Financial Officer	Bob Williams
International Manager	Nina Skriloff
General Management Associates	Rina Saltzman, Stephen Spadaro
Associate to the Weisslers	Brett England
Assistant to Mrs. Weissler	Nikki Pelazza
Manager of Accounting/Admin.	Marian Albarracin
Receptionist	Michelle Coleman
Messenger	Victor Ruiz
Executive Assistant	Cristina Boccitto
Accounting Associate	Marion Taylor

To learn more about the production, please visit
www.pippinthemusical.com

CREDITS
Show control and scenic motion control featuring stage command systems and scenery fabrication by PRG-Scenic Technologies, a division of Production Resource Group, LLC, New Windsor, NY. Lighting equipment from PRG Lighting. Sound equipment by Masque Sound®, Sunshine Studios. Costumes provided by Jennifer Love Costumes, Parsons-Meares, Studio Rouge, Martin Izquierdo, Rachel Navarro, David Thompson, John Furrow, Bra*Tenders. Shoes by LaDuca. Wigs by Tom Watson. Thanks to Gibson Guitar.

SPECIAL THANKS
Diane Borger, Chris De Camillis, Haley Bennett, Nassib El Husseini

 THE SHUBERT ORGANIZATION, INC.

Board of Directors

Philip J. Smith	**Robert E. Wankel**
Chairman	President
Wyche Fowler, Jr.	**Diana Phillips**
Lee J. Seidler	**Michael I. Sovern**
Stuart Subotnick	

Chief Financial Officer	Elliot Greene
Sr. Vice President, Ticketing	David Andrews
Vice President, Finance	Juan Calvo
Vice President, Human Resources	Cathy Cozens
Vice President, Facilities	John Darby
Vice President, Theatre Operations	Peter Entin
Vice President, Marketing	Charles Flateman
Vice President, Audit	Anthony LaMattina
Vice President, Ticket Sales	Brian Mahoney
Vice President, Creative Projects	D.S. Moynihan
Vice President, Real Estate	Julio Peterson
House Manager	Jonathan Schulman

The Rascals: Once Upon a Dream

First Preview: April 15, 2013. Opened: April 16, 2013.
Limited Engagement. Closed May 5, 2013 **after** 1 Preview and 14 Performances.

A Broadway stop on the reunion tour for this 1960s Rock and Roll Hall of Fame group that produced #1 hits "Good Lovin'," "Groovin'" and "People Got to Be Free," plus the #3 "A Beautiful Morning." In addition to performances by the band members, the show includes a multi-media salute to the times that produced them (originally as "The Young Rascals"), and a history of the band.

BAND

FELIX CAVALIERE ....Keyboard/Vocals
EDDIE BRIGATI ....Vocals
DINO DANELLI..............................Drums
GENE CORNISH ....Guitar

BACKING BAND

MARK ALEXANDER ....Keyboard
MARK PRENTICE ....Bass/Music Director

SINGERS

SHARON BRYANT
ANGELA CLEMMONS
DENNIS COLLINS

Narrator/Fat Frankie ....VINNY PASTORE
Felix ....ALEXANDER NEIL MILLER
Eddie ....PETER EVANGELISTA
Dino ....RYAN BOUDREAU
Gene ....BRANDON WOOD
Pam Sawyer ....MAUREEN VAN ZANDT
Lori Burton ....CRYSTAL ARNETTE
Arif Mardin ....PENNY BITTONE
Tom Dowd...........................ALLEN ENLOW

Continued on next page

RICHARD RODGERS THEATRE
UNDER THE DIRECTION OF JAMES M. NEDERLANDER AND JAMES L. NEDERLANDER

STEVEN VAN ZANDT AND MAUREEN VAN ZANDT
PRESENT

THE RASCALS
ONCE UPON A DREAM

STARRING

DINO DANELLI   **EDDIE BRIGATI**   **GENE CORNISH**   **FELIX CAVALIERE**

DIRECTED AND PRODUCED BY
STEVEN VAN ZANDT AND MARC BRICKMAN

PRODUCED BY
LARRY MAGID AND BASE ENTERTAINMENT

WRITTEN BY
STEVEN VAN ZANDT

MUSIC AND LYRICS BY
FELIX CAVALIERE AND EDDIE BRIGATI

www.RascalsBway.com

4/16/13

(L-R): Dino Danelli, Felix Cavaliere, Steven Van Zandt, Eddie Brigati, Gene Cornish

Photo courtesy of the production

The Rascals: Once Upon a Dream

Photo courtesy of the production

The Rascals

Ruby ....ANNIE CHANG
Young Eddie ....CHASE LONGORDO
Young Billy ....SEAN MARTIN
Flower Child (young) ....ISABELLA CARTER
Flower Child (teenage) .GABRIELLE LUND BLOM

"Once Upon a Dream" sung by
SOFIE ZAMCHICK

Steven Van Zandt
Producer/Writer/
Director/Music
Producer

Maureen Van Zandt
Producer

Marc Brickman
Producer/Director/
Production Designer

Larry Magid
Producer

Scott Zeiger
Base Entertainment
Producer

Scott Prisand
Associate Producer

Billy Rapaport
Associate Producer/
Assistant Director

Lori Santoro
Costume Design

A NOTE FROM THE AUTHOR

The opportunity to reunite The Rascals has been a lifelong dream of mine.

They were the first band I ever saw, and their influence on me and my generation set standards we are still trying to meet.

Three years ago Maureen and I were honored at the Kristin Ann Carr fundraiser, and we wanted to do something special in the spirit of Kristin at the event. Maureen suggested I give the impossible one last try, and it happened. The one historic rock reunion nobody thought they'd ever see, the four original Rascals played an amazing hour-long set.

After that I was determined to bring them back permanently, but even a great concert didn't feel like enough after 40 years. I wanted future generations to know their history and their cultural significance. I also wanted to thank them. To show my gratitude for their amazing inspiration.

The show would have to be as big as their original vision and as big as the '60's era it came from, because the Rascals' singles uniquely expressed the first-person American '60's. From the soul music dance explosion to the British Invasion, folk rock, the psychedelic era, the Civil Rights struggle and the Vietnam War, from the pain of conflict and disappointment to the enlightenment of love and forgiveness, from the idealism of the summer of love, to the end of the decade's winter of discontent.

The result is "Once Upon a Dream."

It's a concert with the four original members, in fact, at 28 songs, the most comprehensive concert they've ever done, combined with their story and the major events of the era, told by way of pre-filmed segments on a giant screen.

The rhythm of the show is the rhythm of Broadway, different than a typical concert, but I promise you by the end of the show you will have experienced one of the great bands of all time having given their greatest, most definitive concert ever, and a lot more.

I want to thank co-director, co-producer Marc Brickman for providing the incredible visual design and environment of the show and for his encouragement of the project over the last three years, along with the great work of his team; Peter Shapiro for providing the magnificent Capitol Theatre in Port Chester as the perfect venue to preview the show; Larry Magid and Scott Zeiger for their hard work and faith in the show; Jimmy Nederlander, Nick Scandalios and the whole Nederlander Organization for providing the perfect theatre, the legendary Richard Rodgers, for our Broadway premiere; Renegade Nation for their loyal, tireless work no matter how crazy the idea; my wife Maureen for sharing the vision, her eternal patience and constant inspiration; and the Rascals for trusting me.

Steven Van Zandt

The Rascals: Once Upon a Dream

Darryl DeAngelo
Costume Design

Maggie Brohn
Bespoke Theatricals
General Management

Amy Jacobs
Bespoke Theatricals
General Management

Devin Keudell
Bespoke Theatricals
General Management

Nina Lannan
Bespoke Theatricals
General Management

Photo by Brian Mapp

DOORMAN
Angelo Gonzalez

Photos by Brian Mapp

MUSICIANS/VOCALISTS
Front Row (L-R): Mark Alexander (Keyboards), Mark Prentice (Music Director/Bass), Dennis Collins (Background Vocals)
Back Row (L-R): Sharon Bryant (Background Vocals), Eddie Brigati (Vocals), Dino Danelli (Drums), Gene Cornish (Guitar), Felix Cavaliere (Vocals, Keyboards), Angela Clemmons (Background Vocals)

CREW
Front Row (L-R): Ponzer Berkman (Backline), Ryan Blumstein (Backline), Joel Feitzinger (Teleprompter), Brian Kingman (A2), Steve Carver (House Electrician), John Carton, Andy Catron (Electrics), Mike Ward (Electrics), Geoff Sanoff (Click Track Operator)
Back Row (L-R): John Barone (Backline), Darryl DeAngelo (Costume Designer), Lori Santoro (Costume Designer), Kim Prentice (Wardrobe), Billy Rapaport (Associate Producer), Megan Napoletano (Production Coordinator), Ron Knox (Flyman), Kevin Camus (House Carpenter), Angelo Grasso (Carpenter), John Senter (Electrician), Chris Edwards (A1), Anthony Fransen (Lighting Director), Brian Frankel (Electrician), Steve DeVerna (House Props), Mark Hutchins (Monitor Mixer), Elisha L. Griego (Production Manager)

The Rascals: Once Upon a Dream

SCRAPBOOK

Correspondent: Elisha Griego, "Production Manager"
Memorable Opening Night Letter or Note: Good Lovin' signs from other Broadway casts!
Opening Night Gifts: Party at Sardi's.
Most Exciting Celebrity Visitor and What They Did/Said: Too many to name, but here are a few—Bruce Springsteen, Bill Murray, Graham Nash, Pierce Brosnan, Sid Bernstein, Patti LuPone.
Special Backstage Rituals: The Pre-Show Group Huddle on stage with stage crew, techs and band, led by Billy Rapaport, Spiritual Guru.
Favorite Moment During Each Performance: Top of show/Kabuki Drop…each night is an adventure!!!
Favorite In-Theatre Gathering Place: Production Office… sometimes there are treats.
Favorite Off-Site Hangouts: Lattanzi, Sofia's, Pergola Des Artistes.
Favorite Snack Food: Grapefruit, Bombolini

donuts from Corso, Baked By Melissa mini cupcakes.
Mascot: Eddie in his apron.
Favorite Therapy: Lemon-Ginger Tea with cracked black pepper, Grether's Blackcurrant Pastilles.
Most Memorable Ad-Lib: Our on-stage announcement pre-show: "Please use your handheld devices, take as many pictures as you want, Facebook them, Tweet them, YouTube them, basically tonight… Do whatever the f@$% you want…."
Memorable Press Encounter: CBS This Morning coming to cover just a portion of rehearsal and staying and rocking through the entire set.
Memorable Stage Door Fan Encounter: Any of the "Senior" groupies from the Sixties.
Who Wore the Heaviest/Hottest Costume: Mark Prentice (The Morpheus/Interview with a Vampire get-up).

Who Wore the Least: Angela Clemmons (Go-go dancer get-up).
Memorable Directorial Note: "Make It Nice," "How's the Family?," "That's right, you're a little baby flower girl from the sixties."
Company In-Jokes: "Make It Nice," "How's the Family?"
Nicknames: Little Steven, Veals, G-off, Jo-elle, Sarge, Daddy Rock, Bando.
Embarrassing Moments: Kabuki getting caught on various stage equipment and performers on certain nights.
Superstitions That Turned Out to Be True: We are still waiting…
Coolest Thing About Being in This Show: Everyone leaves the house feeling 17 again.
Any Other Stories or Memories You'd Like To Add!: "In reflection it was a magnificent, amazing experience… Life is on the stage… everything else is just waiting!" (Dino Danelli).

STAFF FOR *THE RASCALS*

GENERAL MANAGEMENT
BESPOKE THEATRICALS
Maggie Brohn
Amy Jacobs   Devin Keudell   Nina Lannan
Associate General Manager .... David Roth

PRODUCTION MANAGEMENT
Elisha L. Griego

COMPANY MANAGER
Carol M. Oune

GENERAL PRESS REPRESENTATIVE
THE HARTMAN GROUP
Michael Hartman   Wayne Wolfe
Emily McGill   Whitney Holden Gore

CASTING
Meredith Tucker

PRODUCTION STAFF
Associate Producer .... Billy Rapaport
Tour Manager .... Michael Bandolik
Production Coordinator .... Megan Napoletano
Costume Design .... Lori Santoro, Darryl DeAngelo
NY Technical Supervisor .... Neil A. Mazzella
Advertising .... Serino/Coyne
    Tom Callahan, Zack Kinney,
    Angelo Desimini, Roger Micone,
    Nick Nolte, Nathaniel Hill
Opening Night Coordination .... Serino/Coyne Events
    Suzanne Tobak, Chrissann Gasparro
Archival Photographs .... George Rodriguez
Legal Counsel .... Howard Siegel
Insurance .... J. Coulter & Co, Inc.
Accounting .... JSP Associates, Inc.
Merchandise .... Perryscope Productions, LLC

LIVE PRODUCTION STAFF
Lighting Director .... Anthony Fransen
Monitor Mixer .... Mark Hutchins
FOH Mixer .... Chris Edwards
Backline Tech Chief .... John Barone
Backline Tech .... Ponzer Berkman,
    Ryan Blumstein
Click Track Operator .... Geoff Sanoff
A2 .... Brian Kingman
Teleprompter Operator .... Joel Feitzinger

VIDEO PRODUCTION STAFF
Film Sequences
    Assistant Director .... Billy Rapaport
Director of Photography/
    Editor .... Nicholas Militello
3D Content/Editing .... Dietrich Juengling
Video Content and additional
    filmed footage .... Jonathan K. Bendis
Additional Editing .... Matthew O'Brien
Video Content .... Michael Sherlock,
    Vidaroo, Michael Bandolik,
    Robert Issen, Rick Broat
Animation Sequence
    "A Girl Like You" .... Flash Rosenberg
New Jersey
    Turnpike Graphic .... David Rogers/
        Creative Group
Assistant Video Editor .... Peter Ochs
Consulting Historian .... Andy Babiuk
Wardrobe .... Maureen Van Zandt

RENEGADE NATION
Recording Engineer .... Geoff Sanoff
Art Director .... Louis Arzonico
Video Editing .... Alexander Vail
Video Content .... Darryl DeAngelo
Assistant to Mr. Van Zandt .... Paul Osmolskis
Chief Financial Officer/
    Business Manager .... Jerome Eisner
Production Assistants .... Jeremy Tufano,
    Dennis Mortensen, Jenna Antonacci
Promotion .... Scott Hueston
Studio Assistant .... Joel Feitzinger
Finance Assistant .... Devanshi Kapadia

Assistant to Mr. Magid .... Taylor Morganti
Executive Producer/
    BASE Entertainment .... Jayna Neagle
Chief Operating Officer/
    BASE Entertainment .... Kris Anderson
Chief Financial Officer/
    BASE Entertainment .... David Collins
Vice President of Finance/
    BASE Entertainment .... Scott Levine
Production Associate/
    BASE Entertainment .... Liz Shumate
General Management Associate/
    Bespoke Theatricals .... Jimmy Wilson

CREDITS
Scenery constructed by Hudson Scenic. Lighting equipment from Hudson/Christie Lighting. Video equipment from Screenworks. Audio equipment from Sound Associates. Softgoods by Sew What? Inc. Portions of the video used were filmed at American Movie Company.

SPECIAL THANKS
The production would like to acknowledge the invaluable artistic contributions made by Arif Mardin (music arrangement and additional production), Tom Dowd (engineering) and David Brigati (background vocal arrangement) on the original Rascals recordings. Thanks to all of our families, The Rascals archivist Joe Russon, Jimmy at Trash and Vaudeville, Twilla Duncan, Sandy Hicks, Joseph Gargano, George Rodriguez, all of the Kickstarter donors and everyone who has helped make this dream become a reality.

Special thanks to Peter Shapiro.

NEDERLANDER

Chairman	**James M. Nederlander**
President	**James L. Nederlander**

Executive Vice President
Nick Scandalios

Vice President	Senior Vice President
Corporate Development	Labor Relations
Charlene S. Nederlander	**Herschel Waxman**

Vice President	Chief Financial Officer
Jim Boese	**Freida Sawyer Belviso**

HOUSE STAFF FOR
THE RICHARD RODGERS THEATRE
House Manager .... Timothy Pettolina
Box Office Treasurer .... Fred Santore Jr.
Assistant Treasurer .... Corinne Russ
Electrician .... Steve Carver
Carpenter .... Kevin Camus
Propertymaster .... Stephen F. DeVerna
Engineer .... Sean Quinn

Rock of Ages

First Preview: March 17, 2009. Opened: April 7, 2009.
Still running as of May 31, 2013.

Drew and Sherrie are two starry-eyed kids who arrive in Los Angeles with dreams of becoming long-haired head-banging rock stars, but they have to learn a lot about life—and help save a rock club destined for the wrecker's ball—before their dreams can come true. This musical has an original story but a score of classic 1980s rock hits.

CAST

(in order of appearance)

Lonny	GENSON BLIMLINE
Justice	MICHELE MAIS
Dennis	NICK CORDERO
Drew	JUSTIN MATTHEW SARGENT
Sherrie	ASHLEY SPENCER
Father	JEREMY WOODARD
Mother	MICHELE MAIS
Regina	JOSEPHINE ROSE ROBERTS
Mayor	ANDRE WARD
Hertz	PAUL SCHOEFFLER
Franz	CODY SCOTT LANCASTER
Stacee Jaxx	JEREMY WOODARD
Waitress #1	TESSA ALVES
Reporter	NEKA ZANG
Ja'Keith Gill	ANDRE WARD
Record Company Men	GENSON BLIMLINE/ NICK CORDERO
Sleazy Producer	JOEY CALVERI
Joey Primo	JOEY CALVERI
Candi	JOSEPHINE ROSE ROBERTS
Strip Club DJ	ANDRE WARD
Young Groupie	CASSIE SILVA

Continued on next page

THE HELEN HAYES THEATRE

MARTIN MARKINSON　　　**DONALD TICK**

MATTHEW WEAVER　CARL LEVIN　JEFF DAVIS　BARRY HABIB　SCOTT PRISAND
MICHAEL COHL　REAGAN SILBER　S2BN ENTERTAINMENT　RELATIVITY MEDIA

in association with

JANET BILLIG RICH　　HILLARY WEAVER
CORNER STORE FUND　RYAN KAVANAUGH　TONI HABIB
PAULA DAVIS　SIMON AND STEFANY BERGSON/JENNIFER MALONEY　CHARLES ROLECEK
SUSANNE BROOK　CRAIG COZZA　ISRAEL WOLFSON　SARA MERCER　JAYSON RAITT　MAX GOTTLIEB
MICHAEL MINARIK　DAVID KAUFMAN/JAY FRANKS　MICHAEL WITTLIN　PROSPECT PICTURES
LAURA SMITH/BILL BODNAR　WIN SHERIDAN　HAPPY WALTERS　MICHELE CARD　NEIL CANELL/JAY CANELL　MARIANO TOLENTINO
MARC BELL and THE ARACA GROUP

present

book by
CHRIS D'ARIENZO

starring

ASHLEY SPENCER　JUSTIN MATTHEW SARGENT　NICK CORDERO　CODY SCOTT LANCASTER
MICHELE MAIS　JOSEPHINE ROSE ROBERTS　PAUL SCHOEFFLER with GENSON BLIMLINE and JEREMY WOODARD

TESSA ALVES　JOEY CALVERI　ERICKA HUNTER　TONY LePAGE　LAURALYN McCLELLAND　RALPH MEITZLER
MICHAEL MINARIK　JENNIFER RIAS　JOSH SASSANELLA　CASSIE SILVA　ANDRE WARD　NEKA ZANG

scenery based on an original design by BEOWULF BORITT	*costume design* GREGORY GALE	*lighting design* JASON LYONS	*sound design* PETER HYLENSKI	*projection design* ZAK BOROVAY

hair/wig design TOM WATSON	*make-up design* ANGELINA AVALLONE	*casting* TELSEY + COMPANY TIFFANY LITTLE CANFIELD, CSA	*production stage manager* MATTHEW DICARLO

assistant director ADAM JOHN HUNTER	*associate choreographer* ROBERT TATAD	*associate producer* DAVID GIBBS

general management ROY GABAY	*press representative* THE HARTMAN GROUP	*advertising & marketing* aka	*technical supervisor* TECH PRODUCTION SERVICES

music director HENRY ARONSON	*music coordinator* JOHN MILLER	*original arrangements* DAVID GIBBS

music supervision, arrangements & orchestrations by
ETHAN POPP

choreographed by
KELLY DEVINE

directed by
KRISTIN HANGGI

10/1/12

The fall 2012 cast of *Rock of Ages*

Photo by Paul Kolnik

Rock of Ages

Photo by Paul Kolnik

Cast Continued

THE ENSEMBLE

TESSA ALVES, JOEY CALVERI, CASSIE SILVA, ANDRE WARD, NEKA ZANG

OFFSTAGE VOCALS

TONY LePAGE

UNDERSTUDIES

For Sherrie: TESSA ALVES, ERICKA HUNTER, CASSIE SILVA
For Drew: CODY SCOTT LANCASTER, TONY LePAGE, JOSH SASSANELLA
For Franz: TONY LePAGE, JOSH SASSANELLA
For Hertz: TONY LePAGE, RALPH MEITZLER, MICHAEL MINARIK
For Stacee Jaxx: JOEY CALVERI, TONY LePAGE, JOSH SASSANELLA
For Lonny/Dennis: JOEY CALVERI, TONY LePAGE, MICHAEL MINARIK
For Regina/Justice: TESSA ALVES, LAURALYN McCLELLAND, JENNIFER RIAS

SWINGS

ERICKA HUNTER, TONY LePAGE, LAURALYN McCLELLAND, RALPH MEITZLER, MICHAEL MINARIK, JENNIFER RIAS, JOSH SASSANELLA

DANCE CAPTAIN

JENNIFER RIAS

BAND

Conductor/Keyboard: HENRY ARONSON
Guitar 1: JOEL HOEKSTRA
Guitar 2: TOMMY KESSLER
Drums: JON WEBER
Bass: WINSTON ROYE

Synthesizer Programming: RANDY COHEN
Music Coordinator: JOHN MILLER
Copyist: FIREFLY MUSIC SERVICE/ BRIAN ALLAN HOBBS

Jeremy Woodard as Stacee Jaxx

Ashley Spencer
Sherrie

Justin Matthew Sargent
Drew

Jeremy Woodard
Stacee Jaxx/Father

Genson Blimline
Lonny

Nick Cordero
Dennis

Cody Scott Lancaster
Franz

Michele Mais
Justice/Mother

Josephine Rose Roberts
Regina/Candi

Paul Schoeffler
Hertz

Tessa Alves
Ensemble

Joey Calveri
Ensemble

Ericka Hunter
Swing

Tony LePage
Swing

Lauralyn McClelland
Swing

Ralph Meitzler
Swing

Michael Minarik
Swing

Jennifer Rias
Swing, Dance Captain

Josh Sassanella
Swing

Cassie Silva
Ensemble

Andre Ward
Ensemble

Rock of Ages

Neka Zang
Ensemble

Henry Aronson
Music Direction, Keyboard

Joel Hoekstra
Guitar

Tommy Kessler
Guitar

Winston Roye
Bass

Jon Weber
Drums

Chris D'Arienzo
Book

Kristin Hanggi
Director

Kelly Devine
Choreographer

Beowulf Boritt
Original Scenery Design

Gregory Gale
Costume Design

Jason Lyons
Lighting Design

Peter Hylenski
Sound Design

Zachary Borovay
Projection Designer

Tom Watson
Hair and Wig Design

Angelina Avallone
Make-up Designer

Peter Fulbright
Tech Production Services
Technical Supervisor

Ethan Popp
Music Supervisor, Arranger, Orchestrator

John Miller
Music Coordinator

David Gibbs
Original Arrangements

Bernard Telsey
Telsey + Company
Casting

Robert Tatad
Associate Choreographer

Adam John Hunter
Associate Director

Roy Gabay
General Manager

Matthew Weaver
Producer

Carl Levin
Producer

Jeff Davis
Producer

Barry Habib
Producer

Scott Prisand
Producer

Michael Cohl
Producer

Ryan Kavanaugh
Relativity Media, LLC (RML)
Producer

Janet Billig Rich
Producer

Toni Habib
Producer

Paula Kaminsky Davis
Producer

Stefany Bergson
Producer

Rock of Ages

Jennifer Maloney
Producer

Jayson Raitt
Producer

Bill Bodnar
Producer

Mariano Tolentino
Producer

Marc Bell
Producer

Michael Rego, Hank Unger, Matthew Rego
The Araca Group
Producer

Adam Dannheisser
*Dennis, Record
Company Man*

Katie Webber
*Sherrie, Waitress,
Ensemble*

Jake Boyd
Swing

Andrew Call
*Joey Primo, Sleazy
Producer, Ensemble*

Adam Dannheisser
*Dennis, Record
Company Man*

Lindsay Janisse
Swing

Kate Rockwell
Sherrie

Teresa Stanley
Justice, Mother

Matthew Stocke
Hertz

Bret Tuomi
Hertz

Photo by Brian Mapp

CREW
(L-R): Robert Etter, Doug Purcell, Rob Lindsay, Matt Nieski, Joseph Beck, Anthony Moritz, Dave Robinson

Rock of Ages

Photo by Brian Mapp

FRONT OF HOUSE
Front Row (L-R): Berd Vaval, Marcos Acosta, Kyle Yuvienco, Andria Acunis, Linda Maley, Dylan Maley-Biancamano
Back Row (L-R): Alan R. Markinson (House Manager), Shani Murfin, Brett Ricci, Natasha Thomas, Kimberly DeAndrade, Chiyo Sakai, Margaret Flanagan, Shykia Fields, Diane Scott

Photo courtesy of the production

STAGE MANAGEMENT
(L-R): Matthew DiCarlo (Production Stage Manager), Francesca Russell (Assistant Stage Manager), Justin Scribner (Stage Manager)

Photo by Brian Mapp

DOORMAN
Anthony Bethea

Photo by Brian Mapp

BAND
Sitting: Tommy Kessler
Standing (L-R): Aurelien Budynek, Henry Aronson, Jon Weber, Ivan Bodley

Rock of Ages

COMPANY MANAGEMENT
(L-R): Chris Aniello, Daniel Kuney, Roy Gabay

BOX OFFICE
(L-R): David Heveran, Kenny Klein

STAFF FOR *ROCK OF AGES*

GENERAL MANAGEMENT
ROY GABAY PRODUCTIONS
Roy Gabay   Mandy Tate
Bruce Kagel   Mark Gagliardi   Sophie Aung

COMPANY MANAGER
Daniel Kuney
Associate Company Manager ....Chris Aniello

GENERAL PRESS REPRESENTATIVE
THE HARTMAN GROUP
Michael Hartman
Leslie Papa   Whitney Holden Gore

CASTING
TELSEY + COMPANY
Bernie Telsey CSA, Will Cantler CSA,
David Vaccari CSA, Bethany Knox CSA,
Craig Burns CSA, Tiffany Little Canfield CSA,
Rachel Hoffman CSA, Justin Huff CSA,
Patrick Goodwin CSA, Abbie Brady-Dalton CSA,
David Morris, Cesar A. Rocha, Andrew Femenella,
Karyn Casl, Kristina Bramhall, Jessie Malone

TECHNICAL SUPERVISOR
TECH PRODUCTION SERVICES
Peter Fulbright
Colleen Houlehen   Mary Duffe
Kaitlyn Anderson

Production Stage Manager ....Matthew DiCarlo
Stage Manager ....Justin Scribner
Assistant Stage Manager ....Francesca Russell
Associate Director ....Adam John Hunter
Resident Director ....Adam Dannheisser
Production Manager ....Peter Fulbright
Production Management Associate ......Colleen Houlehen
Associate Scenic Designer.....................Jo Winiarski
Assistant Scenic Designers ....Maiko Chii,
     Alexis Distler, Buist Bickley
Associate Costume Designer ....Karl Ruckdeschel
Assistant Costume Designers ....Julia Broer,
     Colleen Kesterson
Associate Lighting Designer ....Grant Wilcoxen

Assistant Lighting Designer ....Sean Beach
Assistant Lighting Designer ....Driscoll Otto
Assistant to Mr. Lyons ....Zach Pizza
Moving Light Programmer ....Marc Polimeni
Associate Sound Designer ....Keith Caggiano
Assistant Sound Designer ....Drew Levy
Associate Projection Designer ....Daniel Brodie
Assistant Projection Designer ....Austin Switser
Associate Choreographer ....Robert Tatad
Creative Advisor ....Wendy Goldberg
Production Carpenter ....Doug Purcell
Advance Production Carpenter ....Brian Munroe
Production Electrician...........................Joseph Beck
Production Sound ....Phil Lojo
Head Mixer ....Robert Etter
Monitor Mixer ....Robert Lindsay
Spot Operator ....Matt Nieski
Head Propman ....Al Toth
Propmen ....Joseph Moritz, Anthony Moritz
Wardrobe Supervisor ....Wendall Goings
Dressers ....Stacey Haynes, Renee Mariotti,
     Ryan Moller, James Cavenaugh
Internal Swing/Laundry..................Mikey Goodmark
Stitchers ....Pierre Parisi, Raven Jakubowski,
     Jay Cole, Erik Bergrin
Daywork/Band Dresser ....Thom Carlson
Intern/Shopper ....John Dunnett
Hair & Wig Supervisor ....Renee Kelly
Production Assistant ....Shelley Miles
Production Intern ....Ashley Zednick
Script Supervisor ....Justin Mabardi
Executive for
   Corner Store Entertainment ....Tom Pelligrini
Production Associate ....Rebecca Breithaupt
Assistant to Mr. Levin ....Alexandra Bisker
Music Director/Conductor ....Henry Aronson
Music Coordinator ....John Miller
Assistant to John Miller ....Nichole Jennino
Production Vocal Coach ....Liz Caplan
Synthesizer Programmer ....Randy Cohen
Music Copying/
   Music Preparation ....Anixter Rice Music Service
Advertising & Marketing ....aka/
     Scott A. Moore, Clint Bond, Jr.,
     Liz Furze, Joshua Lee Poole,
     Janette Roush, Adam Jay, Jenna Bissonnette,

     Jacob Matsumiya, Trevor Sponseller
Internet Marketing and Strategy 87AM/
     Adam Cunningham, Lisa Egan,
     Alexandra Bisker
Press Associates ....Nicole Capatasto,
     Tom D'Ambrosio, Juliana Hannett,
     Bethany Larsen, Emily McGill,
     Colgan McNeil, Matt Ross,
     Frances White, Wayne Wolfe
Production Photography ....Joan Marcus
Insurance ....Ventura Insurance Brokerage/
     Tick and Co.
Legal Counsel ....Sendroff and Baruch, LLP/
     Jason Baruch
Banking..................................City National Bank
Payroll Service ....Checks and Balances
Accounting ....Fried & Kowgios Partners, CPAs, LLP
Bookkeeper ....Galbraith & Company
Additional New York
   Rehearsal ....Manhattan Theatre Club
Group Sales ....Broadway Inbound

CREDITS AND ACKNOWLEDGEMENTS
Avalon Salon & Day Spa, Gibson, Ernie Ball, Baldwin Piano, Vic Firth, Vans and The Spoon Group. Audio and video provided by PRG Secaucus. Scenery and automation by Showmotion, Inc., Milford, CT. Lighting equipment from Hudson/Christie Lighting, Mimi Bilinski. Costumes constructed by Jennifer Love Costumes. Custom leatherwear by www.rawhides.com. Shoes and boots constructed by T.O. Dey and Worldtone. Fabric painting and costume crafts by Jeffrey Fender. Hosiery and undergarments by Bra*Tenders. Keyboards by Yamaha. Additional scenery by Daddy-O. Dany Margolies

A special thanks to Trash and Vaudeville
for the rock 'n' roll gear.

Makeup provided by M•A•C.

MUSIC CREDITS
"Anyway You Want It" written by Steve Perry and Neal Schon. © Published by Lacey Boulevard Music and Weed High Nightmare Music.
"Beaver Hunt" written by David Gibbs and Chris Hardwick. Published by Feed the Pony Songs and Fish

Rock of Ages

Ladder, Inc. (BMI).

"Can't Fight This Feeling" written by Kevin Cronin. © Published by Fate Music (ASCAP).

"Cum on Feel the Noize" written by Neville Holder and James Lea. © Barn Publishing (Slade) Ltd.

"Don't Stop Believin'" written by Jonathan Cain, Stephen Ray Perry, Neal J. Schon © Published by Weed High Nightmare Music and Lacey Boulevard Music.

"Every Rose Has Its Thorn" written by Bobby Dall, Bruce Anthony Johannesson, Bret Michaels, Rikki Rocket. © All rights owned or administered by Universal Music-Z Songs on behalf of Cyanide Publ./BMI. Used by permission.

"The Final Countdown" written by Joey Tempest. © Screen Gems-EMI Music Inc.

"Harden My Heart" written by Marvin Webster Ross. © 1980 WB Music Corp. (ASCAP), Narrow Dude Music (ASCAP) and Bonnie Bee Good Music. All rights administered by WB Music Corp. All rights reserved. Used by permission.

"Heat of the Moment" written by Geoffrey Downes and John K. Wetton. © 1982 WB Music Corp. (ASCAP), Almond Legg Music Corp (ASCAP) and Pallan Music. All rights on behalf of itself and Almond Legg Music Corp. administered by WB Music Corp. All rights reserved. Used by permission.

"Heaven" written by Jani Lane, Erik Turner, Jerry Dixon, Steven Sweet and Joey Allen ©.

"Here I Go Again" written by David Coverdale and Bernard Marsden. © 1982 C.C. Songs Ltd. (PRS) and Seabreeze Music Ltd. Administered by WB Music Corp. (ASCAP). All rights reserved. Used by permission.

"High Enough" written by Jack Blades, Ted Nugent and Tommy R. Shaw. © Published by Bicycle Music Company, Broadhead Publishing and Wixen Music.

"Hit Me With Your Best Shot" written by E. Schwartz. © Sony/ATV Tunes LLC/ASCAP.

"I Hate Myself for Loving You" written by Desmond Child and Joan Jett. © All rights owned or administered by Universal-PolyGram Int. Publ., Inc./ASCAP. Used by permission.

"I Wanna Rock" written by Daniel Dee Snider. © All rights owned or administered by Universal Music-Z Melodies on behalf of Snidest Music/SESAC. Used by permission.

"I Want to Know What Love Is" written by Michael Leslie Jones. © Published by Somerset Songs Publishing, Inc.

"Just Like Paradise" written by David Lee Roth and Brett Tuggle. © Diamond Dave Music c/o RS Plane Music.

"Keep on Lovin' You" written by Kevin Cronin. © Published by Fate Music (ASCAP).

"Kiss Me Deadly" written by Mick Smiley. © Published by The Twin Towers Co. and Mike Chapman Publishing Enterprises.

"More Than Words" written by Nuno Bettencourt and Gary F. Cherone. © All rights owned or administered by Almo Music Corp. on behalf of Color Me Blind Music/ASCAP. Used by permission.

"Nothin' But a Good Time" written by Bobby Dall, Bruce Anthony Johannesson, Bret Michaels, Rikki Rocket. © All rights owned or administered by Universal Music-Z Songs on behalf of Cyanide Publ./BMI. Used by permission.

"Oh Sherrie" written by Steve Perry, Randy Goodrum, Bill Cuomo, Craig Krampf. © Published by Street Talk Tunes, April Music Inc & Random Notes, Pants Down Music and Phosphene Music.

"Renegade" written by Tommy Shaw. © All rights owned or administered by Almo Music Corp. on behalf of itself and Stygian Songs /ASCAP. Used by permission.

"The Search Is Over" written by Frank Sullivan and Jim Peterik. © Published by Ensign Music LLC (BMI). Used by permission. All rights reserved.

"Shadows of the Night" written by D.L. Byron. © Zen Archer/ASCAP.

"Sister Christian" written by Kelly Keagy. © Published by Bicycle Music Company.

"To Be With You" written by David Grahame and Eric Martin. ©EMI April Music, Inc. obo itself, Dog Turner Music and Eric Martin Songs (ASCAP).

"Too Much Time on My Hands" written by Tommy Shaw. © Stygian Songs/ASCAP.

"Waiting for a Girl Like You" written by Michael Leslie Jones and Louis Gramattico. © Published by Somerset Songs Publishing, Inc.

"Wanted Dead or Alive" written by Jon Bon Jovi and Richard S. Sambora. © All rights owned or administered by Universal-Polygram Int. Publ., Inc. on behalf of itself and Bon Jovi Publishing/ASCAP. Used by permission.

"We Built This City" written by Dennis Lambert, Martin George Page, Bernie Taupin and Peter Wolf. © All rights owned or administered by Universal-Polygram Int. Publ., Inc. on behalf of Little Mole Music Inc./ASCAP. Used by permission.

"We're Not Gonna Take It" written by Daniel Dee Snider. © All rights owned or administered by Universal Music-Z Melodies on behalf of Snidest Music/SESAC. Used by permission.

THE HELEN HAYES THEATRE STAFF
Owned and Operated by Little Theatre Group LLC
Martin Markinson and Jeffrey Tick

General Manager and Counsel	Susan S. Myerberg
House Manager	Alan R. Markinson
Engineer	Hector Angulo
Treasurer	David Heveran
Assistant Treasurer	Kenny Klein
Assistant General Manager	Lindsay M. Stringfellow
Head Ushers	Linda Maley, Berd Vaval, John Biancamano
Stage Door	Ernest J. Paylor; Anthony Bethea; Stephen Skipper, Jr.; Kelly Washington
Accountant	Chen-Win Hsu, CPA, PC

Helen Hayes Theatre is a proud member of the
Broadway Green Alliance.

Kate Rockwell and Justin Matthew Sargent

The cast of *Rock of Ages*

(L-R): Genson Blimline and Adam Dannheisser

Photos by Paul Kolnik

Rock of Ages

Scrapbook

Correspondent: Josephine Rose Roberts, "Regina," "Candi"

Memorable Fan Letter: After our surprise midnight performance for Tom Cruise at the Friars Club, Tom sent us a huge bouquet of flowers and a handwritten note addressed to each of us.

Milestone Celebrations: The *Rock of Ages* Softball Team brought home the Broadway Softball League Championship trophy for the second consecutive year! Genson Blimline and his wife, Jacqueline, welcomed their first child, Sophia James Blimline. Super Swing, and Canadian Tony LePage and his wife Natalie Roy received their Green Cards. And to top it all off, *Rock of Ages* broke into the Top 50 list of Longest Running Broadway Shows in History!

Most Exciting Celebrity Visitors: Celebrity chef Guy Fieri did a walk-on role in *ROA* to celebrate the opening of our new neighborhood bar on 44th street, Guy's American Kitchen. On "Military Appreciation Night," Purple Heart recipient Jon Moldovan was awarded a mortgage-free home, thanks to the Boot Campaign, right on our stage following the show. We had visits from Tim Tebow, Clay Matthews, Hayden Panettiere and Mark Sanchez (his tenth time at the show!) as well, but the most exciting was when New York Yankee Mark Teixeira made his Broadway debut in the show, and ROCKED it! We had a blast hanging out with him. He's a really fun guy.

Actor Who Performs the Most Roles: Our Super Swing, Tony LePage. He covers all eight male roles, as well as sings in the vocal booth every night.

Special Backstage Rituals: Andre Ward and I always sit on the stage right steps before the show and talk about everything from philosophy to the business.

Favorite Moment During Each Performance: "Here I Go Again." The band is rocking so hard —especially the drums—all the characters are going through major shit, the audience starts screaming and losing their minds….it's just the perfect way to close an act.

Favorite In-Theatre Gathering Places: At the Hayes, we all live downstairs in a little basement where the dressing rooms have little to no walls. Everything you say, everyone hears! If you want fashion advice and dance music, you head to the women's ensemble room; for sports talk, you head to the principal men's room; for spiritual guidance, you head to the men's ensemble room; for candy and snacks, take your pick!

Favorite Off-Site Hangout: Our favorite after-show hang out spot is Glass House on 47th Street near our old theatre, the Brooks Atkinson. We go there so often, Michele Mais (Justice) has her own leopard martini glass they keep on-site for her.

Favorite Snack Foods: We love the Duane-

Lead guitarist Joel Hoekstra gets close to the crowd.

Photos by Monica Simoes

Reade peanut-butter pretzel nuggets and Cody Scott Lancaster has a secret candy stash (that we all secretly know about). Our all time favorite, however, is "Schmackary Sundays," when a cast member volunteers to pick up a variety of Schmackary's cookies to celebrate our last show of the weekend.

Favorite Therapies: We are big fans of Throat-Coat, Prednisone, and napping. However, the best therapy comes from the hands of Ali and Chris at Adept Physical Therapy on Tuesdays and Saturdays.

Memorable Ad-Lib: "I once had a circle jerk with Menudo?"

Technology Issues During a Performance: We don't get many annoying cell phone calls or texts here at *Rock*, due to our fantastic David Coverdale opening announcement. However, we do have occasional 'incidences' when audience members are partying a bit TOO hard —but

Yearbook correspondent Josephine Rose Roberts in costume as "Regina."

how can we blame them? We are "Broadway's Best Party," after all!

Memorable Press Encounter: The *Rock of Ages* cast rang in the 2012 New Year with millions of people in Times Square, performing live on FOX's All-American New Year's Eve Celebration. We also performed in the New York Giants' 2012 Super Bowl Victory Parade!

Memorable Stage Door Fan Encounters: Any time we're asked to sign a body part…also, the time a fan got a tattoo of James Carpinello as Stacee Jaxx.

Web Buzz on the Show: We love our social media here at *Rock of Ages*. People from all over the world can be seen on our Facebook page sharing their kickass memories of their experiences at *ROA*. We even have a 'drunk dial' number….

Fastest Costume Change: Sherrie Christian at the end of Act I. She goes from "Sweet Midwestern Girl" to "Hot Stripper" with a complete costume, shoe, and hair change, all in under 30 seconds.

Heaviest/Hottest Costume: Joey Primo (Andrew Call). Joey wears a $30,000 green, reptile skin coat with feathered wings, studded pants and five-inch platform boots.

Who Wore the Least: Only every girl in the show.

Catchphrase Only the Company Would Recognize: "Snowfall in L.A."

Orchestra Members Who Played the Most Instruments: Arsenal, our kick-ass onstage band, is comprised of three guitarists, one piano player, who doubles as our conductor and musical director, and a drummer who plays in a glass-enclosed cage complete with the sign, "Don't Feed the Animals."

Best In-House Parody Lyric: From "I've Been Waiting for a Girl Like You": "Feels so right, so warm, and Drew…."
From "Sister Christian": "It's Drewwww…yea, yea"

Memorable Directorial Note: "Less tongue in the opening please."

Company In-Jokes: "I've got a one-show voice on a two-show day." —Andre Ward

Understudy Anecdote: Understudy for Justice, during Journey's "Anyway You Want It":
"She loves to sing; She loves to dance; She's a fancy pants."

Coolest Thing About Being in This Show: *ROA* has the hardest working cast and crew on Broadway. In our little theatre, our little family—through equal parts work and fun—helps audiences remember some of the best times of their lives. There is nothing like singing "Don't Stop Believing" with 600 people every night, knowing the best time of OUR lives is right now.

Rodgers + Hammerstein's Cinderella

First Preview: January 25, 2013. Opened: March 3, 2013.
Still running as of May 31, 2013.

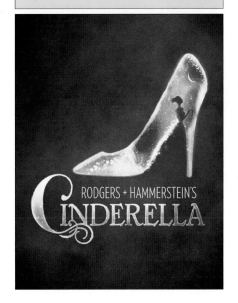

PLAYBILL

RODGERS + HAMMERSTEIN'S
CINDERELLA

Originally written as a 1957 television special, this musical adaptation of the classic Grimm Brothers fairytale retells the story of a young woman's unhappy life with her evil stepmother and stepsisters, and how, with the help of a fairy godmother, she attends a dress ball at a palace where she meets a handsome prince who falls in love with her. For Broadway the show got a new libretto by Douglas Carter Beane with many innovative plot twists, magical costumes by William Ivey Long, and several Rodgers and Hammerstein trunk songs to beef up the score.

CAST OF CHARACTERS

(in order of appearance)

Ella .... LAURA OSNES
Woodland Creature .... PETER NELSON
Topher .... SANTINO FONTANA
Lord Pinkleton .... PHUMZILE SOJOLA
Sebastian .... PETER BARTLETT
Marie .... VICTORIA CLARK
Jean-Michel .... GREG HILDRETH
Madame .... HARRIET HARRIS
Gabrielle .... MARLA MINDELLE
Charlotte .... ANN HARADA
Fox .... HEIDI GIBERSON
Raccoon .... LAURA IRION
Footman .... ANDY MILLS
Driver .... CODY WILLIAMS
Lady of Ridicule .... JILL ABRAMOVITZ
Knights, Townspeople, Lords &
  Ladies of the Court,
  Peasants .... JILL ABRAMOVITZ,
    KRISTINE BENDUL, HEIDI GIBERSON,

Continued on next page

BROADWAY THEATRE

1681 Broadway
A Shubert Organization Theatre
Philip J. Smith, *Chairman*   **Robert E. Wankel,** *President*

ROBYN GOODMAN   JILL FURMAN   STEPHEN KOCIS

EDWARD WALSON   VENETIAN GLASS PRODUCTIONS   THE ARACA GROUP
LUIGI CAIOLA & ROSE CAIOLA   ROY FURMAN   WALT GROSSMAN
PETER MAY/SANFORD ROBERTSON   GLASS SLIPPER PRODUCTIONS LLC/ERIC SCHMIDT
TED LIEBOWITZ/JAMES SPRY   BLANKET FORT PRODUCTIONS
IN ASSOCIATION WITH
CENTER THEATRE GROUP

PRESENT

RODGERS + HAMMERSTEIN'S
CINDERELLA

MUSIC BY RICHARD RODGERS
LYRICS BY OSCAR HAMMERSTEIN II
NEW BOOK BY DOUGLAS CARTER BEANE
ORIGINAL BOOK BY OSCAR HAMMERSTEIN II

STARRING

LAURA OSNES   SANTINO FONTANA
PETER BARTLETT   ANN HARADA   GREG HILDRETH
MARLA MINDELLE   PHUMZILE SOJOLA
WITH
HARRIET HARRIS
AND
VICTORIA CLARK

JILL ABRAMOVITZ   KRISTINE BENDUL   DREW FRANKLIN   HEIDI GIBERSON
STEPHANIE GIBSON   SHONICA GOODEN   KENDAL HARTSE   ROBERT HARTWELL
LAURA IRION   ADAM JEPSEN   ANDY JONES   ANDY MILLS   LINDA MUGLESTON
ALESSA NEECK   PETER NELSON   NICK SPANGLER   KIRSTIN TUCKER
CODY WILLIAMS   BRANCH WOODMAN   KEVIN WORLEY

SCENIC DESIGN	COSTUME DESIGN	LIGHTING DESIGN	SOUND DESIGN
ANNA LOUIZOS	WILLIAM IVEY LONG	KENNETH POSNER	NEVIN STEINBERG
HAIR AND WIG DESIGN	MUSIC DIRECTOR AND CONDUCTOR	MUSIC COORDINATOR	PRODUCTION STAGE MANAGER
PAUL HUNTLEY	ANDY EINHORN	HOWARD JOINES	IRA MONT
CASTING	TECHNICAL SUPERVISION	FIGHT DIRECTOR	ASSOCIATE DIRECTOR	ASSOCIATE CHOREOGRAPHER
CINDY TOLAN	HUDSON THEATRICAL	THOMAS SCHALL	GINA RATTAN	LEE WILKINS
ADAM CALDWELL	ASSOCIATES			
ASSOCIATE PRODUCER	PRESS REPRESENTATIVE	COMPANY MANAGER	GENERAL MANAGEMENT
CHARLES SALAMENO	SAM RUDY MEDIA RELATIONS	BRIG BERNEY	RICHARDS/CLIMAN, INC.

ORCHESTRATIONS
DANNY TROOB

MUSIC ADAPTATION, SUPERVISION AND ARRANGEMENTS
DAVID CHASE

CHOREOGRAPHED BY
JOSH RHODES

DIRECTED BY
MARK BROKAW

THE PRODUCERS WISH TO EXPRESS THEIR APPRECIATION TO THE THEATRE DEVELOPMENT FUND FOR ITS SUPPORT OF THIS PRODUCTION
PRODUCED BY ARRANGEMENT WITH RODGERS & HAMMERSTEIN: AN IMAGEM COMPANY

3/3/12

Santino Fontana
and Laura Osnes

Photo by Carol Rosegg

Rodgers + Hammerstein's Cinderella

MUSICAL NUMBERS

ACT I

Overture ....Orchestra
Prologue
Rocky Glen
  "Me, Who Am I?" ....Topher, Sebastian, Lord Pinkleton, Knights, Pages
Outside the Cottage
  "In My Own Little Corner" ....Ella
Throne Room of the Royal Palace
Town Square
  "Now Is the Time" ....Jean-Michel
  "The Prince Is Giving a Ball" ....Lord Pinkleton, Townspeople,
                                    Madame, Charlotte, Gabrielle, Ella, Marie
Inside the Cottage
  "Cinderella March" ....Orchestra
Outside the Cottage
  "In My Own Little Corner (Reprise)/Fol-De-Rol" ....Ella, Marie
  "Impossible" ....Marie, Ella
Flight to the Castle
  "It's Possible" ....Marie, Ella
Ballroom
  "Gavotte" ....Sebastian, Topher, Lord Pinkleton, Madame,
                              Charlotte, Gabrielle, Lords & Ladies of the Court
  "Ten Minutes Ago" ....Topher, Ella
  "Waltz for a Ball" ....Orchestra
  "Ten Minutes Ago" (Reprise) ....Topher, Ella, Lords & Ladies of the Court
Palace Steps

ACT II

Entr'acte ....Orchestra
Palace Steps
  "Stepsister's Lament" ....Charlotte, Ladies of the Court
Forest
  "The Pursuit" ....Topher, Lord Pinkleton, Lords of the Court,
                                          Pages, Ella, Footman, Driver
Inside the Cottage
  "When You're Driving Through the Moonlight" ....Ella, Madame,
                                                Charlotte, Gabrielle
  "A Lovely Night" ....Ella, Madame, Charlotte, Gabrielle
  "A Lovely Night" (Reprise) ....Ella, Gabrielle
Forest
  "Loneliness of Evening" ....Topher, Ella
Throughout the Kingdom
  "The Prince Is Giving a Ball" (Reprise) ....Sebastian, Lord Pinkleton,
                                                     Heralds, Madame
Inside the Cottage
  "There's Music in You" ....Marie
Palace Steps
  "Now Is the Time" (Reprise) ....Jean-Michel, Gabrielle
  "Do I Love You Because You're Beautiful?" ....Topher, Ella
Palace
  "Ten Minutes Ago" (Reprise) ....Topher, Ella, The Company
Royal Gardens
  "Finale" ....Marie, The Company

Cast Continued

STEPHANIE GIBSON, SHONICA GOODEN,
KENDAL HARTSE, ROBERT HARTWELL,
LAURA IRION, ANDY JONES, ANDY MILLS,
LINDA MUGLESTON, PETER NELSON,
NICK SPANGLER, CODY WILLIAMS,
BRANCH WOODMAN, KEVIN WORLEY

SWINGS
DREW FRANKLIN, ADAM JEPSEN,
ALESSA NEECK, KIRSTIN TUCKER

DANCE CAPTAIN
DREW FRANKLIN

UNDERSTUDIES
For Ella:
HEIDI GIBERSON, ALESSA NEECK
For Woodland Creature, Footman, Driver:
DREW FRANKLIN, ADAM JEPSEN
For Topher:
ANDY JONES, NICK SPANGLER,
  CODY WILLIAMS
For Lord Pinkleton:
BRANCH WOODMAN, KEVIN WORLEY
For Sebastian:
PHUMZILE SOJOLA, BRANCH WOODMAN
For Marie, Madame:
JILL ABRAMOVITZ, LINDA MUGLESTON
For Jean-Michel:
CODY WILLIAMS, KEVIN WORLEY
For Gabrielle:
STEPHANIE GIBSON, KENDAL HARTSE
For Charlotte:
STEPHANIE GIBSON, LAURA IRION
For Fox, Raccoon, Lady of Ridicule:
ALESSA NEECK, KIRSTIN TUCKER

ORCHESTRA
Music Supervisor: DAVID CHASE
Music Director/Conductor: ANDY EINHORN
Associate Conductor/Keyboard: MATT PERRI
Piccolo/Flute/Alto Flute: KATHERINE FINK
Oboe/English Horn: LYNNE COHEN
Clarinet/E-flat Clarinet/
  Bass Clarinet: JONATHAN LEVINE
Bassoon/Flute/Clarinet: DANIEL SULLIVAN
French Horns: ADAM KRAUTHAMER,
  DAVID BYRD-MARROW
Trumpet 1/Flugelhorn/Piccolo Trumpet:
  DOMINIC DERASSE
Trumpet/Flugelhorn: GARETH FLOWERS
Trombone/Bass Trombone: JOHN ALLRED
Percussion: BILL HAYES
Drums: RICH ROSENZWEIG
Harp: SUSAN JOLLES

Continued on next page

Rodgers + Hammerstein's Cinderella

Cast Continued

Violin/Concertmaster:
EMILY BRUSKIN YARBROUGH
Violins: LISA MATRICARDI, MAXIM MOSTON,
  MINEKO YAJIMA
Viola: JJ JOHNSON
Cello: SARAH SEIVER
Bass: MARK VANDERPOEL
Music Copying: Anixter Rice Music Service/
RUSSELL ANIXTER and DONALD RICE
Synthesizer Programming: JEFF MARDER
Music Assistant: BRENDAN WHITING
Music Coordinator: HOWARD JOINES
Additional Orchestrations by BILL ELLIOTT,
  DOUG BESTERMAN
  and LARRY HOCHMAN

Additional lyrics by DOUGLAS CARTER BEANE
  and DAVID CHASE

Laura Osnes
Ella

Santino Fontana
Topher

Victoria Clark
Marie

Harriet Harris
Madame

Peter Bartlett
Sebastian

Ann Harada
Charlotte

Greg Hildreth
Jean-Michel

Marla Mindelle
Gabrielle

Phumzile Sojola
*Lord Pinkleton;
u/s Sebastian*

Jill Abramovitz
*Ensemble;
u/s Marie, Madame*

Kristine Bendul
Ensemble

Drew Franklin
*Swing/
Dance Captain*

Heidi Giberson
Ensemble; u/s Ella

Stephanie Gibson
*Ensemble;
u/s Gabrielle,
Charlotte*

Shonica Gooden
Ensemble

Kendal Hartse
*Ensemble;
u/s Gabrielle*

Robert Hartwell
Ensemble

Laura Irion
*Ensemble;
u/s Charlotte*

Adam Jepsen
Swing

Andy Jones
*Ensemble;
u/s Topher*

Andy Mills
Ensemble

Linda Mugleston
*Ensemble; u/s Marie,
Madame*

Alessa Neeck
Swing; u/s Ella

Peter Nelson
Ensemble

Nick Spangler
*Ensemble;
u/s Topher*

Kirstin Tucker
Swing

Cody Williams
*Ensemble;
u/s Topher,
Jean-Michel*

Branch Woodman
*Ensemble;
u/s Lord Pinkleton*

Kevin Worley
*Ensemble;
u/s Jean-Michel,
Lord Pinkleton*

Rodgers + Hammerstein's Cinderella

(L-R): Harriet Harris, Ann Harada, Marla Mindelle and Laura Osnes

Photo by Carol Rosegg

Richard Rodgers & Oscar Hammerstein II
Music, Lyrics, Original Book

Douglas Carter Beane
New Book

Mark Brokaw
Director

Josh Rhodes
Choreographer

Anna Louizos
Scenic Design

William Ivey Long
Costume Design

Kenneth Posner
Lighting Design

Nevin Steinberg
Sound Design

Paul Huntley
Hair/Wig Design

David Chase
Musical Supervisor/ Arranger

Danny Troob
Orchestrations

Andy Einhorn
Music Director/ Conductor

Howard Joines
Music Coordinator

Tom Schall
Fight Director

Gina Rattan
Associate Director

Lee Wilkins
Associate Choreographer

Rodgers + Hammerstein's Cinderella

Neil A. Mazzella
Hudson Theatrical
Associates
Technical Supervisor

Brig Berney
Company Manager

David R. Richards
and Tamar Haimes
Richards/Climan, Inc.
General Manager

Robyn Goodman
*Producer/
Aged In Wood*

Jill Furman
Producer

Stephen Kocis
Producer

Carl Moellenberg
Venetian Glass
Productions
Producer

Wendy Federman
Venetian Glass
Productions
Producer

Sharon A. Carr
Venetian Glass
Productions
Producer

Ricardo Hornos
Venetian Glass
Productions
Producer

Jamie deRoy
Venetian Glass
Productions
Producer

Richard Winkler
Venetian Glass
Productions
Producer

Van Dean
Venetian Glass
Productions
Producer

Kenny Howard
Venetian Glass
Productions
Producer

Michael Filerman
Venetian Glass
Productions
Producer

Dan Frishwasser
Venetian Glass
Productions
Producer

Michael Rego, Hank Unger, Matthew Rego
The Araca Group
Producer

Luigi Caiola and Rose Caiola
Producers

Roy Furman
Producer

Walt Grossman
Producer

Peter May
Producer

Michael Ritchie
Artistic Director
Center Theatre
Group
Producer

Edward L. Rada
Managing Director
Center Theatre
Group
Producer

Douglas C. Baker
Producing Director
Center Theatre
Group
Producer

Brandon Leffler
Swing

STAGE AND COMPANY MANAGEMENT
(L-R): Alexis Shorter (Stage Manager), Ira Mont (Production Stage Manager),
Allison A. Lee (Assistant Stage Manager), Brig Berney, James Viggiano

SOUND
(L-R): Scott Silvian (Assistant Sound),
Justin Rathbun (Production Sound Engineer),
Jake Scudder (Advance Sound)

Photos by Brian Mapp

Rodgers + Hammerstein's Cinderella

DOORMAN
Ellsworth Butts

FRONT OF HOUSE
Standing: Russ Ramsey
Bottom Row (L-R): Mario Carillo, Mattie Robinson, Billy Pena, Mae Park, Maria Lugo
Middle Row (L-R): William Phelan, Lori Bokun (Head Usher), Carmen Walker, Lana Pinkhas, Fran Lenihan
Top Row: (L-R): Isaac Trujillo, Freddy Matos, Luis Santiago, John Hall, Lisa Maisonet, Nathaniel Wright

CREW
Front Row (L-R): Scott Silvian, Bob Beimers, Justin Rathbun, Jake Scudder, Margo Lawless, Tamara Kopko
Middle Row (L-R): Michael Berglund, Chad Hershey, Peter Becker, Herb Ouellette, Caitlin Johnson, Tina Clifton, Lauren Gallitelli, Nanette Golia, Casey Cameron
Back Row (L-R): Bill Colgan, Rick DalCortivo, Jr., Rick DalCortivo, Eric Castaldo, Vicki Grecki, Pete Drummond, Vivienne Crawford, Lisa Preston, Jaymes Gill

Rodgers + Hammerstein's Cinderella

Rodgers + Hammerstein's Cinderella
SCRAPBOOK

Correspondent: Ann Harada, "Charlotte"

Memorable Opening Night: Our festivities began onstage before the show with Nick Spangler showing a "making of *Cinderella*" video to everyone, and presentations of gifts to the creative team. Josh Rhodes and Lee Wilkins gave us pennies to throw into Cinderella's well and make wishes! The party was at Gotham Hall, complete with a gigantic glass slipper made of ice.

Who Got the Gypsy Robe?: The incomparable Linda Mugleston.

Who Has Done the Most Shows in Their Career?: On seniority alone, I'm gonna say Peter Bartlett.

Special Backstage Rituals: Kevin Worley jumps rope. Kristine Bendul works out at a special barre they set up for her. Peter Nelson climbs down on the escape ladder from the 4th floor to the stage before he straps into his cumbersome Woodland Creature outfit. Santino Fontana tries to catch the shoe I throw offstage in "Stepsister's Lament"—the crew keeps a tally of catches, misses, and wild pitches on the back of the set. Laura Osnes does a cartwheel as she leaves the stage after "Loneliness of Evening." Several of the dressers and hair crew do planks during the forest scene that follows it.

Favorite Moment During Each Performance: Well, I know Harriet Harris's favorite moment is the entrance of the Woodland Creature. She, Greg Hildreth and I watch from the stage left wing as the soldiers and the Creature enter from the stage right wing, screaming and yelling. We especially enjoy Robert Hartwell's track. Then, as Peter Nelson is liberated from his costume on stage left, he shares a high five or hug with Victoria Clark.

Favorite In-Theatre Gathering Place: Santino's dressing room (aka Topher's Tower, decorated by Robert Hartwell).

Favorite Off-Site Hangout: Glass House Tavern, aka Greg Hildreth's house.

Favorite Snack Food: Twizzlers, jellybeans, Starbursts, swedish fish, peanut butter pretzels — basically anything that's put on the shelving unit upstage right and commandeered by Brian "Hutch" Hutchinson, the house carpenter.

Mascots: Baby Yvonne (the doll), Herman (the pet fish Laura gave Santino on opening night).

Most Memorable Ad-Lib So Far: "She's a witch!" (Nick Spangler)

Record Number of Things Having to Do With a Cell Phone: Marla Mindelle, by a landslide.

Fastest Costume Change: Marla Mindelle (off stage), Laura Osnes (onstage).

Who Wore the Heaviest/Hottest Costume: 1) Peter Nelson as Woodland Creature; 2) Victoria Clark in full Fairy Godmother rig; 3) Me, Ann Harada, in the corduroy dress; 4) Greg Hildreth in the corduroy suit (but he has short pants).

Who Wore the Least: Tie between Heidi Giberson as the Fox and Laura Irion as the Raccoon ("Respect the unitard").

Catchphrases Only the Company Would Recognize: Duck walk! Macaroons! Twizzlers! Barbra Streisand! Anika Noni Rose! Let's take it from Alice Ripley, I mean Marin Mazzie! Stop when you get to crotchballs! Buy your tickets now!

Which Orchestra Member Played the Most Consecutive Performances Without a Sub: Daniel Sullivan on bassoon (and flute and clarinet)! Congratulations, man!

Best In-House Parody Lyrics: Nothing that can be printed in a family publication.

Memorable Directorial Note: Verbal life! It makes SUCH a difference!

Company In-Jokes: The Merry Jesters of Oberammergau. She-crab salad. The Griffin.

Understudy Anecdote: Some of the understudies went to do a press event at the airport, singing for the passengers. They were publicized by a sign that read, "FAIRYTALES COME TRUE AT JFK TERMINAL 8." Hmm.

Unique Talents: Greg Hildreth can sing or speak anything with a trident lisp (where it makes a whistling noise on the "s"). Linda Mugleston is an expert whistler (of tunes). Branch Woodman and Laura Osnes are champion bakers. Vicki Clark and Greg Hildreth can both do spot-on impressions of Buttercup, Prince Topher's horse. Not

Buttercup whinnying; Buttercup gliding.

Nicknames: Brie (Stephanie Gibson).

Sweethearts Within the Company: Josh Rhodes (Choreographer) and Lee Wilkins (Associate Choreographer) are married.

Coolest Thing About Being in This Show: Being in a new Rodgers and Hammerstein show in 2013! Also, listening to the magnificent orchestra. Nothing will ever beat live music on Broadway.

Also: Santino Fontana and the cast created a notable YouTube video "Glass Slippers Are So Back" (http://youtu.be/CIZK2GBzD60) a parody of the rap video "Baby Got Back."

1. Laura Osnes, in a stunning William Ivey Long creation, and Santino Fontana at the opening night curtain call.
2. (L-R): Greg Hildreth, Marla Mindelle, Victoria Clark, Laura Osnes, Santino Fontana, Peter Bartlett, Ann Harada, Harriet Harris and Phumzile Sojola during the cast album recording session.
3. (L-R): Victoria Clark, Santino Fontana, Douglas Carter Beane, Mark Brokaw, Laura Osnes and Rodgers and Hammerstein at the opening night curtain call.

Photos by Joseph Marzullo/WENN

Scandalous: The Life and Trials of Aimee Semple McPherson

First Preview: October 13, 2012. Opened: November 15, 2012.
Closed December 9, 2012 after 31 Previews and 29 Performances.

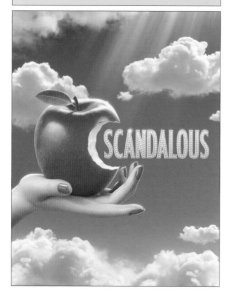

This musical charts the rise, fall and resurrection of the career of seminal 1920s evangelist Aimee Semple McPherson who overcame her initial skepticism about religion to become a traveling preacher and then founder of a massive Los Angeles church built on an amalgam of vaudeville and the Bible. Along the way McPherson goes through three marriages and a torrid affair that nearly proves her undoing. The pet project of talk show host Kathie Lee Gifford, this show asks how much of McPherson's ministry was showbiz and how much was truly the Holy Spirit.

CAST

Aimee Semple McPherson	CAROLEE CARMELLO
Minnie Kennedy	CANDY BUCKLEY
James Kennedy	GEORGE HEARN
Robert Semple	EDWARD WATTS
Harold McPherson	ANDREW SAMONSKY
Boxer	SAM STRASFELD
Boxing Ring Announcer	JOSEPH DELLGER
Emma Jo Schaeffer	ROZ RYAN
Mayor Cryer	JOSEPH DELLGER
Kenneth Ormiston	ANDREW SAMONSKY
Brother Bob	GEORGE HEARN
David Hutton	EDWARD WATTS
Eve	BILLIE WILDRICK
Louella Parsons	ELIZABETH WARD LAND
William Randolph Hearst	JOSEPH DELLGER
Charlie Chaplin	SAM STRASFELD
Myrtle	BILLIE WILDRICK
Asa Keyes	BENJAMIN HOWES
Peggy Rae Wharton	ALISON LUFF

Continued on next page

NEIL SIMON THEATRE
UNDER THE DIRECTION OF JAMES M. NEDERLANDER AND JAMES L. NEDERLANDER

Betsy & Dick DeVos   Foursquare Foundation
Cantinas Ranch Foundation   The Stand Up Group

IN ASSOCIATION WITH
The 5th Avenue Theatre
David Armstrong, Executive Producer and Artistic Director;
Bernadine Griffin, Managing Director; Bill Berry, Producing Director

Jeffrey Finn, Executive Producer

PRESENT

Carolee Carmello

SCANDALOUS
The Life And Trials Of Aimee Semple McPherson

BOOK, LYRICS & ADDITIONAL MUSIC BY	MUSIC BY
Kathie Lee Gifford	David Pomeranz
	AND
	David Friedman

Candy Buckley   Edward Watts   Roz Ryan   Andrew Samonsky

Nick Cartell   Joseph Dellger   Erica Dorfler   Carlos L. Encinias
Hannah Florence   Corey Greenan   Benjamin Howes   Karen Hyland
Elizabeth Ward Land   Alison Luff   Jesse Nager   Sam Strasfeld
Betsy Struxness   Billie Wildrick   Dan'yelle Williamson   Matt Wolfe

AND

George Hearn

SCENIC DESIGN BY	COSTUME DESIGN BY	LIGHTING DESIGN BY	SOUND DESIGN BY
Walt Spangler	Gregory A. Poplyk	Natasha Katz	Ken Travis
HAIR DESIGN BY	**ORCHESTRATIONS**	**DANCE & INCIDENTAL MUSIC ARRANGEMENTS**	**ADDITIONAL VOCAL ARRANGEMENTS**
Paul Huntley Enterprises, Inc.	Bruce Coughlin	Sam Davis	Paul Raiman

MUSIC COORDINATOR	PRODUCTION STAGE MANAGER	ASSOCIATE DIRECTOR
Howard Joines	Amber White	Stephen Sposito
ADVERTISING	**MARKETING**	**PRESS REPRESENTATIVE**
Serino/Coyne	Type A Marketing Anne Rippey	Jeremy Shaffer The Publicity Office
CASTING BY	**PRODUCTION MANAGER**	**GENERAL MANAGEMENT**
Tara Rubin Casting	Juniper Street Productions	Foresight Theatrical Mark Shacket

MUSIC DIRECTION & VOCAL ARRANGEMENTS BY
Joel Fram

CHOREOGRAPHY BY
Lorin Latarro

DIRECTED BY
David Armstrong

Originally Produced at the Signature Theatre, Arlington, VA
Eric Schaeffer, Artistic Director. Maggie Boland, Managing Director

The Producers wish to express their appreciation to Theatre Development Fund for its support of this production.

11/15/12

(L-R): Roz Ryan and Carolee Carmello

Photo by Jeremy Daniel

Scandalous: The Life and Trials of Aimee Semple McPherson

MUSICAL NUMBERS

Setting: Angelus Temple, Los Angeles, 1927

ACT I

"Stand Up!"	Aimee and Ensemble
"Minnie's Prayer"	Minnie
"Why Can't I?"	Aimee
"He Will Be My Home"	Robert and Aimee
"Come Whatever May"	Robert and Aimee
"He Will Be My Home" (Reprise)	Robert, Aimee, James and Minnie
"That Sweet Lassie From Cork"	Ensemble
"Come Whatever May" (Reprise)	Robert, Aimee and Ensemble
"How Could You?"	Aimee
"You Have a Fire"	Aimee and James
"Minnie's Prayer" (Reprise)	Minnie
"Follow Me" (Part 1)	Aimee and Ensemble
"A Girl's Gotta Do What a Girl's Gotta Do"	Emma Jo and Girls
"Follow Me" (Part 2)	Aimee and Ensemble
"For Such a Time As This"	Aimee and Ensemble

ACT II

"Hollywood Aimee"	Reporters
"Adam and Eve"	Aimee, David and Eve
"Foursquare March"	Aimee and Ensemble
"Samson and Delilah"	Aimee, David and Ensemble
"Hollywood Aimee" (Reprise)	Reporters
"Moses and Pharaoh"	Aimee, David, Emma Jo and Ensemble
"It's Just You"	Kenneth and David
"The Coconut Grove"	Aimee, David and Ensemble
"No Other Choice"	Minnie
"Hollywood Aimee" (Reprise)	Ensemble
"Lost or Found?"	Aimee, Asa and Ensemble
"What Does It Profit?"	Aimee
"I Have a Fire"	Aimee and Ensemble
Finale	Company

ORCHESTRA

Musical Director/Conductor: JOEL FRAM
Music Coordinator: HOWARD JOINES
Assoc. Conductor/Keyboard 1: ALVIN HOUGH
Assist. Conductor/Keyboard 2: MATT PERRI
Violin: HIROKO TAGUCHI
Cello: SUMMER BOGGESS
Reeds: VITO CHIAVUZZO, GREG THYMIUS,
JACQUELINE HENDERSON
Trumpets: MATT PETERSON, JEFF WILFORE
French Horn: WILL DE VOS
Bass Trombone: JENNIFER WHARTON
Bass: BRIAN HAMM
Percussion: BILLY MILLER
Drums: STEVE BARTOSIK

Music Copying: Kaye-Houston Music/
ANNE KAYE & DOUG HOUSTON
Keyboard Programming: Synthlink LLC/JIM HARP

Cast Continued

Ensemble .... NICK CARTELL,
JOSEPH DELLGER, ERICA DORFLER,
CARLOS L. ENCINIAS, HANNAH FLORENCE,
BENJAMIN HOWES,
ELIZABETH WARD LAND, ALISON LUFF,
JESSE NAGER, SAM STRASFELD,
BETSY STRUXNESS, BILLIE WILDRICK,
DAN'YELLE WILLIAMSON, MATT WOLFE

DANCE CAPTAIN
KAREN HYLAND

SWINGS
COREY GREENAN
KAREN HYLAND

UNDERSTUDIES
For Aimee Semple McPherson:
ALISON LUFF, BILLIE WILDRICK
For James Kennedy/Brother Bob:
JOSEPH DELLGER, MATT WOLFE
For Minnie Kennedy: ELIZABETH WARD LAND
For Robert Semple/David Hutton:
NICK CARTELL, COREY GREENAN
For Emma Jo Schaeffer: ERICA DORFLER,
DAN'YELLE WILLIAMSON
For Harold McPherson/Kenneth Ormiston:
NICK CARTELL, BENJAMIN HOWES

For All Other Roles:
COREY GREENAN, KAREN HYLAND

Carolee Carmello and Edward Watts

Photo by Jeremy Daniel

Scandalous: The Life and Trials of Aimee Semple McPherson

Carolee Carmello
*Aimee Semple
McPherson*

George Hearn
*James Kennedy/
Brother Bob*

Candy Buckley
Minnie Kennedy

Edward Watts
*Robert Semple/
David Hutton*

Roz Ryan
Emma Jo Schaeffer

Andrew Samonsky
*Harold McPherson/
Kenneth Ormiston*

Nick Cartell
*Ensemble, u/s
Robert Semple/
David Hutton, Harold
McPherson/Kenneth
Ormiston*

Joseph Dellger
*Ensemble, u/s James
Kennedy/Brother
Bob*

Erica Dorfler
*Ensemble, u/s Emma
Jo Schaeffer*

Carlos L. Encinias
Ensemble

Hannah Florence
Ensemble

Corey Greenan
*Swing; u/s Robert
Semple/David Hutton*

Benjamin Howes
*Ensemble, u/s
Harold
McPherson/Kenneth
Ormiston*

Karen Hyland
Swing

Elizabeth Ward Land
*Ensemble, u/s
Minnie Kennedy*

Alison Luff
*Ensemble, u/s Aimee
Semple McPherson*

Jesse Nager
Ensemble

Sam Strasfeld
Ensemble

Betsy Struxness
Ensemble

Billie Wildrick
*Ensemble, u/s Aimee
Semple McPherson*

Dan'yelle Williamson
*Ensemble, u/s Emma
Jo Schaeffer*

Matt Wolfe
*Ensemble, u/s James
Kennedy/Brother
Bob*

Kathie Lee Gifford
*Book, Lyrics,
Additional Music*

David Pomeranz
Music

David Friedman
Music

David Armstrong
Director

Lorin Latarro
Choreographer

Joel Fram
*Music Direction &
Vocal Arrangements*

Walt Spangler
Scenic Design

Gregory A. Poplyk
Costume Design

Natasha Katz
Lighting Design

Ken Travis
Sound Design

Paul Huntley
Hair Design

Bruce Coughlin
Orchestrations

Sam Davis
*Dance and
Incidental Music
Arrangements*

Scandalous: The Life and Trials of Aimee Semple McPherson

Paul Raiman
Additional Vocal Arrangements

Howard Joines
Music Coordinator

Tara Rubin
Tara Rubin Casting
Casting

Amber White
Production Stage Manager

Kevin Bertolacci
Stage Manager

Stephen Sposito
Associate Director

Barrett Martin
Associate Choreographer

Ana Rose Green, Guy Kwan, Joseph DeLuise, Hillary Blanken
Juniper Street Productions
Production Management

Alan Wasser
Foresight Theatrical
General Manager

Allan Williams
Foresight Theatrical
General Manager

David Armstrong
The 5th Avenue Theatre
Producer

Bernadine Griffin
The 5th Avenue Theatre
Producer

Bill Berry
The 5th Avenue Theatre
Producer

Eric Schaeffer
The Signature Theatre
Original Production

Jeffrey Finn
Executive Producer

Kathie Lee Gifford and Regis Philbin on opening night.

Photos by Joseph Marzullo/WENN

(L-R): Composers David Pomeranz and David Friedman

STAFF FOR *SCANDALOUS*

GENERAL MANAGEMENT
FORESIGHT THEATRICAL
Alan Wasser   Allan Williams
Aaron Lustbader   Mark Shacket

COMPANY MANAGER
Cathy Kwon

MARKETING DIRECTOR
Thomas Mygatt

PRESS REPRESENTATIVE
THE PUBLICITY OFFICE
Jeremy Shaffer
Marc Thibodeau   Michael S. Borowski

MARKETING
TYPE A MARKETING
Anne Rippey   Elyce Henkin
John McCoy   Kelly Stotmeister

CASTING
TARA RUBIN CASTING
Tara Rubin CSA   Eric Woodall CSA
Merri Sugarman CSA   Dale Brown CSA
Stephanie Yankwitt
Lindsay Levine   Kaitlin Shaw

PRODUCTION MANAGEMENT
JUNIPER STREET PRODUCTIONS
Hillary Blanken   Guy Kwan
Ana Rose Greene   Joe DeLuise

Production Stage Manager ....Amber White
Stage Manager ....Kevin Bertolacci
Assistant Stage Manager ....Libby Unsworth
Associate Company Manager ....Daniel Hoyos

Associate Choreographer ....Barrett Martin
Dance Captain ....Karen Hyland
Assistant to the Choreographer ....Paul McGill
Assistant Scenic Designer ....Melissa Shakun
Associate Costume Designer ....Sara Jean Tosetti
Assistant Costume Designers................Sarah Cubbage,
                        Justin Hall, Katie Irish,
                            Aaron Mastin
Costume Design Intern ....Talia Hermesh
Associate Lighting Designers ....Peter Hoerburger,
                            Aaron Spivey
Assistant Lighting Designer ....Craig Stelzenmuller
Associate Sound Designer ....Tony Smolenski IV
Moving Lights Programmer ....Victor Seastone
Assistant Wig Designer ....Edward J. Wilson
Makeup Designer ....Angelina Avallone
Assistant Makeup Designer ....Robbie Amodeo
Dialect Coach ....Stephen Gabis
Fight Director ....Ron Piretti
Production Carpenter ....Erik E. Hansen
Flyman ....Scott "Gus" Poitras
Automation Carpenter ....Chad Woerner
Advance Carpenter ....Jack Anderson
Production Electrician ....J. Michael Pitzer
Head Electrician ....Jeremy Wahlers
Production Properties Supervisor ....Michael Pilipski
Head Properties Supervisor ....John H. Paull III
Assistant Props Supervisor ....Diego Irizarry
Production Sound Engineer ....Phillip Lojo
Sound Engineer ....Lucas Indelicato
Deck Audio ....Charles Grieco
Wardrobe Supervisor ....Rory Powers
Assistant Wardrobe Supervisor ....Kyle Wesson
Dressers ....Shana Albery, John Dias, Billy Hipkins,
                      Lizz Hirons, Melissa Kaul,
             Antoinette Martinez, Pamela Pierzina
Wardrobe Crew ....Meghan Gaber, Kim Kaldenberg,
              Keiko Obremski, Graziella Zapata
Hair and Wig Supervisor ....Carmel Vargyas

Scandalous: The Life and Trials of Aimee Semple McPherson

(L-R): Curtain call with George Hearn, Roz Ryan, Carolee Carmello, Candy Buckley, Edward Watts

Assistant Hair and Wig Supervisor . . . . . . .Kevin R. Maybee
Hair Stylist . . . . .Bobbie Cliffton Zlotnik
Music Assistant . . . . .Neil Reilly
Assistant to
   Kathie Lee Gifford . . . . .Christine Gardner
Assistant to Jeffrey Finn . . . . .Jamie Kaye-Phillips
Advertising . . . . .Serino/Coyne/
   Angelo Desimini, Tom Callahan,
   Matt Upshaw, Lauren Houlberg,
   David Molina, Christina Hernandez
Digital Outreach & Website . . . . .Serino/Coyne/
   Jim Glaub, Chip Meyrelles,
   Laurie Conner, Kevin Keating,
   Ian Weiss, Jenna Lauren Freed,
   Emily Genduso, Joe Reckley
Ticketing Analytics . . . . .Serino/Coyne/Mike Rafael
Theatre Displays . . . . .King Displays
Production Legal
   Counsel . . . . .Frankfurt Kurnit Klein & Selz P.C./
   Mark A. Merriman Esq.
Accounting . . . . .Rosenberg, Neuwirth & Kuchner/
   Chris Cacace
General Management Associates . . . . .Lane Marsh,
   Mark Barna, Jake Hirzel
General Management Office . . . . .Jennifer O'Connor,
   Kaitlin Boland, Nina Lutwick
Production Photographer . . . . .Jeremy Daniel
Production Assistants . . . . .Lindsey Alexander,
   Rachel Bury, John Egan
Insurance . . . . .Ventura Insurance Brokerage
Banking . . . . .Signature Bank/
   Barbara von Borstel, Margaret Monigan
Payroll . . . . .Castellana Services, Inc.

Opening Night Coordination . . . . .Serino/Coyne, LLC/
   Suzanne Tobak
Group Sales . . . . .Group Sales Box Office

The production wishes to thank Barbara and Emery Olcott for their contribution to the production.

CREDITS AND ACKNOWLEDGEMENTS

Scenery fabricated and painted by Global Scenic Services, Inc. Bridgeport, CT. Scenery and scenic effects built, painted, electrified and automated by Show Motion, Inc., Milford, CT. Scenery automation and show control by Show Motion, Inc., Milford, CT, using the AC^2 computerized motion control system. Scenery constructed and show control and scenic motion control featuring Stage Command® Systems by PRG Scenic Technologies, a division of Production Resource Group, LLC, New Windsor, NY. Additional scenery by Shock Studios, New Windsor NY. Lighting equipment from PRG Lighting. Audio equipment from PRG Audio. Soft goods manufactured by iWeiss, Fairview, NJ. Props by prop N spoon, Rahway, NJ. Additional props by Tom Carroll Scenery, Jersey City, NJ. Costumes by Carelli Costumes, Cygnet Studio, John Kristiansen, Jennifer Love Costumes, English American Tailoring. Millinery by Scott Coppock, Arnold S. Levine. Hosiery and undergarments provided by Bra*Tenders. Dyeing and distressing by Hochi Asiatico.

SPECIAL THANKS

Patrick Wiley, TDF Costume Collection, Ellen Pilipski,
5th Avenue Costume Shop

Makeup provided by M•A•C Cosmetics
Hair care and styling products provided by
Pravana International.

Rehearsed at Ripley-Grier Studios and
the New 42nd Street Studios

Souvenir merchandise designed and created by
The Araca Group

www.ScandalousOnBroadway.com

NEDERLANDER

Chairman . . . .**James M. Nederlander**
President . . . .**James L. Nederlander**

Executive Vice President
Nick Scandalios

Vice President	Senior Vice President
Corporate Development	Labor Relations
Charlene S. Nederlander	**Herschel Waxman**

| Vice President | Chief Financial Officer |
| **Jim Boese** | **Freida Sawyer Belviso** |

STAFF FOR THE NEIL SIMON THEATRE

Theatre Manager . . . . .David Jannone
Treasurer . . . . .Eddie Waxman
Associate Treasurer . . . . .Marc Needleman
House Carpenter . . . . .John Gordon
Flyman . . . . .Douglas McNeill
House Electrician . . . . .James Travers, Sr.
House Propman . . . . .Danny Viscardo
House Engineer . . . . .John Astras

Spider-Man Turn Off the Dark

First Preview: November 28, 2010. Opened: June 14, 2011.
Still running as of May 31, 2013.

PLAYBILL

Given extraordinary powers by the bite of a genetically enhanced spider, Peter Parker resolves to do battle with the forces of evil and his nemesis, the Green Goblin, as Spider-Man in this musical based on the comic book character of the same name.

CAST
(in order of appearance)

Peter Parker/Spider-Man	REEVE CARNEY
Arachne	KATRINA LENK
Mary Jane Watson	REBECCA FAULKENBERRY
Mrs. Gribrock	ISABEL KEATING
The Bullies	
Flash	MATTHEW WILKAS
Kong	AARON LaVIGNE
Meeks	CHRISTOPHER W. TIERNEY
Boyle	DWAYNE CLARK
Uncle Ben	KEN MARKS
Aunt May	ISABEL KEATING
MJ's Father	TIMOTHY WARMEN
Norman Osborn/	
Green Goblin	ROBERT CUCCIOLI
Emily Osborn	LAURA BETH WELLS
Danny, Lab Assistant	TIMOTHY WARMEN
Ring Announcer	TIMOTHY WARMEN
Ring Girl	KOURTNI LIND
Trainer	BRETT THIELE
First Gangster	AARON LaVIGNE
Second Gangster	DWAYNE CLARK
Third Gangster	MATTHEW WILKAS
Hero Flyer	CHRISTOPHER W. TIERNEY
Purse Lady	ISABEL KEATING

Continued on next page

FOXWOODS THEATRE
A LIVE NATION VENUE

Michael Cohl & Jeremiah J. Harris
Land Line Productions, Hello Entertainment/David Garfinkle/Tony Adams, Sony Pictures Entertainment
Norton Herrick and Herrick Entertainment, Billy Rovzar & Fernando Rovzar, Stephen Bronfman
Jeffrey B. Hecktman, Omneity Entertainment/Richard G. Weinberg
James L. Nederlander, Terry Allen Kramer, S2BN Entertainment, Jam Theatricals
The Mayerson/Gould/Hauser/Tysoe Group, Patricia Lambrecht, and Paul McGuinness

by arrangement with
Marvel Entertainment

present

SPIDER-MAN
TURN OFF THE DARK

Music and Lyrics by
Bono and The Edge

Book by
**Julie Taymor, Glen Berger
& Roberto Aguirre-Sacasa**

Starring
Reeve Carney   Rebecca Faulkenberry   Katrina Lenk
and Robert Cuccioli as Norman Osborn/Green Goblin

Featuring
Michael Mulheren   Ken Marks   Isabel Keating   Timothy Warmen   Jake Epstein
Laura Beth Wells   Matthew Wilkas   Dwayne Clark   Aaron LaVigne

with
Ashley Adamek   Kevin Aubin   Marcus Bellamy   Julius C. Carter   Adam Ray Dyer   Drew Heflin
Craig Henningsen   Dana Marie Ingraham   Kourtni Lind   Ari Loeb   Kevin C. Loomis   Kristen Martin
Jodi McFadden   Monette McKay   Jessica McRoberts   Jake Odmark   Kristen Faith Oei   Maxx Reed   Adam Roberts
Brandon Rubendall   Jennifer Sanchez   Josh Sassanella   Whitney Sprayberry   Cassandra Taylor   Brett Thiele   Christopher W. Tierney

Scenic Design **George Tsypin**	Lighting Design **Donald Holder**	Costume Design **Eiko Ishioka**	Sound Design **Jonathan Deans**
Projection Design **Kyle Cooper**	Mask Design **Julie Taymor**	Hair Design **Campbell Young Associates** **Luc Verschueren**	Make-up Design **Judy Chin**
Aerial Design **Scott Rogers**	Aerial Rigging Design **Jaque Paquin**	Media Design **Howard Werner**	Prosthetics Design **Louie Zakarian**
Arrangements & Orchestrations **David Campbell**	Music Supervision **Teese Gohl**	Music Producer **Paul Bogaev**	Music Direction **Kimberly Grigsby**
Music Coordinator **Antoine Silverman**	Vocal Arrangements **David Campbell, Teese Gohl** **Kimberly Grigsby**		Additional Arrangements / Vocal Arrangements **Dawn Kenny & Rori Coleman**
Associate Scenic Design **Rob Bissinger**	Associate Director **Keith Batten**	Resident Choreographer **Jason Snow**	Production Stage Manager **Theresa A. Bailey**
Casting Director **Telsey + Company**	Marketing Director **Len Gill**	Marketing **Keith Hurd**	Associate Producer **Anne Tanaka**
Press Representation **O & M Co.**	Production Management **Juniper Street Productions &** **MB Productions**	General Management **Foresight Theatrical** **Aaron Lustbader Allan Williams**	Executive Producers **Glenn Orsher** **Stephen Howard** **Martin McCallum** **Adam Silberman**

Choreography and Aerial Choreography by
Daniel Ezralow

Additional Choreography by
Chase Brock

Directed by
Philip Wm. McKinley

Original Direction by
Julie Taymor

12/8/12

Robert Cuccioli (C)
as Norman Osborn
with the Viper Executives

Photo by Jacob Cohl

Spider-Man Turn Off the Dark

MUSICAL NUMBERS

ACT I

"The Myth of Arachne"	Peter
"Behold and Wonder"	Arachne, Ensemble
"Bullying by Numbers"	Peter, Bullies, High School Students
"No More"	Peter, Mary Jane
"D.I.Y. World"	Norman, Emily, Peter, Mary Jane, High School Students, Lab Assistants
"Venom"	Bullies
"Bouncing Off the Walls"	Peter, High School Students
"Rise Above"	Peter, Arachne, Ensemble
"Pull the Trigger"	Norman, Emily, Viper Executives, Soldiers
"Picture This"	Peter, Mary Jane, Norman, Emily

ACT II

"A Freak Like Me Needs Company"	Green Goblin, Ensemble
"If the World Should End"	Mary Jane, Peter
"Sinistereo"	Reporters
"Spider-Man!"	Citizens of New York
"Turn Off the Dark"	Arachne, Peter
"I Just Can't Walk Away"	Mary Jane, Peter
"Boy Falls From the Sky"	Peter
"I'll Take Manhattan"	Green Goblin
"Finale – A New Dawn"	Full Company

Cast Continued

Purse Snatcher	JULIUS C. CARTER
J. Jonah Jameson	MICHAEL MULHEREN

Reporters

Buttons	KEN MARKS
Bud	MATTHEW WILKAS
Stokes	TIMOTHY WARMEN
Maxie	ISABEL KEATING
Travis	AARON LaVIGNE
Robertson	DWAYNE CLARK
Viper Executives	DWAYNE CLARK, AARON LaVIGNE, KEN MARKS, TIMOTHY WARMEN

The Sinister Six

Swarm	DREW HEFLIN
The Lizard	JULIUS C. CARTER
Electro	MAXX REED

Kraven

The Hunter	CHRISTOPHER W. TIERNEY
Carnage	ADAM ROBERTS
Swiss Miss	BRANDON RUBENDALL
Marbles	LAURA BETH WELLS
Receptionist	LAURA BETH WELLS
Exterminator Flyer	CRAIG HENNINGSEN
Newsboy	MATTHEW WILKAS
MJ's Friend	LAURA BETH WELLS
Green Goblin Flyer	ADAM ROBERTS
Citizens, Weavers, Students, Lab Assistants, Reporters, Puppeteers, Spider-Men, Secretaries, Soldiers	ASHLEY ADAMEK,

MARCUS BELLAMY, JULIUS C. CARTER, DWAYNE CLARK, DREW HEFLIN, CRAIG HENNINGSEN, ISABEL KEATING, AARON LaVIGNE, KOURTNI LIND, KEN MARKS, KRISTEN MARTIN, JODI McFADDEN, MONETTE McKAY, KRISTEN FAITH OEI, MAXX REED, ADAM ROBERTS, BRANDON RUBENDALL, WHITNEY SPRAYBERRY, CASSANDRA TAYLOR, BRETT THIELE, CHRISTOPHER W. TIERNEY, TIMOTHY WARMEN, LAURA BETH WELLS, MATTHEW WILKAS

Ensemble Aerialists .... ASHLEY ADAMEK, KEVIN AUBIN, MARCUS BELLAMY, JULIUS C. CARTER, ADAM RAY DYER, DREW HEFLIN, CRAIG HENNINGSEN, DANA MARIE INGRAHAM, KOURTNI LIND, ARI LOEB, KRISTEN MARTIN, JODI McFADDEN, MONETTE McKAY, JESSICA McROBERTS, KRISTEN FAITH OEI, ADAM ROBERTS, BRANDON RUBENDALL, JOSH SASSANELLA, WHITNEY SPRAYBERRY, CASSANDRA TAYLOR, BRETT THIELE, CHRISTOPHER W. TIERNEY

At certain performances, the role of
Peter Parker/Spider-Man will be played by
JAKE EPSTEIN.

UNDERSTUDIES

For Peter Parker/Spider-Man: MATTHEW WILKAS

For Mary Jane Watson: KRISTEN MARTIN, KRISTEN FAITH OEI

For Norman Osborn/ Green Goblin: TIMOTHY WARMEN

For Arachne: JODI McFADDEN, JENNIFER SANCHEZ

For J. Jonah Jameson: KEVIN C. LOOMIS, KEN MARKS, TIMOTHY WARMEN

For Mrs. Gribrock: JESSICA McROBERTS, JENNIFER SANCHEZ

For Flash: AARON LaVIGNE, JAKE ODMARK, JOSH SASSANELLA, CHRISTOPHER W. TIERNEY

For Boyle: JULIUS C. CARTER, AARON LaVIGNE, JOSH SASSANELLA

For Kong: JAKE ODMARK, JOSH SASSANELLA

For Meeks: ADAM RAY DYER, AARON LaVIGNE, JOSH SASSANELLA

For Uncle Ben: KEVIN C. LOOMIS, TIMOTHY WARMEN

For Aunt May: JESSICA McROBERTS, JENNIFER SANCHEZ

For MJ's Father: AARON LaVIGNE, KEVIN C. LOOMIS

For Emily Osborn: JESSICA McROBERTS, JENNIFER SANCHEZ

For First Gangster: KEVIN AUBIN, ARI LOEB, JAKE ODMARK, JOSH SASSANELLA

For Second Gangster: KEVIN AUBIN, ARI LOEB, JOSH SASSANELLA

For Third Gangster: KEVIN AUBIN, ARI LOEB, JAKE ODMARK, JOSH SASSANELLA

For Purse Lady: DANA MARIE INGRAHAM, JESSICA McROBERTS, JENNIFER SANCHEZ

For Purse Snatcher: KEVIN AUBIN, ADAM RAY DYER, ARI LOEB

For Buttons: KEVIN C. LOOMIS, JOSH SASSANELLA

For Bud: MARCUS BELLAMY, AARON LaVIGNE, KEVIN C. LOOMIS, JAKE ODMARK, JOSH SASSANELLA

For Stokes: KEVIN C. LOOMIS, JOSH SASSANELLA

For Maxie: JESSICA McROBERTS, JENNIFER SANCHEZ

For Travis: KEVIN C. LOOMIS, JAKE ODMARK, JOSH SASSANELLA

For Robertson: JULIUS C. CARTER, AARON LaVIGNE, KEVIN C. LOOMIS, JOSH SASSANELLA

For Viper Executives: AARON LaVIGNE, KEVIN C. LOOMIS, JAKE ODMARK, JOSH SASSANELLA, MATTHEW WILKAS

Continued on next page

Spider-Man Turn Off the Dark

Cast Continued

For Danny, Lab Assistant: KEVIN C. LOOMIS,
 JOSH SASSANELLA
For Ring Announcer: KEVIN C. LOOMIS,
 JOSH SASSANELLA
For Ring Girl: DANA MARIE INGRAHAM,
 JESSICA McROBERTS
For Trainer: KEVIN AUBIN, DREW HEFLIN,
 ARI LOEB
For Carnage: KEVIN AUBIN
For Electro: ARI LOEB, BRETT THIELE
For Kraven the Hunter: KEVIN AUBIN,
 ADAM RAY DYER, CRAIG HENNINGSEN,
 ARI LOEB, JOSH SASSANELLA
For The Lizard: KEVIN AUBIN, ARI LOEB
For Swarm: MARCUS BELLAMY, ARI LOEB
For Swiss Miss: KEVIN AUBIN
For Marbles: JESSICA McROBERTS,
 JENNIFER SANCHEZ
For Receptionist: JESSICA McROBERTS,
 JENNIFER SANCHEZ
For Newsboy: MARCUS BELLAMY,
 AARON LaVIGNE, JAKE ODMARK,
 JOSH SASSANELLA
For MJ's Friend: JESSICA McROBERTS,
 JENNIFER SANCHEZ

Dance Captain: DANA MARIE INGRAHAM
Assistant Dance Captain: DREW HEFLIN

SWINGS

KEVIN AUBIN, ADAM RAY DYER,
DANA MARIE INGRAHAM, ARI LOEB,
KEVIN C. LOOMIS, JESSICA McROBERTS,
JAKE ODMARK, JENNIFER SANCHEZ,
JOSH SASSANELLA

ORCHESTRA

Conductor: KIMBERLY GRIGSBY
Associate Conductor: CHARLES duCHATEAU
Guitars: ZANE CARNEY, MATT BECK,
 BEN BUTLER
Basses: AIDEN MOORE,
 RICHARD HAMMOND
Drums: JON EPCAR
Keyboards: BILLY JAY STEIN,
 CHARLES duCHATEAU
Percussion: JOHN CLANCY
Hammered Dulcimer/Percussion: BILL RUYLE
Concertmaster: ANTOINE SILVERMAN
Viola/Violin: CHRISTOPHER CARDONA
Cello: ANJA WOOD
Trumpets: DON DOWNS, TONY KADLECK
French Horn: THERESA MacDONNELL
Trombone/Tuba: MARCUS ROJAS
Reeds: AARON HEICK

Electronic Music Design: BILLY JAY STEIN
Music Coordination: ANTOINE SILVERMAN
Music Copying Supervisor: STEVEN M. ALPER
Music Copyists: BETTIE ROSS,
 RUSSELL ANIXTER, STEVEN COHEN,
 JODY JAROWEY, DON RICE,
 ROY WILLIAMS, DAVID WOLFSON
Piano Vocal Score Coordination: MARK BAECHLE

Reeve Carney
*Peter Parker/
Spider-Man*

Robert Cuccioli
*Norman Osborn/
Green Goblin*

Rebecca
Faulkenberry
Mary Jane Watson

Katrina Lenk
Arachne

Michael Mulheren
J. Jonah Jameson

Ken Marks
*Uncle Ben, Buttons,
Viper Executive,
Ensemble*

Isabel Keating
*Aunt May, Mrs.
Gribrock, Maxie,
Purse Lady*

Timothy Warmen
*MJ's Father, Danny,
Ring Announcer,
Stokes, Viper
Executive*

Jake Epstein
*Peter Parker/
Spider-Man
Alternate*

Laura Beth Wells
*Emily Osborn,
Marbles,
Receptionist, MJ's
Friend, Ensemble*

Matthew Wilkas
*Flash, Third
Gangster, Bud,
Newsboy, Ensemble,
u/s Peter Parker/
Spider-Man*

Dwayne Clark
*Boyle, Second
Gangster, Robertson,
Viper Executive,
Ensemble*

Aaron LaVigne
*Kong, First Gangster,
Travis, Viper
Executive, Ensemble*

Ashley Adamek
Ensemble

Kevin Aubin
Swing

Marcus Bellamy
Ensemble

Julius C. Carter
The Lizard, Ensemble

Adam Ray Dyer
Swing

Drew Heflin
*Swarm, Ensemble,
Assistant Dance
Captain*

Craig Henningsen
Ensemble

Spider-Man Turn Off the Dark

Dana Marie
Ingraham
*Dance Captain,
Swing*

Kourtni Lind
Ring Girl, Ensemble

Ari Loeb
Swing

Kevin C. Loomis
*u/s J. Jonah
Jameson, Swing*

Kristen Martin
*Ensemble, u/s Mary
Jane Watson*

Jodi McFadden
*Ensemble,
u/s Arachne*

Monette McKay
Ensemble

Jessica McRoberts
Swing

Jake Odmark
Swing

Kristen Faith Oei
*Ensemble,
u/s Mary Jane
Watson*

Maxx Reed
Electro, Ensemble

Adam Roberts
*Carnage, Green
Goblin Flyer,
Ensemble*

Brandon Rubendall
*Swiss Miss,
Ensemble*

Jennifer Sanchez
u/s Arachne, Swing

Josh Sassanella
Swing

Whitney Sprayberry
Ensemble

Cassandra Taylor
Ensemble

Brett Thiele
Trainer, Ensemble

Christopher W.
Tierney
*Meeks, Kraven the
Hunter, Hero Flyer,
Ensemble*

Julie Taymor
*Co-Book Writer,
Original Direction,
Mask Designer*

Bono
Music & Lyrics

The Edge
Music & Lyrics

Philip Wm. McKinley
Director

Glen Berger
Co-Book Writer

Roberto
Aguirre-Sacasa
Co-Book Writer

Daniel Ezralow
*Choreographer,
Aerial
Choreographer*

Chase Brock
*Additional
Choreography*

George Tsypin
Scenic Designer

Donald Holder
Lighting Designer

Eiko Ishioka
Costume Designer

Jonathan Deans
Sound Designer

Kyle Cooper
Projections Designer

Campbell Young
Campbell Young
Associates
Hair Designers

Luc Verschueren
Campbell Young
Associates
Hair Designers

Judy Chin
Make-up Designer

Spider-Man Turn Off the Dark

Scott Rogers
Aerial Designer

Jaque Paquin
Aerial Rigging Designer

Howard Werner
Media Design

Rob Bissinger
Associate Scenic Designer

Keith Batten
Associate Director

David Ruttura
Resident Director

Jason Snow
Associate/Resident Choreographer

Jason Brouillard
Assistant Stage Manager

Sandra M. Franck
Assistant Stage Manager

Valerie Lau-Kee Lai
Assistant Stage Manager

Jenny Slattery
Assistant Stage Manager

Michael Wilhoite
Assistant Stage Manager

David Campbell
Arrangements and Orchestrations, Vocal Arrangements

Teese Gohl
Music Supervisor

Paul Bogaev
Music Producer

Kimberly Grigsby
Music Director

Antoine Silverman
Music Coordinator

Rori Coleman
Additional Arangements/Vocal Arrangements

Dawn Kenny
Additional Arrangements/Vocal Arrangements

Billy Jay Stein
Electronic Music Designer

Bernard Telsey
Telsey + Company Casting

Keith Hurd
Marketing

Ana Rose Greene, Guy Kwan, Joe DeLuise, Hillary Blanken
Juniper Street Productions
Production Management

Mike Bauder
MB Productions
Production Management

Fred Gallo
Technical Director

Alan Wasser
Foresight Theatrical
General Manager

Allan Williams
Foresight Theatrical
General Manager

Aaron Lustbader
Foresight Theatrical
General Manager

Michael Cohl
Producer

Jeremiah J. Harris
Producer

David Garfinkle
Hello Entertainment
Producer

Norton Herrick
Producer

Billy Rovzar
Producer

Fernando Rovzar
Producer

Spider-Man Turn Off the Dark

Stephen Bronfman
Producer

Jeffrey B. Hecktman
Producer

Richard G. Weinberg
Omneity
Entertainment
Producer

James L.
Nederlander
Producer

Terry Allen Kramer
Producer

Arny Granat
Jam Theatricals
Producer

Steve Traxler
Jam Theatricals
Producer

Frederic H.
Mayerson
The Mayerson/
Gould/ Hauser/
Tysoe Group
Producer

James M. Gould
The Mayerson/
Gould/ Hauser/
Tysoe Group
Producer

Ron Tysoe
The Mayerson/
Gould/ Hauser/
Tysoe Group
Producer

Paul McGuinness
Producer

Glenn Orsher
Executive Producer

Stephen Howard
Executive Producer

Adam Silberman
Executive Producer

Hettie Barnhill
Ring Girl, Ensemble

Emmanuel Brown
*Meeks, Kraven the
Hunter, Ensemble*

Jeb Brown
*Standby Norman
Osborn/Green Goblin*

Matt Caplan
*Peter Parker/
Spider-Man
Alternate*

Luther Creek
*Kong, First Gangster,
Travis, Viper
Executive, Ensemble*

Daniel Curry
*Swing, Ensemble
Aerialist*

Ayo Jackson
Ensemble Aerialist

Elizabeth Judd
*Ensemble, u/s Mary
Jane Watson*

Reed Kelly
*Swiss Miss,
Ensemble*

Megan Lewis
u/s Arachne, Swing

Natalie Lomonte
*Ensemble Aerialist,
Dance Captain,
Swing*

India McGee
*Ensemble,
Ensemble Aerialist*

Paul McGill
*Swing, Ensemble
Aerialist*

Bethany Moore
*Ring Girl, Ensemble,
Ensemble Aerialist*

Patrick Page
*Norman Osborn/
Green Goblin*

Kyle Post
Swing

Jennifer Savelli
Ensemble, Swing

Emily Shoolin
*Emily Osborn,
Marbles,
Receptionist, MJ's
Friend, Ensemble*

Dollar Tan
Trainer, Ensemble

Joey Taranto
Swing

Spider-Man Turn Off the Dark

Matthew James
Thomas
*Peter Parker/Spider-
Man Alternate*

Stephen Lee
Anderson
*Uncle Ben, Buttons,
Viper Executive,
Ensemble*

David Armstrong
*Exterminator Flyer,
Ensemble*

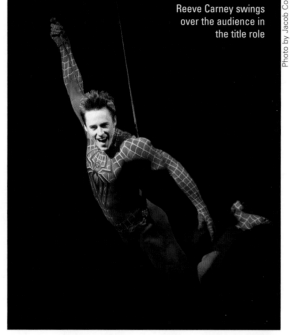

Reeve Carney swings
over the audience in
the title role

Photo by Jacob Cohl

Gerald Avery
Swarm, Ensemble

Emmanuel Brown
*Kraven the Hunter,
Ensemble*

Daniel Curry
Swing

Christina DeCicco
Arachne

Reed Kelly
*Swiss Miss,
Ensemble*

Natalie Lomonte
Ensemble

Paul McGill
Swing

Jamison Scott
Swing

Dan Sharkey
*MJ's Father, Danny,
Stokes; u/s Osborn/
Green Goblin,
Uncle Ben*

Emily Shoolin
*Emily Osborn,
Marbles,
Receptionist, MJ's
Friend, Ensemble*

Joey Taranto
Swing

STAFF FOR
SPIDER-MAN TURN OFF THE DARK

GENERAL MANAGEMENT
FORESIGHT THEATRICAL
Alan Wasser   Allan Williams
Aaron Lustbader   Mark Shacket

PRODUCTION MANAGEMENT
JUNIPER STREET PRODUCTIONS
Hillary Blanken   Kevin Broomell
Guy Kwan   Ana Rose Greene   Alexandra Paull
Joseph DeLuise

MB PRODUCTIONS
Mike Bauder
Sonya Duveneck

TECHNICAL DIRECTOR
Fred Gallo

CASTING
TELSEY + COMPANY
Bernard Telsey CSA, Will Cantler CSA,
David Vaccari CSA
Bethany Knox CSA, Craig Burns CSA,
Tiffany Little Canfield CSA, Rachel Hoffman CSA,

Justin Huff CSA, Patrick Goodwin CSA,
Abbie Brady-Dalton CSA, David Morris, Cesar A. Rocha

COMPANY MANAGER
Doug Gaeta

GENERAL PRESS REPRESENTATIVE
O&M CO.
Rick Miramontez
Elizabeth Wagner   Ryan Ratelle
Andy Snyder

Production Stage Manager ....Theresa A. Bailey
Stage Manager ....Andrew Neal
Assistant Stage Managers ....Jason Brouillard,
           Sandra M. Franck, Valerie Lau-Kee Lai,
           Jenny Slattery, Michael Wilhoite
Sub Stage Managers ....Samantha Preiss,
           Jeffrey Rodriguez
Associate Company Manager ....Thom Mitchell
Assistant Company Manager ....Lisa Guzman
Assistant Director ....Eileen F. Haggerty
Resident Director ....David Ruttura
Assistant Original Direction ....Dodd Loomis
Assistant Choreographer ....Cherice Barton
Production Aerial Supervisor ....Angela Phillips

Flight Instructor ....Gonzalo Brea
UK Casting ....Gillian Hawser

Set Design Creative Team:
Associate Scenic Designer ....Rob Bissinger
Pop-up and Dimensional Design ....Arturs Virtmanis
Illustration and Graphics ....Baiba Baiba
Cityscape Graphics ....Sergei Goloshapov

Assistant Set Design Team:
First Assistant Set Design ....Anita La Scala
Graphic Art ....Sia Balabanova, Rafael Kayanan
Pop-ups ....Nathan Heverin
Model Makers ....Eric Beauzay, Catherine Chung,
           Rachel Short Janocko, Damon Pelletier,
           Daniel Zimmerman
Draftsmen ....Robert John Andrusko, Toni Barton,
           Larry W. Brown, Mark Fitzgibbons,
           Jonathan Spencer, Josh Zangen
Assistant Set Design ....Tijana Bjelajac,
           Szu-Feng Chen, Heather Dunbar,
           Mimi Lien, Qin (Lucy) Lu, Robert Pyzocha,
           Chsato Uno, Frank McCullough
Previsualization ....Lily Twining
Associate Costume
   Designer ....Mary Nemecek Peterson

Spider-Man Turn Off the Dark

Assistant Costume Designers ....Angela M. Kahler,
Katie Irish, Michael Hannah
Costume Shoppers ....Jennifer Adams, Dana Burkart,
Cathy Parrott, Jen Raskopf
Associate Makeup Designer ....Angela Johnson
Associate Lighting Designer ....Vivien Leone
Assistant Lighting Designers ....Caroline Chao,
Carolyn Wong, Michael Jones
Assistant to the
Lighting Designer ....Porsche McGovern
Automated Lighting Programmer ....Richard Tyndall
Assistant Video Designer ....Sarah Jakubasz
Video Programmer ....Phil Gilbert
Associate Sound Designers ....Brian Hsieh,
Keith Caggiano
Puppet and Mask
Production Supervisor ....Louis Troisi
Assistant Puppet and
Mask Coordinator ....Curran Banach
Automated Flying Programmer ....Jason Shupe
Production Carpenter ....Jack Anderson
Assistant Carpenters ....Andrew Elman, Dave Fulton,
Hugh Hardyman, Kris Keene,
Matthew J. Lynch, Mike Norris,
Geoffrey Vaughn
Production Electricians ....Randall Zaibek,
James Fedigan
Head Electrician ....Ron Martin
Production Video Electricians ....Jason Lindahl,
Chris Herman
Production Sound Engineer ....Simon Matthews
Head Sound Engineer ....John Sibley
Assistant Sound Engineer ....Scott Sanders
Production Properties
Supervisor ....Joseph P. Harris, Jr.
Associate Properties Supervisor ....Timothy M. Abel
E-Stop Personnel ....Gonzalo Brea
Production Wardrobe Supervisor ....Michael D. Hannah
Assistant Wardrobe Supervisors ....Christel Murdock,
Sonya Wysocki
Dressers ....Robert Belopede, Dana Burkart,
Diana Calderazzo, Jackie Freeman,
Lyle Jones, Carrie Kamerer,
Rosemary Keough, Shannon McDowell,
Leslie Moulton, Daniel Mura, Evelina Nervil,
Kyle O'Connor, Michael Piscitelli,
Lacie Pulido, Jack Scott, Kyle Stewart,
Ron Tagert, Cheryl Widner
Seamstress ....Alejandra Rubinos
Laundry ....David Gilleo
Hair Supervisor ....Ruth Carsch
Assistant Hair Supervisor ....Lisa Weiss
Assistant Hair Designer ....Cory McCutcheon
Hairstylists ....Brian Hennings, Stacy Schneiderman
Production Makeup Supervisor ....Angela Johnson
Assistant Makeup Supervisor ....Tiffany Hicks
Production Photographer/
Videographer ....Jacob Cohl
Video Crew ....Ben Nabors, Matt Kazman,
Nora Tennessen
Cover Photo ....Jacob Cohl
Lead Guitar Technician ....Dallas Schoo
Additional Guitar Technician ....Mike Vegas
Workshop Audio Engineers ....Carl Glanville, Angie Teo
Vocal Coach ....Don Lawrence
Dialect Coach ....Deborah Hecht
Acting Coach ....Sheila Grey

Technical Production Assistants ....Sue Barsoum,
Steve Chazaro, Kate DellaFera,
Sonya Duveneck, Ania Parks,
Alexandra Paull, Melissa Spengler,
Kim Straatemeier
Production Assistants ....Allison Cottrell,
Hannah Dorfman, Amanda Johnson,
Gregory Murray, Samantha Preiss,
Danya Taymor, Raynelle Wright
Costume Interns ....Yingshi June Lin,
Tomke Von Gawinski
Orthopedist ....David S. Weiss, MD
Physical Therapist ....Heidi Green
Official Athletic Trainer ....Prime Blueprint/
Dr. Edyth Heus
Consulting Producer ....Jeffery Auerbach
Producing Consultant ....Carl Pasbjerg
Executive Assistant to Michael Cohl ....Jamie Forshaw
Executive Assistant to
Jeremiah J. Harris ....Stella Morelli
Executive Assistant to Glenn Orsher ....Tricia Olson
Marketing Director ....Len Gill
Marketing ....Keith Hurd
Marketing Associate ....Mary Caitlin Barrett
Advertising & Marketing ....aka/
Scott Moore, Pippa Bexon,
Danielle Barchetto, Kyle Hall, Adam Jay,
Jacob Matsumiya, Janette Roush,
Trevor Sponseller
Website Design &
Internet Marketing ....Situation Interactive/
Damian Bazadona, John Lanasa,
Jeremy Kraus, Victoria Gettler,
Chris Powers
National Public Relations ....Ken Sunshine/
Sunshine, Sachs & Associates
Sponsorship Consultant ....Cary Chevat
Press Associates ....Sarah Babin, Molly Barnett,
Scott Braun, Philip Carrubba,
Jon Dimond, Joyce Friedmann,
Michael Jorgensen, Yufen Kung,
Chelsea Nachman, Marie Pace,
Pete Sanders
Press Interns ....Valentina Berger Maurette,
Tori Piersanti
Legal Counsel ....Ron Feiner, Esq.,
Beigelman, Feiner & Feldman
Joseph T. Moldovan, Esq., Jack Levy, Esq.,
Joshua D. Saviano, Esq.,
Morrison Cohen LLP
Dale Cendali, Esq.;
Courtney Farkas, Esq.
Kirkland & Ellis LLP
Accounting ....Rosenberg, Neuwirth & Kuchner/
Chris Cacace, Marina Flom,
Kirill Baytalskiy
General Management Associates ....Mark Barna,
Jake Hirzel
General Management Office ....Julia Barnett,
Kaitlin Boland, Lauren Friedlander,
Nina Lutwick
Insurance ....DeWitt Stern Group/Pete Shoemaker
Banking ....Signature Bank/Barbara von Borstel,
Margaret Monigan, Mary Ann Fanelli,
Janett Urena
Payroll ....Castellana Services, Inc.

Transportation and
Housing ....Road Rebel Touring and
Travel Services,
Alternative Business Accommodations,
The Mansfield Hotel

Group Sales
Broadway.com/1-800-Broadway

CREDITS AND ACKNOWLEDGMENTS

Scenery and scenic effects built and electrified by PRG Scenic
Technologies, New Windsor, NY. Scenery painted by Scenic
Art Studios, Cornwall, NY. Show control and scenic motion
control featuring Stage Command Systems® by PRG Scenic
Technologies, New Windsor, NY. Aerial effects equipment
provided by Fisher Technical Services Inc. Video projection
equipment, lighting equipment and sound equipment
provided by PRG, Secaucus, NJ. Special effects executed by
Excitement Technologies, Addison, TX. Softgoods built by I.
Weiss and Sons Inc., Fairview, NJ. Props executed by the
Spoon Group, Rahway, NJ; the Rollingstock Company,
Sarasota, FL; the Paragon Innovation Group Inc., Toronto,
ON; Illusion Projects, Las Vegas, NV; Beyond Imagination,
Newburgh, NY; Cigar Box Studios Inc., Newburgh, NY;
Czinkota Studios, Gardiner, NY; and Hamilton Scenic
Specialty Inc., Dundas, ON. Media content created by
Prologue Films. Puppets executed by Nathan Heverin, New
Paltz, NY; Michael Curry Design Inc., Portland, OR; the
Paragon Innovation Group Inc., Toronto, ON; Igloo
Projects/Philip Cooper, Brooklyn, NY. Puppet assistance by
Ilya Vett. Hauling by Clark Transfer Inc.; Michael O'Brien &
Sons, Bronx, NY; and Prop Transport, New York, NY.
Excerpt from "Manhattan" written by Richard Rodgers,
Lorenz Hart, used by permission of Piedmont Music
Company, publisher. "The Boy Falls From the Sky" lyrics by
Bono and The Edge, music by U2, used by permission.

Costumes constructed by Parsons-Meares Ltd.

Additional costumes by Bill Hargate Costumes; Tom Talmon
Studios; Artur & Tailors Ltd.; Danielle Gisiger; Valentina
Kozhecksy; Arel Studio; Costume Armour, Cornwall, NY;
Maria Ficalora Knitwear; and Jon Gellman Designs.
Millinery by Monica Vianni, Arnold Levine. Costume crafts
by Paragon Innovation Group Inc., Toronto, ON; James
Chai, Philip Cooper, New York, NY; Signs and Shapes
International. Custom shirts by L. Allmeier. Custom shoes
by Jitterbug Boy, LaDuca Shoes, Montana Leather, Capri
Shoes and World Tone. Digital printing and screen printing
by Gene Mignola. Costume painting by Parmalee Welles-
Tolkan, Mary Macy, Margaret Peot, Virginia Clow, Claudia
Dzundza. Additional printing by Jeff Fender. Development
painting by Hochi Asiatico.

IN MEMORY OF
Tony Adams

SPECIAL THANKS

Stan Lee, Anne Runolfsson, Thomas Schumacher, William
Court Cohen, Trevor Bowen, Keryn Kaplan, Shan Lui, Liz
Devlin, Catriona Garde, Susan Hunter, Missy Iredell,
Michelle Lieu, Jennifer McManus, Principle Management
Dublin and New York, Steve Lillywhite, David Toraya, Allen
Grubman, Gil Karson, Larry Shire, Paul Wachter, Seth
Gelblum, Michael West, Elliot Goldenthal, Rick Rubin, Jon
Kilik, Michael Arndt, Bill Flanagan, Jennifer Lyne, Colin
Farrell, Susan Stroman, Eoin Colfer, Jake Bell, Don Lasker,
Darryl Scherba, William Dailey, Michael O'Brien and Sons,

Spider-Man Turn Off the Dark

Derek Mouton of MCD, Vox Amplification, Fender Guitars, Rickenbacker Guitars, to NS Design for the loan of the electric violin and cello, Roland, Tekserve, James Jones Hammered Dulcimers, Bruce Glikas

The Chrysler Building and its image are trademarks of Tishman Speyer Properties, LP and its affiliates and is used herein with permission.

Makeup provided by M·A·C Cosmetics

Rehearsed at the New 42nd Street Studios

Souvenir merchandise designed and created by
S2BN Entertainment
Norman Perry   Brahma Jade   Pete Milano
www.SpiderManOnBroadwaystore.com

Energy efficient washer/dryer courtesy of
LG Electronics

**To learn more about the production please visit
www.SpiderManOnBroadway.com**

HISTORY OF THE FOXWOODS THEATRE

The Foxwoods Theatre combines architectural preservation with state-of-the-art construction and technology. The spirit and character of New York's grandest historic theatres has been maintained and united with the technical amenities of a modern facility.

In 1997 the Ford Center for the Performing Arts was erected on the site of the legendary Lyric Theatre (1903; 1,261 seats) and Apollo Theatre (1920; 1,194 seats). The auditorium's interior design is based on historic elements from the Apollo Theatre. The Apollo's original ceiling dome, proscenium arch, and side boxes were removed, restored and re-installed (upon expansion for the larger scale of the new theatre) in the new auditorium. The side wall panels were created for acoustical considerations and designed to complement the historic features. New murals were commissioned to form a frieze over the new side boxes. Informally titled "Wings of Creativity," they were inspired by ancient Greek myths of Apollo, patron god of musicians and poets.

The lobby's design is based on historical elements of the Lyric Theatre. An elliptical dome from the Lyric was reproduced as the centerpiece of a new two-story atrium. The grand limestone staircase was designed to provide the flow and spirit of a grand theatre or opera house. The staircase railings feature lyre designs that were recreated from the original 43rd Street façade balcony rails. In the floor is a magnificent mosaic featuring comedy and tragedy masks inspired by sculptures on the historic 43rd St. façade. The 650-sq.-ft. mosaic includes 172,800 hand-cut pieces of marble from all over the world. At the top of the stairs is a medallion with the head of Zeus, taken from the Lyric's auditorium, and on the dress circle level, cold-painted windows (a stained glass technique) featuring a cupid design have been restored. The lighting in the lobby features the bare carbon filament light bulb, utilized in the early 20th century, to create a warm candlelight glow.

At 1,932 seats, the new theatre is one of Broadway's largest. The Ford Center opened with the acclaimed musical *Ragtime*, followed by the Broadway revival of *Jesus Christ Superstar* and the award-winning revival of *42nd Street*. In 2005, the Ford Center was renamed the Hilton Theatre. Its premiere production was the musical *Chitty Chitty Bang Bang*, followed by the dance-inspired musical *Hot Feet*, the holiday spectacular *Dr. Seuss' How the Grinch Stole Christmas:*

Robert Cuccioli as Green Goblin

The Musical, The Pirate Queen and the new Mel Brooks' musical *Young Frankenstein*. In 2010, the Hilton Theatre was renamed the Foxwoods Theatre. We are pleased to welcome *Spider-Man Turn Off The Dark* to the Foxwoods stage.

TICKET INFORMATION

There is an $.90 surcharge added to the price of each ticket purchased, in support of the New 42nd Street's not-for-profit projects on 42nd Street. An additional $1.10 project support surcharge is added to the price of each ticket by the Foxwoods Theatre. Proceeds earned by the Foxwoods Theatre are used for maintenance of the historic Theatre.

FOXWOODS THEATRE GUEST INFORMATION

FOOD & BEVERAGE: Concessions are available throughout the lobbies during pre-show and intermission and is permitted in the auditorium. Persons under the age of 21 will not be served alcoholic beverages. Outside food and beverages are not permitted in the facility.

CURTAIN CALL: Please remain in your seat until the performance has ended completely and the auditorium lights

Katrina Lenk as Arachne

have been raised.

HEARING ASSISTANCE: The Foxwoods Theatre is equipped with an Infrared System to assist hearing-impaired patrons. A limited number of listening headsets are available at the Coat Check. A deposit of driver's license or credit card is required.

LOST & FOUND: Items are taken to our stage door reception area following the performance. Please call (212) 556-4750.

MEDICAL EMERGENCIES: Medical emergencies should be reported to any uniformed staff member.

ELECTRONIC DEVICES: Please silence cellular phones, beepers, wristwatch alarms and similar devices.

NO SMOKING: This is a smoke-free facility. No smoking applies to all areas of the theatre.

SOUVENIRS: Gift Kiosks are located throughout the theatre. The merchandise store offers collectables from the show and is centrally located on the Orchestra Level. Most major credit cards are accepted.

THEATRE RENTALS/RECEPTIONS/TOURS: The Foxwoods Theatre's auditorium and other facilities are available to rent for special events, meetings, lectures, films and private receptions. For more information please call (212) 556-4750.

FOXWOODS THEATRE

VP Theatrical/General Manager ....Erich Jungwirth
Assistant General Manager ....Sue Barsoum
House Manager ....Eric Paris
Facility Manager ....Jeff Nuzzo
Assistant Facility Manager ....David Dietsch
Box Office Treasurer ....Spencer Taustine
Assistant Box Office Treasurer ....Michelle Smith
Head Carpenter ....James C. Harris
Head Electrician ....Art J. Friedlander
Head of Properties ....Joseph P. Harris Jr.
Head of Sound ....John R. Gibson
Staff Accountant ....Jill Johnson
Office Manager ....Brian Mahoney
Shipping/Receiving ....Dinara Kratsch

FOXWOODS THEATRE
A Live Nation Venue

LIVE NATION ENTERTAINMENT

President and
    Chief Executive Officer ....Michael Rapino
President,
    North America Concerts, North ....Mark Campana
President, North America Concerts, South ....Bob Roux
President, North Atlantic ....Alan Ostfield
Regional President, New York ....Jim Koplik
Vice President Ticketing Operations ....Wayne Goldberg
President of Live Nation Network ....Russell Wallach
Chief Financial Officer ....Kathy Willard
Senior Vice-President,
    North America Finance ....Kathy Porter
Vice President, Finance ....Dan Casale
Director of Accounting, Northeast ....Lisa Bashi

About Live Nation Entertainment

Live Nation Entertainment (NYSE-LYV) is the largest live entertainment company in the world, connecting 200 million fans to 100,000 events in more than 40 countries, which has made Ticketmaster.com the number-three eCommerce website in the world. For additional information, visit www.livenation.com/investors.

Spider-Man Turn Off the Dark
SCRAPBOOK

Correspondent: Isabel Keating, "Aunt May," "Mrs. Gribrock," "Maxie," "Purse Lady"

Most Exciting Celebrity Visitors: We've had quite the parade come through here, to be sure: a veritable who's who from all walks of life and from all over the world, including President Bill Clinton. There are far too many to list, but a tiny sampling of names includes movie stars such as Jamie Foxx, Ben Stiller, Harry Belafonte, and my fave (for obvious reasons) Hugh Jackman, along with their families. Rock stars, of course: Jon Bon Jovi and family, Alice Cooper, Lou Reed. Pop stars too: One Direction, the Jonas Brothers. Comedians Steve Martin, Mike Myers, Joan Rivers; sports superstars Amar'e Stoudemire, Danell Leyva, John McEnroe; supermodels Tyra Banks and Cindy Crawford and their families. Ad infinitum.... So, you see, we've all become inured to a constant stream of notables. HOWEVER. Nothing prepared me for the excitement caused by the visit we had from our First Lady Michelle Obama and Sasha and Malia! That was something else entirely: one for the history books. I didn't get a chance to meet them after the show, but I could see their smiling faces in the audience. That was a special day.

Memorable Ad-Lib: Another night we had Donald Trump in the house. For once, he didn't have the stage, but brilliant Patrick Page, our Green Goblin at the time, shouted him out during his improv at the top of the second act. After introducing Mr. Trump by pointing him out to the crowd, Patrick asked: "What's that you say, Donald? You need to see my birth certificate?" Needless to say, it brought the house down. Mr. Trump took it all with grace and good humor.

Actor Who Performed the Most Roles in This Show: Most of us in the cast of *Spider-Man* play multiple roles (an integral part of the concept of the show) which entail many costume, wig and make-up changes. All of this would be impossible were it not for our ninja-like wardrobe, hair and makeup specialists, who see to it that we each make all of our lightning-quick changes with the greatest of ease! Ah, the magic of theatre! I myself play five different roles, and my changes are possible thanks to Jackie, Tiffany, Ruth, Carrie, Danny and Rose. I love each and every one of my characters, but I do have an extra-special fondness for "Bunny Van Wyck" (also known as "Izzy") who goes through an ordeal involving her purse, and is rescued by Spider-Man. I wear one of the five magnificently detailed masks that Julie (Taymor) crafted for us based on our individual physiognomies, in extreme caricature: heightened, beautiful, funny. I love Bunny/Izzy so much.

Special Backstage Rituals: We have a very special ritual we perform as a company before every single performance. At our "places" call, the cast gathers on deck, stage right. We hold hands to form a circle in order to offer each other well wishes for a good show. This circle originated early in our process as an invocation of gratitude

and protection. For a time, it included moments where anyone who wished would speak from the heart and dedicate a few special words. It evolved to become a ritual of remembrance and inclusion, our "TICK CIRCLE." Every time an actor departs the company, he or she adds a word or sound with a movement to the existing choreography. The TICK CIRCLE is so named because one night company member Dollar Tan spontaneously launched into one of his signature moves and voiced a simple "tick, tick, BOOM, BOOM, BOOM" with coordinated foot-stomps. It has since grown (and continues to grow!) into a lengthy stream of words and sounds accompanied by specific moves which we execute with alacrity and occasional grace, nightly, just before the curtain goes up.

Favorite In-Theatre Gathering Place: For most of us, there is very little time in the course of the

Olympian gymnast Danell Leyva (C) meets Reeve Carney (far R) and the other Spider-Men
Photo by Joseph Marzullo/WENN

show for socializing. But for the moments we do have, the PT room (physical therapy room) seems to be the social hub, whether for a pit stop; for strengthening, stretching, rolling out; and usually, especially, laughing.

Favorite Off-Site Hangout: We all practically live at Green Symphony (43rd Street near Eighth Avenue)! Jay and Joy and the staff take really good care of us with plenty of healthy options to replenish the massive energy we all use putting on the show. They even named one of their smoothies "The Webslinger!" We tend to spread the post-show hangouts equitably around the neighborhood. I love Bar Centrale, and Sardi's holds a special place in my heart. Angus is great, especially if we're a larger group, and we bridge the divide and cross over to The Lambs Club and Tony's di Napoli. Pre-show I favor Orso: it's a great sunny space to talk shop. And where would we be without Joe Allen?!

Favorite Snack Foods: I think it must be birthday cake! With such a large company, we have at least one birthday a week!

Mascot: That would be...um, Spider-Man!

Favorite Therapy: To each his own, but I can't live without "Myos" (that's my pet name for my myofascial roller). Myos is MAGIC! That and massage and Epsom salts baths. AND FOOD! Food therapy is really the best. Oh, yes, there is also this very rare and beneficial therapy called SLEEP!

Memorable Stage Door Fan Encounter: We have such incredible fans! One Spider-Fan, Christine Antosca, has been to the show 200

times! And one of our youngest fans is Suzu, who attends with her mom and knows most of the words to the songs. I wouldn't be surprised if she could perform the choreography too.

Who Wore the Heaviest/Hottest Costumes: I believe the SuperVillains of the Sinister Six vie for heaviest and hottest (in all senses of the words): Kraven the Hunter (Manny Brown), Carnage (Adam Roberts), Swiss Miss (Brandon Rubendall), Swarm (Gerald Avery), The Lizard (Julius Carter) and Electro (Maxx Reed).

Catchphrase Only the Company Would Recognize: "Get me the shoes."

Orchestra Member Who Played the Most Consecutive Performances Without a Sub: We have a world-class band! There is no traditional orchestra pit at the Foxwoods, so these musicians play from two separate rooms below the stage. One room houses the rhythm section with our conductor Kimberly Grigsby, the other, strings and brass who follow Kim from a video screen. I, and a few others in the cast, often find a moment during the show to sit in the rooms with the musicians so we can listen to the incredible sound of the music close-up and acoustically. It is INCREDIBLE! The power! The talent! Each of our orchestra members is a star in his/her own right, and therefore, each is in great demand. For the sake of keeping the art and their identities fresh and visible, it is imperative, and indeed encouraged, that they accept work outside the show while also maintaining their "chairs." That said, these star musicians love playing the show live nightly, so there is usually a good ratio of original band members to subs (who, it must be said, are also world-class musicians).

Company In-Joke: Every so often we quote our original intrepid production stage manager C. Randall White: "And...we're gonna hold."

Coolest Thing About Being in This Show: I have the opportunity to work with some of the most talented, multifaceted, forward-thinking, eclectic artists I've yet encountered, from the creatives and designers to the acrobats, dancers and actors, to the makeup, hair, and wardrobe crew, to the technicians, engineers, backstage crew, stage managers, musicians, and ultimately, our audiences. And I get to be Peter Parker's Aunt May. I mean, really, it doesn't get any cooler. It's thrilling. It's *Spider-Man*!

Addendum: In the course of bringing *Spider-Man* to life, our company has seen quite a few births and deaths, metaphorically certainly, but also literally: several babies have been born among cast and crew; others of us have grieved the deaths of parents, grandparents, siblings. We've shared these great joys and great sorrows. We've endured. And, like our company, *Spider-Man*—the play—is something very special and strong and resilient. The story, and its inherent messages, are ones I find valuable for my own life: one can overcome difficulty, one can rise above. That's a powerful, uplifting and illuminating realization, especially in the darkest times we all encounter.

The Testament of Mary

First Preview: March 26, 2013. Opened: April 22, 2013.
Closed May 5, 2013 after 27 Previews and 16 Performances.

PLAYBILL®

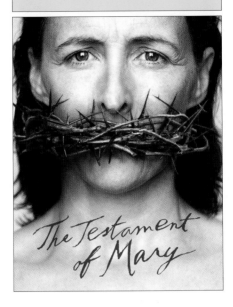

Fiona Shaw portrays the mother of Jesus Christ in the period following the crucifixion of her son. In contrast to the traditional serene Blessed Virgin Mother seen in religious art, Tóibín's character is angry ordinary woman coping with the trauma of the event, questioning her role, questioning the politics of the situation, and especially questioning how she and her son are being put into history. This production was picketed by religious groups.

Fiona Shaw

⑨ WALTER KERR THEATRE
A JUJAMCYN THEATRE

JORDAN ROTH, *President*
ROCCO LANDESMAN, *President Emeritus*
PAUL LIBIN, *Executive Vice President*   **JACK VIERTEL**, *Senior Vice President*

SCOTT RUDIN   STUART THOMPSON
JON B. PLATT   ROGER BERLIND   BROADWAY ACROSS AMERICA   SCOTT M. DELMAN
JEAN DOUMANIAN   ROY FURMAN   STEPHANIE P. McCLELLAND
SONIA FRIEDMAN PRODUCTIONS/TULCHIN BARTNER PRODUCTIONS
THE ARACA GROUP   HENI KOENIGSBERG   DARYL ROTH   ELI BUSH

PRESENT

Fiona Shaw

IN

The Testament of Mary

BY

Colm Tóibín

SCENERY DESIGNED BY	COSTUME DESIGNED BY	LIGHTING DESIGNED BY
TOM PYE	ANN ROTH	JENNIFER TIPTON

ORIGINAL MUSIC AND SOUND DESIGN BY	PRODUCTION STAGE MANAGER	PRESS REPRESENTATIVE
MEL MERCIER	MICHAEL J. PASSARO	PHILIP RINALDI

PRODUCTION MANAGEMENT	GENERAL MANAGEMENT
AURORA PRODUCTIONS	STP/MARSHALL B. PURDY

DIRECTED BY

Deborah Warner

THE PRODUCERS WISH TO EXPRESS THEIR APPRECIATION TO THEATRE DEVELOPMENT FUND FOR ITS SUPPORT OF THIS PRODUCTION.

4/22/13

CAST
FIONA SHAW

SETTING
Now

Fiona Shaw is appearing
with the permission of
Actors' Equity Association.

Fiona Shaw

Photos by Paul Kolnik

The Testament of Mary

Fiona Shaw and Deborah Warner

This year marks the 25-year anniversary of the working partnership between Fiona Shaw and Deborah Warner. They first worked together on a landmark production of *Electra* at the Royal Shakespeare Company in 1988 (Olivier and London Critics' Awards, Best Actress). Further productions together have included *The Good Person of Sichuan* (National Theatre; Olivier and London Critics' Awards, Best Actress), *Hedda Gabler* (Abbey Theatre, Dublin and West End; London Critics' Award, Best Actress, Laurence Olivier Award for Direction and Production), *Footfalls* (Garrick Theatre, West End), *Richard II* (NT, Paris, Salzburg; French Critics Best Foreign Production), *The Waste Land* (Brussels, Dublin, Paris, Toronto, Montreal, Cork, London, Adelaide, Perth, Dublin, Bergen, Madrid and New York; two Drama Desk Awards, Best Director Obie Award); *Medea* (Abbey Theatre, Dublin, West End, BAM, Paris and Broadway; Evening Standard Award for Best Actress and Best Director; Tony Award nominations for Best Actress and Best Director and two Obie Awards), *The Powerbook* (NT), *Readings* (Paris; a poetry show), *Julius Caesar* (Barbican, Paris, Madrid and Luxembourg), *Happy Days* (NT, Epidaurus, where it made history as the first 20th century text to be performed in the ancient theatre, Amsterdam, Paris, Dublin, BAM), *Dido and Aeneas* (Vienna, Opera Comique – Paris, Amsterdam), Tony Kushner's translation of *Mother Courage and Her Children* (NT) and *Peace Camp* for the London 2012 Cultural Olympics.

Fiona Shaw

Colm Tóibín
Author

Deborah Warner
Director

Tom Pye
Set Designer

Ann Roth
Costume Designer

Jennifer Tipton
Lighting Designer

Mel Mercier
Composer/ Sound Designer

Gene O'Donovan
Aurora Productions
Production Management

Ben Heller
Aurora Productions
Production Management

Marshall B. Purdy
General Manager

Scott Rudin
Producer

Stuart Thompson
Producer

Jon B. Platt
Producer

Roger Berlind
Producer

John Gore
Broadway Across America
Producer

Beth Williams
Broadway Across America
Producer

Scott M. Delman
Producer

Jean Doumanian
Producer

Roy Furman
Producer

Stephanie P. McClelland
Producer

Sonia Friedman
Sonia Friedman Productions
Producer

Norman Tulchin
Tulchin/Bartner Productions
Producer

Heni Koenigsberg
Producer

The Testament of Mary

Michael Rego, Hank Unger, Matthew Rego
The Araca Group
Producer

Daryl Roth
Producer

MANAGEMENT
(L-R): Christopher Taggart
(Management Associate),
Jeff Siebert
(Production Assistant),
Michael J. Passaro
(Production Stage Manager),
Pat Sosnow (Stage Manager),
Michael Bolgar
(Company Manager)

Photos by Brian Mapp

BOX OFFICE
(L-R): Harry Jaffie,
Gail Yerkovich

CREW
Front Row (L-R): Brian Veith, Shelby Wong, T.J. D'Angelo, Alison Traynor, Juliett Cipriati, Kendra McDuffie
Back Row (L-R): Heather Jewels, Kaiser Akram, David Fraiden, Leslie Morgenstern, Laura Kaye

CREW
Front Row (L-R): Stephen Schroettnig, Bobby Horvath with Pinhead (the vulture), Vincent J. Valvo
Back Row (L-R): Timothy Bennet, Paul Jepson, George E. Fullum, Laura Beattie, Paul Valvo, Darin Stillman
Not Pictured: Dan Coey, Richard M. Fullum

The Testament of Mary

STAFF FOR *THE TESTAMENT OF MARY*

SCOTT RUDIN PRODUCTIONS

Steven Cardwell   Andrew Coles   Peter Cron
Taylor Hess   Robert Hoffman   David Rogers
Jason Sack   Chelsea Salyer   Dan Sarrow
Jason Shrier   Christopher Verone

GENERAL MANAGEMENT
STUART THOMPSON PRODUCTIONS
Stuart Thompson   Marshall B. Purdy
Patrick Gracey   David Turner
Kevin Emrick   Christopher Taggart
Andrew Lowy   Brittany Weber
Matthew Wright   James Yandoli

COMPANY MANAGER
Michael Bolgar

PRODUCTION MANAGEMENT
AURORA PRODUCTIONS
Gene O'Donovan   Ben Heller
Stephanie Sherline   Jarid Sumner   Anita Shah
Anthony Jusino   Liza Luxenberg
G. Garrett Ellison   Troy Pepicelli   Gayle Riess
Catherine Nelson   Melissa Mazdra

PRESS REPRESENTATIVE
PHILIP RINALDI PUBLICITY
Philip Rinaldi   Ryan Hallett
Amanda Dekker Kaus   Zoe Tarmy

Production Stage Manager ....Michael J. Passaro
Stage Manager ....Pat Sosnow
UK Management Consultant ....James Triner
Associate Scenic Designers ....Ben Gerlis,
Christine Peters
Associate Costume Designer ....Matthew Pachtman
Associate Lighting Designer ....Alan Edwards
Associate Sound Designer ....David Sanderson
Production Carpenter ....Steve Schroettnig
Advance Carpenter ....Erik Yans
Production Properties ....Paul Jepson
UK Props Supervisor ....Lizzie Frankl
U.S. Props Supervisor ....Faye Armon-Troncoso
Production Electrician ....Dan Coey
Moving Light Programmer ....Michael Hill
Production Sound Engineer ....Darin Stillman
Wardrobe Supervisor ....Laura Beattie
UK Production Associate ....Emma Cameron
Production Assistant ....Jeff Siebert
General Management Intern ....Zachary Spitzer
Production Intern ....Elizabeth Goodman
Props Assistants ....Jessica Provenzale, Polina Minchuk
Advertising ....Serino/Coyne/
Nancy Coyne, Greg Corradetti,
Carolyn London, Jason Zammit,
Elyse Familetti
Marketing ....Serino/Coyne/
Leslie Barrett, Diana Salameh,
Mike Rafael, Catherine Herzog
Digital Outreach & Website ....Serino/Coyne/
Jeff Carroll, Whitney Creighton,
Crystal Chase, Sumeet Bharati
Logo and Artwork Design .....BLT Communications, Inc.

Production Photographer ....Paul Kolnik
London Rehearsal Photography ....Hugo Glendinning
Fiona Shaw Portrait by ....Brigitte Lacombe
Accountant ....Fried & Kowgios CPAs LLP/
Robert Fried, CPA
Controller ....Galbraith & Company, Inc./Kenny Noth
Insurance ....DeWitt Stern Group
Legal Counsel ....Loeb & Loeb, LLP/
Seth Gelblum, Esq.
Banking ....City National Bank/Michele Gibbons
Payroll ....Castellana Services, Inc.
Theatre Displays ....Fine Art Imaging
Transportation ....IBA Limousine
Travel ....Tzell Travel/Andi Henig
Housing ....Road Concierge/Lisa Morris,
ABA-IDEAL/Elizabeth Helke

PRODUCTION CREDITS
Scenery constructed and automated by Showman Fabricators Inc., Long Island City, NY. Lighting equipment from PRG Lighting, a division of Production Resource Group, LLC, New Windsor, NY. Sound equipment by Sound Associates. Properties built or supplied by Nic Payne Ceramics, The Raptor Project, Hawk on the Wild Side, Vauxhall City Farm, SAS Armouries, Tarver Productions, Al Frankl, Will Gaskell, Kristine Omlid and Vik Fifield. Tree made by Claire Karoff and Lillian Clements and perch made by Nicholas Sainz Xatzis. Special thanks to Lincoln Center Theater. UK rehearsal scenery built by Paul Hennessey. Costumes by Studio Rouge, Inc. Custom fabric painting by Jeff Fender Studios. Special thanks to Noe Eccles, Kate Ellis, Alastair Goolden, Arja Kastinen, Lia Pantazopoulou, Outi Pulkkinen, Nick Roth, Francesco Turrisi, Dimitris Varelopoulos, Olesya Zdorovetska, Ray Barron Studios and The Rise Studios.

Developed by
the Dublin Theatre Festival and
Landmark Productions with the support of
Irish Theatre Trust.

Rehearsed at
the New 42nd Street Studios and the Jerwood Space

www.testamentonbroadway.com

JUJAMCYN THEATERS

JORDAN ROTH
President
ROCCO LANDESMAN
President Emeritus

PAUL LIBIN	**JACK VIERTEL**
Executive Vice President	Senior Vice President
MEREDITH VILLATORE	**JENNIFER HERSHEY**
Chief Financial Officer	Vice President,
	Building Operations
MICAH HOLLINGWORTH	**HAL GOLDBERG**
Vice President,	Vice President,
Company Operations	Theatre Operations

Director of Business Affairs ....Albert T. Kim
Director of Human Resources ....Michele Louhisdon
Director of Ticketing Services ....Justin Karr

Theatre Operations Managers ....Willa Burke,
Susan Elrod, Emily Hare,
Jeff Hubbard, Albert T. Kim
Theatre Operations Associates ....Carrie Jo Brinker,
Brian Busby, Michael Composto,
Anah Jyoti Klate
Accounting ....Cathy Cerge, Amy Frank,
Tariq Hamami, Alexander Parra
Executive Producer, Red Awning ....Nicole Kastrinos
Director of Sales, Givenik.com ....Karen Freidus
Building Operations Associate ....Erich Bussing
Ticketing and Pricing Associate ....Jonathon Scott
Executive Coordinator ....Ed Lefferson
Executive Assistants ....Clark Mims Tedesco,
Beth Given, Julia Kraus
Receptionist ....Lisa Perchinske
Sales Associate, Givenik.com ....Taylor Kurpiel
Maintenance ....Ralph Santos, Ramon Zapata
Security ....Rasim Hodzic, Terone Richardson
Interns ....Kimille Howard, Amy Larrowe,
Christopher Luner, Lana Percival, Steven Rowe

STAFF FOR THE WALTER KERR THEATRE FOR
THE TESTAMENT OF MARY

Theatre Manager ....Susan Elrod
Associate Theatre Manager ....Brian Busby
Treasurer ....Harry Jaffie
Head Carpenter ....George E. Fullum
Head Propertyman ....Timothy Bennet
Follow Spot Operator ....Paul Valvo
Head Electrician ....Vincent J. Valvo
Flyman ....Richard M. Fullum
Engineer ....Zaim Hodzic
Assistant Treasurers ....Michael Loiacono,
Joseph Smith, Gail Yerkovich
Head Usher .................................T.J. D'Angelo
Director ....Michelle Fleury
Ticket Takers ....Alison Traynor, Robert Zwaschka
Ushers ....Florence Arcaro,
Juliett Cipriati, Aaron Kendall,
Manuel Sandridge, Mallory Simms,
Ilir Velovich, Shelby Wong
Doormen ....Brandon Houghton, Kevin Wallace
Head Porter ....Marcio Martinez
Porter ....Rudy Martinez
Head Cleaner ....Sevdija Pasukanovic
Cleaner ....Lourdes Perez

Security provided by GBA Consulting, Inc.

This live vulture, Pinhead, appeared onstage during the pre-show sequence.

Photo by Brian Mapp

The Trip to Bountiful

First Preview: March 30, 2013. Opened: April 23, 2013.
Still running as of May 31, 2013.

PLAYBILL®

THE TRIP TO BOUNTIFUL

A revival of Horton Foote's 1953 play about elderly widow Carrie Watts who is sick of living in the city with her bossy daughter-in-law and milquetoast son, and longs to return once more to Bountiful, Texas, the small town where she grew up. Carrie boards a bus with the help of a sympathetic young woman who appears to her as the daughter she never got to have. A coming-of-age story for an octogenarian, the odyssey satisfies Carrie's yearnings in ways she did not expect.

CAST
(in order of appearance)

Mrs. Carrie Watts ....CICELY TYSON
Ludie Watts....................CUBA GOODING JR.
Jessie Mae Watts ....VANESSA WILLIAMS
Thelma ....CONDOLA RASHAD
Houston Ticket Agent ....DEVON ABNER
Second Houston Ticket Agent ..CURTIS BILLINGS
Roy ....ARTHUR FRENCH
Sheriff.......................................TOM WOPAT
Travelers and
Houston Bus Station Employees ..DEVON ABNER,
CURTIS BILLINGS, PAT BOWIE,
LEON ADDISON BROWN,
SUSAN HEYWARD, BILL KUX,
LINDA POWELL, CHARLES TURNER

UNDERSTUDIES

For Mrs. Carrie Watts: PAT BOWIE
For Ludie Watts: LEON ADDISON BROWN
For Jessie Mae Watts: LINDA POWELL

Continued on next page

STEPHEN SONDHEIM THEATRE

NELLE NUGENT
PAULA MARIE BLACK   DAVID R. WEINREB   KENNETH TEATON   STEPHEN BYRD   ALIA M. JONES
CAROLE L. HABER/PHILIP GEIER   WENDY FEDERMAN/CARL MOELLENBERG/RICARDO HORNOS
FIFTY CHURCH STREET PRODUCTIONS/HALLIE FOOTE

IN ASSOCIATION WITH

KEVIN LILES   JOSEPH SIROLA   HOWARD AND JANET KAGAN/CHARLES SALAMENO   SHARON A. CARR/PATRICIA R. KLAUSNER
RAYMOND GASPARD   WILLETTE MURPHY KLAUSNER/REGINALD M. BROWNE

PRESENT

CICELY TYSON   CUBA GOODING JR.   VANESSA WILLIAMS

IN

THE TRIP TO BOUNTIFUL

BY

HORTON FOOTE

ALSO STARRING

CONDOLA RASHAD

AND

TOM WOPAT

WITH

DEVON ABNER   CURTIS BILLINGS   ARTHUR FRENCH
PAT BOWIE   LEON ADDISON BROWN   SUSAN HEYWARD   BILL KUX   LINDA POWELL   CHARLES TURNER

SCENIC DESIGN	COSTUME DESIGN	LIGHTING DESIGN	ORIGINAL MUSIC AND SOUND DESIGN
JEFF COWIE	VAN BROUGHTON RAMSEY	RUI RITA	JOHN GROMADA

HAIR DESIGN	MAKE-UP DESIGN	ADVERTISING & MARKETING	CASTING
PAUL HUNTLEY	ANGELINA AVALLONE	AKA	CAPARELLIOTIS CASTING

TECHNICAL SUPERVISION	PRESS REPRESENTATIVE	COMPANY MANAGER	PRODUCTION STAGE MANAGER
HUDSON THEATRICAL ASSOCIATES	THE HARTMAN GROUP	JENNIFER HINDMAN KEMP	ROBERT BENNETT

ASSOCIATE PRODUCERS	ASSOCIATE DIRECTOR	GENERAL MANAGER
FRANCESCA ZAMBELLO FAITH GAY	DAVID ALPERT	PETER BOGYO

DIRECTED BY

MICHAEL WILSON

The Producers wish to express their appreciation to Theatre Development Fund for its support of this production.

4/23/13

(L-R): Cicely Tyson and Cuba Gooding Jr.

Photo by Joan Marcus

The Trip to Bountiful

Cast Continued

For Thelma: SUSAN HEYWARD
For Roy: CHARLES TURNER
For Sheriff: DEVON ABNER
For Houston Ticket Agent: BILL KUX
For Second Houston Ticket Agent: BILL KUX

SETTING

Houston, Harrison and a country place in Texas
March, 1953

MUSICIANS

Conductor and Piano: LYNNE SHANKEL
Cello: DANIEL MILLER
Clarinet, Flute: RICHARD HECKMAN
Trumpet: ROBERT MILLIKAN
Bass: DAVID PHILLIPS
Vocals: AISHA de HAAS

Cicely Tyson
Mrs. Carrie Watts

Cuba Gooding Jr.
Ludie Watts

Vanessa Williams
Jessie Mae Watts

Condola Rashad
Thelma

Tom Wopat
Sheriff

Devon Abner
Houston Ticket Agent; u/s Sheriff

Curtis Billings
Second Houston Ticket Agent

Pat Bowie
Ensemble; u/s Mrs. Carrie Watts

Leon Addison Brown
Ensemble; u/s Ludie Watts

Arthur French
Roy

Susan Heyward
Ensemble; u/s Thelma

Bill Kux
Ensemble; u/s Houston Ticket Agent

Linda Powell
Ensemble; u/s Jessie Mae Watts

Charles Turner
Ensemble; u/s Roy

Horton Foote
Playwright

Michael Wilson
Director

Rui Rita
Lighting Design

John Gromada
Composer/ Sound Design

Paul Huntley
Wig Design

Kate Wilson
Voice Coach

David Caparelliotis
Caparelliotis Casting
Casting

Neil A. Mazzella
Hudson Theatrical Associates
Technical Supervision

Peter Bogyo
General Manager

David Alpert
Associate Director

Paula Marie Black
Producer

Stephen C. Byrd
Producer

The Trip to Bountiful

Alia M. Jones
Producer

Carole Haber
Producer

Philip H. Geier
Producer

Wendy Federman
Federman/
Moellenberg/Hornos
Producer

Carl Moellenberg
Federman/
Moellenberg/Hornos
Producer

Ricardo Hornos
Federman/
Moellenberg/Hornos
Producer

Rick Costello
Fifty Church Street
Productions
Producer

Hallie Foote
Producer

Kevin Liles
Producer

Joseph Sirola
Producer

Howard & Janet Kagan
Producers

Sharon A. Carr
Producer

Patricia R. Klausner
Producer

Raymond Gaspard
Producer

Reginald M. Browne
Producer

Francesca Zambello
Producer

Faith Gay
Producer

(L-R): Cicely Tyson and Condola Rashad

Photo by Joan Marcus

(L-R): Vanessa Williams and Cuba Gooding Jr.

Photo by Joan Marcus

2012-2013 AWARDS

TONY AWARD
Best Performance by an Actress
in a Leading Role in a Play
(Cicely Tyson)

DRAMA DESK AWARD
Outstanding Actress in a Play
(Cicely Tyson)

OUTER CRITICS CIRCLE AWARD
Outstanding Actress in a Play
(Cicely Tyson)

The Trip to Bountiful

BOX OFFICE
(L-R): Ronnie Tobia,
Jaime Perlman

Photos by Brian Mapp

GOTHAM SECURITY
Front (L-R): Joe Lopez, Brandon Blakes
Back (L-R): Keith Edwards, Carlos Ortiz

FRONT OF HOUSE
Left Side (Bottom to Top): Diana Trent Vargas, Molly McQuilkin, Karen Murray,
Kristopher Kaye, Roger Darbaise, Trevor Rex, Travis Navarra, Justin Brown
Right Side (Bottom to Top): Johannah-Joy Magyawe, Candice Schnurr,
Linda Gjonbalaj, Brian Nicholas Rossi, Nicole Ramirez, Jessica Alverson

HAIR/WARDROBE
(L-R): Katherine Sorg (Dresser),
Eileen Miller (Wardrobe Supervisor),
Daniel Koye (Hair & Makeup Supervisor),
Mary Ann Lewis-Oberpriller (Dresser)

CREW
Front (L-R): Alex Neumann (Associate Sound Designer), Paul Ashton, Jocelyn Smith,
Ed Chapman (Sound Engineer), Andrew Sullivan
Back (L-R): Eileen Miller, William Craven, Rebecca Heroff, Steve Beers, Josh Weitzman, Andrew Forste,
Donald "Buck" Roberts

STAGE MANAGEMENT
Front: Jereme Kyle Lewis (Production Asst.)
Back (L-R): Robert Bennett (Production Stage
Manager), Diane DiVita (Stage Manager)

The Trip to Bountiful
Scrapbook

Correspondent: Bill Kux, Ensemble
Memorable Opening Night Letter, Fax or Note: We received a Fax from many Broadway companies, but most memorably from the Australian Touring Company of *Driving Miss Daisy* signed by Angela Lansbury and James Earl Jones.
Most Exciting Celebrity Visitor and What They Did/Said: We've had an array of celebrities including Jessye Norman, Barbara Cook, Audra McDonald, Hal Holbrook, Garrett Morris, Ruby Dee, Bill Duke, Isaiah Thomas, Blair Underwood and Tom Cruise (with two security guards). Two who made a big impression because of their heartfelt reactions were Liza Minnelli and Tony Bennett.
Special Backstage Rituals: The company warm-ups were often led by the indefatigable Kate Wilson. "My mind is my own," "The lips the teeth the tip of the tongue," "Show me the money." One evening we saw a spontaneous break dance demonstration by Cuba Gooding, Jr., who still has the moves.
Favorite Moment During Each Performance: We always listen to Miss Tyson, possessed by the spirit and breaking into "Blessed Assurance" during the Harrison bus station scene and taking the audience along with her. There was such a response every night that the New York Times featured this phenomenon on the front page of the Tuesday, May 28 paper.
Favorite Snack Food: I provide freshly baked cakes (KuxCakes: I'm just a Broadway Baker) every week. The favorite seemed to be Kentucky Bourbon Cake judging by how quickly it's devoured.
Most Memorable Ad-Lib: In the last moments of the play, Mother Watts suddenly remembers where she has hidden the all-important pension check and dips into her décolletage to retrieve it. At an early preview, Miss Tyson dipped but came up empty. She dipped to the right, left and further south to the delighted screams of laughter from the audience. No check. She finally said to Vanessa Williams as Jessie Mae, "When I find it I'll give it to you" and Vanessa, without missing a beat, said, "And I'll give it right back."
Nicknames: "Dirty Half Dozen" for the Men's Dressing Room.
Catchphrases Only the Company Would Recognize: "Are we walking yet?" "MOTHER WATTS!" "Feel that dirt."
Memorable Directorial Note: When Michael turned the show over to the company at the end of the preview period, bursting with emotion, love and tremendous pride.
Also: We love to hear the gentle crooning of Tom Wopat singing Joni Mitchell in the dressing room next door, interspersed with groans, oaths and shrieks of despair when the Brewers miss a play.

STAFF LISTING FOR *THE TRIP TO BOUNTIFUL*

GENERAL MANAGER
Peter Bogyo

COMPANY MANAGER
Jennifer Hindman Kemp

GENERAL PRESS REPRESENTATIVE
THE HARTMAN GROUP
Michael Hartman   Tom D'Ambrosio   Frances White

CASTING
David Caparelliotis, CSA

PRODUCTION STAGE MANAGER .....Robert Bennett
Stage Manager ....Diane DiVita
Associate Director ....David Alpert
Associate Set Designer ....Aimee B. Dombo
Associate Costume Designer ....Leon Dobkowski
Associate Lighting Designer ....John Viesta III
Associate Sound Designer ....Alex Neumann
Production Coordinator ....Patrick Mediate
Automated Light Programmer ....Jay Penfield
Assistant to the
    General Manager ....Anthony McDonald
Production Assistants ....Jereme Kyle Lewis,
    Wade Dooley
SDC Foundation Observer ....Sydney Chatman
Assistant to Lighting Designer ....Mandi Effpie
Sound Design Intern ....Kristin Rizzo
Production Carpenter.......................Geoffrey Quart
Production Electrician ....James Maloney
Production Sound Engineer ....Ed Chapman
Production Assistant Sound ....Alex Neumann
Production Properties Coordinator ....Propaganda LLC
Wardrobe Supervisor ....Eileen Miller
Dressers ....Mary Ann Lewis-Oberpriller,
    Katherine Sorg
Hair & Makeup Supervisor ....Daniel Koye
Voice Coach ....Kate Wilson
Singing Consultant ....Deborah Lapidus
Movement Consultants ....Mark Olsen, Hope Clark

Scenery Graphics Designer ....Aimee Dombo
Advertising/Marketing/Digital ....AKA/
    Elizabeth Furze, Scott A. Moore,
    Bashan Aquart, Melissa Marano,
    Danielle Barchetto, Sarah Borenstein,
    Adam Jay, Jamaal Parham, Flora Pei,
    Janette Roush, Sara Rosenzweig, Jen Taylor
Marketing Consultants ....UniWorld Group, Inc.
Web Design/Maintenance ....AKA
Special Promotions ....Jeffrey Solis
Accountant ....Fried & Kowigos CPA's LLP/
    Robert Fried, CPA
Controller ....Galbraith & Company, Inc./
    Tabitha Falcone
Banking ....First Republic Bank/Marianne Johnson
Insurance ....DeWitt Stern/Peter Shoemaker
Legal Counsel ....David H. Friedlander, Esq.
Production Photography ....Joan Marcus
Inhouse Photography ....Lisa Pacino
Opening Night Coordination ....Serino/Coyne LLC/
    Suzanne Tobak
Payroll Service ....Castellana Services Inc.
Rehearsal Space ....Chelsea Studios
Theatre Displays ....BAM Signs, Inc./Adam Miller

THE FOXBORO COMPANY, INC.

Nelle Nugent ....President and CEO
Kenneth Teaton ....SVP Production and Creative Affairs
Patrick Mediate ....Development Manager

CREDITS

Scenery fabrication by Hudson Scenic Studio, Inc. Lighting equipment from PRG Lighting. Sound equipment by Sound Associates. Costumes for Miss Tyson, Miss Williams and Miss Rashad by Eric Winterling, Inc. Uniforms and costumes by Western Costume Co. Custom shoes by Western Costume Co. Millinery by Lynne Mackey Studio. Custom shirts by Cego. Additional costumes from the Costume House and Helen Uffner Vintage Clothing.

MUSIC CREDITS

"**Satin Doll**" written by Duke Ellington. Courtesy of Sony/ATV Music Publishing, LLC. "**Blue Moon**" written by Richard Rodgers and Lorenz Hart. Courtesy of Sony/ATV Music Publishing, LLC. "**Don't Let the Stars Get in Your Eyes**" written by Slim Willet, Kenneth Burns and Henry Haynes. Courtesy of Sony/ATV Music Publishing, LLC. "**I Apologize**" written by Al Hoffman, Al Goodhart and Ed Nelson. Courtesy of Warner/Chappell Music, Inc. Music clearance by BZ/Rights & Permissions, Inc.

SPECIAL THANKS

Charles Davis, Myrtis Outlar, Betty Joyce Sikora, Rosa and Spencer Green, Reverend Ruiel Taylor, Robert Garcia, Robert Nelson, Josh Fitts, Diane Woods, Mary Nelle Wiley, Betty Jo Dickerson, Frankie Mangum, Dorothy Randle, Millard McQueen, Mr. and Mrs. Dale McCrohan, David Woolard, Russell Martin, Robert Garcia, Millard McQueen & Cynthia Franco of the Horton Foote Papers at Southern Methodist University's DeGolyer Library

For all tickets, including groups, please contact
Telecharge.com: (212) 239-6200
Outside of New York: 1-800- 432-7250
or www.telecharge.com

STEPHEN SONDHEIM THEATRE
SYDNEY BEERS   GREG BACKSTROM
General Manager   Associate Managing Director
VALERIE SIMMONS
Operations Manager

STEPHEN SONDHEIM THEATRE STAFF
House Manager ....Johannah-Joy G. Magyawe
Assistant House Manager ....Molly McQuilkin
Treasurer ....Jaime Perlman
House Carpenter ....Steve Beers
House Electrician ....Josh Weitzman
House Properties ....Andrew Forste
Assistant Treasurers ....Andrew Clements,
    Carlos Morris, Ronnie Tobia
Engineer ....Deosarran
Security ....Gotham Security
Maintenance ....Juan Hernandez
Lobby Refreshments by ....Sweet Hospitality Group

Vanya and Sonia and Masha and Spike

First Preview: March 5, 2013. Opened: March 14, 2013.
Still running as of May 31, 2013.

PLAYBILL®

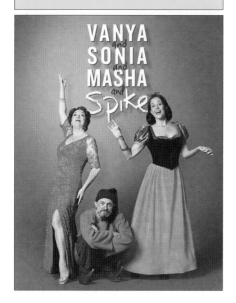

Christopher Durang pokes fun at both Anton Chekhov and modern showbiz in this comedy about two grown siblings who welcome a visit from their movie-star sister at their country house, only to find she has brought along her buff boy-toy—and her epic ego. The characters and situations are contemporary, yet manage to echo those from Chekhov plays The Seagull, The Three Sisters, The Cherry Orchard *and Uncle Vanya. The play is notable for its series of show-stopping comic speeches for each of the characters.*

CAST
(in order of appearance)

Vanya .... DAVID HYDE PIERCE
Sonia .... KRISTINE NIELSEN
Cassandra .... SHALITA GRANT
Masha .... SIGOURNEY WEAVER
Spike .... BILLY MAGNUSSEN
Nina .... GENEVIEVE ANGELSON

TIME and PLACE

Set in the present, in a lovely farmhouse
in Bucks County

UNDERSTUDIES

For Sonia and Masha: LINDA MARIE LARSON
For Cassandra: HEATHER ALICIA SIMMS
For Spike: CREED GARNICK
For Nina: LIESEL ALLEN YEAGER

---

⑤ GOLDEN THEATRE
A Shubert Organization Theatre
Philip J. Smith, *Chairman*   **Robert E. Wankel,** *President*

JOEY PARNES   LARRY HIRSCHHORN

JOAN RAFFE/JHETT TOLENTINO   MARTIN PLATT & DAVID ELLIOTT   PAT FLICKER ADDISS   CATHERINE ADLER   JOHN O'BOYLE
JOSHUA GOODMAN   JAMIE DEROY/RICHARD WINKLER   CRICKET HOOPER JIRANEK/MICHAEL PALITZ
MARK S. GOLUB & DAVID S. GOLUB   RADIO MOUSE ENTERTAINMENT   SHADOWCATCHER ENTERTAINMENT   MARY COSSETTE/BARBARA MANOCHERIAN
MEGAN SAVAGE/MEREDITH LYNSEY SCHADE   HUGH HYSELL/RICHARD JORDAN   CHERYL WIESENFELD/RON SIMONS
S.D. WAGNER   JOHN JOHNSON

IN ASSOCIATION WITH
McCARTER THEATRE CENTER   LINCOLN CENTER THEATER

PRESENT

SIGOURNEY WEAVER   DAVID HYDE PIERCE

IN

VANYA and SONIA
and MASHA and Spike

A NEW COMEDY BY
CHRISTOPHER DURANG

WITH
KRISTINE NIELSEN

AND
BILLY MAGNUSSEN

SHALITA GRANT   GENEVIEVE ANGELSON

SCENIC DESIGN	COSTUME DESIGN	LIGHTING DESIGN	ORIGINAL MUSIC & SOUND DESIGN
DAVID KORINS	EMILY REBHOLZ	JUSTIN TOWNSEND	MARK BENNETT
CASTING	PRODUCTION STAGE MANAGER	PRESS REPRESENTATIVE	ADVERTISING & MARKETING
DANIEL SWEE	DENISE YANEY	O&M CO.	SPOTCO

DIRECTED BY
NICHOLAS MARTIN

ORIGINALLY COMMISSIONED AND PRODUCED BY McCARTER THEATRE, PRINCETON, N.J. EMILY MANN, ARTISTIC DIRECTOR; TIMOTHY J. SHIELDS, MANAGING DIRECTOR; MARA ISAACS, PRODUCING DIRECTOR
AND PRODUCED BY LINCOLN CENTER THEATER, NEW YORK CITY, UNDER THE DIRECTION OF ANDRE BISHOP AND BERNARD GERSTEN, IN 2012.

THE PRODUCERS WISH TO EXPRESS THEIR APPRECIATION TO THEATRE DEVELOPMENT FUND FOR ITS SUPPORT OF THIS PRODUCTION.

3/14/13

(L-R): Billy Magnussen, Kristine Nielsen, Sigourney Weaver, Genevieve Angelson, and David Hyde Pierce

Photo by Carol Rosegg

Vanya and Sonia and Masha and Spike

Sigourney Weaver
Masha

David Hyde Pierce
Vanya

Kristine Nielsen
Sonia

Billy Magnussen
Spike

Shalita Grant
Cassandra

Genevieve Angelson
Nina

Creed Garnick
u/s Spike

Linda Marie Larson
u/s Sonia, Masha

Heather Alicia Simms
u/s Cassandra

Liesel Allen Yeager
u/s Nina

Christopher Durang
Playwright

Nicholas Martin
Director

David Korins
Sets

Emily Rebholz
Costumes

Justin Townsend
Lighting

Mark Bennett
Original Music and Sound

Daniel Swee
Casting Director

Leah J. Loukas
Wig Designer

Joey Parnes
Producer

Larry Hirschhorn
Producer

Joan Raffe
Producer

Jhett Tolentino
Producer

Martin Platt
Producer

David Elliott
Producer

Pat Flicker Addiss
Producer

Catherine Adler
Producer

John O'Boyle
Producer

Joshua Goodman
Producer

Jamie deRoy
Producer

Richard Winkler
Producer

Cricket Hooper Jiranek
Producer

Michael Palitz
Producer

Mark S. Golub
Producer

David S. Golub
Producer

M. Kilburg Reedy
Radio Mouse Entertainment
Producer

Vanya and Sonia and Masha and Spike

Jason E. Grossman
Radio Mouse
Entertainment
Producer

Mary Cossette
Producer

Barbara
Manocherian
Producer

Megan Savage
Producer

Meredith Lynsey
Schade
Producer

Hugh Hysell
Producer

Richard Jordan
Producer

Cheryl Wiesenfeld
Producer

Ron Simons
Producer

S.D. Wagner
Producer

John Johnson
Producer

Emily Mann
*Artistic Director
McCarter Theatre
Center*

Timothy J. Shields
*Managing Director
McCarter Theatre
Center*

André Bishop
*Artistic Director
Lincoln Center
Theater*

Bernard Gersten
*Executive Producer
Lincoln Center
Theater*

Amelia McClain
u/s Nina

Photo by Brian Mapp

BOX OFFICE TREASURERS
(L-R): Diane Lettieri, Gary Powers

(L-R): Sigourney Weaver, Kristine Nielsen
and Billy Magnussen

Photo by Carol Rosegg

2012-2013 AWARDS

TONY AWARD
Best Play

NEW YORK DRAMA CRITICS' CIRCLE AWARD
Best Play

DRAMA DESK AWARD
Outstanding Play

OUTER CRITICS CIRCLE AWARDS
Outstanding New Broadway Play
Outstanding Featured Actress in a Play
(Kristine Nielsen)

DRAMA LEAGUE AWARD
Distinguished Production
of a Play

RICHARD SEFF AWARD
Outstanding Character Actor
50 Years of Age or Older
(Kristine Nielsen)

THEATRE WORLD AWARD
For Outstanding Broadway
or Off-Broadway Debut
(Shalita Grant)

Vanya and Sonia and Masha and Spike

Photo by Brian Mapp

CREW

Sitting on Floor (L-R): Esther Vasquez (Usher), Sylvia Yoshioka (Head Electrician), Jeannie Naughton (Dresser), Ruddi Almonte (Usher), Edytha Harlin (Usher)
Sitting in Chairs (L-R): Rita Russell (Ticket Taker), Denise Yaney (Stage Manager)
Standing (L-R): Dylan Foley (Production Props), Patricia Byrne (Usher), Margie Howard (Asst. Stage Manager), Sheila Staffney (Usher), Terry McGarty (Head Carpenter), Deborah McIntyre (Usher), Carolyne A. Jones-Barnes (House Manager), Thomas Mitchell (Head Props), Yolanda Ramsay (Hair/Wigs Supervisor), Wayne Smith (Sound), Julia Gonzalez (Usher), Yuri Fernandez (Porter), Helen Bentley (Chief Usher), Mae Smith (Asst. Chief Usher), Audrey Maher (Dresser)

STAFF FOR
VANYA AND SONIA AND MASHA AND SPIKE

GENERAL MANAGEMENT
JOEY PARNES PRODUCTIONS
Joey Parnes
John Johnson   S.D. Wagner
Chie Morita

COMPANY MANAGER
Kit Ingui

PRESS REPRESENTATIVE
O&M CO.
Rick Miramontez   Andy Snyder
Marie Pace

Production Stage Manager ....Denise Yaney
Stage Manager .................................M.A. Howard
Assistant Director ....Bryan Hunt
Associate Set Designer ....Rod Lemmond
Assistant Costume Designer ....Ren Ladassor
Associate Lighting Designer ....Chris Thielking
Associate Sound Designer ....Josh Liebert
Associate Sound Designer ....Charles Coes
Wig Designer ....Leah J. Loukas
Production Carpenter ....Larry Morley
Production Properties ....Mike Smanko
Production Electrician...........................Dan Coey
Audio Engineer ....Wayne Smith
Wardrobe Supervisor ....Lynn Bowling
Dressers ....Audrey Maher, Jean Marie Naughton
Hair/Wig Supervisor ....Yolanda Ramsay
Outside Props ....James Keane
Production Assistant ....Emily DaSilva
Casting Associate ....Camille Hickman

Advertising/Marketing/Interactive ....SpotCo/
Drew Hodges, Jim Edwards,
Tom Greenwald, Nick Pramik,
Stephen Sosnowski, Beth Watson,
Ryan Zatcoff, Kristen Rathbun,
Julie Wechsler, Sheila Collins
Press Associates ....Sarah Babin, Molly Barnett,
Scott Braun, Philip Carrubba,
Jon Dimond, Joyce Friedmann,
Michael Jorgensen, Yufen Kung,
Chelsea Nachman, Ryan Ratelle,
Pete Sanders, Elizabeth Wagner
Press Interns ....Valentina Berger Maurette,
Clio McConnell
Legal Counsel ....Lazarus & Harris LLP/
Scott Lazarus, Esq., Robert Harris, Esq.
Accountants ....Marks Paneth & Shron LLP/
Mark A. D'Ambrosi, Patricia M. Pedersen,
Petrina Moritz
Banking ....City National Bank/
Stephanie Dalton, Michele Gibbons
Insurance ....AON/Albert G. Ruben/
George Walden, Claudia B. Kaufman
Payroll ....Castellana Services Inc./
Lance Castellana, James Castellana,
Norman Sewell
Physical Therapy ....PhysioArts
Production Photographer ....Carol Rosegg
Production Videographer ....Fresh Produce Productions/
Frank Basile
Opening Night Coordination ....The Lawrence Company/
Michael Lawrence

CREDITS

Scenery fabricated and painted by Global Scenic Services, Inc., Bridgeport, CT. Lighting equipment by PRG. Sound equipment by Masque Sound. "Here Comes the Sun" written by George Harrison, published by Wixen Music Publishing, Inc.

Souvenir merchandise provided by
Encore Merchandising, Inc.

Rehearsed at the New 42nd Street Rehearsal Studios.

SPECIAL THANKS
Mara Isaacs, Adam Siegel, Patrick Herold

THE SHUBERT ORGANIZATION, INC.
Board of Directors

Philip J. Smith   Robert E. Wankel
Chairman   President

Wyche Fowler, Jr.   Diana Phillips

Lee J. Seidler   Michael I. Sovern

Stuart Subotnick

Chief Financial Officer ....Elliot Greene
Sr. Vice President, Ticketing ....David Andrews
Vice President, Finance ....Juan Calvo
Vice President, Human Resources ....Cathy Cozens
Vice President, Facilities ....John Darby
Vice President, Theatre Operations ....Peter Entin
Vice President, Marketing ....Charles Flateman
Vice President, Audit ....Anthony LaMattina
Vice President, Ticket Sales ....Brian Mahoney
Vice President, Creative Projects ............D.S. Moynihan
Vice President, Real Estate ....Julio Peterson

---

House Manager ....Carolyne A. Jones-Barnes

Vanya and Sonia and Masha and Spike
SCRAPBOOK

①

Correspondent: Genevieve Angelson, "Nina"

Opening Night Gifts: Chris Durang gave me a hat with a Hootie Owl from Bucks County that I love and wear out of the theatre every night.

Most Exciting Celebrity Visitor and What They Did/Said: We were all pretty stunned by meeting Carol Burnett. But I was personally pretty jazzed to meet Oliver Platt! His performance in *The Impostors*... unforgettable. And of course I get to meet my favorite celebrity every night as Nina: Masha Hardwicke!

Sampling of the Many Ways the Title Has Been Mangled by Fans: They always leave the "Nina" out of the title. What's up with that?

Special Backstage Rituals: When we opened at the McCarter, David gave all of us little stuffed Blue Herons that make real Blue Heron bird calls. Kristine and Sigourney and Shalita and I used to make the birds call to each other when we shared a dressing room (at LCT and the McCarter), saying nothing else. I miss that now that we have our own dressing rooms.

Favorite Moment During Each Performance: Mr. Durang wrote a beautiful play, but I must confess, I can't think of any theatrical experience that would trump my daily head massage from Hair/Wig specialist Yolanda Ramsay or loving visits with dresser Jeannie Naughton.

Favorite In-Theatre Gathering Place: The conversation in the understudy-girls-dressing-room can get pretty graphic and juicy!!! Makes the boy understudies blush.

Favorite Off-Site Hangout: We hang out

1. (L-R): *Yearbook* Correspondent Genevieve Angelson, Sigourney Weaver, Billy Magnussen, David Hyde Pierce, Kristine Nielsen and Shalita Grant take a bow on opening night.
2. A kiss from Christopher Durang at curtain call.
3. At the opening night party, Magnussen gets to the heart of director Nicholas Martin.
4. After the opening night show with Durang (C) and cast (L-R) Billy Magnussen, Genevieve Angelson, Sigourney Weaver, David Hyde Pierce, Kristine Nielsen and Shalita Grant.

③

every Sunday on-site for brunch!! And we throw the best birthday parties on Broadway. I'm talking streamers.

Favorite Snack Food: ANY birthday cake ever made by our amazing ASM Margie Howard. Also, every Sunday we cheer for QUICHE by DENICHE!!! (Stage Manager.)

Mascot: People, lions, eagles, partridges, raccoons, porpoises, opossums, hedgehogs, woodchucks, geese, spiders, octopuses, foxes, wild turkeys, frogs, blue herons, and Tommy Kirk, one of the Hardy Boys on the Mickey Mouse Show. We don't discriminate.

Favorite Therapy: Sarah from Physio Arts, Grether's Pastilles, Andrzej Leszczynski from Holsome in our days back at the McCarter. Billy eats about 80 wintergreen Altoids every show.

Record Number of Cell Phone Rings, Cell Phone Photos or Texting Incidents During a Performance: Almost never because that's a particularly enormous faux pas in our play. The few times it has happened I thought David might go on a killing rampage. And he almost never does that.

Memorable Fan Encounter: Once an old man kissed me and said I was a beautiful Roman princess.

Busiest Day at the Box Office: At our first preview there was a line around the block and my heart soared with the Broadway magic of it.

Fastest Quick Change: Sigourney into Snow White. That was basically all we stopped for in our tech rehearsals, which were otherwise criminally easy and painless. It's an impressive change.

Who Wore the Least: Nicky Martin.

Nicknames: My personal favorite is Sigo-go Wee-Wee.

Sweethearts Within the Company: There have been rumors about Creed Garnick and Keith Reddin.

Embarrassing Moments: Last week I fell on my face in a giant pink princess costume. I've been less embarrassed.

Ghostly Encounters Backstage: I thought that only happened at the Belasco!

Superstition That Turned Out To Be True: People can actually break legs on stage. Christopher Durang did it just before our transfer!

Coolest Thing About Being in This Show: The pride of representing Chris Durang.

④

War Horse

First Preview: March 15, 2011. Opened: April 14, 2011.
Closed January 6, 2013 after 33 Previews and 718 Performances.

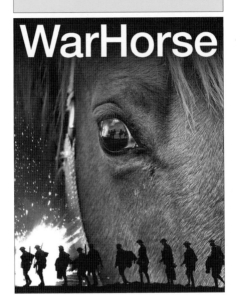

PLAYBILL

A young man braves the battlefields of World War I in order to retrieve his pet horse who has been sold to the cavalry. Lincoln Center Theater's transfer of the hit National Theatre production is notable for its arresting physical design, especially the horses—huge puppets manipulated by multiple puppeteers simultaneously.

CAST

THE HORSES

Joey as a foal ....HUNTER CANNING,
DAVID PEGRAM, HANNAH SLOAT
Joey ....TOBY BILLOWITZ, LUTE BREUER,
JOEL REUBEN GANZ, ARIEL HELLER,
ALEX HOEFFLER, LEAH HOFMANN,
JESLYN KELLY, TOM LEE,
JONATHAN CHRISTOPHER MacMILLAN,
JONATHAN DAVID MARTIN, JUDE SANDY,
or ISAAC WOOFER
Topthorn ....TOBY BILLOWITZ,
LUTE BREUER, JOEL REUBEN GANZ,
ARIEL HELLER, ALEX HOEFFLER,
LEAH HOFMANN, JESLYN KELLY, TOM LEE,
JONATHAN CHRISTOPHER MacMILLAN,
JONATHAN DAVID MARTIN, JUDE SANDY,
or ISAAC WOOFER
Coco ....TOBY BILLOWITZ, LUTE BREUER,
JOEL REUBEN GANZ, ALEX HOEFFLER,
JESLYN KELLY, TOM LEE,
JONATHAN DAVID MARTIN,
or ISAAC WOOFER
Heine ....NAT McINTYRE, TOMMY SCHRIDER
Continued on next page

**LINCOLN CENTER THEATER
AT THE VIVIAN BEAUMONT**

under the direction of
André Bishop and **Bernard Gersten**

NATIONAL THEATRE OF GREAT BRITAIN
under the direction of
Nicholas Hytner and **Nick Starr**
in association with
Bob Boyett **War Horse LP**
presents
National Theatre of Great Britain production

WarHorse

based on the novel by **Michael Morpurgo**
adapted by **Nick Stafford**
in association with **Handspring Puppet Company**
with (in alphabetical order)

Stephen James Anthony   Toby Billowitz   Alyssa Bresnahan   Lute Breuer   Hunter Canning
Anthony Cochrane   Richard Crawford   Sanjit De Silva   Andrew Durand   Joel Reuben Ganz
Ben Graney   Ariel Heller   Alex Hoeffler   Leah Hofmann   Ben Horner   Brian Lee Huynh
Jeslyn Kelly   Tessa Klein   David Lansbury   Tom Lee   Jonathan Christopher MacMillan
David Manis   Jonathan David Martin   Nat McIntyre   Andy Murray   David Pegram
Kate Pfaffl   Jude Sandy   Tommy Schrider   Hannah Sloat   Jack Spann   Elliot Villar
Isaac Woofer   Katrina Yaukey   Madeleine Rose Yen

sets, costumes & drawings	puppet design, fabrication and direction	lighting
Rae Smith	**Adrian Kohler** with **Basil Jones** for Handspring Puppet Company	**Paule Constable**

director of movement and horse movement	animation & projection design
Toby Sedgwick	**59 Productions**

music	songmaker	sound	music director
Adrian Sutton	**John Tams**	**Christopher Shutt**	**Greg Pliska**

associate puppetry director	artistic associate	production stage manager	casting
Mervyn Millar	**Samuel Adamson**	**Rick Steiger**	**Daniel Swee**

NT technical producer	NT producer	NT associate producer	NT marketing	Boyett Theatricals producer
Katrina Gilroy	**Chris Harper**	**Robin Hawkes**	**Karl Westworth**	**Tim Levy**

managing director	production manager	executive director of development & planning	director of marketing	general press agent
Adam Siegel	**Jeff Hamlin**	**Hattie K. Jutagir**	**Linda Mason Ross**	**The Hartman Group**

directed by
Marianne Elliott and **Tom Morris**

Leadership Support from The Jerome L. Greene Foundation.
Major Support from Ellen and Howard Katz in honor of Marianne Elliott,
Florence and Robert Kaufman, The Blanche and Irving Laurie Foundation,
and The National Endowment for the Arts.
Generous Support from Laura Pels International Foundation for Theater and
The Henry Nias Foundation courtesy of Dr. Stanley Edelman.
National Theatre is supported by Arts Council England

Sponsor

American Airlines
250 Cities. 40 Countries.
Official Airline

Supported by
**ARTS COUNCIL
ENGLAND**

10/8/12

(L-R): Andrew Durand, "Joey" and Leah Hofmann

Photo by Paul Kolnik

War Horse

THE FIRST WORLD WAR — also known as The Great War and The War to End All Wars — took place mainly in Europe between August 1914 and November 1918. The assassination of Archduke Franz Ferdinand of Austria on June 28, 1914, triggered a chain of events that systematically severed the economic alliances and blood ties that held the royal houses of Europe in a mutually beneficial peace. An estimated 10 million soldiers lost their lives during the resulting war, which began with German troops sweeping into Luxembourg and Belgium on August 4.

The United Kingdom, France, Russia, and later Italy and the United States headed the Allied Powers which defeated the Central Powers, led by the Austro-Hungarian, German and Ottoman Empires. World War I caused the disintegration of the Austro-Hungarian, German, Ottoman and Russian Empires, and the cost of the war also began the breakup of the British Empire and left France devastated for more than 25 years. Unresolved questions of who was to blame and who suffered the most in the Great War continued to trouble the old and new nations of Europe, sowing the seeds for the start of World War II more than 20 years later.

Although American involvement in the war was relatively short, the U.S. suffered more than 300,000 casualties. Nonetheless, the U.S. involvement was a decisive factor in the Allied victory of 1918.

The war's western front, which stretched 440 miles from the Swiss border to the North Sea and where the action of *War Horse* takes place, was a line of trenches, dug-outs and barbed-wire fences, with an area known as "no man's land" between them.

The engagement of war was revolutionized during World War I when the surprise, speed, precision and ruthlessness of the horse cavalry was upended by the introduction of barbed wire and automatic machine guns. And towards the end of the war a new weapon emerged. It was mobile, deflected machine gun bullets and crushed barb wire. The horse had been replaced by the tank.

A total of eight million horses died during World War I. One million English horses were taken to France to be used by the British Army. Only 62,000 of them were brought back to England.

UNDERSTUDIES

For Joey as a Foal: BEN GRANEY, BRIAN LEE HUYNH, TESSA KLEIN

For Song Woman, Song Man: KATRINA YAUKEY

For Lt. Nicholls or Cpt. Stewart: BEN GRANEY, TOMMY SCHRIDER

For Arthur: ANTHONY COCHRANE, RICHARD CRAWFORD

For Billy: HUNTER CANNING, DAVID PEGRAM

For Albert: STEPHEN JAMES ANTHONY, HUNTER CANNING

For Ted: ANTHONY COCHRANE, NAT McINTYRE

For Chapman Carter: DAVID LANSBURY, ELLIOT VILLAR

For Allan: BEN HORNER, DAVID LANSBURY

For Thomas Bone: BEN HORNER, DAVID PEGRAM, JACK SPANN

For Rose: TESSA KLEIN, KATRINA YAUKEY

For Priest: TOMMY SCHRIDER, ELLIOT VILLAR

For Sgt. Thunder: ANTHONY COCHRANE, ANDY MURRAY

For Pvt. Taylor: HUNTER CANNING, BEN GRANEY

For Paulette: HANNAH SLOAT, KATRINA YAUKEY

For Soldat Schnabel: SANJIT DE SILVA, NAT McINTYRE, JACK SPANN

For Hauptmann Müller: DAVID MANIS, ELLIOT VILLAR

For Soldat Klausen: SANJIT DE SILVA, BEN HORNER

For Dr. Schweyk or Taff: BEN HORNER, NAT McINTYRE

For Oberst Strauss: BEN HORNER, ANDY MURRAY, JACK SPANN

For Sgt. Fine: BRIAN LEE HUYNH, NAT McINTYRE

For Unteroffizier Klebb: RICHARD CRAWFORD, TOMMY SCHRIDER, JACK SPANN

For Emilie: KATE PFAFFL, HANNAH SLOAT

For Manfred: DAVID MANIS, ANDY MURRAY

For Matron Callaghan: ALYSSA BRESNAHAN, TESSA KLEIN

For Annie: TESSA KLEIN, KATE PFAFFL

For Vet. Ofc. Martin: SANJIT DE SILVA, ELLIOT VILLAR

For Heine: BEN HORNER, JACK SPANN

Ensemble: HARLAN BENGEL, MATT DICKSON

Cast Continued

THE PEOPLE (*in order of speaking*)

Song Woman	KATE PFAFFL
Song Man	JACK SPANN
Lieutenant James Nicholls	SANJIT DE SILVA
Arthur Narracott	DAVID MANIS
Billy Narracott	STEPHEN JAMES ANTHONY
Albert Narracott	ANDREW DURAND
Ted Narracott	ANDY MURRAY
Chapman Carter	ANTHONY COCHRANE
Allan	ELLIOT VILLAR
Thomas Bone	NAT McINTYRE
John Greig	JOEL REUBEN GANZ, ALEX HOEFFLER, JONATHAN DAVID MARTIN, or ISAAC WOOFTER
Rose Narracott	ALYSSA BRESNAHAN
Priest	DAVID LANSBURY
Captain Charles Stewart	BRIAN LEE HUYNH
Sergeant Thunder	RICHARD CRAWFORD
Private David Taylor	DAVID PEGRAM
Paulette	TESSA KLEIN
Soldat Schnabel	BEN GRANEY
Hauptmann Friedrich Müller	DAVID LANSBURY
Soldat Klausen	ELLIOT VILLAR
Doctor Schweyk	TOMMY SCHRIDER
Oberst Strauss	NAT McINTYRE
Emilie	MADELEINE ROSE YEN
Unteroffizier Klebb	SANJIT DE SILVA
Sergeant Fine	BEN GRANEY
Taff	TOMMY SCHRIDER
Manfred	ANTHONY COCHRANE
Matron Callaghan	KATRINA YAUKEY
Annie Gilbert	HANNAH SLOAT
Veterinary Officer Martin	BEN HORNER
Goose	JESLYN KELLY, TOM LEE JONATHAN CHRISTOPHER MacMILLAN, or JUDE SANDY

Villagers of Devon, Soldiers, Infantry played by Members of the Company.

Assistant Stage Managers .... AMY MARSICO, CHRISTOPHER R. MUNNELL

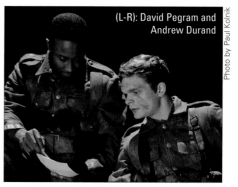

(L-R): David Pegram and Andrew Durand

Photo by Paul Kolnik

War Horse

Stephen James
Anthony
Billy Narracott

Toby Billowitz
Joey, Topthorn, Coco

Alyssa Bresnahan
Rose Narracott

Lute Breuer
Joey, Topthorn, Coco

Hunter Canning
Joey as a foal

Anthony Cochrane
*Chapman Carter,
Manfred*

Richard Crawford
Sergeant Thunder

Sanjit De Silva
*Lieutenant James
Nicholls,
Unteroffizier Klebb*

Andrew Durand
Albert Narracott

Joel Reuben Ganz
*Joey, Topthorn,
Coco, John Greig*

Ben Graney
*Soldat Schnabel,
Sergeant Fine*

Ariel Heller
Joey, Topthorn

Alex Hoeffler
*Joey, Topthorn,
Coco, John Greig*

Leah Hofmann
Joey, Topthorn

Ben Horner
*Veterinary Officer
Martin*

Brian Lee Huynh
*Captain Charles
Stewart*

Jeslyn Kelly
*Joey, Topthorn,
Coco, Goose*

Tessa Klein
Paulette

David Lansbury
*Priest, Hauptmann
Friedrich Müller*

Tom Lee
*Joey, Topthorn,
Coco, Goose*

Jonathan
Christopher
MacMillan
*Joey, Topthorn,
Goose*

David Manis
Arthur Narracott

Jonathan David
Martin
*Joey, Topthorn,
Coco, John Greig*

Nat McIntyre
*Heine, Thomas Bone,
Oberst Strauss*

Andy Murray
Ted Narracott

David Pegram
*Joey as a foal,
Private David Taylor*

Kate Pfaffl
Song Woman

Jude Sandy
*Joey, Topthorn,
Goose*

Tommy Schrider
*Heine, Doctor
Schweyk, Taff*

Hannah Sloat
*Joey as a foal,
Annie Gilbert*

Jack Spann
Song Man

Elliot Villar
*Allan, Soldat
Klausen*

Isaac Woofter
*Joey, Topthorn,
Coco, John Greig*

Katrina Yaukey
Matron Callaghan

Madeleine Rose Yen
Emilie

War Horse

Harlan Bengel
Understudy

Matt Dickson
Understudy

Michael Morpurgo
Author

Nick Stafford
Adaptor

Adrian Kohler
Handspring Puppet
Company
*Puppet Direction,
Design and
Fabrication*

Basil Jones
Handspring Puppet
Company
*Puppet Direction,
Design and
Fabrication*

Marianne Elliott
Director

Tom Morris
Director

Rae Smith
*Set, Costumes,
Drawings*

Paule Constable
Lighting

Toby Sedgwick
*Director of
Movement and
Horse Sequences*

Leo Warner
59 Productions
*Animation and
Projection Design*

Mark Grimmer
59 Productions
*Animation and
Projection Design*

Lysander Ashton
59 Productions
*Animation and
Projection Design*

Peter Stenhouse
59 Productions
*Animation and
Projection Design*

Adrian Sutton
Music

John Tams
Songmaker

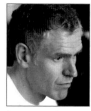

Christopher Shutt
Sound

Greg Pliska
Music Director

Mervyn Millar
*Associate Puppetry
Director*

Samuel Adamson
Artistic Associate

Benjamin Endsley
Klein
Resident Director

Matt Acheson
*Resident Puppetry
Director*

Paul Huntley
*Hair and Wig
Designer*

Thomas Schall
Fight Director

Gillian Lane-Plescia
Dialect Coach

Kate Wilson
Vocal Coach

Bob Boyett

Nicholas Hytner
*Director, National
Theatre of Great
Britain*

Edgar Wallner
*Chairman
National Angels
Limited*

Michael Linnit
*Managing Director
National Angels
Limited*

André Bishop
*Artistic Director
Lincoln Center
Theater*

Bernard Gersten
*Executive Producer
Lincoln Center
Theater*

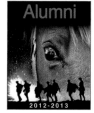

Geoffrey Allen
Murphy
Understudy

War Horse

Enrico D. Wey
Joey, Topthorn

Jessica Tyler Wright
Song Woman

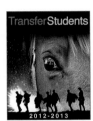

Joby Earle
Understudy

Geoffrey Allen
Murphy
Understudy

Enrico D. Wey
Joey, Topthorn

LINCOLN CENTER THEATER

ANDRÉ BISHOP   BERNARD GERSTEN
ARTISTIC DIRECTOR   EXECUTIVE PRODUCER

ADMINISTRATIVE STAFF

MANAGING DIRECTOR ....ADAM SIEGEL
General Manager ....Jessica Niebanck
Associate General Manager ....Meghan Lantzy
General Management Assistant ....Laura Stuart
Facilities Manager ....Alex Mustelier
Associate Facilities
  Manager....................Michael Assalone
GENERAL PRESS AGENT ....PHILIP RINALDI
Press Associate ....Amanda Dekker
PRODUCTION MANAGER ....JEFF HAMLIN
Associate Production Manager ....Paul Smithyman
EXECUTIVE DIRECTOR OF DEVELOPMENT
  & PLANNING ....HATTIE K. JUTAGIR
Associate Director of
  Development ....Rachel Norton
Manager of Special Events and
  LCT Young Angels ....Karin Schall
Grants Writer ....Neal Brilliant
Manager, Patron Program ....Sheilaja Rao
Assistant to the Executive Director of
  Development & Planning ....Raelyn R. Lagerstrom
Development Associate/
  Special Events & LCT
  Young Angels ....Jennifer H. Rosenbluth-Stoll
Development Assistant/
  Patron Program ....Sydney Rais-Sherman
DIRECTOR OF FINANCE ....DAVID S. BROWN
Controller ....Susan Knox
Systems Manager ....Stacy Valentine
Finance Assistant ....Kristen Parker
DIRECTOR OF
  MARKETING ....LINDA MASON ROSS
Associate Director of Marketing ....Ashley Dunn
Digital Marketing Associate ....Rebecca Leshin
Marketing Assistant ....David Cannon
DIRECTOR OF EDUCATION ....KATI KOERNER
Associate Director
  of Education ....Alexandra Lopez
Education Assistant ....Jennifer Wintzer
Assistant to the
  Executive Producer ....Barbara Hourigan
Office Manager ....Brian Hashimoto
Messenger ....Esau Burgess
Reception ....Anna Strasser, Michelle Metcalf

ARTISTIC STAFF

ASSOCIATE
  DIRECTORS ....GRACIELA DANIELE,

NICHOLAS HYTNER,
JACK O'BRIEN,
SUSAN STROMAN,
DANIEL SULLIVAN
RESIDENT DIRECTOR .... BARTLETT SHER
DRAMATURG and DIRECTOR,
  LCT DIRECTORS LAB ....ANNE CATTANEO
CASTING DIRECTOR ....DANIEL SWEE, CSA
MUSICAL THEATER
  ASSOCIATE PRODUCER ....IRA WEITZMAN
ARTISTIC DIRECTOR/LCT3 .... PAIGE EVANS
Artistic Administrator ....Julia Judge
Casting Associate ....Camille Hickman
LCT3 Associate ....Natasha Sinha
Lab Assistant ....Kate Marvin

HOUSE STAFF

HOUSE MANAGER ....RHEBA FLEGELMAN
Production Carpenter ....William Nagle
Production Electrician ....Patrick Merryman
Production Soundman ....Marc Salzberg
Production Propertyman ....Karl Rausenberger
Production Flyman ....John Weingart
House Technician ....Linda Heard
Chief Usher ..................................M.L. Pollock
Box Office Treasurer ....Fred Bonis
Assistant Treasurer ....Robert A. Belkin

SPECIAL SERVICES

Advertising ....SpotCo/
  Drew Hodges, Jim Edwards,
  Tom Greenwald, Jim Aquino,
  Ryan Zatcoff, Cory Spinney
Online Marketing ....SpotCo/
  Marc Mettler, Christina Sees
Marketing ....SpotCo/
  Nick Pramik, Kristen Rathbun,
  Stephen Santore, Julie Wechsler,
  Caroline Newhouse

General Press Representative ....The Hartman Group/
  Michael Hartman, Matt Ross,
  Nicole Capatasto
Principal Poster Artist ....James McMullan
Counsel ....Charles H. Googe, Esq.;
  Carol Kaplan, Esq.; and
  Caroline Barnard, Esq. of
  Paul, Weiss, Rifkind, Wharton & Garrison
Counsel ....Lazarus & Harris LLP
Immigration Counsel ....Theodore Ruthizer, Esq.;
  Mark D. Koestler, Esq.
  of Kramer, Levin, Naftalis & Frankel LLP
Labor Counsel ....Michael F. McGahan, Esq.
  of Epstein, Becker & Green, P.C.
Auditor ....Frederick Martens, C.P.A.
  Lutz & Carr, L.L.P.
Insurance ....Jennifer Brown of
  DeWitt Stern Group
Photographer ....Paul Kolnik
Video Services ....Fresh Produce Productions/
  Frank Basile
Consulting Architect ....Hugh Hardy,
  H3 Hardy Collaboration Architecture
Construction Manager ....Yorke Construction
Payroll Service ....Castellana Services, Inc.
Merchandising ....Marquee Merchandise, LLC/
  Matt Murphy
Lobby Refreshments ....Sweet Concessions

STAFF FOR *WAR HORSE*

COMPANY MANAGER ....MATTHEW MARKOFF
Assistant Company Manager ....Rachel Scheer
Associate Puppetry Director ....Mervyn Millar
Resident Director ....Benjamin Endsley Klein
Resident Puppetry Director ....Matt Acheson
Movement Associate ....Adrienne Kapstein
US Associate Set Designer ....Frank McCullough

Continued on page 401

Continued on page 401

"Joey as a foal" (L-R): Hunter Canning,
David Pegram, Hannah Sloat

Photo by Paul Kolnik

War Horse

STAGE MANAGEMENT
From Top (L-R):
Karen Evanouskas
(Production Assistant),
Rick Steiger
(Production Stage Manager),
Brian Bogin
(Assistant Stage Manager),
Christopher R. Munnell
(Assistant Stage Manager)

FRONT OF HOUSE
Front Row (L-R): Susan Lehman, Diane Nottle, Mim Pollock,
Margareta Shakeridge, Paula Gallo
Back Row (L-R): Jerry Sodano, Officer Douglas Charles, Nick Andors,
Jeff Goldstein, Catherine Thorpe

WARDROBE
Front Row (L-R): Adam Adelman,
Terry LaVada, Sarah Rochford
Back Row (L-R): Donna Holland,
Peggy Danz Kazdan, Patti Luther,
Joe Godwin, Holly Nissen,
Greg Holtz, Abby Bailey

Not pictured:
Lynn Bowling (Wardrobe Supervisor),
James Nadeaux, Ros Wells (dressers)

**MAKE-UP DESIGNER
AND HAIR SUPERVISOR**
Cynthia Demand

CREW
Front Row (L-R): Bruce Rubin (Electrician/Board Operator), Luis Lojo (Deck Sound), Adam Smolenski (Deck Sound), Brant Underwood (Deck Automation),
Greg Cushna (Flyman), Kyle Barrineau (Props), Nick Irons (Follow Spot), Rudy Wood (Props), Andrew Belits (Carpenter)
Back Row (L-R): Marc Salzberg (Production Soundman), Bill Burke (Projection Technician), John Weingart (Production Flyman), Mark Dignam (Props),
Frank Linn (Automation Tech), Joe Pizzuto (Pyro Technician), Pat Merryman (Production Electrician), Jeff Ward (Follow Spot Operator), Kevin McNeill (Carpenter),
Bill Nagle (Production Carpenter), Karl Rausenberger (Production Propman)
Not Pictured: Dan Rich (Follow Spot Operator), John Ross (Props), John Howie (Carpenter), Ray Skillin (Deck Carpenter)

War Horse
SCRAPBOOK

Correspondent: Katrina Yaukey, "Matron Callaghan"

Most Vivid Memory of the Final Performance: Walking downstage for the final chorus of "Only Remembered."

Farewell Party: Lincoln Center hosted a farewell party at PJ Clarke's where current and past cast and crew celebrated.

Most Exciting Celebrity Visitors: Courtney B. Vance came with his kid just to watch fight call. Angela Lansbury came to see her nephew David Lansbury in the show. Karl Rove in the house.

Special Backstage Rituals: Ordering Burrito Box. Butt grabs. Hugs from Jude. "Do I need to shave?" Crosswords in the hair room. Circle of vomit after mud. Poker. Dancing with Joe stage-right pre-plough. Shooting the shit with Rudy.

Favorite Moments During the Final Weeks: David Manis created a video called *Barely Remembered* that jokes about *War Horse* in year three. Naked fight call where the puppeteers ran through fight call in their underwear. The New Year's Eve dance party. Lute breaking the crow puppet's nose. The cart breaking in the first show of the re-cast and then again during the final week. Listening to the show backstage. Last shave. Being in good health. The head and heart crow tracks realizing that they'll never have to hold a pole ever again.

Favorite In-Theatre Gathering Places: The greenroom for birthday events. The stables for after-show cool down. Large rehearsal room for Ballee. Upstairs for Catan between shows. Dressing room ten for cards.

Understudy Anecdote: Matt Dickson's pole work in the beginning.

Favorite Off-Site Hangouts: YMCA for racket ball. Indie. Lincoln Park. Emerald Inn. Bowling at Frames. Ollie's.

Favorite Snack Foods: Protein shakes. Fruit. Burrito Box. Halal cart. Dark chocolate-covered raisins. Tea and toast. Grapefruit. Gourmet Garage. Snacks from stage management. Mo's goodies. Gatorade, pastilles, and Celtic music before the show and Philip Glass at intermission.

Mascots: Charger and Bruce.

Favorite Therapies: Massage. Acupuncture. Physical therapy. Bourbon. Poker. Trips to Beaver Mountain with Bangs and Serena. Moscow mules.

Memorable Ad-Libs: "Her farm has been desecrated." "No shootings please." "Yeehaw." "Gefreit wee wee." "Did I get him?" "That was a pain in the arse." "Ja ja the Fuhrer's impeccable strategy." "What about your BIG tommy knife?"

Memorable Run-in With Technology: Our second to last Sunday someone took flash photos throughout the entire first act.

Memorable Press Encounters: Joey meets Mr. Met and Chip the horse at Citifield. Photo shoot where we had third-string Canadian Albert with our cast.

Memorable Stage Door Fan Encounter: Sigourney Weaver fans outside our door.

Fastest Costume Change: Changing from a clean English soldier to a dirty German soldier. Record time 19 seconds (JD Martin).

Catchphrases Only the Company Would Recognize: "Full o' dreams." "Explorate." "May the horse be with you." "Only dismembered." "Yes we Catan. "You can pet my cat." "You charmed them." "That's Ballee."

Sweethearts Within the Company: Joel Reuben Ganz and Katrina Yaukey met on the show.

Best In-House Parody Lyrics: "Barely remembered for what we have done." "A horse that will kill your brother." "Come on 'me."

Memorable Directorial Notes: "Joey's night was terrifying."
"Stop wearing your helmet like a bonnet."
"Elliot, I could hear you whipping your horses."
"Could you act more like a man?"
To a female, "Could you moan more like a man when you're lying on the floor?"

Nicknames: "Copper full of dreams." "Mr. Chickens." "Mr. Buckets." "Other Asian." Crow track nicknames: "Edgar Allen Crow," "Crownan the Barbarian," "Juicy Crowture," "Crow J. Simpson," "Crow Ella DaVille, "Crow Crow Chanel."

Embarrassing Moments: Geoffrey Murphy, "I had a stroke." Albert's mom revealed her thong. Albert had to hand a leg back to baby Joey when the horse was too far away and said, "here ya go boy." When the guns don't fire and people have to find ways to kill people, like stab them or something. Dying halfway off the revolve. The lift didn't go up for the first show this year. Tommy Schrider saying, "What's up, Bangs?" rather than, "Good morning, Bangs." Andy Murray losing the whip and having to hit the horse with his hand.

Coolest Things About Being in This Show: The horses. Jude Sandy. Andrew Durand, "getting to have a pet horse," The Lincoln Center showers and Japanese toilets. Performing consistently in front of one thousand people every night.

Continued from page 399

UK Associate Costume Designer ....Johanna Coe
US Associate Costume Designer ....Sarah Laux
UK Associate Lighting Designer ....Nick Simmons
US Associate Lighting Designer ....Karen Spahn
UK Associate Sound Designer ....John Owens
US Assistant Sound Designer ....Bridget O'Connor
UK Puppetry Technician ....Ed Dimbleby
Automated Light Programmer ....Victor Seastone
Projection Programmer ....Benjamin Pearcy
Props ....Faye Armon
Fight Captain ....Elliot Villar
Make-Up Designer ....Cynthia Demand
Wardrobe Supervisor ....Lynn Bowling
Dressers ....Adam Adelman, Abby Bailey,
Joe Godwin, Donna Holland,
Greg Holtz, Peggy Danz Kazdan,
Terry LaVada, Patti Luther,
James Nadeaux, Holly Nissen,
Sarah Rochford, Rosie Wells
Hair Supervisor ....Cynthia Demand
Physical Therapy ....PhysioArts/Jennifer Green
Orthopedist ....David S. Weiss, MD
Production Assistant ....Karen Evanouskas
Child Guardian ....Krystal Rowley

Fight Director ....Thomas Schall

Dialect Coach ....Gillian Lane-Plescia

Vocal Coach ....Kate Wilson

Hair and Wig Design ....Paul Huntley

Official Accordion Sponsorship by Saltarelle

Incidental Music

Recorded at Sear Sound, NY
Recording Engineer: Gary Maurer
Copyist: Steve Cohen

Jim Lake ....Trumpet, Cornet
Angela Gosse ....Trumpet, Cornet
Judy Yin-Chi Lee ....Horn, Alto Horn
Hitomi Yakata ....Trombone, Euphonium
Richard Heckman ....Clarinet, Flute

NATIONAL THEATRE

John Makinson ....Chairman of the Board
Nicholas Hytner ....Director
Nick Starr...............................Executive Director
Lisa Burger ....Chief Operating Officer
Chris Harper ....Producer
Katrina Gilroy ....Technical Producer

Robin Hawkes....................Administrative Producer
Karl Westworth ....Marketing Manager

Supported by the National Theatre's
War Horse Production Office.

Additional thanks to the National Theatre's Marketing, Digital, Graphics and Finance departments.

CREDITS

Scenery by Hudson Scenic Studio. Tank by Scott Fleary. Costumes by National Theatre Costume department. Officer uniform tailoring by Mark Costello. Tailoring by Roxy Cressy. Additional tailoring by Kirstie Robinson. Footwear supervision by National Theatre Footware department. English and German uniforms supplied by Khaki Devil. U.S. alterations by James Nadeaux. Additional U.S. alterations by John Kristiansen, NY. Additional costume supplies by Costume Store, Vintage Shirt Company and Silvermans. Costume aging and distressing by Jeff Fender Studio. Sound and video equipment by Sound Associates. Lighting equipment from PRG Lighting. Props by National Theatre Props department. Technical drawings by Tim Crowdy. Violin provided by David Gage String Instruments.

Visit WarHorseOnBroadway.com

Wicked

First Preview: October 8, 2003. Opened: October 30, 2003.
Still runnning as of May 31, 2013.

This imaginative "prequel" to The Wizard of Oz *traces the friendship of two young women of Oz, Elphaba and Glinda, and how events beyond their control transform them into the familiar Wicked Witch of the West and Good Witch of the North. Dorothy, the Scarecrow and other beloved Oz characters don't arrive until nearly the end, but reveal fascinating backstories of their own. The show also offers a surprise from the early life of the Wizard himself, and explores what it really means to be "wicked."*

THE CAST

(in order of appearance)

Glinda	ALLI MAUZEY
Witch's Father	MICHAEL DeVRIES
Witch's Mother	KRISTEN GORSKI-WERGELES
Midwife	KATHY SANTEN
Elphaba	WILLEMIJN VERKAIK
Nessarose	CATHERINE CHARLEBOIS
Boq	F. MICHAEL HAYNIE
Madame Morrible	RANDY DANSON
Doctor Dillamond	TOM FLYNN
Fiyero	KYLE DEAN MASSEY
Ozian Official	MICHAEL DeVRIES
The Wonderful Wizard of Oz	ADAM GRUPPER
Chistery	MARK SHUNKEY

Monkeys, Students, Denizens of the Emerald City, Palace Guards and
Other Citizens of Oz .... NOVA BERGERON, JERAD BORTZ, MICHAEL DeVRIES, MAIA EVWARAYE-GRIFFIN, KRISTEN GORSKI-WERGELES, JESSE JP JOHNSON, BRANDON LEFFLER,

Continued on next page

GERSHWIN THEATRE

UNDER THE DIRECTION OF
JAMES M. NEDERLANDER AND JAMES L. NEDERLANDER

Marc Platt
Universal Pictures
The Araca Group   and   Jon B. Platt
David Stone

present

WICKED

Music and Lyrics
Stephen Schwartz

Book
Winnie Holzman

Based on the novel by **Gregory Maguire**

starring

Willemijn Verkaik   Alli Mauzey

also starring

Kyle Dean Massey

Catherine Charlebois   Tom Flynn   F. Michael Haynie

Alicia L. Albright Nova Bergeron Jerad Bortz Michael DeVries
Maia Evwaraye-Griffin Jenny Florkowski Kristen Gorski-Wergeles Jesse JP Johnson
Brandon Leffler Colby Q. Lindeman Jonathan McGill Brian Munn
Vicki Noon Lindsay K. Northen Rhea Patterson Eddie Pendergraft Alexander Quiroga
Constantine Rousouli Adam Sanford Kathy Santen Mark Shunkey
Heather Spore Brian Wanee Jonathan Warren Betsy Werbel Robin Wilner

and

Randy Danson   Adam Grupper

Settings	Costumes	Lighting	Sound
Eugene Lee	**Susan Hilferty**	**Kenneth Posner**	**Tony Meola**
Projections	Wigs & Hair	Production Supervisor	Technical Supervisor
Elaine J. McCarthy	**Tom Watson**	**Thom Widmann**	**Jake Bell**
Music Arrangements	Associate Music Supervisor	Dance Arrangements	Music Coordinator
Alex Lacamoire &	**Dominick Amendum**	**James Lynn Abbott**	**Michael Keller**
Stephen Oremus			
Associate Set Designer	Special Effects	Associate Choreographer	Associate Director
Edward Pierce	**Chic Silber**	**Corinne McFadden Herrera**	**Lisa Leguillou**
Casting	Production Stage Manager	General Management	Press	Executive Producers
Telsey + Company	**Marybeth Abel**	**321 Theatrical**	**The Hartman Group**	**Marcia Goldberg**
Craig Burns, CSA		**Management**		**& Nina Essman**

Orchestrations
William David Brohn

Music Supervisor
Stephen Oremus

Musical Staging by
Wayne Cilento

Directed by
Joe Mantello

Grammy Award-winning Original Cast Recording on DECCA BROADWAY

2/11/13

Alli Mauzey
as Glinda

Photo by Joan Marcus

Willemijn Verkaik
as Elphaba

Photos by Brinkoff-Mögenburg

Wicked

MUSICAL NUMBERS

ACT I

"No One Mourns the Wicked" ....Glinda and Citizens of Oz
"Dear Old Shiz" ....Students
"The Wizard and I" ....Morrible, Elphaba
"What Is This Feeling?" ....Galinda, Elphaba and Students
"Something Bad" ....Dr. Dillamond and Elphaba
"Dancing Through Life" ....Fiyero, Galinda, Boq, Nessarose, Elphaba and Students
"Popular" ....Galinda
"I'm Not That Girl" ....Elphaba
"One Short Day" ....Elphaba, Glinda and Denizens of the Emerald City
"A Sentimental Man" ....The Wizard
"Defying Gravity" ....Elphaba, Glinda, Guards and Citizens of Oz

ACT II

"No One Mourns the Wicked" (reprise) ....Citizens of Oz
"Thank Goodness" ....Glinda, Morrible and Citizens of Oz
"The Wicked Witch of the East" ....Elphaba, Nessarose and Boq
"Wonderful" ....The Wizard and Elphaba
"I'm Not That Girl" (reprise) ....Glinda
"As Long As You're Mine" ....Elphaba and Fiyero
"No Good Deed" ....Elphaba
"March of the Witch Hunters" ....Boq and Citizens of Oz
"For Good" ....Glinda and Elphaba
"Finale" ....All

ORCHESTRA

Conductor: DOMINICK AMENDUM
Associate Conductor: DAVID EVANS
Assistant Conductor: BEN COHN
Concertmaster: CHRISTIAN HEBEL
Violin: VICTOR SCHULTZ
Viola: KEVIN ROY
Cello: DANNY MILLER
Harp: LAURA SHERMAN
Lead Trumpet: JON OWENS
Trumpet: TOM HOYT
Trombones: DALE KIRKLAND,
    DOUGLAS PURVIANCE
Flute: HELEN CAMPO
Oboe: TUCK LEE

Clarinet/Soprano Sax: JOHN MOSES
Bassoon/Baritone Sax/Clarinets: CHAD SMITH
French Horns: THEO PRIMIS,
    CHAD YARBROUGH
Drums: MATT VANDERENDE
Bass: KONRAD ADDERLEY
Piano/Synthesizer: BEN COHN
Keyboards: PAUL LOESEL, DAVID EVANS
Guitars: RIC MOLINA, GREG SKAFF
Percussion: ANDY JONES
Music Coordinator: MICHAEL KELLER

Wicked uses Yamaha Pianos exclusively.

Cast Continued

COLBY Q. LINDEMAN, JONATHAN McGILL,
VICKI NOON, LINDSAY K. NORTHEN,
RHEA PATTERSON, EDDIE PENDERGRAFT,
ALEXANDER QUIROGA,
CONSTANTINE ROUSOULI,
ADAM SANFORD, KATHY SANTEN,
MARK SHUNKEY, HEATHER SPORE,
BRIAN WANEE, BETSY WERBEL,
ROBIN WILNER

UNDERSTUDIES AND STANDBYS

Standby for Glinda:
TIFFANY HAAS
Understudy for Elphaba:
VICKI NOON
Understudy for Glinda:
LINDSAY K. NORTHEN, HEATHER SPORE
For Fiyero:
JERAD BORTZ, CONSTANTINE ROUSOULI
For the Wizard and Dr. Dillamond:
MICHAEL DeVRIES, BRIAN MUNN
For Madame Morrible:
KATHY SANTEN, BETSY WERBEL
For Boq:
JESSE JP JOHNSON, EDDIE PENDERGRAFT
For Nessarose and Midwife:
ALICIA L. ALBRIGHT, JENNY FLORKOWSKI
For Chistery:
BRIAN WANEE, JONATHAN WARREN
For Witch's Father and Ozian Official:
BRIAN MUNN, ALEXANDER QUIROGA
For Witch's Mother:
ALICIA L. ALBRIGHT, ROBIN WILNER
For Midwife:
ROBIN WILNER

SWINGS

Jenny Florkowski, Brian Munn

Dance Captains/Swings:
JONATHAN WARREN, ALICIA L. ALBRIGHT

Willemijn Verkaik is appearing with the permission
of Actors' Equity Association.

Willemijn Verkaik
Elphaba

Alli Mauzey
Glinda

Randy Danson
Madame Morrible

Adam Grupper
The Wizard

Kyle Dean Massey
Fiyero

Catherine Charlebois
Nessarose

Tom Flynn
Dr. Dillamond

Wicked

F. Michael Haynie
Boq

Tiffany Haas
Glinda Standby

Alicia L. Albright
Dance Captain; Swing; u/s Nessarose/Midwife/ Witch's Mother

Nova Bergeron
Ensemble

Jerad Bortz
Ensemble; u/s Fiyero

Michael DeVries
Witch's Father/ Ozian Official; u/s Wizard/ Dillamond

Maia Evwaraye-Griffin
Ensemble

Jenny Florkowski
Swing; u/s Nessarose/ Midwife

Kristen Gorski-Wergeles
Witch's Mother, Ensemble

Jesse JP Johnson
Ensemble; u/s Boq

Brandon Leffler
Ensemble

Colby Q. Lindeman
Ensemble

Jonathan McGill
Ensemble

Brian Munn
Swing; u/s Wizard/Dillamond/ Witch's Father/ Ozian Official

Vicki Noon
Ensemble; u/s Elphaba

Lindsay K. Northen
Ensemble; u/s Glinda

Rhea Patterson
Ensemble

Eddie Pendergraft
Ensemble; u/s Boq

Alexander Quiroga
Ensemble; u/s Witch's Father/ Ozian Official

Constantine Rousouli
Ensemble; u/s Fiyero

Adam Sanford
Ensemble

Kathy Santen
Midwife; u/s Morrible

Mark Shunkey
Chistery

Heather Spore
Ensemble; u/s Glinda

Brian Wanee
Ensemble; u/s Chistery

Jonathan Warren
Dance Captain, Swing, Fight Captain; u/s Chistery

Betsy Werbel
Ensemble; u/s Morrible

Robin Wilner
Ensemble; u/s Witch's Mother/ Midwife

Stephen Schwartz
Music and Lyrics

Winnie Holzman
Book

Joe Mantello
Director

Wayne Cilento
Musical Staging

Eugene Lee
Scenic Designer

Susan Hilferty
Costume Designer

Kenneth Posner
Lighting Designer

Wicked

Tony Meola
Sound Designer

Elaine J. McCarthy
Projections Designer

Tom Watson
Hair and Wig Design

Joe Dulude II
Make-up Designer

Thom Widmann
*Production
Supervisor*

Jake Bell
Technical Supervisor

Stephen Oremus
*Music Supervisor/
Arranger*

William David Brohn
Orchestrations

Alex Lacamoire
Music Arrangements

Dominick Amendum
*Associate Music
Supervisor/
Conductor*

James Lynn Abbott
*Dance
Arrangements*

Michael Keller
Music Coordinator

Edward Pierce
*Associate Scenic
Designer*

Chic Silber
Special Effects

Corinne McFadden
Herrera
*Associate
Choreographer*

Lisa Leguillou
Associate Director

Bernard Telsey
Telsey + Company
Casting

Gregory Maguire
*Author of Original
Novel*

Marcia Goldberg, Nancy Nagel Gibbs
and Nina Essman
321 Theatrical Management
General Management

Marc Platt
Producer

Mark Rego, Hank Unger and Matthew Rego
The Araca Group
Producer

Jon B. Platt
Producer

David Stone
Producer

ALUMNI
2012-2013

Todd Anderson
Swing; u/s Chistery

Etai BenShlomo
Boq

Richard H. Blake
Fiyero

Caroline Bowman
*Ensemble;
u/s Elphaba*

Jackie Burns
Elphaba

Dioni Michelle
Collins
*Ensemble;
u/s Morrible*

Jennifer DiNoia
Elphaba

Kate Fahrner
Standby for Glinda

Jenny Fellner
Nessarose

Wicked

Kristina Fernandez
Ensemble

Tess Ferrell
Swing

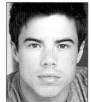
David Hull
Ensemble; u/s Fiyero

Lindsay Janisse
*Witch's Mother,
Ensemble*

Kevin Jordan
Swing; u/s Chistery

Kelly Lafarga
*Swing; u/s Midwife/
Witch's Mother*

Desi Oakley
Swing; u/s Midwife

Nathan Peck
Ensemble

Casey Quinn
Ensemble

Amanda Rose
Swing

John Schiappa
*Swing; u/s Wizard/
Dillamond, Witch's
Father/Ozian Official*

Chandra Lee
Schwartz
Glinda

Libby Servais
Swing

Lindsay Wood
Swing

TRANSFER
STUDENTS
2012-2013

Todd Anderson
Swing; u/s Chistery

Larkin Bogan
Swing; u/s Boq

James Brown III
Ensemble

Katie Rose Clarke
Glinda

Anna Eilinsfeld
*Ensemble;
u/s Elphaba*

Tess Ferrell
*Swing;
u/s Nessarose/
Midwife*

Spencer Jones
*Assistant Dance
Captain, Swing;
u/s Chistery*

Derek Klena
Fiyero

Kelly Lafarga
*Swing; u/s Midwife/
Witch's Mother*

Sean McCourt
*Witch's Father/Ozian
Official; u/s Wizard,
Dillamond*

Emily Mechler
Ensemble; u/s Glinda

Lindsay Mendez
Elphaba

Casey Quinn
Ensemble

Amanda Rose
Swing

Michael McCorry
Rose
Ensemble; u/s Fiyero

John Schiappa
Dr. Dillamond

Carla Stickler
*Ensemble
u/s Elphaba*

Ron Todorowski
Ensemble

Lindsay Wood
*Swing; u/s Witch's
Mother/Midwife*

Briana Yacavone
*Swing;
u/s Nessarose/
Midwife*

Wicked

FRONT OF HOUSE

Front Row (L-R): Mariana Casanova, Michele Belmond, Carmen Rodriguez, Lorraine Lowrey, Jean Logan, Susan Sunday, Rick Kaye, Jacob Korder, Marilyn Luby, Albert Cruz, Brenda Denaris

Back Row (L-R): Joyce Pena, Peggy Boyles, Heather Farrell, Leonila Guity, Greg Woolard, Eileen Roig, Eric Brown, Alex Kehr, Joe Ortenzio, David Pena, Siobhan Dunne, Philippa Koopman

STAGE AND COMPANY MANAGEMENT

Top Row (L-R): Shawn Pennington, Jennifer Marik
Bottom Row (L-R): Adam Jackson, Christy Ney, Susan Sampliner

WARDROBE

Front Row (L-R): Kevin Hucke, Kathe Mull, Randy Witherspoon, James Byrne
Back Row (L-R): Karen Lloyd, Bobbye Sue Albrecht, Laurel Parrish, Teri Pruitt, Michael Michalski, Alyce Gilbert

HAIR AND MAKE-UP

(L-R): Barbara Rosenthal, Nora Martin, Brittnye Batchelor, Craig Jessup, Rob Harmon, Cheri Tiberio

Wicked

CREW
(L-R): Jeff Sigler, Henry L. Brisen, Neil McShane, Kevin Anderson, Augie Mericola (with magic potion), Steve Caputo, Larry Doby, John Riggins, Mark Illo

Wicked

SCRAPBOOK

Correspondents: Jonathan Warren (Dance Captain/Swing/Fight Captain) and Alicia Albright (Dance Captain/Swing/Understudy)

Fun Facts: In 2012, *Wicked* had the highest grossing week in Broadway history. *Wicked* grossed $2.947 million the week between Christmas and New Year's. *Wicked* ended 2012 as the highest grossing Broadway show for the ninth consecutive year.

Memorable Press Encounter: Tiffany Haas and Donna Vivino had a fabulous time at the National Museum of American History-Smithsonian in Washington D.C., honoring *Wicked*'s Tony Award-winning costume designer, Susan Hilferty. Her stunning, detailed design of the famous Act II Elphaba gown was inducted into the Museum. Tiff and Viv sang some of their favorite *Wicked* tunes for the honoree as well as an enthusiastic crowd. It was certainly an event they will never forget! They felt wickedly popular to be included!

Celebrity Visitors: Tim Tebow came to see *Wicked* before starting his run with the Jets. It was his first Broadway show. Also, Kim and Kanye had a date night at *Wicked*!

Memorable Stage Door Encounter: Alicia Albright, our dance captain/swing, while leaving the stage door, received screams, accolades, well wishes, and a beautiful bouquet of flowers for her performance in the show. After accepting the flowers, she realized they thought that she was Glinda (which she does not play). She let the adoring fans know that she is in fact the dance

Backstage at Christmas 2012, wearing our paper crowns with Jonathan McGill (top) as Father Christmas.

captain—to which they responded by asking for the flowers back. WaaWaa.

Heaviest/Hottest Costume: We are all wearing upholstery fabric in the opening number… beautiful, but hot and heavy!

Who Wore the Least: There is nothing skimpy in Oz. We are covered head to toe!

Holiday Gift from Producers: The cast and crew received an elegant thermos in an embossed leather sleeve.

Actor Who Performed the Most Roles in the Show: Brian Wanee, our onstage swing, performs all twelve male ensemble roles and performs every night onstage.

Memorable Ad-Lib: "APPROVED!!"

Special Backstage Ritual: Every new company member must prick their finger and drop the blood in the Elphaba bucket…wink wink!

Actor Who Has Done the Most Broadway Shows: Adam Grupper—nine.

Favorite Moment During Each Performance: The end of Act I!

Favorite In-Theatre Gathering Place: Marybeth Abel's office.

Favorite Off-Site Hangouts: Lillie's, Medi Winebar, McHale's.

Favorite Snack Foods: Anything gluten free—it's an epidemic!!

Mascot: The scrappy rat who died in the deck. His scent comes to visit us when the smoke comes onto the stage.

Favorite Therapy: Mark Hunter-Hall of Encore PT.

Catchphrases Only the Company Would Know: Anything Constantine Rousouli says. He is a walking catchphrase.

Sweethearts Within the Company: Three women in the ensemble gave birth to girls in 2012, born two months apart.

Fun Holiday Traditions: Father Christmas (Jonathan McGill) comes to visit us and spread Christmas cheer every year. We love to make/decorate gingerbread houses for Christmas. Every year for Christmas and Easter, Alyce Gilbert, our wardrobe supervisor, gives everyone in the company a loaf of bread. At Christmas everyone also receives a traditional English Christmas Cracker, which includes a game and a paper crown.

Makeup provided by MAC Cosmetics

MARC PLATT PRODUCTIONS
Adam Siegel, Greg Lessans, Joey Levy, Jared LeBoff, Nik Mavinkurve, Conor Welch, Claire Wihnyk, Keri DeVos

STONE PRODUCTIONS
David Stone   Patrick Catullo   Aaron Glick

321 THEATRICAL MANAGEMENT
Mattea Cogliano-Benedict, Tara Geesaman, Tracy Geltman, Andrew Hartman, Brent McCreary, Amy Merlino, Alex Owen, Rebecca Peterson, Ken Silverman, Haley Ward

UNIVERSAL PICTURES
President & COO,
Universal Studios ....Ron Meyer
Chairman ....Adam Fogelson
Co-Chairman ....Donna Langley
Vice-Chairman ....Rick Finkelstein
President, Universal Pictures ....Jimmy Horowitz

Wicked is a proud member of the
Broadway Green Alliance

To find out more about the world of *Wicked*
and to take our Broadway survey,
visit www.wickedthemusical.com.

CREDITS
Scenery built by F&D Scene Changes, Calgary, Canada. Show control and scenic motion control featuring Stage Command Systems© and scenery fabrication by Scenic Technologies, a division of Production Resource Group, New Windsor, NY. Lighting and certain special effects equipment from Fourth Phase and sound equipment from ProMix, both divisions of Production Resource Group LLC. Other special effects equipment by Sunshine Scenic Studios and Aztec Stage Lighting. Video projection system provided by Scharff Weisberg Inc. Projections by Vermilion Border Productions. Costumes by Barbara Matera Ltd., Parsons-Meares Ltd., Scafati, TRICORNE New York City and Eric Winterling. Millinery by Rodney Gordon and Lynne Mackey. Shoes by T.O. Dey, Frederick Longtin, Pluma, LaDuca Shoes NYC, and J.C. Theatrical. Flatheads and monkey wings built by Michael Curry Design Inc. Masks and prosthetics by W.M. Creations, Inc., Matthew W. Mungle and Lloyd Matthews; lifecasts by Todd Kleitsch. Fur by Fur & Furgery. Undergarments and hosiery by Bra*Tenders, Inc. Antique jewelry by Ilene Chazanof. Specialty jewelry and tiaras by Larry Vrba. Custom Oz accessories by LouLou Button. Custom screening by Gene Mignola. Certain props by John Creech Designs and Den Design Studio. Energy-efficient washers courtesy of LG Electronics. Additional hand props courtesy of George Fenmore. Confetti supplied by Artistry in Motion. Puppets by Bob Flanagan. Musical instruments from Manny's and Carroll Musical Instrument Rentals. Drums and other percussion equipment from Bosphorus, Black Swamp, PTECH, D'Amico and Vater. Emer'gen'C provided by Alacer Corp. Rehearsed at the Lawrence A. Wien Center, 890 Broadway, and the Ford Center for the Performing Arts.

NEDERLANDER
Chairman ....James M. Nederlander
President ....James L. Nederlander

Executive Vice President
Nick Scandalios

Vice President Corporate Development	Senior Vice President Labor Relations
Charlene S. Nederlander	**Herschel Waxman**

Vice President	Chief Financial Officer
Jim Boese	**Freida Sawyer Belviso**

STAFF FOR THE GERSHWIN THEATRE
Manager ....Richard D. Kaye
Assistant Manager ....Susan Sunday
Treasurer ....John Campise
Assistant Treasurer ....Anthony Rossano
Carpenter ....John Riggins
Electrician ....Henry L. Brisen
Property Master ....Mark Illo
Flyman ....Dennis Fox
Fly Automation Carpenter ....Michael J. Szymanski
Head Usher ....Martha McGuire Boniface

Short Runs

First Preview:
February 14, 2012.
Opened: March 15, 2012.
Limited Engagement.
Closed June 2, 2012 after
30 Previews and
78 Performances.

First Preview:
March 19, 2012.
Opened: April 2, 2012.
Closed August 19, 2012 after
16 Previews and
160 Performances.

First Preview:
March 1, 2012.
Opened: March 22, 2012.
Closed July 1, 2012 after
24 Previews and
116 Performances.

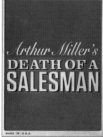

First Preview:
April 4, 2012.
Opened: April 25, 2012.
Limited Engagement.
Closed July 8, 2012 after
23 Previews and
86 Performances.

First Preview:
March 30, 2012.
Opened: April 26, 2012.
Limited Engagement.
Closed June 17, 2012 after
32 Previews and
61 Performances.

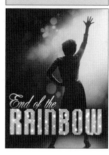

First Preview:
October 13, 2011.
Opened: November 7, 2011.
Closed June 24, 2012 after
30 Previews and
264 Performances.

These shows closed shortly after the start of the 2012-2013 season with virtually no changes to their casts from the previous year's Playbill Broadway Yearbook. For complete details and photographs from these shows, please consult the 2011-2012 edition.

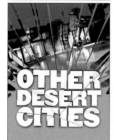

First Preview:
February 28, 2011.
Opened: March 20, 2011.
Closed June 24, 2012 after
23 Previews and
526 Performances.

First Preview:
April 3, 2012.
Opened: April 22, 2012.
Limited Engagement.
Closed July 22, 2012 after
23 Previews and
105 Performances.

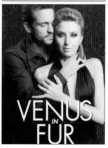

First Preview:
October 12, 2011.
Opened: November 3, 2011.
Closed June 17, 2012 after
25 Previews and
261 Performances.

First Preview:
March 24, 2011.
Opened: April 20, 2011.
Closed August 26, 2012 after
28 Previews and
561 Performances.

First Preview:
October 13, 2011.
Opened: November 8, 2011.
Closed June 17, 2012 after
37 Previews and
191 Performances.

Broadway Bares XXII: "Happy Endings"

June 17, 2012 at Roseland Ballroom

Photo courtesy Broadway Cares/Equity Fights AIDS. Photo by Peter James Zielinski

B roadway Bares XXII: Happy Endings, raised $1,254,176, breaking the previous year's record for the third year in a row. The burlesque-style benefit for Broadway Cares/Equity Fights AIDS featured 227 New York dancers transforming "favorite fairytales into crazy-hot, spectacular come-to-life stories" in an evening conceived by director Lee Wilkins with associate director Michael Lee Scott.

Kyle Dean Massey portrayed a young man lost in a world where he didn't fit in until Miriam Shor appeared as his fairy godmother, showing him that fairytales can have happy endings. Choreographers who took part included Marc Kimelman and aerialist choreographer Brandon Perayda ("Sleeping Beauty"), Stephanie Klemons ("Rapunzel"), Lorin Latarro ("Pinocchio"), Josh Rhodes and Lee Wilkins ("Snow White") and Charlie Williams ("Mirror, Mirror"). Making special appearances were Academy Award-nominee Jennifer Tilly and drag queen Lady Bunny.

Photo by Joseph Marzullo/WENN

Photo by Joseph Marzullo/WENN

1. "The Pied Piper" Marty Lawson (*How to Succeed...*) and his magic flute.
2. Andy Mills (*Memphis*) had more than three bears to deal with in this "Goldilocks."
3. Jerry Mitchell, creator of Broadway Bares, and Judith Light (*The Assembled Parties*).
4. Fairy Godmother Miriam Shor (TV's "GCB") and Kyle Dean Massey (*Next to Normal*) with the not-so-grim book of fairytales.
5. Kyle Dean Massey and the Damnettes in the opening number, "Happy Endings," written by Chad Beguelin and Matthew Sklar (*Elf, The Wedding Singer*).

The Playbill Broadway Yearbook 2012-2013

24th Annual "Gypsy of the Year"

December 3 and 4, 2012 at the New Amsterdam Theatre

The gypsies of *The Lion King* performed "Tossed Around," an athletic dance number that sent them whirling over sets of wooden chairs, earning that show the title honor at the 24th Annual Gypsy of the Year competition. The Broadway Cares/Equity Fights AIDS fundraising event collected a grand total of $3,902,608 during a six-week appeal.

Host Seth Rudetsky did one of his trademark "deconstructions" of one of his own youthful recordings featuring a tragically misguided attempt at bluesing-up "Tomorrow" from *Annie*. To cleanse the audience's palate Rudetsky brought out Broadway's new Annie, Lilla Crawford, to show how to do it right. That brought a huge hand. But then, in an only-at-"Gypsy" moment, she was joined by now-adult Andrea McArdle—the original Annie of 1977—for a duet on the show's signature anthem.

1. Ricky Martin and fellow *Evita* cast mates.
2. Seth Rudetsky deconstructs... *himself!*
3. *The Book of Mormon* tour takes the top fundraising prize with $478,130.
4. David Hyde Pierce and Debra Monk with the reunited cast of *Curtains* paid tribute to late lyricist and BC/EFA benefactor Fred Ebb.
5. The cast of *The Lion King* in "Tossed Around."
6. Two Annies: The original, Andrea McArdle, and the current, Lilla Crawford.

Fundraising awards were handed out by Chita Rivera, Ricky Martin and Katie Holmes. Top fundraiser was the national tour of *The Book of Mormon*, which brought in $478,130. Other fundraising awards were *Once* with $232,770, *Evita* with $224,105, *The Book of Mormon* with $209,265, and *Wicked* with $165,370.

Other top national tour fundraisers: *Wicked* (Emerald City Tour) with $357,379, *Wicked* (Munchkinland Tour) with $252,152, and *Les Misérables* with $172,290.

Top Broadway play fundraiser was *The Heiress* with $50,204. The top fundraisers among Off-Broadway shows were *Avenue Q* with $24,940 and *Vanya and Sonia and Masha and Spike* with $20,700.

Gypsy Robe

Presented on the opening night of a new musical

On the opening night of *Pippin*, Stephanie Pope models the Gypsy Robe with keepsakes from other shows this season

The ritual of the Gypsy Robe began in 1950 when Bill Bradley, in the chorus of *Gentlemen Prefer Blondes*, persuaded Florence Baum, a chorus member, to let him have her dressing gown. He sent it to a friend in the chorus of *Call Me Madam*, Arthur Partington, on opening night, telling him it had been worn by all of the *Ziegfeld Follies* beauties. Arthur added a rose from Ethel Merman's gown and sent it to a chorus member in the next show to open, *Guys and Dolls*. It continued this way, passing from show to show, until a specific ceremony was begun with rules on how the Robe is to be presented, worn and paraded onstage. The Robe goes only to a musical with a chorus and to the chorus member with the most Broadway Chorus credits. An artifact from the show is attached to the Robe, which is signed by the recipient and cast members. The recipient attends the next musical opening and presents the Robe to the gypsy in that show. Numerous robes have been filled and retired over the years.

The recipients of the Gypsy Robe for the 2012-13 season were:
Timothy J. Alex, *Elf*
Michael Arnold, *Motown*
Carlos L. Encinias, *Scandalous*
Merwin Foard, *Annie*
Lisa Gajda, *Chaplin*
Rod Harrelson, *Bring It On*
Nadine Isenegger, *Matilda The Musical*
Linda Mugleston, *Rodgers + Hammerstein's Cinderella*
Stephanie Pope, *Pippin*
Eric Sciotto, *The Mystery of Edwin Drood*
Charlie Sutton, *Kinky Boots*
Jason Wooten, *Jekyll & Hyde*
Kirsten Wyatt, *A Christmas Story*

42nd Annual Theater Hall of Fame Ceremony

January 28, 2013 in Gershwin Theatre's North Rotunda

The 42nd Annual Theater Hall of Fame Ceremony was held in the Gershwin Theatre's North Rotunda. The 2012 inductees: actors Betty Buckley and Sam Waterston, directors Trevor Nunn and Michael Kahn, producer/director André Bishop, playwrights Paula Vogel and Christopher Durang and, posthumously, costume designer Martin Pakledinaz. Tyne Daly (a 2011 inductee) hosted the ceremony, which was produced by Terry Hodge Taylor. After the induction, a dinner was held at the New York Friars Club.

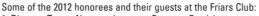

Some of the 2012 honorees and their guests at the Friars Club:
1. Director Trevor Nunn and actress Suzanne Bertish.
2. Peter Manning and producer/director André Bishop.
3. A family affair: Katherine Waterston, Sam Waterston, and Elisabeth Waterston.
4. Playwrights Sara Ruhl and Paula Vogel.
5. Director Michael Kahn and publicist Shirley Herz.

The 27th Annual Easter Bonnet Competition

April 22-23, 2013 at the Minskoff Theatre

The 27th annual Broadway Cares/Equity Fights AIDS Easter Bonnet Competition raised an all-time record of $4,250,542 in six weeks of nightly curtain-call appeals. The number was revealed at the April 23 performance of skits, songs, dances and giant hats that make up the unique fundraiser-show, at the Minskoff Theatre.

This year's top fundraising award went to the Tom Hanks starrer *Lucky Guy*, which raised $301,549, an unusual win for a non-musical play.

The total leaped ahead of the $3,734,129 previous record set in pre-recession 2007. This year's total was raised by 47 participating Broadway, Off-Broadway and touring shows.

Special guests Hanks, plus Cyndi Lauper and Harvey Fierstein (both of *Kinky Boots*) presented the fundraising, performance and bonnet design at the Minskoff following the two Easter Bonnet performances.

The 2013 Bonnet competition resulted in a first-ever tie for Outstanding Bonnet Design: *Spider-Man: Turn Off the Dark* and *The Lion King* shared the event's signature accolade—*Lion King* for a smoke-breathing lion mask hat, *Spider-Man* for its salute to *Pippin*: a circus tent hat with a spider web design traced out in light on the top.

Kinky Boots took the prize for Outstanding Bonnet Presentation with "Your Truest Colors," a parody of some of the more serious dance numbers that grace (and often win) the Bonnet competition. Members of the *Boots* company, several of them clearly not dancers, danced in form-fitting body suits to composer Lauper's "True Colors." Lauper herself appeared at the song's climax to model the show's bonnet, an inverted red pump.

Runner-up for the Outstanding Bonnet Presentation was an audience favorite, a collaboration between the orphans of *Annie* and the newsboys of *Newsie*s, in which they pretended to compete in the categories of rap, evilest villain (helped by the adult villains of the two shows), and best Roosevelt, as one show features Teddy, the other Franklin D.

Among national touring companies, the two *Wicked* tours were finally knocked off their perennial pedestal by the tour of *Book of Mormon*, which collected $278,054 in the fight against AIDS. The Off-Broadway shows that raised the most were *Avenue Q* at $33,426 and *My Name Is Asher Lev* at $33,149.

1. (L-R): Ann Harada, Marin Mazzie and Seth Rudetsky in the opening number with new lyrics by Seth set to *Mame*'s "It's Today."
2. Outstanding Bonnet Design co-winner *Spider-Man* in its salute to *Pippin*.
3. Jennifer Chicheportiche representing Momix and Dancers Responding to AIDS in her beaded headdress.
4. Lilla Crawford of *Annie* accepts the runner-up award for Outstanding Bonnet Presention, a joint effort between her show and *Newsies*.
5. *The Lion King*'s smoking mask, co-winner of Outstanding Bonnet Design.
6. Tom Hanks (R) from *Lucky Guy*, the top fundraiser, with Harvey Fierstein (L) and Cyndi Lauper.
7. Lauper in the *Kinky Boots* entry, winner of Outstanding Bonnet Presentation.
8. And the tally is...the largest amount ever raised in a single year.

The Antoinette Perry (Tony) Awards

June 9, 2013 at Radio City Music Hall

Kinky Boots, Vanya and Sonia and Masha and Spike, Pippin and Edward Albee's Who's Afraid of Virginia Woolf? won the major production categories at the 2013 Antoinette Perry "Tony" Awards.

The 67th annual awards, representing excellence in Broadway theatre for the 2012-2013 season, were presented at Radio City Musical Hall in a ceremony hosted by Neil Patrick Harris and broadcast on CBS-TV.

The nominees and recipients of the 67th Annual Tony Awards follow. Winners are listed in boldface, with an asterisk (*).

Best Musical
Bring It On: The Musical
A Christmas Story, The Musical
Kinky Boots
Matilda The Musical

Best Play
The Assembled Parties, Richard Greenberg
Lucky Guy, Nora Ephron
The Testament of Mary, Colm Tóibín
Vanya and Sonia and Masha and Spike, **Christopher Durang**

Best Revival of a Musical
Annie
The Mystery of Edwin Drood
Pippin
Rodgers + Hammerstein's Cinderella

Best Revival of a Play
Golden Boy
Orphans
The Trip to Bountiful
Edward Albee's Who's Afraid of Virginia Woolf?

Best Performance by an Actor in a Leading Role in a Musical
Bertie Carvel, Matilda The Musical
Santino Fontana, Rodgers + Hammerstein's Cinderella
Rob McClure, Chaplin
Billy Porter, Kinky Boots
Stark Sands, Kinky Boots

Best Performance by an Actress in a Leading Role in a Musical
Stephanie J. Block, The Mystery of Edwin Drood
Carolee Carmello, Scandalous
Valisia LeKae, Motown The Musical

Patina Miller, Pippin
Laura Osnes, Rodgers + Hammerstein's Cinderella

Best Performance by an Actor in a Leading Role in a Play
Tom Hanks, Lucky Guy
Nathan Lane, The Nance
Tracy Letts, Edward Albee's Who's Afraid of Virginia Woolf?
David Hyde Pierce, Vanya and Sonia and Masha and Spike
Tom Sturridge, Orphans

Best Performance by an Actress in a Leading Role in a Play
Laurie Metcalf, The Other Place
Amy Morton, Edward Albee's Who's Afraid of Virginia Woolf?
Kristine Nielsen, Vanya and Sonia and Masha and Spike
Holland Taylor, Ann
Cicely Tyson, The Trip to Bountiful

Best Performance by an Actor in a Featured Role in a Musical
Charl Brown, Motown The Musical
Keith Carradine, Hands on a Hardbody
Will Chase, The Mystery of Edwin Drood
Gabriel Ebert, Matilda The Musical
Terrence Mann, Pippin

Best Performance by an Actress in a Featured Role in a Musical
Annaleigh Ashford, Kinky Boots
Victoria Clark, Rodgers + Hammerstein's Cinderella
Andrea Martin, Pippin
Keala Settle, Hands on a Hardbody
Lauren Ward, Matilda The Musical

1. Patina Miller, Best Actress in a Musical, Pippin.
2. Pam MacKinnon, Best Director of a Play, Edward Albee's Who's Afraid of Virginia Woolf?
3. Tracy Letts, Best Actor in a Play, Edward Albee's Who's Afraid of Virginia Woolf?
4. Diane Paulus, Best Director of a Musical, Pippin.
5. Cicely Tyson, Best Actress in a Play, The Trip to Bountiful.
6. Billy Porter, Best Actor in a Musical, Kinky Boots.

Best Performance by an Actress in a Leading Role in a Musical

The Tony Awards

Shalita Grant, *Vanya and Sonia and Masha and Spike*
Judith Ivey, *The Heiress*
*Judith Light, *The Assembled Parties*
Condola Rashad, *The Trip to Bountiful*

Best Direction of a Musical
Scott Ellis, *The Mystery of Edwin Drood*
Jerry Mitchell, *Kinky Boots*
Diane Paulus, *Pippin*
Matthew Warchus, *Matilda The Musical*

Best Direction of a Play
*Pam MacKinnon, *Edward Albee's Who's Afraid of Virginia Woolf?*
Nicholas Martin, *Vanya and Sonia and Masha and Spike*
Bartlett Sher, *Golden Boy*
George C. Wolfe, *Lucky Guy*

Best Performance by an Actor in a Featured Role in a Play
Danny Burstein, *Golden Boy*
Richard Kind, *The Big Knife*
Billy Magnussen, *Vanya and Sonia and Masha and Spike*
Tony Shalhoub, *Golden Boy*
*Courtney B. Vance, *Lucky Guy*

Best Performance by an Actress in a Featured Role in a Play
Carrie Coon, *Edward Albee's Who's Afraid of Virginia Woolf?*

Best Choreography
Andy Blankenbuehler, *Bring It On: The Musical*
Peter Darling, *Matilda The Musical*
*Jerry Mitchell, *Kinky Boots*
Chet Walker, *Pippin*

Best Scenic Design of a Musical
*Rob Howell, *Matilda The Musical*
Anna Louizos, *The Mystery of Edwin Drood*

Scott Pask, *Pippin*
David Rockwell, *Kinky Boots*

Best Scenic Design of a Play
*John Lee Beatty, *The Nance*
Santo Loquasto, *The Assembled Parties*
David Rockwell, *Lucky Guy*
Michael Yeargan, *Golden Boy*

Best Costume Design of a Musical
Gregg Barnes, *Kinky Boots*
Rob Howell, *Matilda The Musical*

1. Judith Light, Best Actress in a Featured Role in a Play, *The Assembled Parties*.
2. Courtney B. Vance, Best Actor in a Featured Role in a Play, *Lucky Guy*.
3. Cyndi Lauper, Best Original Score, *Kinky Boots*.
4. Gabriel Ebert, Best Actor in a Featured Role in a Musical, *Matilda The Musical*.
5. Andrea Martin, Best Actress in a Featured Role in a Musical, *Pippin*.

Photos by Joseph Marzullo/WENN

The Tony Awards

Photos by Joseph Marzullo/WENN

Dominique Lemieux, *Pippin*
**William Ivey Long, *Rodgers +
Hammerstein's Cinderella***

Best Costume Design of a Play
Soutra Gilmour, *Cyrano de Bergerac*
Ann Roth, *The Nance*
Albert Wolsky, *The Heiress*
Catherine Zuber, *Golden Boy*

Best Lighting Design of a Musical
Kenneth Posner, *Kinky Boots*
Kenneth Posner, *Pippin*
Kenneth Posner, *Rodgers + Hammerstein's
Cinderella*
*Hugh Vanstone, *Matilda The Musical*

Best Lighting Design of a Play
***Jules Fisher & Peggy Eisenhauer,
*Lucky Guy***
Donald Holder, *Golden Boy*
Jennifer Tipton, *The Testament of Mary*
Japhy Weideman, *The Nance*

Best Sound Design of a Musical
Jonathan Deans & Garth Helm, *Pippin*
Peter Hylenski, *Motown The Musical*
*John Shivers, *Kinky Boots*

Nevin Steinberg, *Rodgers + Hammerstein's
Cinderella*

Best Sound Design of a Play
John Gromada, *The Trip to Bountiful*
Mel Mercier, *The Testament of Mary*
*Leon Rothenberg, *The Nance*
Peter John Still and Marc Salzberg, *Golden Boy*

Best Book of a Musical
A Christmas Story, The Musical,
Joseph Robinette
Kinky Boots, Harvey Fierstein
*Matilda The Musical, Dennis Kelly
Rodgers + Hammerstein's Cinderella,
Douglas Carter Beane

**Best Original Score (Music and/or Lyrics)
Written for the Theatre**
A Christmas Story, The Musical Music and
Lyrics: Benj Pasek and Justin Paul
Hands on a Hardbody, Music: Trey Anastasio
and Amanda Green, Lyrics: Amanda Green
***Kinky Boots, Music & Lyrics:
Cyndi Lauper**
Matilda The Musical, Music & Lyrics:
Tim Minchin

Best Orchestrations
Chris Nightingale, *Matilda The Musical*
*Stephen Oremus, *Kinky Boots*
Ethan Popp & Bryan Crook, *Motown The
Musical*
Danny Troob, *Rodgers + Hammerstein's
Cinderella*

**Special Tony Award for Lifetime
Achievement in the Theatre**
Bernard Gersten
Ming Cho Lee
Paul Libin

Tony Honors for Excellence in the Theatre
New York City Mayor Michael R. Bloomberg
Career Transition for Dancers
William "Bill" Craver
Peter Lawrence
The Lost Colony
The four actresses who created the title role of

Matilda The Musical on Broadway:
Sophia Gennusa, Oona Laurence,
Bailey Ryon and Milly Shapiro
Isabelle Stevenson Award
Larry Kramer

Regional Theatre Tony Award
The Huntington Theatre Company
of Boston, Massachusettes

Here's a tally of the 2013 Tony Award winners:
Kinky Boots 6
Matilda The Musical 4
Pippin 4
*Edward Albee's Who's Afraid
of Virginia Woolf?* 3
The Nance 3
Lucky Guy 2
Vanya and Sonia and Masha and Spike 1
Rodgers + Hammerstein's Cinderella 1
The Assembled Parties 1
The Trip to Bountiful 1

1. Daryl Roth and Hal Luftig, lead producers of the
Best Musical, *Kinky Boots*.
2. Jerry Mitchell, Best Choreography, *Kinky Boots*.
3. Larry Hirschhorn (lead producer), Emily Mann
(Artistic Director, McCarter Theatre Center),
playwright Christopher Durang and Joey Parnes
(lead producer), representing the Best Play, *Vanya
and Sonia and Masha and Spike*.
4. Fran and Barry Weissler, two of the lead
producers of the Best Musical Revival, *Pippin*.

Other Theatre Awards

Covering the 2012-2013 Broadway Season

PULITZER PRIZE FOR DRAMA
Disgraced by Ayad Akhtar (Off-Broadway)

NY DRAMA CRITICS' CIRCLE AWARDS
Best Play: *Vanya and Sonia and Masha and Spike*
Best Musical: *Matilda the Musical*
Special Citations: Soho Rep; New York City Center's Encores! series; John Lee Beatty

DRAMA DESK AWARDS
Outstanding Play: *Vanya and Sonia and Masha and Spike*
Outstanding Musical: *Matilda the Musical*
Outstanding Revival of a Play: *Edward Albee's Who's Afraid of Virginia Woolf?*
Outstanding Revival of a Musical: *Pippin*
Outstanding Actor in a Play: Tracy Letts, *Edward Albee's Who's Afraid of Virginia Woolf?*
Outstanding Actress in a Play: Cicely Tyson, *The Trip to Bountiful*
Outstanding Actor in a Musical: Billy Porter, *Kinky Boots*
Outstanding Actress in a Musical: Laura Osnes, *Rodgers + Hammerstein's Cinderella*

Outstanding Music in a Play: Glen Kelly, *The Nance*
Outstanding Revue: *Old Hats* (OB)
Outstanding Set Design: Rob Howell, *Matilda the Musical*
Outstanding Costume Design: William Ivey Long, *Rodgers + Hammerstein's Cinderella*
Outstanding Lighting Design: Justin Townsend, *Here Lies Love* (OB)
Outstanding Projection Design: Peter Nigrini, *Here Lies Love* (OB)
Outstanding Sound Design in a Musical (Three-way tie): Steve Canyon Kennedy, *Hands on a Hardbody*; Scott Lehrer and Drew Levy, *Chaplin: The Musical*; Tony Meola, *The Mystery of Edwin Drood*
Outstanding Sound Design in a Play: Mel Mercier, *The Testament of Mary*
Outstanding Solo Performance: Michael Urie, *Buyer & Cellar* (OB)
Unique Theatrical Experience: *Cirque Du Soleil: Totem* (OB)
Outstanding Ensemble Performance: The cast of *Working: A Musical* (Marie-France Arcilla, Joe Cassidy, Donna Lynne Champlin, Jay Armstrong Johnson, Nehal Joshi and Kenita R. Miller) (OB)
Special Award to The New York Musical Theatre Festival/Isaac Robert Hurwitz, Executive Director and Producer (OB)

Outstanding Featured Actor in a Play: Richard Kind, *The Big Knife*
Outstanding Featured Actress in a Play: Judith Light, *The Assembled Parties*
Outstanding Featured Actor in a Musical: Bertie Carvel, *Matilda the Musical*
Outstanding Featured Actress in a Musical: Andrea Martin, *Pippin*
Outstanding Director of a Play: Pam MacKinnon, *Edward Albee's Who's Afraid of Virginia Woolf?*
Outstanding Director of a Musical: Diane Paulus, *Pippin*
Outstanding Choreography: Chet Walker and Gypsy Snider, *Pippin*
Outstanding Music: David Byrne and Fatboy Slim, *Here Lies Love* (OB)
Outstanding Lyrics: Tim Minchin, *Matilda the Musical*
Outstanding Book of a Musical: Dennis Kelly, *Matilda the Musical*
Outstanding Orchestrations: Danny Troob, *Rodgers + Hammerstein's Cinderella*

Special Award to Wakka Wakka (Gabrielle Brechner, Kirjan Waage, and Gwendolyn Warnock) (OB)
Special Award to Jayne Houdyshell
Special Award to Samuel D. Hunter (OB)
Sam Norkin Off-Broadway Award to Maruti Evans

OUTER CRITICS CIRCLE AWARDS
Outstanding New Broadway Play: *Vanya and Sonia and Masha and Spike*
Outstanding New Broadway Musical: *Kinky Boots*
Outstanding New Off-Broadway Play: *My Name is Asher Lev*
Outstanding New Off-Broadway Musical: *Here Lies Love*
Outstanding Book of a Musical (Broadway or OB): *Matilda the Musical*
Outstanding New Score (Broadway or OB): *Kinky Boots*
Outstanding Revival of a Play (Broadway or OB): *Edward Albee's Who's Afraid of Virginia Woolf?*

Outstanding Revival of a Musical (Broadway or OB): *Pippin*
Outstanding Director of a Play (Lucille Lortel Award): Jack O'Brien, *The Nance*
Outstanding Director of a Musical: Diane Paulus, *Pippin*
Outstanding Choreographer: Chet Walker, *Pippin*
Outstanding Set Design (Play or Musical): Rob Howell, *Matilda the Musical*
Outstanding Costume Design (Play or Musical): William Ivey Long, *Rodgers + Hammerstein's Cinderella*
Outstanding Lighting Design (Play or Musical): Kenneth Posner, *Pippin*

Drama Desk Award Winners:
1. Laura Osnes, Outstanding Actress in a Musical.
2. Bertie Carvel, Outstanding Featured Actor in a Musical.
3. Richard Kind, Outstanding Featured Actor in a Play.
4. Kristine Nielsen accepts her Outer Critics Circle Award.

Other Theatre Awards

Covering the 2012-2013 Broadway Season

Outstanding Actor in a Play: Nathan Lane, *The Nance*
Outstanding Actress in a Play: Cicely Tyson, *The Trip to Bountiful*
Outstanding Actor in a Musical: Billy Porter, *Kinky Boots*
Outstanding Actress in a Musical: Patina Miller, *Pippin*
Outstanding Featured Actor in a Play: Tom Sturridge, *Orphans*
Outstanding Featured Actress in a Play: Kristine Nielsen, *Vanya and Sonia and Masha and Spike*
Outstanding Featured Actor in a Musical: Terrence Mann, *Pippin*
Outstanding Featured Actress in a Musical: Andrea Martin, *Pippin*
Outstanding Solo Performance: Holland Taylor, *Ann*
John Gassner Award (New American Play): Aaron Posner, *My Name is Asher Lev* (OB)
Special Achievement Award: Irish Repertory Theatre, Charlotte Moore (Artistic Director) and Ciarán O'Reilly (Producing Director) in recognition of 25 years of producing outstanding theatre.

THE DRAMA LEAGUE AWARDS
Distinguished Production of a Play: *Vanya and Sonia and Masha and Spike*
Distinguished Production of a Musical: *Kinky Boots*
Outstanding Revival of a Broadway or Off-Broadway Play: *Edward Albee's Who's Afraid of Virginia Woolf?*
Distinguished Revival of a Musical: *Pippin*
Distinguished Performance Award: Nathan Lane, *The Nance*
Distinguished Achievement in Musical Theatre Award: Bernadette Peters
Founders Award for Excellence in Directing: Jerry Mitchell
Unique Contribution to the Theatre Award: Madison Square Garden Entertainment and the Rockettes

THEATRE WORLD AWARDS
For Outstanding Broadway or Off-Broadway debuts:
Bertie Carvel, *Matilda the Musical*
Carrie Coon, *Edward Albee's Who's Afraid of Virginia Woolf?*
Brandon J. Dirden, *The Piano Lesson* (OB)
Shalita Grant, *Vanya and Sonia and Masha and Spike*
Tom Hanks, *Lucky Guy*
Valisia LeKae, *Motown: The Musical*
Rob McClure, *Chaplin: The Musical*
Ruthie Ann Miles, *Here Lies Love* (OB)
Conrad Ricamora, *Here Lies Love* (OB)
Keala Settle, *Hands on a Hardbody*
Yvonne Strahovski, *Golden Boy*
Tom Sturridge, *Orphans*
Dorothy Loudon Award for Excellence in the Theatre: Jonny Orsini, *The Nance*

John Willis Award for Lifetime Achievement in the Theatre: Alan Alda

CLARENCE DERWENT AWARDS
From Actors' Equity for "most promising female and male performers on the New York metropolitan scene."
Annaleigh Ashford, *Kinky Boots* (Broadway) & *Dogfight* (OB)
Michael Urie, *Buyer & Cellar* (OB)

RICHARD SEFF AWARDS
From Actors' Equity, to "female and male character actors 50 years of age or older."
Kristine Nielsen, *Vanya and Sonia and Masha and Spike*
Lewis J. Stadlen, *The Nance*

OTHER ACTORS' EQUITY AWARDS
Joe A. Callaway Award for best performances in a classic play in the New York metropolitan area: Merritt Wever of *Uncle Vanya* (OB) and Michael Shannon of *Uncle Vanya* (OB)
St. Clair Bayfield Award for the best supporting performance by an actor in a Shakespearean play in the New York metropolitan area: David Furr, *As You Like It* (OB)
ACCA Award for Outstanding Broadway

Chorus: the cast of *Newsies*
Paul Robeson Award for "a person who best exemplifies the principles by which Mr. Robeson lived": Director/producer/writer William Greaves

FRED EBB AWARD
Sam Willmott

THE TDF/IRENE SHARAFF AWARDS
From the Theatre Development Fund, for outstanding costume design
Robert L.B. Tobin Award for Sustained Excellence in Theatrical Design: Desmond Heeley
Artisan Award: Lawrence Vrba
Lifetime Achievement Award for Costume Design: David Toser
Young Master Award: Daniel Lawson
Special Memorial Tribute: Martin Pakledinaz

FRED AND ADELE ASTAIRE AWARDS
Outstanding Choreography of a Broadway Show: Chet Walker, *Pippin;* Patricia Wilcox & Warren Adams, *Motown*
Outstanding Choreography in a Feature Film: Sidi Larbi Cherkaoui, *Anna Karenina*
Outstanding Female Dancer in a Broadway Show: Charlotte d'Amboise, *Pippin*
Outstanding Male Dancer in a Broadway Show: Eric LaJuan Summers, *Motown*
Douglas Watt Lifetime Achievement Award: Marge Champion
Outstanding Achievement in the Preservation of Musical Theatre Award: Ted Chapin

HENRY HEWES DESIGN AWARDS
Announced in October 2012 for work in the 2011-2012 Season
Scenic Design: David Korins for *Chinglish*
Costume Design: Gregg Barnes for *Follies*
Lighting Design: Brian MacDevitt for *Death of a Salesman*
Notable Effects: Daniel Kluger for sound design for *Tribes* (OB)

STAGE DIRECTORS AND CHOREOGRAPHERS FOUNDATION
"Mr. Abbott" Award: Jerry Mitchell

KLEBAN PRIZE IN MUSICAL THEATRE
Promising Musical Theatre Lyricist: Daniel Maté
Promising Musical Theatre Librettist: Alan Gordon

GRAMMY AWARD
Best Musical Theatre Album: *Once*

1. Theatre World Award winners Jonny Orsini and Shalita Grant.
Fred and Adele Astaire Award honorees:
2. Ted Chapin.
3. Marge Champion.

Faculty

The Playbill Broadway Yearbook | 2012 • 9 • 2013

Teachers in Broadway Shows This Season: Top Images (L-R): Elizabeth Marvel in *Picnic* (photo by Joan Marcus); Amy Morton and Tracy Letts in *Edward Albee's Who's Afraid of Virginia Woolf* (photo by Michael Brosilow). Bottom Images (Clockwise from upper left): Lauren Ward in *Matilda* (photo by Joan Marcus); John Schiappa in *Wicked* (photo by Joan Marcus); Caroline O'Connor in *A Christmas Story* (photo by Carol Rosegg); Bertie Carvel in *Matilda* (photo by Joan Marcus) .

Faculty

The Shubert Organization

Philip J. Smith
Chairman and co-CEO

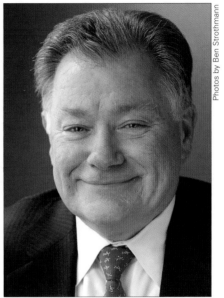

Robert E. Wankel
President and co-CEO

Photos by Ben Strothmann

Coalition of Broadway Unions and Guilds (COBUG)

Photo by Brian Mapp

Seated (L-R): John Seid (Local 306), K.C. Boyle (Local 802 AFM), Andy Friedman (Local 32BJ), Carol Bokun (Local 306), David Faux (Dramatists Guild), Dan Dashman (Local 798 Makeup/Hair), Angela Johnson (Local 798 Makeup/Hair)
Standing (L-R): Deborah Allton-Maher (AGMA), Nick Kaledin (ATPAM), Barbara Wolkoff (SDC), Gene McElwain (Local 751), Kimberly Rimbold (AEA), Carl Mulert (USA 829), Tony DePaulo (IATSE), Pat White (Local 764 Wardrobe), Elizabeth Miller (SDC), Frank Gallagher (Local 764 Wardrobe), Larry Lorczak (AEA)

Faculty

The Nederlander Organization

James M. Nederlander
Chairman

James L. Nederlander
Chairman

Nick Scandalios
Executive Vice President

Freida Belviso
Chief Financial Officer

Jim Boese
Vice President

Susan Lee
Chief Marketing Officer

Jack Meyer
Vice President Programming

Charlene S. Nederlander
Vice President Corporate Development

Kathleen Raitt
Vice President Corporate Relations

Herschel Waxman
Senior Vice President Labor Relations

Tony Awards Staff

Photo by Brian Mapp

Seated (L-R): Heather Hitchens, Elisa Shevitz, Rachel Schwartz, Ben Pesner, Kendra Srebro, Suzanne Tobak
Standing (L-R): Jan Svendsen, Charlotte St. Martin, Joanna Sheehan, Margaret Crisostomo, Lindsey Brown, Shawn Purdy, Carl Levin, Erica Ryan, Josh Cacchione, Leslie Dock, Ian Weiss, Chrissann Gasparro, Jean Kroeper

Faculty

JUJAMCYN THEATERS

Faculty

The Broadway League

Seated (L-R): Julia Davis, Laura Fayans, Elisa Shevitz, Kendra Srebro, Kayla Kreidell, Jean Kroeper, Jason Laks
Middle Row (L-R): Erica Ryan, Charlotte St. Martin, Chris Brucato, Robin Fox, Tom Ferrugia, Ben Pesner, Jennifier Stewart, Ed Sandler, Jan Svendsen
Back Row (L-R): Chris Brockmeyer, Colin Gibson, Josh Cacchione, Neal Freeman, Rachel Reiner, Leslie Dock, Elizabeth Rublein, Robert Davis, Seth Popper

Manhattan Theatre Club

Front Row (L-R): Laura Petrucci, Emily Yowell, Caitlin Baird, Heather Gallagher, Lindsey Sag, Samantha Kindler, Stephanie Dolce, Mark Bowers,
Rosanna Consalvo Sarto, Nicki Hunter, Darragh Garvey, Scott Kaplan
Second Row (L-R): Aubrie Fennecken, Amy Loe, David Shookhoff, Mandy Greenfield (Artistic Producer), Lynne Meadow (Artistic Director),
Barry Grove (Executive Producer), Jerry Patch, Nancy Piccione
Third Row (L-R): Debra Waxman, Kim Oria, Melanie Sovern, Ben Ferber, Annie MacRae, Elizabeth Rothman, Ryan Guhde, Amber Wilkerson, Thatcher Stevens,
Kelly Gillespie, Emily Fleisher, Sarah DeStefano
Back Row (L-R): Amy Harris, Patricia Leonard, Jason Fritzsch, Jessica Adler, Kevin Sullivan, Becca Goland-Van Ryn, Derrick Olson, Lynne Randall, Molly Clarke,
Tim Salamandyk, Mallory Triest, Josh Martinez-Nelson

Faculty

The Roundabout Theatre Company

Seated (L-R): Sydney Beers, Julia Levy (Executive Director), Todd Haimes (Artistic Director), Harold Wolpert (Managing Director), Tom O'Connor
Standing (L-R): Daniel Gomez, Jennifer DiBella, Jill Rafson, Susan Neiman, Nicholas Caccavo, Valerie Simmons, Greg Backstrom, Denise Cooper, Wendy Hutton

Dodgers

Front Row (L-R): Flora Johnstone, Brandon Smithey, Anne Ezell, Ann E. Van Nostrand, Tony Lance, Priya Iyer, Andrew Serna
Middle Row (L-R): Sally Campbell Morse, Linda Wright, Mariann Fresiello, Paula Maldonado, Laurinda Wilson, Jessica Morris, Ben Cohen, Pamela Lloyd
Back Row (L-R): Michael David, Scott Dennis, Lyndsey Goode, Richard Hester, Dana Sherman, John Haber, Abigail Kornet, Tim Sulka, Daniel Kogan, Jeff Parvin, Ashley Tracey, Lauren Mitchell
Not Pictured: Sandra Carlson, Jessica Ludwig, Lauren Freed, Jennie Mamary, Edward Strong, Jennifer Vaughan

Faculty

IATSE Local One, Stagehands

Seated (L-R): Paul F. Dean, Jr., Chairman, Board of Trustees; Robert C. Score, Recording-Corresponding Secretary; James J. Claffey, Jr., President; William Walters, Vice President; Robert McDonough, Treasurer
Standing (L-R): Edward J. McMahon, III, Television Business Manager; Mickey Fox, Theatre Business Manager; Kevin McGarty, Theatre Business Manager; Robert C. Nimmo, Television Business Manager; Daniel D. Dashman, Trustee; William Ngai, Trustee

Stage Directors and Choreographers Society

Seated (L-R): Laura Penn (Executive Director), Sharon Ott, John Rando, Rick Lombardo, Tom Moore, Karen Azenberg (President),
Kristy Cummings (SDC Staff), Michele Holmes (SDC Staff)
Standing Front Row (L-R): Ronald H. Shechtman (Counsel), Nicole Herrington (SDC Staff), Barbara Wolkoff (SDC Staff),
Doug Hughes (Executive Vice President), Linda Hartzell, Adam Levi (SDC Staff), Robert Moss, Seret Scott, Walter Bobbie, Lena Abrams (SDC Staff)
Standing Middle Row (L-R): Randy Anderson (SDC Staff), Ethan McSweeny (Treasurer), Christopher Ashley, Dan Knechtges, Kim Rogers (SDC Staff),
Michelle Sokolowski (SDC Staff)
Standing Back Row (L-R): Mauro Melleno (SDC Staff), Elizabeth Miller (SDC Staff), Lisa Peterson, Amy Morton, Cole Jordan (SDC Staff)

Faculty

Actors' Equity Association

Photo by Stephanie Masucci

Nick Wyman
President

Photo by Stephanie Masucci

Mary McColl
Executive Director

NATIONAL COUNCIL

Paige Price
1st Vice President

Rebecca Kim Jordan
2nd Vice President

Ira Mont
3rd Vice President

Sandra Karas
Secretary-Treasurer

Melissa Robinette
Eastern Regional Vice President

Dev Kennedy
Central Regional Vice President

Doug Carfrae
Western Regional Vice President

Photo by Brian Mapp

AEA STAFF
Front Row (L-R): Stephanie Masucci, Anne Fortuno, Jenifer Hills, Kimberly Rimbold, David Lotz
Middle Row (L-R): Timothy Try, Joan Glazer, Karen Nothmann, Russell Lehrer, Lawrence Lorczak, Steven DiPaola, Chris Williams
Back Row (L-R): Andrea Murray, Tom Miller, Robert Fowler, Doug Beebe, Joseph Garber (LA office), Adriana Douzos

Photo by Brian Mapp

AEA STAFF
Sitting (L-R): Karlene Laemmie, Kristine Arwe, Stephanie Schwartz
Standing (L-R): Calandra Hackney, Elisabeth Stern, Courtney Godan, Dave Thorn

AEA STAFF
Front Row (L-R): Sylvina Persaud, Catherine Jayne, Kathy Mercado, Zalina Hoosein, Beverly Sloan
Middle Row (L-R): Diane Raimondi, Tripp Chamberlain, Joanna Spencer, Nicholas Neipert, Kathleen Munroe, Elly Deutsch
Back Row (L-R): Michelle Kelts, Tatiana Kouloumbis, Matthew Conti, Dragica Dabo, Stuart Levy, Gary Dimon

Photo by Brian Mapp

Photo by Brian Mapp

AEA STAFF
Front Row (L-R): Jennifer Camp, Mary Kate Gilrein, Pearl Brady, Adeola Adegbola, Michelle Lehrman, Toni Stanton
Middle Row (L-R): Jillian Moss, Tom Kaub, Maria Cameron, Valerie LaVarco, Chris Bennett, Megan Rogers, Lara Schuman, Louise Foisy
Back Row (L-R): Barry Rosenberg, Jonathan Donahue, Robert Druitt, Buckly Stephens, Walt Kiskaddon, Jeffrey Bateman, David Westphal, Thomas Carpenter

Faculty

Dramatists Guild

STAFF
Front (L-R): Amy VonVett, Rebecca Stump, Rachel Routh, Gary Garrison, Roland Tec, Brandon Piper, Deborah Murad, Seth Cotterman
Back (L-R): Ralph Sevush, David Faux, Caterina Bartha, Tari Stratton, Patrick Shearer, Jenn Bushinger, Joey Stocks

DRAMATISTS GUILD COUNCIL/STEERING COMMITTEE
Seated (L-R): Doug Wright (Secretary), Theresa Rebeck (Treasurer)
Middle Row (L-R): Julia Jordan, Stephen Schwartz (President), John Weidman, Marsha Norman, David Lindsay-Abaire, Peter Parnell (Vice President)
Back Row (L-R): David Auburn, David Ives, Craig Carnelia

Association of Theatrical Press Agents and Managers

Seated (L-R): Jonathan Shulman, Adam Miller, Gregg Arst, Nick Kaledin (Secretary/Treasurer), Rina Saltzman, Susan Elrod (Manager Chapter Chair)
Standing (L-R): David Gersten (Press Agent Chapter Chair), Maury Collins (Chicago Steward), Don Tirabassi (Boston Steward), Jim Payne (California Steward), Kevin McAnarney, Barbara Carroll, Shirley Herz, Jeremy Shaffer
Not Pictured: David Calhoun (President), Penny Daulton (Vice-President), Robert Nolan, Steven Schnepp

Faculty

Theatrical Teamsters, Local 817

EXECUTIVE BOARD
(L-R): James Leavey (Recording Secretary), Charles Spillane, Jr. (Trustee), James Fanning (Vice President), Francis J. Connolly, Jr. (Secretary Treasurer), Thomas J. O'Donnell (President), Michael Hyde (Trustee), Gene O'Neill (Trustee)

OFFICE STAFF
(L-R): Tina Gusmano, Christine Harkerss, Margie Vaeth, Allison Hammond, Marg Marklin

Local 829 United Scenic Artists

Seated (L-R): Carl Baldasso, Caitlin McConnell, Beverly Miller, Cecilia Friederichs, Cathy Santucci Keator, Cynthia Parker Frye
Standing (L-R): F. Mitchell Dana, Patrick Langevin, Carl Mulert

Faculty

IATSE Local 751, Treasurers & Ticket Sellers Union

Photos by Brian Mapp

EXECUTIVE COUNCIL
Sitting (L-R): Diane Heatherington, Noreen Morgan, Karen Winer
Standing (L-R): Harry Jaffie, Lawrence Paone (Secretary-Treasurer/Business Agent),
Fred Bonis, Matthew Fearon (Vice President), Stanley Shaffer, Michael Loiacono,
Gene McElwain (President), Peter Attanasio and Dave Heveran

OFFICERS AND STAFF
Sitting (L-R): Stephanie Swisher-Lajoie, Patricia Quiles
Standing (L-R): James Sita, Lawrence Paone (Secretary-Treasurer/Business Agent),
Gene McElwain (President)

Theatrical Wardrobe Union, IATSE Local 764

Photo by Brian Mapp

First Row (L-R): Paula Inocent, Paula Cohen, Barbara Hladsky, Peggy Danz Kazdan, Monica Belucci, Olivia Booth, Angela Lehrer,
Shannon Koger (Secretary/Treasurer), Mary Ferry (Funds Administrator)
Second Row (L-R): Dennis Birchall, Pam Pierzina, Rosemary Taylor, Chris Lavin, Steve Epstein, Rick Ortiz, Denise Martin, Corey Groom, Tian Thoon, Pat Sullivan (Trustee)
Third Row (L-R): Julie Fernandez, Shelly Friedman (Trustee), Keiko Obremski, Steve Taylor, Elizabeth Ensminger, Alexa Burt, Danajean Cicerchi, Emma Atherton,
Holly Nissen, Jennifer Woods, Pat White (President)
Fourth Row (L-R): Ashley Green, Warren Wernick, Robert Harrington, David Besser, Kristen Gardner, Ricky Yates, Ray Panelli, Marcia Moore, John Furrow, Scott
Harrington (Trustee), Jenna Krempel (Vice-President), Terry LaVada (Sergeant-at-Arms), Rita Santi, Frank Gallagher (Business Representative)

Faculty

American Federation of Musicians, Local 802

Sitting (L-R): Financial Vice President Tom Olcott, President Tino Gagliardi, Recording Vice President John O'Connor
Standing (L-R): Executive Board Members Gail Kruvand, Bob Cranshaw, Jay Brandford, Martha Hyde, Bud Burridge, Clint Sharman, Pat Dougherty, Andy Schwartz
Not pictured: Executive Board Member Sara Cutler

IATSE Local 306 Motion Picture Projectionists, Video Technicians and Allied Crafts (Ushers)

Sitting (L-R): Cheryl Budd (Sergeant-at-Arms), Carol Bokun (Theatrical Business Agent), Lorraine Lowrey (Secretary-Treasurer), Ken Costigan (Executive Board)
Standing (L-R): John Seid (President), Alfie (Mascot), Joe Rivierzo (Executive Board), Tim Barrett (Executive Board), Barry Garfman (Traditional Business Agent), Helen Bentley (Executive Board)

International Union of Operating Engineers Local 30

BUSINESS MANAGER
John T. Ahern

Faculty

Broadway Cares/Equity Fights AIDS

First Row (L-R): Mo Brady, Carol Ingram, Frank Conway, Yvonne Ghareeb, Keith Bullock, Scott Stevens, Tom Viola
Second Row (L-R): Joy Nelson, Sarah Cardillo, Cat Domiano, Madeline Reed, Ngoc Bui, Andy Halliday, Dennis Henriquez, Denise Roberts Hurlin, Dan Perry
Third Row (L-R): Aaron Waytkus, Skip Lawing, Josh Blye, Danny Whitman, Lane Beauchamp, Joe Norton, Chris Gizzi, Chris DeLuise, Chris Kenney, Chris Davis, Peter Borzotta
Top Row (L-R): Dex Ostling, Ryan Walls, Larry Cook, Nathan Hurlin, Michael Graziano

American Theatre Wing

Seated (L-R): Sondra Gilman, Ted Chapin (Vice Chairman), Heather A. Hitchens (Executive Director), William Ivey Long (Chairman), Dasha Epstein, Peter Schneider (Vice Chairman), David Henry Hwang, Rachel Schwartz, Nicole Mitzel Gardner
Standing (L-R): David Brown, Enid Nemy (Secretary), Michael Price (Treasurer), Bill Craver, Marva Smalls, Binta Niambi Brown, Pamela Zilly, Raisa Ushomirsky, Mark Abrahams, Joanna Sheehan, Megan Kolb, Kenny Gallo

Faculty

Theatre Development Fund and TKTS

TDF STAFF
First Row, Kneeling (L-R): Jennifer Hurlbert, Max Freedman, Vickie Alvarez, Mark Runion, Michael Buffer, Patrick Berger
Second Row, Sitting (L-R): Stephen Cabral, Lisa Carling, Michael Naumann, Victoria Bailey, Joy Cooper, Eric Sobel
Third Row (L-R): Jane Pfeffer, Tina Kirsimae, Howard Marren, Kim Midkiff, Allison Taylor, Jonathan Calindas, Lea Wulferth, Richard Price, David LeShay
Fourth Row (L-R): Michael Yaccarino, Tom Westerman, Rob Neely, Craig Stekeur, Tymand Staggs, Fran Polino, Sarah Aziz, Julie Williams, Denyse Owens, Joseph Cali
Back Row (L-R): Daniel Renner, Ginger Meagher, Mark Blankenship, Joanne Haas, Thomas Adkins, Costas Michalopoulos, Michelle St. Hill, Robert Gore

TKTS TREASURERS
Front: William Castellano (Head Treasurer)
Second Row (L-R): Michael McCarthy,
Gale Sprydon, Rajesh Sharma
Back Row (L-R): Charles Stuis, Jr., Craig Henniger,
John Cinelli

TDF COSTUME COLLECTION
(L-R): Mark Runion, Stephen Cabral, Joanne Haas, Jennifer Hurlbert, Joey Haws, Craig Stekeur

Faculty

The Actors Fund

Photo by Brian Mapp

BOARD OF TRUSTEES
Seated (L-R): Jomarie Ward, Janice Reals Ellig, Charlotte St. Martin, Vice Chair Philip J. Smith, Paul Libin, Honey Waldman, Kate Edelman Johnson
Standing (L-R): Vice Chair Philip S. Birsh, Merle Debuskey, Ebs Burnough, Stewart F. Lane, Assistant Treasurer Lee H. Perlman, Jeffrey Bolton, Tom Viola, Secretary Marc Grodman, M.D., Joyce Gordon, James J. Claffey, Jr.

Not pictured: Chairman of the Board Brian Stokes Mitchell, Assistant Secretary Abby Schroeder, Treasurer Steve Kalafer, Alec Baldwin, Annette Bening, Jed W. Bernstein, John Breglio, Nancy Coyne, Rick Elice, Teresa Eyring, Mark Hostetter, Ken Howard, David Henry Hwang, Anita Jaffe, Michael Kerker, Chris Keyser, Matthew Loeb, Kristen Madsen, Kevin McCollum, Lin-Manuel Miranda, James L. Nederlander, Martha Nelson, Phyllis Newman, Harold Prince, Roberta Reardon, Thomas Schumacher, David Steiner, Edward D. Turen, Joseph H. Wender, David White, BD Wong, Nick Wyman, George Zuber

NEW YORK STAFF
Sitting (L-R): Joy Pascua-Kim, Lynnell Herzer, Dalin Rivera, Ryan Dietz, Jay Haddad, Sylvia Gonzalez, Jean Lee, Alice Vienneau, Amy Wilder
Standing (L-R): Jennifer Anglade, Sam Smith, Judy Fish, Rebecca Sauer, Barbara Toy, David Engelman, Cassandra Kohilakis, Stephen Joseph, Holly Wheeler, Robyn Cucurullo, Susan Varon, Allison Hooban, Gloria Jones, Tim Pinckney, Tamar Shapiro, Renata Marinaro, Risa Neuwirth, Darren Robertson, Liliana Lustig
Chicago Office: Steven Haught
Not pictured: Joseph P. Benincasa (President & CEO), Barbara Davis (COO), Connie Yoo (CFO), Thomas Exton (CAO)

Photo by Brian Mapp

WESTERN COUNCIL
Sitting (L-R): James Karen, Ilyanne Morden Kichaven, Charlotte Rae, Marguerite Ray, Jane A. Johnston Shearing, Mary Lou Westerfield, Bridget Hanley
Standing (L-R): Jomarie Ward (Trustee), Joseph Ruskin, Hollace Davids, Dan Guerrero, B. Harlan Boll, Barbara Allyne Bennet, William Thomas, Theodore Bikel, Michael Medico, Ken Werther, Daniel Henning, Pam Dixon, Martin Wiviott, Vice Chair Ilene Graff, John Bowab, Kate Edelman Johnson (Trustee)

Not pictured: Chair John Holly, Vice Chair David Rambo, John Acosta, Joni Berry, Budd Friedman, Katherine Fugate, Danny Goldman, Richard Herd, Scott Roth, Bryan Unger, David Young, Robby Benson (Emeritus), Henry Polic II (Emeritus), Lynn Wood (Emeritus)

LOS ANGELES STAFF
Sitting (L-R): Dan Kitowski, Tina Hookom, Ze'ev Korn, Keith McNutt, Meg Thomas, Jan-Kees Van Der Gaag
Standing (L-R): Ted Abenheim, Gregory Polcyn, Emmanuel Freeman, Miata Edoga, Amanda Steele, Joey Shanley, Heather Vanian, Robin LaBorwit, Amy Hammond, Angelique Prahalis, Caitlin Sorenson, Joanne Webb, Laura Campbell, Frank Salamone, TaNisha Harris

Photo by Scott Appel

Faculty

Boneau/Bryan-Brown

Chris Boneau

Adrian Bryan-Brown

Jim Byk

Michelle Farabaugh

Jackie Green

Kelly Guiod

Linnae Hodzic

Kevin Jones

Amy Kass

Holly Kinney

Emily Meagher

Aaron Meier

Christine Olver

Joe Perrotta

Amanda Sales

Heath Schwartz

Michael Strassheim

Susanne Tighe

Faculty

Lincoln Center Theater

First Row (L-R): Bartlett Sher, Kati Koerner, Jeff Hamlin, Karin Schall, Josh Lowenthal, Adam Siegel, Paul Smithyman
Second Row (L-R): Amanda Kaus, Natasha Sinha, Laura Stuart, David Cannon, Linda Mason Ross, Nikki Vera, Jenny Rosenbluth-Stoll
Third Row (L-R): Neal Brilliant, Sydney Rais-Sherman, Rachel Norton, Ashley Dunn, Meghan Lantzy, Matthew Markoff, Sheilaja Rao
Fourth Row (L-R): Zoe Tarmy, Jessica Niebanck, Mike Assalone, Ira Weitzman, Julia Judge
Fifth Row (L-R): Anne Cattaneo, Kira Rice, Jerry Less, Jessica Perlmeter Cochrane

The Hartman Group

Front Row (L-R): Tom D'Ambrosio, Michael Hartman, Colgan McNeil
Back Row (L-R): Emily McGill, Bethany Larsen, Wayne Wolfe, Frances White, Nicole Capatasto, Whitney Holden Gore, Matt Ross

Faculty

Richard Kornberg & Associates

Photo by Brian Mapp

Richard Kornberg

Photo by Brian Mapp

Danielle McGarry

Photo by Ben Strothmann

Don Summa

Photo by Brian Mapp

Billy Zavelson

The Publicity Office

Photo by Andrew Cole

Seated (L-R): Marc Thibodeau, Michael Borowski
Standing: Jeremy Shaffer

Jeffrey Richards Associates

Photo by Brian Mapp

Seated (L-R):
Christopher Pineda,
Irene Gandy, Jeffrey Richards,
Franco, Alana Karpoff, Skye,
Michael Crea
Standing (L-R): Will Trice,
Wally Hays, PJ Miller,
Thomas Raynor,
Andy Drachenberg

Keith Sherman & Associates

Photo by Brian Mapp

Front: Pat Reiher
Back (L-R): Logan Metzler, Scott Klein, Brett Oberman, Keith Sherman

Polk & Company

Photo by Brian Mapp

Front (L-R): Layne McNish, Ryan Hallett
Back (L-R): Matt Polk, Jessica Johnson

Faculty

RICK MIRAMONTEZ   SARAH BABIN   MOLLY BARNETT   SCOTT BRAUN   PHILIP CARRUBBA

JON DIMOND   JOYCE FRIEDMANN   MICHAEL JORGENSEN   CHELSEA NACHMAN   MARIE PACE

RYAN RATELLE   PETE SANDERS   ANDY SNYDER

Faculty

A. BAKER
BRUNCH CLUB

K. BARDWIL
KEY CLUB

S. BARTON
CHEERLEADING

W. BEISHIR
DETENTION

A. BIZJAK
JAZZ TEAM

C. BLONDEL
WRESTLING

J. BODLEY
ROCK BAND

A. BOND
SANDWICH CLUB

J. BOOR
STUDENT COUNCIL

K. CAROTHERS
HEAD OF THE PLASTICS

A. CATALA
ABSTINENCE CLUB

R. COHEN
MUSIC CONSERVATORY

J. COOPER
COMIC BOOK CLUB

J. COOPER
BANJO CLUB

T. COPPOLA
BREAKFAST CLUB

D. COX
HISTORICAL SOCIETY

G. CRADDOCK
EAGLE SCOUTS

T. CREWS
VALEDICTORIAN

M. CROWLEY
THESPIANS

A. CRUZ
GLEE CLUB

M. CURRY
URBAN ACHIEVER

A. DAVIS
BLACK HISTORY CLUB

M. DELMORE
BABYSITTERS CLUB

A. EISENHOWER
SWIM TEAM

T. FALOTICO
WATER POLO

D. FORKIN
SCIENTOLOGY

J. FOX
A.M. ANNOUNCEMENTS

J. FRAENKEL
HILLEL

L. FRAENKEL
SMALL PEOPLE CLUB

T. FRANCIS
STUDY CLUB

R. GASKINS
DRILL TEAM

C. GOFF
MOST TALKATIVE

G. GREEN
PEP SQUAD

E. HAMMERMAN
DEAD POETS SOCIETY

J. HANNETT
DRAMA SOCIETY

SpotCo Class of 2013

L. HU
SCIENCE OLYMPIAD

J. HUBBELL
COMPUTER CLUB

P. JEFFREY
SCI-FI BOOK CLUB

L. JOHNSON
DANCE TEAM

D. HODGES
PRINCIPAL

J. EDWARDS
VICE PRINCIPAL

B. BERK
DEAN OF STUDENTS

T. GREENWALD
AV SQUAD

I. ROSEN
GUIDANCE COUNSELOR

R. KOLB
TAXIDERMY

S. LADD
TEACHER'S PET

N. LINDEMAN
PING PONG

M. McCRACKEN
NERD

J. McGOWAN
A CAPPELLA

J. McNICHOLAS
BROADCAST CLUB

Z. MEISNER
BENCHWARMER

B. MORAN
CABER TOSS

T. MOSER
BRAVO CLUB

M. PIHAKIS
ICE SKATING

N. PRAMIK
LINGUISTICS

D. PRESTON
MATHLETES

K. RATHBUN
QUIZ BOWL CAPTAIN

A. ROTHENBERG
COLOR GUARD

V. SAINATO
DEBATE

S. SANTORE
CROSS COUNTRY

C. SCHERER
RESIDENT DJ

B. SCHULTZ
HOME ECONOMICS

C. SCHWITZ
FIRST TEAM ALL-STATE

D. SELLERS
JAZZ BAND

C. SHALOIKO
SKI CLUB

D. SNYPE
BALLET FOLKLORICO

C. SOGLIUZZO
TEAM SPIRIT

S. SOSNOWSKI
FENCING

C. SPINNEY
QUEEN BEE

H. TROY
PUNK

N. VENNERA
BOXING CLUB

B. WATSON
YOUNG DEMOCRATS

J. WECHSLER
SPEED-WALKING CLUB

H. WILSON
BEST DRESSED

E. WU
CLUB

K. YOUNG
MASCOT

R. ZATCOFF
HOMEROOM REP

Faculty

ANDY APOSTOLIDES · HAILEY APTER · LESLIE BARRETT · DAVID BARRINEAU · WILLIAM BELL · SUMEET BHARATI · CHRISTY BORG

SIMONE BOYD-DeCASTRO · DANIELLE BOYLE · MATT BRITT · DENISE BROWN · TOM CALLAHAN · JEFF CARROLL · JON CHAMBERS

CRYSTAL CHASE · MICHAEL CLAEYS · NICK COBURN · LAURIE CONNOR · MONICA CORONEL · GREG CORRADETTI · BRUCE COUNCIL

NANCY COYNE · WHITNEY CREIGHTON · GRAY CRENSHAW · ANDREA CUEVAS · RANDY CUMBERBATCH · ANTHONY CUTAJAR · ANGELO DESIMINI · BRIAN DeVITO · ALEX DIAZ · DOUG ENSIGN

JON ERWIN · ELYSE FAMILETTI · JOE FIGLIOLA · CHERI FONTANEZ · JENNA FREED · CHRISSANN GASPARRO · EMILY GENDUSO · JIM GLAUB · IFAT GOLAN · RYAN GREER

PETER GUNTHER · CHRISTINA HERNANDEZ · MIKHAIL HERRERA · CATHERINE HERZOG · KIM HEWSKI · NATHANIEL HILL · KEVIN HIRST · ISABEL HITTLEMAN · LAUREN HOULBERG · ARTURO IRIZARRY

VANESSA JAVIER · KARA JENKINS · SCOTT JOHNSON · ROBERT JONES · JACQUI KAISER · LEORA KANNER · KEVIN KEATING · MARY KEKLLAS · ZACK KINNEY · ZHANNA KIRTSMAN

JONATHAN LAPRADE · JIM LAZOS · ADINA LEVIN · CAROLYN LONDON · AGATHA MACIEJEWSKI · SARAH MARCUS · KAT MAROTTA · CHRIS MARTIN · UMA MCCROSSON · RYAN MCPHEE

KEVIN MEERE · MARCI MEYERS · CHIP MEYRELLES · ROGER MICONE · CATHERINE MIGUEIS · BRANDON MIKOLASKI · STEPHANIE MOISE · DAVID MOLINA · ROSA MONSERRAT · SHAWNA MONSON

JARED NARBER · DREW NEBRIG · SOFIA NISNEVICH · RAY NOELLE · NICK NOLTE · ANDREI OLEINIK · TEE PANTON · BRAD PATTINIAN · MIKE RAFAEL · JOE RECKLEY

CATHERINE REID · SCOTT RITCHEY · JIM RUSSEK · DIANA SALAMEH · BETH SCHEFFLAN · MARK SEELEY · BEN SKINNER · GERRI STERNE · CHARLOTTE TANCINCO · CAROLINE THOMPSON

SUZANNE TOBAK · ALHAGIE TOURAY · MATTHEW UPSHAW · KARA WEINTRAUB · IAN WEISS · GINGER WITT · ABBY WOLBE · SCOTT YAMBOR · JASON ZAMMIT · DANA ZELL

SERINO/COYNE 2012-2013
It's **SHOW** TIME.

Faculty

Faculty

Playbill

Philip S. Birsh
Publisher

Arthur T. Birsh
Chairman

Clifford S. Tinder
*Senior Vice President/
Publisher, Classic Arts
Division*

Joan Alleman Birsh
*Corporate Vice
President*

Blake Ross
*Editor-in-Chief
Playbill*

SALES
Sitting (L-R): Clara Barragán, Glenn Asciutto, Jeff Nicholson, Glenn Shaevitz
Standing (L-R): Stephanie Bradbury, Jim Cairl, Ari Ackerman, Diane Niedzialek, Yadira Mitchell, Cliff S. Tinder, Talaura Harms
Not Pictured: Jolie Schaffzin

OFFICE MANAGEMENT
Sitting (L-R): Oldyna Dynowska, Dolly Reyes, Wanda Young
Standing (L-R): Tiffany Feo, Anderson Peguero, Esvard D'Haiti, Arturo Gonzalez

PRODUCTION / ARTISTIC / EDITORIAL
Sitting (L-R): Harry Haun, Blake Ross, Damian Fowler
Standing (L-R): Alex Near, Diana Leidel, Cliff S. Tinder, Maude Popkin
Not pictured: Brian Libfeld, Kesler Thibert

442

Faculty

Playbill

ONLINE EDITORIAL / PLAYBILL.COM
Sitting (L-R): Blake Ross, Andrew Gans, Matt Blank, David Gewirtzman
Standing (L-R): Joseph Marzullo, Jennifer Brown, Kenneth Jones, Adam Hetrick, Mark Ezovski, Michael Gioia, Andrew Ku, Jon Goldman

EDU / VIP / VAULT / MEMORY BANK / PLAYBILL PRO
Front Row (L-R): Andrew Ku, Danny Hatch, Jennifer Brown
Middle Row: (L-R): Robert Viagas, Kelechi Ezie, Brad Gumbel, David Gewirtzman
Back Row (L-R): Megan Dekic, Brynn Cox, Steven McCasland, Sarah Jane Arnegger, Jill Boriss, Robbie Rozelle, Jon Goldman, Frank Dain

Louis Botto	Harry Haun	Jennifer Lanter	Carey Purcell	Mervyn Rothstein	Seth Rudetsky	Mark Shenton	Robert Simonson	Steven Suskin
Columnist 1924-2012	*Columnist*	*Columnist*	*Staff Writer*	*Columnist*	*Columnist*	*London Correspondent*	*Senior Correspondent*	*Columnist*

Faculty

Playbill

ACCOUNTING
Sitting (L-R): John Locascio, Theresa Bernstein, Jim Eastman
Standing (L-R): Lewis Cole, JoAnn D'Amato, Patrick Pizzolorusso
Not Pictured: Andy Montero

Carolina Diaz
*Florida Production
Manager*

Regional Advertising Salespersons

Kenneth R. Back
*Sales Manager
Cincinnati*

Elaine Bodker
*Sales
St. Louis*

Bob Caulfield
*Sales
San Francisco*

Margo Cooper
*Sales Manager
St. Louis*

Ron Friedman
*Sales Manager
Columbus*

Tom Green
*Sales
Florida/Texas, etc.*

Betsy Gugick
*Sales Manager
Dallas*

Ed Gurien
*Sales
Florida/Dallas*

Karen Kanter
*Sales Director
California*

Michel Manzo
*Sales Manager
Philadelphia*

Marilyn A. Miller
*Sales Manager
Minneapolis*

Judy Pletcher
*Sales Manager
Washington, DC*

Donald Roberts
*Sales Manager
Florida*

Kenneth Singer
*Sales Manager
Houston*

Jill Wettersten
*Sales Manager
Chicago*

Not Pictured: Leslie J. Feldman, Nancy Hardin

Faculty

Playbill / Woodside Offices

PRODUCTION
Sitting (L-R): Benjamin Hyacinthe, Patrick Cusanelli, Amy Asch
Standing (L-R): Sean Kenny, Judy Samelson
Not pictured: David Porrello

PROGRAM EDITORS/PRODUCTION
Sitting (L-R): Joseph Conroy, Sean Kenny, Patrick Cusanelli, Bill Reese
Standing (L-R): Pam Karr, Scott Hale, Matt Bonnano, Claire Mangan, Benjamin Hyacinthe,
Judy Samelson, Amy Asch
Not pictured: Diane Kolack

PLAYBILLSTORE.COM
Front Row (L-R): Yajaira Marrero, Craig Fogel, Rebeca Miller
Back Row (L-R): Phil Newsom, Bruce Stapleton

DAY SHIFT MANUFACTURING
Front Row (L-R): John Matthews, James Anticona,
Rodrigo Garcia, David Rodriguez, Francisco Montero
Middle Row (L-R): Janet Moti, Nancy Galarraga,
Mike Holder, Scott Cipriano
Back Row: (L-R): Lidia Yagual, Larry Przetakiewicz,
Frank Divirgilio, Steve Ramlall, Arnold Jaklitsch,
Steven Ryder, Robert Cusanelli
Not pictured: Ray Sierra

NIGHT SHIFT MANUFACTURING
Front Row (L-R): Bernard Morgan, Elias Garcia,
Kenneth Gomez, Joe Gurrieri
Standing (L-R): Sneider Cahuana, Ana Rincon,
Pablo Yagual, Frank Dunn, Juan Burgos, James Ayala

In Memoriam

June 2012 to May 2013

Richard Adler
Paul Ainsley
John Aman
Christine L. Anderson
Patty Andrews
Allan Arbus
R.G. Armstrong
Victor Arnold
Lisa Jalowetz Aronson
David Atkinson
Conrad Bain
Shirley Ballard
Billy Barnes
Daniel Barton
Ralph Beaumont
Steve Ben Israel
David Berk
Eddie Bert
Lois Bewley
Herbert Blau
Ernest Borgnine
Louis Botto
Beverley Bozeman
Richard Briers
Stephen Brockway
Jacqueline Brookes
Brian Brownlee
Betty Ann Busch
Helena Carroll
Janet Carroll
Dorothy Ateca Carter
Rudy Challenger
Marianne Challis
William Chapman
Shirley Chester
Sybil Christopher
David Connell
Sam Crothers
Edward Crotty
Hal David
Audrey Dearden
Vincent DeMarco
Henry Denker
Phyllis Diller
Shana Dowdeswell
Jacquelyn Dubois
Victor Duntiere
Charles Durning
Burt Edwards
Christopher "Shadow" Edwards
Valerie Eliot
Nora Ephron
Patrick Farrelly
Doris Faye
Peter Flint
Pyotr Fomenko
Steve Forrest
Manheim Fox

Broadway Dims Its Lights

Broadway theatres dimmed their marquee lights this season upon the passing of the following theatre personalities, listed here along with the date the honor was accorded: Actor Charles Durning, December 27, 2012. Composer Marvin Hamlisch, August 8, 2012. Actress Celeste Holm, July 18, 2012. Actor Jack Klugman, December 28, 2012. Costume designer Martin Pakledinaz, July 12, 2012. Producer Martin Richards, November 27, 2012. Playwright Gore Vidal, August 3, 2012.

Vanya Franck
Bonnie Franklin
Frederick Franklin
Ulrich Franzen
Al Freeman, Jr.
Jonathan Frid
Noel Friedman
Luigi Gasparinetti
Robin Gibb
Virginia Gibson
Ben Gillespie
Don Grady
Kevin Gray
Michael Gray
Martha Greenhouse
Andy Griffith
Richard Griffiths
James Grout
Larry Hagman
Marvin Hamlisch
Arthur Hammer
William Hanley
Paul Harris
Sherman Hemsley
Susan Hight

Celeste Holm
Howard Honig
John Horn
Scott Hunter
George Ives
Barney Johnston
Fay Kanin
John Kerr
Kenny Kerr
Jerome Kilty
Archer King
Larry L. King
Jack Klugman
Garrett Lewis
Karl Light
Ralph Linn
Robert Litz
Herbert Lom
Susan Luckey
Morgan MacKay
Lori March
Albert Marre
Sid Marshall
Joel Marston
Matt Mattox

James McGill
Jaylee Mead
Patricia Medina
Roy Miller
Kathi Moss
Leonard A. Mulhern
Lou Myers
Frederick Neumann
Barbara Newman
John Newton
Patricia Northrop
William Nuss
Jeremy Nussbaum
Frank O'Brien
Mike O'Carroll
Mark O'Donnell
Michael O'Hare
Dale C. Olson
Lupe Ontiveros
George Ormiston
Milo O'Shea
Martin Pakledinaz
Ron Palillo
Larry Payton
John R. Powers
Phil Ramone
Martin Richards
Jack Richardson
Fred Ridgeway
Joan Roberts
Steve Roland
Marty Ross
Frank Savino
Ravi Shankar
Gloria Hope Sher
Robert Sickinger
Lee Silver
Carrie Smith
Victor Spinetti
Joan Stein
Arthur Storch
Ian Stuart
Anne Sullivan
Donna Summer
Willy Switkes
Maria Tallchief
Phyllis Thaxter
Susan Tyrrell
Porter Van Zandt
Gore Vidal
Evelyn Ward
Simon Ward
Fran Warren
Andy Williams
William Windom
Eugene V. Wolsk
Jean Sincere Zambello

Photo by Robert Viagas

Louis Botto, one of the best-known and best-loved *Playbill* writers, died November 4, 2012 at age 88 after a long illness. A *Playbill* employee from 1971 to his retirement in 2012, he authored three columns simultaneously for the Broadway programs: "Backward Glances," filled with stage legends and vintage glamour; the chatty "Passing Stages"; and his masterwork, "At This Theatre," the story-packed history of each Broadway theatre, later collected as a book of the same title. Botto saw his first Broadway show, *White Horse Inn*, in 1937.

Index

Index

Index

Index

Index

Index

Index

Index

Index

Index

Index

Index

Index

Index

Index

Index

Index

Index

Index

Index

Index

Index

Index

Index